THE L LIBRARY
SANFORD, CAROLINA
SIGN
HERE
— PRE BY —
Drs. E eth and
John erer

THE COLLECTED WORKS OF
ABRAHAM LINCOLN

THE COLLECTED WORKS OF
ABRAHAM LINCOLN

THE ABRAHAM LINCOLN ASSOCIATION
SPRINGFIELD, ILLINOIS

III

ROY P. BASLER, *EDITOR*
MARION DOLORES PRATT AND LLOYD A. DUNLAP
ASSISTANT EDITORS

RUTGERS UNIVERSITY PRESS
NEW BRUNSWICK, NEW JERSEY

THE HISTORY BOOK CLUB EDITION

COMPOSED IN INTERTYPE WAVERLEY
BY H. WOLFF BOOK MANUFACTURING COMPANY, NEW YORK CITY,
PRINTED BY MURRAY PRINTING COMPANY, FORGE VILLAGE, MASSACHUSETTS,
AND BOUND BY THE HADDON CRAFTSMEN, SCRANTON, PENNSYLVANIA

TITLE PAGE WOOD ENGRAVING BY STANLEY RICE
DESIGN BY P. J. CONKWRIGHT

SOURCES AND LOCATION SYMBOLS

DESCRIPTION OF SOURCES

The following symbols provide a description of sources as cited at the beginning of the first footnote to each item. In addition to the customary symbols for describing manuscripts, the editors have employed symbols or single words to identify other sources which have been cited repeatedly in the first footnote.

AD	Autograph Document
ADS	Autograph Document Signed
ADf	Autograph Draft
ADfS	Autograph Draft Signed
AE	Autograph Endorsement
AES	Autograph Endorsement Signed
AL	Autograph Letter
ALS	Autograph Letter Signed
ALS copy	Autograph Letter Signed, copied by Lincoln and preserved in his papers
Copy	Copy not by Lincoln
D	Document
DS	Document Signed
Df	Draft
DfS	Draft Signed
ES	Endorsement Signed
F	Facsimile—following any of the preceding symbols
LS	Letter Signed
P	Photostat—following any of the preceding symbols

Angle	*New Letters and Papers of Lincoln.* Compiled by Paul M. Angle. Boston and New York: Houghton Mifflin Company, 1930.
Herndon	*Herndon's Lincoln: The True Story of a Great Life.* By William H. Herndon and Jesse W. Weik. 3 volumes. Chicago, New York, and San Francisco: Belford, Clarke & Company, [1889].
Hertz	*Abraham Lincoln: A New Portrait.* By Emanuel Hertz. 2 volumes. New York: Horace Liveright, Inc., 1931.
Lapsley	*The Writings of Abraham Lincoln.* Edited by Arthur Brooks Lapsley. 8 volumes. New York: P. F. Collier and Son, 1905.

SOURCES

NH	*Complete Works of Abraham Lincoln.* Edited by John G. Nicolay and John Hay. 12 volumes. New York: Francis D. Tandy Company, 1905.
OR	*The War of the Rebellion: A Compilation of the Official Records of the Union and Confederate Armies.* 4 series; 70 "volumes"; 128 books. Washington: Government Printing Office, 1880-1901. Roman numerals are used for Series, Volume, and Part (if any); pages are in arabic.
Tarbell	*The Life of Abraham Lincoln. . . .* By Ida M. Tarbell. 2 volumes. New York: The Doubleday & McClure Company, 1900.
Tracy	*Uncollected Letters of Abraham Lincoln.* Edited by Gilbert A. Tracy. Boston and New York: Houghton Mifflin Company, 1917.
Wilson	*Uncollected Works of Abraham Lincoln.* Edited by Rufus Rockwell Wilson. 2 volumes. Elmira, New York: Primavera Press, 1947-1948.

LOCATION SYMBOLS

CCamStJ	St. John's Seminary Library, Camarillo, Calif.
CLCM	Los Angeles County Museum Library, Los Angeles, Calif.
CSmH	Henry E. Huntington Library, San Marino, Calif.
CoHi	State Historical Society of Colorado, Denver, Colo.
CoU	University of Colorado Library, Boulder, Colo.
Ct	Connecticut State Library, Hartford, Conn.
CtHi	Connecticut Historical Society, Hartford, Conn.
CtLHi	Litchfield Historical Society, Litchfield, Conn.
CtSoP	Pequot Library, Southport, Conn.
CtWat	Watertown Library Association, Watertown, Conn.
CtY	Yale University Library, New Haven, Conn.
DLC	Library of Congress, Washington, D. C.
DLC-HW	Herndon-Weik Collection, Library of Congress
DLC-RTL	The Robert Todd Lincoln Collection of the Papers of Abraham Lincoln, Library of Congress
DLM	Lincoln Museum, Ford's Theatre, National Park Service, Washington, D. C.
DNA	National Archives, Washington, D. C. All additional abbreviations and numbers given with this symbol are those employed by the National Archives at the time the manuscript was located.
DNM	National Museum Library, Washington, D. C.

DeHi	Historical Society of Delaware Library, Wilmington, Del.
DeWI	Wilmington Institute Free Library, Wilmington, Del.
I-Ar	Archives Division, Illinois State Library, Springfield, Ill.
IBloHi	McLean County Historical Society, Bloomington, Ill.
ICHi	Chicago Historical Society, Chicago, Ill.
ICU	University of Chicago Library, Chicago, Ill.
IDecJ	James Millikin University Library, Decatur, Ill.
IFre	Freeport Public Library, Freeport, Ill.
IHi	Illinois State Historical Library, Springfield, Ill.
IJI	Illinois College Library, Jacksonville, Ill.
ISLA	The Abraham Lincoln Association, Springfield, Ill.
IU	University of Illinois Library, Urbana, Ill.
IaCrM	Iowa Masonic Library, Cedar Rapids, Iowa
IaDaM	Davenport Public Museum, Davenport, Iowa
IaHA	Iowa State Department of History and Archives, Des Moines, Iowa
In	Indiana State Library, Indianapolis, Ind.
InFtwL	Lincoln National Life Foundation, Fort Wayne, Ind.
InHi	Indiana Historical Society, Indianapolis, Ind.
InLTHi	Tippecanoe County Historical Association, Lafayette, Ind.
InU	Indiana University Library, Bloomington, Ind.
KyBC	Berea College Library, Berea, Ky.
KyU	University of Kentucky Library, Lexington, Ky.
LU	Louisiana State University Library, Baton Rouge, La.
MB	Boston Public Library, Boston, Mass.
MCon	Free Public Library, Concord, Mass.
MFai	Millicent Library, Fairhaven, Mass.
MH	Harvard University Library, Cambridge, Mass.
MHi	Massachusetts Historical Society, Boston, Mass.
MS	Springfield Library Association, Springfield, Mass.
MSHi	Connecticut Valley Historical Society, Springfield, Mass.
MdAA	Hall of Records, State of Maryland, Annapolis, Md.
MdHi	Maryland Historical Society, Baltimore, Md.
MeHi	Maine Historical Society, Portland, Me.
MiD	Detroit Public Library, Detroit, Mich.
MiK-M	Kalamazoo Public Library Museum, Kalamazoo, Mich.
MiU-C	William L. Clements Library, University of Michigan, Ann Arbor, Mich.

MiU-Hi	Michigan Historical Collection, University of Michigan, Ann Arbor, Mich.
MnHi	Minnesota Historical Society, St. Paul, Minn.
MnSM	Macalester College Library, St. Paul, Minn.
MoHi	State Historical Society of Missouri, Columbia, Mo.
MoSHi	Missouri Historical Society, St. Louis, Mo.
N	New York State Library, Albany, N. Y.
NAuE	Fred L. Emerson Foundation, Auburn, N. Y.
NBLiHi	Long Island Historical Society, Brooklyn, N. Y.
NBuG	Grosvenor Library, Buffalo, New York
NBuHi	Buffalo Historical Society, Buffalo, N. Y.
NDry	Southworth Library, Dryden, N. Y.
NHi	New-York Historical Society, New York City
NIC	Cornell University Library, Ithaca, N. Y.
NN	New York Public Library, New York City
NNC	Columbia University Library, New York City
NNP	Pierpont Morgan Library, New York City
NRU	University of Rochester Library, Rochester, N. Y.
NSh	John Jermain Memorial Library, Sag Harbor, N. Y.
NSk	Skaneateles Library Association, Skaneateles, N. Y.
NWM	U. S. Military Academy Library, West Point, N. Y.
NbO	Omaha Public Library, Omaha, Nebr.
NcGu	Guilford College Library, Guilford, N. C.
NhExP	Phillips Exeter Academy, Exeter, N. H.
NjP	Princeton University Library, Princeton, N. J.
OCHP	Historical and Philosophical Society of Ohio, Cincinnati, Ohio
OClCS	Case Institute of Technology, Cleveland, Ohio
OClWHi	Western Reserve Historical Society, Cleveland, Ohio
OFH	Hayes Memorial Library, Fremont, Ohio
OMC	Marietta College Library, Marietta, Ohio
ORB	Oliver R. Barrett Collection, Chicago, Ill.*
OSHi	Clark County Historical Society, Springfield, Ohio
OrHi	Oregon Historical Society, Portland, Ore.
PHC	Haverford College Library, Haverford, Pa.
PHi	Historical Society of Pennsylvania, Philadelphia, Pa.

* After the *Collected Works* was in press, the collection of the late Oliver R. Barrett was sold at auction by Parke-Bernet Galleries (Catalog 1315) on February 19-20, 1952. It has been impossible to trace all new owners of the more than two hundred items, and impracticable to change the source citations for those which are known, but many of the more important items went to such well-known collections as those in the Library of Congress (Debates Scrapbook, purchased for the Alfred Whital Stern Collection) and Illinois State Historical Library (letters to Joshua F. Speed, etc.).

PMA	Allegheny College Library, Meadville, Pa.
PP	Free Library of Philadelphia, Philadelphia, Pa.
PPDrop	Dropsie College Library, Philadelphia, Pa.
PSt	Pennsylvania State College Library, State College, Pa.
PU	University of Pennsylvania Library, Philadelphia, Pa.
RPAB	Annmary Brown Memorial Library, Providence, R. I.
RPB	Brown University Library, Providence, R. I.
THaroL	Lincoln Memorial University, Harrogate, Tenn.
THi	Tennessee Historical Society, Nashville, Tenn.
ViU	University of Virginia Library, Charlottesville, Va.
VtU	University of Vermont Library, Burlington, Vt.
WBeloHi	Beloit Historical Society, Beloit, Wis.
WHi	State Historical Society of Wisconsin, Madison, Wis.
WvU	West Virginia University Library, Morgantown, W. Va.

Courtesy of Frederick Hill Meserve

OCTOBER 4, 1859 (*c.*)
By Alexander Hesler

THE COLLECTED WORKS OF

ABRAHAM LINCOLN

THE COLLECTED WORKS OF
ABRAHAM LINCOLN

First Debate with Stephen A. Douglas at Ottawa, Illinois[1]

August 21, 1858

First joint debate:—August 21– 1858, at Ottawa, Illinois. Senator Douglas' two speeches taken from the Chicago Times; Mr. Lincoln's, from the Press & Tribune.[2]

MR. DOUGLAS' SPEECH.

Ladies and gentlemen: I appear before you to-day for the purpose of discussing the leading political topics which now agitate the public mind. By an arrangement between Mr. Lincoln and myself, we are present here to-day for the purpose of having a joint discussion as the representatives of the two great political parties of the State and Union, upon the principles in issue between these parties and this vast concourse of people, shows the deep feeling which pervades the public mind in regard to the questions dividing us.

Prior to 1854 this country was divided into two great political parties, known as the Whig and Democratic parties. Both were national and patriotic, advocating principles that were universal in their application. An old line Whig could proclaim his principles in Louisiana and Massachusetts alike. Whig principles had no boundary sectional line, they were not limited by the Ohio river, nor by the Potomac, nor by the line of the free and slave States, but applied and were proclaimed wherever the Constitution ruled or the American flag waved over the American soil. (Hear him, and three cheers.) So it was, and so it is with the

[1] Debates Scrapbook, ORB. Although Lincoln deleted cheering and interruptions throughout the scrapbook, the editors have retained these deleted portions. Lincoln's corrections and insertions are indicated in footnotes. Typographical errors not corrected in the scrapbook have been corrected by the editors. All brackets are in the source.

[2] Lincoln's prefatory note in the debates scrapbook.

great Democratic party, which, from the days of Jefferson until this period, has proven itself to be the historic party of this nation. While the Whig and Democratic parties differed in regard to a bank, the tariff, distribution, the specie circular and the sub-treasury, they agreed on the great slavery question which now agitates the Union. I say that the Whig party and the Democratic party agreed on this slavery question while they differed on those matters of expediency to which I have referred. The Whig party and the Democratic party jointly adopted the Compromise measures of 1850 as the basis of a proper and just solution of this slavery question in all its forms. Clay was the great leader, with Webster on his right and Cass on his left, and sustained by the patriots in the Whig and Democratic ranks, who had devised and enacted the Compromise measures of 1850.

In 1851, the Whig party and the Democratic party united in Illinois in adopting resolutions endorsing and approving the principles of the compromise measures of 1850, as the proper adjustment of that question. In 1852, when the Whig party assembled in Convention at Baltimore for the purpose of nominating a candidate for the Presidency, the first thing it did was to declare the compromise measures of 1850, in substance and in principle, a suitable adjustment of that question. (Here the speaker was interrupted by loud and long continued applause.) My friends, silence will be more acceptable to me in the discussion of these questions than applause. I desire to address myself to your judgment, your understanding, and your consciences, and not to your passions or your enthusiasm. When the Democratic convention assembled in Baltimore in the same year, for the purpose of nominating a Democratic candidate for the Presidency, it also adopted the compromise measures of 1850 as the basis of Democratic action. Thus you see that up to 1853-'54, the Whig party and the Democratic party both stood on the same platform with regard to the slavery question. That platform was the right of the people of each State and each Territory to decide their local and domestic institutions for themselves, subject only to the federal constitution.

During the session of Congress of 1853-'54, I introduced into the Senate of the United States a bill to organize the Territories of Kansas and Nebraska on that principle which had been adopted in the compromise measures of 1850, approved by the Whig party and the Democratic party in Illinois in 1851, and endorsed by the Whig party and the Democratic party in national convention in 1852. In order that there might be no misunderstanding in relation to the principle involved in the Kansas and Nebraska bill, I put forth the true intent and meaning of the act in these words: "It is the true intent and meaning of this act not to legislate slavery into any State or Territory, or to exclude it therefrom, but to leave the people thereof perfectly free to form and regulate their domestic institutions in their own way, subject only to the federal constitution." Thus, you see, that up to 1854, when the Kansas and Nebraska bill was brought into Congress for the purpose of carrying out the principles which both parties had up to that time endorsed and approved, there had been no division in this country in regard to that principle except the opposition of the abolitionists. In the House of Representatives of the Illinois Legislature, upon a resolution asserting that principle, every Whig and every Democrat in the House voted in the affirmative, and only four men voted against it, and those four were old line Abolitionists. (Cheers.)

In 1854, Mr. Abraham Lincoln and Mr. Trumbull entered into an arrangement, one with the other, and each with his respective friends, to dissolve the old Whig party on the one hand, and to dissolve the old Democratic party on the other, and to connect the members of both into an Abolition party under the name and disguise of a Republican party. (Laughter and cheers, hurrah for Douglas.) The terms of that arrangement between Mr. Lincoln and Mr. Trumbull have been published to the world by Mr. Lincoln's special friend, James H. Matheny, Esq., and they were that Lincoln should have Shields' place in the U.S. Senate, which was then about to become vacant, and that Trumbull should have my seat when my term expired. (Great laughter.) Lincoln went to work to abolitionize the Old Whig party all over the State, pretending that he was then as good a Whig as ever; (laughter) and Trumbull went to work in his part of the State preaching Abolitionism in its milder and lighter form, and trying to abolitionize the Democratic party, and bring old Democrats handcuffed and bound hand and foot into the Abolition camp. ("Good," "hurrah for Douglas," and cheers.) In pursuance of the arrangement, the parties met at Springfield in October, 1854, and proclaimed their new platform. Lincoln was to bring into the Abolition camp the old line Whigs, and transfer them over to Giddings, Chase, Ford, Douglass and Parson Lovejoy,[3] who were ready to receive them and christen them in their new faith. (Laughter and cheers.) They laid down on that occasion a platform for their new Republican party, which was to be thus constructed. I have the resolutions of their State convention then held, which was the first

[3] Joshua R. Giddings, U.S. representative from Ohio, and Thomas H. Ford, Ohio Know-Nothing and Abolitionist, have not been previously identified.

mass State Convention ever held in Illinois by the Black Republican party, and I now hold them in my hands and will read a part of them, and cause the others to be printed. Here is the most important and material resolution of this Abolition platform.

1. *Resolved,* That we believe this truth to be self-evident, that when parties become subversive of the ends for which they are established, or incapable of restoring the government to the true principles of the constitution, it is the right and duty of the people to dissolve the political bands by which they may have been connected therewith, and to organize new parties upon such principles and with such views as the circumstances and exigencies of the nation may demand.

2. *Resolved,* That the times imperatively demand the reorganization of parties, and repudiating all previous party attachments, names and predilections, we unite ourselves together in defence of the liberty and constitution of the country, and will hereafter co-operate as the Republican party, pledged to the accomplishment of the following purposes: to bring the administration of the government back to the control of first principles; to restore Nebraska and Kansas to the position of free territories; that, as the constitution of the United States, vests in the States, and not in Congress, the power to legislate for the extradition of fugitives from labor, to repeal and entirely abrogate the fugitive slave law; to restrict slavery to those States in which it exists; to prohibit the admission of any more slave States into the Union; to abolish slavery in the District of Columbia; to exclude slavery from all the territories over which the general government has exclusive jurisdiction; and to resist the acquirements of any more territories unless the practice of slavery therein forever shall have been prohibited.

3. *Resolved,* That in furtherance of these principles we will use such constitutional and lawful means as shall seem best adapted to their accomplishment, and that we will support no man for office, under the general or State government, who is not positively and fully committed to the support of these principles, and whose personal character and conduct is not a guaranty that he is reliable, and who shall not have abjured old party allegiance and ties.

(The resolutions, as they were read, were cheered throughout.)

Now, gentlemen, your Black Republicans have cheered every one of those propositions, ("good and cheers,") and yet I venture to say that you cannot get Mr. Lincoln to come out and say that he is now in favor of each one of them. (Laughter and applause. "Hit him again.") That these propositions, one and all, constitute the platform of the Black Republican party of this day, I have no doubt, ("good") and when you were not aware for what purpose I was reading them, your Black Republicans cheered them as good Black Republican doctrines. ("That's it," etc.) My object in reading these resolutions, was to put the question to Abraham Lincoln this day, whether he now stands and will stand by each article in that creed and carry it out. ("Good." "Hit him again.") I desire to know whether Mr. Lincoln to-day stands as he did in 1854, in favor of the unconditional repeal of the fugitive slave law. I desire him to answer whether he stands pledged to-day, as he did in 1854, against the admission of any more slave States into the Union, even if the people want them. I want to know whether he stands pledged against the admission of a new State into the Union with such a constitution as the people of that State may see fit to make. ("That's it;" "put it at him.") I want to know whether he stands to-day pledged to the abolition of slavery in the District of Columbia. I desire him to answer whether he stands pledged to the prohibition of the slave trade between the different States. ("He does.") I desire to know whether he stands pledged to prohibit slavery in all the territories of the United States, North as well as South of the Missouri Compromise line, ("Kansas too.") I desire him to answer whether he is opposed to the acquisition of any more territory unless slavery is first prohibited therein. I want his answer to these questions. Your affirmative cheers in favor of this Abolition platform is not satisfactory. I ask Abraham Lincoln to answer these questions, in order that when I trot him down to lower Egypt I may put the same questions to him. (Enthusiastic applause.) My principles are the same everywhere. (Cheers, and "hark.") I can proclaim them alike in the North, the South, the East, and the West. My principles will apply wherever the Constitution prevails and the American flag waves. ("Good," and applause.) I desire to know whether Mr. Lincoln's principles will bear transplanting from Ottawa to Jonesboro? I put these questions to him to-day distinctly, and ask an answer. I have a right to an answer ("that's so," "he can't dodge you," etc.), for I quote from the platform of the Republican party, made by himself and others at the time that party was formed, and the bargain made by Lincoln to dissolve and kill the old Whig party, and transfer its members, bound hand and foot, to the Abolition party, under the direction of Giddings and Fred Douglass. (Cheers.) In the remarks I have made on this platform, and the position of Mr. Lincoln upon it, I mean nothing personally disrespectful or unkind to that gentleman. I have known him for nearly twenty-five years. There were many points of sympathy between us when we first got acquainted. We were both comparatively boys, and both struggling with poverty in a strange land. I was a school-teacher in the town of Winchester, and he a flourishing grocery-keeper in the town of Salem. (Applause and laughter.) He was more successful in his occupation than I was in mine, and hence more fortunate in this world's goods. Lincoln is one of those peculiar men who perform with admirable skill everything which they undertake. I made as good a school-teacher as I could and when a cabinet maker I made a good bedstead and tables, although my old boss said I succeeded better with bureaus and secretaries than anything else; (cheers,) but I believe that Lincoln was always more successful in business than I, for his business enabled him to get into the Legislature. I met him there, however, and had a sympathy with him, because of the up hill struggle we both had in life. He was then just as good at telling an anecdote as now. ("No doubt.") He could beat any of the boys wrestling, or running a foot race, in pitching quoits or tossing a copper, could ruin more liquor than all the boys of the town together, (uproarious laughter,) and the dignity and impartiality with which he presided at a horse race or fist fight, excited the admiration and won the praise of everybody that was present and participated. (Renewed laughter.) I sympathised with him, because he was struggling with difficulties and so was I. Mr. Lincoln served with me in the Legislature in 1836, when we both retired, and he subsided, or became submerged, and he was lost sight of as a public man for some years. In 1846, when Wilmot introduced his celebrated proviso, and the Abolition tornado swept over the country, Lincoln again turned up as a member of Congress from the Sangamon district. I was then in the Senate of the United States, and was glad to welcome my old friend and companion. Whilst in Congress, he distinguished himself by his opposition to the Mexican war, taking the side of the common enemy against his own country; ("that's true,") and when he returned home he found that the indignation of the people followed him everywhere, and he was again submerged or obliged to retire into private life, forgotten by his former friends. ("And will be again.") He came up again in 1854, just in time to make this Abolition or Black Republican platform, in company with Giddings, Lovejoy, Chase, and Fred Douglass for the Republican party to stand upon. (Laughter, "Hit him again," &c.) Trumbull, too, was one of our own contemporaries. He was born and raised in old Connecticut, was bred a federalist, but removing to Georgia, turned nullifier when nullification was popular, and as soon as he disposed of his clocks and wound up his business, migrated to Illinois, (laughter,) turned politician and lawyer here, and made his appearance in 1841, as a member of the Legislature. He became noted as the author of the scheme to repudiate a large portion of the State debt of Illinois, which, if successful, would have brought infamy and disgrace upon the fair escutcheon of our glorious State. The odium attached to that measure consigned him to oblivion for a time. I helped to do it. I walked into a public meeting in the hall of the House of Representatives and replied to his repudiating speeches, and resolutions were carried over his head denouncing repudiation, and asserting the moral and legal obligation of Illinois to pay every dollar of the debt she owed and every bond that bore her seal. ("Good," and cheers.) Trumbull's malignity has followed me since I thus defeated his infamous scheme.

These two men having formed this combination to abolitionize the old Whig party and the old Democratic party, and put themselves into the Senate of the United States, in pursuance of their bargain, are now carrying out that arrangement. Matheny states that Trumbull broke faith; that the bargain was that Lincoln should be the Senator in Shields' place, and Trumbull was to wait for mine; (laughter and cheers,) and the story goes, that Trumbull cheated Lincoln, having control of four or five abolitionized Democrats who were holding over in the Senate; he would not let them vote for Lincoln, and which obliged the rest of the Abolitionists to support him in order to secure an Abolition Senator. There are a number of authorities for the truth of this besides Matheny, and I suppose that even Mr. Lincoln will not deny it. (Applause and laughter.)

Mr. Lincoln demands that he shall have the place intended for Trumbull, as Trumbull cheated him and got his, and Trumbull is stumping the State traducing me for the purpose of securing that position for Lincoln, in order to quiet him. ("Lincoln can never get it, &c.") It was in consequence of this arrangement that the Republican Convention was empanelled to instruct for Lincoln and nobody else, and it was on this account that they passed resolutions that he was their first, their last, and their only choice. Archy Williams was nowhere, Browning was nobody, Wentworth was not to be considered, they had no man in the Republican party for the place except Lincoln, for the reason that he demanded that they should carry out the arrangement. ("Hit him again.")

Having formed this new party for the benefit of deserters from Whiggery, and deserters from Democracy, and having laid down the Abolition platform which I have read, Lincoln now takes his stand and proclaims his Abolition doctrines. Let me read a part of them. In his speech at Springfield to the convention which nominated him for the Senate, he said:

In my opinion it will not cease until a crisis shall have been reached and passed. "A house divided against itself cannot stand." I believe this

Government *cannot endure permanently half Slave and half Free.* I do not expect the Union to be dissolved—I do not expect the house to fall—*but I do expect it will cease to be divided.* It will become all one thing, or all the other. Either the opponents of Slavery *will arrest the further spread of it,* and place it where the public mind shall rest in the belief *that it is in the course of ultimate extinction;* or its advocates *will push it forward till it shall become alike lawful in all the States*—old as well as new, North as well as South.

("Good," "good," and cheers.)

I am delighted to hear you Black Republicans say "good." (Laughter and cheers.) I have no doubt that doctrine expresses your sentiments ("hit them again," "that's it,") and I will prove to you now, if you will listen to me, that it is revolutionary and destructive of the existence of this Government. ("Hurrah for Douglas," "good," and cheers.) Mr. Lincoln, in the extract from which I have read, says that this Government cannot endure permanently in the same condition in which it was made by its framers—divided into free and slave States. He says that it has existed for about seventy years thus divided, and yet he tells you that it cannot endure permanently on the same principles and in the same relative condition in which our fathers made it. ("Neither can it.") Why can it not exist divided into free and slave States? Washington, Jefferson, Franklin, Madison, Hamilton, Jay, and the great men of that day, made this Government divided into free States and slave States, and left each State perfectly free to do as it pleased on the subject of slavery. ("Right, right.") Why can it not exist on the same principles on which our fathers made it? ("It can.") They knew when they framed the Constitution that in a country as wide and broad as this, with such a variety of climate, production and interest, the people necessarily required different laws and institutions in different localities. They knew that the laws and regulations which would suit the granite hills of New Hampshire would be unsuited to the rice plantations of South Carolina, ("right, right,") and they, therefore, provided that each State should retain its own Legislature, and its own sovereignty with the full and complete power to do as it pleased within its own limits, in all that was local and not national. (Applause.) One of the reserved rights of the States, was the right to regulate the relations between Master and Servant, on the slavery question. At the time the Constitution was formed, there were thirteen States in the Union, twelve of which were slaveholding States and one a free State. Suppose this doctrine of uniformity preached by Mr. Lincoln, that the States should all be free or all be slave had prevailed and what would have been the result? Of course, the twelve slaveholding States would have overruled the one free State, and slavery would have been fastened by a Constitutional provision on every inch of the American Republic, instead of being left as our fathers wisely left it, to each State to decide for itself. ("Good, good," and three cheers for Douglas.) Here I assert that uniformity in the local laws and institutions of the different States is neither possible or desirable. If uniformity had been adopted when the government was established, it must inevitably have been the uniformity of slavery everywhere, or else the uniformity of negro citizenship and negro equality everywhere.

We are told by Lincoln that he is utterly opposed to the Dred Scott decision, and will not submit to it, for the reason that he says it deprives the negro of the rights and privileges of citizenship. (Laughter and applause.) That is the first and main reason which he assigns for his warfare on the Supreme Court of the United States and its decision. I ask you, are you in favor of conferring upon the negro the rights and privileges of citizenship? ("No, no.") Do you desire to strike out of our State Constitution that clause which keeps slaves and free negroes out of the State, and allow the free negroes to flow in, ("never,") and cover your prairies with black settlements? Do you desire to turn this beautiful State into a free negro colony, ("no, no,") in order that when Missouri abolishes slavery she can send one hundred thousand emancipated slaves into Illinois, to become citizens and voters, on an equality with yourselves? ("Never," "no.") If you desire negro citizenship, if you desire to allow them to come into the State and settle with the white man, if you desire them to vote on an equality with yourselves, and to make them eligible to office, to serve on juries, and to adjudge your rights, then support Mr. Lincoln and the Black Republican party, who are in favor of the citizenship of the negro. ("Never, never.") For one, I am opposed to negro citizenship in any and every form. (Cheers.) I believe this government was made on the white basis. ("Good.") I believe it was made by white men, for the benefit of white men and their posterity for ever, and I am in favor of confining citizenship to white men, men of European birth and descent, instead of conferring it upon negroes, Indians and other inferior races. ("Good for you." "Douglas forever.")

Mr. Lincoln, following the example and lead of all the little Abolition orators, who go around and lecture in the basements of schools and churches, reads from the Declaration of Independence, that all men were created equal, and then asks how can you deprive a negro of that equality which God and the Declaration of Independence awards to him. He and they maintain that negro equality is guarantied by the laws of God, and that it is asserted in the Declaration of Independence. If they think so, of course they have a right to say so, and so vote. I do not question Mr. Lincoln's conscientious belief that the negro was made his equal, and hence is his brother, (laughter,) but for my own part, I do not regard the negro as my equal, and positively deny that he is my brother or any kin to me whatever. ("Never." "Hit him again," and cheers.) Lincoln has evidently learned by heart Parson Lovejoy's catechism. (Laughter and applause.) He can repeat it as well as Farnsworth,[4] and he is worthy of a medal from father Giddings and Fred Douglass for his Abolitionism. (Laughter.) He holds that the negro was born his equal and yours, and that he was endowed with equality by the Almighty, and that no human law can deprive him of these rights which were guarantied to him by the Supreme ruler of the Universe. Now, I do not believe that the Almighty ever intended the negro to be the equal of the white man. ("Never, never.") If he did, he has been a long time demonstrating the fact. (Cheers.) For thousands of years the negro has been a race upon the earth, and during all that time, in all latitudes and climates, wherever he has wandered or been taken, he has been inferior to the race which he has there met. He belongs to an inferior race, and must always occupy an inferior position. ("Good," "that's so," &c.) I do not hold that because the negro is our inferior that therefore he ought to be a slave. By no means can such a conclusion be drawn from what I have said. On the contrary, I hold that humanity and christianity both require that the negro shall have and enjoy every right, every privilege, and every immunity consistent with the safety of the society in which he lives. (That's so.) On that point, I presume, there can be no diversity of opinion. You and I are bound to extend to our inferior and dependent being every right, every privilege, every facility and immunity consistent with the public good. The question then arises what rights and privileges are consistent with the public good. This is a question which each State and each Territory must decide for itself—Illinois has decided it for herself. We have provided that the negro shall not be a slave, and we have also provided that he shall not be a citizen, but protect him in his civil rights, in his life, his person and his property, only depriving him of all political rights whatsoever, and refusing to put him on an equality with the white man. ("Good.") That policy of Illinois is satisfactory to the Democratic party and to me, and if it were to the Republicans,

[4] U.S. Representative John F. Farnsworth of Chicago.

there would then be no question upon the subject; but the Republicans say that he ought to be made a citizen, and when he becomes a citizen he becomes your equal, with all your rights and privileges. ("He never shall.") They assert the Dred Scott decision to be monstrous because it denies that the negro is or can be a citizen under the Constitution. Now, I hold that Illinois had a right to abolish and prohibit slavery as she did, and I hold that Kentucky has the same right to continue and protect slavery that Illinois had to abolish it. I hold that New York had as much right to abolish slavery as Virginia has to continue it, and that each and every State of this Union is a sovereign power, with the right to do as it pleases upon this question of slavery, and upon all its domestic institutions. Slavery is not the only question which comes up in this controversy. There is a far more important one to you, and that is, what shall be done with the free negro? We have settled the slavery question as far as we are concerned; we have prohibited it in Illinois forever, and in doing so, I think we have done wisely, and there is no man in the State who would be more strenuous in his opposition to the introduction of slavery than I would; (cheers) but when we settled it for ourselves, we exhausted all our power over that subject. We have done our whole duty, and can do no more. We must leave each and every other State to decide for itself the same question. In relation to the policy to be pursued towards the free negroes, we have said that they shall not vote; whilst Maine, on the other hand, has said that they shall vote. Maine is a sovereign State, and has the power to regulate the qualifications of voters within her limits. I would never consent to confer the right of voting and of citizenship upon a negro, but still I am not going to quarrel with Maine for differing from me in opinion. Let Maine take care of her own negroes and fix the qualifications of her own voters to suit herself, without interfering with Illinois, and Illinois will not interfere with Maine. So with the State of New York. She allows the negro to vote provided he owns two hundred and fifty dollars' worth of property, but not otherwise. While I would not make any distinction whatever between a negro who held property and one who did not; yet if the sovereign State of New York chooses to make that distinction it is her business and not mine, and I will not quarrel with her for it. She can do as she pleases on this question if she minds her own business, and we will do the same thing. Now, my friends, if we will only act conscientiously and rigidly upon this great principle of popular sovereignty which guarantees to each State and Territory the right to do as it pleases on all things local and domestic instead of Congress interfering, we will continue at peace one with another. Why should Illinois be at war with Missouri, or Kentucky with Ohio, or Virginia with New York, merely because their institutions differ? Our fathers intended that our institutions should differ. They knew that the North and the South having different climates, productions and interests, required different institutions. This doctrine of Mr. Lincoln's of uniformity among the institutions of the different States is a new doctrine, never dreamed of by Washington, Madison, or the framers of this Government. Mr. Lincoln and the Republican party set themselves up as wiser than these men who made this government, which has flourished for seventy years under the principle of popular sovereignty, recognizing the right of each State to do as it pleased. Under that principle, we have grown from a nation of three or four millions to a nation of about thirty millions of people; we have crossed the Allegheny mountains and filled up the whole North West, turning the prairie into a garden, and building up churches and schools, thus spreading civilization and christianity where before there was nothing but savage-barbarism. Under that principle we have become from a feeble nation, the most powerful on the face of the earth, and if we only adhere to that principle, we can go forward increasing in territory, in power, in strength and in glory until the Republic of America shall be the North Star that shall guide the friends of freedom throughout the civilized world. ("Long may you live," and great applause.) And why can we not adhere to the great principle of self-government, upon which our institutions were originally based. ("We can.") I believe that this new doctrine preached by Mr. Lincoln and his party will dissolve the Union if it succeeds. They are trying to array all the Northern States in one body against the South, to excite a sectional war between the free States and the slave States, in order that the one or the other may be driven to the wall.

I am told that my time is out. Mr. Lincoln will now address you for an hour and a half, and I will then occupy a half hour in replying to him. (Three times three cheers were here given for Douglas.)

MR. LINCOLN'S REPLY.

Mr. Lincoln then came forward and was greeted with loud and protracted cheers from fully two-thirds of the audience. This was admitted by the Douglas men on the platform. It was some minutes before he could make himself heard, even by those on the stand. At last he said:

MY FELLOW-CITIZENS: When a man hears himself somewhat misrepresented, it provokes him—at least, I find it so with myself; but when the misrepresentation becomes very gross and palpable, it is more apt to amuse him. [Laughter.] The first thing I see fit to notice, is the fact that Judge Douglas alleges, after running through the history of the old Democratic and the old Whig parties, that Judge Trumbull and myself made an arrangement in 1854, by which I was to have the place of Gen. Shields in the United States Senate, and Judge Trumbull was to have the place of Judge Douglas. Now all I have to say upon that subject is, that I think no man—not even Judge Douglas—can prove it, *because it is not true*. [Cheers.] I have no doubt he is "*conscientious*" in saying it. [Laughter.] As to those resolutions that he took such a length of time to read, as being the platform of the Republican party in 1854, I say I never had anything to do with them, and I think Trumbull never had. [Renewed laughter.] Judge Douglas cannot show that either one of us ever did have any thing to do with them. I believe *this* is true about those resolutions: There was a call for a Convention to form a Republican party at Springfield, and I think that my friend Mr. Lovejoy, who is here upon this stand, had a hand in it. I think this is true, and I think if he will remember accurately, he will be able to recollect that he tried to get me into it, and I would not go in. [Cheers and laughter.] I believe it is also true, that I went away from Springfield when the Convention was in session, to attend court in Tazewell County. It is true they did place my name, though without authority, upon the Committee, and afterwards wrote me to attend the meeting of the Committee, but I refused to do so, and I never had anything to do with that organization. This is the plain truth about all that matter of the resolutions.

Now, about this story that Judge Douglas tells of Trumbull bargaining to sell out the old Democratic party, and Lincoln agreeing to sell out the old Whig party, I have the means of *knowing* about that; [laughter] Judge Douglas cannot have; and I know there is no substance to it whatever. [Applause.] Yet I have no doubt he is "*conscientious*" about it. [Laughter.] I know that after Mr. Lovejoy got into the Legislature that winter, he complained of me that I had told all the old Whigs in his district that the old Whig party was good enough for them, and some of them voted against him because I told them so. Now I have no means of totally disproving such charges as this which the Judge makes. A man cannot prove a negative, but he has a right to claim that when a man makes an affirmative charge, he must offer some proof to show the truth of what he says. I certainly cannot introduce testimony to show the negative about things, but I have a right to claim that if a man says he *knows* a thing, then he must show *how* he knows it. I always have a right to claim this, and it is not satisfactory to me that he may be "conscientious" on the subject. [Cheers and Laughter.]

Now gentlemen, I hate to waste my time on such things, but in regard to that general abolition tilt that Judge Douglas makes, when he says that I was engaged at that time in selling out and abolitionizing the old Whig party—I hope you will permit me to read a part of a printed speech that I made then at Peoria, which will show altogether a different view of the position I took in that contest of 1854.

VOICE—Put on your specs.

MR. LINCOLN—Yes, sir, I am obliged to do so. I am no longer a young man. [Laughter.]

This is the *repeal* of the Missouri Compromise.* The foregoing history may not be precisely accurate in every particular; but I am sure it is sufficiently so, for all the uses I shall attempt to make of it, and in it, we have before us, the chief materials[5] enabling us to correctly judge whether the repeal of the Missouri Compromise is right or wrong.

I think, and shall try to show, that it is wrong; wrong in its direct effect, letting slavery into Kansas and Nebraska—and wrong in its prospective principle, allowing it to spread to every other part of the wide world, where men can be found inclined to take it.

This *declared* indifference, but as I must think, covert *real* zeal for the spread of slavery, I can not but hate. I hate it because of the monstrous injustice of slavery itself. I hate it because it deprives our republican example of its just influence in the world—enables the enemies of free institutions, with plausibility, to taunt us as hypocrites—causes the real friends of freedom to doubt our sincerity, and especially because it forces so many really good men amongst ourselves into an open war with the very fundamental principles of civil liberty—criticising the Declaration of Independence, and insisting that there is no right principle of action but *self-interest.*

Before proceeding, let me say I think I have no prejudice against the Southern people. They are just what we would be in their situation. If slavery did not now exist amongst them, they would not introduce it. If it did now exist amongst us, we should not instantly give it up. This I believe of the masses north and south. Doubtless there are individuals, on both sides, who would not hold slaves under any circum-

* This extract from Mr. Lincoln's Peoria Speech of 1854, was read by him in the Ottawa debate, but was not reported fully or accurately, in either the Times or Press & Tribune. It is inserted now as necessary to a complete report of the debate. [Footnote written by Lincoln in the margin of the debates scrapbook.]

5 "Materially" corrected by Lincoln to "materials."

stances; and others who would gladly introduce slavery anew, if it were out of existence. We know that some southern men do free their slaves, go north, and become tip-top abolitionists; while some northern ones go south, and become most cruel slave-masters.

When southern people tell us they are no more responsible for the origin of slavery, than we; I acknowledge the fact. When it is said that the institution exists, and that it is very difficult to get rid of it, in any satisfactory way, I can understand and appreciate the saying. I surely will not blame them for not doing what I should not know how to do myself. If all earthly power were given me, I should not know what to do, as to the existing institution. My first impulse would be to free all the slaves, and send them to Liberia,—to their own native land. But a moment's reflection would convince me, that whatever of high hope, (as I think there is) there may be in this, in the long run, its sudden execution is impossible. If they were all landed there in a day, they would all perish in the next ten days; and there are not surplus shipping and surplus money enough in the world to carry them there in many times ten days. What then? Free them all, and keep them among us as underlings? Is it quite certain that this betters their condition? I think I would not hold one in slavery, at any rate; yet the point is not clear enough to me to denounce people upon. What[6] next? Free them, and make them politically and socially, our equals? My own feelings will not admit of this; and if mine would, we well know that those of the great mass of white people will not. Whether this feeling accords with justice and sound judgment, is not the sole question, if indeed, it is any part of it. A universal feeling, whether well or ill-founded, can not be safely disregarded. We can not, then, make them equals. It does seem to me that systems of gradual emancipation might be adopted; but for their tardiness in this, I will not undertake to judge our brethren of the south.

When they remind us of their constitutional rights, I acknowledge them, not grudgingly, but fully, and fairly; and I would give them any legislation for the reclaiming of their fugitives, which should not, in its stringency, be more likely to carry a free man into slavery, than our ordinary criminal laws are to hang an innocent one.

But all this; to my judgment, furnishes no more excuse for permitting slavery to go into our own free territory, than it would for reviving the African slave trade by law. The law which forbids the bringing of slaves *from* Africa; and that which has so long forbid the taking them *to* Nebraska, can hardly be distinguished on any moral principle; and the repeal of the former could find quite as plausible excuses as that of the latter.

I have reason to know that Judge Douglas *knows* that I said this. I think he has the answer here to one of the questions he put to me. I do not mean to allow him to catechise me unless he pays back for it in kind. I will not answer questions one after another unless he reciprocates, but as he made this inquiry and I have an-

6 "Whas" corrected by Lincoln to "What."

swered it before, he has got it without my getting anything in return. He has got my answer on the Fugitive Slave Law.

Now gentlemen, I don't want to read at any greater length, but this is the true complexion of all I have ever said in regard to the institution of slavery and the black race. This is the whole of it, and anything that argues me into his idea of perfect social and political equality with the negro, is but a specious and fantastic arrangement of words, by which a man can prove a horse chestnut to be a chestnut horse. [Laughter.] I will say here, while upon this subject, that I have no purpose directly or indirectly to interfere with the institution of slavery in the States where it exists. I believe I have no lawful right to do so, and I have no inclination to do so. I have no purpose to introduce political and social equality between the white and the black races. There is a physical difference between the two, which in my judgment will probably forever forbid their living together upon the footing of perfect equality, and inasmuch as it becomes a necessity that there must be a difference, I, as well as Judge Douglas, am in favor of the race to which I belong, having the superior position. I have never said anything to the contrary, but I hold that notwithstanding all this, there is no reason in the world why the negro is not entitled to all the natural rights enumerated in the Declaration of Independence, the right to life, liberty and the pursuit of happiness. [Loud cheers.] I hold that he is as much entitled to these as the white man. I agree with Judge Douglas he is not my equal in many respects—certainly not in color, perhaps not in moral or intellectual endowment. But in the right to eat the bread, without leave of anybody else, which his own hand earns, *he is my equal and the equal of Judge Douglas, and the equal of every living man.* [Great applause.]

Now I pass on to consider one or two more of these little follies. The Judge is wofully at fault about his early friend Lincoln being a "grocery keeper." [Laughter.] I don't know as it would be a great sin, if I had been, but he is mistaken. Lincoln never kept a grocery anywhere in the world. [Laughter.] It is true that Lincoln did work the latter part of one winter in a small still house, up at the head of a hollow. [Roars of laughter.] And so I think my friend, the Judge, is equally at fault when he charges me at the time when I was in Congress of having opposed our soldiers who were fighting in the Mexican war. The Judge did not make his charge very distinctly but I can tell you what he can prove by referring to the record. You remember I was an old Whig, and whenever the Democratic party tried to get me to vote that the war had been righteously begun by the President, I would not do it. But whenever they asked for any money, or land warrants, or anything to pay the soldiers there, during all that time, I gave the same votes that Judge Douglas did. [Loud applause.] You can think as you please as to whether that was consistent. Such is the truth; and the Judge has the right to make all he can out of it. But when he, by a general charge, conveys the idea that I withheld supplies from the soldiers who were fighting in the Mexican war, or did anything else to hinder the soldiers, he is, to say the least, grossly and altogether mistaken, as a consultation of the records will prove to him.

As I have not used up so much of my time as I had supposed, I will dwell a little longer upon one or two of these minor topics upon with the Judge has spoken. He has read from my speech in Springfield, in which I say that "a house divided against itself cannot stand." Does the Judge say it *can* stand? [Laughter.] I don't know whether he does or not. The Judge does not seem to be attending to me just now, but I would like to know if it is his opinion that a house divided against itself *can stand*. If he does, then there is a question of veracity, not between him and me, but between the Judge and an authority of a somewhat higher character. [Laughter and applause.]

Now, my friends, I ask your attention to this matter for the purpose of saying something seriously. I know that the Judge may readily enough agree with me that the maxim which was put forth by the Saviour is true, but he may allege that I misapply it; and the Judge has a right to urge that, in my application, I do misapply it, and then I have a right to show that I do *not* misapply it. When he undertakes to say that because I think this nation, so far as the question of Slavery is concerned, will all become one thing or all the other, I am in favor of bringing about a dead uniformity in the various States, in all their institutions, he argues erroneously. The great variety of the local institutions in the States, springing from differences in the soil, differences in the face of the country, and in the climate, are bonds of Union. They do not make "a house divided against itself," but they make a house united. If they produce in one section of the country what is called for by the wants of another section, and this other section can supply the wants of the first, they are not matters of discord but bonds of union, true bonds of union. But can this question of slavery be considered as among *these* varieties in the institutions of the country? I leave it to you to say whether, in the history of our government, this institution of slavery has not always failed to be a bond of union, and, on the contrary, been an apple of discord and an element of division in the house. [Cries of "Yes, yes," and applause.] I ask you to consider whether, so long as the moral constitution of men's minds shall continue to be the same, after this generation and assemblage shall sink into the grave, and another race shall arise, with the same moral and intellectual development we have—whether, if that institution is standing in the same irritating position in which it now is, it will not continue an element of division? [Cries of "Yes, yes."] If so, then I have a right to say that in regard to this question, the Union is a house divided against itself, and when the Judge reminds me that I have often said to him that the institution of slavery has existed for eighty years in some States, and yet it does not exist in some others, I agree to the fact, and I account for it by looking at the position in which our fathers originally placed it—restricting it from the new Territories where it had not gone, and legislating to cut off its source by the abrogation of the slave trade, thus putting the seal of legislation *against its spread.* The public mind *did* rest in the belief that it was in the course of ultimate extinction. [Cries of "Yes, yes."] But lately, I think—and in this I charge nothing on the Judge's motives—lately, I think, that he, and those acting with him, have placed that institution on a new basis, which looks to the *perpetuity and nationalization of slavery.* [Loud cheers.] And while it is placed upon this new basis, I say, and I have said, that I believe we shall not have peace upon the question until the opponents of slavery arrest the further spread of it, and place it where the public mind shall rest in the belief that it is in the course of ultimate extinction; or, on the other hand, that its advocates will push it forward until it shall become alike lawful in all the States, old as well as new, North as well as South. Now, I believe if we could arrest the spread, and place it where Washington, and Jefferson, and Madison placed it, it *would be* in the course of ultimate extinction, and the public mind *would,* as for eighty years past, believe that it was in the course of ultimate extinction. The crisis would be past and the institution might be let alone for a hundred years, if it should live so long, in the States where it exists, yet it would be going out of existence in the way best for both the black and the white races. [Great cheering.]

A VOICE—Then do you repudiate Popular Sovereignty?

MR. LINCOLN—Well, then, let us talk about Popular Sovereignty! [Laughter.] What is Popular Sovereignty? [Cries of "A humbug," "a humbug."] Is it the right of the people to have

Slavery or not have it, as they see fit, in the territories? I will state—and I have an able man to watch me—my understanding is that Popular Sovereignty, as now applied to the question of Slavery, does allow the people of a Territory to have Slavery if they want to, but does not allow them *not* to have it if they *do not* want it. [Applause and laughter.] I do not mean that if this vast concourse of people were in a Territory of the United States, any one of them would be obliged to have a slave if he did not want one; but I do say that, as I understand the Dred Scott decision, if any one man wants slaves, all the rest have no way of keeping that one man from holding them.

When I made my speech at Springfield, of which the Judge complains, and from which he quotes, I really was not thinking of the things which he ascribes to me at all. I had no thought in the world that I was doing anything to bring about a war between the free and slave States. I had no thought in the world that I was doing anything to bring about a political and social equality of the black and white races. It never occurred to me that I was doing anything or favoring anything to reduce to a dead uniformity all the local institutions of the various States. But I must say, in all fairness to him, if he thinks I am doing something which leads to these bad results, it is none the better that I did not mean it. It is just as fatal to the country, if I have any influence in producing it, whether I intend it or not. But can it be true, that placing this institution upon the original basis—the basis upon which our fathers placed it—can have any tendency to set the Northern and the Southern States at war with one another, or that it can have any tendency to make the people of Vermont raise sugar cane, because they raise it in Louisiana, or that it can compel the people of Illinois to cut pine logs on the Grand Prairie, where they will not grow, because they cut pine logs in Maine, where they do grow? [Laughter.] The Judge says this is a new principle started in regard to this question. Does the Judge claim that he is working on the plan of the founders of government? I think he says in some of his speeches—indeed I have one here now—that he saw evidence of a policy to allow slavery to be south of a certain line, while north of it it should be excluded, and he saw an indisposition on the part of the country to stand upon that policy, and therefore he set about studying the subject upon *original principles*, and upon *original principles* he got up the Nebraska bill! I am fighting it upon these "original principles"—fighting it in the Jeffersonian, Washingtonian, and Madisonian fashion. [Laughter and applause.]

Now my friends I wish you to attend for a little while to one or two other things in that Springfield speech. My main object was to show, so far as my humble ability was capable of showing to the people of this country, what I believed was the truth—that there was a *tendency*, if not a conspiracy among those who have engineered this slavery question for the last four or five years, to make slavery perpetual and universal in this nation. Having made that speech principally for that object, after arranging the evidences that I thought tended to prove my proposition, I concluded with this bit of comment:

> We cannot absolutely know that these exact adaptations are the result of pre-concert, but when we see a lot of framed timbers, different portions of which we know have been gotten out at different times and places, and by different workmen—Stephen, Franklin, Roger and James, for instance—and when we see these timbers joined together, and see they exactly make the frame of a house or a mill, all the tenons and mortices exactly fitting and all the lengths and proportions of the different pieces exactly adapted to their respective places and not a piece too many or too few—not omitting even the scaffolding—or if a single piece be lacking we see the place in the frame exactly fitted and prepared yet to bring such piece in—in such a case we feel it impossible not to believe that Stephen and Franklin, and Roger and James, all understood one another from the beginning, and all worked upon a common plan or draft drawn before the first blow was struck. [Great cheers.]

When my friend, Judge Douglas, came to Chicago, on the 9th of July, this speech having been delivered on the 16th of June, he made an harangue there, in which he took hold of this speech of mine, showing that he had carefully read it; and while he paid no attention to *this* matter at all, but complimented me as being a "kind, amiable, and intelligent gentleman," notwithstanding I had said this; he goes on and eliminates, or draws out, from my speech this tendency of mine to set the States at war with one another, to make all the institutions uniform, and set the niggers and white people to marrying together. [Laughter.] Then, as the Judge had complimented me with these pleasant titles, (I must confess to my weakness,) I was a little "taken," [laughter] for it came from a great man. I was not very much accustomed to flattery, and it came the sweeter to me. I was rather like the Hoosier, with the gingerbread, when he said he reckoned he loved it better than any other man, and got less of it. [Roars of laughter.] As the Judge had so flattered me, I could not make up my mind that he meant to deal unfairly with me; so I went to work to show him that he misunderstood the whole scope of my speech, and that I really never intended to set the people at war with one another. As an illustration, the next time I met him, which was at Springfield, I used this expression, that I claimed no right under the Constitution, nor had I any inclination, to enter into the Slave States and interfere with the institutions of slavery. He says upon that: Lincoln will not enter into the Slave States, but will go to the banks of the Ohio, on this side, and shoot over! [Laughter.] He runs on, step by step, in the horse-chestnut style of argument, until in the Springfield speech, he says, "Unless he shall be successful in firing his batteries until he shall have extinguished slavery in all the States, the Union shall be dissolved." Now I don't think that was exactly the way to treat a kind, amiable, intelligent gentleman. [Roars of laughter.] I know if I had asked the Judge to show when or where it was I had said that, if I didn't succeed in firing into the Slave States until slavery should be extinguished, the Union should be dissolved, he could not have shown it. I understand what he would do. He would say, "I don't mean to quote from you, but this was the *result* of what you say." But I have the right to ask, and I do ask now, Did you not put it in such a form that an ordinary reader or listener would take it as an expression *from me*? [Laughter.]

In a speech at Springfield, on the night of the 17th, I thought I might as well attend to my own business a little, and I recalled his attention as well as I could to this charge of conspiracy to nationalize Slavery. I called his attention to the fact that he had acknowledged, in my hearing twice, that he had carefully read the speech, and, in the language of the lawyers, as he had twice read the speech, and still had put in no plea or answer, I took a default on him. I insisted that I had a right then to renew that charge of conspiracy. Ten days afterwards, I met the Judge at Clinton—that is to say, I was on the ground, but not in the discussion—and heard him make a speech. Then he comes in with his plea to this charge, for the first time, and his plea when put in, as well as I can recollect it, amounted to this: that he never had any talk with Judge Taney or the President of the United States with regard to the Dred Scott decision before it was made. I (Lincoln) ought to know that the man who makes a charge without knowing it to be true, falsifies as much as he who knowingly tells a falsehood; and lastly, that he would pronounce the whole thing a falsehood; but he would make no personal application of the charge of falsehood, not because of any regard for the "kind, amiable, intelligent gentleman," but because of his own personal self-respect! [Roars of laughter.] I have understood since then, (but [turning to Judge

Douglas] will not hold the Judge to it if he is not willing) that he has broken through the "self-respect," and has got to saying the thing *out*. The Judge nods to me that it is so. [Laughter.] It is fortunate for me that I can keep as good-humored as I do, when the Judge acknowledges that he has been trying to make a question of veracity with me. I know the Judge is a great man, while I am only a small man, but *I feel that I have got him.* [Tremendous cheering.] I demur to that plea. I waive all objections that it was not filed till after default was taken, and demur to it upon the merits. What if Judge Douglas never did talk with Chief Justice Taney and the President, before the Dred Scott decision was made, does it follow that he could not have had as perfect an understanding without talking, as with it? I am not disposed to stand upon my legal advantage. I am disposed to take his denial as being like an answer in chancery, that he neither had any knowledge, information or belief in the existence of such a conspiracy. I am disposed to take his answer as being as broad as though he had put it in these words. And now, I ask, even if he has done so, have not I a right to *prove it on him*, and to offer the evidence of more than two witnesses, by whom to prove it; and if the evidence proves the existence of the conspiracy, does his broad answer denying all knowledge, information, or belief, disturb the fact? It can only show that he was *used* by conspirators, and was not a *leader* of them. [Vociferous cheering.]

Now in regard to his reminding me of the moral rule that persons who tell what they do not know to be true, falsify as much as those who knowingly tell falsehoods. I remember the rule, and it must be borne in mind that in what I have read to you, I do not say that I *know* such a conspiracy to exist. To that, I reply *I believe it*. If the Judge says that I do *not* believe it, then *he* says what *he* does not know, and falls within his own rule, that he who asserts a thing which he does not know to be true, falsifies as much as he who knowingly tells a falsehood. I want to call your attention to a little discussion on that branch of the case, and the evidence which brought my mind to the conclusion which I expressed as my *belief*. If, in arraying that evidence, I had stated anything which was false or erroneous, it needed but that Judge Douglas should point it out, and I would have taken it back with all the kindness in the world. I do not deal in that way. If I have brought forward anything not a fact, if he will point it out, it will not even ruffle me to take it back. But if he will not point out anything erroneous in the evidence, is it not rather for him to show, by a comparison of the evidence that I have *reasoned* falsely, than to call the "kind, amiable, intelligent gentleman," a liar? [Cheers and laughter.] If I have reasoned to a false conclusion, it is the vocation of an able debater to show by argument that I have wandered to an erroneous conclusion. I want to ask your attention to a portion of the Nebraska Bill, which Judge Douglas has quoted: "It being the true intent and meaning of this act, not to legislate slavery into any Territory or State, nor to exclude it therefrom, but to leave the people thereof perfectly free to form and regulate their domestic institutions in their own way, subject only to the Constitution of the United States." Thereupon Judge Douglas and others began to argue in favor of "Popular Sovereignty"—the right of the people to have slaves if they wanted them, and to exclude slavery if they did not want them. "But," said, in substance, a Senator from Ohio, (Mr. Chase, I believe,) "we more than suspect that you do not mean to allow the people to exclude slavery if they wish to, and if you do mean it, accept an amendment which I propose expressly authorizing the people to exclude slavery." I believe I have the amendment here before me, which was offered, and under which the people of the Territory, through their proper representatives, might if they saw fit, prohibit the existence of slavery thereïn. And now I state it as a *fact*, to be taken back if there is any mistake about it, that Judge Douglas and those acting with him, *voted that amendment down.* [Tremendous applause.] I now think that those men who voted it down, had a *real reason* for doing so. They know what that reason was. It looks to us, since we have seen the Dred Scott decision pronounced holding that "under the Constitution" the people cannot exclude slavery—I say it looks to outsiders, poor, simple, "amiable, intelligent gentlemen," [great laughter,] as though the niche was left as a place to put that Dred Scott decision in—[laughter and cheers]—a niche which would have been spoiled by adopting the amendment. And now, I say again, if *this* was not the reason, it will avail the Judge much more to calmly and good-humoredly point out to these people what that *other* reason was for voting the amendment down, than, swelling himself up, to vociferate that he may be provoked to call somebody a liar. [Tremendous applause.]

Again: there is in that same quotation from the Nebraska bill this clause—"It being the true intent and meaning of this bill not to legislate slavery into any Territory or *State*." I have always been puzzled to know what business the word "State" had in that connection. Judge Douglas knows. *He put it there.* He knows what he put it there for. We outsiders cannot say what he put it there for. The law they were passing was not about States, and was not making provisions for States. What was it placed there for? After seeing the Dred Scott decision, which holds that the people cannot exclude slavery from a *Territory*, if another Dred Scott decision shall come, holding that they cannot exclude it from a *State*, we shall discover that when the word was originally put there, it was in view of something which was to come in due time, we shall see that it was the *other half* of something. [Applause.] I now say again, if there is any different reason for putting it there, Judge Douglas, in a good-humored way, without calling anybody a liar, *can tell what the reason was.* [Renewed cheers.]

When the Judge spoke at Clinton, he came very near making a charge of falsehood against me. He used, as I found it printed in a newspaper, which I remember was very nearly like the real speech, the following language:

> I did not answer the charge [of conspiracy] before, for the reason that I did not suppose there was a man in America with a heart so corrupt as to believe such a charge could be true. I have too much respect for Mr. Lincoln to suppose he is serious in making the charge.

I confess this is rather a curious view, that out of respect for me he should consider I was making what I deemed rather a grave charge in fun. [Laughter.] I confess it strikes me rather strangely. But I let it pass. As the Judge did not for a moment believe that there was a man in America whose heart was so "corrupt" as to make such a charge, and as he places me among the "men in America" who have hearts base enough to make such a charge, I hope he will excuse me if I hunt out another charge very like this; and if it should turn out that in hunting I should find that other, and it should turn out to be Judge Douglas himself who made it, I hope he will reconsider this question of the deep corruption of heart he has thought fit to ascribe to me. [Great applause and laughter.] In Judge Douglas' speech of March 22d, 1858, which I hold in my hand, he says:

> In this connection there is another topic to which I desire to allude. I seldom refer to the course of newspapers, or notice the articles which they publish in regard to myself; but the course of the Washington *Union* has been so extraordinary, for the last two or three months, that I think it well enough to make some allusion to it. It has read me out of the Democratic party every other day, at least for two or three months, and keeps reading me out, (laughter;) and, as if it had not succeeded still continues to read me out, using such terms as "traitor," "renegade," "deserter," and other kind and polite epithets of that nature. Sir, I have no vindication to make of my democracy against the Washington *Union*, or any other newspapers. I am willing to allow my history and action for the last twenty years to speak for themselves as

to my political principles, and my fidelity to political obligations. The Washington *Union* has a personal grievance. When its editor was nominated for Public Printer I declined to vote for him, and stated that at some time I might give my reasons for doing so. Since I declined to give that vote, this scurrilous abuse, these vindictive and constant attacks have been repeated almost daily on me. Will my friend from Michigan read the article to which I allude.

This is a part of the speech. You must excuse me from reading the entire article of the Washington *Union*, as Mr. Stuart[7] read it for Mr. Douglas. The Judge goes on and sums up, as I think correctly:

Mr. President, you here find several distinct propositions advanced boldly by the Washington *Union* editorially and apparently *authoritatively*, and every man who questions any of them is denounced as an Abolitionist, a Free-Soiler, a fanatic. The propositions are, first, that the primary object of all government at its original institution is the protection of person and property; second, that the Constitution of the United States declares that the citizens of each State shall be entitled to all the privileges and immunities of citizens in the several States; and that, therefore, thirdly, all State laws, whether organic or otherwise, which prohibit the citizens of one State from settling in another with their slave property, and especially declaring it forfeited, are direct violations of the original intention of the Government and Constitution of the United States; and fourth, that the emancipation of the slaves of the northern States was a gross outrage on the rights of property, inasmuch as it was involuntarily done on the part of the owner.

Remember that this article was published in the *Union* on the 17th of November, and on the 18th appeared the first article giving the adhesion of the *Union* to the Lecompton constitution. It was in these words:

"KANSAS AND HER CONSTITUTION.—The vexed question is settled. The problem is solved. The dread point of danger is passed. All serious trouble to Kansas affairs is over and gone."

And a column, nearly of the same sort. Then, when you come to look into the Lecompton Constitution, you find the same doctrine incorporated in it which was put forth editorially in the *Union*. What is it?

"ARTICLE 7, *Section* 1. The right of property is before and higher than any constitutional sanction; and the right of the owner of a slave to such slave and its increase is the same and as inviolable as the right of the owner of any property whatever."

Then in the schedule is a provision that the Constitution may be amended after 1864 by a two-thirds vote.

"But no alteration shall be made to affect the right of property in the ownership of slaves."

It will be seen by these clauses in the Lecompton Constitution that they are identical in spirit with this *authoritative* article in the Washington *Union* of the day previous to its indorsement of this Constitution.

7 U.S. Senator Charles E. Stuart ("my friend from Michigan").

I pass over some portions of the speech, and I hope that any one who feels interested in this matter will read the entire section of the speech, and see whether I do the Judge injustice. He proceeds:

> When I saw that article in the *Union* of the 17th of November, followed by the glorification of the Lecompton Constitution on the 18th of November, and this clause in the Constitution asserting the doctrine that a State has no right to prohibit slavery within its limits, I saw that there was a *fatal blow* being struck at the sovereignty of the States of this Union.

I stop the quotation there, again requesting that it may all be read. I have read all of the portion I desire to comment upon. What is this charge that the Judge thinks I must have a very corrupt heart to make? It was a purpose on the part of certain high functionaries to make it impossible for the people of one State to prohibit the people of any other State from entering it with their "property," so called, and making it a slave State. In other words, it was a charge implying a design to make the institution of slavery national. And now I ask your attention to what Judge Douglas has himself done here. I know he made that part of the speech as a reason why he had refused to vote for a certain man for public printer, but when we get at it, the charge itself is the very one I made against him, that he thinks I am so corrupt for uttering. Now whom does he make that charge against? Does he make it against that newspaper editor merely? No; he says it is identical in spirit with the Lecompton Constitution, and so the framers of that Constitution are brought in with the editor of the newspaper in that "fatal blow being struck." He did not call it a "conspiracy." In his language it is a "fatal blow being struck." And if the words carry the meaning better when changed from a "conspiracy" into a "fatal blow being struck," I will change *my* expression and call it "fatal blow being struck." [Cheers and laughter.] We see the charge made not merely against the editor of the *Union* but all the framers of the Lecompton Constitution; and not only so, but the article was an *authoritative* article. By whose authority? Is there any question but he means it was by the authority of the President, and his Cabinet—the Administration?

Is there any sort of question but he means to make that charge? Then there are the editors of the *Union*, the framers of the Lecompton Constitution, the President of the United States and his Cabinet, and all the supporters of the Lecompton Constitution in Congress and out of Congress, who are all involved in this "fatal blow being struck." I commend to Judge Douglas' consideration the question of *how corrupt a man's heart must be to make such a charge*! [Vociferous cheering.]

Now my friends, I have but one branch of the subject, in the little time I have left, to which to call your attention, and as I shall come to a close at the end of that branch, it is probable that I shall not occupy quite all the time allotted to me. Although on these questions I would like to talk twice as long as I have, I could not enter upon another head and discuss it properly without running over my time. I ask the attention of the people here assembled and elsewhere, to the course that Judge Douglas is pursuing every day as bearing upon this question of making slavery national. Not going back to the records but taking the speeches he makes, the speeches he made yesterday and day before and makes constantly all over the country—I ask your attention to them. In the first place what is necessary to make the institution national? Not war. There is no danger that the people of Kentucky will shoulder their muskets and with a young nigger stuck on every bayonet march into Illinois and force them upon us. There is no danger of our going over there and making war upon them. Then what is necessary for the nationalization of slavery? It is simply the next Dred Scott decision. It is merely for the Supreme Court to decide that no *State* under the Constitution can exclude it, just as they have already decided that under the Constitution neither Congress nor the Territorial Legislature can do it. When that is decided and acquiesced in, the whole thing is done. This being true, and this being the way as I think that slavery is to be made national, let us consider what Judge Douglas is doing every day to that end. In the first place, let us see what influence he is exerting on public sentiment. In this and like communities, public sentiment is everything. With public sentiment, nothing can fail; without it nothing can succeed. Consequently he who moulds public sentiment, goes deeper than he who enacts statutes or pronounces decisions. He makes statutes and decisions possible or impossible to be executed. This must be borne in mind, as also the additional fact that Judge Douglas is a man of vast influence, so great that it is enough for many men to profess to believe anything, when they once find out that Judge Douglas professes to believe it. Consider also the attitude he occupies at the head of a large party—a party which he claims has a majority of all the voters in the country. This man sticks to a decision which forbids the people of a Territory from excluding slavery, and he does so not because he says it is right in itself—he does not give any opinion on that—but because it has been *decided by the court*, and being decided by the court, he is, and you are bound to take it in your political action as *law*—not that he judges at all of its merits, but because a decision of the court is to him a "*Thus saith the Lord.*" [Applause.] He places it on that ground alone, and you will bear in mind that thus committing himself unreservedly to this decision, *commits him to the next one* just as firmly as to this. He did not commit himself on account of the merit or demerit of the decision, but it is a *Thus saith the Lord.* The next decision, as much as this, will be a *thus saith the Lord.* There is nothing that can divert or turn him away from this decision. It is nothing that I point out to him that his great prototype, Gen. Jackson, did not believe in the binding force of decisions. It is nothing to him that Jefferson did not so believe. I have said that I have often heard him approve of Jackson's course in disregarding the decision of the Supreme Court pronouncing a National Bank constitutional. He says, I did not hear him say so. He denies the accuracy of my recollection. I say he ought to know better than I, but I will make no question about this thing, though it still seems to me that I heard him say it twenty times. [Applause and laughter.] I will tell him though, that he now claims to stand on the Cincinnati platform, which affirms that Congress *cannot* charter a National Bank, in the teeth of that old standing decision that Congress *can* charter a bank. [Loud applause.] And I remind him of another piece of history on the question of respect for judicial decisions, and it is a piece of Illinois history, belonging to a time when the large party to which Judge Douglas belonged, were displeased with a decision of the Supreme Court of Illinois, because they had decided that a Governor could not remove a Secretary of State. You will find the whole story in Ford's History of Illinois, and I know that Judge Douglas will not deny that he was then in favor of overslaughing that decision by the mode of adding five new Judges, so as to vote down the four old ones. Not only so, but it ended in *the Judge's sitting down on that very bench as one of the five new Judges to break down the four old ones.* [Cheers and laughter.] It was in this way precisely that he got his title of Judge. Now, when the Judge tells me that men appointed conditionally to sit as members of a court, will have to be catechised beforehand upon some subject, I say "You know Judge; you have tried it." [Laughter.] When he says a court of this kind will lose the confidence of all men, will be prostituted and disgraced by such a proceeding, I say, "You know best, Judge; you have been through the mill." [Great laughter.] But I cannot shake Judge Douglas' teeth loose from the Dred Scott decision. Like some obstinate animal (I mean no disrespect,) that will hang on when he has once got his teeth fixed, you may cut off a leg, or you may tear away an arm, still he will not relax his hold. And so I may point out to the Judge, and say that he is bespattered all over, from the beginning of his political life to the present time, with attacks upon judicial decisions—I may cut off limb after limb of his public record, and strive to wrench him from a single dictum of the Court—yet I cannot divert him from it. He hangs to the last, to the Dred Scott decision. [Loud cheers.] These things show there is a purpose *strong as death and eternity* for which he adheres to this decision, and for which he will adhere to *all other decisions* of the same Court. [Vociferous applause.]

A HIBERNIAN.—Give us something besides Dred Scott.

MR. LINCOLN.—Yes; no doubt you want to hear something that don't hurt. [Laughter and applause.] Now, having spoken of the Dred Scott decision, one more word and I am done. Henry Clay, my beau ideal of a statesman, the man for whom I fought all my humble life—Henry Clay once said of a class of men who would repress all tendencies to liberty and ultimate emancipation, that they must, if they would do this, go back to the era of our Independence, and muzzle the cannon which thunders its annual joyous return; they must blow out the moral lights around us; they must penetrate the human soul, and eradicate there the love of liberty; and then and not till then, could they perpetuate slavery in this country! [Loud cheers.] To my thinking, Judge Douglas is, by his example and vast influence, doing that very thing in this community, [cheers,] when he says that the negro has nothing in the Declaration of Independence. Henry Clay plainly understood the contrary. Judge Douglas is going back to the era of our Revolution, and to the extent of his ability, muzzling the cannon which thunders its annual joyous return. When he invites any people willing to have slavery, to establish it, he is blowing out the moral lights around us. [Cheers.] When he says he "cares not whether slavery is voted down or voted up,"—that it is a sacred right of self government—he is in my judgment penetrating the human soul and eradicating the light of reason and the love of liberty in this American people. [Enthusiastic and continued applause.] And now I will only say that when, by all these means and appliances, Judge Douglas shall succeed in bringing public sentiment to an exact accordance with his own views—when these vast assemblages shall echo back all these sentiments—when they shall come to repeat his views and to avow his principles, and to say all that he says on these mighty questions—

then it needs only the formality of the second Dred Scott decision, which he endorses in advance, to make Slavery alike lawful in all the States—old as well as new, North as well as South.

My friends, that ends the chapter. The Judge can take his half-hour.

MR. DOUGLAS' REPLY.

MR. DOUGLAS—Fellow citizens: I will now occupy the half hour allotted to me in replying to Mr. Lincoln. The first point to which I will call your attention is, as to what I said about the organization of the Republican party in 1854, and the platform that was formed on the 5th of October, of that year, and I will then put the question to Mr. Lincoln whether or not he approves of each article in that platform ("he answered that already"), and ask for a specific answer. ("He has answered." "You cannot make him answer," &c.) I did not charge him with being a member of the committee which reported that platform. ("Yes, you did.") I charged that that platform was the platform of the Republican party adopted by them. The fact that it was the platform of the Republican party is not denied, but Mr. Lincoln now says, that although his name was on the committee which reported it, that he does not think he was there, but thinks he was in Tazewell, holding court. ("He said he was there.") Gentlemen, I ask your silence, and no interruption. Now, I want to remind Mr. Lincoln that he was at Springfield, when that convention was held, and those resolutions adopted. ("You can't do it." "He wasn't there," &c.)

[MR. GLOVER,[8] chairman of the Republican committee—I hope no Republican will interrupt Mr. Douglas. The masses listened to Mr. Lincoln attentively, and as respectable men we ought now to hear Mr. Douglas, and without interruption.] ("Good.")

MR. DOUGLAS, resuming—The point I am going to remind Mr. Lincoln of is this: that after I had made my speech in 1854, during the fair, he gave me notice that he was going to reply to me the next day. I was sick at the time, but I staid over in Springfield to hear his reply and to reply to him. On that day this very convention, the resolutions adopted by which I have read, was to meet in the Senate chamber. He spoke in the hall of the House; and when he got through his speech—my recollection is distinct, and I shall never forget it—Mr. Codding walked in as I took the stand to reply, and gave notice that the Republican State Convention

[8] This episode is not reported in the *Press and Tribune*, and was deleted by Lincoln in the debates scrapbook.

would meet instantly in the Senate chamber, and called upon the Republicans to retire there and go into this very convention, instead of remaining and listening to me. (Three cheers for Douglas.)

MR. LINCOLN, interrupting, excitedly and angrily—Judge, add that I went along with them. (This interruption was made in a pitiful, mean, sneaking way, as Lincoln floundered around the stand.)

MR. DOUGLAS—Gentlemen, Mr. Lincoln tells me to add that he went along with them to the Senate chamber. I will not add that, because I do not know whether he did or not.

MR. LINCOLN, again interrupting—I know he did not.

[Two of the Republican committee here seized Mr. Lincoln, and by a sudden jerk caused him to disappear from the front of the stand, one of them saying quite audibly, "What are you making such a fuss for. Douglas didn't interrupt you, and can't you see that the people don't like it."]

MR. DOUGLAS—I do not know whether he knows it or not, that is not the point, and I will yet bring him to on the question.[9]

In the first place—Mr. Lincoln was selected by the very men who made the Republican organization, on that day to reply to me. He spoke for them and for that party, and he was the leader of the party; and on the very day he made his speech in reply to me preaching up this same doctrine of negro equality, under the Declaration of Independence, this Republican party met in Convention. (Three cheers for Douglas.) Another evidence that he was acting in concert with them is to be found in the fact that that convention waited an hour after its time of meeting to hear Lincoln's speech, and Codding, one of their leading men marched in the moment Lincoln got through, and gave notice that they did not want to hear me and would proceed with the business of the Convention. ("Strike him again,"—three cheers, etc.) Still another fact. I have here a newspaper printed at Springfield, Mr. Lincoln's own town, in October, 1854, a few days afterwards, publishing these resolutions, charging Mr. Lincoln with entertaining

[9] The five preceding paragraphs composing this digression were deleted by Lincoln in the debates scrapbook. The bias of the *Times* reporter is obvious, but it may be well to note that the episode appears in the *Press and Tribune* as follows:

"MR. LINCOLN—Let the Judge add that Lincoln went along with them.

"JUDGE DOUGLAS.—Mr. Lincoln says let him add that he went along with them to the Senate Chamber. I will not add that for I do not know it.

"MR. LINCOLN.—I do know it.

"JUDGE DOUGLAS.—But whether he knows or not my point is this, and I will yet bring him to his milk on this point."

these sentiments, and trying to prove that they were also the sentiments of Mr. Yates, then candidate for Congress. This has been published on Mr. Lincoln over and over again, and never before has he denied it. (Three cheers.)

But my friends, this denial of his that he did not act on the committee is a miserable quibble to avoid the main issue, (applause.) ("That's so,") which is that this Republican platform declares in favor of the unconditional repeal of the Fugitive Slave Law. Has Lincoln answered whether he endorsed that or not? (No, no.) I called his attention to it when I first addressed you and asked him for an answer and I then predicted that he would not answer. (Bravo, glorious and cheers.) How does he answer. Why that he was not on the committee that wrote the resolutions. (Laughter.) I then repeated the next proposition contained in the resolutions, which was to restrict slavery in those states in which it exists and asked him whether he endorsed it. Does he answer yes, or no? He says in reply, "I was not on the committee at the time; I was up in Tazewell." The next question I put to him was, whether he was in favor of prohibiting the admission of any more slave States into the Union. I put the question to him distinctly, whether, if the people of the Territory, when they had sufficient population to make a State, should form their constitution recognizing slavery, he would vote for or against its admission. ("That's it.") He is a candidate for the United States Senate, and it is possible, if he should be elected, that he would have to vote directly on that question. ("He never will.") I asked him to answer me and you whether he would vote to admit a State into the Union, with slavery or without it, as its own people might choose. ("Hear him," "That's the doctrine," and applause.) He did not answer that question. ("He never will.") He dodges that question also, under the cover that he was not on the Committee at the time, that he was not present when the platform was made. I want to know if he should happen to be in the Senate when a State applied for admission, with a constitution acceptable to her own people, he would vote to admit that State, if slavery was one of its institutions. (That's the question.) He avoids the answer.

MR. LINCOLN—interrupting the third time excitedly, No, Judge —(Mr. Lincoln again disappeared suddenly aided by a pull from behind.)[10]

MR. DOUGLAS. It is true he gives the abolitionists to understand by a hint that he would not vote to admit such a State. And why? He goes on to say that the man who would talk about giving each

[10] This paragraph is not in the *Press and Tribune.*

State the right to have slavery, or not, as it pleased, was akin to the man who would muzzle the guns which thundered forth the annual joyous return of the day of our independence. (Great laughter.) He says that that kind of talk is casting a blight on the glory of this country. What is the meaning of that? That he is not in favor of each State having the right to do as it pleases on the slavery question? ("Stick it to him," "don't spare him," and applause.) I will put the question to him again and again, and I intend to force it out of him. (Immense applause.)

Then again, this platform which was made at Springfield by his own party, when he was its acknowledged head, provides that Republicans will insist on the abolition of slavery in the District of Columbia, and I asked Lincoln specifically whether he agreed with them in that? Did you get an answer? ("No, no.") He is afraid to answer it. ("We will not vote for him.") He knows I will trot him down to Egypt. (Laughter and cheers.) I intend to make him answer there, ("that's right,") or I will show the people of Illinois that he does not intend to answer these questions. ("Keep him to the point," "give us more," etc.) The convention to which I have been alluding goes a little further, and pledges itself to exclude slavery from all the Territories over which the general government has exclusive jurisdiction north of 36 deg. 30 min., as well as South. Now I want to know whether he approves that provision. (He'll never answer and cheers.) I want him to answer, and when he does, I want to know his opinion on another point, which is, whether he will redeem the pledge of this platform and resist the acquirement of any more territory unless slavery therein shall be forever prohibited. I want him to answer this last question. Each of the questions I have put to him are practical questions, questions based upon the fundamental principles of the Black Republican party, and I want to know whether he is the first, last and only choice of a party with whom he does not agree in principle. ("Great applause,") ("Rake him down.") He does not deny but that that principle was unanimously adopted by the Republican party; he does not deny that the whole Republican party is pledged to it; he does not deny that a man who is not faithful to it is faithless to the Republican party, and now I want to know whether that party is unanimously in favor of a man who does not adopt that creed and agree with them in their principles: I want to know whether the man who does not agree with them, and who is afraid to avow his differences and who dodges the issue, is the first, last and only choice of the Republican party. (Cheers.) A VOICE, how about the conspiracy?

MR. DOUGLAS, never mind, I will come to that soon enough. (Bravo, Judge, hurra, three cheers for Douglas.) But the platform which I have read to you not only lays down these principles but it adds:

Resolved, That in furtherance of these principles we will use such constitutional and lawful means as shall seem best adapted to their accomplishment, and that we will support no man for office, under the general or state government, who is not positively and fully committed to the support of these principles, and whose personal character and conduct is not a guarantee that he is reliable, and who shall not have abjured old party allegiance and ties.

("Good," "you have him," &c.)

The Black Republican party stands pledged that they will never support Lincoln until he has pledged himself to that platform, (tremendous applause, men throwing up their hats, and shouting, "you've got him,") but he cannot devise his answer; he has not made up his mind, whether he will or not. (Great laughter.) He talked about everything else he could think of to occupy his hour and a half, and when he could not think of anything more to say, without an excuse for refusing to answer these questions, he sat down long before his time was out. (Cheers.)

In relation to Mr. Lincoln's charge of conspiracy against me, I have a word to say. In his speech to-day he quotes a playful part of his speech at Springfield, about Stephen, and James, and Franklin, and Roger, and says that I did not take exception to it. I did not answer it, and he repeats it again. I did not take exception to this figure of his. He has a right to be as playful as he pleases in throwing his arguments together, and I will not object; but I did take objection to his second Springfield speech, in which he stated that he intended his first speech as a charge of corruption or conspiracy against the Supreme Court of the United States, President Pierce, President Buchanan, and myself. That gave the offensive character to the charge. He then said that when he made it he did not know whether it was true or not (laughter), but inasmuch as Judge Douglas had not denied it, although he had replied to the other parts of his speech three times, he repeated it as a charge of conspiracy against me, thus charging me with moral turpitude. When he put it in that form I did say that inasmuch as he repeated the charge simply because I had not denied it, I would deprive him of the opportunity of ever repeating it again, by declaring that it was in all its bearings an infamous lie. (Three cheers for Douglas.) He says he will repeat it until I answer his folly, and nonsense about Stephen, and Franklin, and Roger, and Bob, and James.

He studied that out, prepared that one sentence with the greatest care, committed it to memory, and put it in his first Springfield speech, and now he carries that speech around and reads that sentence to show how pretty it is. (Laughter.) His vanity is wounded because I will not go into that beautiful figure of his about the building of a house. (Renewed laughter.) All I have to say is, that I am not green enough to let him make a charge which he acknowledges he does not know to be true, and then take up my time in answering it, when I know it to be false and nobody else knows it to be true. (Cheers.)

I have not brought a charge of moral turpitude against him. When he, or any other man, brings one against me, instead of disproving it I will say that it is a lie, and let him prove it if he can. (Enthusiastic applause.)

I have lived twenty-five years in Illinois. I have served you with all the fidelity and ability which I possess, ("That's so," "good," and cheers,) and Mr. Lincoln is at liberty to attack my public action, my votes, and my conduct; but when he dares to attack my moral integrity, by a charge of conspiracy between myself, Chief Justice Taney, and the Supreme Court and two Presidents of the United States, I will repel it. ("Three cheers for Douglas.")

Mr. Lincoln has not character enough for integrity and truth merely on his own *ipse dixit* to arraign President Buchanan, President Pierce, and nine judges of the Supreme Court, not one of whom would be complimented by being put on an equality with him. ("Hit him again, three cheers" &c.) There is an unpardonable presumption in a man putting himself up before thousands of people, and pretending that his *ipse dixit*, without proof, without fact and without truth, is enough to bring down and destroy the purest and best of living men. ("Hear him," "Three cheers.")

Fellow-citizens, my time is fast expiring; I must pass on. Mr. Lincoln wants to know why I voted against Mr. Chase's amendment to the Nebraska Bill. I will tell him. In the first place, the bill already conferred all the power which Congress had, by giving the people the whole power over the subject. Chase offered a proviso that they might abolish slavery, which by implication would convey the idea that they could prohibit by not introducing that institution. Gen. Cass asked him to modify his amendment, so as to provide that the people might either prohibit or introduce slavery, and thus make it fair and equal. Chase refused to so modify his proviso, and then Gen. Cass and all the rest of us, voted it down. (Immense cheering.) These facts appear on the journals and debates of Congress, where Mr. Lincoln found the charge, and if he had told the whole truth, there would have been no necessity for me to occupy your time in explaining the matter. (Laughter and applause.)

Mr. Lincoln wants to know why the word "state," as well as "territory," was put into the Nebraska Bill! I will tell him. It was put there to meet just such false arguments as he has been adducing. (Laughter.) That first, not only the people of the territories should do as they pleased, but that when they come to be admitted as States, they should come into the Union with or without slavery, as the people determined. I meant to knock in the head this Abolition doctrine of Mr. Lincoln's, that there shall be no more slave States, even if the people want them. (Tremendous applause.) And it does not do for him to say, or for any other Black Republican to say, that there is nobody in favor of the doctrine of no more slave States, and that nobody wants to interfere with the right of the people to do as they please. What was the origin of the Missouri difficulty and the Missouri compromise? The people of Missouri formed a constitution as a slave State, and asked admission into the Union, but the Free Soil party of the North being in a majority, refused to admit her because she had slavery as one of her institutions. Hence this first slavery agitation arose upon a State and not upon a Territory, and yet Mr. Lincoln does not know why the word State was placed in the Kansas-Nebraska bill. (Great laughter and applause.) The whole Abolition agitation arose on that doctrine of prohibiting a State from coming in with slavery or not, as it pleased, and that same doctrine is here in this Republican platform of 1854; it has never been repealed; and every Black Republican stands pledged by that platform, never to vote for any man who is not in favor of it. Yet Mr. Lincoln does not know that there is a man in the world who is in favor of preventing a State from coming in as it pleases, notwithstanding. The Springfield platform says that they, the Republican party, will not allow a State to come in under such circumstances. He is an ignorant man. (Cheers.)

Now you see that upon these very points I am as far from bringing Mr. Lincoln up to the line as I ever was before. He does not want to avow his principles. I do want to avow mine, as clear as sunlight in mid-day. (Cheers and applause.) Democracy is founded upon the eternal principle of right. (That is the talk.) The plainer these principles are avowed before the people, the stronger will be the support which they will receive. I only wish I had the power to make them so clear that they would shine in the heavens for every man, woman, and child to read. (Loud cheering.) The first of those principles that I would proclaim would be in opposition to Mr. Lincoln's doctrine of uniformity between the different States, and I would declare instead the sovereign right of each State to decide the slavery question as well as all other domestic questions for themselves, without interference from any other State or power whatsoever. (Hurrah for Douglas.)

When that principle is recognized you will have peace and harmony and fraternal feeling between all the States of this Union; until you do recognize that doctrine there will be sectional warfare agitating and distracting the country. What does Mr. Lincoln propose? He says that the Union cannot exist divided into free and slave States. If it cannot endure thus divided, then he must strive to make them all free or all slave, which will inevitably bring about a dissolution of the Union. (Cries of "he can't do it.")

Gentlemen, I am told that my time is out and I am obliged to stop. (Three times three cheers were here given for Senator Douglas.)

To Joseph O. Cunningham[1]

J. O. Cunningham, Esq | Ottawa,
My Dear Sir | Aug. 22. 1858

Yours of the 18th. signed as Secretary of the Rep. Club, is received. In the matter of making speeches I am a good [deal] pressed by invitations from almost all quarters; and while I hope to be at Urbana sometime during the canvass I cannot yet say when. Can you not see me at Monticello on the 6th. of Sept.?

Douglas and I, for the first time this canvass, crossed swords here yesterday; the fire flew some, and I am glad to know I am yet alive. There was a vast concourse of people—more than could [get] near enough to hear. Yours as ever A. LINCOLN

[1] ALS, IU. Joseph O. Cunningham was editor of the Urbana *Union*.

Speech at Augusta, Illinois[1]

August 25, 1858

At two o'clock the people flocked over to a beautiful grove near the village. . . . It was fully as large as Dug's "3,000 meetings," though I do not put the number of voters present higher than 1,200. Mr. Lincoln spoke about two hours in an earnest, calm, convincing manner. The bulk of his audience were from the Slave

States—and two-thirds of them had been Clay Whigs. The first hour of his speech was devoted to an examination of Clay's principles on the Slavery question, and to repelling the charges, made against the speaker, that he was an "Abolitionist," in favor of "negro equality" and "amalgamation." He made clean work of these points as he went along, and I don't think there was a man on the ground but he satisfied, and pleased, and there were hundreds who voted for Fillmore in 1856. The last hour he spent in showing up the great conspiracy in which Douglas is engaged to Nationalize slavery and Africanize this continent. I will not attempt to give even a synopsis of his arguments. Suffice it to say that he drove home conviction of the truth of his charges into the minds of almost every man who listened to him. His speech will do great good in this section of country. . . .

[1] Chicago *Press and Tribune*, August 28, 1858.

Speech at Macomb, Illinois[1]

August 25, 1858

. . . . Lincoln addressed the Court House full of people in Macomb. His remarks were addressed to the Old Clay Whigs, and to some extent he covered the same ground as in his Augusta speech this afternoon. But he was less formal, and his speech was more like an earnest conversation with his Old Whig friends. The effect produced was excellent, and all went away satisfied and convinced that the Douglasite gabble about the Abolition and Amalgamation principles of the Republican party, was all lies and slander. . . .

[1] Chicago *Press and Tribune*, August 28, 1858. Lincoln spoke at Macomb on the night of August 25.

Second Debate with Stephen A. Douglas at Freeport, Illinois[1]

August 27, 1858

Second joint debate, August 27, 1858 at Freeport, Illinois. Lincoln, as reported in the Press & Tribune. Douglas, as reported in the Chicago Times.[2]

[1] Debates Scrapbook, ORB. Cheering, interruptions, and explanatory matter deleted by Lincoln have been retained in the text. Lincoln's other corrections and insertions have been indicated in footnotes. Typographical errors not corrected in the scrapbook have been corrected by the editors. All brackets are in the source unless footnoted. [2] Lincoln's prefatory note in the scrapbook.

MR. LINCOLN'S SPEECH.

Mr. Lincoln was introduced by Hon. Thomas J. Turner, and was greeted with loud cheers. When the applause had subsided, he said:

LADIES AND GENTLEMEN—On Saturday last, Judge Douglas and myself first met in public discussion. He spoke one hour, I an hour-and-a-half, and he replied for half an hour. The order is now reversed. I am to speak an hour, he an hour-and-a-half, and then I am to reply for half an hour. I propose to devote myself during the first hour to the scope of what was brought within the range of his half hour speech at Ottawa. Of course there was brought within the scope in that half hour's speech something of his own opening speech. In the course of that opening argument Judge Douglas proposed to me seven distinct interrogatories. In my speech of an hour and a half, I attended to some other parts of his speech, and incidentally, as I thought, answered one of the interrogatories then. I then distinctly intimated to him that I would answer the rest of his interrogatories on condition only that he should agree to answer as many for me.[3] He made no intimation at the time of the proposition, nor did he in his reply allude at all to that suggestion of mine. I do him no injustice in saying that he occupied at least half of his reply in dealing with me as though I had *refused* to answer his interrogatories. I now propose that I will answer any of the interrogatories, upon condition that he will answer questions from me not exceeding the same number. I give him an opportunity to respond. The Judge remains silent. I now say to you that I will answer his interrogatories, whether he answers mine or not; [applause] and that after I have done so, I shall propound mine to him. [Applause.]

[Owing to the press of people against the platform, our reporter did not reach the stand until Mr. Lincoln had spoken to this point. The previous remarks were taken by a gentleman in Freeport, who has politely furnished them to us.]

I have supposed myself, since the organization of the Republican party at Bloomington, in May, 1856, bound as a party man by the platforms of the party, then and since. If in any interrogatories which I shall answer I go beyond the scope of what is within these platforms it will be perceived that no one is responsible but myself.

Having said thus much, I will take up the Judge's interrogatories as I find them printed in the Chicago *Times*, and answer them *seriatim*. In order that there may be no mistake about it, I have

[3] "On condition only that he should agree to answer as many for me" is inserted by Lincoln in the margin.

copied the interrogatories in writing, and also my answers to them. The first one of these interrogatories is in these words:

Question 1. "I desire to know whether Lincoln to-day stands, as he did in 1854, in favor of the unconditional repeal of the fugitive slave law?"

Answer. I do not now, nor ever did, stand in favor of the unconditional repeal of the fugitive slave law. [Cries of "Good," "Good."]

Q. 2. "I desire him to answer whether he stands pledged to-day, as he did in 1854, against the admission of any more slave States into the Union, even if the people want them?"

A. I do not now, nor ever did, stand pledged against the admission of any more slave States into the Union.

Q. 3. "I want to know whether he stands pledged against the admission of a new State into the Union with such a Constitution as the people of that State may see fit to make."

A. I do not stand pledged against the admission of a new State into the Union, with such a Constitution as the people of that State may see fit to make. [Cries of "good," "good."]

Q. 4. "I want to know whether he stands to-day pledged to the abolition of slavery in the District of Columbia?"

A. I do not stand to-day pledged to the abolition of slavery in the District of Columbia.

Q. 5. "I desire him to answer whether he stands pledged to the prohibition of the slave trade between the different States?"

A. I do not stand pledged to the prohibition of the slave trade between the different States.

Q. 6. "I desire to know whether he stands pledged to prohibit slavery in all the Territories of the United States, North as well as South of the Missouri Compromise line."

A. I am impliedly, if not expressly, pledged to a belief in the *right* and *duty* of Congress to prohibit slavery in all the United States Territories. [Great applause.]

Q. 7. "I desire him to answer whether he is opposed to the acquisition of any new territory unless slavery is first prohibited therein."

A. I am not generally opposed to honest acquisition of territory; and, in any given case, I would or would not oppose such acquisition, accordingly as I might think such acquisition would or would not agravate [*sic*][4] the slavery question among ourselves. [Cries of good, good.]

Now, my friends, it will be perceived upon an examination of

[4] "Agitate" deleted and "agravate" inserted by Lincoln.

these questions and answers, that so far I have only answered that I was not *pledged* to this, that or the other. The Judge has not framed his interrogatories to ask me anything more than this, and I have answered in strict accordance with the interrogatories, and have answered truly that I am not *pledged* at all upon any of the points to which I have answered. But I am not disposed to hang upon the exact form of his interrogatory. I am rather disposed to take up at least some of these questions, and state what I really think upon them.

As to the first one, in regard to the Fugitive Slave Law, I have never hesitated to say, and I do not now hesitate to say, that I think, under the Constitution of the United States, the people of the Southern States are entitled to a Congressional Fugitive Slave Law. Having said that, I have had nothing to say in regard to the existing Fugitive Slave Law further than that I think it should have been framed so as to be free from some of the objections that pertain to it, without lessening its efficiency. And inasmuch as we are not now in an agitation in regard to an alteration or modification of that law, I would not be the man to introduce it as a new subject of agitation upon the general question of slavery.

In regard to the other question of whether I am pledged to the admission of any more slave States into the Union, I state to you very frankly that I would be exceedingly sorry ever to be put in a position of having to pass upon that question. I should be exceedingly glad to know that there would never be another slave State admitted into the Union; [applause]; but I must add, that if slavery shall be kept out of the Territories during the territorial existence of any one given Territory, and then the people shall, having a fair chance and a clear field, when they come to adopt the Constitution, do such an extraordinary thing as to adopt a Slave Constitution, uninfluenced by the actual presence of the institution among them, I see no alternative, if we own the country, but to admit them into the Union. [Applause.]

The third interrogatory is answered by the answer to the second, it being, as I conceive, the same as the second.

The fourth one is in regard to the abolition of slavery in the District of Columbia. In relation to that, I have my mind very distinctly made up. I should be exceedingly glad to see slavery abolished in the District of Columbia. [Cries of "good, good."] I believe that Congress possesses the constitutional power to abolish it. Yet as a member of Congress, I should not with my present views, be in favor of *endeavoring* to abolish slavery in the District of Columbia, unless it would be upon these conditions. *First*, that the abolition should be gradual. *Second,* that it should be on a vote of the majority of qualified voters in the District, and *third,* that compensation should be made to unwilling owners. With these three conditions, I confess I would be exceedingly glad to see Congress abolish slavery in the District of Columbia, and, in the language of Henry Clay, "sweep from our Capital that foul blot upon our nation." [Loud applause.]

In regard to the fifth interrogatory, I must say here, that as to the question of the abolition of the Slave Trade between the different States, I can truly answer, as I have, that I am *pledged* to nothing about it. It is a subject to which I have not given that mature consideration that would make me feel authorized to state a position so as to hold myself entirely bound by it. In other words, that question has never been prominently enough before me to induce me to investigate whether we really have the Constitutional power to do it. I could investigate it if I had sufficient time, to bring myself to a conclusion upon that subject, but I have not done so, and I say so frankly to you here, and to Judge Douglas. I must say, however, that if I should be of opinion that Congress does possess the Constitutional power to abolish the slave trade[5] among the different States, I should still not be in favor of the exercise of that power unless upon some conservative principle as I conceive it, akin to what I have said in relation to the abolition of slavery in the District of Columbia.

My answer as to whether I desire that slavery should be prohibited in all the Territories of the United States is full and explicit within itself, and cannot be made clearer by any comments of mine. So I suppose in regard to the question whether I am opposed to the acquisition of any more territory unless slavery is first prohibited therein, my answer is such that I could add nothing by way of illustration, or making myself better understood, than the answer which I have placed in writing.

Now in all this, the Judge has me and he has me on the record. I suppose he had flattered himself that I was really entertaining one set of opinions for one place and another set for another place —that I was afraid to say at one place what I uttered at another. What I am saying here I suppose I say to a vast audience as strongly tending to Abolitionism as any audience in the State of Illinois, and I believe I am saying that which, if it would be offensive[6] to any persons and render them enemies to myself, would be offensive to persons in this audience.

[5] "Slavery" deleted and "the slave trade" inserted by Lincoln.
[6] "Affirmed" deleted and "offensive" inserted by Lincoln.

I now proceed to propound to the Judge the interrogatories, so far as I have framed them. I will bring forward a new installment when I get them ready. [Laughter.] I will bring them forward now, only reaching to number four.

The first one is—

Question 1. If the people of Kansas shall, by means entirely unobjectionable in all other respects, adopt a State Constitution, and ask admission into the Union under it, *before* they have the requisite number of inhabitants according to the English Bill—some ninety-three thousand—will you vote to admit them? [Applause.]

Q. 2. Can the people of a United States Territory, in any lawful way, against the wish of any citizen of the United States, exclude slavery from its limits prior to the formation of a State Constitution? [Renewed applause.]

Q. 3. If the Supreme Court of the United States shall decide[7] that States can not exclude slavery from their limits, are you in favor of acquiescing in, adopting and following such decision as a rule of political action? [Loud applause.]

Q. 4. Are you in favor of acquiring additional territory, in disregard of how such acquisition may affect the nation on the slavery question? [Cries of "good," "good."]

As introductory to these interrogatories which Judge Douglas propounded to me at Ottawa, he read a set of resolutions which he said Judge Trumbull and myself had participated in adopting, in the first Republican State Convention held at Springfield, in October, 1854. He insisted that I and Judge Trumbull, and perhaps, the entire Republican party were responsible for the doctrines contained in the set of resolutions which he read, and I understand that it was from that set of resolutions that he deduced the interrogatories which he propounded to me, using these resolutions as a sort of authority for propounding those questions to me. Now I say here to-day that I do not answer his interrogatories because of their springing at all from that set of resolutions which he read. I answered them because Judge Douglas thought fit to ask them. [Applause.] I do not now, nor never did recognize any responsibility upon myself in that set of resolutions. When I replied to him on that occasion, I assured him that I never had anything to do with them. I repeat here to-day, that I never in any possible form had anything to do with that set of resolutions. It turns out, I believe, that those resolutions were never passed in any Convention held in Springfield. [Cheers and Laughter.] It turns out that they were never passed at any Convention or any public meeting

7 "Decree" deleted and "decide" inserted by Lincoln.

that I had any part in. I believe it turns out in addition to all this, that there was not, in the fall of 1854, any Convention holding a session in Springfield, calling itself a Republican State Convention; yet it is true there was a Convention, or assemblage of men calling themselves a Convention, at Springfield, that did pass *some* resolutions. But so little did I really know of the proceedings of that Convention, or what set of resolutions they had passed, though having a general knowledge that there had been such an assemblage of men there, that when Judge Douglas read the resolutions, I really did not know but they had been the resolutions passed then and there. I did not question that they were the resolutions adopted. For I could not bring myself to suppose that Judge Douglas could say what he did upon this subject without *knowing* that it was true. [Cheers and laughter.] I contented myself, on that occasion, with denying, as I truly could, all connection with them, not denying or affirming whether they were passed at Springfield. Now it turns out that he had got hold of some resolutions passed at some Convention or public meeting in Kane County. [Renewed laughter.] I wish to say here that I don't conceive that in any fair and just mind this discovery relieves me at all. I had just as much to do with the Convention in Kane County as that in Springfield. I am just as much responsible for the resolutions at Kane County as those at Springfield, the amount of the responsibility being exactly nothing in either case; no more than there would be in regard to a set of resolutions passed in the moon. [Laughter and loud cheers.]

I allude to this extraordinary matter in this canvass for some further purpose than anything yet advanced. Judge Douglas did not make his statement upon that occasion as matters that he believed to be true, but he stated them roundly as *being true*, in such form as to pledge his veracity for their truth. When the whole matter turns out as it does, and when we consider who Judge Douglas is—that he is a distinguished Senator of the United States—that he has served nearly twelve years as such—that his character is not at all limited as an ordinary Senator of the United States, but that his name has become of world-wide renown—it is *most extraordinary* that he should so far forget all the suggestions of justice to an adversary, or of prudence to himself, as to venture upon the assertion of that which the slightest investigation would have shown him to be wholly false. [Cheers.] I can only account for his having done so upon the supposition that that evil genius which has attended him through his life, giving to him an apparent astonishing prosperity, such as to lead very many good men to doubt there being any advantage in virtue over vice—[Cheers and laughter] I say I can only account for it on the supposition that that evil genius has at last made up its mind to forsake him. [Continued cheers and laughter.]

And I may add that another extraordinary feature of the Judge's conduct in this canvass—made more extraordinary by this incident—is that he is in the habit, in almost all the speeches he makes, of charging falsehood upon his adversaries—myself and others. I now ask whether he is able to find in anything that Judge Trumbull, for instance, has said, or in anything that I have said, a justification at all compared with what we have, in this instance, for that sort of vulgarity. [Cries of "good," "good," "good."]

I have been in the habit of charging as a matter of belief on my part, that, in the introduction of the Nebraska bill into Congress, there was a conspiracy to make slavery perpetual and national. I have arranged from time to time the evidence which establishes and proves the truth of this charge. I recurred to this charge at Ottawa. I shall not now have time to dwell upon it at very great length, but inasmuch as Judge Douglas in his reply of half an hour, made some points upon me in relation to it, I propose noticing a few of them.

The Judge insists that, in the first speech I made, in which I very distinctly made that charge, he thought for a good while I was in fun! that I was playful—that I was not sincere about it—and that he only grew angry and somewhat excited when he found that I insisted upon it as a matter of earnestness. He says he characterised it as a falsehood as far as I implicated his *moral character* in that transaction. Well, I did not know, till he presented that view that I had implicated his moral character. He is very much in the habit, when he argues me up into a position I never thought of occupying, of very cosily saying he has no doubt Lincoln is "conscientious" in saying so. He should remember that I did not know but what *he* was ALTOGETHER "CONSCIENTIOUS" in that matter. [Great Laughter.] I can conceive it possible for men to conspire to do a good thing, and I really find nothing in Judge Douglas' course or arguments that is contrary to or inconsistent with his belief of a conspiracy to nationalize and spread slavery as being a good and blessed thing, [Continued Laughter,] and so I hope he will understand that I do not at all question but that in all this matter he is entirely "conscientious." [More laughter and cheers.]

But to draw your attention to one of the points I made in this case, beginning at the beginning. When the Nebraska bill was introduced, or a short time afterwards, by an amendment I believe, it was provided that it must be considered "the true intent and meaning of this act not to legislate slavery into any State or Territory, or to exclude it therefrom, but to leave the people thereof perfectly free to form and regulate their own domestic institutions in their own way, subject only to the Constitution of the United States." I have called his attention to the fact that when he and some others began arguing that they were giving an increased degree of liberty to the people in the Territories over and above what they formerly had on the question of slavery, a question was raised whether the law was enacted to give such unconditional liberty to the people, and to test the sincerity of this mode of argument, Mr. Chase, of Ohio, introduced an amendment, in which he made the law—if the amendment were adopted—expressly declare that the people of the Territory should have the power to exclude slavery if they saw fit. I have asked attention also to the fact that Judge Douglas and those who acted with him, voted that amendment down, notwithstanding it expressed exactly the thing they said was the true intent and meaning of the law. I have called attention to the fact that in subsequent times, a decision of the Supreme Court has been made in which it has been declared that a Territorial Legislature has no constitutional right to exclude slavery. And I have argued and said that for men who did intend that the people of the territory should have the right to exclude slavery absolutely and unconditionally, the voting down of Chase's amendment is wholly inexplicable. It is a puzzle—a riddle. But I have said that with men who did look forward to such a decision, or who had it in contemplation, that such a decision of the Supreme Court would or might be made, the voting down of that amendment would be perfectly rational and intelligible. It would keep Congress from coming in collision with the decision when it was made. Anybody can conceive that if there was an intention or expectation that such a decision was to follow, it would not be a very desirable party attitude to get into for the Supreme Court—all or nearly all its members belonging to the same party—to decide one way, when the party in Congress had decided the other way. Hence it would be very rational for men expecting such a decision, to keep the niche in that law clear for it. After pointing this out, I tell Judge Douglas that it looks to me as though here was the reason why Chase's amendment was voted down. I tell him that as he did it, and knows why he did it, if it was done for a reason different from this, *he knows what that reason was, and can tell us what it was.* I tell him, also, it will be vastly more satisfactory to the country, for him to give some other plausible, intelligible reason *why* it was voted down than to stand upon his dignity and call people liars. [Loud cheers.] Well, on Saturday he did make his answer, and what do you think it was? He says if I had only taken upon myself to tell the whole truth about that amendment of Chase's no explanation would have been necessary on his part—or words to that effect. Now, I say here, that I am quite unconscious of having suppressed anything material to the case, and I am very frank to admit if there is any sound reason other than that which appeared to me material, it is quite fair for him to present it. What reason does he propose? That when Chase came forward with his amendment expressly authorizing the people to exclude slavery from the limits of every Territory, Gen. Cass proposed to Chase, if he (Chase) would add to his amendment that the people should have the power to *introduce* or exclude, they would let it go. (This is substantially all of his reply.) And because Chase would not do that, they voted his amendment down. Well, it turns out, I believe, upon examination, that General Cass took some part in the little running debate upon that amendment, and then ran away *and did not vote on it at all.* [Laughter.] Is not that the fact? So confident, as I think, was Gen. Cass, that there was a snake somewhere about, he chose to run away from the whole thing. This is an inference I draw from the fact that though he took part in the debate, his name does not appear in the ayes and noes. But does Judge Douglas' reply amount to a satisfactory answer? [Cries of "yes," "yes," and "no," "no."] There is some little difference of opinion here. [Laughter.] But I ask attention to a few more views bearing on the question of whether it amounts to a satisfactory answer. The men, who were determined that that amendment should not get into the bill and spoil the place where the Dred Scott decision was to come in, sought an excuse to get rid of it somewhere. One of these ways—one of these excuses—was to ask Chase to add to his proposed amendment a provision that the people might *introduce* slavery if they wanted to. They very well knew Chase would do no such thing—that Mr. Chase was one of the men differing from them on the broad principle of his insisting that freedom was *better* than slavery—a man who would not consent to enact a law, penned with his own hand, by which he was made to recognize slavery on the one hand and liberty on the other as *precisely equal;* and when they insisted on his doing this, they very well knew they insisted on that which he would not for a moment think of doing, and that they were only bluffing him. I believe (I have not, since he made his answer, had a chance to examine the journals or *Congressional Globe*, and therefore speak from memory)—I believe the state of the bill at that time, according to parliamentary rules, was such that no member could propose an additional amendment to Chase's amendment. I rather think this is the truth—the Judge shakes his head. Very well. I would like to know, then, *if they wanted Chase's amendment fixed over, why somebody else could not have offered to do it?* If they wanted it amended, why did they not offer the amendment? Why did they stand there taunting and quibbling at Chase? [Laughter.] Why did they not *put it in themselves*? But to put it on the other ground; suppose that there was such an amendment offered, and Chase's was an amendment to an amendment; until one is disposed of by parliamentary law, you cannot pile another on. Then all these gentlemen had to do was to vote Chase's on, and then in the amended form in which the whole stood, add their own amendment to it if they wanted it put in that shape. This was all they were obliged to do, and the ayes and noes show that there were 36 who voted it down, against 10 who voted in favor of it. The 36 held entire sway and control. They could in some form or other have put that bill in the exact shape they wanted. If there was a rule preventing their amending it at the time, they could pass that, and then Chase's amendment being merged, put it in the shape they wanted. They did not choose to do so, but they went into a quibble with Chase to get him to add what they knew he would not add, and because he would not, they stand upon that flimsy pretext for voting down what they argued was the meaning and intent of their own bill. They left room thereby for this Dred Scott decision, which goes very far to make slavery national throughout the United States.

I pass one or two points I have because my time will very soon expire, but I must be allowed to say that Judge Douglas recurs again, as he did upon one or two other occasions, [to][8] the enormity of Lincoln—an insignificant individual like Lincoln—upon his *ipse dixit* charging a conspiracy upon a large number of members of Congress, the Supreme Court and two Presidents, to nationalize slavery. I want to say that, in the first place, I have made no charge of this sort upon my *ipse dixit*. I have only arrayed the evidence tending to prove it, and presented it to the understanding of others, saying what I think it proves, but giving you the means of judging whether it proves it or not. This is precisely what I have done. I have not placed it upon my *ipse dixit* at all. On this occasion, I wish to recall his attention to a piece of evidence which I brought forward at Ottawa on Saturday, showing that he had

[8] Not in the source.

made substantially the *same charge* against substantially the *same persons*, excluding his dear self from the category. I ask him to give some attention to the evidence which I brought forward, that he himself had discovered a "fatal blow being struck" against the right of the people to exclude slavery from their limits, which fatal blow he assumed as in evidence in an article in the Washington *Union*, published "by authority." I ask by whose authority? He discovers a similar or identical provision in the Lecompton Constitution. Made by whom? The framers of that Constitution. Advocated by whom? By all the members of the party in the nation, who advocated the introduction of Kansas into the Union under the Lecompton Constitution.

I have asked his attention to the evidence that he arrayed to prove that such a fatal blow was being struck, and to the facts which he brought forward in support of that charge—being identical with the one which he thinks so villainous in me. He pointed it not at a newspaper editor merely, but at the President and his Cabinet and the members of Congress advocating the Lecompton Constitution and those framing that instrument. I must again be permitted to remind him, that although my *ipse dixit* may not be as great as his, yet it somewhat reduces the force of his calling my attention to the *enormity* of my making a like charge against him. [Loud applause.]

Go on, Judge Douglas.

MR. DOUGLAS' SPEECH.

Ladies and Gentlemen—The silence with which you have listened to Mr. Lincoln during his hour is creditable to this vast audience, composed of men of various political parties. Nothing is more honorable to any large mass of people assembled for the purpose of a fair discussion, than that kind and respectful attention that is yielded not only to your political friends, but to those who are opposed to you in politics.

I am glad that at last I have brought Mr. Lincoln to the conclusion that he had better define his position on certain political questions to which I called his attention at Ottawa. He there showed no disposition, no inclination to answer them. I did not present idle questions for him to answer merely for my gratification. I laid the foundation for those interrogatories by showing that they constituted the platform of the party whose nominee he is for the Senate. I did not presume that I had the right to catechise him as I saw proper, unless I showed that his party, or a majority of it, stood upon the platform and were in favor of the propositions upon which my questions were based. I desired simply to know, inasmuch as he had been nominated as the first, last, and only choice of his party, whether he concurred in the platform which that party had adopted for its government. In a few moments I will proceed to review the answers which he has given to these interrogatories; but in order to relieve his anxiety I will first respond to those which he has presented to me. Mark you, he has not presented interrogatories which have ever received the sanction of the party with which I am acting, and hence he has no other foundation for them than his own curiosity. ("That's a fact.")

First, he desires to know if the people of Kansas shall form a constitution by means entirely proper and unobjectionable and ask admission into the Union as a State, before they have the requisite population for a member of Congress, whether I will vote for that admission. Well, now, I regret exceedingly that he did not answer that interrogatory himself before he put it to me, in order that we might understand, and not be left to infer, on which side he is. (Good, good.) Mr. Trumbull, during the last session of Congress, voted from the beginning to the end against the admission of Oregon, although a free State, because she had not the requisite population for a member of Congress. (That's it.) Mr. Trumbull would not consent, under any circumstances, to let a State, free or slave, come into the Union until it had the requisite population. As Mr. Trumbull is in the field, fighting for Mr. Lincoln, I would like to have Mr. Lincoln answer his own question and tell me whether he is fighting Trumbull on that issue or not. (Good, put it to him, and cheers.) But I will answer his question. In reference to Kansas; it is my opinion, that as she has population enough to constitute a slave State, she has people enough for a free State. (Cheers.) I will not make Kansas an exceptional case to the other States of the Union. (Sound, and hear, hear.) I hold it to be a sound rule of universal application to require a territory to contain the requisite population for a member of Congress, before it is admitted as a State into the Union. I made that proposition in the Senate in 1856, and I renewed it during the last session, in a bill providing that no territory of the United States should form a constitution and apply for admission until it had the requisite population. On another occasion I proposed that neither Kansas, or any other territory, should be admitted until it had the requisite population. Congress did not adopt any of my propositions containing this general rule, but did make an exception of Kansas. I will stand by that exception. (Cheers.) Either Kansas must come in as a free State, with whatever population she may have, or the rule must be applied to all the other territories alike. (Cheers.) I therefore answer at once, that it having been decided that Kansas has people enough for a slave State, I hold that she has enough for a free State. ("Good," and applause.) I hope Mr. Lincoln is satisfied with my answer; ("he ought to be," and cheers,) and now I would like to get his answer to his own interrogatory—whether or not he will vote to admit Kansas before she has the requisite population. ("Hit him again.") I want to know whether he will vote to admit Oregon before that Territory has the requisite population. Mr. Trumbull will not, and the same reason that commits Mr. Trumbull against the admission of Oregon, commits him against Kansas, even if she should apply for admission as a free State. ("You've got him," and cheers.) If there is any sincerity, any truth in the argument of Mr. Trumbull in the Senate against the admission of Oregon because she had not 93,420 people, although her population was larger than that of Kansas, he stands pledged against the admission of both Oregon and Kansas until they have 93,420 inhabitants. I would like Mr. Lincoln to answer this question. I would like him to take his own medicine. (Laughter.) If he differs with Mr. Trumbull, let him answer his argument against the admission of Oregon, instead of poking questions at me. ("Right, good, good," laughter and cheers.)

The next question propounded to me by Mr. Lincoln is, can the people of a territory in any lawful way against the wishes of any citizen of the United States; exclude slavery from their limits prior to the formation of a State Constitution? I answer emphatically, as Mr. Lincoln has heard me answer a hundred times from every stump in Illinois, that in my opinion the people of a territory can, by lawful means, exclude slavery from their limits prior to the formation of a State Constitution. (Enthusiastic Applause.) Mr. Lincoln knew that I had answered that question over and over again. He heard me argue the Nebraska bill on that principle all over the State in 1854, in 1855 and in 1856, and he has no excuse for pretending to be in doubt as to my position on that question. It matters not what way the Supreme Court may hereafter decide as to the abstract question whether slavery may or may not go into a territory under the constitution, the people have the lawful means to introduce it or exclude it as they please, for the reason that slavery cannot exist a day or an hour anywhere, unless it is supported by local police regulations. (Right, right.) Those police regulations can only be established by the local legislature, and if the people are opposed to slavery they will elect representatives to that body who will by unfriendly legislation effectually prevent the introduction of it into their midst. If, on the contrary, they are for it, their legislation will favor its extension. Hence, no matter what the decision of the Supreme Court may be on that abstract question, still the right of the people to make a slave territory or a free territory is perfect and complete under the Nebraska bill. I hope Mr. Lincoln deems my answer satisfactory on that point.

[Deacon Bross spoke.][9]

In this connection, I will notice the charge which he has introduced in relation to Mr. Chase's amendment. I thought that I had chased that amendment out of Mr. Lincoln's brain at Ottawa; (laughter) but it seems that it still haunts his imagination, and he is not yet satisfied. I had supposed that he would be ashamed to press that question further. He is a lawyer, and has been a Member of Congress, and has occupied his time and amused you by telling you about parliamentary proceedings. He ought to have known better than to try to palm off his miserable impositions upon this intelligent audience. ("Good," and cheers.) The Nebraska bill provided that the legislative power, and authority of the said Territory, should extend to all rightful subjects of legislation consistent with the organic act and the Constitution of the United States. It did not make any exception as to slavery, but gave all the power that it was possible for Congress to give, without violating the Constitution to the Territorial Legislature, with no exception or limitation on the subject of slavery at all. The language of that bill which I have quoted, gave the full power and the full authority over the subject of slavery, affirmatively and negatively, to introduce it or exclude it, so far as the Constitution of the United States would permit. What more could Mr. Chase give by his amendment? Nothing. He offered his amendment for the identical purpose for which Mr. Lincoln is using it, to enable demagogues in the country to try and deceive the people. ("Good, hit him again," and cheers.)

[Deacon Bross spoke.]

His amendment was to this effect. It provided that the Legislature should have the power to exclude slavery; and General Cass suggested, "why not give the power to introduce as well as exclude?" The answer was, they have the power already in the bill to do both. Chase was afraid his amendment would be adopted if he

9 William Bross of Chicago, who sat on the platform. This and succeeding references to Bross were deleted by Lincoln. They do not appear in the *Press and Tribune*.

put the alternative proposition and so make it fair both ways, but would not yield. He offered it for the purpose of having it rejected. He offered it, as he has himself avowed over and over again, simply to make capital out of it for the stump. He expected that it would be capital for small politicians in the country, and that they would make an effort to deceive the people with it, and he was not mistaken, for Lincoln is carrying out the plan admirably. ("Good, good.") Lincoln knows that the Nebraska bill, without Chase's amendment, gave all the power which the Constitution would permit. Could Congress confer any more? ("No, no.") Could Congress go beyond the Constitution of the country? We gave all, a full grant, with no exception in regard to slavery one way or the other. We left that question as we left all others, to be decided by the people for themselves, just as they pleased. I will not occupy my time on this question. I have argued it before all over Illinois. I have argued it in this beautiful city of Freeport; I have argued it in the North, the South, the East and the West, avowing the same sentiments and the same principles. I have not been afraid to avow my sentiments up here for fear I would be trotted down into Egypt. (Cheers and laughter.)

The third question which Mr. Lincoln presented is, if the Supreme Court of the United States shall decide that a State of this Union cannot exclude slavery from its own limits will I submit to it? I am amazed that Lincoln should ask such a question. ("A school boy knows better.") Yes, a school boy does know better. Mr. Lincoln's object is to cast an imputation upon the Supreme Court. He knows that there never was but one man in America, claiming any degree of intelligence or decency, who ever for a moment pretended such a thing. It is true that the Washington *Union,* in an article published on the 17th of last December, did put forth that doctrine, and I denounced the article on the floor of the Senate, in a speech which Mr. Lincoln now pretends was against the President. The *Union* had claimed that slavery had a right to go into the free States, and that any provision in the Constitution or laws of the free States to the contrary were null and void. I denounced it in the Senate, as I said before, and I was the first man who did. Lincoln's friends, Trumbull, and Seward, and Hale, and Wilson, and the whole Black Republican side of the Senate were silent. They left it to me to denounce it. (Cheers.) And what was the reply made to me on that occasion? Mr. Toombs, of Georgia, got up and undertook to lecture me on the ground that I ought not to have deemed the article worthy of notice, and ought not to have replied to it; that there was not one man, woman or child south of the Potomac, in any slave State, who did not repudiate any such pretension. Mr. Lincoln knows that that reply was made on the spot, and yet now he asks this question. He might as well ask me, suppose Mr. Lincoln should steal a horse would I sanction it; (laughter,) and it would be as genteel in me to ask him, in the event he stole a horse, what ought to be done with him. He casts an imputation upon the Supreme Court of the United States by supposing that they would violate the Constitution of the United States. I tell him that such a thing is not possible. (Cheers.) It would be an act of moral treason that no man on the bench could ever descend to. Mr. Lincoln himself would never in his partizan feelings so far forget what was right as to be guilty of such an act. ("Good, good.")

The fourth question of Mr. Lincoln is, are you in favor of acquiring additional territory in disregard as to how such acquisition may effect the Union on the slavery questions. This question is very ingeniously and cunningly put.

[Deacon Bross here spoke, *sotto voce*,—the reporter understanding him to say, "Now we've got him."]

The Black Republican creed lays it down expressly, that under no circumstances shall we acquire any more territory unless slavery is first prohibited in the country. I ask Mr. Lincoln whether he is in favor of that proposition. Are you (addressing Mr. Lincoln) opposed to the acquisition of any more territory, under any circumstances, unless slavery is prohibited in it? That he does not like to answer. When I ask him whether he stands up to that article in the platform of his party, he turns, yankee-fashion, and without answering it, asks me whether I am in favor of acquiring territory without regard to how it may affect the Union on the slavery question. (Good.) I answer that whenever it becomes necessary, in our growth and progress to acquire more territory, that I am in favor of it, without reference to the question of slavery, and when we have acquired it, I will leave the people free to do as they please, either to make it slave or free territory, as they prefer. [Here Deacon Bross spoke, the reporter believes that he said, "That's bold." It was said solemnly.] It is idle to tell me or you that we have territory enough. Our fathers supposed that we had enough when our territory extended to the Mississippi river, but a few years' growth and expansion satisfied them that we needed more, and the Louisiana territory, from the West branch of the Mississippi, to the British possessions, was acquired. Then we acquired Oregon, then California and New Mexico. We have enough now for the present, but this is a young and a growing nation. It swarms as often as a hive of bees, and as new swarms are turned out each year, there must be hives in which they can gather and make their honey. (Good.) In less than fifteen years, if the same progress that has distinguished this country for the last fifteen years continues, every foot of vacant land between this and the Pacific ocean, owned by the United States, will be occupied. Will you not continue to increase at the end of fifteen years as well as now? I tell you, increase, and multiply, and expand, is the law of this nation's existence. (Good.) You cannot limit this great republic by mere boundary lines, saying, "thus far shalt thou go, and no further." Any one of you gentlemen might as well say to a son twelve years old that he is big enough, and must not grow any larger, and in order to prevent his growth put a hoop around him to keep him to his present size. What would be the result? Either the hoop must burst and be rent asunder, or the child must die. So it would be with this great nation. With our natural increase, growing with a rapidity unknown in any other part of the globe, with the tide of emigration that is fleeing from despotism in the old world to seek a refuge in our own, there is a constant torrent pouring into this country that requires more land, more territory upon which to settle, and just as fast as our interests and our destiny require additional territory in the north, in the south, or on the islands of the ocean, I am for it, and when we acquire it will leave the people, according to the Nebraska bill, free to do as they please on the subject of slavery and every other question. (Good, good, hurra for Douglas.)

I trust now that Mr. Lincoln will deem himself answered on his four points. He racked his brain so much in devising these four questions that he exhausted himself, and had not strength enough to invent the others. (Laughter.) As soon as he is able to hold a council with his advisers, Lovejoy, Farnsworth, and Fred. Douglass, he will frame and propound others. (Good, good, &c. Renewed laughter, in which Mr. Lincoln feebly joined, saying that he hoped with their aid to get seven questions, the number asked him by Judge Douglas, and so make *conclusions* even.) You Black Republicans who say good, I have no doubt think that they are all good men. (White, white.) I have reason to recollect that some people in this country think that Fred. Douglass is a very good man. The last time I came here to make a speech, while talking from the stand to you, people of Freeport, as I am doing to-day, I saw a carriage and a magnificent one it was, drive up and take a position on the outside of the crowd; a beautiful young lady was sitting on the box seat, whilst Fred. Douglass and her mother reclined inside, and the owner of the carriage acted as driver. (Laughter, cheers, cries of right, what have you to say against it, &c.) I saw this in your own town. ("What of it.") All I have to say of it is this, that if you, Black Republicans, think that the negro ought to be on a social equality with your wives and daughters, and ride in a carriage with your wife, whilst you drive the team, you have a perfect right to do so. (Good, good, and cheers, mingled with hooting and cries of white, white.) I am told that one of Fred. Douglass' kinsmen, another rich black negro, is now traveling in this part of the State making speeches for his friend Lincoln as the champion of black men. ("White men, white men," and "what have you got to say against it." That's right, &c.) All I have to say on that subject is that those of you who believe that the negro is your equal and ought to be on an equality with you socially, politically, and legally; have a right to entertain those opinions, and of course will vote for Mr. Lincoln. ("Down with the negro," no, no, &c.)

I have a word to say on Mr. Lincoln's answer to the interrogatories contained in my speech at Ottawa, and which he has pretended to reply to here to-day. Mr. Lincoln makes a great parade of the fact that I quoted a platform as having been adopted by the Black Republican party at Springfield in 1854, which, it turns out, was adopted at another place. Mr. Lincoln loses sight of the thing itself in his ecstasies over the mistake I made in stating the place where it was done. He thinks that that platform was not adopted on the right "spot."

When I put the direct questions to Mr. Lincoln to ascertain whether he now stands pledged to that creed—to the unconditional repeal of the fugitive slave law, a refusal to admit any more slave States into the Union even if the people want them, a determination to apply the Wilmot Proviso not only to all the territory, we now have, but all that we may hereafter acquire, he refused to answer, and his followers say, in excuse, that the resolutions upon which I based my interrogatories were not adopted at the "*right spot.*" (Laughter and applause.) Lincoln and his political friends are great on "*spots.*" (Renewed laughter.) In Congress, as a representative of this State, he declared the Mexican war to be unjust and infamous, and would not support it, or acknowledge his own country to be right in the contest, because he said that American blood was not shed on American soil in the "*right spot.*" (Lay on to him.) And now he cannot answer the questions I put to him at Ottawa because the resolutions I read were not adopted at the "*right spot.*" It may be possible that I was led into an error as to the *spot* on which the resolutions I then read were proclaimed, but I was not, and am not in error as to the fact of their forming the basis of the creed of the Republican party when that party was first organized. [Cheers.] I will state to you the evidence I had, and upon which I relied for my statement that the resolutions in question were adopted at Springfield on the 5th of October, 1854. Although I was aware that such resolutions had been passed in this district, and nearly all the northern Congressional districts and county conventions, I had not noticed whether or not they had been adopted by any State convention. In 1856, a debate arose in Congress between Major Thomas L. Harris, of the Springfield district, and Mr. Norton,[10] of the Joliet district, on political matters connected with our State, in the course of which Major Harris quoted those resolutions as having been passed by the first Republican State Convention that ever assembled in Illinois. I knew that Major Harris was remarkable for his accuracy, that he was a very conscientious and sincere man, and I also noticed that Norton did not question the accuracy of this statement. I therefore took it for granted that it was so, and the other day when I concluded to use the resolutions at Ottawa, I wrote to Charles H. Lanphier, editor of the State Register, at Springfield, calling his attention to them, telling him that I had been informed that Major Harris was lying sick at Springfield, and desiring him to call upon him and ascertain all the facts concerning the resolutions, the time and the place where they were adopted. In reply Mr. Lanphier sent me two copies of his paper, which I have here. The first is a copy of the State Register, published at Springfield, Mr. Lincoln's own town, on the 16th of October 1854, only eleven days after the adjournment of the convention, from which I desire to read the following:

During the late discussions in this city, Lincoln made a speech, to which Judge Douglas replied. In Lincoln's speech he took the broad ground that, according to the Declaration of Independence, the whites and blacks are equal. From this he drew the conclusion, which he several times repeated, that the white man had no right to pass laws for the government of the black man without the nigger's consent. This speech of Lincoln's was heard and applauded by all the Abolitionists assembled in Springfield. So soon as Mr. Lincoln was done speaking, Mr. Codding arose and requested all the delegates to the Black Republican convention to withdraw into the Senate chamber. They did so, and after long deliberation, they laid down the following abolition platform as the platform on which they stood. We call the particular attention of all our readers to it.

10 Jesse O. Norton.

Then follows the identical platform, word for word, which I read at Ottawa. (Cheers.) Now, that was published in Mr. Lincoln's own town, eleven days after the convention was held, and it has remained on record up to this day never contradicted.

When I quoted the resolutions at Ottawa and questioned Mr. Lincoln in relation to them, he said that his name was on the committee that reported them, but he did not serve, nor did he think he served, because he was, or thought he was, in Tazewell county at the time the convention was in session. He did not deny that the resolutions were passed by the Springfield convention. He did not know better, and evidently thought that they were, but afterwards his friends declared that they had discovered that they varied in some respects from the resolutions passed by that convention. I have shown you that I had good evidence for believing that the resolutions had been passed at Springfield. Mr. Lincoln ought to have known better; but not a word is said about his ignorance on the subject, whilst I, notwithstanding the circumstances, am accused of forgery.

Now, I will show you that if I have made a mistake as to the place where these resolutions were adopted—and when I get down to Springfield I will investigate the matter and see whether or not I have—that the principles they enunciate were adopted as the Black Republican platform (white, white,) in the various counties and Congressional Districts throughout the north end of the State in 1854. This platform was adopted in nearly every county that gave a Black Republican majority for the Legislature in that year, and here is a man (pointing to Mr. Denio,[11] who sat on the stand near Deacon Bross,) who knows as well as any living man that it was the creed of the Black Republican party at that time. I would be willing to call Denio as a witness, or any other honest man belonging to that party. I will now read the resolutions adopted at the Rockford Convention on the 30th of August, 1854, which nominated Washburne for Congress. You elected him on the following platform:

Resolved, That the continued and increasing aggressions of slavery in our country are destructive of the best rights of a free people, and that such aggressions cannot be successfully resisted without the united political action of all good men.

Resolved, That the citizens of the United States hold in their hands peaceful, constitutional, and efficient remedy against the encroachments of the slave power, the ballot box, and, if that remedy is boldly and wisely applied, the principles of liberty and eternal justice will be established.

[11] Cyrenius B. Denio, state representative from Jo Daviess County.

Resolved, That we accept this issue forced upon us by the slave power, and, in defense of freedom, will co-operate and be known as Republicans, pledged to the accomplishment of the following purposes:

To bring the Administration of the Government back to the control of first principles; to restore Kansas and Nebraska to the position of free Territories; to repeal and entirely abrogate the fugitive slave law; to restrict slavery to those States in which it exists; to prohibit the admission of any more slave States into the Union; to exclude slavery from all the territories over which the general government has exclusive jurisdiction, and to resist the acquisition of any more territories unless the introduction of slavery therein forever shall have been prohibited.

Resolved, That in furtherance of these principles we will use such constitutional and lawful means as shall seem best adapted to their accomplishment, and that we will support no man for office under the General or State Government who is not positively committed to the support of these principles and whose personal character and conduct is not a guaranty that he is reliable and shall abjure all party allegiance and ties.

Resolved, That we cordially invite persons of all former political parties whatever in favor of the object expressed in the above resolutions to unite with us in carrying them into effect.

[Senator Douglas was frequently interrupted in reading these resolutions by loud cries of "Good, good," "that's the doctrine," and vociferous applause.]

Well, you think that is a very good platform, do you not? ("Yes, yes, all right," and cheers.) If you do, if you approve it now, and think it is all right, you will not join with those men who say that I libel you by calling these your principles, will you? ("Good, good, hit him again," and great laughter and cheers.) Now, Mr. Lincoln complains; Mr. Lincoln charges that I did you and him injustice by saying that this was the platform of your party. (Renewed laughter.) I am told that Washburne made a speech in Galena last night in which he abused me awfully for bringing to light this platform on which he was elected to Congress. He thought that you had forgotten it, as he and Mr. Lincoln desire to. (Laughter.) He did not deny but that you had adopted it, and that he had subscribed to and was pledged to it, but he did not think it was fair to call it up and remind the people that it was their platform.

[Here Deacon Bross spoke.]

But I am glad to find that you are more honest in your abolitionism than your leaders, by avowing that it is your platform, and right in your opinion. (Laughter, "you have them, good, good.")

In the adoption of that platform, you not only declared that you would resist the admission of any more slave States, and work for the repeal of the Fugitive Slave law, but you pledged yourselves not to vote for any man for State or Federal offices who was not committed to these principles. ("Exactly so." Exactly so! Cheers.) You were thus committed. Similar resolutions to those were adopted in your county Convention here, and now with your admissions that they are your platform and embody your sentiments now as they did then, what do you think of Mr. Lincoln, your candidate for the U.S. Senate, who is attempting to dodge the responsibility of this platform, because it was not adopted in the right spot? (Shouts of laughter, hurra for Douglas, &c.) I thought that it was adopted in Springfield, but it turns out it was not, that it was adopted at Rockford and in the various counties which comprise this Congressional District. When I get into the next district, I will show that the same platform was adopted there, and so on through the State, until I nail the responsibility of it upon the back of the Black Republican party throughout the State. ("White, white," three cheers for Douglas.)

(A VOICE—Couldn't you modify and call it brown? Laughter.)

MR. DOUGLAS.—Not a bit. I thought that you were becoming a little brown when your members in Congress voted for the Crittenden-Montgomery bill, but since you have backed out from that position and gone back to Abolitionism, you are black, and not brown. (Shouts of laughter, and a voice, "Can't you ask him another question.")

Gentlemen, I have shown you what your platform was in 1854. You still adhere to it. The same platform was adopted by nearly all the counties where the Black Republican party had a majority in 1854. I wish now to call your attention to the action of your representatives in the Legislature when they assembled together at Springfield. In the first place you must remember that this was the organization of a new party. It is so declared in the resolutions themselves which say that you are going to dissolve all old party ties and call the new party Republican. The old Whig party was to have its throat cut from ear to ear, and the Democratic party was to be annihilated and blotted out of existence, whilst in lieu of these parties the Black Republican party was to be organized on this Abolition platform. You know who the chief leaders were in breaking up and destroying these two great parties. Lincoln on the one hand and Trumbull on the other, being disappointed politicians, (laughter,) and having retired or been driven to obscurity by an outraged constituency because of their political sins, formed a scheme to abolitionize the two parties and lead the Old Line Whigs and Old Line Democrats captive, bound hand and foot into the Abolition camp. Giddings, Chase, Fred. Douglass and Lovejoy were here to christen them whenever they were brought in. (Great laughter.) Lincoln went to work to dissolve the Old Line Whig party. Clay was dead, and although the sod was not yet green on his grave, this man undertook to bring into disrepute those great compromise measures of 1850, with which Clay and Webster were identified. Up to 1854 the old Whig party and the Democratic party had stood on a common platform so far as this slavery question was concerned. You Whigs and we Democrats differed about the bank, the tariff, distribution, the specie circular and the subtreasury, but we agreed on this slavery question and the true mode of preserving the peace and harmony of the Union. The compromise measures of 1850 were introduced by Clay, were defended by Webster, and supported by Cass, and were approved by Fillmore, and sanctioned by the National men of both parties. They constituted a common plank upon which both Whigs and Democrats stood. In 1852 the Whig party in its last national convention at Baltimore endorsed and approved these measures of Clay, and so did the national convention of the Democratic party held that same year. Thus the old line Whigs and the old line Democrats stood pledged to the great principle of self-government, which guarantees to the people of each Territory the right to decide the slavery question for themselves. In 1854 after the death of Clay and Webster, Mr. Lincoln on the part of the Whigs undertook to abolitionize the Whig party, by dissolving it, transferring the members into the Abolition camp and making them train under Giddings, Fred. Douglass, Lovejoy, Chase, Farnsworth, and other abolition leaders. Trumbull undertook to dissolve the Democratic party by taking old Democrats into the abolition camp. Mr. Lincoln was aided in his efforts by many leading Whigs throughout the State. Your member of Congress, Mr. Washburne, being one of the most active. (Good fellow.) Trumbull was aided by many renegades from the Democratic party, among whom were John Wentworth, (laughter,) Tom Turner and others with whom you are familiar.

MR. TURNER, who was one of the moderators, here interposed and said that he had drawn the resolutions which Senator Douglas had read.

MR. DOUGLAS—Yes, and Turner says that he drew these resolutions. ("Hurra for Turner." "Hurra for Douglas.") That is right, give Turner cheers for drawing the resolutions if you approve them. If he drew those resolutions he will not deny that they are the creed of the Black Republican party.

MR. TURNER.—They are our creed exactly. (Cheers.)

MR. DOUGLAS—And yet Lincoln denies that he stands on them.

("Good, good," and laughter.) Mr. Turner says that the creed of the Black Republican party is the admission of no more slave States, and yet Mr. Lincoln declares that he would not like to be placed in a position where he would have to vote for them. All I have to say to friend Lincoln is, that I do not think there is much danger of his being placed in such a position. (More laughter.) As Mr. Lincoln would be very sorry to be placed in such an embarrassing position as to be obliged to vote on the admission of any more slave States, I propose, out of mere kindness, to relieve him from any such necessity. (Renewed laughter and cheers.)

When the bargain between Lincoln and Trumbull was completed for abolitionizing the Whig and Democratic parties, they "spread" over the State, Lincoln still pretending to be an Old Line Whig in order to "rope in" the Whigs, and Trumbull pretending to be as good a Democrat as he ever was in order to coax the Democrats over into the Abolition ranks. ("That's exactly what we want.") They played the part that "decoy ducks" play down on the Potomac river. In that part of the country they make artificial ducks and put them on the water in places where the wild ducks are to be found for the purpose of decoying them. Well, Lincoln and Trumbull played the part of these "decoy ducks" and deceived enough Old Line Whigs and Old Line Democrats to elect a Black Republican Legislature. When that Legislature met, the first thing it did was to elect as Speaker of the House the very man who is now boasting that he wrote the Abolition platform on which Lincoln will not stand ("Good;" "hit him again," and cheers.) I want to know of Mr. Turner whether or not, when he was elected he was a good embodiment of Republican principles?

MR. TURNER—I hope I was then and am now.

MR. DOUGLAS—He answers that he hopes he was then and is now. He wrote that Black Republican platform, and is satisfied with it now. ("Hurrah for Turner," "good," &c.) I admire and acknowledge Turner's honesty. Every man of you know that what he says about these resolutions being the platform of the Black Republican party is true, and you also know that each one of these men who are shuffling and trying to deny it are only trying to cheat the people out of their votes for the purpose of deceiving them still more after the election. ("Good," and cheers.) I propose to trace this thing a little further, in order that you can see what additional evidence there is to fasten this revolutionary platform upon the Black Republican party. When the Legislature assembled, there was an United States Senator to elect in the place of Gen. Shields, and before they proceeded to ballot, Lovejoy insisted on laying down certain principles by which to govern the party. It has been published to the world and satisfactorily proven that there was at the time the alliance was made between Trumbull and Lincoln to abolitionize the two parties, an agreement that Lincoln should take Shields' place in the United States Senate, and Trumbull should have mine so soon as they could conveniently get rid of me. When Lincoln was beaten for Shields' place in a manner I will refer to in a few minutes, he felt very sore and restive; his friends grumbled, and some of them came out and charged that the most infamous treachery had been practised against him; that the bargain was that Lincoln was to have had Shields' place, and Trumbull was to have waited for mine, but that Trumbull having the control of a few abolitionized Democrats, he prevented them from voting for Lincoln, thus keeping him within a few votes of an election until he succeeded in forcing the party to drop him and elect Trumbull. Well, Trumbull having cheated Lincoln, his friends made a fuss, and in order to keep them and Lincoln quiet, the party were obliged to come forward, in advance, at the last State election, and make a pledge that they would go for Lincoln and nobody else. Lincoln could not be silenced in any other way.

Now, there are a great many Black Republicans of you who do not know this thing was done. ("White, white," and great clamor.) I wish to remind you that while Mr. Lincoln was speaking there was not a Democrat vulgar and black-guard enough to interrupt him. (Great applause and cries of hurrah for Douglas.) But I know that the shoe is pinching you. I am clinching Lincoln now and you are scared to death for the result. (Cheers.) I have seen this thing before. I have seen men make appointments for joint discussions, and the moment their man has been heard, try to interrupt and prevent a fair hearing of the other side. I have seen your mobs before, and defy your wrath. (Tremendous applause.) My friends, do not cheer, for I need my whole time. The object of the opposition is to occupy my attention in order to prevent me from giving the whole evidence and nailing this double dealing on the Black Republican party. As I have before said, Lovejoy demanded a declaration of principles on the part of the Black Republicans of the Legislature before going into an election for United States Senator. He offered the following preamble and resolutions which I hold in my hand:

Whereas, human slavery is a violation of the principles of natural and revealed rights; and whereas, the fathers of the Revolution, fully imbued with the spirit of these principles, declared freedom to be the inalienable birthright of all men; and whereas, the preamble to the

Constitution of the United States avers that that instrument was ordained to establish justice, and secure the blessings of liberty to ourselves and our posterity; and whereas, in furtherance of the above principles, slavery was forever prohibited in the old northwest territory, and more recently in all that territory lying west and north of the State of Missouri, by the act of the federal government; and whereas, the repeal of the prohibition, last referred to, was contrary to the wishes of the people of Illinois, a violation of an implied compact, long deemed and held sacred by the citizens of the United States, and a wide departure from the uniform action of the general government in relation to the extension of slavery; therefore,

Resolved, by the House of Representatives, the Senate concurring therein, That our Senators in Congress be instructed, and our Representatives requested, to introduce, if not otherwise introduced, and to vote for a bill to restore such prohibition to the aforesaid territories, and also to extend a similar prohibition to all territory which now belongs to the United States, or which may hereafter come under their jurisdiction.

Resolved, That our Senators in Congress be instructed, and our Representatives requested, to vote against the admission of any State into the Union, the constitution of which does not prohibit slavery, whether the territory out of which such State may have been formed shall have been acquired by conquest, treaty, purchase, or from original territory of the United States.

Resolved, That our Senators in Congress be instructed and our Representatives requested to introduce and vote for a bill to repeal an act entitled "an act respecting fugitives from justice and persons escaping from the service of their masters"; and, failing in that, for such a modification of it as shall secure the right of *habeas corpus* and trial by jury before the regularly-constituted authorities of the State, to all persons claimed as owing service or labor.

(Cries of "good," "good," and cheers.) Yes, you say "good," "good," and I have no doubt you think so. Those resolutions were introduced by Mr. Lovejoy immediately preceding the election of Senator. They declared first, that the Wilmot Proviso must be applied to all territory North of 36 deg., 30 min. Secondly, that it must be applied to all territory South of 36 deg., 30 min. Thirdly, that it must be applied to all the territory now owned by the United States, and finally, that it must be applied to all territory hereafter to be acquired by the United States. The next resolution declares that no more slave States shall be admitted into this Union under any circumstances whatever, no matter whether they are formed out of territory now owned by us or that we may hereafter acquire, by treaty, by Congress, or in any manner whatever. (A VOICE, "That is right.") You say that is right. We will see in a moment. The next resolution demands the unconditional repeal of the fugitive slave law, although its unconditional repeal would leave no provision for carrying out that clause of the Constitution of the United States which guarantees the surrender of fugitives. If they could not get an unconditional repeal, they demanded that that law should be so modified as to make it as nearly useless as possible. Now I want to show you who voted for these resolutions. When the vote was taken on the first resolution it was decided in the affirmative—yeas 41, nays 32. You will find that this is a strict party vote, between the Democrats, on the one hand, and the Black Republicans, on the other. (Cries of white, white, and clamor.) I know your name, and always call things by their right name. The point I wish to call your attention to, is this: that these resolutions were adopted on the 7th day of February, and that on the 8th they went into an election for a U.S. Senator, and on that day every man who voted for these resolutions, with but two exceptions, voted for Lincoln for the U.S. Senate. (Cries of "good, good," and "give us their names.") I will read the names over to you if you want them, but I believe your object is to occupy my time. (Cries of "that is it.")

On the next resolution, the vote stood—yeas 33, nays 40, and on the third resolution—yeas 35, nays 47. I wish to impress it upon you, that every man who voted for those resolutions, with but two exceptions, voted on the next day for Lincoln, for U.S. Senator. Bear in mind that the members who thus voted for Lincoln were elected to the Legislature, pledged to vote for no man for office under the State or federal government who was not committed to this Black Republican platform. (Cries of "white, white," and "good for you.") They were all so pledged. Mr. Turner, who stands by me, and who then represented you, and who says that he wrote those resolutions, voted for Lincoln, when he was pledged not to do so unless Lincoln was committed in favor of those resolutions. I now ask Mr. Turner, (turning to Turner) did you violate your pledge in voting for Mr. Lincoln, or did he commit himself to your platform before you cast your vote for him? (Mr. Lincoln here started forward, and grasping Mr. Turner, shook him nervously, and said, "Don't answer, Turner, you have no right to answer.")

I could go through the whole list of names here and show you that all the Black Republicans in the Legislature, ("white, white,") who voted for Mr. Lincoln, had voted on the day previous for these resolutions. For instance, here are the names of Sargent and Little of Joe Daviess and Carroll; Thomas J. Turner, of Stephenson; Lawrence, of Boone and McHenry; Swan, of Lake; Pinckney, of Ogle county, and Lyman, of Winnebago. Thus you see every member from your Congressional District voted for Mr. Lincoln, and they were pledged not to vote for him unless he was committed to the doctrine of no more slave States, the prohibition of slavery in the Territories, and the repeal of the Fugitive Slave law. Mr. Lincoln tells you to-day that he is not pledged to any such doctrine. Either Mr. Lincoln was then committed to those propositions, or Mr. Turner violated his pledges to you when he voted for him. Either Lincoln was pledged to each one of those propositions, or else every Black Republican—(cries of "white, white,")—representative from this Congressional District violated his pledge of honor to his constituents by voting for him. I ask you which horn of the dilemma will you take? Will you hold Lincoln up to the platform of his party, or will you accuse every representative you had in the Legislature of violating his pledge of honor to his constituents. (VOICES; "we go for Turner," "we go for Lincoln;" "hurrah for Douglas," "hurrah for Turner.") There is no escape for you. Either Mr. Lincoln was committed to those propositions, or your members violated their faith. Take either horn of the dilemma you choose. There is no dodging the question, I want Lincoln's answer. He says he was not pledged to repeal the fugitive slave law, that he does not quite like to do it; he will not introduce a law to repeal it, but thinks there ought to be some law; he does not tell what it ought to be; upon the whole, he is altogether undecided, and don't know what to think or to do. That is the substance of his answer upon the repeal of the fugitive slave law. I put the question to him distinctly, whether he endorsed that part of the Black Republican platform which calls for the entire abrogation and repeal of the fugitive slave law. He answers no! that he does not endorse that, but he does not tell what he is for, or what he will vote for. His answer is, in fact, no answer at all. Why cannot he speak out and say what he is for and what he will do? (Cries of "that's right.")

In regard to there being no more slave States, he is not pledged to that. He would not like, he says, to be put in a position where he would have to vote one way or another upon that question. I pray you do not put him in a position that would embarrass him so much. (Laughter.) Gentlemen, if he goes to the Senate, he may be put in that position, and then which way will he vote?

[A VOICE—How will you vote?]

MR. DOUGLAS—I will vote for the admission of just such a State as by the form of their Constitution the people show they want; if they want slavery, they shall have it; if they prohibit slavery, it shall be prohibited. They can form their institutions to please themselves, subject only to the Constitution; and I for one stand ready to receive them into the Union. ("Three cheers for Douglas.")

Why cannot your Black Republican candidates talk out as plain as that when they are questioned? (Cries of "good, good.")

[Here Deacon Bross spoke.]

I do not want to cheat any man out of his vote. No man is deceived in regard to my principles if I have the power to express myself in terms explicit enough to convey my ideas.

Mr. Lincoln made a speech when he was nominated for the U.S. Senate which covers all these abolition platforms. He there lays down a proposition so broad in its abolitionism as to cover the whole ground.

> In my opinion it (the slavery agitation) will not cease until a crisis shall have been reached and passed. "A house divided against itself cannot stand." I believe this Government cannot endure permanently half Slave and half Free. I do not expect the house to fall—but I do expect it will cease to be divided. It will become all one thing or all the other. Either the opponents of Slavery will arrest the further spread of it, and place it where the public mind shall rest in the belief that it is in the course of ultimate extinction, or its advocates will push it forward till it shall become alike lawful in all the States—old as well as new, North as well as South.

There you find that Mr. Lincoln lays down the doctrine that this Union cannot endure divided as our Fathers made it, with free and slave States. He says they must all become one thing, or all the other; that they must be all free or all slave, or else the Union cannot continue to exist. It being his opinion that to admit any more slave States, to continue to divide the Union into free and slave States, will dissolve it. I want to know of Mr. Lincoln whether he will vote for the admission of another Slave state. (Cries of "Bring him out.")

He tells you the Union cannot exist unless the States are all free or all slave; he tells you that he is opposed to making them all slave, and hence he is for making them all free, in order that the Union may exist; and yet he will not say that he will not vote against the admission of another slave State, knowing that the Union must be dissolved if he votes for it. (Great laughter.) I ask you if that is fair dealing? The true intent and inevitable conclusion to be drawn from his first Springfield speech is, that he is opposed to the admission of any more slave States under any circumstance. If he is so opposed why not say so? If he believes this Union cannot endure divided into free and slave States, that they must all become free in order to save the Union, he is bound, as an honest man, to vote against any more slave States. If he believes it he is bound to do it. Show me that it is my duty in order to save the Union to do a particular act, and I will do it if the constitution does not prohibit it. (Applause.) I am not for the dissolution of the Union under any circumstances. (Renewed applause.) I will pursue no course of conduct that will give just cause for the dissolution of the Union. The hope of the friends of freedom throughout the world rests upon the perpetuity of this Union. The down-trodden and oppressed people who are suffering under European despotism all look with hope and anxiety to the American Union as the only resting place and permanent home of freedom and self-government.

Mr. Lincoln says that he believes that this Union cannot continue to endure with slave States in it, and yet he will not tell you distinctly whether he will vote for or against the admission of any more slave States, but says he would not like to be put to the test. (Laughter.) I do not think he will be put to the test. (Renewed laughter.) I do not think that the people of Illinois desire a man to represent them who would not like to be put to the test on the performance of a high constitutional duty. (Cries of good.) I will retire in shame from the Senate of the United States when I am not willing to be put to the test in the performance of my duty. I have been put to severe tests. (That is so.) I have stood by my principles in fair weather and in foul, in the sunshine and in the rain. I have defended the great principles of self-government here among you when Northern sentiment ran in a torrent against me. (A VOICE,—that is so,) and I have defended that same great principle when Southern sentiment came down like an avalanche upon me. I was not afraid of any test they put to me. I knew I was right —I knew my principles were sound—I knew that the people would see in the end that I had done right, and I knew that the God of Heaven would smile upon me if I was faithful in the performance of my duty. (Cries of good, cheers and laughter.)

Mr. Lincoln makes a charge of corruption against the Supreme Court of the United States, and two Presidents of the United States, and attempts to bolster it up by saying that I did the same against the Washington *Union*. Suppose I did make that charge of corruption against the Washington *Union*, when it was true, does that justify him in making a false charge against me and others? That is the question I would put. He says that at the time the Nebraska bill was introduced, and before it was passed there was a conspiracy between the Judges of the Supreme Court, President Pierce, President Buchanan and myself by that bill, and the decision of the Court to break down the barrier and establish slavery all over the Union. Does he not know that that charge is historically false as against President Buchanan? He knows that Mr. Buchanan was at that time in England, representing this country with distinguished ability at the Court of St. James, that he was there for a long time before and did not return for a year or more after. He knows that to be true, and that fact proves his charge to be false as against Mr. Buchanan. (Cheers.) Then again, I wish to call his attention to the fact that at the time the Nebraska bill was passed the Dred Scott case was not before the Supreme Court at all; it was not upon the docket of the Supreme Court; it had not been brought there, and the Judges in all probability, knew nothing of it. Thus the history of the country proves the charge to be false as against them. As to President Pierce, his high character as a man of integrity and honor is enough to vindicate him from such a charge, (laughter and applause,) and as to myself, I pronounce the charge an infamous lie, whenever and wherever made, and by whomsoever made. I am willing that Mr. Lincoln should go and rake up every public act of mine, every measure I have introduced, report I have made, speech delivered, and criticise them, but when he charges upon me a corrupt conspiracy for the purpose of perverting the institutions of the country, I brand it as it deserves. I say the history of the country proves it to be false, and that it could not have been possible at the time. But now he tries to protect himself in this charge, because I made a charge against the Washington *Union.* My speech in the Senate against the Washington *Union* was made because it advocated a revolutionary doctrine, by declaring that the free States had not the right to prohibit slavery within their own limits. Because I made that charge against the Washington *Union,* Mr. Lincoln says it was a charge against Mr. Buchanan. Suppose it was; is Mr. Lincoln the peculiar defender of Mr. Buchanan? Is he so interested in the federal administration, and so bound to it, that he must jump to the rescue and defend it from every attack that I may make against it? (Great laughter and cheers.) I understand the whole thing. The Washington *Union,* under that most corrupt of all men, Cornelius Wendell, is advocating Mr. Lincoln's claim to the Senate. Wendell was the printer of the last Black Republican House of Representatives; he was a candidate before the present Democratic House, but was ignominiously kicked out, and then he took the money which he had made out of the public printing by means of the Black Republicans, bought the Washington *Union,* and is now publishing it in the name of the Democratic party, and advocating Mr. Lincoln's election to the Senate. Mr. Lincoln therefore considers any attack upon Wendell and his corrupt gang as a personal attack upon him. (Immense cheering and laughter.) This only proves what I have charged, that there is an alliance between Lincoln and his supporters and the federal office-holders of this State, and Presidential aspirants out of it, to break me down at home.

[A VOICE.—That is impossible, and cheering.]

Mr. Lincoln feels bound to come in to the rescue of the Washington *Union*. In that speech which I delivered in answer to the Washington *Union*, I made it distinctly against the *Union*, and against the *Union* alone. I did not choose to go beyond that. If I have occasion to attack the President's conduct, I will do it in language that will not be misunderstood. When I differed with the President, I spoke out so that you all heard me. ("That you did," and cheers.) That question passed away; it resulted in the triumph of my principle by allowing the people to do as they please, and there is an end of the controversy. ("Hear, hear.") Whenever the great principle of self-government—the right of the people to make their own Constitution, and come into the Union with slavery, or without it, as they see proper—shall again arise, you will find me standing firm in defence of that principle, and fighting whoever fights it. ("Right, right." "Good, good," and cheers.) If Mr. Buchanan stands, as I doubt not he will, by the recommendation contained in his message, that hereafter all State constitutions ought to be submitted to the people before the admission of the State into the Union, he will find me standing by him firmly, shoulder to shoulder, in carrying it out. I know Mr. Lincoln's object, he wants to divide the Democratic party, in order that he may defeat me and get to the Senate.

Mr. Douglas' time here expired, and he stopped on the moment.

MR. LINCOLN'S REJOINDER.

As Mr. Lincoln arose he was greeted with vociferous cheers. He said:

My friends, it will readily occur to you that I cannot in half an hour notice all the things that so able a man as Judge Douglas can say in an hour and a half, and I hope, therefore, if there be anything that he has said upon which you would like to hear something from me, but which I omit to comment upon, you will bear in mind that it would be expecting an impossibility for me to go over his whole ground. I can but take up some of the points that he has dwelt upon, and employ my half-hour specially on them.

The first thing I have to say to you is a word in regard to Judge Douglas' declaration about the "vulgarity and blackguardism" in the audience—that no such thing, as he says, was shown by any Democrat while I was speaking. Now, I only wish, by way of reply on this subject, to say that while *I* was speaking *I* used no "vulgarity or blackguardism" towards any Democrat. [Great laughter and applause.]

Now, my friends, I come to all this long portion of the Judge's speech—perhaps half of it—which he has devoted to the various resolutions and platforms that have been adopted in the different counties in the different Congressional districts, and in the Illinois Legislature—which he supposes are at variance with the positions I have assumed before you to-day. It is true that many of these resolutions are at variance with the positions I have here assumed. All I have to ask is that we talk reasonably and rationally about it. I happen to know, the Judge's opinion to the contrary notwithstanding, that I have never tried to conceal my opinions, nor tried to deceive any one in reference to them. He may go and examine all the members who voted for me for United States Senator in 1855, after the election of 1854. They were pledged to certain things here at home, and were determined to have pledges from me, and if he will find any of these persons who will tell him anything inconsistent with what I say now, I will resign, or rather retire from the race, and give him no more trouble. [Applause.] The plain truth is this: At the introduction of the Nebraska policy, we believed there was a new era being introduced in the history of the Republic, which tended to the spread and perpetuation of slavery. But in our opposition to that measure we did not agree with one another in everything. The people in the north end of the State were for stronger measures of opposition than we of the central and southern portions of the State, but we were all opposed to the Nebraska doctrine. We had that one feeling and that one sentiment in common. You at the north end met in your Conventions and passed your resolutions. We in the middle of the State and further south did not hold such Conventions and pass the same resolutions, although we had in general a common view and a common sentiment. So that these meetings which the Judge has alluded to, and the resolutions he has read from were local and did not spread over the whole State. We at last met together in 1856 from all parts of the State, and we agreed upon a common platform. You, who held more extreme notions either yielded those notions, or if not wholly yielding them, agreed to yield them practically, for the sake of embodying the opposition to the measures which the opposite party were pushing forward at that time. We met you then, and if there was anything yielded, it was for practical purposes. We agreed then upon a platform for the party throughout the entire State of Illinois, and now we are all bound as a party, *to that platform*. And I say here to you, if any one expects of me—in the case of my election—that I will do anything not signified by our Republican platform and my answers here to-day, I tell you very frankly that person will be deceived. I do not ask for the vote of any one who supposes that I have secret purposes or pledges that I dare not speak out. Cannot the Judge be satisfied? If he fears, in the unfortunate case of my election, [Laughter] that my going to Washington will enable me to advocate sentiments contrary to those which I expressed when you voted for and elected me, I assure him that his fears are wholly needless and groundless. Is the Judge really afraid of any such thing? [Laughter.] I'll tell you what he is afraid of. *He is afraid we'll all pull together*. [Applause, and cries of "we will, we will."] This is what alarms him more than anything else. [Laughter.] For my part, I do hope that all of us, entertaining a common sentiment in opposition to what appears to us a design to nationalize and perpetuate slavery, will waive minor differences on questions which either belong to the dead past or the distant future, and all pull together in this struggle. What are your sentiments? ["We will, we will," and loud cheers.] If it be true, that on the ground which I occupy—ground which I occupy as frankly and boldly as Judge Douglas does his—my views, though partly coinciding with yours, are not as perfectly in accordance with your feelings as his are, I do say to you in all candor, Go for him and not for me. I hope to deal in all things fairly with Judge Douglas, and with the people of the State, in this contest. And if I should never be elected to any office, I trust I may go down with no stain of falsehood upon my reputation,—notwithstanding the hard opinions Judge Douglas chooses to entertain of me. [Laughter.]

The Judge has again addressed himself to the abolition tendencies of a speech of mine, made at Springfield in June last. I have so often tried to answer what he is always saying on that melancholy theme, that I almost turn with disgust from the discussion—from the repetition of an answer to it. I trust that nearly all of this intelligent audience have read that speech. ["We have; we have."] If you have, I may venture to leave it to you to inspect it closely, and see whether it contains any of those "bugaboos" which frighten Judge Douglas. [Laughter.]

The Judge complains that I did not fully answer his questions. If I have the sense to comprehend and answer those questions, I have done so fairly. If it can be pointed out to me how I can more fully and fairly answer him, I aver I have not the sense to see how it is to be done. He says I do not declare I would in any event vote for the admission of a slave State into the Union. If I have been fairly reported he will see that I did give an explicit answer to his interrogatories. I did not merely say that I would dislike to be put to the test; but I said clearly, if I were put to the test, and a Territory from which slavery had been excluded should present herself with a State Constitution sanctioning slavery—a most extraordinary thing and wholly unlikely ever to happen—I did not see how I could avoid voting for her admission. But he refuses to understand that I said so, and he wants this audience to understand that I did not say so. Yet it will be so reported in the printed speech that he cannot help seeing it.

He says if I should vote for the admission of a Slave State I would be voting for a dissolution of the Union, because I hold that the Union can not permanently exist half slave and half free. I repeat that I do not believe this Government *can* endure permanently half slave and half free, yet I do not admit, nor does it at all follow, that the admission of a single Slave State will permanently fix the character and establish this as a universal slave nation. The Judge is very happy indeed at working up these quibbles. [Laughter and cheers.] Before leaving the subject of answering questions I aver as my confident belief, when you come to see our speeches in print, that you will find every question which he has asked me more fairly and boldly and fully answered than he has answered those which I put to him. Is not that so? [Cries of yes, yes.] The two speeches may be placed side by side; and I will venture to leave it to impartial judges whether his questions have not been more directly and circumstantially answered than mine.

Judge Douglas says he made a charge upon the editor of the Washington *Union*, *alone*, of entertaining a purpose to rob the States of their power to exclude slavery from their limits. I undertake to say, and I make the direct issue, that he did *not* make his charge against the editor of the *Union* alone. [Applause.] I will undertake to prove by the record here, that he made that charge against more and higher dignitaries than the editor of the Washington *Union*. I am quite aware that he was shirking and dodging around the form in which he put it, but I can make it manifest that he leveled his "fatal blow" against more persons than this Washington editor. Will he dodge it now by alleging that I am trying to defend Mr. Buchanan against the charge? Not at all. Am I not making the same charge myself? [Laughter and applause.] I am trying to show that you, Judge Douglas, are a witness on my side. [Renewed Laughter.] I am not defending Buchanan, and I will tell Judge Douglas that in my opinion, when he made that charge, he had an eye farther North than he was to-day. He was then fighting against people who called *him* a Black Republican and an Abolitionist. It is mixed all through his speech, and it is tolerably manifest that his eye was a great deal farther North than it is to-day. [Cheers and laughter.] The Judge says that though he made this charge Toombs got up and declared there was not a man in the United States, except the editor of the *Union*, who was in favor of the doctrines put forth in that article. And thereupon, I understand that the Judge withdrew the charge. Although he had taken extracts from the newspaper, and then from the Lecompton Constitution, to show the existence of a conspiracy to bring about a "fatal blow," by which the States were to be deprived of the right of excluding slavery, it all went to pot as soon as Toombs got up and told him it was not true. [Laughter.] It reminds me of the story that John Phoenix, the California railroad surveyor, tells. He says they started out from the Plaza to the Mission of Dolores. They had two ways of determining distances. One was by a chain and pins taken over the ground. The other was by a "go-it-ometer"—an invention of his own—a three-legged instrument, with which he computed a series of triangles between the points. At night he turned to the chain-man to ascertain what distance they had come, and found that by some mistake he had merely dragged the chain over the ground without keeping any record. By the "go-it-ometer" he found he had made ten miles. Being skeptical about this, he asked a drayman who was passing how far it was to the plaza. The drayman replied it was just half a mile, and the surveyor put it down in his book—just as Judge Douglas says, after he had made his calculations and computations, he took Toombs' statement. [Great laughter.] I have no doubt that after Judge Douglas had made his charge, he was as easily satisfied about its truth as the surveyor was of the drayman's statement of the distance to the plaza. [Renewed laughter.] Yet it is a fact that the man who put forth all that matter which Douglas deemed a "fatal blow" at State sovereignty, was elected by the Democrats as public printer.

Now, gentlemen, you may take Judge Douglas' speech of March 22d, 1858, beginning about the middle of page 21, and reading to the bottom of page 24, and you will find the evidence on which I say that he did not make his charge against the editor of the *Union* alone. I cannot stop to read it, but I will give it to the reporters. Judge Douglas said:

Mr. President, you here find several distinct propositions advanced boldly by the Washington *Union* editorially and apparently *authoritatively*, and every man who questions any of them is denounced as an abolitionist, a Free-Soiler, a fanatic. The propositions are, first, that the primary object of all government at its original institution is the protection of persons and property; second, that the Constitution of the United States declares that the citizens of each State shall be entitled to all the privileges and immunities of citizens in the several States; and that, therefore, thirdly, all State laws, whether organic or otherwise, which prohibit the citizens of one State from settling in another with their slave property, and especially declaring it forfeited, are direct violations of the original intention of the Government and Constitution of the United States; and fourth, that the emancipation of the slaves of the Northern States was a gross outrage on the rights of property, inasmuch as it was involuntarily done on the part of the owner.

Remember that this article was published in the *Union* on the 17th of November, and on the 18th appeared the first article giving the adhesion of the *Union* to the Lecompton Constitution. It was in these words:

"KANSAS AND HER CONSTITUTION.—The vexed question is settled. The problem is solved. The dread point of danger is passed. All serious trouble to Kansas affairs is over and gone."

And a column, nearly, of the same sort. Then, when you come to look into the Lecompton Constitution, you find the same doctrine incorporated in it which was put forth editorially in the *Union*. What is it?

"ARTICLE 7. *Section* 1. The right of property is before and higher than any constitutional sanction; and the right of the owner of a slave to such slave and its increase is the same and as inviolable as the right of the owner of any property whatever."

Then in the schedule is a provision that the Constitution may be amended after 1864 by a two-thirds vote.

"But no alteration shall be made to affect the right of property in the ownership of slaves."

It will be seen by these clauses in the Lecompton Constitution that they are identical in spirit with this *authoritative* article in the Washington *Union* of the day previous to its indorsement of this Constitution.

When I saw that article in the *Union* of the 17th of November, followed by the glorification of the Lecompton Constitution on the 18th of November, and this clause in the Constitution asserting the doctrine that a State has no right to prohibit slavery within its limits, I saw that there was a *fatal blow* being struck at the sovereignty of the States of this Union.

Here he says, "Mr. President, you here find several distinct propositions advanced boldly, and apparently *authoritatively*." By whose authority, Judge Douglas? [Great cheers and laughter.] Again, he says in another place, "It will be seen by these clauses in the Lecompton Constitution, that they are identical in spirit with this *authoritative* article." *By whose authority?* [Renewed cheers.] Who do you mean to say authorized the publication of these articles? He knows that the Washington *Union* is considered the organ of the Administration. *I* demand of Judge Douglas *by whose au-*

thority he meant to say those articles were published, if not by the authority of the President of the United States and his Cabinet? I defy him to show whom he referred to, if not to these high functionaries in the Federal Government. More than this, he says the articles in that paper and the provisions of the Lecompton Constitution are "identical," and being identical, he argues that the authors are co-operating and conspiring together. He does not use the word "conspiring," but what other construction can you put upon it? He winds up with this:

> When I saw that article in the *Union* of the 17th of November, followed by the glorification of the Lecompton Constitution on the 18th of November, and this clause in the Constitution asserting the doctrine that a State has no right to prohibit slavery within its limits, I saw that there was a *fatal blow* being struck at the sovereignty of the States of this Union.

I ask him if all this fuss was made over the editor of this newspaper. [Laughter.] It would be a terribly "*fatal* blow" indeed which a single man could strike, when no President, no Cabinet officer, no member of Congress, was giving strength and efficiency to the movement. Out of respect to Judge Douglas' good sense I must believe he didn't manufacture his idea of the "fatal" character of that blow out of such a miserable scapegrace as he represents that editor to be. But the Judge's eye is farther south now. [Laughter and cheers.] Then, it was very peculiarly and decidedly North. His hope rested on the idea of visiting the great "Black Republican" party, and making it the tail of his new kite. [Great laughter.] He knows he was then expecting from day to day to turn Republican and place himself at the head [of][12] our organization. He has found that these despised "Black Republicans" estimate him by a standard which he has taught them none too well. Hence he is crawling back into his old camp, and you will find him eventually installed in full fellowship among those whom he was then battling, and with whom he now pretends to be at such fearful variance. [Loud applause and cries of "go on, go on."] I cannot, gentlemen, my time has expired.

[12] Not in the source.

Speech at Tremont, Illinois[1]

August 30, 1858

. . . . About one half of his time was pleasantly, and we can but think profitably, occupied in talking familiarly and often eloquently to his old Whig friends He went through with a rapid account of the times when he had advocated the doctrines of the Whig party in Tazewell County during the successive campaigns of 1840-'44-'48 and '52, and alluded to the fact that he had often met Douglas upon the very steps upon which he was speaking, before as now to oppose his political doctrines. He then entered into a comparison of the principles of the Whig party as expounded by its great leader, Henry Clay, and those of the Republican party of the present day, showing that there was no difference. He then remarked that he was opposing slavery on account of the new aspect in which it was being placed by its upholders, and then branched out with a comprehensive view of the great issues involved in this canvass.

[1] Chicago *Press and Tribune*, September 2, 1858, copied from the Peoria *Transcript*, August 31, 1858.

Speech at Carlinville, Illinois[1]

August 31, 1858

He [Lincoln] said the question is often asked, why this fuss about niggers? It is dictated that their position is a small matter, but let us inquire whether it is or not. His speech at the June convention had been much commented upon, and he read an extract from it, and showed wherein it had been misrepresented as to the ultimate triumph or extinction of slavery; that, although the agitation of the question was commenced in '54 with the avowed object of putting a stop to it, yet, the agitation was still increasing. The policy then adopted professed to leave the subject to the people of the territories and save politicians further trouble. Buchanan and Douglas have often promised us that this agitation would cease, but it is still going on, and only last winter was the hottest of any time yet.

The measures of '50 settled it for a time, only to be reopened in '54 in a worse and more malignant form in a territory where it had been previously at rest. Clay, Webster, Calhoun and Benton have gone but we still have the slavery agitation, and will have it till a more conservative and less aggressive party gains power. The north is not alone to blame—for churches and families divided upon this question—is it then a little thing?

In view of its importance and aggressive nature, I think it must come to a crisis—that it will become national by court verdicts or local by the popular voice. We have no idea of interfering with it in any manner. I am standing up to our bargain for its mainte-

[1] Carlinville *Democrat*, September 2, 1858.

nance where it lawfully exists. Our fathers restricted its spread and stopped the importation of negroes, with the hope that it would remain in a dormant condition till the people saw fit to emancipate the negroes. There is no allusion to slavery in the constitution—and Madison says it was omitted that future generations might not know such a thing ever existed—and that the constitution might yet be a "national charter of freedom." And Keitt[2] of S.C., once admitted that nobody ever thought it would exist to this day.

If placed in the former attitude we should have peace. But it is now advancing to become lawful everywhere. The Nebraska bill introduced this era—and it was gotten up by a man who twice voted for the Wilmot Proviso and the extension of the Missouri Compromise line to the Pacific. This change in our national policy is decided to be constitutional—although the court would not decide the only question before them—whether Dred Scott was a slave or not—and did decide, too, that a territorial legislature cannot exclude slavery in behalf of the people, and if their premises be correct a state cannot exclude it—for they tell us that the negro is property anywhere in the light that horses are property, and if the constitution gives the master a right of property in negroes above the jurisdiction of the territorial laws, enacted in the sovereignty of the people—it only requires another case and another favorable decision from the same court to make the rights of property alike in states as well as territories, and that by virtue of the constitution and in disregard of local laws to the contrary—Buchanan takes this position now. Sustain these men and negro equality will be abundant, as every white laborer will have occasion to regret when he is elbowed from his plow or his anvil by slave niggers.

Douglas insists that I am in favor of perfect uniformity in the institutions of all the states. I believe in their right to do just as they please in this matter. But he is not quite so vain as to say that the good man uttered a falsehood when he said, "A house divided against itself cannot stand." Does he believe this thing will always stand as it now is—neither expand or diminish?

In '32, I voted for Henry Clay, in '36 for the Hugh L. White ticket, in '40 for "Tip and Tyler." In '44 I made the last great effort for "Old Harry of the West" with my friend there, Dr. Heaton.[3] But we got gloriously whipped. Taylor was elected in '48, and we fought nobly for Scott in '52. But now Douglas snatches

[2] Congressman Laurence M. Keitt.

[3] Probably Dr. O. B. Heaton, who practiced in Greene and Macoupin counties.

the robes of Clay and dubs me an abolitionist! How do the principles of the two men agree? Clay always opposed the rightfulness of slavery—Douglas always took the opposite, or kept mum. I can express all my views on the slavery question by quotations from Henry Clay. Doesn't this look like we are akin?

Douglas tries to make capital by charges of negro equality against me. My speeches have been printed and before the country for some time on this question, and Douglas knows the utter falsity of such a charge. To prove it Mr. L. read from a speech of his at Peoria in '54 in reply to Douglas as follows:

"Shall we free them and make them politically and socially our equals? MY OWN FEELINGS WILL NOT ADMIT OF THIS, and if they would the feelings of the great mass of white people would not. Whether this accords with strict justice or not is not the sole question. A universal feeling, whether well or ill-founded, cannot safely be disregarded. We cannot then make them our equals. . . . When they remind us of their constitutional rights I acknowledge them fully and freely, and I would give them any legislation for the recovery of their fugitives, which would not be more likely, in the stringency of its provisions, to take a man into slavery than our ordinary criminal laws are to hang an innocent man."

There is no reason in favor of sending slavery to Kansas that might not be adduced in support of the African slave trade. Each are demanded by the profitableness of the traffic thus made in opening a new slave mart, and not from the rightfulness of it. They are upon a common basis, and should be alike condemned. The compromises of the constitution we must all stand by, but where is the justness of extending the institution to compete with white labor and thus to degrade it? Is it not rather our duty to make labor more respectable by preventing all black competition, especially in the territories? Mr. L. then read from another speech of his in '54, showing that Douglas there attempted to gain the public favor by pandering to the prejudices of the masses, in disregard of truth. Negroes have natural rights however, as other men have, although they cannot enjoy them here, and even Taney once said that "the Declaration of Independence was broad enough for all men." But though it does not declare that all men are equal in their attainments or social position, yet no sane man will attempt to deny that the African upon his own soil has all the natural rights that instrument vouchsafes to all mankind. It has proved a stumbling block to tyrants, and ever will, unless brought into contempt by its pretended friends. Douglas says no man can defend it except on the hypothesis that it only referred to British white subjects, and that no other white men are included—that it does not speak alike to the down trodden of all nations—German, French, Spanish, etc., but simply meant that the English were born equal and endowed by their Creator with certain natural or equal rights among which are life, liberty and the pursuit of happiness, and that it meant nobody else. Are Jeffersonian Democrats willing to have the gem taken from the magna charta of human liberty in this shameful way? Or will they maintain that its declaration of equality of natural rights among all nations is correct?

Douglas pretends to be horrified at amalgamation, yet had he not opened the way for slavery in Kansas, could there have been any amalgamation there? If you keep the two races separate is there any danger of amalgamation? Is not slavery the great source of it? You know that Virginia has more mulattoes than all the northern states! Douglas says he does not care whether they vote slavery up or down in Kansas; then I submit it to this audience which is the most favorable to amalgamation, he who would not raise his finger to keep it out, or I who would give my vote and use my lawful means to prevent its extension. Clay and other great men were ever ready to express their abhorrence of slavery—but we of the north dare not use his noble language when he said, to force its perpetuation and extension you must muzzle the cannon that annually proclaims liberty, and repress all tendencies in the human heart to justice and mercy. We can no longer express our admiration for the Declaration of Independence without their petty sneers. And it is thus they are fast bringing that sacred instrument into contempt. These men desire that slavery should be perpetual and that we should not foster all lawful moves toward emancipation, and to gain their end they will endeavor to impress upon the public mind that the negro is not human, and even upon his own soil he has no rights which white men are bound to respect. Douglas demands that we shall bow to all decisions. If the courts are to decide upon political subjects, how long will it be till Jefferson's fears of a political despotism are realized? He denounces all opposed to the Dred Scott opinions, in disregard to his former opposition to real decisions and the fact that he got his title of Judge by breaking down a decision of our supreme court. He has an object in these denunciations, and is it not to prepare our minds for acquiescence in the next decision declaring slavery to exist in the states? If Douglas can make you believe that slavery is a sacred right—if we are to swallow Dred Scottism that the right of property in negroes is not confined to those states where it is established by local law—if by special sophisms he can make you believe that no nation except the English are born equal and are entitled to life, liberty, and the pursuit of happiness, upon their own soil, or when they are not constitutionally divested of the God-given rights to enjoy the fruits of their own labor, then may we truly despair of the universality of freedom, or the efficacy of those sacred principles enunciated by our fathers—and give in our adhesion to the perpetuation and unlimited extension of slavery.

Speeches at Clinton, Illinois[1]

September 2, 1858

Mr. Lincoln responded briefly.[2] He said he was not vain enough to suppose that his personal popularity was sufficient to call out the large and enthusiastic crowd which surrounded him. He felt certain that the Great Cause in which he was engaged was dear to the hearts of all true lovers of freedom, and that the thousands of voters in his hearing, though they might be somewhat partial to him, had a greater reverence for a Principle than for a Man. He closed his brief remarks by thanking his hearers for their numbers and enthusiasm, and saying that he would address them at length on the regular speaking ground.

The questions are sometimes asked, "What is all this fuss that is being made about negroes?—what does it amount to?—and where will it end?" These questions imply that those who ask them consider the slavery question a very insignificant matter—they think that it amounts to little or nothing, and that those who agitate it are extremely foolish. Now it must be admitted that if the great question which has caused so much trouble *is* insignificant, we are very foolish to have anything to do with it—if it is of no

[1] Bloomington *Pantagraph,* September 3, 1858. These speeches have been heretofore misdated September 8, 1858 (NH, III, 349-56). Tradition has come to attribute to the Clinton speeches one of Lincoln's most famous utterances—"You can fool all the people some of the time and some of the people all the time, but you cannot fool all the people all the time." In 1905 testimony was gathered by the Chicago *Tribune* and Brooklyn *Eagle* to prove that Lincoln used the epigram at Clinton. The testimony was conflicting and dubious in some particulars, but the epigram has remained a favorite in popular usage. Neither the report in the *Pantagraph* which provides the text of the Clinton speeches, nor any other contemporary Lincoln reference located by the present editors, makes any reference to the epigram.

[2] This brief speech was made to a crowd which gathered at a "mound a short distance northwest of the court house" as the parade moved toward the grove "west of Clinton" where the speaker's stand had been erected. Lincoln responded to a welcoming speech by Lawrence Weldon, prominent DeWitt County Republican. Upon arriving at the grove, Lincoln delivered his prepared speech, of which only a short excerpt appears in the *Pantagraph.*

importance we had better throw it aside and busy ourselves about something else. But let us inquire a little into this *insignificant* matter, as it is called by some, and see if it is not important enough to demand the close attention of every well-wisher of the Union. In one of Douglas' recent speeches I find a reference to a speech which was made by me in Springfield sometime ago. The Judge makes one quotation from that speech that requires some little notice from me at this time. I regret that I have not my Springfield speech before me, but the Judge has quoted one particular part of it so often that I think I can recollect it. It runs, I think, as follows:

> We are now far into the fifth year since a policy was initiated with the avowed object and confident promise of putting an end to slavery agitation. Under the operation of that policy that agitation has not only not ceased, but has constantly augmented. In my opinion it will not cease until a crisis shall have been reached and passed.
>
> "A house divided against itself cannot stand." I believe this government cannot endure permanently, half slave and half free. I do not expect the Union to be dissolved—I do not expect the house to fall—but I do expect it will cease to be divided. It will become all one thing, or all the other. Either the opponents of slavery will arrest the further spread of it, and place it where the public mind shall rest in the belief that it is in the course of ultimate extinction; or its advocates will push it forward till it shall become alike lawful in *all* the States, old as well as new—*North* as well as *South.*

Judge Douglas makes use of the above quotation, and finds a great deal of fault with it. He deals unfairly with me, and tries to make the people of this State believe that I advocated dangerous doctrines in my Springfield speech. Let us see if that portion of my Springfield speech which Judge Douglas complains of so bitterly, is as objectionable to others as it is to him: We are, certainly, far into the fifth year since a policy was initiated with the avowed object and confident promise of putting an end to slavery agitation. On the 4th day of January, 1854, Judge Douglas introduced the Kansas-Nebraska bill. He initiated a new policy, and that policy, so he says, was to put an end to the agitation of the slavery question. Whether that was his object or not I will not stop to discuss, but at all events *some* kind of a policy was initiated; and what has been the result? Instead of the quiet times and good feeling which was promised us by the self-styled author of Popular Sovereignty, we have had nothing but ill-feeling and agitation. According to Judge Douglas, the passage of the Nebraska bill would tranquilize the whole country—there would be no more slavery agitation in or out of Congress, and the vexed question would be left entirely to the people of the territories. Such was the opinion of Judge Douglas, and such were the opinions of the leading men of the Democratic Party. Even as late as the spring of 1856, Mr. Buchanan said, a short time subsequent to his nomination by the Cincinnati Convention, that the Territory of Kansas would be tranquil in less than six weeks. Perhaps he thought so, but Kansas has not been and is not tranquil, and it may be a long time before she will be so.

We all know how fierce the agitation was in Congress last winter, and what a narrow escape Kansas had from being admitted into the Union with a Constitution that was detested by ninety-nine hundredths of her citizens. Did the angry debates which took place at Washington during the last session of Congress lead you to suppose that the slavery agitation was settled?

An election was held in Kansas in the month of August,[3] and the Constitution which was submitted to the people was voted down by a large majority. So Kansas is still out of the Union, and there is a probability that she will remain out for some time. But Judge Douglas says the slavery question is settled. He says the bill which he introduced into the Senate of the United States on the 4th day of January, 1854, settled the slavery question forever! Perhaps he can tell us *how* that bill settled the slavery question, for if he is able to settle a question of such great magnitude he ought to be able to explain the manner in which he does it. He knows and you know that the question is *not* settled, and that his ill-timed *experiment* to settle it has made it worse than it ever was before.

And now let me say a few words in regard to Douglas' great hobby of negro equality. He thinks—he says at least—that the Republican party is in favor of allowing whites and blacks to intermarry, and that a man can't be a good Republican unless he is willing to elevate black men to office and to associate with them on terms of perfect equality. He knows that we advocate no such doctrines as those, but he cares not how much he misrepresents us if he can gain a few votes by so doing. To show you what my opinion of negro equality was in times past, and to prove to you that I stand on that question where I always stood, I will read you a few extracts from a speech that was made by me in Peoria in 1854. It was made in reply to one of Judge Douglas' speeches.

[Mr. Lincoln then read a number of extracts which had the ring of the true metal. We have rarely heard anything with which we have been more pleased. And the audience, after hearing the extracts read, and comparing their conservative sentiments with those now advocated by Mr. Lincoln, testified their approval by loud applause. How any *reasonable* man can hear one of Mr. Lin-

[3] August 2, 1858.

coln's speeches without being converted to Republicanism, is something that we can't account for.][4]

Slavery, continued Mr. Lincoln, is not a matter of little importance: it overshadows every other question in which we are interested. It has divided the Methodist and Presbyterian Churches, and has sown discord in the American Tract Society. The churches have split, and the Society will follow their example before long. So it will be seen that slavery is agitated in the religious as well as in the political world.

Judge Douglas is very much afraid that the triumph of the Republican party will lead to a general mixture of the white and black races. Perhaps I am wrong in saying that he *is* afraid; so I will correct myself by saying that he *pretends* to fear that the success of our party will result in the amalgamation of blacks and whites. I think I can show plainly, from documents now before me, that Judge Douglas' fears are groundless. The census of 1850 tells us that in that year there were over four hundred thousand mulattoes in the United States. Now let us take what is called an Abolition State—the Republican, slavery-hating State of New Hampshire—and see how many mulattoes we can find within her borders. The number amounts to just one hundred and eighty-four. In the Old Dominion—in the Democratic and aristocratic State of Virginia—there were a few more mulattoes than the census-takers found in New Hampshire. How many do you suppose there were? Seventy-nine thousand seven hundred and seventy-five—twenty-three thousand more than there were in all the free States! In the slave States there were, in 1850, three hundred and forty-eight thousand mulattoes—all of home production; and in the free States there were less than sixty thousand mulattoes—and a large number of them were imported from the South.

[4] Brackets are in the source.

To William Fithian[1]

Bloomington, Sept. 3. 1858

Dear Doctor Yours of the 1st. was received this morning, as also one from Mr. Harmon, and one from Hiram Beckwith on the same subject.[2] You will see by the Journal that I have appointed to speak at Danville on the 22nd. of Sept.—the day *after* Douglas speaks there. My recent experience shows that speaking at the same place the next day after D. is the very thing—it is, in fact, a concluding speech on him. Please show this to Messrs. Harmon &

Beckwith; and tell them they must excuse me from writing seperate letters to them. Yours as ever A. LINCOLN

P.S. Give full notice to all surrounding counties. A. L.

[1] ALS-P, ISLA.

[2] Hiram W. Beckwith and Oscar F. Harmon were lawyers and active Republicans at Danville, Illinois, who had written that Lincoln should come to Danville (DLC-RTL).

Speech at Bloomington, Illinois[1]

September 4, 1858

After briefly expressing his acknowledgments to the speaker and the audience for the highly complimentary reception with which they had honored him, and remarking that he well knew that this great crowd had not assembled to do honor to him personally, but to the great cause of which he was an humble advocate,—Mr. L. took up Mr. Douglas' Bloomington speech of July 16th, and remarked that he was now here to fulfill his promise then made, of replying to that speech.

There were probably many of his (L's) friends in this audience, who did not need arguments addressed to them. There were also some friends of Douglas who could not be convinced by any argument that could be made. There was probably still a third class, whose minds were not fully made up, and who were yet open to conviction. To that class he wished chiefly to address himself. If such a class there was, it probably consisted for the most part of old line Whigs. He (Mr. L.) was also an old line Whig, and had stood by the party as long as it had a being. He had first appeared in this town twenty years ago, when John T. Stewart[2] was the Whig candidate for Congress, and Stephen A. Douglas the Democratic candidate,—and he had then done such service as he was able, in behalf of Stewart. Again in 1840 he had spoken for Harrison, with Douglas contending on the other side. In 1844 he had canvassed with his best ability for Clay, both here and in Indiana, while Douglas was doing his utmost for the Democratic nominee. In 1848 he was again in the field for Taylor, while Douglas was leading on the Democracy to the support of Cass. And in 1852 he (L.) was supporting Scott, while Douglas was the leader of the supporters of Pierce. That was the last Whig battle, for in 1856 Fillmore did not run as a Whig, and was not supported as such. He (Mr. L.) thought therefore that he was fairly entitled to ask

[1] Bloomington *Pantagraph*, September 6, 1858. Lincoln was introduced by Leonard Swett. Brackets are in the source. [2] John T. Stuart.

of old Whigs at least a fair and impartial hearing. *That* he did ask, and he asked nothing more on account of his former position as an old Whig.

Douglas, in his Bloomington speech, after complimenting himself pretty highly for his services to popular sovereignty, devotes a large portion of his time to an attack upon me. He charges that I am trying to produce uniformity of local institutions throughout the States, to produce an entire equality of the white and black races, and to make war between the north and the south. He finds the evidence for these charges in my Springfield speech of June 16th. Not that I have ever *said* any such things, but he infers them from what I did say. I admit that if my course tends to such results, it makes no difference whether I *intended* them or not, I am equally responsible. But I think the Judge's inferences far-fetched and unwarranted.

Mr. L. then quoted the paragraphs of his Springfield speech of June 16th to which Douglas chiefly takes exception, as follows:

> If we could know where we are, and whither we are tending, we could then better judge what to do, and how to do it. We are now far into the fifth year since a policy was initiated with the avowed object and confident promise of putting an end to slavery agitation. Under the operation of that policy that agitation has not only not ceased, but has constantly augmented. In my opinion it will not cease until a crisis shall have been reached and passed.
>
> "A house divided against itself cannot stand." I believe this government cannot endure permanently, half slave and half free. I do not expect the Union to be dissolved—I do not expect the house to fall—but I do expect it will cease to be divided. It will become all one thing, or all the other. Either the opponents of slavery will arrest the further spread of it, and place it where the public mind shall rest in the belief that it is in the course of ultimate extinction; or its advocates will push it forward till it shall become alike lawful in *all* the States, old as well as new—*North* as well as *South.*

He proceeded to show that it *is* now, the fifth year since the Kansas-Nebraska bill was introduced; that it *was* introduced "with the avowed object and confident promise of putting an end to slavery agitation;" and he asked whether the agitation had not augmented instead of *ceasing*. A dozen times had the slavery question been declared to be *settled* forever. It was so when the Missouri Compromise was passed, when the Nullification Compromise was adopted, when Texas was admitted, when the Compromises of 1850 were adopted. Yet the agitation was always soon renewed. All these were merely settlements of small phases of the question, not of the question itself. The Lecompton question was another phase, and it was claimed that the English bill had settled *that*. Douglas says it is settled. *What* is settled? *The Lecompton Constitution* undoubtedly is *settled*, [loud applause and laughter,] but is the Kansas question settled? Has Kansas a constitution? Is it settled how she is to come in? No: the whole thing is to be done over again. We are just where we were when we started. We have only been *settling* one *settlement* of the question, and we have only got back to where we were four years ago. Certainly, if the question is ever to be settled, we are four or five years nearer the time of the settlement of it than we were when the Nebraska bill was introduced, —but that is all. The bill was to give the people of Kansas the right of self-government. Now was there ever in the world a territory whose people have had *so little* control of their own affairs, and have been *so much* interfered with by outsiders of all kinds, as this same Kansas? The whole thing has been a lie.

This agitation springs from the same old cause which has agitated the nation all through our history. It is not merely an agitation got up to help men into office. No *such* agitation could call together such crowds as this, year after year, and generation after generation. The same cause has rent asunder the great Methodist and Presbyterian churches, and is now disturbing the Tract Society. It is not a temporary or trifling cause. It will not cease until a crisis has been reached and passed. When the public mind rests in the belief that the evil is in a course of ultimate extinction, it will become quiet. We have no right to interfere with slavery in the States. We only want to restrict it to where it is. We have never had an agitation except when it was endeavored to spread it. Will war follow from adopting the policy which was originally adopted by the Government, and from which war never *did* follow, —from which no trouble came? The framers of the Constitution prohibited slavery (not *in* the Constitution, but the *same men* did it) north of the Ohio river, where it did not exist, and did not prohibit it south of that river, where it *did* exist. By the Kansas-Nebraska bill it is placed in a position to become alike lawful in all the States. Brooks of South Carolina said in one of his speeches that at the formation of the Constitution nobody expected slavery to last till now, but we have more experience of it, and the invention of the cotton gin has taught us that slavery must be permanent and spreading. I, (said Mr. L.) fight it in its *advancing* phase, and wish to place it in the same attitude that the framers of the government did.

Mr. L. briefly referred to Douglas' charge of wishing to bring about an entire uniformity in all the domestic regulations of the

States, and exposed its fallacy. That charge springs from the error of regarding slavery in the same light with the ordinary matters of police regulations in the different States. The differences of soil, productions and pursuits in the different States are but cements of union, not matters tending to disunion. Is not slavery, on the contrary, and has it not always been, an apple of discord, always tending to divide the house and overthrow it?

The charge of favoring the equality of the races was taken up, and replied to by reading an extract from a speech made by Mr. L. at Peoria, in 1854, *in debate with Mr. Douglas himself.* [The extract was the same which Mr. L. quoted in his Ottawa speech, and declares that his feelings and those of the great mass of the white race will not admit of making the negroes politically and socially our equals, &c. We have heretofore published it.]

There is no moral argument that can be made for carrying slaves into new territory, which will not also stand good in favor of the African slave trade. If a Kentuckian may take his slave into a new territory, any other citizen of the United States may. If he has no slaves, he may buy one for the purpose, and may buy him where he can buy him cheapest. Certainly he can buy him cheaper in Africa than in Kentucky. It may be said that the Kentucky slave is a slave already, and his condition is not altered by taking him to the territory. So is the African a slave already. The trader does not find him a free man when he goes to Africa for his cargo, but finds him already a slave in the custody of a master who has captured him in the interior and brought him to the coast. There is no argument justifying the taking of slaves to new territory which will not equally justify the African slave trade. That trade will be reopened if this thing continues to go on,—unless indeed the prohibition be continued as a measure of protection to *home production.*

Mr. L. then read at considerable length from another of his published speeches, on the subject of negro equality, and contrasting the Declaration of Independence with Douglas' version of it, which confines its meaning to an assertion of the equality of British subjects in America with British subjects in England. Referring to the "amalgamation" humbug, he inquired where the mulattoes came from, and quoted the census figures, showing that nearly the whole of them are from slave States; that New Hampshire, whose laws approach nearest to negro equality, contains scarcely any mulattoes, while Virginia has several thousand more than all the free States combined. And he inquired which party was practically in favor of amalgamation, we who wish to exclude negroes from the territory, or those who wish to mix them in with the whites there.

Mr. L. said he held the same views on slavery as Henry Clay. Douglas had seized the dead statesman's mantle, wrapped it around him, and with its ends trailing fifty feet behind him, was claiming it as his own, and would allow no one else to share it. Yet Clay always denounced slavery as unjust; Douglas has never once said in public whether he thought slavery right or wrong. Henry Clay said of a class of men who would repress all tendencies to liberty and ultimate emancipation, that they must, if they would do this, go back to the era of our independence and muzzle the cannon which thunders its annual joyous return; they must blow out the moral lights around us; they must penetrate the human soul, and eradicate there the love of liberty; and then, and not till then, could they perpetuate slavery in this country. Henry Clay called slavery "the greatest of human evils," and spoke of the slaves as "that unhappy race in bondage." When has Douglas ever used such words in speaking of this institution? Mr. L. quoted numerous passages from Clay's speeches, showing him to be in favor of the ultimate extinction of slavery, and in favor of excluding it in the formation of new States where it did not exist. He then remarked that the body and soul of the Republican movement was to keep slavery away from where it does not exist, and asked what milder way there could be to place it in course of ultimate extinction.

Mr. L. reminded those Democrats who are now repeating Douglas' ideas about restricting the Declaration of Independence to white people, that until within five years past, *nobody* held or avowed such opinions. He then took up popular sovereignty, or the right of the people to govern themselves, and quoted the Declaration of Independence to show that the idea was clearly set forth there, long before Douglas was born. Douglas' invention was that popular sovereignty was the right to do what you please with yourself and so many slaves as you can buy. The people of the territories have gained the right to have slaves if they want them, but not the right *not* to have them if they don't want them.

Mr. L. then briefly examined the Dred Scott decision, and declared that nothing now was wanting to nationalize slavery but a decision of the Supreme Court that no State could exclude slavery, and acquiescence in it by the people. The tenacity with which Douglas clings to the Dred Scott decision, not because he argues it to be right, but because of the source from which it comes, commits him to the next decision also, and looks as if he *anticipated* that decision, legalizing slavery in the States, and wished to prepare the public mind for it. Could he more effectually mould the public mind for that decision than he is doing, if that were really his object? When the public mind *is* prepared for it, the decision will come. And when you have stricken down the principles of the Declaration of Independence, and thereby consigned the negro to hopeless and eternal bondage, are you *quite* sure that the demon will not turn and rend you? Will not the people then be ready to go down beneath the tread of any tyrant who may wish to rule them?

[This idea was most eloquently wrought out in Mr. L's peroration, and we regret much that we cannot give a verbatim report of it.

The speech was about two hours long, and was listened to with undivided attention throughout, by as many as could hear. We shall finish our account, by giving some account of the evening speeches, tomorrow.]

To John C. Bagby[1]

John C. Bagby, Esq — Springfield,
My dear Sir: — Sep. 6. 1858

Mr. Hatch[2] tells me you write rather in a discouraged tone as to your own election. That wont do. You *must* be elected. *Must* is the word. Make known to the committee at Chicago the *amount* and *nature* of the help you can make available, and I expect they will furnish it. But, by all means, dont say "if I can"; say "*I will*."

Yours truly — A. LINCOLN

[1] ALS, owned by Francis C. Bagby, Detroit, Michigan.
[2] Probably Ozias M. Hatch.

Speech at Paris, Illinois[1]

September 7, 1858

Let us inquire (said Mr. Lincoln) what Judge Douglas really invented when he introduced, and drove through Congress, the Nebraska bill. He called it "Popular Sovereignty." What does Popular Sovereignty mean? Strictly and literally it means the Sovereignty of the People over their own affairs—in other words, the Right of the People of every nation and community to govern themselves. Did Mr. Douglas invent this? Not quite. The idea of Popular Sovereignty was floating about the world several ages before the author of the Nebraska bill saw daylight—indeed, before Columbus set foot on the American continent. In the year 1776 it took tangible form in the noble words which you are all familiar with: "We hold these truths to be self-evident: That all men are created equal; That they are endowed by their Creator with certain inalienable rights; That among these are life, liberty and the pursuit of happiness; That to secure these rights governments were instituted among men, *deriving their just powers from the consent of the governed.*" Was not this the origin of Popular Sovereignty as applied to the American people? Here we are told that governments are instituted among men to secure certain rights, and that they derive their just powers *from the consent of the governed.* If that is not Popular Sovereignty, then I have no conception of the meaning of words.

Then if Mr. Douglas did not invent *this* kind of Sovereignty, let us pursue the inquiry and find out what the invention really was. Was it the right of emigrants in Kansas and Nebraska to govern themselves and a gang of niggers too, if they wanted them? Clearly this was no invention of his, because Gen. Cass put forth the same doctrine in 1848, in his so-called Nicholson letter, six years before Douglas thought of such a thing. Gen. Cass could have taken out a patent for the idea, if he had chosen to do so, and have prevented his Illinois rival from reaping a particle of benefit from it. Then what was it, I ask again, that this "Little Giant" invented? It never occurred to Gen. Cass to call his discovery by the odd name of "Popular Sovereignty." He had not the *impudence* to say that the *right of people to govern niggers* was the *right of people to govern themselves.* His notions of the fitness of things were not moulded to the brazen degree of calling the right to put a hundred niggers through under the lash in Nebraska, a "*sacred right of self-government.*" And here, I submit to this intelligent audience and the whole world, was Judge Douglas' discovery, and the whole of it. He invented a *name* for Gen. Cass' old Nicholson letter dogma. He discovered that the right of the white man to breed and flog niggers in Nebraska was POPULAR SOVEREIGNTY!

1 Chicago *Press and Tribune*, September 11, 1858. This speech has been heretofore incorrectly dated September 8, 1858 (NH, XI, 105-106). Lincoln spoke at Tolono and Mattoon, Illinois, on the morning of September 7, and at Paris that afternoon. No reports of the Tolono and Mattoon speeches have been located.

Speech at Edwardsville, Illinois[1]

September 11, 1858

I have been requested to give a concise statement, as I understand it, of the difference between the Democratic and the Repub-

1 Alton *Weekly Courier*, September 16, 1858. Brackets are in the source unless otherwise noted.

lican parties on the leading issues of this campaign. The question has just been put to me by a gentleman whom I do not know. I do not even know whether he is a friend of mine or a supporter of Judge Douglas in this contest; nor does that make any difference. His question is a pertinent one and, though it has not been asked me anywhere in the State before, I am very glad that my attention has been called to it to-day. Lest I should forget it, I will give you my answer before proceeding with the line of argument I had marked out for this discussion.

The difference between the Republican and the Democratic parties on the leading issue of this contest, as I understand it, is, that the former consider slavery a moral, social and political wrong, while the latter *do not* consider it either a moral, social or political wrong; and the action of each, as respects the growth of the country and the expansion of our population, is squared to meet these views. I will not allege that the Democratic party consider slavery morally, socially and politically *right;* though their tendency to that view has, in my opinion, been constant and unmistakable for the past five years. I prefer to take, as the accepted maxim of the party, the idea put forth by Judge Douglas, that he "don't care whether slavery is voted down or voted up." I am quite willing to believe that many Democrats would prefer that slavery be always voted down, and I am sure that some prefer that it be always "voted up"; but I have a right to insist that their action, especially if it be their *constant and unvärying* action, shall determine their ideas and preferences on the subject. Every measure of the Democratic party of late years, bearing directly or indirectly on the slavery question, has corresponded with this notion of utter indifference whether slavery or freedom shall outrun in the race of empire across the Pacific—every measure, I say, up to the Dred Scott decision, where, it seems to me, the idea is boldly suggested that slavery is *better* than freedom. The Republican party, on the contrary, hold that this government was instituted to secure the blessings of freedom, and that slavery is an unqualified evil to the negro, to the white man, to the soil, and to the State. Regarding it an evil, they will not molest it in the States where it exists; they will not overlook the constitutional guards which our forefathers have placed around it; they will do nothing which can give proper offence to those who hold slaves by legal sanction; but they will use every constitutional method to prevent the evil from becoming larger and involving more negroes, more white men, more soil, and more States in its deplorable consequences. They will, if possible, place it where the public mind shall rest in the belief that it is in course of ultimate peaceable extinction, in God's own good time. And to this end they will, if possible, restore the government to the policy of the fathers—the policy of preserving the new territories from the baneful influence of human bondage, as the Northwestern territories were sought to be preserved by the ordinance of 1787 and the compromise act of 1820. They will oppose, in all its length and breadth, the modern Democratic idea that slavery is as good as freedom, and ought to have room for expansion all over the continent, if people can be found to carry it. All, or very nearly all, of Judge Douglas' arguments about "Popular Sovereignty," as he calls it, are logical if you admit that slavery is as good and as right as freedom; and not one of them is worth a rush if you deny it. This is the difference, as I understand it, between the Republican and the Democratic parties; and I ask the gentleman, and all of you, whether his question is not satisfactorily answered.—[Cries of "Yes, yes."]

OPINIONS OF HENRY CLAY.

In this connection let me read to you the opinions of our old leader Henry Clay, on the question of whether slavery *is* as good as freedom. The extract which I propose to read is contained [in][2] a letter written by Mr. Clay in his old age, as late as 1849. The circumstances which called it forth were these. A convention had been called to form a new constitution for the State of Kentucky. The old Constitution had been adopted in the year 1799—half a century before, when Mr. Clay was a young man just rising into public notice. As long ago as the adoption of the old Constitution, Mr. Clay had been the earnest advocate of a system of gradual emancipation and colonization of the state of Kentucky. And again in his old age, in the maturity of his great mind, we find the same wise project still uppermost in his thoughts. Let me read a few passages from his letter of 1849: "I know there are those who draw an argument in favor of slavery from the alleged intellectual inferiority of the black race. Whether this argument is founded in fact or not, I will not now stop to inquire, but merely say that if it proves anything at all, it proves too much. It proves that among the white races of the world any one might properly be enslaved by any other which had made greater advances in civilization. And, if this rule applies to nations there is no reason why it should not apply to individuals; and it might easily be proved that the wisest man in the world could rightfully reduce all other men and women to bondage," &c., &c. [Mr. Lincoln read at considerable

[2] Not in the source.

length from Mr. Clay's letter—earnestly pressing the material advantages and moral considerations in favor of gradual emancipation in Kentucky.]

"POPULAR SOVEREIGNTY,"
WHAT DID DOUGLAS REALLY INVENT?

Let us inquire, what Douglas really invented, when he introduced, and drove through Congress, the Nebraska bill. He called it "Popular Sovereignty." What does Popular Sovereignty mean? Strictly and literally it means the sovereignty of the people over their own affairs—in other words, the right of the people of every nation and community to govern themselves. Did Mr. Douglas invent this? Not quite. The idea of Popular Sovereignty was floating about the world several ages before the author of the Nebraska bill saw daylight—indeed before Columbus set foot on the American continent. In the year 1776 it took tangible form in the noble words which you are all familiar with: "We hold these truths to be self-evident: That all men are created equal; That they are endowed by their Creator with certain inalienable rights; That among these are life, liberty and the pursuit of happiness; That to secure these rights governments are instituted among men, *deriving their just powers from the consent of the governed.*" Was not this the origin of Popular Sovereignty as applied to the American people? Here we are told that Governments are instituted among men to secure certain rights, and that they derive their just powers *from the consent of the governed.* If that is not Popular Sovereignty, then I have no conception of the meaning of words.

Then, if Mr. Douglas did not invent *this* kind of sovereignty, let us pursue the inquiry and find out what the invention really was. Was it the right of emigrants in Kansas and Nebraska to govern themselves and a gang of niggers too, if they wanted them? Clearly this was no invention of his, because Gen. Cass put forth the same doctrine in 1848, in his so-called Nicholson letter—six whole years before Douglas thought of such a thing. Gen. Cass could have taken out a patent for the idea, if he had chosen to do so, and have prevented his Illinois rival from reaping a particle of benefit from it. Then what was it, I ask again, that this "Little Giant" invented? It never occurred to Gen. Cass to call his discovery by the odd name of "Popular Sovereignty." He had not the *impudence* to say that the *right of people to govern niggers* was the *right of people to govern themselves.* His notions of the fitness of things were not moulded to the brazen degree of calling the right to put a hundred niggers through under the lash in Nebraska, a "*sacred right of self-government.*" And here, I submit to this intelligent audience and the whole world, was Judge Douglas' discovery, and the whole of it. He invented a *name* for Gen. Cass' old Nicholson letter dogma. He discovered that the right of the white man to breed and flog niggers in Nebraska was POPULAR SOVEREIGNTY!—[Great applause and laughter.]

WHAT MAY WE LOOK FOR AFTER THE NEXT DRED SCOTT DECISION?

My friends, I have endeavored to show you the logical consequences of the Dred Scott decision, which holds that the people of a Territory cannot prevent the establishment of Slavery in their midst. I have stated what cannot be gainsayed—that the grounds upon which this decision is made are equally applicable to the Free States as to the Free Territories, and that the peculiar reasons put forth by Judge Douglas for endorsing this decision, commit him in advance to the next decision, and to all other decisions emanating from the same source. Now, when by all these means you have succeeded in dehumanizing the negro; when you have put him down, and made it forever impossible for him to be but as the beasts of the field; when you have extinguished his soul, and placed him where the ray of hope is blown out in darkness like that which broods over the spirits of the damned; are you quite sure the demon which you have roused *will not turn and rend you*? What constitutes the bulwark of our own liberty and independence? It is not our frowning battlements, our bristling sea coasts, the guns of our war steamers, or the strength of our gallant and disciplined army. These are not our reliance against a resumption of tyranny in our fair land. All of them may be turned against our liberties, without making us stronger or weaker for the struggle. Our reliance is in the *love of liberty* which God has planted in our bosoms. Our defense is in the preservation of the spirit which prizes liberty as the heritage of all men, in all lands, every where. Destroy this spirit, and you have planted the seeds of despotism around your own doors. Familiarize yourselves with the chains of bondage, and you are preparing your own limbs to wear them. Accustomed to trample on the rights of those around you, you have lost the genius of your own independence, and become the fit subjects of the first cunning tyrant who rises. And let me tell you, all these things are prepared for you with the logic of history, if the elections shall promise that the next Dred Scott decision and all future decisions will be quietly acquiesced in by the people.—[Loud applause.]

Speech at Greenville, Illinois[1]

September 13, 1858

In a most able manner did Mr. Lincoln clear up and refute the charges that he was an Abolitionist, and an Amalgamationist, and in favor of placing negroes upon a social and political equality with the whites. He asserted positively, and proved conclusively by his former acts and speeches that he was not in favor of interfering with slavery in the States where it exists, nor ever had been. That he was not even in favor of abolishing slavery in the District of Columbia, unless a majority of the people of the District should be in favor of it, and remuneration should be made to masters who might be unwilling to give up their slaves without compensation; and even then he would want it done gradually. He also showed clearly, what nobody but the Democrats deny, that slavery is a great moral, social, and political evil, and was so looked upon by all the fathers of the Government—that the institution was considered a foul blot on the Nation, which would at some future day be removed. Mr. Lincoln said he had always believed as the fathers did, that it would in the course of time be entirely removed from our country, until the new policy of nationalizing it had been set on foot. Since that time he had believed it would either become alike lawful in all the States, or that eventually, in God's own good time and way, it would finally disappear. But whether it should ever become extinct or not, he was in favor of living up to all the guarantees of the Constitution. Whatever constitutional rights the slaveholders might have, he was in favor of protecting them.

On the other hand, he was opposed to the new doctrine that the Constitution carries slavery into all the Territories, and protects it there against the wishes of the people. It had always, until lately, been held that slavery was a creature of positive local legislation, and did not legally exist anywhere, in the absence of such legislation. Yet he admitted that practically it would exist where there was no legislation in regard to it; that it had been so planted where ever it has existed. That it would be taken into new Territories, and there permitted to remain, until legislation would become necessary to protect it, when such legislation would be enacted, and it would thereby become legalized.

[1] Greenville *Advocate,* September 16, 1858.

Fragment: Notes for Speeches[1]

[c. September 15, 1858]

At Freeport I propounded four distinct interrogations to Judge Douglas, all which he assumed to answer. I say he assumed to answer them; for he did not very distinctly answer any of them.

To the first, which is in these words, "If the people of Kansas shall, by means entirely unobjectionable in all other respects, adopt a State constitution, and ask admission into the Union under it, before they have the requisite number of inhabitants according to the English bill,—some ninety-three thousand,—will you vote to admit them?" the judge did not answer "Yes" or "No," "I would" or "I would not," nor did he answer in any other such distinct way. But he did so answer that I infer he would vote for the admission of Kansas in the supposed case stated in the interrogatory—that, other objections out of the way, he would vote to admit Kansas before she had the requisite population according to the English bill. I mention this now to elicit an assurance that I correctly understood the judge on this point.

To my second interrogatory, which is in these words, "Can the people of a United States Territory, in any lawful way, against the wish of any citizen of the United States, exclude slavery from their limits, prior to the formation of a State constitution?" the judge answers that they can, and he proceeds to show how they can exclude it. The how, as he gives it, is by withholding friendly legislation and adopting unfriendly legislation. As he thinks, the people still can, by doing nothing to help slavery and by a little unfriendly leaning against it, exclude it from their limits. This is his position. This position and the Dred Scott decision are absolutely inconsistent. The judge furiously indorses the Dred Scott decision; and that decision holds that the United States Constitution guarantees to the citizens of the United States the right to hold slaves in the Territories, and that neither Congress nor a territorial legislature can destroy or abridge that right. In the teeth of this, where can the judge find room for his unfriendly legislation against their right? The members of a territorial legislature are sworn to sup-

[1] NH, IV, 203-12. As in the instance of the similar fragment, c. August 21, 1858, *supra*, the manuscript of this piece is no longer among the Lincoln Papers, and no portion of it has been located. Presumably Nicolay and Hay had access to it intact for the *Complete Works*, where it is dated [October 1, 1858?]. Since the argument closely agrees with the central portion of Lincoln's reply in the Jonesboro Debate, *infra*, which deals with Douglas' replies to the questions propounded by Lincoln at Freeport, one may infer that Lincoln prepared this portion of the Jonesboro Debate in advance and that this fragment represents what he intended to say when he went to Jonesboro.

port the Constitution of the United States. How dare they legislate unfriendly to a right guaranteed by that Constitution? And if they should how quickly would the courts hold their work to be unconstitutional and void! But doubtless the judge's chief reliance to sustain his proposition that the people can exclude slavery, is based upon non-action—upon withholding friendly legislation. But can members of a territorial legislature, having sworn to support the United States Constitution, conscientiously withhold necessary legislative protection to a right guaranteed by that Constitution?

Again, will not the courts, without territorial legislation, find a remedy for the evasion of a right guaranteed by the United States Constitution? It is a maxim of the courts that "there is no right without a remedy." But, as a matter of fact, non-action, both legislative and judicial, will not exclude slavery from any place. It is of record that Dred Scott and his family were held in actual slavery in Kansas without any friendly legislation or judicial assistance. It is well known that other negroes were held in actual slavery at the military post in Kansas under precisely the same circumstances. This was not only done without any friendly legislation, but in direct disregard of the congressional prohibition,—the Missouri Compromise,—then supposed to be valid, thus showing that it requires positive law to be both made and executed to keep actual slavery out of any Territory where any owner chooses to take it. Slavery having actually gone into a territory to some extent, without local legislation in its favor, and against congressional prohibition, how much more will it go there now that by a judicial decision that congressional prohibition is swept away, and the constitutional guaranty of property declared to apply to slavery in the Territories.

But this is not all. Slavery was originally planted on this continent without the aid of friendly legislation. History proves this. After it was actually in existence to a sufficient extent to become, in some sort, a public interest, it began to receive legislative attention, but not before. How futile, then, is the proposition that the people of a Territory can exclude slavery by simply not legislating in its favor. Learned disputants use what they call the *argumentum ad hominem*—a course of argument which does not intrinsically reach the issue, but merely turns the adversary against himself. There are at least two arguments of this sort which may easily be turned against Judge Douglas's proposition that the people of a Territory can lawfully exclude slavery from their limits prior to forming a State constitution. In his report of the 12th of March,

1856, on page 28, Judge Douglas says: "The sovereignty of a Territory remains in abeyance, suspended in the United States, in trust for the people, until they shall be admitted into the Union as a State." If so,—if they have no active living sovereignty,—how can they readily enact the judge's unfriendly legislation to slavery?

But in 1856, on the floor of the Senate, Judge Trumbull asked Judge Douglas the direct question, "Can the people of a Territory exclude slavery prior to forming a State constitution?"—and Judge Douglas answered, "That is a question for the Supreme Court." I think he made the same answer to the same question more than once. But now, when the Supreme Court has decided that the people of a Territory cannot so exclude slavery, Judge Douglas shifts his ground, saying the people can exclude it, and thus virtually saying it is not a question for the Supreme Court.

I am aware Judge Douglas avoids admitting in direct terms that the Supreme Court have decided against the power of the people of a Territory to exclude slavery. He also avoids saying directly that they have not so decided; but he labors to leave the impression that he thinks they have not so decided. For instance, in his Springfield speech of July 17, 1858, Judge Douglas, speaking of me says: "He infers that it [the court] would decide that the territorial legislatures could not prohibit slavery. I will not stop to inquire whether the courts will carry the decision that far or not." The court has already carried the decision exactly that far, and I must say I think Judge Douglas very well knows it has. After stating that Congress cannot prohibit slavery in the Territories, the court adds: "And if Congress itself cannot do this, if it be beyond the powers conferred on the Federal Government, it will be admitted, we presume, that it could not authorize a territorial government to exercise them, it could confer no power on any local government, established by its authority, to violate the provisions of the Constitution."

Can any mortal man misunderstand this language? Does not Judge Douglas equivocate when he pretends not to know that the Supreme Court has decided that the people of a Territory cannot exclude slavery prior to forming a State constitution?

My third interrogatory to the judge is in these words: "If the Supreme Court of the United States shall decide that States cannot exclude slavery from their limits, are you in favor of acquiescing in, adopting, and following such decision as a rule of political action?" To this question the judge gives no answer whatever. He disposes of it by an attempt to ridicule the idea that the Supreme

Court will ever make such a decision. When Judge Douglas is drawn up to a distinct point, there is significance in all he says, and in all he omits to say. In this case he will not, on the one hand, face the people and declare he will support such a decision when made, nor on the other will he trammel himself by saying he will not support it.

Now I propose to show, in the teeth of Judge Douglas's ridicule, that such a decision does logically and necessarily follow the Dred Scott decision. In that case the court holds that Congress can legislate for the Territories in some respects, and in others it cannot; that it cannot prohibit slavery in the Territories, because to do so would infringe the "right of property" guaranteed to the citizen by the fifth amendment to the Constitution, which provides that "no person shall be deprived of life, liberty, or property without due process of law." Unquestionably there is such a guaranty in the Constitution, whether or not the court rightfully apply it in this case. I propose to show, beyond the power of quibble, that that guaranty applies with all the force, if not more, to States than it does to Territories. The answers to two questions fix the whole thing: to whom is this guaranty given? and against whom does it protect those to whom it is given? The guaranty makes no distinction between persons in the States and those in the Territories; it is given to persons in the States certainly as much as, if not more than, to those in the Territories. "No person," under the shadow of the Constitution, "shall be deprived of life, liberty, or property without due process of law."

Against whom does this guaranty protect the rights of property? Not against Congress alone, but against the world—against State constitutions and laws, as well as against acts of Congress. The United States Constitution is the supreme law of the land; this guaranty of property is expressly given in that Constitution, in that supreme law; and no State constitution or law can override it. It is not a case where power over the subject is reserved to the States, because it is not expressly given to the General Government; it is a case where the guaranty is expressly given to the individual citizen, in and by the organic law of the General Government; and the duty of maintaining that guaranty is imposed upon that General Government, overriding all obstacles.

The following is the article of the Constitution containing the guaranty of property upon which the Dred Scott decision is based:

ARTICLE V. No person shall be held to answer for a capital or otherwise infamous crime, unless on a presentment or indictment by a grand jury, except in cases arising in the land or naval forces, or in the militia when in actual service, in time of war or public danger; nor shall any person be subject for the same offense to be twice put in jeopardy of life or limb; nor shall be compelled, in any criminal case, to be a witness against himself, nor be deprived of life, liberty, or property without due process of law; nor shall private property be taken for public use without just compensation.

Suppose, now, a provision in a State constitution should negative all the above propositions, declaring directly or substantially that "any person may be deprived of life, liberty, or property without due process of law," a direct contradiction—collision—would be pronounced between the United States Constitution and such State constitution. And can there be any doubt but that which is declared to be the supreme law would prevail over the other to the extent of the collision? Such State constitution would be unconstitutional.

There is no escape from this conclusion but in one way, and that is to deny that the Supreme Court, in the Dred Scott case, properly applies this constitutional guaranty of property. The Constitution itself impliedly admits that a person may be deprived of property by "due process of law," and the Republicans hold that if there be a law of Congress or territorial legislature telling the slaveholder in advance that he shall not bring his slave into the Territory upon pain of forfeiture, and he still will bring him, he will be deprived of his property in such slave by "due process of law." And the same would be true in the case of taking a slave into a State against a State constitution or law prohibiting slavery.

Notes for the Debate at Jonesboro, Illinois[1]

September 15, 1858

Brief answer to his opening.
Put in the Democratic Resolutions.
Examine his answers to my questions.[2]

"If the people of Kansas shall, by means entirely unobjectionable in all other respects, adopt a State Constitution, and ask admission into the Union under it *before* they have the requisite number of inhabitants according to the English Bill—some ninety three thousand—will you vote to admit them?"

[1] AD, IHi. The single sheet of notes was picked up from the platform and preserved by John T. Stuart. [2] See Fragment: Notes for Speeches, *supra*.

Third Debate with Stephen A. Douglas at Jonesboro, Illinois[1]

September 15, 1858

MR. DOUGLAS' SPEECH.

Ladies and Gentlemen: I appear before you to-day in pursuance of a previous notice, and have made arrangements with Mr. Lincoln to divide time and discuss with him the leading political topics that now agitate the country.

Prior to 1854 this country was divided into two great political parties known as Whig and Democratic. These parties differed from each other on certain questions which were then deemed to be important to the best interests of the republic. Whigs and Democrats differed about a bank, the tariff, distribution, the specie circular and the sub-treasury. On those issues we went before the country and discussed the principles, objects and measures of the two great parties. Each of the parties could proclaim its principles in Louisiana as well as in Massachusetts, in Kentucky as well as in Illinois. Since that period, a great revolution has taken place in the formation of parties, by which they now seem to be divided by a geographical line, a large party in the North being arrayed under the abolition or republican banner in hostility to the Southern States, Southern people, and Southern institutions. It becomes important for us to inquire how this transformation of parties has occurred, made from those of national principles to geographical factions. You remember that in 1850, this country was agitated from its centre to its circumference about this slavery question, it became necessary for the leaders of the great Whig party and the leaders of the great Democratic party to postpone, for the time being, their particular disputes and unite first to save the Union before they should quarrel as to the mode in which it was to be governed. During the Congress of 1849, '50, Henry Clay was the leader of the Union men, supported by Cass and Webster and the leaders of the democracy and the leaders of the Whigs, in opposition to Northern abolitionists or Southern disunionists. That great contest of 1850 resulted in the establishment of the compromise

[1] Debates Scrapbook, ORB. Although Lincoln did not provide this debate with the prefatory note that precedes the first and second debates, the same sources provide the text of the speeches—the Chicago *Times* for Douglas and the Chicago *Press and Tribune* for Lincoln. As in the first two debates, Lincoln's deletions of cheering and interruptions have not been followed. His corrections and insertions in the margin have been indicated by footnotes. Bracketed passages are in the source unless otherwise noted. Typographical errors not corrected in the scrapbook have been corrected by the editors.

measures of that year, which measures rested on the great principle that the people of each State and each territory of this Union ought to be permitted to regulate their own domestic institutions in their own way subject to no other limitation than that which the Federal Constitution imposes.

I now wish to ask you whether that principle was right or wrong which guaranteed to every State and every community the right to form and regulate their domestic institutions to suit themselves. These measures were adopted, as I have previously said, by the joint action of the Union Whigs and Union Democrats, in opposition to Northern Abolitionists and Southern Disunionists. In 1858, when the Whig party assembled at Baltimore, in national convention for the last time, they adopted the principle of the Compromise measures of 1850 as their rule of party action in the future. One month thereafter the Democrats assembled at the same place to nominate a candidate for the Presidency, and declared the same great principle as the rule of action by which the Democracy would be governed. The Presidential election of 1852 was fought on that basis. It is true that the Whigs claimed special merit for the adoption of those measures, because they asserted that their great Clay originated them, their God-like Webster defended them, and their Fillmore signed the bill making them the law of the land; but on the other hand the Democrats claimed special credit for the Democracy, upon the ground that we gave twice as many votes in both Houses of Congress for the passage of these measures as the Whig party.

Thus you see that in the Presidential election of 1852, the Whigs were pledged by their platform and their candidate to the principle of the Compromise measures of 1850, and the Democracy were likewise pledged by our principles, our platform, and our candidate to the same line of policy, to preserve peace and quiet between the different sections of this Union. Since that period the Whig party has been transformed into a sectional party, under the name of the Republican party, whilst the Democratic party continues the same national party it was at that day. All sectional men, all men of Abolition sentiments and principles, no matter whether they were old Abolitionists or had been Whigs or Democrats, rally under the sectional Republican banner, and consequently all national men; all Union loving men, whether Whigs, Democrats, or by whatever name they have been known, ought to rally under the stars and stripes in defence of the Constitution, as our fathers made it, and of the Union as it has existed under the Constitution.

How has this departure from the faith of the Democracy and the faith of the Whig party been accomplished? In 1854, certain restless, ambitious, and disappointed politicians throughout the land took advantage of the temporary excitement created by the Nebraska bill to try and dissolve the old Whig party and the old Democratic party, to abolitionize their members and lead them, bound hand and foot, captives into the abolition camp. In the State of New York a convention was held by some of these men and a platform adopted, every plank of which was as black as night, each one relating to the negro, and not one referring to the interests of the white man. That example was followed throughout the Northern States, the effect being made to combine all the free States in hostile array against the slave States. The men who thus thought that they could build up a great sectional party, and through its organization control the political destinies of this country, based all their hopes on the single fact that the North was the stronger division of the nation, and hence, if the North could be combined against the South, a sure victory awaited their efforts. I am doing no more than justice to the truth of history when I say that in this State Abraham Lincoln, on behalf of the Whigs, and Lyman Trumbull, on behalf of the Democrats, were the leaders who undertook to perform this grand scheme of abolitionizing the two parties to which they belonged. They had a private arrangement as to what should be the political destiny of each of the contracting parties before they went into the operation. The arrangement was that Mr. Lincoln was to take the old line Whigs with him, claiming that he was still as good a Whig as ever, over to the Abolitionists, and Mr. Trumbull was to run for Congress in the Belleville district, and, claiming to be a good Democrat, coax the old Democrats into the Abolition camp, and when, by the joint efforts of the abolitionized Whigs, the abolitionized Democrats, and the old line Abolition and Free Soil party of this State, they should secure a majority in the legislature. Lincoln was then to be made United States Senator in Shields' place, Trumbull remaining in Congress until I should be accommodating enough to die or resign, and give him a chance to follow Lincoln. (Laughter, applause, and cries of "don't die.") That was a very nice little bargain so far as Lincoln and Trumbull were concerned, if it had been carried out in good faith, and friend Lincoln had attained to senatorial dignity according to the contract. They went into the contest in every part of the State, calling upon all disappointed politicians to join in the crusade against the Democracy, and appealed to the prevailing sentiments and prejudices in all the northern counties of the State. In three Congressional districts in the north end of the State they adopted, as the platform of this new party thus formed by Lincoln and Trumbull in the connection with the Abolitionists, all of those principles which aimed at a warfare on the part of the North against the South. They declared in that platform that the Wilmot proviso was to be applied to all the territories of the United States, North as well as South of 36 deg. 30 min., and not only to all the territory we then had, but all that we might hereafter acquire; that hereafter no more slave States should be admitted into this Union, even if the people of such State desired slavery; that the fugitive slave law should be absolutely and unconditionally repealed; that slavery should be abolished in the District of Columbia; that the slave trade should be abolished between the different States, and, in fact, every article in their creed related to this slavery question, and pointed to a Northern geographical party in hostility to the Southern States of this Union. Such were their principles in Northern Illinois. A little further south they became bleached and grew paler just in proportion as public sentiment moderated and changed in this direction. They were Republicans or Abolitionists in the north, anti-Nebraska men down about Springfield, and in this neighborhood they contented themselves with talking about the inexpediency of the repeal of the Missouri compromise. (Shouts of laughter.) In the extreme northern counties they brought out men to canvass the State whose complexion suited their political creed, and hence Fred Douglass, the negro, was to be found there, following General Cass, and attempting to speak on behalf of Lincoln, Trumbull and abolitionism against that illustrious Senator. (Renewed laughter.) Why, they brought Fred Douglass to Freeport when I was addressing a meeting there in a carriage driven by the white owner, the negro sitting inside with the white lady and her daughter. (Shame.) When I got through canvassing the northern counties that year and progressed as far south as Springfield, I was met and opposed in discussion by Lincoln, Lovejoy, Trumbull, and Sidney Breese, who were on one side. (Laughter.) Father Giddings, the high priest of abolitionism, had just been there, and Chase came about the time I left. ("Why didn't you shoot him?") I did take a running shot at them, but as I was single-handed against the white, black and mixed drove, I had to use a short gun and fire into the crowd instead of taking them off singly with a rifle. (Great laughter and cheers.) Trumbull had for his lieutenants, in aiding him to abolitionize the democracy, such men as John Wentworth, of Chicago, Gov. Reynolds, of Belleville, Sidney Breese, of Carlisle, and John Dougherty, of Union, ("good," "good," "give it to them," &c.,) each of whom modified his opinions to suit the particular locality he was in. Dougherty, for instance, would not go much further than to talk about the inexpediency of the Nebraska bill, whilst his allies at Chicago, advocated negro citizenship and negro equality, putting the white man and the negro on the same basis under the law. (Never, never.) Now these men, four years ago, were engaged in a conspiracy to break down the democracy; to-day they are again acting together for the same purposes. They do not hoist the same flag; they do not own the same principles, or profess the same faith; but conceal their union for the sake of policy. In the northern counties, you find that all the conventions are called in the name of the Black Republican party; at Springfield, they dare not call a Republican Convention, but invite all the enemies of the democracy to unite, and when they get down into Egypt, Trumbull issues notices calling upon the "*free democracy*" to assemble and hear him speak. I have one of the handbills calling a Trumbull meeting at Waterloo the other day, which I received there, which is in the following language:

> A meeting of the Free Democracy will take place in Waterloo, on Monday, Sept. 13th inst., whereat Hon. Lyman Trumbull, Hon. John Baker and others will address the people upon the different political topics of the day. Members of all parties are cordially invited to be present, and hear and determine for themselves.
>
> THE MONROE FREE DEMOCRACY.

What is that name of "Free Democrats" put forth for unless to deceive the people, and make them believe that Trumbull and his followers are not the same party as that which raises the black flag of Abolitionism in the northern part of this State, and makes war upon the Democratic party throughout the State. When I put that question to them at Waterloo on Saturday last, one of them rose and stated that they had changed their name for political effect in order to get votes. There was a candid admission. Their object in changing their party organization and principles in different localities was avowed to be an attempt to cheat and deceive some portion of the people until after the election. Why cannot a political party that is conscious of the rectitude of its purposes and the soundness of its principles declare them every where alike. I would disdain to hold any political principles that I could not avow in the same terms in Kentucky that I declared in Illinois, in Charleston as well as in Chicago, in New Orleans as well as in New York. (Cheers.) So long as we live under a constitution common to all the States, our political faith ought to be as broad, as liberal, and just as that constitution itself, and should be proclaimed alike in every portion of the Union. (Hear, hear.) But it is apparent that our opponents find it necessary, for partizan effect, to change their colors in different counties in order to catch the popular breeze, and hope with these discordant materials combined together to secure a majority in the legislature for the purpose of putting down the Democratic party. This combination did succeed in 1854 so far as to elect a majority of their confederates to the legislature, and the first important act which they performed was to elect a Senator in the place of the eminent and gallant Senator Shields. His term expired in the United States Senate at that time, and he had to be crushed by the abolition coalition for the simple reason that he would not join in their conspiracy to wage war against one-half of the Union. That was the only objection to Gen. Shields. He had served the people of the State with ability in the legislature, he had served you with fidelity and ability as auditor, he had performed his duties to the satisfaction of the whole country as head of the Land Department at Washington, he had covered the State and the Union with immortal glory on the bloody fields of Mexico in defence of the honor of our flag, and yet he had to be stricken down by this unholy combination. And for what cause? Merely because he would not join a combination of one-half of the States to make war upon the other half, after having poured out his heart's blood for all the States in the Union. Trumbull was put in his place by abolitionism. How did Trumbull get there? Before the Abolitionists would consent to go into an election for United States Senator they required all the members of this new combination to show their hands upon this question of abolitionism. Lovejoy, one of their high priests, brought in resolutions defining the abolition creed, and required them to commit themselves on it by their votes—yea or nay. In that creed, as laid down by Lovejoy, they declared first, that the Wilmot proviso must be put on all the territories of the United States north as well as south of 36 deg. 30 min., and that no more territory should ever be acquired unless slavery was at first prohibited therein; second, that no more States should ever be received into the Union unless slavery was first prohibited, by constitutional provision, in such States; third, that the fugitive slave law must be immediately repealed, or, failing in that, then such amendments were to be made to it as would render it useless and inefficient for the objects for which it was passed, &c. The next day after these resolutions were offered they were voted upon, part of them carried, and the others defeated, the same men who voted for them, with only two exceptions, voting soon after for Abraham Lincoln as their candidate for the United States Senate. He came within one or two votes of being elected, but he could not quite get the number required, for the simple reason that his friend Trumbull, who was a party to the bargain by which Lincoln was to take Shields' place, controlled a few abolitionized Democrats in the legislature, and would not allow them all to vote for him, thus wronging Lincoln by permitting him on each ballot to be almost elected, but not quite, until he forced them to drop Lincoln and elect him (Trumbull), in order to unite the party. (Immense laughter.) Thus you find, that although the legislature was carried that year by the bargain between Trumbull, Lincoln, and the Abolitionists, and the union of these discordant elements in one harmonious party; yet Trumbull violated his pledge, and played a yankee trick on Lincoln when they came to divide the spoils. (Laughter and cheers. Mr. Lincoln greatly agitated, his face buried in his hands.) Perhaps you would like a little evidence on this point. If you would, I will call Col. Jas. H. Matheny, of Springfield, to the stand, Mr. Lincoln's especial confidential friend for the last twenty years, and see what he will say upon the subject of this bargain. Matheny is now the Black Republican or Abolition candidate for Congress in the Springfield district against the gallant Col. Harris, and is making speeches all over that part of the State against me and in favor of Lincoln, in concert with Trumbull. He ought to be a good witness, and I will read an extract from a speech which he made in 1856, when he was mad because his friend Lincoln had been cheated. It is one of numerous speeches of the same tenor that were made about that time, exposing this bargain between Lincoln, Trumbull, and the Abolitionists. Matheny then said:

> The Whigs, Abolitionists, Know Nothings, and renegade Democrats made a solemn compact for the purpose of carrying this State against the Democracy, on this plan: 1st. That they would all combine and elect Mr. Trumbull to Congress, and thereby carry his district for the legislature, in order to throw all the strength that could be obtained into that body against the Democrats. 2d. That when the legislature should meet, the officers of that body, such as speaker, clerks, doorkeepers, &c., would be given to the Abolitionists; and 3d, That the Whigs were to have the United States Senator. That, accordingly, in good faith, Trumbull was elected to Congress, and his district carried for the legislature, and, when it convened, the Abolitionists got all the officers of that body, and thus far the "bond" was fairly executed. The Whigs, on their part, demanded the election of Abraham Lincoln to the United States Senate, that the bond might be fulfilled, the other parties to the contract having already secured to themselves all that was called for. But, in the most perfidious manner, they refused to

elect Mr. Lincoln; and the mean, low-lived, sneaking Trumbull succeeded, by pledging all that was required by any party, in thrusting Lincoln aside and foisting himself, an excrescence from the rotten bowels of the Democracy, into the United States Senate: and thus it has ever been, that an *honest* man makes a bad bargain when he conspires or contracts with rogues.

Matheny thought that his friend Lincoln made a bad bargain when he conspired and contracted with such rogues as Trumbull and his abolition associates in that campaign. (Great cheers and laughter; Lincoln looking very miserable.) Lincoln was shoved off the track, and he and his friends all at once began to mope, became sour and mad, (laughter,) and disposed to tell, but dare not; (shouts of laughter;) and this they stood for a long time until the Abolitionists coaxed and flattered him back by their assurances that he should certainly be a Senator in Douglas' place. (Roars of laughter, Lincoln looking as if he had not a friend on earth, although Herr Kriesman[2] whispered "never mind" into his ear.) In that way the Abolitionists have been enabled to hold Lincoln to the alliance up to this time, and now they have brought him into a fight against me, and he is to see if he is again to be cheated by them. Lincoln this time though required more of them than a promise, and holds their bond, if not security, that Lovejoy shall not cheat him as Trumbull did. (Renewed shouts of laughter.)

When the Republican convention assembled at Springfield in June last for the purpose of nominating State officers only, the Abolitionists could not get Lincoln and his friends into it until they would pledge themselves that Lincoln should be their candidate for the Senate; and you will find, in proof of this, that that convention passed a resolution unanimously declaring that Abraham Lincoln was the "first, last and only choice" of the Republicans for United States Senator. He was not willing to have it understood that he was merely their first choice, or their last choice, but their *only* choice. The Black Republican party had nobody else. Browning was nowhere, Gov. Bissell was of no account, Archie Williams was not to be taken into consideration, John Wentworth was not worth mentioning, John M. Palmer was degraded, and their party presented the extraordinary spectacle of having but one—the first, last, and only choice for the Senate. (Laughter.) Suppose Lincoln should die, what a horrible condition the Republican party would be in. (A groan from Lincoln, and great laughter.) They would have nobody left. They have no

[2] Probably Herman Kreismann, German Republican of Chicago who traveled widely and spoke to German audiences in the campaign.

other choice, and it was necessary for them to put themselves before the world in this ludicrous, ridiculous attitude of having no other choice in order to quiet Lincoln's suspicions, and assure him that he was not to be cheated by Lovejoy, and the trickery by which Trumbull out generalled him. Well, gentlemen, I think they will have a nice time of it before they get through. I do not intend to give them any chance to cheat Lincoln at all this time. (Cheers.) I intend to relieve him and them from all anxiety upon that subject, and spare them the mortification of more exposures of contracts violated, and the pledged honor of rogues forfeited. (Great applause.)

But I wish to invite your attention to the chief points at issue between Mr. Lincoln and myself in this discussion. Mr. Lincoln, knowing that he was to be the candidate of his party on account of the arrangement of which I have already spoken, knowing that he was to receive the nomination of the Convention for the United States Senate, had his speech, accepting that nomination, all written and committed to memory, ready to be delivered the moment the nomination was announced. Accordingly, when it was made he was in readiness, and delivered his speech, a portion of which I will read, in order that I may state his political principles fairly, by repeating them in his own language.

> We are now far into the fifth year since a policy was instituted for the avowed object, and with the confident promise of putting an end to slavery agitation; under the operation of that policy, that agitation had only not ceased, but had constantly augmented. I believe it will not cease until a crisis shall have been reached and passed. A house divided against itself cannot stand. I believe this government cannot endure permanently half slave and half free. I do not expect the Union to be dissolved. I do not expect the house to fall, but I do expect it will cease to be divided. It will become all one thing or all the other. Either, the opponents of slavery will arrest the spread of it and place it where the public mind shall rest in the belief that it is in the course of ultimate extinction, or its advocates will push it forward until it shall become alike lawful in all the States North as well as South.

There you have Mr. Lincoln's first and main proposition, upon which he bases his claims, stated in his own language. He tells you that this Republic cannot endure permanently divided into slave and free States, as our fathers made it. He says that they must all become free or all become slave, that they must all be one thing or all be the other, or this government cannot last. Why can it not last if we will execute the government in the same spirit and upon the same principles upon which it is founded. Lincoln, by his proposition, says to the South, "If you desire to maintain your institutions as they are now, you must not be satisfied with minding your own business, but you must invade Illinois and all the other northern States, establish slavery in them and make it universal;" and in the same language he says to the north, "you must not be content with regulating your own affairs and minding your own business, but if you desire to maintain your freedom you must invade the Southern States, abolish slavery there and everywhere, in order to have the States all one thing or all the other." I say that this is the inevitable and irresistible result of Mr. Lincoln's argument inviting a warfare between the North and the South, to be carried on with ruthless vengeance, until the one section or the other shall be driven to the wall and become the victim of the rapacity of the other. What good would follow such a system of warfare? Suppose the North should succeed in conquering the South, how much would she be the gainer, or suppose the South should conquer the North, could the Union be preserved in that way? Is this sectional warfare to be waged between Northern States and Southern States until they all shall become uniform in their local and domestic institutions merely because Mr. Lincoln says that a house divided against itself cannot stand, and pretends that this scriptural quotation, this language of our Lord and Master, is applicable to the American Union and American constitution? Washington and his compeers in the convention that framed the constitution, made this government divided into free and slave States. It was composed then of thirteen sovereign and independent States, each having sovereign authority over its local and domestic institutions, and all bound together by the federal constitution. Mr. Lincoln likens that bond of the federal constitution joining free and slave States together to a house divided against itself, and says that it is contrary to the law of God and cannot stand. When did he learn, and by what authority does he proclaim, that this government is contrary to the law of God, and cannot stand? It has stood thus divided into free and slave States from its organization up to this day. During that period we have increased from four millions to thirty millions of people; we have extended our territory from the Mississippi to the Pacific ocean; we have acquired the Floridas and Texas and other territory sufficient to double our geographical extent; we have increased in population, in wealth, and in power beyond any example on earth; we have risen from a weak and feeble power to become the terror and admiration of the civilized world; and all this has been done under a constitution which Mr. Lincoln, in substance, says is in violation of the law of God, and under a union divided into free and slave States, which Mr. Lincoln thinks, because of such division, cannot stand. Surely, Mr. Lincoln is a wiser man than those who framed the government. Washington did not believe, nor did his compatriots, that the local laws and domestic institutions that were well adapted to the green mountains of Vermont were suited to the rice plantations of South Carolina; they did not believe at that day that in a republic so broad and expanded as this, containing such a variety of climate, soil and interest, that uniformity in the local laws and domestic institutions were either desirable or possible. They believed then as our experience has proved to us now, that each locality, having different interests, a different climate and different surroundings, required different local laws; local policy and local institutions adapted to the wants of that locality. Thus our government was formed on the principle of diversity in the local institutions and laws and not on that of uniformity.

As my time flies, I can only glance, at these points and not present them as fully as I would wish, because I desire to bring all the points in controversy between the two parties before you in order to have Mr. Lincoln's reply. He makes war on the decision of the Supreme Court in the case known as the Dred Scott case, I wish to say to you, fellow-citizens, that I have no war to make on that decision, or any other ever rendered by the Supreme Court. I am content to take that decision as it stands delivered by the highest judicial tribunal on earth, a tribunal established by the Constitution of the United States for that purpose, and hence that decision becomes the law of the land, binding on you, on me, and on every other good citizen, whether we like it or not. Hence I do not choose to go into an argument to prove, before this audience, whether or not Chief Justice Taney understood the law better than Abraham Lincoln. (Laughter.)

Mr. Lincoln objects to that decision, first and mainly because it deprives the negro of the rights of citizenship. I am as much opposed to his reason for that objection as I am to the objection itself. I hold that a negro is not and never ought to be a citizen of the United States. (Good, good, and tremendous cheers.) I hold that this government was made on the white basis, by white men, for the benefit of white men and their posterity forever, and should be administered by white men and none others. I do not believe that the Almighty made the negro capable of self-government. I am aware that all the abolition lecturers that you find traveling about through the country are in the habit of reading the Declaration of Independence to prove that all men were created equal and endowed by their Creator with certain inalienable rights, among which are life, liberty, and the pursuit of happiness. Mr. Lincoln is very much in the habit of following in the track of Lovejoy in this particular, by reading that part of the Declaration of Independence to prove that the negro was endowed by the Almighty with the inalienable right of equality with white men. Now, I say to you, my fellow-citizens, that in my opinion the signers of the Declaration had no reference to the negro whatever when they declared all men to be created equal. They desired to express by that phrase, white men, men of European birth and European descent, and had no reference either to the negro, the savage Indians, the Fejee, the Malay, or any other inferior and degraded race, when they spoke of the equality of men. One great evidence that such was their understanding, is to be found in the fact that at that time every one of the thirteen colonies was a slaveholding colony, every signer of the Declaration represented a slave-holding constituency, and we know that no one of them emancipated his slaves, much less offered citizenship to them when they signed the Declaration, and yet, if they had intended to declare that the negro was the equal of the white man, and entitled by divine right to an equality with him, they were bound, as honest men, that day and hour to have put their negroes on an equality with themselves. (Cheers.) Instead of doing so, with uplifted eyes to Heaven they implored the Divine blessing upon them, during the seven years' bloody war they had to fight to maintain that Declaration, never dreaming that they were violating divine law by still holding the negroes in bondage and depriving them of equality.

My friends, I am in favor of preserving this government as our fathers made it. It does not follow by any means that because a negro is not your equal or mine that hence he must necessarily be a slave. On the contrary, it does follow that we ought to extend to the negro every right, every privilege, every immunity which he is capable of enjoying consistent with the good of society. When you ask me what these rights are, what their nature and extent is, I tell you that that is a question which each State of this Union must decide for itself. Illinois has already decided the question. We have decided that the negro must not be a slave within our limits, but we have also decided that the negro shall not be a citizen within our limits; that he shall not vote, hold office, or exercise any political rights. I maintain that Illinois, as a sovereign State, has a right thus to fix her policy with reference to the relation between the white man and the negro; but while we had the right to decide the question for ourselves we must recognize the same right in Kentucky and in every other State to make the same decision, or a different one. Having decided our own policy with reference to the black race, we must leave Kentucky and Missouri and every other State perfectly free to make just such a decision as they see proper on that question.

Kentucky has decided that question for herself. She has said that within her limits a negro shall not exercise any political rights, and she has also said that a portion of the negroes under the laws of that State shall be slaves. She had as much right to adopt that as her policy as we had to adopt the contrary for our policy. New York has decided that in that State a negro may vote if he has $250 worth of property, and if he owns that much he may vote upon an equality with the white man. I, for one, am utterly opposed to negro suffrage anywhere and under any circumstances; yet, inasmuch as the Supreme Court have decided in the celebrated Dred Scott case that a State has a right to confer the privilege of voting upon free negroes, I am not going to make war upon New York because she has adopted a policy repugnant to my feelings. (That's good.) But New York must mind her own business, and keep her negro suffrage to herself and not attempt to force it upon us. (Great applause.)

In the State of Maine they have decided that a negro may vote and hold office on an equality with a white man. I had occasion to say to the Senators from Maine in a discussion last session, that if they thought that the white people within the limits of their State were no better than negroes, I would not quarrel with them for it, but they must not say that my white constituents of Illinois were no better than negroes, or we would be sure to quarrel. (Cheers.)

The Dred Scott decision covers the whole question, and declares that each State has the right to settle this question of suffrage for itself, and all questions as to the relations between the white man and the negro. Judge Taney expressly lays down the doctrine. I receive it as law, and I say that while those States are adopting regulations on that subject disgusting and abhorrent, according to my views, I will not make war on them if they will mind their own business and let us alone. (Bravo, and cheers.)

I now come back to the question, why cannot this Union exist forever divided into free and slave States as our fathers made it? It can thus exist if each State will carry out the principles upon which our institutions were founded, to wit: the right of each State to do as it pleases, without meddling with its neighbors. Just act upon that great principle, and this Union will not only live forever, but it will extend and expand until it covers the whole continent, and make this confederacy one grand ocean-bound republic. We must bear in mind that we are yet a young nation growing with a rapidity unequalled in the history of the world, that our national increase is great, and that the emigration from the old world is increasing, requiring us to expand and acquire new territory from time to time in order to give our people land to live upon. If we live upon the principle of State rights and State sovereignty, each State regulating its own affairs and minding its own business, we can go on and extend indefinitely, just as fast and as far as we need the territory. The time may come, indeed has now come, when our interests would be advanced by the acquisition of the island of Cuba. (Terrific applause.) When we get Cuba we must take it as we find it, leaving the people to decide the question of slavery for themselves, without interference on the part of the federal government, or of any State of this Union. So, when it becomes necessary to acquire any portion of Mexico or Canada, or of this continent or the adjoining islands, we must take them as we find them, leaving the people free to do as they please, to have slavery or not, as they choose. I never have inquired and never will inquire whether a new State applying for admission has slavery or not for one of her institutions. If the constitution that is presented be the act and deed of the people and embodies their will, and they have the requisite population, I will admit them with slavery or without it just as the people shall determine. (That's good. That's right, and cheers.) My objection to the Lecompton constitution did not consist in the fact that it made Kansas a slave State. I would have been as much opposed to its admission under such a constitution as a free State as I was opposed to its admission under it as a slave State. I hold that that was a question which that people had a right to decide for themselves, and that no power on earth ought to have interfered with that decision. In my opinion, the Lecompton constitution was not the act and deed of the people of Kansas, and did not embody their will, and the recent election in that Territory, at which it was voted down by nearly ten to one, shows conclusively that I was right in saying when the constitution was presented, that it was not the act and deed of the people, and did not embody their will.

If we wish to preserve our institutions in their purity, and transmit them unimpaired to our latest posterity, we must preserve with religious good faith that great principle of self government which guarantees to each and every State, old and new, the right to make just such constitutions as they deserve, and come into the Union with their own constitution and not one palmed upon them. (Cheers.) Whenever you sanction the doctrine that Congress may crowd a constitution down the throats of an unwilling people against their consent, you will subvert the great fundamental principle upon which all our free institutions rest. In the future I have no fear that the attempt will ever be made. President Buchanan declared in his annual message, that hereafter the rule adopted in the Minnesota case, requiring a constitution to be submitted to the people, should be follcwed in all future cases, and if he stands by that recommendation there will be no division in the Democratic party on that principle in the future. Hence, the great mission of the Democracy is to unite the fraternal feeling of the whole country, restore peace and quiet by teaching each State to mind its own business, and regulate its own domestic affairs, and all to unite carrying out the constitution as our fathers made it, and thus to preserve the Union and render it perpetual in all time to come. Why should we not act as our fathers who made the government? There was no sectional strife in Washington's army. They were all brethren of a common confederacy, they fought under a common flag that they might bestow upon their posterity a common destiny, and to this end they poured out their blood in common streams and shared in some instances a common grave. (Three hearty cheers for Douglas.)

MR. LINCOLN'S REPLY.

Mr. Lincoln was then introduced to the audience by D. L. Phillips, Esq., and was greeted with three cheers, and then "three more;" after which he said:

LADIES AND GENTLEMEN: There is very much in the principles that Judge Douglas has here enunciated that I most cordially approve, and over which I shall have no controversy with him. In so far as he has insisted that all the States have the right to do exactly as they please about all their domestic relations, including that of slavery, I agree entirely with him. He places me wrong in spite of all I can tell him, though I repeat it again and again, insisting that I have no difference with him upon this subject. I have made a great many speeches, some of which have been printed, and it will be utterly impossible for him to find anything that I have ever put in print contrary to what I now say upon this subject. I hold myself under constitutional obligations to allow the people in all the States without interference, direct or indirect, to do exactly as they please, and I deny that I have any inclination to interfere with them, even if there were no such constitutional obligation. I can only say again that I am placed improperly—altogether improperly in spite of all I can say—when it is insisted that I entertain any other view or purposes in regard to that matter.

While I am upon this subject, I will make some answers briefly to certain propositions that Judge Douglas has put. He says, "Why can't this Union endure permanently, half slave and half free?" I have said that I supposed it could not, and I will try, before this new audience, to give briefly some of the reasons for entertaining that opinion. Another form of his question is, "Why can't we let it stand as our fathers placed it?" That is the exact difficulty between us, I say that Judge Douglas and his friends have changed them from the position in which our fathers originally placed it. I say in the way our fathers originally left the slavery question, the institution was in the course of ultimate extinction, and the public mind rested in the belief that it *was* in the course of ultimate extinction. I say when this government was first established it was the policy of its founders to prohibit the spread of slavery into the new Territories of the United States, where it had not existed. But Judge Douglas and his friends have broken up that policy and placed it upon a new basis by which it is to become national and perpetual. All I have asked or desired anywhere is that it should be placed back again upon the basis that the fathers of our government originally placed it upon. I have no doubt that it *would* become extinct, for all time to come, if we but re-adopted the policy of the fathers by restricting it to the limits it has already covered—restricting it from the new Territories.

I do not wish to dwell at great length on this branch of the subject at this time, but allow me to repeat one thing that I have stated before. Brooks, the man who assaulted Senator Sumner on the floor of the Senate, and who was complimented with dinners and silver pitchers, and gold-headed canes, and a good many other things for that feat, in one of his speeches declared that when this Government was originally established nobody expected that the institution of slavery would last until this day. That was but the opinion of one man, but it was such an opinion as we can never get from Judge Douglas or anybody in favor of slavery in the North at all. You *can* sometimes get it from a Southern man. He said at the same time that the framers of our Government did not have the knowledge that experience has taught us—that experience and the invention of the cotton-gin have taught us that the perpetuation of slavery is a necessity. He insisted, therefore, upon its being changed from the basis upon which the Fathers of the Government left it to the basis of its perpetuation and nationalization.

I insist that this is the difference between Judge Douglas and myself—that Judge Douglas is helping that change along. I insist upon this Government being placed where our fathers originally placed it.

I remember Judge Douglas once said that he saw the evidences on the statute books of Congress, of a policy in the origin of government to divide slavery and freedom by a geographical line—that he saw an indisposition to maintain that policy, and therefore he set about studying up a way to settle the institution on the right basis—the basis which he thought it ought to have been placed upon at first; and in that speech he confesses that he seeks to place it not upon the basis that the fathers placed it upon, but upon one gotten up on "original principles." When he asks me why we cannot get along with it in the attitude where our fathers placed it he had better clear up the evidences that he has himself changed it from that basis; that he has himself been chiefly instrumental in changing the policy of the fathers. [Applause.] Any one who will read his speech of the 22d of last March, will see that he there makes an open confession, showing that he set about fixing the institution upon an altogether different set of principles. I think I have fully answered him when he asks me why we cannot let it alone upon the basis where our fathers left it, by showing that he has himself changed the whole policy of the Government in that regard.

Now, fellow citizens, in regard to this matter about a contract that was made between Judge Trumbull and myself, and all that long portion of Judge Douglas' speech on this subject—I wish simply to say what I have said to him before, that he cannot know whether it is true or not, and I *do know* that there is not a word of truth in it. [Applause.] And I have told him so before. [Continued applause. "That's right." "Hit him again."] I don't want any harsh language indulged in, but I do not know how to deal with this persistent insisting on a story that I know to be utterly without truth. It used to be a fashion amongst men that when a charge was made some sort of proof was brought forward to establish it, and if no proof was found to exist, the charge was dropped. I don't know how to meet this kind of an argument. I don't want to have a fight with Judge Douglas, and I have no way of making an argument up into the consistency of a corn-cob and stopping his mouth with it. [Laughter and applause.] All I can do is, good-humoredly to say that from the beginning to the end of all that story about a bargain between Judge Trumbull and myself, *there is not a word of truth in it*. [Applause.] I can only ask him to show some sort of evidence of the truth of his story. He brings forward here and reads from what he contends is a speech by James H. Matheny charging such a bargain between Trumbull and myself. My own opinion is that Matheny did do some such immoral thing as to tell a story that he knew nothing about. I believe he did. I contradicted it instantly and it has been contradicted by Judge Trumbull, while nobody has produced any proof, because there is none. Now whether the speech which the Judge brings forward here is really the one Matheny made I do not know, and I hope the Judge will pardon me for doubting the genuineness of this document since his production of those Springfield Resolutions at Ottawa. [Laughter and cheers.] I do not wish to dwell at any great length upon this matter. I can say nothing when a long story like this is told except it is not true, and demand that he who insists upon it shall produce some proof. That is all any man can do, and I leave it in that way for I know of no other way of dealing with it.

The Judge has gone over a long account of the old Whig and Democratic parties, and it connects itself with this charge against Trumbull and myself. He says that they agreed upon a compromise in regard to the slavery question in 1850; that in a National Democratic Convention resolutions were passed to abide by that compromise as a finality upon the slavery question. He also says that the Whig party in National Convention agreed to abide by and regard as a finality, the compromise of 1850. I understand the Judge to be altogether right about that; I understand that part of the history of the country as stated by him to be correct. I recollect that I, as a member of that party, acquiesced in that compromise. I recollect in the Presidential election which followed, when we had General Scott up for the Presidency, Judge Douglas was around berating us Whigs as Abolitionists, precisely as he does to-day—not a bit of difference. I have often heard him. We could do nothing when the old Whig party was alive that was not Abolitionism, but it has got an extremely good name since it has passed away. [Laughter.]

When that compromise was made it did not repeal the old Missouri Compromise. It left a region of United States territory half as large as the present territory of the United States, North of the line of 36° 30′ in which slavery was prohibited by act of Congress. This compromise did not repeal that one. It did not affect or propose to repeal it. But at last it became Judge Douglas's duty, as he thought (and I find no fault with him) as Chairman of the Committee on Territories, to bring in a bill for the organization of a territorial government—first of one, then of two territories north of that line.

When he did so it ended in his inserting a provision substantially repealing the Missouri Compromise. That was because the compromise of 1850 *had not* repealed it. And now I ask why he could not have let that compromise alone? We were quiet from the agitation of the slavery question. We were making no fuss about it. All had acquiesced in the compromise measures of 1850. We never had been seriously disturbed by any abolition agitation before that period. When he came to form governments for the territories North of the line of 36° 30′, why could he not have let that matter stand as it was standing? [Applause.] Was it necessary to the organization of a territory? Not at all. Iowa lay North of the line and had been organized as a territory and had come into the Union as a State without disturbing that Compromise. There was no sort of necessity for destroying it to organize these territories. But gentlemen, it would take up all my time to meet all the little quibbling arguments of Judge Douglas to show that the Missouri Compromise was repealed by the Compromise of 1850. My own opinion is that a careful investigation of all the arguments to sustain the position that that Compromise was virtually repealed by the Compromise of 1850 would show that they are the merest fallacies. I have the report that Judge Douglas first brought into Congress at the time of the introduction of the Nebraska bill, which in its original form *did not* repeal the Missouri Compromise, and he there expressly stated that he had forborne to do so *because it had not been done by the Compromise of* 1850. I close this part of the discussion on my part by asking him the question again "Why when we had peace under the Missouri Compromise could you not have let it alone?"

In complaining of what I said in my speech at Springfield in which he says I accepted my nomination for the Senatorship, (where by the way he is at fault, for if he will examine it he will find no acceptance in it;) he again quotes that portion in which I said that "a house divided against itself cannot stand." Let me say a word in regard to that matter.

He tries to persuade us that there must be a variety in the different institutions of the States of the Union; that that variety necessarily proceeds from the variety of soil, climate, of the face of the country and the difference in the natural features of the States. I agree to all that. Have these very matters ever produced any difficulty amongst us? Not at all. Have we ever had any quarrel over the fact that they have laws in Louisiana designed to regulate the commerce that springs from the production of sugar? Or because we have a different class relative to the production of flour in this State? Have they produced any differences? Not at all. They are the very cements of this Union. They don't make the house a house divided against itself. They are the props that hold up the house and sustain the Union.

But has it been so with this element of slavery? Have we not always had quarrels and difficulties over it? And when will we cease to have quarrels over it? Like causes produce like effects. It is worth while to observe that we have generally had comparative peace upon the slavery question and that there has been no cause for alarm until it was excited by the effort to spread it into new territory. Whenever it has been limited to its present bounds and there has been no effort to spread it, there has been peace. All the trouble and convulsion has proceeded from efforts to spread it over more territory. It was thus at the date of the Missouri Compromise. It was so again with the annexation of Texas; so with the territory acquired by the Mexican war, and it is so now. Whenever there has been an effort to spread it there has been agitation and resistance. Now I appeal to this audience, (very few of whom are my political friends,) as national men, whether we have reason to expect that the agitation in regard to this subject will cease while the causes that tend to reproduce agitation are actively at work? Will not the same cause that produced agitation in 1820 when the Missouri Compromise was formed—that which produced the agitation upon the annexation of Texas and at other times—work out the same results always? Do you think that the nature of man will be changed—that the same causes that produced agitation at one time will not have the same effect at another?

This has been the result so far as my observation of the Slavery question and my reading in history extends. What right have we then to hope that the trouble will cease—that the agitation will come to an end—until it shall either be placed back where it originally stood and where the fathers originally placed it, or on the other hand until it shall entirely master all opposition. This is the view I entertain, and this is the reason I entertained it, as Judge Douglas has read from my Springfield speech.

Now, my friends, there is one other thing that I feel myself under some sort of obligation to mention. Judge Douglas has here to-day—in a very rambling way, I was about saying—spoken of the platforms for which he seeks to hold me responsible. He says, "Why can't you come out and make an open avowal of principles in all places alike?" and he reads from an advertisement that he says was used to notify the people of a speech to be made by Judge Trumbull at Waterloo. In commenting on it he desires to know whether we cannot speak frankly and manfully as he and his friends do! How,

I ask, do his friends speak out their own sentiments? A Convention of his party in this State met on the 21st of April, at Springfield, and passed a set of resolutions which they proclaim to the country as their platform. This does constitute their platform, and it is because Judge Douglas claims it is his platform—that these are his principles and purposes—that he has a right to declare he speaks his sentiments "frankly and manfully." On the 9th of June, Col. John Dougherty, Gov. Reynolds and others, calling themselves National Democrats, met in Springfield and adopted a set of resolutions which are as easily understood, as plain and as definite in stating to the country and to the world what they believed in and would stand upon, as Judge Douglas' platform. Now, what is the reason, that Judge Douglas is not willing that Col. Dougherty and Gov. Reynolds should stand upon their own written and printed platform as well as he upon his? Why must he look farther than their platform when he claims himself to stand by his platform?

Again, in reference to our platform; On the 16th of June the Republicans had their Convention and published their platform, which is as clear and distinct as Judge Douglas'. In it they spoke their principles as plainly and as definitely to the world. What is the reason that Judge Douglas is not willing I should stand upon that platform? Why must he go around hunting for some one who is supporting me, or has supported me at some time in his life, and who has said something at some time contrary to that platform? Does the Judge regard that rule as a good one? If it turn out that the rule is a good one for me—that I am responsible for any and every opinion that any man has expressed who is my friend—then it is a good rule for him. I ask, is it not as good a rule for him as it is for me? In my opinion, it is not a good rule for either of us. Do you think differently, Judge?

Mr. Douglas—I do not.

Mr. Lincoln—Judge Douglas says he does not think differently. I am glad of it. Then can he tell me why he is looking up resolutions of five or six years ago, and insisting that they were my platform, notwithstanding my protest that they are not, and never were my platform, and my pointing out the platform of the State Convention which he delights to say nominated me for the Senate? I cannot see what he means by parading these resolutions, if it is not to hold me responsible for them in some way. If he says to me here, that he does not hold the rule to be good, one way or the other, I do not comprehend how he could answer me more fully if he answered me at greater length. I will therefore put in as my answer to the resolutions that he has hunted up against me, what I, as a lawyer, would call a good plea to a bad declaration. [Laughter.] I understand that it is a maxim of law, that a poor plea may be a good plea to a bad declaration. I think that the opinions the Judge brings from those who support me, yet differ from me, is a bad declaration against me; but if I can bring the same things against him, I am putting in a good plea to that kind of declaration, and now I propose to try it.

At Freeport Judge Douglas occupied a large part of his time in producing resolutions and documents of various sorts, as I understood to make me somehow responsible for them; and I propose now doing a little of the same sort of thing for him. In 1850 a very clever gentleman by the name of Thompson Campbell, a personal friend of Judge Douglas and myself, a political friend of Judge Douglas and opponent of mine, was a candidate for Congress in the Galena District. He was interrogated as to his views on this same slavery question. I have here before me the interrogatories and Campbell's answers to them. I will read them:

INTERROGATORIES.

1st. Will you, if elected, vote for and cordially support a bill prohibiting slavery in the Territories of the United States?

2d. Will you vote for and support a bill abolishing slavery in the District of Columbia?

3d. Will you oppose the admission of any Slave States which may be formed out of Texas or the Territories?

4th. Will you vote for and advocate the repeal of the Fugitive Slave Law passed at the recent session of Congress?

5th. Will you advocate and vote for the election of a Speaker of the House of Representatives who shall be willing to organize the Committees of that House, so as to give the Free States their just influence in the business of legislation?

6th. What are your views not only as to the constitutional right of Congress to prohibit the slave trade between the States, but also as to the expediency of exercising that right immediately?

CAMPBELL'S REPLY.

To the first and second interrogatories, I answer unequivocally in the affirmative.

To the third interrogatory I reply, that I am opposed to the admission of any more slave States into the Union, that may be formed out of Texan or any other Territory.

To the fourth and fifth interrogatories I unhesitatingly answer in the affirmative.

To the sixth interrogatory I reply, that so long as the slave States continue to treat slaves as articles of commerce, the Constitution confers power on Congress to pass laws regulating that peculiar COMMERCE, and that the protection of Human Rights imperatively demands the interposition of every constitutional means to prevent this most inhuman and iniquitous traffic. T. CAMPBELL.

I want to say here that Thompson Campbell was elected to Congress on that platform as the Democratic candidate in the Galena District, against Martin P. Sweet.

JUDGE DOUGLAS.—Give me the date of the letter.

MR. LINCOLN.—The time Campbell ran was in 1850. I have not the exact date here. It was some time in 1850 that these interrogatories were put and the answer given. Campbell was elected to Congress, and served out his term. I think a second election came up before he served out his term and he was not re-elected. Whether defeated or not nominated, I do not know. [Mr. Campbell was nominated for re-election by the Democratic party, by acclamation.] At the end of his term his very good friend, Judge Douglas, got him a high office from President Pierce, and sent him off to California. Is not that the fact? Just at the end of his term in Congress it appears that our mutual friend Judge Douglas got our mutual friend Campbell a good office, and sent him to California upon it. And not only so, but on the 27th of last month when Judge Douglas and myself spoke at Freeport in joint discussion, there was his same friend Campbell, come all the way from California, to help the Judge beat me; and there was poor Martin P. Sweet standing on the platform, trying to help poor me to be elected. [Laughter.] That is true of one of Judge Douglas' friends.

So again, in that same race of 1850, there was a Congressional Convention assembled at Joliet, and it nominated R. S. Molony, for Congress, and unanimously adopted the following resolutions:

Resolved, That we are uncompromisingly opposed to the extension of slavery; and while we would not make such opposition a ground of interference with the interests of the States where it exists, yet we moderately but firmly insist that it is the duty of Congress to oppose its extension into Territory now free, by all means compatible with the obligations of the Constitution, and with good faith to our sister States; that these principles were recognized by the Ordinance of 1787, which received the sanction of Thomas Jefferson, who is acknowledged by all to be the great oracle and expounder of our faith.

Subsequently the same interrogatories were propounded to Dr. Molony which had been addressed to Campbell, as above, with the exception of the 6th respecting the Inter-State slave trade, to which Dr. Molony, the Democratic nominee for Congress, replied as follows:

I received the written interrogatories this day, and as you will see by the LaSalle *Democrat* and Ottawa *Free Trader*, I took at Peru on the 5th and at Ottawa on the 7th the affirmative side of interrogatories 1st and 2d, and in relation to the admission of any more Slave States from Free Territory, my position taken at these meetings as correctly reported in said papers was *emphatically* and *distinctly* opposed to it. In relation to the admission of any more Slave States from Texas whether I shall go against it or not will depend upon the opinion that I may hereafter form of the true meaning and nature of the Resolutions of Annexation. If, by said resolutions, the honor and good faith of the nation is pledged to admit more Slave States from Texas when she (Texas) may apply for the admission of such State then I should; if in Congress, vote for their admission. But if not so PLEDGED and bound by sacred contract, then a bill for the admission of more Slave States from Texas would *never* receive my vote.

To your 4th interrogatory I answer *most decidedly* in the affirmative, and for reasons set forth in my reported remarks at Ottawa last Monday.

To your 5th interrogatory I also reply in the affirmative *most cordially*, and that I will use my utmost exertions to secure the nomination and election of a man who will accomplish the objects of said interrogatories. I most cordially approve of the resolutions adopted at the union meeting held at Princeton on the 27th September ult. Yours, &c., R. S. MOLONY.

All I have to say in regard to Dr. Molony, is that he was the regularly nominated Democratic candidate for Congress in his District—was elected at that time, at the end of his term was appointed to a Land Office at Danville. (I never heard anything of Judge Douglas' instrumentality in this.) He held this office a considerable time, and when we were at Freeport the other day, there were hand bills scattered about notifying the public that after our debate was over, R. S. Molony would make a Democratic speech in favor of Judge Douglas. That is all I know of my own personal knowledge. It is added here to this resolution, and truly I believe that—

"Among those who participated in the Joliet Convention, and who supported its nominee, with his platform as laid down in the resolution of the Convention and in his reply as above given, we call at random the following names, all of which are recognized at this day as leading Democrats:"

"COOK COUNTY—E. B. Williams, Charles McDonell, Arno Voss, Thomas Hoyne, Isaac Cook."

I reckon we ought to except Cook. [Laughter.]

"F. C. Sherman."

"WILL—Joel A. Matteson, S. W. Bowen."

"KANE—B. F. Hall, G. W. Renwick, A. M. Herrington, Elijah Wilcox."

"McHENRY—W. M. Jackson, Enos W. Smith, Neil Donnelly."

"LASALLE—John Hise, William Reddick."

William Reddick! another one of Judge Douglas' friends that stood on the stand with him at Ottawa, at the time the Judge says my knees trembled so that I had to be carried away. [Laughter.] The names are all here:

"DuPage—Nathan Allen."

"DeKalb—Z. B. Mayo."

Here is another set of resolutions which I think are apposite to the matter in hand.

On the 28th of February of the same year, a Democratic District Convention was held at Naperville, to nominate a candidate for Circuit Judge. Among the delegates were Bowen and Kelly, of Will; Captain Naper, H. H. Cody, Nathan Allen, of DuPage; W. M. Jackson, J. M. Strode, P. W. Platt and Enos W. Smith, of McHenry; J. Horsman and others, of Winnebago. Col. Strode presided over the Convention. The following resolutions were unanimously adopted—the first on motion of P. W. Platt, the second on motion of William M. Jackson.

Resolved, That this Convention is in favor of the Wilmot Proviso, both in *Principle* and *Practice,* and that we know of no good reason why any *person* should oppose the largest latitude in *Free Soil, Free Territory* and *Free Speech.*

Resolved, That in the opinion of this Convention the time has arrived when *all men should be free,* whites as well as others.

Judge Douglas—What is the date of those resolutions?

Mr. Lincoln—I understand it was in 1850, but I do not *know* it. I do not state a thing and say I know it, when I do not. But I have the highest belief that this is so. I know of no way to arrive at the conclusion that there is an error in it. I mean to put a case no stronger than the truth will allow. But what I *was* going to comment upon is an extract from a newspaper in DeKalb County, and it strikes me as being rather singular, I confess, under the circumstances. There is a Judge Mayo in that county, who is a candidate for the Legislature, for the purpose, if he secures his election, of helping to re-elect Judge Douglas. He is the editor of a newspaper [DeKalb County *Sentinel*], and in that paper I find the extract I am going to read. It is part of an editorial article in which he was electioneering as fiercely as he could for Judge Douglas and against me. It was a curious thing, I think, to be in such a paper. I will agree to that, and the Judge may make the most of it:

Our education has been such, that we have ever been rather *in favor of the equality of the blacks; that is, that they should enjoy all the privileges of the whites where they reside.* We are aware that this is not a very popular doctrine. We have had many a confab with some who are now strong "Republicans," we taking the broad ground of equality and they the opposite around.

We were brought up in a State where blacks were voters, and we do not know of any inconvenience resulting from it, though perhaps it would not work as well where the blacks are more numerous. We have no doubt of the right of the whites to guard against such an evil, if it is one. Our opinion is that it would be best for all concerned to have the colored population in a State by themselves [In this I agree with him]; but if within the jurisdiction of the United States, *we say by all means they should have the right to have their Senators and Representatives in Congress, and to vote for President.* With us "worth makes the man, and want of it the fellow." We have seen many a "nigger" that we thought more of than some white men.

That is one of Judge Douglas' friends. Now I do not want to leave myself in an attitude where I can be misrepresented, so I will say I do not think the Judge is responsible for this article; but he is quite as responsible for it, as I would be if one of my friends had said it. I think that is fair enough. [Cheers.]

I have here also a set of resolutions placed by a Democratic State Convention in Judge Douglas' own good old State of Vermont, that I think ought to be good for him too:

Resolved, That liberty is a right inherent and inalienable in man, and that herein *all men are equal.*

Resolved, That we claim no authority in the Federal Government to abolish slavery in the several States, but we do claim for it constitutional power perpetually to prohibit the introduction of slavery into territory now free, and abolish it wherever, under the jurisdiction of Congress it exists.

Resolved, That this power ought immediately to be exercised in prohibiting the introduction and existence of slavery in New Mexico and California, in abolishing slavery and the slave trade in the District of Columbia, on the high seas, and wherever else, under the Constitution, it can be reached.

Resolved, That no more slave States should be admitted into the Federal Union.

Resolved, That the Government ought to return to its ancient policy, not to extend, nationalize or encourage, but to limit, localize and discourage slavery.

At Freeport I answered several interrogatories that had been propounded to me by Judge Douglas at the Ottawa meeting. The Judge has yet not seen fit to find any fault with the position that I took in regard to those seven interrogatories, which were certainly broad enough, in all conscience, to cover the entire ground. In my answers, which have been printed, and all have had the opportunity of seeing, I take the ground that those who elect me must expect that I will do nothing which is not in accordance with those answers. I have some right to assert that Judge Douglas has no fault to find with them. But he chooses to still try to thrust me upon different ground without paying any attention to my answers, the obtaining of which from me cost him so much trouble and concern. At the same time, I propounded four interrogatories to him, claiming it as a right that he should answer as many interrogatories for me as I did for him, and I would reserve myself for a future installment when I got them ready. The Judge in answering me upon that occasion, put in what I suppose he intends as answers to all four of my interrogatories. The first one of these interrogatories I have before me, and it is in these words:

Question 1. If the people of Kansas shall, by means entirely unobjectionable in all other respects, adopt a State Constitution, and ask admission into the Union under it, *before* they have the requisite number of inhabitants according to the English Bill—some ninety-three thousand—will you vote to admit them?

As I read the Judge's answer in the newspaper, and as I remember it as pronounced at the time, he does not give any answer which is equivalent to yes or no—I will or I won't. He answers at very considerable length, rather quarreling with me for asking the question, and insisting that Judge Trumbull had done something that I ought to say something about; and finally getting out such statements as induce me to infer that he means to be understood he will, in that supposed case, vote for the admission of Kansas. I only bring this forward now for the purpose of saying that if he chooses to put a different construction upon his answer he may do it. But if he does not, I shall from this time forward assume that he will vote for the admission of Kansas in disregard of[3] the English bill. He has the right to remove any misunderstanding I may have. I only mention it now that I may hereafter assume this to be the true construction of his answer, if he does not now choose to correct me.

The second interrogatory that I propounded to him, was this:

Q. 2. Can the people of a United States Territory, in any lawful way, against the wish of any citizen of the United States, exclude slavery from its limits prior to the formation of a State Constitution?

To this Judge Douglas answered that they can lawfully exclude slavery from the Territory prior to the formation of a constitution. He goes on to tell us how it can be done. As I understand him, he holds that it can be done by the Territorial Legislature refusing to make any enactments for the protection of slavery in the Territory, and especially by adopting unfriendly legislation to it. For the sake of clearness I state it again; that they can exclude slavery from the Territory, 1st, by withholding what he assumes to be an indispensable assistance to it in the way of legislation; and 2d, by unfriendly

[3] "According to" corrected by Lincoln to "in disregard of."

legislation. If I rightly understand him, I wish to ask your attention for a while to his position.

In the first place, the Supreme Court of the United States has decided that any Congressional prohibition of slavery in the Territories is unconstitutional—that they have reached this proposition as a conclusion from their former proposition that the Constitution of the United States expressly recognizes property in slaves, and from that other constitutional provision that no person shall be deprived of property without due process of law. Hence they reach the conclusion that as the Constitution of the United States expressly recognizes property in slaves, and prohibits any person from being deprived of property without due process of law, to pass an act of Congress by which a man who owned a slave on one side of a line would be deprived of him if he took him on the other side, is depriving him of that property without due process of law. That I understand to be the decision of the Supreme Court. I understand also that Judge Douglas adheres most firmly to that decision; and the difficulty is, how is it possible for any power to exclude slavery from the Territory unless in violation of that decision? That is the difficulty.

In the Senate of the United States, in 1856, Judge Trumbull in a speech, substantially if not directly, put the same interrogatory to Judge Douglas, as to whether the people of a Territory had the lawful power to exclude slavery prior to the formation of a constitution? Judge Douglas then answered at considerable length, and his answer will be found in the *Congressional Globe*, under date of June 9th, 1856. The Judge said that whether the people could exclude slavery prior to the formation of a constitution or not *was a question to be decided by the Supreme Court*. He put that proposition, as will be seen by the *Congressional Globe*, in a variety of forms, all running to the same thing in substance—that it was a question for the Supreme Court. I maintain that when he says, after the Supreme Court have decided the question, that the people may yet exclude slavery by any means whatever, he does virtually say, that it is *not* a question for the Supreme Court [Applause.] He shifts his ground. I appeal to you whether he did not say it was a question for the Supreme Court. Has not the Supreme Court decided that question? When he now says the people *may* exclude slavery, does he not make it a question for the people? Does he not virtually shift his ground and say that it is *not* a question for the Court, but for the people? This is a very simple proposition—a very plain and naked one. It seems to me that there is no difficulty in deciding it. In a variety of ways he said that it was a question for the Supreme Court. He did not stop then to tell us that whatever the Supreme Court decides the people can by withholding necessary "police regulations" keep slavery out. He did not make any such answer. I submit to you now, whether the new state of the case has not induced the Judge to sheer away from his original ground. [Applause.] Would not this be the impression of every fair-minded man?

I hold that the proposition that slavery cannot enter a new country without police regulations is historically false. It is not true at all. I hold that the history of this country shows that the institution of slavery was originally planted upon this continent *without* these "police regulations" which the Judge now thinks necessary for the actual establishment of it. Not only so, but is there not another fact —how came this Dred Scott decision to be made? It was made upon the case of a negro being taken and actually held in slavery in Minnesota Territory, claiming his freedom because the act of Congress prohibited his being so held there. *Will the Judge pretend that Dred Scott was not held there without police regulations?* There is at least one matter of record as to his having been held in slavery in the Territory, not only without police regulations, but in the teeth of Congressional legislation supposed to be valid at the time. This shows that there is vigor enough in Slavery to plant itself in a new country even against unfriendly legislation. It takes not only law but the *enforcement* of law to keep it out. That is the history of this country upon the subject.

I wish to ask one other question. It being understood that the Constitution of the United States guarantees property in slaves in the Territories, if there is any infringement of the right of that property, would not the United States Courts, organized for the government of the Territory, apply such remedy as might be necessary in that case? It is a maxim held by the Courts, that there is no wrong without its remedy; and the Courts have a remedy for whatever is acknowledged and treated as a wrong.

Again: I will ask you my friends, if you were elected members of the Legislature, what would be the first thing you would have to do before entering upon your duties? *Swear to support the Constitution of the United States.* Suppose you believe, as Judge Douglas does, that the Constitution of the United States guarantees to your neighbor the right to hold slaves in that Territory—that they are his property—how can you clear your oaths unless you give him such legislation as is necessary to enable him to enjoy that property? What do you understand by supporting the Constitution of a State or of the United States? Is it not to give such constitutional helps to the rights established by that Constitution as may be practically needed? Can you, if you swear to support the Constitution, and believe that the Constitution establishes a right, clear your oath, without giving it support? Do you support the Constitution if, knowing or believing there is a right established under it which needs specific legislation, you withhold that legislation? Do you not violate and disregard your oath? I can conceive of nothing plainer in the world. There can be nothing in the words "support the constitution," if you may run counter to it by refusing support to any right established under the constitution. And what I say here will hold with still more force against the Judge's doctrine of "unfriendly legislation." How could you, having sworn to support the Constitution, and believing it guaranteed the right to hold slaves in the Territories, assist in legislation *intended to defeat that right?* That would be violating your own view of the constitution. Not only so, but if you were to do so, how long would it take the courts to hold your votes unconstitutional and void? Not a moment.

Lastly I would ask—is not Congress, itself, under obligation to give legislative support to any right that is established under the United States Constitution? I repeat the question—is not Congress, itself, bound to give legislative support to any right that is established in the United States Constitution? A member of Congress swears to support the Constitution of the United States, and if he sees a right established by that Constitution which needs specific legislative protection, can he clear his oath without giving that protection? Let me ask you why many of us who are opposed to slavery upon principle give our acquiescence to a fugitive slave law? Why do we hold ourselves under obligations to pass such a law, and abide by it when it is passed? Because the Constitution makes provision that the owners of slaves shall have the right to reclaim them. It gives the right to reclaim slaves, and that right is, as Judge Douglas says, a barren right, unless there is legislation that will enforce it.

The mere declaration "No person held to service or labor in one State under the laws thereof, escaping into another, shall in consequence of any law or regulation therein be discharged from such service or labor, but shall be delivered up on claim of the party to whom such service or labor may be due" is powerless without specific legislation to enforce it. Now on what ground would a member of Congress who is opposed to slavery in the abstract vote for a fugitive law, as I would deem it my duty to do? Because there is a Constitutional right which needs legislation to enforce it. And although it is distasteful to me, I have sworn to support the Constitution, and having so sworn I cannot conceive that I do support it if I withheld from that right any necessary legislation to make it practical. And if that is true in regard to a fugitive slave law, is the right to have fugitive slaves reclaimed any better fixed in the Constitution than the right to hold slaves in the Territories? For this decision is a just exposition of the Constitution as Judge Douglas thinks. Is the one right any better than the other? Is there any man who while a member of Congress would give support to the one any more than the other? If I wished to refuse to give legislative support to slave property in the Territories, if a member of Congress, I could not do it holding the view that the Constitution establishes that right. If I did it at all, it would be because I deny that this decision properly construes the Constitution. But if I acknowledge with Judge Douglas that this decision properly construes the Constitution, I cannot conceive that I would be less than a perjured man if I should refuse in Congress to give such protection to that property as in its nature it needed.

At the end of what I have said here I propose to give the Judge my fifth interrogatory which he may take and answer at his leisure. My fifth interrogatory is this: If the slaveholding citizens of a United States Territory should need and demand Congressional legislation for the protection of their slave property in such territory, would you, as a member of Congress, vote for or against such legislation?

JUDGE DOUGLAS—Will you repeat that? I want to answer that question.

MR. LINCOLN—If the slaveholding citizens of a United States Territory should need and demand Congressional legislation for the protection of their slave property in such Territory, would you, as a member of Congress vote for or against such legislation?

I am aware that in some of the speeches Judge Douglas has made, he has spoken as if he did not know or think that the Supreme Court had decided that a territorial Legislature cannot exclude slavery. Precisely what the Judge would say upon the subject—whether he would say definitely that he does not understand they have so decided, or whether he would say he does understand that the Court have so decided, I do not know; but I know that in his speech at Springfield he spoke of it as a thing they had not decided yet; and in his answer to me at Freeport, he spoke of it so far again as I can comprehend it, as a thing that had not yet been decided. Now I hold that if the Judge does entertain that view I think he is not mistaken in so far as it can be said that the Court has not decided anything save the mere question of jurisdiction. I know the legal arguments that can be made—that after a court has decided that it cannot take jurisdiction of a case, it then has decided all that is before it, and that is the end of it. A plausible argument can be made in favor of that proposition, but I know that Judge Douglas has said in one of his speeches that the court went forward *like honest men as they were* and decided all the points in the case. If any points are really extrajudicially decided because not necessarily before them, then this one as to the power of the Territorial Legislature to exclude slavery is one of them, as also the one that the Missouri Compromise was null and void. They are both extra-judicial or neither is according as the Court held that they had no jurisdiction in the case between the parties, because of want of capacity of one party to maintain a suit in that Court. I want, if I have sufficient time, to show that the Court did *pass its opinion*, but that is the only thing actually done in the case. If they did not decide, they showed what they were ready to decide whenever the matter was before them. What is that opinion? After having argued that Congress had no power to pass a law excluding slavery from a United States Territory, they then used language to this effect:—that inasmuch as Congress itself could not exercise such a power, it followed as a matter of course that it could not authorize a territorial government to exercise it, for the Territorial Legislature can do no more than Congress could do. Thus it expressed its opinion emphatically against the power of a Territorial Legislature to exclude slavery, leaving us in just as little doubt on that point as upon any other point they really decided.

Now, my fellow citizens, I will detain you only a little while longer. My time is very nearly out. I find a report of a speech made by Judge Douglas at Joliet, since we last met at Freeport—published I believe in the *Missouri Republican*—on the 9th of this month, in which Judge Douglas says:

> You know at Ottawa, I read this platform, and asked him if he concurred in each and all of the principles set forth in it. He would not answer these questions. At last I said frankly, I wish you to answer them, because when I get them up here where the color of your principles is a little darker than in Egypt, I intend to trot you down to Jonesboro. The very notice that I was going to take him down to Egypt made him tremble in the knees so that he had to be carried from the platform. He laid up seven days, and in the meantime held a consultation with his political physicians, they had Lovejoy and Farnsworth and all the leaders of the Abolition party, they consulted it all over, and at last Lincoln came to the conclusion that he would answer, so he came up to Freeport last Friday.

Now that statement altogether furnishes a subject for philosophical contemplation. [Laughter.] I have been treating it in that way, and I have really come to the conclusion that I can explain it in no other way than by believing the Judge is crazy. [Renewed laughter.] If he was in his right mind, I cannot conceive how he would have risked disgusting the four or five thousand of his own friends who stood there, and knew, as to my having been carried from the platform, that there was not a word of truth in it.

JUDGE DOUGLAS—Didn't they carry you off?

MR. LINCOLN—There; that question illustrates the character of this man Douglas, exactly. He smiles now and says, "Didn't they carry you off?" But he says then, *"He had to be carried off;"* and he said it to convince the country that he had so completely broken me down by his speech that I had to be carried away. Now he seeks to dodge it, and asks, "Didn't they carry you off?" Yes, they did. *But, Judge Douglas, why didn't you tell the truth?* [Great laughter and cheers.] I would like to know why you didn't tell the truth about it. [Continued laughter.] And then again, "He laid up seven days." He puts this in print for the people of the country to read as a serious document. I think if he had been in his sober senses he would not have risked that barefacedness in the presence of thousands of his own friends, who knew that I made speeches within six of the seven days at Henry, Marshall County; Augusta, Hancock County, and Macomb, McDonough County, including all the necessary travel to meet him again at Freeport at the end of the six days. Now, I say, there is no charitable way to look at that statement, except to conclude that he is actually crazy. [Laughter.] There is another thing in that statement that alarmed me very greatly as he states it, that he was going to "trot me down to Egypt." Thereby he would have you to infer that I would not come to Egypt unless he forced me—that I could not be got here, unless he, giant-like, had hauled me down here. [Laughter.] That statement he makes, too, in the teeth of the knowledge that I had made the stipulation to come down here, *and that he himself had been very reluctant to enter into the stipulation.* [Cheers and laughter.] More than all this, Judge Douglas, when he made that statement must have been crazy, and wholly out of his sober senses, or else he would have known that when he got me down here—that promise—that windy promise—of his powers to annihilate me, wouldn't amount to anything. Now, how little do I look like being carried away trembling? Let the Judge go on, and after he is done with his half hour, I want you all, if I can't go home myself, to let me stay and rot here; and if anything happens to the Judge, if I cannot carry him to the hotel and put him to bed, let me stay here and rot. [Great laughter.] I say, then, there is something *extraordinary* in this statement? I ask you if you know any other living man who would make such a statement? [Cries of "No," "no." "Yes," "yes."] I will ask my friend Casey, over there, if he would do such a thing? [Casey dropped his head and said nothing.] Would he send that out and have his men take it as the truth? Did the Judge talk of trotting me down to Egypt to scare me to death? Why, I know this people better than he does. I was raised just a little east of here. I am a part of this people. But the Judge was raised further north, and perhaps he has some horrid idea of what this people might be induced to do. [Roars of laughter and cheers.] But really I have talked about this matter perhaps longer than I ought, for it is no great thing, and yet the smallest are often the most difficult things to deal with. The Judge has set about seriously trying to make the impression that when we meet at different places I am literally in his clutches—that I am a poor, helpless, decrepit mouse, and that I can do nothing at all. This is one of the ways he has taken to create that impression. I don't know any other way to meet it, except this. I don't want to quarrel with him—to call him a liar—but when I come square up to him I don't know what else to call him, if I must tell the truth out. [Cheers and laughter.] I want to be at peace, and reserve all my fighting powers for necessary occasions. My time, now, is very nearly out, and I give up the trifle that is left to the Judge to let him set my knees trembling again, if he can.

MR. DOUGLAS' REPLY.

Mr. Douglas on again taking the stand was greeted with thundering applause. He said:

My friends, while I am very grateful to you for the enthusiasm which you show for me, I will say in all candor, that your quietness will be much more agreeable than your applause, inasmuch as you deprive me of some part of my time whenever you cheer. (All right, go ahead, we won't interrupt, &c.)

I will commence where Mr. Lincoln left off, and make a remark upon this serious complaint of his about my speech at Joliet. I did say there in a playful manner that when I put these questions to Mr. Lincoln at Ottawa he failed to answer, and that he trembled and had to be carried off the stand, and required seven days to get up his reply. (Laughter.) That he did not walk off from that stand he will not deny. That when the crowd went away from the stand with me, a few persons carried him home on their shoulders and laid him down, he will admit. (Shouts of laughter.) I wish to say to you that whenever I degrade my friends and myself by allowing them to carry me on their backs along through the public streets when I am able to walk I am willing to be deemed crazy. ("All right, Douglas," laughter and applause. Lincoln chewing his nails in a rage in a back corner.) I did not say whether I beat him or he beat me in the argument. It is true I put these questions to him, and I put them not as mere idle questions, but showed that I based them upon the creed of the Black Republican party as declared by their conventions in that portion of the State which he depends upon to elect him, and desired to know whether he endorsed that creed. He would not answer. When I reminded him that I intended bringing him into Egypt and renewing my questions if he refused to answer, he then consulted and did get up his answers one week after,—answers which I may refer to in a few minutes and show you how equivocal they are. My object was to make him avow whether or not he stood by the platform of his party; the resolutions I then read, and upon which I based my questions, had been adopted by his party in the Galena Congressional district, and the Chicago and Bloomington Congressional districts, composing a large majority of the counties in this State that give Republican or Abolition majorities. Mr. Lincoln cannot and will not deny that the doctrines laid down in these resolutions were in substance put forth in Lovejoy's resolutions which were voted for by a majority of his party, some of them, if not all, receiving the support of every man of his party. Hence, I laid a foundation for my questions to him before I asked him whether that was or was not the platform of his party. He says that he answered by questions. One of them was whether he would vote to admit any more slave States into the Union. The creed of the Republican party as set forth in the resolutions of their various conventions was that they would under no circumstances vote to admit another slave State. It was put forth in the Lovejoy resolutions in the legislature, it was put forth and passed in a majority of all the counties of this State which give Abolition or Republican majorities, or elect members to the legislature of that school of politics. I had a right to know whether he would vote for or against the admission of another slave State in the event the people wanted it. He first answered that he was not pledged on the subject, and then said, "In regard to the other question of whether I am pledged to the admission of any more slave States into the Union, I state to you very frankly that I would be exceedingly sorry ever to be put in the position of having to pass on that question. ("No doubt," and laughter. Mr. Lincoln looks savagely into the crowd for the man who said "no doubt.") I should be exceedingly glad to know that there would never be another slave State admitted into the Union; but I must add that if slavery shall be kept out of the territories during the territorial existence of any one given territory, and then the people, having a fair chance and clean field when they come to adopt a constitution, do such an extraordinary thing as adopt a slave constitution, uninfluenced by the actual presence of the institution among them, I see no alternative, if we own the country, but to admit them into the Union."

Now analyze that answer. In the first place he says he would be exceedingly sorry to be put in a position where he would have to vote on the question of the admission of a slave State. Why is he a candidate for the Senate if he would be sorry to be put in that position? I trust the people of Illinois will not put him in a position which he would be so sorry to occupy. ("There's no danger," &c.) The next position he takes is that he would be glad to know that there would never be another slave State, yet, in certain contingencies, he might have to vote for one. What is that contingency? "If Congress keeps slavery out by law while it is a territory, and then the people should have a fair chance and should adopt slavery, uninfluenced by the presence of the institution," he supposes he would have to admit the State. Suppose Congress should not keep slavery out during their territorial existence, then how would he vote when the people applied for admission into the Union with a slave constitution? That he does not answer, and that is the condition of every territory we have now got. Slavery is not kept out of Kansas by act of Congress, and when I put the question to Mr. Lincoln whether he will vote for the admission with or without slavery, as her people may desire, he will not answer, and you have not got an answer from him. In Nebraska slavery is not prohibited by act of Congress, but the people are allowed, under the Nebraska bill, to do as they please on the subject; and when I ask him whether he will vote to admit Nebraska with a slave constitution if her people desire it, he will not answer. So with New Mexico, Washington territory, Arizona, and the four new States to be admitted from Texas. You cannot get an answer from him to these questions. His answer only applies to a given case, to a condition—things which he knows do not exist in any one territory in the Union. He tries to give you to understand that he would allow the people to do as they please, and yet he dodges the question as to every territory in the Union. I now ask why cannot Mr. Lincoln answer to each of these territories? He has not done it, and he will not do it. The Abolitionists up North understand that this answer is made with a view of not committing himself on any one territory now in existence. It is so understood there, and you cannot expect an answer from him on a case that applies to any one territory, or applies to the new States which by compact we are pledged to admit out of Texas, when they have the requisite population and desire admission. I submit to you whether he has made a frank answer, so that you can tell how he would vote in any one of these cases. "He would be sorry to be put in the position." Why would he be sorry to be put in this position if his duty required him to give the vote? If the people of a territory ought to be permitted to come into the Union as a State, with slavery or without it, as they pleased, why not give the vote admitting them cheerfully? If in his opinion they ought not to come in with slavery, even if they wanted to, why not say that he would cheerfully vote against their admission? His intimation is that conscience would not let him vote. "No," and he would be sorry to do that which his conscience would compel him to do as an honest man. (Laughter and cheers.)

In regard to the contract or bargain between Trumbull, the Abolitionists and him, which he denies, I wish to say that the charge can be proved by notorious historical facts. Trumbull, Lovejoy, Giddings, Fred Douglass, Hale, and Banks,[4] were traveling the State at that time making speeches on the same side and in the same cause with him. He contents himself with the simple denial that no such thing occurred. Does he deny that he, and Trumbull, and Breese, and Giddings, and Chase, and Fred Douglass, and Lovejoy, and all those Abolitionists and deserters from the Democratic party, did make speeches all over this State in the same common cause? Does he deny that Jim Matheny was then and is now his confidential friend, and does he deny that Matheny made the charge of the bargain and fraud in his own language, as I have read it from his printed speech. Matheny spoke of his own personal knowledge of that bargain existing between Lincoln, Trumbull, and the Abolitionists. He still remains Lincoln's confidential friend, and is now a candidate for Congress, and is canvassing the Springfield district for Lincoln. I assert that I can prove the charge to be true in detail if I can ever get it where I can summon and compel the attendance of witnesses. I have the statement of another man to the same effect as that made by Matheny, which I am not permitted to use yet, but Jim Matheny is a good witness on that point, and the history of the country is conclusive upon it. That Lincoln up to that time had been a Whig, and then under-

[4] Nathaniel P. Banks and John P. Hale.

took to Abolitionize the Whigs and bring them into the Abolition camp, is beyond denial; that Trumbull up to that time had been a Democrat, and deserted, and undertook to Abolitionize the Democracy, and take them into the Abolition camp, is beyond denial; that they are both now active, leading, distinguished members of this Abolition Republican party, in full communion, is a fact that cannot be questioned or denied.

But Lincoln is not willing to be responsible for the creed of his party. He complains because I hold him responsible, and in order to avoid the issue, he attempts to show that individuals in the Democratic party, many years ago, expressed abolition sentiments. It is true that Tom Campbell, when a candidate for Congress in 1850, published the letter which Lincoln read. When I asked Lincoln for the date of that letter he could not give it. The date of the letter has been suppressed by other speakers who have used it, though I take it for granted that Lincoln did not know the date. If he will take the trouble to examine, he will find that the letter was published only two days before the election, and was never seen until after it, except in one county. Tom Campbell would have been beat to death by the Democratic party if that letter had been made public in his district. As to Molony, it is true he uttered sentiments of the kind referred to by Mr. Lincoln, and the best democrats would not vote for him for that reason. I returned from Washington after the passage of the Compromise measures in 1850, and when I found Molony running under John Wentworth's tutelage, and on his platform, I denounced him, and declared that he was no democrat. In my speech at Chicago, just before the election that year, I went before the infuriated people of that city and vindicated the Compromise measures of 1850. Remember the city council had passed resolutions nullifying acts of Congress and instructing the police to withhold their assistance from the execution of the laws, and as I was the only man in the city of Chicago who was responsible for the passage of the Compromise measures, I went before the crowd, justified each and every one of those measures, and let it be said to the eternal honor of the people of Chicago, that when they were convinced by my exposition of those measures that they were right and they had done wrong in opposing them, they repealed their nullifying resolutions and declared that they would acquiesce in and support the laws of the land. These facts are well known, and Mr. Lincoln can only get up individual instances, dating back to 1849, '50, which are contradicted by the whole tenor of the democratic creed.

But Mr. Lincoln does not want to be held responsible for the

Black Republican doctrine of no more slave States. Farnsworth is the candidate of his party to-day in the Chicago district, and he made a speech in the last Congress in which he called upon God to palsy his right arm if he ever voted for the admission of another slave State, whether the people wanted it or not. Lovejoy is making speeches all over the State for Lincoln now, and taking ground against any more slave States. Washburne, the Black Republican candidate for Congress in the Galena district, is making speeches in favor of this same abolition platform declaring no more slave States. Why are men running for Congress in the northern districts, and taking that abolition platform for their guide, when Mr. Lincoln does not want to be held to it down here in Egypt and in the centre of the State, and objects to it so as to get votes here. (He can't get any.) Let me tell Mr. Lincoln that his party in the northern part of the State hold to that abolition platform, and that if they do not in the south and in the centre they present the extraordinary spectacle of a house divided against itself, and hence cannot stand. (Hurra.) I now bring down upon him the vengeance of his own scriptural quotation, and give it a more appropriate application than he did, when I say to him that his party, abolition in one end of the State and opposed to it in the other, is a house divided against itself, and cannot stand, and ought not to stand, for it attempts to cheat the American people out of their votes by disguising its sentiments. (Cheers.)

Mr. Lincoln attempts to cover up and get over his abolitionism by telling you that he was raised a little east of you, (laughter,) beyond the Wabash in Indiana, and he thinks that makes a mighty sound and good man of him on all these questions. I do not know that the place where a man is born or raised has much to do with his political principles. The worst Abolitionists I have ever known in Illinois have been men who have sold their slaves in Alabama and Kentucky, and have come here and turned Abolitionists whilst spending the money got for the negroes they sold, (that's so, and laughter,) and I do not know that an Abolitionist from Indiana or Kentucky ought to have any more credit because he was born and raised among slaveholders. (Not a bit, not as much, &c.) I do not know that a native of Kentucky is more excusable because raised among slaves, his father and mother having owned slaves, he comes to Illinois, turns Abolitionist, and slanders the graves of his father and mother, and breathes curses upon the institutions under which he was born, and his father and mother bred. True, I was not born out west here. I was born away down in Yankee land, (good,) I was born in a valley in Vermont (all right,) with the high mountains around me. I love the old green mountains and valleys of Vermont, where I was born, and where I played in my childhood. I went up to visit them some seven or eight years ago, for the first time for twenty odd years. When I got there they treated me very kindly. They invited me to the commencement of their college, placed me on the seats with their distinguished guests, and conferred upon me the degree of L.L.D. in latin, (doctor of laws,) the same as they did on old Hickory, at Cambridge, many years ago, and I give you my word and honor I understood just as much of the latin as he did. (Laughter.) When they got through conferring the honorary degree, they called upon me for a speech, and I got up with my heart full and swelling with gratitude for their kindness, and I said to them, "My friends, Vermont is the most glorious spot on the face of this globe for a man to be born in, *provided* he emigrates when he is very young. (Uproarious shouts of laughter.)

I emigrated when I was very young. I came out here when I was a boy, and I found my mind liberalized, and my opinions enlarged when I got on these broad prairies, with only the Heavens to bound my vision, instead of having them circumscribed by the little narrow ridges that surrounded the valley where I was born. But, I discard all flings of the land where a man was born. I wish to be judged by my principles, by those great public measures and constitutional principles upon which the peace, the happiness and the perpetuity of this republic now rest.

Mr. Lincoln has framed another question, propounded it to me, and desired my answer. As I have said before, I did not put a question to him that I did not first lay a foundation for by showing that it was a part of the platform of the party whose votes he is now seeking, adopted in a majority of the counties where he now hopes to get a majority, and supported by the candidates of his party now running in those counties. But I will answer his question. It is as follows: "If the slaveholding citizens of a United States territory should need and demand congressional legislation for the protection of their slave property in such territory, would you, as a member of Congress, vote for or against such legislation?" I answer him that it is a fundamental article in the Democratic creed that there should be non-interference and non-intervention by Congress with slavery in the States or territories. (Immense cheering.) Mr. Lincoln could have found an answer to his question in the Cincinnati platform, if he had desired it. (Renewed applause.) The Democratic party have always stood by that great principle of non-interference and non-intervention by Congress with slavery in the

States and territories alike, and I stand on that platform now. (Cheer after cheer was here given for Douglas.)

Now I desire to call your attention to the fact that Lincoln did not define his own position in his own question. ("He can't, it's too far South," and laughter.) How does he stand on that question? He put the question to me at Freeport whether or not I would vote to admit Kansas into the Union before she had 93,420 inhabitants. I answered him at once that it having been decided that Kansas had now population enough for a slave State, she had population enough for a free State. ("Good; that's it," and cheers.)

I answered the question unequivocally, and then I asked him whether he would vote for or against the admission of Kansas before she had 93,420 inhabitants, and he would [not][5] answer me. To-day he has called attention to the fact that in his opinion my answer on that question was not quite plain enough, and yet he has not answered it himself. (Great Laughter.) He now puts a question in relation [to][6] Congressional interference in the territories to me. I answer him direct, and yet he has not answered the question himself. I ask you whether a man has any right, in common decency, to put questions in these public discussions, to his opponent, which he will not answer himself, when they are pressed home to him. I have asked him three times, whether he would vote to admit Kansas whenever the people applied with a constitution of their own making and their own adoption, under circumstances that were fair, just and unexceptionable, but I cannot get an answer from him. Nor will he answer the question which he put to me, and which I have just answered in relation to Congressional interference in the territories, by making a slave code there.

It is time that he goes on to answer the question by arguing that under the decision of the Supreme Court it is the duty of a man to vote for a slave code in the territories. He says that it is his duty, under the decision that the court has made, and if he believes in that decision he would be a perjured man if he did not give the vote. I want to know whether he is not bound to a decision which is contrary to his opinions just as much as to one in accordance with his opinions. (Certainly.) If the decision of the Supreme Court, the tribunal created by the constitution to decide the question, is final and binding, is he not bound by it just as strongly as if he was for it instead of against it originally. Is every man in this land allowed to resist decisions he does not like, and only support those that meet his approval? What are important courts worth unless their decisions are binding on all good citizens? It is the fun-

[5] Not in source. [6] Not in source.

damental principles of the judiciary that its decisions are final. It is created for that purpose so that when you cannot agree among yourselves on a disputed point you appeal to the judicial tribunal which steps in and decides for you, and that decision is then binding on every good citizen. It is the law of the land just as much with Mr. Lincoln against it as for it. And yet he says that if that decision is binding he is a perjured man if he does not vote for a slave code in the different territories of this Union. Well, if you (turning to Mr. Lincoln) are not going to resist the decision, if you obey it, and do not intend to array mob law against the constituted authorities, then, according to your own statement, you will be a perjured man if you do not vote to establish slavery in these territories. My doctrine is, that even taking Mr. Lincoln's view that the decision recognizes the right of a man to carry his slaves into the territories of the United States, if he pleases, yet after he gets there he needs affirmative law to make that right of any value. The same doctrine not only applies to slave property, but all other kinds of property. Chief Justice Taney places it upon the ground that slave property is on an equal footing with other property. Suppose one of your merchants should move to Kansas and open a liquor store; he has a right to take groceries and liquors there, but the mode of selling them, and the circumstances under which they shall be sold, and all the remedies must be prescribed by local legislation, and if that is unfriendly it will drive him out just as effectually as if there was a constitutional provision against the sale of liquor. So the absence of local legislation to encourage and support slave property in a territory excludes it practically just as effectually as if there was a positive constitutional provision against it. Hence, I assert that under the Dred Scott decision you cannot maintain slavery a day in a territory where there is an unwilling people and unfriendly legislation. If the people are opposed to it, our right is a barren, worthless, useless right, and if they are for it, they will support and encourage it. We come right back, therefore, to the practical question, if the people of a territory want slavery they will have it, and if they do not want it you cannot force it on them. And this is the practical question, the great principle upon which our institutions rest. ("That's the doctrine.") I am willing to take the decision of the Supreme Court as it was pronounced by that august tribunal without stopping to inquire whether I would have decided that way or not. I have had many a decision made against me on questions of law which I did not like, but I was bound by them just as much as if I had had a hand in making them, and approved them. Did you ever see a lawyer or a client lose his case that he approved the decision of the court. They always think the decision unjust when it is given against them. In a government of laws like ours we must sustain the constitution as our fathers made it, and maintain the rights of the States as they are guaranteed under the constitution, and then we will have peace and harmony between the different States and sections of this glorious Union. (Prolonged cheering.)

To Martin P. Sweet[1]

Hon: M. P. Sweet Centralia,
My dear Sir Sept. 16 1858

Yesterday Douglas and I met at Jonesboro. A very trifling thing occurred which gives me a little uneasiness. I was, at the suggestion of friends, putting in, some resolutions and the like of abolition caste, passed by Douglas friends, some time ago, as a Set-off to his attempts of a like character against me. Among others I put the questions to T. Campbell and his answers to them, in 1850 when you and he ran for Congress. As my attention was divided, half lingering upon that case, and half advancing to the next one, I mentioned your name, as Campbell's opponent, in a confused [confound?] sentence, which, when I heard it myself, struck me as having something disparaging to you in it. I instantly corrected it, and asked the reporters to suppress it; but my fear now is that those villainous reporters Douglas has with him will try to make something out of it. I do not myself exactly remember what it was, so little connection had it with any distinct thought in my my [*sic*] mind, and I really hope no more may be heared of it; but if there should, I write this to assure you that nothing can be farther from me than to *feel*, much less, intentionally *say* anything disrespectful to you.

I sincerely hope you may hear nothing of it except what I have written. Yours very truly, A. LINCOLN

[1] ALS, IHi.

To Elihu B. Washburne[1]

Hon: E. B. Washburne Centralia,
Dear Sir Sept. 16, 1858–

Yesterday at Jonesborough, Douglas, by way of placing you and me on different ground, alledged that you were every where, pledging yourself unconditionally against the admission of any more

Slave States. If his allegation be true, burn this without answering it. If it be untrue, write me such a letter as I may make public with which to contradict him. Yours truly A. LINCOLN

Address to Springfield.

[1] ALS, owned by Hempstead Washburne, Chicago, Illinois. Apparently Washburne did not reply to this by letter, for in the Lincoln Papers there are no Washburne letters between May 31, 1858 and May 20, 1860.

Fourth Debate with Stephen A. Douglas at Charleston, Illinois[1]

September 18, 1858

Fourth joint debate September 18. 1858. Lincoln, as reported in the Press & Tribune. Douglas, as reported in the Chicago Times.[2]

MR. LINCOLN'S SPEECH.

Mr. Lincoln took the stand at a quarter before three, and was greeted with vociferous and protracted applause; after which, he said:

LADIES AND GENTLEMEN: It will be very difficult for an audience so large as this to hear distinctly what a speaker says, and consequently it is important that as profound silence be preserved as possible.

While I was at the hotel to-day an elderly gentleman called upon me to know whether I was really in favor of producing a perfect equality between the negroes and white people. [Great laughter.] While I had not proposed to myself on this occasion to say much on that subject, yet as the question was asked me I thought I would occupy perhaps five minutes in saying something in regard to it. I will say then that I am not, nor ever have been in favor of bringing about in any way the social and political equality of the white and black races, [applause]—that I am not nor ever have been in favor of making voters or jurors of negroes, nor of qualifying them to hold office, nor to intermarry with white people; and I will say in addition to this that there is a physical difference between the white and black races which I believe will for ever forbid the two races living together on terms of social and

[1] Debates Scrapbook, ORB. As in the preceding debates, the editors have not followed Lincoln's deletion of cheering and interruptions. Insertions and corrections made by Lincoln are indicated in footnotes. Typographical errors not corrected in the scrapbook have been corrected by the editors. Bracketed passages are in the source unless otherwise noted.

[2] Lincoln's prefatory note in the debates scrapbook.

political equality. And inasmuch as they cannot so live, while they do remain together there must be the position of superior and inferior, and I as much as any other man am in favor of having the superior position assigned to the white race. I say upon this occasion I do not perceive that because the white man is to have the superior position the negro should be denied everything. I do not understand that because I do not want a negro woman for a slave I must necessarily want her for a wife. [Cheers and laughter.] My understanding is that I can just let her alone. I am now in my fiftieth year, and I certainly never have had a black woman for either a slave or a wife. So it seems to me quite possible for us to get along without making either slaves or wives of negroes. I will add to this that I have never seen to my knowledge a man, woman or child who was in favor of producing a perfect equality, social and political, between negroes and white men. I recollect of but one distinguished instance that I ever heard of so frequently as to be entirely satisfied of its correctness—and that is the case of Judge Douglas' old friend Col. Richard M. Johnson.[3] [Laughter.] I will also add to the remarks I have made, (for I am not going to enter at large upon this subject,) that I have never had the least apprehension that I or my friends would marry negroes if there was no law to keep them from it, [laughter] but as Judge Douglas and his friends seem to be in great apprehension that they might, if there were no law to keep them from it, [roars of laughter] I give him the most solemn pledge that I will to the very last stand by the law of this State, which forbids the marrying of white people with negroes. [Continued laughter and applause.] I will add one further word, which is this, that I do not understand there is any place where an alteration of the social and political relations of the negro and the white man can be made except in the State Legislature—not in the Congress of the United States—and as I do not really apprehend the approach of any such thing myself, and as Judge Douglas seems to be in constant horror that some such danger is rapidly approaching, I propose as the best means to prevent it that the Judge be kept at home and placed in the State Legislature to fight the measure. [Uproarious laughter and applause.] I do not propose dwelling longer at this time on this subject.

When Judge Trumbull, our other Senator in Congress, returned to Illinois in the month of August, he made a speech at Chicago in

[3] Richard M. Johnson, U.S. representative from Kentucky, 1807-1819 and 1829-1837; U.S. senator, 1819-1829; vice-president of the United States, 1837-1841.

which he made what may be called *a charge* against Judge Douglas, which I understand proved to be very offensive to him. The Judge was at that time out upon one of his speaking tours through the country, and when the news of it reached him, as I am informed, he denounced Judge Trumbull in rather harsh terms for having said what he did in regard to that matter. I was traveling at that time and speaking at the same places with Judge Douglas on subsequent days, and when I heard of what Judge Trumbull had said of Douglas and what Douglas had said back again, I felt that I was in a position where I could not remain entirely silent in regard to the matter. Consequently upon two or three occasions I alluded to it, and alluded to it in no other wise than to say that in regard to the charge brought by Trumbull against Douglas, I *personally* knew nothing and sought to say nothing about it—that I did personally know Judge Trumbull—that I believed him to be a man of veracity—that I believed him to be a man of capacity sufficient to know very well whether an assertion he was making as a conclusion drawn from a set of facts, was true or false; and as a conclusion of my own from that, I stated it as my belief, if Trumbull should ever be called upon he would prove everything he had said. I said this upon two or three occasions. Upon a subsequent occasion, Judge Trumbull spoke again before an audience at Alton, and upon that occasion not only repeated his charge against Douglas, but arrayed the evidence he relied upon to substantiate it. This speech was published at length; and subsequently at Jacksonville Judge Douglas alluded to the matter. In the course of his speech, and near the close of it, he stated in regard to myself what I will now read: "Judge Douglas proceeded to remark that he should not hereafter occupy his time in refuting such charges made by Trumbull, but that Lincoln having indorsed the character of Trumbull for veracity, he should hold him (Lincoln) responsible for the slanders." I have done simply what I have told you, to subject me to this invitation to notice the charge. I now wish to say that it had not originally been my purpose to discuss that matter at all. But inasmuch as it seems to be the wish of Judge Douglas to hold me responsible for it, then for once in my life I will play General Jackson and to the just extent I take the responsibility. [Great applause and cries of "good, good," "hurrah for Lincoln," etc.]

I wish to say at the beginning that I will hand to the reporters that portion of Judge Trumbull's Alton speech which was devoted to this matter, and also that portion of Judge Douglas' speech made at Jacksonville in answer to it. I shall thereby furnish the readers of this debate with the complete discussion between Trumbull and

Douglas. I cannot now read them, for the reason that it would take half of my first hour to do so. I can only make some comments upon them. Trumbull's charge is in the following words: "Now, the charge is, that there was a plot entered into to have a constitution formed for Kansas and put in force without giving the people an opportunity to vote upon it, and that Mr. Douglas was in the plot." I will state, without quoting further, for all will have an opportunity of reading it hereafter, that Judge Trumbull brings forward what he regards as sufficient evidence to substantiate this charge.[4]

[The extracts handed to our reporter by Mr. Lincoln are quite too lengthy to appear in this number of the PRESS AND TRIBUNE. Judge Trumbull's speech at Alton has already had a place in our columns, and Senator Douglas' remarks at Jacksonville are faithfully repeated in his portion of this (Charleston) debate.]

It will be perceived Judge Trumbull shows that Senator Bigler,[5] upon the floor of the Senate, had declared there had been a conference among the Senators, in which conference it was determined to have an Enabling Act passed for the people of Kansas to form a Constitution under, and in this conference it was agreed among them that it was best not to have a provision for submitting the Constitution to a vote of the people after it should be formed. He then brings forward to show, and showing, as he deemed, that Judge Douglas reported the bill back to the Senate with that clause stricken out. He then shows that there was a new clause inserted into the bill, which would in its nature *prevent* a reference of the Constitution back for a vote[6] of the people—if, indeed, upon a mere silence in the law, it could be assumed that they had the right to vote upon it. These are the general statements that he has made.

I propose to examine the points in Judge Douglas' speech, in which he attempts to answer that speech of Judge Trumbull's. When you come to examine Judge Douglas' speech, you will find that the first point he makes is—"Suppose it were true that there was such a change in the bill, and that I struck it out—is that a proof of a plot to force a Constitution upon them against their will?" His striking out such a provision, if there was such a one in the bill, he argues does not establish the proof that it was stricken out for the purpose of robbing the people of that right. I

[4] Lincoln's asterisk at this point identifies the clippings from Lyman Trumbull's speech and Douglas' speech in reply, which Lincoln pasted in the debates scrapbook. Both extracts appear following the debate.

[5] Senator William Bigler of Pennsylvania.

[6] "A vote" inserted in scrapbook.

would say, in the first place, that that would be a *most manifest* reason for it. It is true, as Judge Douglas states, that many Territorial bills have passed without having such a provision in them. I believe it is true, though I am not certain, that in some instances, Constitutions framed, under such bills have been submitted to a vote of the people, with the law silent upon the subject, but it does not appear that they once had their Enabling Acts framed with an express provision *for* submitting the Constitution to be framed, to a vote of the people, and then that they were stricken out when Congress did not mean to alter the effect of the law. That there have been bills which never had the provision in, I do not question; but when was that provision taken out of one that it was in? More especially does this evidence tend to prove the proposition that Trumbull advanced, when we remember that the provision was stricken out of the bill almost simultaneously with the time that Bigler says there was a conference among certain Senators, and in which it was agreed that a bill should be passed leaving that out. Judge Douglas, in answering Trumbull, omits to attend to the testimony of Bigler, that there was a meeting in which it was agreed they should so frame the bill that there should be no submission of the Constitution to a vote of the people. The Judge does not notice this part of it. If you take this as one piece of evidence, and then ascertain that simultaneously Judge Douglas struck out a provision that did require it to be submitted, and put the two together, I think it will make a pretty fair show of proof that Judge Douglas did, as Trumbull says, enter into a plot to put in force a Constitution for Kansas without giving the people any opportunity of voting upon it.

But I must hurry on. The next proposition that Judge Douglas puts is this: "But upon examination it turns out that the Toombs bill never did contain a clause requiring the Constitution to be submitted." This is a mere question of fact, and can be determined by evidence. I only want to ask this question—Why did not Judge Douglas say that these words were not stricken out of the Toombs bill, or this bill from which it is alleged the provision was stricken out—a bill which goes by the name of Toombs, because he originally brought it forward? I ask why, if the Judge wanted to make a direct issue with Trumbull, did he not take the exact proposition Trumbull made in his speech, and say it was not stricken out? Trumbull has given the exact words that he says were in the Toombs bill, and he alleges that when the bill came back, they were stricken out. Judge Douglas does not say that the words which Trumbull says were stricken out, were not so stricken out, but he says there was no provision in the Toombs bill to submit the Constitution to a vote of the people. We see at once that he is merely making an issue upon the meaning of the words. He has not undertaken to say that Trumbull tells a lie about these words being stricken out; but he is really, when pushed up to it, only taking an issue upon the meaning of the words. Now, then, if there be any issue upon the meaning of the words, or if there be upon the question of fact as to whether these words were stricken out, I have before me what I suppose to be a genuine copy of the Toombs bill, in which it can be shown that the words Trumbull says were in it, were, in fact, originally there. If there be any dispute upon the fact, I have got the documents here to show they were there. If there be any controversy upon the sense of the words—whether these words which were stricken out really constituted a provision for submitting the matter to a vote of the people, as that is a matter of argument, I think I may as well use Trumbull's own argument. He says that the proposition is in these words:

> That the following propositions be and the same are hereby offered to the said convention of the people of Kansas when formed, for their free acceptance or rejection; which, if accepted by the convention *and ratified by the people at the election for the adoption of the Constitution*, shall be obligatory upon the United States and the said State of Kansas.

Now, Trumbull alleges that these last words were stricken out of the bill when it came back, and he says this was a provision for submitting the Constitution to a vote of the people, and his argument is this: "Would it have been possible to ratify the land propositions at the election for the adoption of the Constitution, unless such an election was to be held?" [Applause and laughter.] That is Trumbull's argument. Now Judge Douglas does not meet the charge at all, but he stands up and says there was no such proposition in that bill for submitting the Constitution to be framed to a vote of the people. Trumbull admits that the language is not a direct provision for submitting it, but it is a provision necessarily implied from another provision. He asks you how it is possible to ratify the land proposition at the election for the adoption of the Constitution, if there was no election to be held for the adoption of the Constitution. And he goes on to show that it is not any less a law because the provision is put in that indirect shape than it would be if it was put directly. But I presume I have said enough to draw attention to this point, and I pass it by also.

Another one of the points that Judge Douglas makes upon

Trumbull, and at very great length, is, that Trumbull, while the bill was pending, said in a speech in the Senate that he supposed the Constitution to be made would have to be submitted to the people. He asks, if Trumbull thought so then, what ground is there for anybody thinking otherwise now? Fellow citizens, this much may be said in reply: That bill had been in the hands of a party to which Trumbull did not belong. It had been in the hands of the Committee at the head of which Judge Douglas stood. Trumbull perhaps had a printed copy of the original Toombs bill. I have not the evidence on that point, except a sort of inference I draw from the general course of business there. What alterations, or what provisions in the way of altering, were going on in committee, Trumbull had no means of knowing, until the altered bill was reported back. Soon afterwards, when it was reported back, there was a discussion over it, and perhaps Trumbull in reading it hastily in the altered form did not perceive all the bearings of the alterations. He was hastily borne into the debate, and it does not follow that because there was something in it Trumbull did not perceive, that something did not exist. More than this, is it true that what Trumbull did can have any effect on what Douglas did? [Applause.] Suppose Trumbull had been in the plot with these other men, would that let Douglas out of it? [Applause and laughter.] Would it exonerate Douglas that Trumbull didn't then perceive he was in the plot? He also asks the question: Why didn't Trumbull propose to amend the bill if he thought it needed any amendment? Why, I believe that everything Judge Trumbull had proposed, particularly in connection with this question of Kansas and Nebraska, since he had been on the floor of the Senate, had been promptly voted down by Judge Douglas and his friends. He had no promise that an amendment offered by him to anything on this subject would receive the slightest consideration. Judge Trumbull did bring to the notice of the Senate at that time the fact that there was no provision for submitting the Constitution about to be made for the people of Kansas, to a vote of the people. I believe I may venture to say that Judge Douglas made some reply to this speech of Judge Trumbull's, *but he never noticed that part of it at all.* And so the thing passed by. I think, then, the fact that Judge Trumbull offered no amendment, does not throw much blame upon him; and if it did, it does not reach the question of fact *as to what Judge Douglas was doing.* [Applause.] I repeat that if Trumbull had himself been in the plot, it would not at all relieve the others who were in it from blame. If I should be indicted for murder, and upon the trial it should be discovered that I had been implicated in that murder, but that the prosecuting witness was guilty too, that would not at all touch the question of my crime. It would be no relief to my neck that they discovered this other man who charged the crime upon me to be guilty too.

Another one of the points Judge Douglas makes upon Judge Trumbull is, that when he spoke in Chicago he made his charge to rest upon the fact that the bill had the provision in it for submitting the Constitution to a vote of the people, when it went into his (Judge Douglas') hands, that it was missing when he reported it to the Senate, and that in a public speech he had subsequently said the alteration in the bill was made while it was in committee, and that they were made in consultation between him (Judge Douglas) and Toombs. And Judge Douglas goes on to comment upon the fact of Trumbull's adducing in his Alton speech the proposition that the bill not only came back with that proposition stricken out, but with another clause and another provision in it, saying that "until the complete execution of this act there shall be no election in said Territory,"—which Trumbull argued was not only taking the provision for submitting to a vote of the people out of the bill, but was adding an affirmative one, in that it prevented the people from exercising the right under a bill that was merely silent on the question. Now in regard to what he says, that Trumbull shifts the issue—that he shifts his ground—and I believe he uses the term, that "it being proven false, he has changed ground" —I call upon all of you, when you come to examine that portion of Trumbull's speech, (for it will make a part of mine,) to examine whether Trumbull has shifted his ground or not. I say he did not shift his ground, but that he brought forward his original charge and the evidence to sustain it yet more fully, but precisely as he originally made it. Then, in addition thereto, he brought in a new piece of evidence. He shifted no ground. He brought no new piece of evidence inconsistent with his former testimony, but he brought a new piece, tending, as he thought, and as I think, to prove his proposition. To illustrate: A man brings an accusation against another, and on trial the man making the charge introduces A and B to prove the accusation. At a second trial he introduces the same witnesses, who tell the same story as before, and a third witness, who tells the same thing, and in addition, gives further testimony corroborative of the charge. So with Trumbull. There was no shifting of ground, nor inconsistency of testimony between the new piece of evidence and what he originally introduced.

But Judge Douglas says that he himself moved to strike out that last provision of the bill, and that on his motion it was stricken out and a substitute inserted. That I presume is the truth. I presume it is true that that last proposition was stricken out by Judge Douglas. Trumbull has not said it was not. Trumbull has himself said that it was so stricken out. He says: "I am speaking of the bill as Judge Douglas reported it back. It was amended somewhat in the Senate before it passed, but I am speaking of it as he brought it back." Now when Judge Douglas parades the fact that the provision was stricken out of the bill when it came back, he asserts nothing contrary to what Trumbull alleges. Trumbull has only said that he originally put it in—not that he did not strike it out. Trumbull says it was not in the bill when it went to the committee. When it came back it was in, and Judge Douglas said the alterations were made by him in consultation with Toombs. Trumbull alleges therefore as his conclusion that Judge Douglas put it in. Then if Douglas wants to contradict Trumbull and call him a liar, let him say he did not put it in, and not that he didn't take it out again. It is said that a bear is sometimes hard enough pushed to drop a cub, and so I presume it was in this case. [Loud applause.] I presume the truth is that Douglas put it in and afterwards took it out. [Laughter and cheers.] That I take it is the truth about it. Judge Trumbull says one thing; Douglas says another thing, and the two don't contradict one another at all. The question is, what did he put it in for? In the first place what did he take the other provision out of the bill for?—the provision which Trumbull argued was necessary for submitting the Constitution to a vote of the people? What did he take that out for, and having taken it out, what did he put this in for? I say that in the run of things it is not unlikely forces conspire, to render it vastly expedient for Judge Douglas to take that latter clause out again. The question that Trumbull has made is that Judge Douglas put it in, and he don't meet Trumbull at all unless he denies that.

In the clause of Judge Douglas' speech upon this subject he uses this language towards Judge Trumbull. He says: "He forges his evidence from beginning to end, and by falsifying the record he endeavors to bolster up his false charge." Well, that is a pretty serious statement. Trumbull forges his evidence from beginning to end. Now upon my own authority I say that it is not true. [Great cheers and laughter.] What is a forgery? Consider the evidence that Trumbull has brought forward. When you come to read the speech, as you will be able to, examine whether the evidence is a forgery from beginning to end. He had the bill or document in his hand like that [holding up a paper]. He says that is a copy of the Toombs bill—the amendment offered by Toombs. He says that is a copy of the bill as it was introduced and went into Judge Douglas' hands. Now, does Judge Douglas say that is a forgery? That is one thing Trumbull brought forward. Judge Douglas says he forged it from beginning to end! That is the "beginning," we will say. Does Douglas say that is a forgery? Let him say it to-day and we will have a subsequent examination upon this subject. [Loud applause.] Trumbull then holds up another document like this and says that is an exact copy of the bill as it came back in the amended form out of Judge Douglas' hands. Does Judge Douglas say that is a forgery? Does he say it in his general sweeping charge? Does he say so now? If he does not, then take this Toombs bill and the bill in the amended form and it only needs to compare them to see that the provision is in the one and not in the other; it leaves the inference inevitable that it was taken out. [Applause.]

But while I am dealing with this question let us see what Trumbull's other evidence is. One other piece of evidence I will read. Trumbull says there are in this original Toombs bill these words: "That the following propositions be, and the same are hereby offered to the said convention of the people of Kansas, when formed, for their free acceptance or rejection; which, if accepted by the convention and ratified by the people at the election for the adoption of the constitution, shall be obligatory upon the United States and the said State of Kansas." Now, if it is said that this is a forgery, we will open the paper here and see whether it is or not. Again, Trumbull says as he goes along, that Mr. Bigler made the following statement in his place in the Senate, December 9, 1857.

I was present when that subject was discussed by Senators before the bill was introduced, and the question was raised and discussed, whether the constitution, when formed, should be submitted to a vote of the people. It was held by those most intelligent on the subject, that in view of all the difficulties surrounding that Territory, the danger of any experiment at that time of a popular vote, it would be better there should be no such provision in the Toombs bill; and it was my understanding, in all the intercourse I had, that the Convention would make a constitution, and send it here without submitting it to the popular vote.

Then Trumbull follows on: "In speaking of this meeting again on the 21st December, 1857, (*Congressional Globe*, same vol., page 113,) Senator Bigler said:

Nothing was further from my mind than to allude to any social or confidential interview. The meeting was not of that character. Indeed, it was semi-official and called to promote the public good. My recollection was clear that I left the conference under the impression that it had been deemed best to adopt measures to admit Kansas as a State through the agency of one popular election, and that for delegates to this Convention. This impression was stronger because I thought the spirit of the bill infringed upon the doctrine of non-intervention, to which I had great aversion; but with the hope of accomplishing a great good, and as no movement had been made in that direction in the Territory, I waived this objection, and concluded to support the measure. I have a few items of testimony as to the correctness of these impressions, and with their submission I shall be content. I have before me the bill reported by the Senator from Illinois on the 7th of March, 1856, providing for the admission of Kansas as a State, the third section of which reads as follows:

"That the following propositions be, and the same are hereby offered to the said Convention of the people of Kansas, when formed, for their free acceptance or rejection; which if accepted by the Convention and ratified by the people at the election for the adoption of the Constitution, shall be obligatory upon the United States and the said State of Kansas."

The bill read in his place by the Senator from Georgia, on the 25th of June, and referred to Committee on Territories, contained the same section, word for word. Both these bills were under consideration at the conference referred to; but, Sir, when the Senator from Illinois reported the Toombs bill to the Senate with amendments, the next morning it did not contain that portion of the third section which indicated to the Convention that the Constitution should be approved by the people. The words "AND RATIFIED BY THE PEOPLE AT THE ELECTION FOR THE ADOPTION OF THE CONSTITUTION," had been stricken out.

Now these things Trumbull says were stated by Bigler upon the floor of the Senate on certain days, and that they are recorded in the "Congressional Globe" on certain pages. Does Judge Douglas say this is a forgery? Does he say there is no such thing in the "Congressional Globe?" What does he mean when he says Judge Trumbull forges his evidence from beginning to end? So again he says in another place, that Judge Douglas, in his speech Dec. 9, 1857, ("Congressional Globe," part 1, page 15) stated:

That during the last session of Congress I [Mr. Douglas] reported a bill from the Committee on Territories, to authorize the people of Kansas to assemble and form a Constitution for themselves. Subsequently the Senator from Georgia [Mr. Toombs] brought forward a substitute for my bill, which, *after having been modified by him and myself in consultation*, was passed by the Senate.

Now Trumbull says this is a quotation from a speech of Douglas, and is recorded in the "Congressional Globe." Is *it* a forgery? Is it there or not? It may not be there, but I want the Judge to take these pieces of evidence, and distinctly say they are forgeries if he dare do it. [Great applause.]

A VOICE—"He will."

Mr. Lincoln—Well, sir, you had better not commit him. [Cheers and laughter.] He gives other quotations—another from Judge Douglas. He says:

I will ask the Senator to show me an intimation, from any one member of the Senate, in the whole debate on the Toombs bill, and in the Union, from any quarter, that the Constitution was not to be submitted to the people. I will venture to say that on all sides of the chamber it was so understood at the time. If the opponents of the bill had understood it was not, they would have made the point on it; and if they had made it, we should certainly have yielded to it; and put in the clause. That is a discovery made since the President found out that it was not safe to take it for granted that that would be done, which ought in fairness to have been done.

Judge Trumbull says Douglas made that speech and it is recorded. Does Judge Douglas say it is a forgery and was not true? Trumbull says somewhere, and I propose to skip it, but it will be found by any one who will read this debate, that he did distinctly bring it to the notice of those who were engineering the bill, that it lacked that provision, and then he goes on to give another quotation from Judge Douglas, where Judge Trumbull uses this language:

Judge Douglas, however, on the same day and in the same debate, probably recollecting or being reminded of the fact that I had objected to the Toombs bill when pending that it did not provide for a submission of the Constitution to the people, made another statement, which is to be found in the same volume of the *Globe*, page 22, in which he says:

"That the bill was silent on this subject was true, and my attention was called to that about the time it was passed; and I took the fair construction to be, that powers not delegated were reserved, and that of course the Constitution would be submitted to the people."

Whether this statement is consistent with the statement just before made, that had the point been made it would have been yielded to, or that it was a new discovery, you will determine.

So I say, I do not know whether Judge Douglas will dispute this, and yet maintain his position that Trumbull's evidence "was forged from beginning to end." I will remark that I have not got these Congressional Globes with me. They are large books and difficult to carry about, and if Judge Douglas shall say that on these points where Trumbull has quoted from them, there are no such passages there, I shall not be able to prove they are there upon this occasion, but I will have another chance. Whenever he points out the forgery and says, "I declare that this particular thing which Trumbull has uttered is not to be found where he says it is," then my attention will be drawn to that, and I will arm myself for the contest—stating now that I have not the slightest doubt on earth that I will find every quotation just where Trumbull says it is. Then the question is, how can Douglas call that a forgery? How can he make out that it is a forgery? What is a forgery? It is the bringing forward something in writing or in print purporting to be of certain effect when it is altogether untrue. If you come forward with my note for one hundred dollars when I have never given such a note, there is a forgery. If you come forward with a letter purporting to be written by me which I never wrote, there is another forgery. If you produce anything in writing or print saying it is so and so, the document not being genuine, a forgery has been committed. How do you make this a forgery when every piece of the evidence is genuine? If Judge Douglas does say these documents and quotations are false and forged he has a full right to do so, but until he does it specifically we don't know how to get at him. If he does say they are false and forged, I will then look further into it, and I presume I can procure the certificates of the proper officers that they are genuine copies. I have no doubt each of these extracts will be found exactly where Trumbull says it is. Then I leave it to you if Judge Douglas, in making his sweeping charge that Judge Trumbull's evidence is forged from beginning to end, at all meets the case—if that is the way to get at the facts. I repeat again, if he will point out which one is a forgery, I will carefully examine it, and if it proves that any one of them is really a forgery it will not be me who will hold to it any longer. I have always wanted to deal with every one I meet candidly and honestly. If I have made any assertion not warranted by facts, and it is pointed out to me, I will withdraw it cheerfully. But I do not choose to see Judge Trumbull calumniated, and the evidence he has brought forward branded in general terms, "a forgery from beginning to end." This is not the legal way of meeting a charge, and I submit to all intelligent persons, both friends of Judge Douglas and of myself, whether it is.

Now coming back—how much time have I left?

The Moderator—Three minutes.

Mr. Lincoln—The point upon Judge Douglas is this. The bill that went into his hands had the provision in it for a submission of the constitution to the people; and I say its language amounts to an express provision for a submission, and that he took the provision out. He says it was known that the bill was silent in this particular; *but I say, Judge Douglas, it was not silent when you got it.* [Great applause.] It was vocal with the declaration when you got it, for a submission of the constitution to the people. And now, my direct question to Judge Douglas is, to answer why, if he deemed the bill silent on this point, he found it necessary to strike out those particular harmless words. If he had found the bill silent and without this provision, he might say what he does now. If he supposed it was implied that the constitution would be submitted to a vote of the people, how could these two lines so encumber the statute as to make it necessary to strike them out? How could he infer that a submission was still implied, after its express provision had been stricken from the bill? I find the bill vocal with the provision, while he silenced it. He took it out, and although he took out the other provision preventing a submission to a vote of the people, I ask, *why did you first put it in*? I ask him whether he took the original provision out, which Trumbull alleges was in the bill? If he admits that he did take it, *I ask him what he did it for*? It looks to us as if he had altered the bill. If it looks differently to him—if he has a different reason for his action from the one we assign him—he can tell it. I insist upon knowing why he made the bill silent upon that point when it was vocal before he put his hands upon it.

I was told, before my last paragraph, that my time was within three minutes of being out. I presume it is expired now. I therefore close. [Three tremendous cheers were given as Mr. Lincoln retired.]

SENATOR DOUGLAS' SPEECH.

LADIES AND GENTLEMEN:—I had supposed that we assembled here to-day for the purpose of a joint discussion between Mr. Lincoln and myself upon the political questions that now agitate the whole country. The rule of such discussions is, that the opening speaker shall touch upon all the points he intends to discuss in order that his opponent, in reply, shall have the opportunity of answering them. Let me ask you what questions of public policy relating to the welfare of this State or the Union, has Mr. Lincoln discussed before you? (None, none, and great applause.) Gentlemen, allow me to suggest that silence is the best compliment you can pay me. I need my whole time, and your cheering only occupies it. Mr. Lincoln simply contented himself at the outset by saying, that he was not in favor of social and political equality between the white man and the negro, and did not desire the law so changed as to make the latter voters or eligible to office. I am glad that I have at last succeeded in getting an answer out of him upon this question of negro citizenship and eligibility to office, for I have been trying to bring him to the point on it ever since this canvass commenced.

I will now call your attention to the question which Mr. Lincoln has occupied his entire time in discussing. He spent his whole hour in retailing a charge made by Senator Trumbull against me. The circumstances out of which that charge was manufactured, occurred prior to the last Presidential election, over two years ago. If the charge was true, why did Trumbull make it in 1856, when I was discussing the questions of that day all over this State with Lincoln and him, and when it was pertinent to the then issue. He was then as silent as the grave on the subject. If that charge was true, the time to have brought it forward was the canvass of 1856, the year when the Toombs bill passed the Senate. When the facts were fresh in the public mind, when the Kansas question was the paramount question of the day, and when such a charge would have had a material bearing on the election. Why did he and Lincoln remain silent then, knowing that such a charge could be made and proven if true? Were they not false to you and false to the country in going through that entire campaign, concealing their knowledge of this enormous conspiracy which, Mr. Trumbull says, he then knew and would not tell? (Laughter.) Mr. Lincoln intimates in his speech, a good reason why Mr. Trumbull would not tell, for, he says, that it might be true, as I proved that it was at Jacksonville, that Trumbull was also in the plot, yet that the fact of Trumbull's being in the plot would not in any way relieve me. He illustrates this argument by supposing himself on trial for murder, and says that it would be no extenuating circumstance if, on his trial, another man was found to be a party to his crime. Well, if Trumbull was in the plot, and concealed it in order to escape the odium which would have fallen upon himself, I ask you whether you can believe him now when he turns State's evidence, and avows his own infamy in order to implicate me. (He is a liar, and a traitor. We couldn't believe Lyman Trumbull under oath, &c.) I am amazed that Mr. Lincoln should now come forward and endorse that charge, occupying his whole hour in reading Mr. Trumbull's speech in support of it. Why, I ask, does not Mr. Lincoln make a speech of his own instead of taking up his time reading Trumbull's speech at Alton? (Cheers.) I supposed that Mr. Lincoln was capable of making a public speech on his own account, or I should not have accepted the banter from him for a joint discussion. (Cheers, and voices: "How about the charges?") Do not trouble yourselves, I am going to make my speech in my own way, and I trust as the Democrats listened patiently and respectfully to

Mr. Lincoln, that his friends will not interrupt me when I am answering him. When Mr. Trumbull returned from the East, the first thing he did when he landed at Chicago was to make a speech wholly devoted to assaults upon my public character and public action. Up to that time I had never alluded to his course in Congress, or to him directly or indirectly, and hence his assaults upon me were entirely without provocation and without excuse. Since then he has been traveling from one end of the State to the other repeating his vile charge. I propose now to read it in his own language:

> Now, fellow citizens, I make the distinct charge, that there was a preconcerted arrangement and plot entered into by the very men who now claim credit for opposing a constitution formed and put in force without giving the people any opportunity to pass upon it. This, my friends, is a serious charge, but I charge it to-night that the very men who traverse the country under banners proclaiming popular sovereignty, by design concocted a bill on purpose to force a constitution upon that people.

In answer to some one in the crowd, who asked him a question, Trumbull said:

> And you want to satisfy yourself that he was in the plot to force a constitution upon that people? I will satisfy you. I will cram the truth down any honest man's throat until he cannot deny it. And to the man who does deny it, I will cram the lie down his throat till he shall cry enough. (Voices, "shameful," "that's decency for you," &c.)
>
> It is preposterous—it is the most damnable effrontery that man ever put on, to conceal a scheme to defraud and cheat the people out of their rights and then claim credit for it.

That is the polite language Senator Trumbull applied to me, his colleague, when I was two hundred miles off. (That's like him.) Why did he not speak out as boldly in the Senate of the United States, and cram the lie down my throat when I denied the charge, first made by Bigler, and made him take it back. You all recollect how Bigler assaulted me when I was engaged in a hand to hand fight, resisting a scheme to force a constitution on the people of Kansas against their will. He then attacked me with this charge; but I proved its utter falsity; nailed the slander to the counter, and made him take the back track. There is not an honest man in America who read that debate who will pretend that the charge is true. (Hurra for Douglas.) Trumbull was then present in the Senate, face to face with me, and why did he not then rise and repeat the charge, and say he would cram the lie down my throat. (He was afraid.) I tell you that Trumbull then knew it was a lie. He knew that Toombs denied that there ever was a clause in the bill he brought forward calling for and requiring a submission of the Kansas constitution to the people. I will tell you what the facts of the case were. I introduced a bill to authorize the people of Kansas to form a constitution, and come into the Union as a State whenever they should have the requisite population for a member of Congress, and Mr. Toombs proposed a substitute, authorizing the people of Kansas, with their then population of only 25,000, to form a constitution, and come in at once. The question at issue was, whether we would admit Kansas with a population of 25,000, or, make her wait until she had the ratio entitling her to a representative in Congress, which was 93,420. That was the point of dispute in the Committee of Territories, to which both my bill and Mr. Toombs' substitute had been referred. I was overruled by a majority of the committee, my proposition rejected, and Mr. Toombs' proposition to admit Kansas then, with her population of 25,000, adopted. Accordingly, a bill to carry out his idea of immediate admission was reported as a substitute for mine—the only points at issue being, as I have already said, the question of population, and the adoption of safeguards against frauds at the election. Trumbull knew this—the whole Senate knew it—and hence he was silent at that time. He waited until I became engaged in this canvass, and finding that I was showing up Lincoln's Abolitionism and negro equality doctrines (cheers), that I was driving Lincoln to the wall, and white men would not support his rank Abolitionism, he came back from the East and trumped up a system of charges against me, hoping that I would be compelled to occupy my entire time in defending myself, so that I would not be able to show up the enormity of the principles of the Abolitionists. Now, the only reason, and the true reason, why Mr. Lincoln has occupied the whole of his first hour in this issue between Trumbull and myself is, to conceal from this vast audience the real questions which divide the two great parties. (That's it; and cheers.)

I am not going to allow them to waste much of my time with these personal matters. I have lived in this State twenty-five years, most of that time have been in public life, and my record is open to you all. If that record is not enough to vindicate me from these petty, malicious assaults, I despise ever to be elected to office by slandering my opponents and traducing other men. (Cheers.) Mr. Lincoln asks you to elect him to the United States Senate to-day solely because he and Trumbull can slander me. Has he given any other reason? (No, no.) Has he avowed what he was desirous to do in Congress on any one question? (No, no.) He desires to ride into office not upon his own merits, not upon the merits and soundness of his principles, but upon his success in fastening a stale old slander upon me. ("That's the truth." "Hear, hear.")

I wish you to bear in mind that up to the time of the introduction of the Toombs bill, and after its introduction, there had never been an act of Congress for the admission of a new State which contained a clause requiring its constitution to be submitted to the people. The general rule made the law silent on the subject, taking it for granted that the people would demand and compel a popular vote on the ratification of their constitution. Such was the general rule under Washington, Jefferson, Madison, Jackson and Polk, under the Whig Presidents and the Democratic Presidents from the beginning of the government down, and nobody dreamed that an effort would ever be made to abuse the power thus confided to the people of a territory. For this reason our attention was not called to the fact of whether there was or was not a clause in the Toombs bill compelling submission, but it was taken for granted that the constitution would be submitted to the people whether the law compelled it or not.

Now, I will read from the report made by me as Chairman of the Committee on Territories at the time I reported back the Toombs substitution to the Senate. It contained several things which I had voted against in committee, but had been overruled by a majority of the members, and it was my duty as chairman of the committee to report the bill back as it was agreed upon by them. The main point upon which I had been overruled was the question of population. In my report accompanying the Toombs bill, I said:

> In the opinion of your committee, whenever a constitution shall be formed in any territory, preparatory to its admission into the Union as a State, justice, the genius of our institutions, the whole theory of our republican system imperatively demand that the voice of the people shall be fairly expressed, and their will embodied in that fundamental law, without fraud, or violence, or intimidation, or any other improper or unlawful influence, and subject to no other restrictions than those imposed by the Constitution of the United States. (Cheers.)

There you find that we took it for granted that the constitution was to be submitted to the people whether the bill was silent on the subject or not. Suppose I had reported it so, following the example of Washington, Adams, Jefferson, Madison, Monroe, Adams, Jackson, Van Buren, Harrison, Tyler, Polk, Taylor, Fillmore, and Pierce, would that fact have been evidence of a conspiracy to force a constitution upon the people of Kansas against their will? (A unanimous "No!") If the charge which Mr. Lincoln makes be true against me, it is true against Zachary Taylor, Millard Fillmore, and every Whig President as well as every Democratic President, and against Henry Clay, who, in the Senate or the House, for forty years advocated bills similar to the one I reported, no one of them containing a clause compelling the submission of the constitution to the people. Are Mr. Lincoln and Mr. Trumbull prepared to charge upon all those eminent men from the beginning of the government down to the present day, that the absence of a provision compelling submission, in the various bills passed by them authorizing the people of territories to form State constitutions, is evidence of a corrupt design on their part to force a constitution upon an unwilling people? ("We'll skin them if they dare to.")

I ask you to reflect on these things, for I tell you that there is a conspiracy to carry this election for the Black Republicans by slander, and not by fair means. Mr. Lincoln's speech this day is conclusive evidence of the fact. He has devoted his entire time to an issue between Mr. Trumbull and myself, and has not uttered a word about the politics of the day. Are you going to elect Mr. Trumbull's colleague upon an issue between Mr. Trumbull and me? (Laughter, and "No, no!") I thought I was running against Abraham Lincoln, that he claimed to be my opponent, had challenged me to a discussion of the public questions of the day with him, and was discussing these questions with me; but it turns out that his only hope is to ride into office on Trumbull's back, who will carry him by falsehood. (Cheers.)

Permit me to pursue this subject a little further. An examination of the record proves that Trumbull's charge—that the Toombs bill originally contained a clause requiring the constitution to be submitted to the people—*is false.* The printed copy of the bill which Mr. Lincoln held up before you, and which he pretends contains such a clause, merely contains a clause requiring a submission of the land grant, and *there is no clause in it requiring a submission of the constitution.* Mr. Lincoln can not find such a clause in it. My report shows that we took it for granted that the people would require a submission of the constitution, and secure it for themselves. There never was a clause in the Toombs bill requiring the constitution to be submitted; Trumbull knew it at the time, and his speech made on the night of its passage discloses the fact that he knew it was silent on the subject; Lincoln pretends, and tells you that Trumbull has not changed his evidence in support of his charge since he made his speech in Chicago. Let us see. The Chicago TIMES took up Trumbull's Chicago speech, compared it with the official records of Congress, and proved that speech to be false in its charge that the original Toombs bill required a submission of the constitution to the people. Trumbull then saw that he was caught—and his falsehood exposed—and he went to Alton, and, under the very walls of the penitentiary, (laughter,) made a new speech, in which he predicated his assault upon me in the allegation that I had caused to be voted into the Toombs bill a clause which prohibited the convention from submitting the constitution to the people, and quoted what he pretended was the clause. Now, has not Mr. Trumbull entirely changed the evidence on which he bases his charge? ("Yes, yes!" "Lincoln's as big a liar as Trumbull," &c.) The clause which he quoted in his Alton speech (which he has published and circulated broadcast over the State) as having been put into the Toombs bill by me is in the following words:

> And until the complete execution of this act, no other election shall be held in said territory.

Trumbull says that the object of that amendment was to prevent the convention from submitting the constitution to a vote of the people.

Now, I will show you that when Trumbull made that statement at Alton he knew it to be untrue. I read from Trumbull's speech in the Senate on the Toombs bill on the night of its passage. He then said:

> There is nothing said in this bill, so far as I have discovered, about submitting the constitution which is to be formed, to the people for their sanction or rejection. Perhaps the convention will have the right to submit it, if it should think proper, but it is certainly not compelled to do so according to the provisions of the bill.

Thus you see that Trumbull, when the bill was on its passage in the Senate, said that it was silent on the subject of submission, and that there was nothing in the bill one way or the other on it. In his Alton speech he says that there was a clause in the bill preventing its submission to the people, and that I had it voted in as an amendment. Thus I convict him of falsehood and slander by quoting from him on the passage of the Toombs' bill in the Senate of the United States, his own speech, made on the night of July 2, 1856, and reported in the *Congressional Globe* for the 1st session 34th Congress, Vol. 33. What will you think of a man who makes a false charge and falsifies the records to prove it? I will now show you that the clause which Trumbull says was put in the bill on my motion, was never put in at all by me, but was stricken out on my motion and another substituted in its place. I call your attention to the same volume of the *Congressional Globe* to which I have already referred, page 795, where you will find the following in the report of the proceedings of the Senate:

> MR. DOUGLAS—I have an amendment to offer from the committee on territories. On page 8, section 11, strike out the words "until the complete execution of this act no other election shall be held in said territory," and insert the amendment which I hold in my hand.

You see from this that I moved to strike out the very words that Trumbull says I put in. The committee on territories overruled me in committee and put the clause in, but as soon as I got the bill back into the Senate I moved to strike it out and put another clause in its place. On the same page you will find that my amendment was agreed to *unanimously*. I then offered another amendment, recognizing the right of the people of Kansas under the Toombs bill, to order just such elections as they saw proper. You can find it on page 796 of the same volume. I will read it.

> MR. DOUGLAS—I have another amendment to offer from the committee, to follow the amendment which has been adopted. The bill reads now, "And until the complete execution of this act, no other election shall be held in said territory." It has been suggested that it should be modified in this way, "And to avoid conflict in the complete execution of this act, all other elections in said territory are hereby postponed until such time as said convention shall appoint," so that they can appoint the day in the event that there should be a failure to come into the Union.

The amendment was *unanimously* agreed to—clearly and distinctly recognizing the right of the convention to order just as many elections as they saw proper in the execution of the act. Trumbull concealed in his Alton speech the fact that the clause he quoted had been stricken out in my motion, and the other fact that this other clause was put in the bill on my motion, and made the false charge that I incorporated into the bill a clause preventing submission, in the face of the fact, that on my motion, the bill was so amended before it passed as to recognize in express words the right and duty of submission.

On this record that I have produced before you, I repeat my charge that Trumbull did falsify the public records of the country, in order to make his charge against me, ("it's plain," and tremendous applause,) and I tell Mr. Abraham Lincoln that if he will examine these records, he will then know that what I state is true. Mr. Lincoln has this day endorsed Mr. Trumbull's veracity after he had my word for it that that veracity was proved to be violated and forfeited by the public records. It will not do for Mr. Lincoln in parading his calumnies against me to put Mr. Trumbull between him and the odium and responsibility which justly attaches to such calumnies. I tell him that I am as ready to persecute the endorser as the maker of a forged note. (Cheers.) I regret the necessity of occupying my time with these petty personal matters. It is unbecoming the dignity of a canvass for an office of the character for which we are candidates. When I commenced the canvass at Chicago, I spoke of Mr. Lincoln in terms of kindness as an old friend—I said that he was a good citizen, of unblemished character, against whom I had nothing to say. I repeated these complimentary remarks about him in my successive speeches, until he became the endorser for these and other slanders against me. If there is anything personally disagreeable, uncourteous or disreputable in these personalities, the sole responsibility rests on Mr. Lincoln, Mr. Trumbull, and their backers.

I will show you another charge made by Mr. Lincoln against me, as an offset to his determination of willingness to take back anything that is incorrect, and to correct any false statement he may have made. He has several times charged that the Supreme Court, President Pierce, President Buchanan and myself, at the time I introduced the Nebraska bill in January, 1854, at Washington, entered into a conspiracy to establish slavery all over this country. I branded this charge as a falsehood, and then he repeated it, asked me to analyze its truth and answer it. I told him, "Mr. Lincoln, I know what you are after—you want to occupy my time in personal matters, to prevent me from showing up the revolutionary principles which the Abolition party—whose candidate you are—have proclaimed to the world." But he asked me to analyze his proof, and I did so. I called his attention to the fact that at the time the Nebraska bill was introduced, there was no such case as the Dred Scott case pending in the Supreme Court, nor was it brought there for years afterwards, and hence that it was impossible there could have been any such conspiracy between the Judges of the Supreme Court and the other parties involved. I proved by the record that the charge was false, and what did he answer? Did he take it back like an honest man and say that he had been mistaken? No, he repeated the charge, and said, that although there was no such case pending that year, that there was an understanding between the Democratic owners of Dred Scott and the Judges of the Supreme Court and other parties involved that the case should be brought up. I then demanded to know who these Democratic owners of Dred Scott were. He could not or would not tell; he did not know. In truth, there were no Democratic owners of Dred Scott on the face of the land. (Laughter.)

Dred Scott was owned at that time by the Rev. Dr. Chaffee, an Abolition member of Congress from Springfield, Massachusetts, and his wife, (immense laughter and applause,) and Mr. Lincoln ought to have known that Dred Scott was so owned, for the reason that as soon as the decision was announced by the court, Dr. Chaffee and his wife executed a deed emancipating him, and put that deed on record. (Cheers.) It was a matter of public record, therefore, that at the time the case was taken to the Supreme Court, Dred Scott was owned by an Abolition member of Congress, a friend of Lincoln's, and a leading man of his party, while the defence was conducted by Abolition lawyers—and thus the Abolitionists managed both sides of the case. I have exposed these facts to Mr. Lincoln, and yet he will not withdraw his charge of conspiracy. I now submit to you whether you can place any confidence in a man who continues to make a charge when its utter falsity is proven by the public records. I will state another fact to show how utterly reckless and unscrupulous this charge against the Supreme Court, President Pierce, President Buchanan and myself is. Lincoln says that President Buchanan was in the conspiracy at Washington in the winter of 1854, when the Nebraska bill was introduced. The history of this country shows that James Buchanan was at that time representing this country at the court of St. James, Great Britain, with distinguished ability and usefulness, that he had not been in the United States for nearly a year previous, and that he did not return until about three years after. (Cheers.) Yet Mr. Lincoln keeps repeating this charge of conspiracy against Mr. Buchanan, when the public records prove it to be untrue. Having proved it to be false as far as the Supreme Court and President Buchanan are concerned, I drop it, leaving the public to say whether I, by myself, without their concurrence, could have gone into a conspiracy with them. (Laughter and cheers.) My friends, you see that the object clearly is to conduct the canvass on personal matters, and hunt me down with charges that are proven to be false by the public records of the country. I am willing to throw open my whole public and private life to the inspection of any man, or all men who desire to investigate it. Having resided among you twenty-five years, during nearly the whole of which time a public man, exposed to more assaults, perhaps more abuse than any man living of my age, or who ever did live, and having survived it all and still commanded your confidence, I am willing to trust to your knowledge of me and my public conduct without making any more defence against these assaults. (Great cheering.)

Fellow-citizens, I came here for the purpose of discussing the leading political topics which now agitate the country. I have no charges to make against Mr. Lincoln, none against Mr. Trumbull, and none against any man who is a candidate, except in repelling their assaults upon me. If Mr. Lincoln is a man of bad character, I leave you to find it out; if his votes in the past are not satisfactory, I leave others to ascertain the fact; if his course on the Mexican war was not in accordance with your notions of patriotism and fidelity to our own country as against a public enemy, I leave you to ascertain the fact. I have no assaults to make upon him except to trace his course on the questions that now divide the country and engross so much of the people's attention.

You know that prior to 1854 this country was divided into two great political parties, one the Whig, the other the Democratic. I, as a Democrat for twenty years prior to that time, had been in public discussions in this State as an advocate of Democratic principles, and I can appeal with confidence to every old line Whig within the hearing of my voice to bear testimony that during all that period I fought you Whigs like a man on every question that separated the two parties. I had the highest respect for Henry Clay as a gallant party leader, as an eminent statesman, and as one of the bright ornaments of this country; but I conscientiously believed that the Democratic party was right on the questions which separated the Democrats from the Whigs. The man does not live who can say that I ever personally assailed Henry Clay or Daniel Webster, or any one of the leaders of that great party, whilst I combatted with all my energy the meaures they advocated. What did we differ about in those days? Did Whigs and Democrats differ about this slavery question. On the contrary, did we not, in 1850, unite to a man in favor of that system of compromise measures which Mr. Clay introduced, Webster defended, Cass supported, and Fillmore approved and made the law of the land by his signature. While we agreed on those compromise measures we differed about a bank, the tariff, distribution, the specie circular, the sub-treasury, and other questions of that description. Now let me ask you which one of those questions on which Whigs and Democrats then differed now remains to divide two great parties. Every one of those questions which divide Whigs and Democrats has passed away, the country has out-grown them, they have passed into history. Hence it is immaterial whether you were right or I was right on the bank, the sub-treasury, and other questions, because they no longer continue living issues. What then has taken the place of those questions about which we once differed? The slavery question has now become the leading and controlling issue; that question on which you and I agreed, on which the Whigs and Democrats united, has now become the leading issue between the national Democracy on the one side, and the Republican or Abolition party on the other.

Just recollect for a moment the memorable contest of 1850, when this country was agitated from its centre to its circumference by the slavery agitation. All eyes in this nation were then turned to the three great lights that survived the days of the revolution. They looked to Clay, then in retirement at Ashland, and to Webster and Cass in the United States Senate. Clay had retired to Ashland, having, as he supposed, performed his mission on earth, and was preparing himself for a better sphere of existence in another world. In that retirement he heard the discordant, harsh and grating sounds of sectional strife and disunion, and he aroused and came forth and resumed his seat in the Senate, that great theatre of his great deeds. From the moment that Clay arrived among us he became the leader of all the Union men whether whigs or democrats. For nine months we each assembled, each day, in the council chamber, Clay in the chair, with Cass upon his right hand and Webster upon his left, and the democrats and whigs gathered around, forgetting differences, and only animated by one common, patriotic sentiment to devise means and measures by which we could defeat the mad and revolutionary scheme of the northern abolitionists and southern disunionists. (Cheers.) We did devise those means. Clay brought them forward, Cass advocated them, the Union democrats and Union whigs voted for them, Fillmore signed them, and they gave peace and quiet to the country. Those Compromise measures of 1850 were founded upon the great fundamental principle that the people of each State and each territory ought to be left free to form and regulate their own domestic institutions in their own way subject only to the Federal Constitution. (Cheers. Hear, hear.) I will ask every old line Democrat and every old line Whig within the hearing of my voice, if I have not truly stated the issues as they then presented themselves to the country. You recollect that the abolitionists raised a howl of indignation and cried for vengeance and the destruction of Democrats and Whigs both, who supported those Compromise measures of 1850. When I returned home to Chicago, I found the citizens inflamed and infuriated against the authors of those great measures. Being the only man in that city who was held responsible for affirmative votes on all those measures, I came forward and addressed the assembled inhabitants, defended each and every one of Clay's Compromise measures as they passed the Senate and the House and were approved by President Fillmore. Previous to that time, the city council had passed resolutions nullifying the act of Congress and instructing the police to withhold all assistance from its execution; but the people of Chicago listened to my defense, and like candid, frank, conscientious men, when they became convinced that they had done an injustice to Clay, Webster, Cass, and all of us who had supported those measures, they repealed their nullifying resolutions and declared that the laws should be executed and the supremacy of the constitution maintained. Let it always be recorded in history to the immortal honor of the people of Chicago, that they returned to their duty when they found that they were wrong, and did justice to those whom they had blamed and abused unjustly. When the legislature of this State assembled that year, they proceeded to pass resolutions approving the Compromise measures of 1850. When the Whig party assembled in 1852 at Baltimore in National Convention for the last time, to nominate Scott for the Presidency, they adopted as a part of their platform the Compromise measures of 1850 as the cardinal plank upon which every Whig would stand and by which he would regulate his future conduct. When the democratic party assembled at the same place one month after to nominate General Pierce, we adopted the same platform so far as those Compromise measures were concerned, agreeing that we would stand by those glorious measures as a cardinal article in the democratic faith. Thus you see that in 1852 all the old Whigs and all the old Democrats stood on a common plank so far as this slavery question was concerned, differing on other questions.

Now, let me ask how is it, that since that time so many of you Whigs have wandered from the true path marked out by Clay and carried out broad and wide by the great Webster? How is it that so many old line Democrats have abandoned the old faith of their party and joined with Abolitionism and Freesoilism to overturn the platform of the old Democrats, and the platform of the old Whigs? You cannot deny that since 1854, there has been a great revolution on this one question. How has it been brought about? I answer, that no sooner was the sod grown green over the grave of the immortal Clay, no sooner was the rose planted on the tomb of the Godlike Webster, than many of the leaders of the Whig party, such as Seward, of New York and his followers, led off and attempted to abolitionize the Whig party, and transfer all your old Whigs bound hand and foot into the abolition camp. Seizing hold of the temporary excitement produced in this country by the introduction of the Nebraska bill, the disappointed politicians in the Democratic party, united with the disappointed politicians in the Whig party, and endeavored to form a new party composed of all the abolitionists, of abolitionized Democrats and abolitionized Whigs, banded together in an abolition platform.

And who led that crusade against National principles in this State? I answer, Abraham Lincoln on behalf of the Whigs, and Lyman Trumbull on behalf of the Democrats, formed a scheme by which they would abolitionize the two great parties in this State on condition that Lincoln should be sent to the United States Senate in place of Gen. Shields, and that Trumbull should go to Congress from the Belleville district, until I would be accommodating enough either to die or resign for his benefit, and then he was to go to the Senate in my place. You all remember that during the year 1854 these two worthy gentlemen, Mr. Lincoln and Mr. Trumbull, one an Old Line Whig and the other an Old Line Democrat, were hunting in partnership to elect a legislature against the Democratic party. I canvassed the State that year from the time I returned home until the election came off, and spoke in every county that I could reach during that period. In the northern part of the State I found Lincoln's ally, in the person of FRED. DOUGLASS, THE NEGRO, preaching abolition doctrines, while Lincoln was discussing the same principles down here, and Trumbull, a little farther down, was advocating the election of members to the legislature who would act in concert with Lincoln's and Fred. Douglass' friends. I witnessed an effort made at Chicago by Lincoln's then associates, and now supporters, to put Fred. Douglass, the negro, on the stand at a Democratic meeting to reply to the illustrious Gen. Cass when he was addressing the people there. (Shame on them.) They had the same negro hunting me down, and they now have a negro traversing the northern counties of the State, and speaking in behalf of Lincoln. (Hit him again; he's a disgrace to the white people, &c.) Lincoln knows that when we were at Freeport in joint discussion, there was a distinguished colored friend of his there then who was on the stump for him, (shouts of laughter,) and who made a speech there the night before we spoke, and another the night after, a short distance from Freeport, in favor of Lincoln, and in order to show how much interest the colored brethren felt in the success of their brother Abe. (Renewed laughter.) I have with me here, and would read if it would not occupy too much of my time, a speech made by Fred. Douglass in Poughkeepsie, N.Y., a short time since to a large convention, in which he conjures all the friends of negro equality and negro citizenship to rally as one man around Abraham Lincoln, the perfect embodiment of their principles, and by all means to defeat Stephen A. Douglas. (It can't be done, &c.) Thus you find that this Republican party in the northern part of the State had colored gentlemen for their advocates in 1854, in company with Lincoln and Trumbull, as they have now. When in October, 1854, I went down to Springfield to attend the State fair, I found the leaders of this party all assembled together under the title of an Anti-Nebraska meeting. It was Black Republicans up north, and Anti-Nebraska at Springfield. I found Lovejoy, a high priest of Abolitionism, and Lincoln one of the leaders who was towing the old line Whigs into the abolition camp, and Trumbull, Sidney Breese, and Gov. Reynolds, all making speeches against the Democratic party and myself, at the same place and in the same cause. (They're all birds of a feather, shun them.) The same men who are now fighting the Democratic party and the regular Democratic nominees in this State were fighting us then. They did not then acknowledge that they had become abolitionists, and many of them deny it now. Breese, Dougherty, and Reynolds were then fighting the Democracy under the title of Anti-Nebraska men, and now they are fighting the Democracy under the pretence that they are *simon pure* Democrats. (Laughter.) Saying that they are authorized to have every office-holder in Illinois beheaded who prefers the election of Douglas to that of Lincoln, or the success of the Democratic ticket in preference to the Abolition ticket for members of Congress, State officers, members of the Legislature, or any office in the State. They canvassed the State against us in 1854, as they are doing now, owning different names and different principles in different localities, but having a common object in view, viz: the defeat of all men holding national principles in opposition to this sectional Abolition party. They carried the legislature in 1854, and when it assembled in Springfield they proceeded to elect a United States Senator, all voting for Lincoln with one or two exceptions, which exceptions prevented them from quite electing him. And why should they not elect him? Had not Trumbull agreed that Lincoln should have Shields' place? Had not the abolitionists agreed to it? Was it not the solemn compact, the condition on which Lincoln agreed to abolitionize the old Whigs that he should be Senator? Still, Trumbull having control of a few abolitionized Democrats, would not allow them all to vote for Lincoln on any one ballot, and thus kept him for some time within one or two votes of an election until he worried out Lincoln's friends, and compelled them to drop him and elect Trumbull in violation of the bargain. (Cheers.) I desire to read you a piece of testimony in confirmation of the notoriously public facts which I have stated to you. Col. Jas. H. Matheny, of Springfield, is and for twenty years has been the confidential personal and political friend and manager of Mr. Lincoln. Matheny is this very day the candidate of the Republican or Abolition party for Congress against the gallant Major Thos. L. Harris, in the Springfield district, and is making speeches for Lincoln and against me. I will read you the testimony of Matheny about this bargain between Lincoln and Trumbull when they undertook to abolitionize Whigs and Democrats only four years ago. Matheny being mad at Trumbull for having played a Yankee trick on Lincoln, exposed the bargain in a public speech two years ago, and I will read the published report of that speech, the correctness of which Mr. Lincoln will not deny:

> The Whigs, Abolitionists, Know Nothings, and renegade Democrats, made a solemn compact for the purpose of carrying this State against the Democracy on this plan: 1st, That they would all combine and elect Mr. Trumbull to Congress, and thereby carry his district for the legislature, in order to throw all the strength that could be obtained into that body against the Democrats. 2d. That when the legislature should meet, the officers of that body, such as speaker, clerks, door-keepers, &c, would be given to the Abolitionists; and 3d, That the Whigs were to have the United States Senator. Thus, accordingly, in good faith, Trumbull was elected to Congress, and his district carried for the Legislature, and when it convened the Abolitionists got all the officers of that body, and thus far the "bond" was fairly executed. The Whigs, on their part, demanded the election of Abraham Lincoln to the United States Senate, that the bond might be fulfilled, the other parties to the contract having already secured to themselves all that was called for. But, in the most perfidious manner, they refused to elect Mr. Lincoln; and the mean, low-lived, sneaking Trumbull succeeded by pleading all that was required by any party, in thrusting Lincoln aside and foisting himself, an excresence from the rotten bowels of the Democracy into the United States Senate: and thus it has ever been, that an *honest* man makes a bad bargain when he conspires or contracts with rogues.

Lincoln's confidential friend, Matheny, thought that Lincoln made a bad bargain when he conspired with such rogues as Trumbull and the Abolitionists. (Great laughter.) I would like to know whether Lincoln had as high an opinion of Trumbull's veracity when the latter agreed to support him for the Senate, and then cheated him as he does now, (renewed laughter,) when Trumbull comes forward and makes charges against me. You could not then prove Trumbull an honest man either by Lincoln, by Matheny, or by any of Lincoln's friends. They charged everywhere that Trumbull had cheated them out of the bargain, and Lincoln found sure enough that it was a *bad bargain* to contract and conspire with rogues. (Laughter.)

And now I will explain to you what has been a mystery all over the State and Union, the reason why Lincoln was nominated for the United States Senate by the Black Republican convention. You know it has never been usual for any party, or any convention to nominate a candidate for United States Senator. Probably this was the first time that such a thing was ever done. The Black Republican convention had not been called for that purpose, but to nominate a State ticket, and every man was surprised and many disgusted when Lincoln was nominated. Archie Williams thought he was entitled to it. Browning knew that he deserved it, Wentworth was certain that he would get it, Peck had hopes, Judd felt sure that he was the man, and Palmer had claims and had made arrangements to secure it; but to their utter amazement, Lincoln was nominated by the convention, (laughter,) and not only that, but he received the nomination unanimously, by a resolution declaring that Abraham Lincoln was "the first, last, and only choice" of the Republican party. How did this occur? Why, because they could not get Lincoln's friends to make another bargain with "rogues," (laughter,) unless the whole party would come up as one man and pledge their honor that they would stand by Lincoln first, last and all the time, and that he should not be cheated by Lovejoy this time, as he was by Trumbull before. Thus, by passing this resolution, the Abolitionists are all for him, Lovejoy and Farnsworth are canvassing for him, Giddings is ready to come here in his behalf, and the negro speakers are already on the stump for him, and he is sure not to be cheated this time. He would not go into the arrangement until he got their bond for it, and Trumbull is compelled now to take the stump, get up false charges against me, and travel all over the State to try and elect Lincoln, in order to keep Lincoln's friends quiet about the bargain in which Trumbull cheated them four years ago. You see, now, why it is that Lincoln and Trumbull are so mighty fond of each other. (Tremendous laughter.) They have entered into a conspiracy to break me down by these assaults on my public character, in order to draw my attention from a fair exposure of the mode in which they attempted to abolitionize the old Whig and the old Democratic parties and lead them captive into the Abolition camp. (That's so, and hear, hear.) Do you not all remember that Lincoln went around here four years ago making speeches to you, and telling you that you should all go for the Abolition ticket, and swearing that he was as good a Whig as he ever was; (laughter;) and that

Trumbull went all over the State making pledges to the old Democrats, and trying to coax them into the Abolition camp, swearing by his Maker, with the uplifted hand, that he was still a Democrat, always intended to be, and that never would he desert the Democratic party. (Laughter.) He got your votes to elect an Abolition legislature, which passed Abolition resolutions, attempted to pass Abolition laws, and sustained Abolitionists for office, State and national. Now, the same game is attempted to be played over again. Then Lincoln and Trumbull made captives of the old Whigs and old Democrats and carried them into the Abolition camp where Father Giddings, the high priest of Abolitionism, received and christened them in the dark cause just as fast as they were brought in. (Hear, hear.) Giddings found the converts so numerous that he had to have assistance, and he sent for John P. Hale, N. P. Banks, Chase, and other Abolitionists, and they came on, and with Lovejoy and Fred. Douglass, the negro, helped to baptize these new converts as Lincoln, Trumbull, Breese, Reynolds, and Dougherty could capture them and bring them within the Abolition clutch. Gentlemen, they are now around making the same kind of speeches. Trumbull was down in Monroe county the other day assailing me and making a speech in favor of Lincoln, and I will show you under what notice his meeting was called. You see these people are Black Republicans or Abolitionists up North, while at Springfield to-day, they dare not call their convention "Republican," but are obliged to say "a convention of all men opposed to the Democratic party," and in Monroe county and lower Egypt Trumbull advertises their meetings as follows:

> A meeting of the Free Democracy will take place at Waterloo, on Monday, September 12th inst., whereat Hon. Lyman Trumbull, Hon. John Baker, and others, will address the people upon the different political topics of the day. Members of all parties are cordially invited to be present, and hear and determine for themselves.
>
> September 9, 1858. THE FREE DEMOCRACY.

Did you ever before hear of this new party called the "Free Democracy?"

What object have these Black Republicans in changing their name in every county? (To cheat people.) They have one name in the North, another in the centre, and another in the South. When I used to practice law before my distinguished judicial friend, whom I recognize in the crowd before me, if a man was charged with horse stealing and the proof showed that he went by one name in Stephenson county, another in Sangamon, a third in Monroe, and a fourth in Randolph, we thought that the fact of his changing his name so often to avoid detection, was pretty strong evidence of his guilt. I would like to know why it is that this great free soil abolition party is not willing to avow the same name in all parts of the State? (They dare not.) If this party believes that its course is just, why does it not avow the same principle in the North, and in the South, in the East and in the West, wherever the American flag waves over American soil. (Cheers.)

A VOICE—The party does not call itself Black Republican in the North.

MR. DOUGLAS—Sir, if you will get a copy of the paper published at Waukegan, fifty miles from Chicago, which advocates the election of Mr. Lincoln, and has his name flying at its mast-head, you will find that it declares that "this paper is devoted to the cause of *Black Republicanism*. (Good, hit him again, and cheers.) I had a copy of it and intended to bring it down here into Egypt to let you see what name the party rallied under up in the Northern part of the State, and to convince you that their principles are as different in the two sections of the State as is their name. I am sorry that I have mislaid it and have not got it here. Their principles in the North are jet black, (laughter,) in the centre they are in color a decent mulatto, (renewed laughter,) and in lower Egypt they are almost white. (Shouts of laughter.) Why, I admired many of the white sentiments contained in Lincoln's speech at Jonesboro, and could not help but contrast them with the speeches of the same distinguished orator made in the Northern part of the State. Down here he denies that the Black Republican party is opposed to the admission of any more slave States, under any circumstances, and says that they are willing to allow the people of each State when it wants to come into the Union, to do just as it pleases on the question of slavery. In the North, you find Lovejoy, their candidate for Congress in the Bloomington district, Farnsworth, their candidate in the Chicago district, and Washburne, their candidate in the Galena district, all declaring that never will they consent, under any circumstances, to admit another slave State, even if the people want it. (That's so.) Thus, while they avow one set of principles up there, they avow another and entirely different set down here. And here let me recall to Mr. Lincoln the scriptural quotation which he has applied to the federal government, that a house divided against itself cannot stand, and ask him how does he expect this Abolition party to stand when in one-half of the State it advocates a set of principles which it has repudiated in the other half. (Laughter and applause.)

I am told that I have but eight minutes more. I would like to talk to you an hour and a half longer, but I will make the best use I can of the remaining eight minutes. Mr. Lincoln said in his first remarks that he was not in favor of the social and political equality of the negro with the white man. Everywhere up north he has declared that he was not in favor of the social and political equality of the negro, but he would not say whether or not he was opposed to negroes voting and negro citizenship. I want to know whether he is for or against negro citizenship? He declared his utter opposition to the Dred Scott decision, and advanced as a reason that the court had decided that it was not possible for a negro to be a citizen under the constitution of the United States. If he is opposed to the Dred Scott decision for that reason he must be in favor of conferring the right and privilege of citizenship upon the negro! I have been trying to get an answer from him on that point, but have never yet obtained one, and I will show you why. In every speech he made in the north he quoted the Declaration of Independence to prove that all men were created equal, and insisted that the phrase "all men," included the negro as well as the white man, and that the equality rested upon Divine law. Here is what he said on that point:

> I should like to know if, taking this old declaration of independence, which declares that all men are equal upon principle, and making exceptions to it where will it stop. If one man says it does not mean a negro, why may not another say it does not mean some other man? If that declaration is not the truth let us get the statute book in which we find it and tear it out!

Lincoln maintains there that the Declaration of Independence asserts that the negro is equal to the white man, and that under Divine law, and if he believes so it was rational for him to advocate negro citizenship, which, when allowed, puts the negro on an equality under the law. (No negro equality for us; down with Lincoln.) I say to you in all frankness, gentlemen, that in my opinion a negro is not a citizen, cannot be, and ought not to be, under the constitution of the United States. (That's the doctrine.) I will not even qualify my opinion to meet the declaration of one of the Judges of the Supreme Court in the Dred Scott case, "that a negro descended from African parents, who was imported into this country as a slave, is not a citizen, and cannot be." I say that this government was established on the white basis. It was made by white men, for the benefit of white men and their posterity forever, and never should be administered by any except white men. (Cheers.) I declare that a negro ought not to be a citizen, whether his parents were imported into this country as slaves or not, or whether or not he was born here. It does not depend upon the place a negro's parents were born, or whether they were slaves or not, but upon the fact that he is a negro, belonging to a race incapable of self government, and for that reason ought not to be on an equality with white men. (Immense applause.)

My friends, I am sorry that I have not time to pursue this argument further, as I might have done but for the fact that Mr. Lincoln compelled me to occupy a portion of my time in repelling those gross slanders and falsehoods that Trumbull has invented against me and put in circulation. In conclusion, let me ask you why should this government be divided by a geographical line—arraying all men North in one great hostile party against all men South? Mr. Lincoln tells you, in his speech at Springfield, "that a house divided against itself cannot stand; that this government, divided into free and slave States, cannot endure permanently; that they must either be all free or all slave; all one thing or all the other." Why cannot this government endure divided into free and slave States, as our fathers made it? When this government was established by Washington, Jefferson, Madison, Jay, Hamilton, Franklin, and the other sages and patriots of that day, it was composed of free States and slave States, bound together by one common constitution. We have existed and prospered from that day to this thus divided, and have increased with a rapidity never before equalled in wealth, the extension of territory, and all the elements of power and greatness, until we have become the first nation on the face of the globe. Why can we not thus continue to prosper? We can if we will live up to and execute the government upon those principles upon which our fathers established it. During the whole period of our existence Divine Providence has smiled upon us, and showered upon our nation richer and more abundant blessings than have ever been conferred upon any other.

Senator Douglas' time here expired, and he stopped on the minute, amidst deafening applause.

MR. LINCOLN'S REJOINDER.

As Mr. Lincolon stepped forward, the crowd sent up three rousing cheers.

MR. LINCOLN said:

Fellow Citizens—It follows as a matter of course that a half-hour answer to a speech of an hour-and-a-half can be but a very hurried one. I shall only be able to touch upon a few of the points suggested by Judge Douglas, and give them a brief attention, while I shall have to totally omit others for the want of time.

Judge Douglas has said to you that he has not been able to get from me an answer to the question whether I am in favor of negro-citizenship. So far as I know, the Judge never asked me the question before. [Applause.] He shall have no occasion to ever ask it again, for I tell him very frankly that I am not in favor of negro citizenship. [Renewed applause.] This furnishes me an occasion for saying a few words upon the subject. I mentioned in a certain speech of mine which has been printed, that the Supreme Court had decided that a negro could not possibly be made a citizen, and without saying what was my ground of complaint in regard to that, or whether I had any ground of complaint, Judge Douglas has from that thing manufactured nearly every thing that he ever says about my disposition to produce an equality between the negroes and the white people. [Laughter and applause.] If any one will read my speech, he will find I mentioned that as one of the points decided in the course of the Supreme Court opinions, but I did not state what objection I had to it. But Judge Douglas tells the people what my objection was when I did not tell them myself. [Loud applause and laughter.] Now my opinion is that the different States have the power to make a negro a citizen under the Constitution of the United States if they choose. The Dred Scott decision decides that they have not that power. If the State of Illinois had that power I should be opposed to the exercise of it. [Cries of "good," "good," and applause.] That is all I have to say about it.

Judge Douglas has told me that he heard my speeches north and my speeches south—that he had heard me at Ottawa and at Freeport in the north, and recently at Jonesboro in the south, and there was a very different cast of sentiment in the speeches made at the different points. I will not charge upon Judge Douglas that he wilfully misrepresents me, but I call upon every fair-minded man to take these speeches and read them, *and I dare him to point out any difference between my printed speeches north and south.* [Great cheering.] While I am here perhaps I ought to say a word, if I have the time, in regard to the latter portion of the Judge's speech, which was a sort of declamation in reference to my having said I entertained the belief that this government would not endure, half slave and half free. I have said so and I did not say it without what seemed to me to be good reasons. It perhaps would require more time than I have now to set forth these reasons in detail; but let me ask you a few questions. Have we ever had any peace on this slavery question? [No, no.] When are we to have peace upon it if it is kept in the position it now occupies? [Never.] How are we ever to have peace upon it? That is an important question. To be sure if we will all stop and allow Judge Douglas and his friends to march on in their present career until they plant the institution all over the nation, here and wherever else our flag waves, and we acquiesce in it, there will be peace. But let me ask Judge Douglas how he is going to get the people to do that? [Applause.] They have been wrangling over this question for at least forty years. This was the cause of the agitation resulting in the Missouri Compromise—this produced the troubles at the annexation of Texas, in the acquisition of the territory acquired in the Mexican war. Again, this was the trouble which was quieted by the Compromise of 1850, when it was settled "*forever*," as both the great political parties declared in their National Conventions. That "forever" turned out to be just four years, [laughter] *when Judge Douglas himself re-opened it.* [Immense applause, cries of "hit him again," &c.] When is it likely to come to an end? He introduced the Nebraska bill in 1854 to put *another end* to the slavery agitation. He promised that it would finish it all up immediately, and he has never made a speech since until he got into a quarrel with the President about the Lecompton Constitution, in which he has not declared that we are *just at the end* of the slavery agitation. But in one speech, I think last winter, he did say that he didn't quite see when the end of the slavery agitation would come. [Laughter and cheers.] Now he tells us again that it is all over, and the people of Kansas have voted down the Lecompton Constitution. How is it over? That was only one of the attempts at putting an end to the slavery agitation—one of these "final settlements." [Renewed laughter.] Is Kansas in the Union? Has she formed a Constitution that she is likely to come in under? Is not the slavery agitation still an open question in that Territory? Has the voting down of that Constitution put an end to all the trouble? Is that more likely to settle it than every one of these previous attempts to settle the slavery agitation. [Cries of "No," "No."] Now, at this day in the history of the world we can no more foretell where the end of this slavery agitation will be than we can see the end of the world itself. The Nebraska-Kansas bill was introduced four years and a half ago, and if the agitation is ever to come to an end, we may say we are four years and a half nearer the end. So, too, we can say we are four years and a half nearer the end of the world; and we can just as clearly see the end of the world as we can see the end of this agitation. [Applause.] The Kansas settlement did not conclude it. If Kansas should sink to-day, and leave a great vacant space in the earth's surface, this vexed question would still be among us. I say, then, there is no way of putting an end to the slavery agitation amongst us but to put it back upon the basis where our fathers placed it, [applause] no way but to keep it out of our new Territories [renewed applause]—to restrict it forever to the old States where it now exists. [Tremendous and prolonged cheering; cries of "That's the doctrine," "Good," "Good," &c.] Then the public mind *will* rest in the belief that it is in the course of ultimate extinction. That is one way of putting an end to the slavery agitation. [Applause.]

The other way is for us to surrender and let Judge Douglas and his friends have their way and plant slavery over all the States—cease speaking of it as in any way a wrong—regard slavery as one of the common matters of property, and speak of negroes as we do of our horses and cattle. But while it drives on in its state of progress as it is now driving, and as it has driven for the last five years, I have ventured the opinion, and I say to-day, that we will have no end to the slavery agitation until it takes one turn or the other. [Applause.] I do not mean that when it takes a turn towards ultimate extinction it will be in a day, nor in a year, nor in two years. I do not suppose that in the most peaceful way ultimate extinction would occur in less than a hundred years at the least; but that it will occur in the best way for both races in God's own good time, I have no doubt. [Applause.] But, my friends, I have used up more of my time than I intended on this point.

Now, in regard to this matter about Trumbull and myself having made a bargain to sell out the entire Whig and Democratic parties in 1854—Judge Douglas brings forward no evidence to sustain his charge, except the speech Matheny is said to have made in 1856, in which he told a cock-and-bull story of that sort, upon the same moral principles that Judge Douglas tells it here to-day. [Loud applause.] This is the simple truth. I do not care greatly for the story, but this is the truth of it, and I have twice told Judge Douglas to his face, that from beginning to end there is not one word of truth in it. [Thunders of applause.] I have called upon him for the proof, and he does not at all meet me as Trumbull met him upon that of which we were just talking, by producing the record. He didn't bring the record, because there was no record for him to bring. [Cheers and laughter.] When he asks if I am ready to indorse Trumbull's veracity after he has broken a bargain with me, I reply that if Trumbull *had* broken a bargain with me, I would not be likely to indorse his veracity [laughter and applause]; but I am ready to indorse his veracity because *neither in that thing, nor in any other, in all the years that I have known Lyman Trumbull, have I known him to fail of his word or tell a falsehood, large or small.* [Great cheering.] It is for that reason that I indorse Lyman Trumbull.

MR. JAMES BROWN—(*Douglas Post Master*).—What does Ford's history say about him?[7]

MR. LINCOLN—Some gentleman asks me what Ford's History says about him. My own recollection is, that Ford speaks of Trumbull in very disrespectful terms in several portions of his book, *and that he talks a great deal worse of Judge Douglas.* [Roars of laughter and applause.] I refer you, sir, to the history for examination. [Cheers.]

Judge Douglas complains, at considerable length, about a disposition on the part of Trumbull and myself to attack him personally. I want to attend to that suggestion a moment. I don't want to be unjustly accused of dealing illiberally or unfairly with an adversary, either in court, or in a political canvass, or anywhere else. I would despise myself if I supposed myself ready to deal less liberally with an adversary than I was willing to be treated myself. Judge Douglas, in a general way, without putting it in a direct shape, revives the old charge against me, in reference to the Mexican War. He does not take the responsibility of putting it in a very definite form, but makes a general reference to it. That charge is more than ten years old. He complains of Trumbull and myself, because he says we bring charges against him one or two years old. He knows, too, that in regard to the Mexican War story, the more respectable papers of his own party throughout the State have been compelled to take it back and acknowledge that it was a lie. [Continued and vociferous applause.]

Here Mr. Lincoln turned to the crowd on the platform, and selecting Hon. Orlando B. Ficklin, led him forward and said:

I do not mean to do anything with Mr. Ficklin except to present his face and tell you that *he personally knows it to be a lie!* He was a member of Congress at the only time I was in Congress, and he (Ficklin) knows that whenever there was an attempt to procure a vote of mine which would indorse the origin and justice of the war, I refused to give such indorsement, and voted against it; but I never voted against the supplies for the army, and he knows, as well as Judge Douglas, that whenever a dollar was asked by way of compensation or otherwise, for the benefit of the soldiers, *I gave all the votes that Ficklin or Douglas did, and perhaps more.* [Loud applause.]

[7] Thomas Ford, *History of Illinois* (1854).

Mr. Ficklin—My friends, I wish to say this in reference to the matter. Mr. Lincoln and myself are just as good personal friends as Judge Douglas and myself. In reference to this Mexican war, my recollection is that when Ashmun's resolution (amendment) was offered by Mr. Ashmun of Massachusetts, in which he declared that the Mexican war was unnecessarily and unconstitutionally commenced by the President—my recollection is that Mr. Lincoln voted for that resolution.

Mr. Lincoln—That is the truth. Now you all remember that was a resolution censuring the President for the manner in which the war was *begun*. You know they have charged that I voted against the supplies, by which I starved the soldiers who were out fighting the battles of their country. I say that Ficklin knows it is false. When that charge was brought forward by the Chicago *Times*, the Springfield *Register* (Douglas organ) reminded the *Times* that the charge really applied to John Henry; and I do know that John Henry *is now making speeches and fiercely battling for Judge Douglas*. [Loud applause.] If the Judge now says that he offers this as a sort of a set-off to what I said to-day in reference to Trumbull's charge, then I remind him that he made this charge before I said a word about Trumbull's. He brought this forward at Ottawa, the first time we met face to face; and in the opening speech that Judge Douglas made, he attacked me in regard to a matter ten years old. Isn't he a pretty man to be whining about people making charges against him only *two* years old. [Cheers.]

The Judge thinks it is altogether wrong that I should have dwelt upon this charge of Trumbull's at all. I gave the apology for doing so in my opening speech. Perhaps it didn't fix your attention. I said that when Judge Douglas was speaking at places where I spoke on the succeeding day, he used very harsh language about this charge. Two or three times afterwards I said I had confidence in Judge Trumbull's veracity and intelligence; and my own opinion was, from what I knew of the character of Judge Trumbull, that he would vindicate his position, and prove whatever he had stated to be true. This I repeated two or three times; and then I dropped it, without saying anything more on the subject for weeks—perhaps a month. I passed it by without noticing it at all till I found at Jacksonville, Judge Douglas, in the plenitude of his power, is not willing to answer Trumbull and let me alone; but he comes out there and uses this language: "He should not hereafter occupy his time in refuting such charges made by Trumbull, but that Lincoln, having indorsed the character of Trumbull for veracity, he should hold him (Lincoln) responsible for the slanders." What was Lincoln to do? [Laughter.] Did he not do right, when he had the fit opportunity of meeting Judge Douglas here, to tell him he was ready for the responsibility? [Enthusiastic cheering, "good, good. Hurrah for Lincoln!"] I ask a candid audience whether in doing thus Judge Douglas was not the assailant rather than I? ["Yes, yes, Hit him again!"] Here I meet him face to face and say I am ready to take the responsibility so far as it rests upon me.

Having done so, I ask the attention of this audience to the question whether I have succeeded in sustaining the charge ["yes," "yes"], and whether Judge Douglas has at all succeeded in rebutting it? [Loud cries of "no, no."] You all heard me call upon him to say *which of these pieces of evidence was a forgery?* Does he say that what I present here as a copy of the original Toombs bill is a forgery? ["No," "no."] Does he say that what I present as a copy of the bill reported by himself is a forgery? ["No," "no," "no."] Or what is presented as a transcript from the *Globe*, of the quotations from Bigler's speech is a forgery? [No, no, no.] Does he say the quotations from his own speech are forgeries? ["No," "no," "no."] Does he say this transcript from Trumbull's speech is a forgery? [Loud cries of "no, no." "He didn't deny one of them."] *I would then like to know how it comes about, that when each piece of a story is true, the whole story turns out false?* [Great cheers and laughter.] I take it these people have some sense; they see plainly that Judge Douglas is playing cuttlefish, [Laughter] a small species of fish that has no mode of defending itself when pursued except by throwing out a black fluid, which makes the water so dark the enemy cannot see it and thus it escapes. [Roars of laughter.] Ain't the Judge playing the cuttlefish? ["Yes, yes," and cheers.]

Now I would ask very special attention to the consideration of Judge Douglas' speech at Jacksonville; and when you shall read his speech of to-day, I ask you to watch closely and see which of these pieces of testimony, every one of which he says is a forgery, he has shown to be such. *Not one of them has he shown to be a forgery.* Then I ask the original question, if each of the pieces of testimony is true, *how is it possible that the whole is a falsehood?* [Loud and continued cheers.]

In regard to Trumbull's charge that he (Douglas) inserted a provision into the bill to prevent the Constitution being submitted to the people, what was his answer? He comes here and reads from the *Congressional Globe* to show that on his motion that provision was struck out of the bill. Why, Trumbull has not said it was not stricken out, but Trumbull says he (Douglas) put it in, and it is no answer to the charge to say he afterwards took it out. Both are perhaps true. It was in regard to that thing precisely that I told him he had dropped the cub. [Roars of laughter.] Trumbull shows you that by his introducing the bill it was his cub. [Laughter.] It is no answer to that assertion to call Trumbull a liar merely because he did not specially say Douglas struck it out. Suppose that were the case, does it answer Trumbull? [No, no.] I assert that you (pointing to an individual,) are here to-day, and you undertake to prove me a liar by showing that you were in Mattoon yesterday. [Laughter.] I say that you took your hat off your head, and you prove me a liar by putting it on your head. [Roars of laughter.] That is the whole force of Douglas' argument.

Now, I want to come back to my original question. Trumbull says that Judge Douglas had a bill with a provision in it for submitting a Constitution to be made to a vote of the people of Kansas. Does Judge Douglas deny that fact? [Cries of "no, no."] Does he deny that the provision which Trumbull reads was put in that bill? ["No, no."] Then Trumbull says he struck it out. Does he dare to deny that? ["No, no, no."] He does not, and I have the right to repeat the question—*why, Judge Douglas took it out?* [Immense applause.] Bigler has said there was a combination of certain Senators, among whom he did not include Judge Douglas, by which it was agreed that the Kansas bill should have a clause in it not to have the Constitution formed under it submitted to a vote of the people. He did not say that Douglas was among them, but we prove by another source that about the same time Douglas comes into the Senate *with that provision stricken out of the bill.* Although Bigler cannot say they were all working in concert, yet it looks very much as if the thing was agreed upon and done with a mutual understanding after the conference; and while we do not know that it was absolutely so, yet it looks so probable that we have a right to call upon the man who knows the true reason why it was done, *to tell what the true reason was.* [Great cheers.] When he will not tell what the true reason was, he stands in the attitude of an accused thief who has stolen goods in his possession, and when called to account, refuses to tell where he got them. [Immense applause.] Not only is this the evidence, but when he comes in with the bill having the provision stricken out, he tells us in a speech, not then but since, that these alterations and modifications in the bill *had been made by* HIM, *in consultation with Toombs, the originator of the bill.* He tells us the same to-day. He says there were certain modifications made in the bill in committee that he did not vote for. I ask you to remember while certain amendments were made which he disapproved of, but which a majority of the committee voted in, he has himself told us that in this particular *the alterations and modifications were made by him upon consultation with Toombs.* [Enthusiastic cheering.] We have his own word that these alterations were made *by him* and not by the committee. ["That's so," "good, good."] Now, I ask what is the reason Judge Douglas is so chary about coming to the exact question? What is the reason he will not tell you anything about HOW it was made, BY WHOM it was made, or that he remembers it being made at all? Why does he stand playing upon the meaning of words, and quibbling around the edges of the evidence? If he can explain all this, but leaves it unexplained, I have a right to infer that Judge Douglas understood it was the purpose of his party, in engineering that bill through, to make a Constitution and have Kansas come into the Union with that Constitution, *without its being submitted to a vote of the people.* ["That's it."] If he will explain his action on this question, by giving a *better reason* for the facts that happened, than he has done, it will be satisfactory. But until he does that—until he gives a better or more plausible reason than he has offered against the evidence in the case—*I suggest to him it will not avail him at all that he swells himself up, takes on dignity, and calls people liars.* [Great applause and laughter.] Why, sir, there is not a word in Trumbull's speech that depends on Trumbull's veracity at all. He has only arrayed the evidence and told you what follows as a matter of reasoning. There is not a statement in the whole speech that depends on Trumbull's word. If you have ever studied geometry, you remember that by a course of reasoning Euclid proves that all the angles in a triangle are equal to two right angles. Euclid has shown you how to work it out. Now, if you undertake to disprove that proposition, and to show that it is erroneous, would you prove it to be false by calling Euclid a liar? [Roars of laughter and enthusiastic cheers.] They tell me that my time is out, and therefore I close.

EXTRACT FROM MR. TRUMBULL'S SPEECH MADE AT ALTON, REFERRED TO BY LINCOLN IN HIS OPENING AT CHARLESTON.[8]

I come now to another extract from a speech of Mr. Douglas, made at Beardstown, and reported in the Missouri Republican. This extract has reference to a statement made by me at Chicago,

[8] Lincoln's headnote to the following extract.

wherein I charged that an agreement had been entered into by the very persons now claiming credit for opposing a Constitution not submitted to the people, to have a Constitution formed and put in force without giving the people of Kansas an opportunity to pass upon it. Without meeting this charge, which I substantiated by a reference to the record my colleague is reported to have said:

> For when this charge was once made in a much milder form, in the Senate of the United States, I did brand it as a lie, in the presence of Mr. Trumbull, and Mr. Trumbull sat and heard it thus branded, without daring to say it was true. I tell you he knew it to be false when he uttered it at Chicago; and yet he says he is going to cram the lie down his throat until he should cry enough. The miserable craven hearted wretch! he would rather have both ears cut off than to use that language in my presence, where I could call him to account. I see the object is to draw me into a personal controversy, with the hope thereby of concealing from the public the enormity of the principles to which they are committed. I shall not allow much of my time in this canvass to be occupied by these personal assaults. I have none to make on Mr. Lincoln; I have none to make on Mr. Trumbull; I have none to make on any other political opponent. If I cannot stand on my own public record, on my own private and public character as history will record it, I will not attempt to rise by traducing the character of other men. I will not make a blackguard of myself by imitating the course they have pursued against me. I have no charges to make against them.

This is a singular statement taken altogether. After indulging in language which would disgrace a loafer in the filthiest purlieus of a fish market, *he winds up by saying that he will not make a blackguard of himself*, that he has no charges to make against me. So I suppose he considers, that to say of another that he knew a thing to be false when he uttered it, that he was a "miserable craven hearted wretch," does not amount to a personal assault, and does not make a man a blackguard. A discriminating public will judge of that for themselves; but as he says he has "no charges to make on Mr. Trumbull." I suppose politeness requires I should believe him. At the risk of again offending this mighty man of war and losing something more than my ears, *I shall have the audacity to again read the record upon him and prove and pin upon him, so that he cannot escape it, the truth of every word I uttered at Chicago*. You, fellow citizens, are the judges to determine whether I do this. My colleague says he is willing to stand on his public record. By that he shall be tried, and if he had been able to discriminate between the exposure of a public act by the record, and a personal attack upon the individual, he would have discovered that there was nothing personal in my Chicago remarks, unless the condemnation of himself by his own public record is personal, and then you must judge who is most to blame for the torture his public record inflicts upon him, he for making, or I for reading it after it was made. As an individual I care very little about Judge Douglas one way or the other. It is his public acts with which I have to do, and if they condemn, disgrace and consign him to oblivion, he has only himself, not me, to blame.

Now, the charge is that *there was a plot entered into to have a Constitution formed for Kansas, and put in force, without giving the people an opportunity to pass upon it, and that Mr. Douglas was in the plot.* This is as susceptible of proof by the record as is the fact that the State of Minnesota was admitted into the Union at the last session of Congress.

On the 25th of June, 1856, a bill was pending in the United States Senate to authorize the people of Kansas to form a Constitution and come into the Union. On that day Mr. Toombs offered an amendment which he intended to propose to the bill which was ordered to be printed, and, with the original bill and other amendments, recommended to the Committee on Territories, of which Mr. Douglas was Chairman. This amendment of Mr. Toombs, printed by order of the Senate, and a copy of which I have here present provided for the appointment of commissioners who were to take a census of Kansas, divide the territory into election districts, and superintend the election of delegates to form a Constitution, and contains a clause in the 18th section which I will read to you, requiring the Constitution which should be formed to be submitted to the people for adoption. It reads as follows:

> That the following propositions be and the same are hereby offered to the said Convention of the people of Kansas, when formed, for their free acceptance or rejection, which, if accepted by the Convention, AND RATIFIED BY THE PEOPLE AT THE ELECTION FOR THE ADOPTION OF THE CONSTITUTION, shall be obligatory on the United States, and upon the said State of Kansas. &c.

It has been contended by some of the newspaper press, that this section did not require the constitution which should be formed to be submitted to the people for approval, and that it was only the land propositions which were to be submitted. You will observe the language is that the propositions are to be "ratified by the people at the election for the adoption of the Constitution." Would it have been possible to ratify the land propositions "AT THE ELECTION FOR THE ADOPTION OF THE CONSTITUTION," unless such an election was to be held?

When one thing is required by a contract or law to be done, the doing of which is made dependent upon and cannot be performed without the doing of some other thing, is not that other thing just as much required by the contract or law as the first? It matters not in what part of the act, nor in what phraseology the intention of the Legislature is expressed, so you can clearly ascertain that it is; and whenever that intention is ascertained from an examination of the language used, such intention is part of and a requirement of the law. Can any candid, fair-minded man, read the section I have quoted, and say that the intention to have the Constitution which should be formed submitted to the people for their adoption is not clearly expressed? In my judgment there can be no controversy among honest men upon a proposition so plain as this. Mr. Douglas has never pretended to deny, so far as I am aware, that the Toombs amendment, as originally introduced, did require a submission of the Constitution to the people. This amendment of Mr. Toombs was referred to the committee of which Judge Douglas was chairman, and reported back by him on the 30th of June, with the words, "*And ratified by the people at the election for the adoption of the Constitution*" STRICKEN OUT. I have here a copy of the bill as reported back by Mr. Douglas to substantiate the statement I make. Various other alterations were also made in the bill to which I shall presently have occasion to call attention. There was no other clause in the original Toombs bill requiring a submission of the Constitution to the people than the one I have read, and there was no clause whatever, after that was struck out, in the bill, as reported back by Judge Douglas requiring a submission. I will now introduce a witness whose testimony cannot be impeached, he acknowledging himself to have been one of the conspirators and privy to the fact about which he testifies.

Senator Bigler alluding to the Toombs bill, as it was called, and which, after sundry amendments, passed the Senate, and to the propriety of submitting the Constitution which should be formed to a vote of the people, made the following statement in his place in the Senate, December 9th, 1857. I read from part I, Congressional Globe of last session, paragraph 21.

> I was present when that subject was discussed by Senators, before the bill was introduced, and the question was raised and discussed whether the Constitution, when formed, should be submitted to a vote of the people. It was held by the most intelligent on the subject, that in view of all the difficulties surrounding that Territory, the danger of any experiment at that time of a popular vote, it would be better that there should be no such provision in the Toombs bill; and it is my understanding, in all the intercourse I had, that that Convention would make a Constitution and send it here without submitting it to the popular vote.

In speaking of this meeting again on the 21st December, 1857 (Congressional Globe, same vol. page 113), Senator Bigler said:

Nothing was farther from my mind than to allude to any social or confidential interview. The meeting was not of that character. Indeed, it was semi-official, and called to promote the public good. My recollection was clear that I left the conference under the impression that it had been deemed best to adopt measures to admit Kansas as a State through the agency of one popular election, and that for delegates to the convention. This impression was the stronger, because I thought the spirit of the bill infringed upon the doctrine of non-intervention, to which I had great aversion; but with the hope of accomplishing great good, and as no movement had been made in that direction in the territory, I waived this objection, and concluded to support the measure. I have a few items of testimony as to the correctness of these impressions, and with their submission I shall be content. I have before me the bill reported by the Senator from Illinois, on the 7th of March, 1856, providing for the admission of Kansas as a State, the third section of which reads as follows:

"That the following propositions be and the same are hereby offered to the said convention of the people of Kansas, when formed, for their free acceptance or rejection; which if accepted by the convention, and ratified by the people at the election for the adoption of the Constitution, shall be obligatory upon the United States, and upon the said State of Kansas."

The bill read in place by the Senator from Georgia, on the 25th of June, and referred to the Committee on Territories, contained the same section word for word. Both these bills were under consideration at the conference referred to, but sir, when the Senator from Illinois reported the Toombs bill to the Senate, with amendments, the next morning, it did not contain that portion of the third section which indicated to the Convention that the Constitution should be approved by the people. The words "AND RATIFIED BY THE PEOPLE AT THE ELECTION FOR THE ADOPTION OF THE CONSTITUTION" had been stricken out.

I am not now seeking to prove that Douglas was in the plot to force a constitution upon Kansas without allowing the people to vote directly upon it. I shall attend to that branch of the subject by and by. My object now is to prove the existence of the plot, what the design was, and I ask if I have not already done so. Here are the facts:

The introduction of a bill on the 7th of March, 1856, providing for the calling of a convention in Kansas, to form a State Constitution, and providing that the Constitution should be submitted to the people for adoption; an amendment to this bill, proposed by Mr. Toombs, containing the same requirement; a reference of these various bills to the Committee on Territories, a consultation of Senators to determine whether it was advisable to have the constitution submitted for ratification; the determination that it was not advisable; and a report of the bill back to the Senate next morning, with the clause providing for the submission stricken out. Could evidence be more complete to establish the first part of the charge I have made, of a plot having been entered into by somebody, to have a constitution adopted without submitting it to the people?

Now, for the other part of the charge, that Judge Douglas was in this plot, whether knowingly or ignorantly, is not material to my purpose. The charge is that he was an instrument co-operating in the project to have a Constitution formed and put into operation, without affording the people an opportunity to pass upon it. The first evidence to sustain the charge is the fact that he reported back the Toombs amendment with the clause providing for the submission stricken out. This, in connection with his speech in the Senate on the 9th of December 1857 (Congressional Globe, Part I, page 14) wherein he stated—

> That during the last Congress, I [Mr. Douglas] reported a bill from the Committee on Territories, to authorize the people of Kansas to assemble and form a Constitution for themselves. Subsequently the Senator from Georgia [Mr. Toombs] brought forward a substitute for my bill, which, AFTER HAVING BEEN MODIFIED BY HIM AND MYSELF IN CONSULTATION, was passed by the Senate.

This of itself ought to be sufficient to show that my colleague was an instrument in the plot to have a constitution put in force without submitting it to the people, and to forever close his mouth from attempting to deny. No man can reconcile his acts and former declarations with his present denial, and the only charitable conclusion would be that he was being used by others without knowing it. Whether he is entitled to the benefit of even this excuse, you must judge on a candid hearing of the facts I shall present. When the charge was first made in the United States Senate, by Mr. Bigler, that my colleague had voted for an enabling act which put a government in operation without submitting the Constitution to the people, my colleague (Cong. Globe last session, part I, p. 21) stated:

> I will ask the Senator to show me an intimation from any one member of the Senate, in the whole debate on the Toombs bill, and in the Union from any quarter, that the Constitution was not to be submitted to the people. I will venture to say that on all sides of the chamber it was so understood at the time: If the opponents of the bill had understood it was not, they would have made the point on it; and if they had made it we should certainly have yielded to it, and put in the clause. That is a discovery made since the President found out that

it was not safe to take it for granted that that would be done, which ought in fairness to have been done.

I knew at the time this statement was made, that I had urged the very objection to the Toombs bill two years before, that it did not provide for the submission of the Constitution. You will find my remarks, made on the 2d of July, 1856, in the appendix to the Congressional Globe of that year, p. 179, urging this very objection. Do you ask why I did not expose him at the time? I will tell you—Mr. Douglas was then doing good service against the Lecompton iniquity. The Republicans were then engaged in a hand to hand fight with the National Democracy, to prevent the bringing of Kansas into the Union as a Slave State against the wishes of its inhabitants, and of course I was unwilling to turn our guns from the common enemy to strike down an ally. Judge Douglas, however on the same day, and in the same debate, probably recollecting, or being reminded of the fact, that I had objected to the Toombs bill when pending, that it did not provide for the submission of the Constitution to the people, made another statement which is to be found in the same volume of the Congressional Globe, page 22, in which he says:

> That the bill was silent on the subject is true, and my attention was called to that about the time it was passed; and I took the fair construction to be, that powers not delegated were reserved, and that of course the Constitution would be submitted to the people.

Whether this statement is consistent with the statement just before made, that had the point been made it would have been yielded to, or that it was a new discovery, you will determine; for if the public records do not convict and condemn him, he may go uncondemned, so far as I am concerned. I make no use here of the testimony of Senator Bigler to show that Judge Douglas must have been privy to the consultation held at his house, when it was determined not to submit the Constitution to the people, because Judge Douglas denies it, and I wish to use his own acts and declarations which are abundantly sufficient for my purpose.

I come to a piece of testimony which disposes of all these various pretences which have been set up for striking out of the original Toombs proposition the clause requiring a submission of the Constitution to the people, and shows that it was not done either by accident, by inadvertence, or because it was believed that the bill being silent on the subject, the constitution would necessarily be submitted to the people for approval. What will you think, after listening to the facts already presented, to show that there was a design with those who concocted the Toombs bill as amended, not to submit the Constitution to the people, if I now bring before you the amended bill as Judge Douglas reported it back, and show the clause of the original bill requiring submission, was not only struck out, but that other clauses were inserted in the bill putting it absolutely out of the power of the convention to submit the Constitution to the people for approval, had they desired to do so? If I can produce such evidence as that, will you not all agree that it clinches and establishes forever, all I charged at Chicago, and more too?

I propose now to furnish that evidence. It will be remembered that Mr. Toombs' bill provided for holding an election for delegates to form a Constitution under the supervision of commissioners to be appointed by the President, and in the bill as reported back by Judge Douglas, these words, *not to be found in the original bill*, are inserted at the close of the 11th section, viz:

> And until the complete execution of this act, no other election shall be held in said Territory.

This clause put it out of the power of the convention to refer to the people for adoption; it absolutely prohibited the holding of any other election than that for the election of delegates, till that act was completely executed, which would not have been till Kansas was admitted as a State, or at all events till her constitution was fully prepared and ready for submission to Congress for admission. Other amendments reported by Judge Douglas to the original Toombs bill, clearly show that the intention was to enable Kansas to become a State without any further action than simply a resolution of admission. The amendment reported by Mr. Douglas, that "until the next Congressional apportionment, the said State shall have one representative," clearly shows this, no such provision being contained in the original Toombs bill. For what other earthly purpose could the clause to prevent any other election in Kansas, except that of delegates, till it was admitted as a State, have been inserted except to prevent a submission of the constitution, when formed, to the people?

The Toombs bill did not pass in the exact shape in which Judge Douglas reported it. Several amendments were made to it in the Senate. I am now dealing with the action of Judge Douglas, as connected with that bill, and speak of the bill as he recommended it. The facts I have stated in regard to this matter appear upon the records, which I have here present to show to any man who wishes to look at them. They establish beyond the power of controversy, all the charges I have made, and show that Judge Douglas was made use of as an instrument by others, or else knowingly was a party to the scheme to have a government put in force over the people of Kansas, without giving them an opportunity to pass upon it. That others high in position in the so called Democratic party were parties to such a scheme is confessed by Gov. Bigler; and the only reason why the scheme was not carried, and Kansas long ago forced into the Union as a Slave State, is the fact, that the Republicans were sufficiently strong in the House of Representatives to defeat the measure.

EXTRACT FROM MR. DOUGLAS' SPEECH MADE AT JACKSONVILLE, & REFERRED TO BY MR. LINCOLN IN HIS OPENING AT CHARLESTON.[9]

I have been reminded by a friend behind me that there is another topic upon which there has been a desire expressed that I should speak. I am told that Mr. Lyman Trumbull, who has the good fortune to hold a seat in the United States Senate, in violation of the bargain between him and Lincoln, was here the other day and occupied his time in making certain charges against me, involving, if they be true, moral turpitude. I am also informed that the charges he made here were substantially the same as those made by him in the city of Chicago, which were printed in the newspapers of that city. I now propose to answer those charges and to annihilate every pretext that an honest man has ever had for repeating them.

In order that I may meet these charges fairly, I will read them, as made by Mr. Trumbull, in his Chicago speech, in his own language. He says:

> Now, fellow-citizens, I make the distinct charge that there was a preconcerted arrangement and plot entered into by the very men who now claim credit for opposing a constitution not submitted to the people, to have a constitution formed and put in force without giving the people an opportunity to pass upon it. This, my friends, is a serious charge, but I charge it to-night, that the very men who traverse the country under banners, proclaiming popular sovereignty, by design, concocted a bill on purpose to force a constitution upon that people.

Again, speaking to some one in the crowd, he says:

> And you want to satisfy yourself that he was in the plot to force a constitution upon that people? I will satisfy you. I will cram the truth down any honest man's throat, until he cannot deny it, and to the man who does deny it, I will cram the lie down his throat till he shall cry enough! It is preposterous—it is the most damnable effrontery that man ever put on to conceal a scheme to defraud and cheat the people out of their rights, and then claim credit for it.

[9] Lincoln's headnote to the following extract.

That is polite and decent language for a Senator of the United States. (A voice—"that's so, if you did not mind what you said.") Remember that that language was used without any provocation whatever from me. I had not alluded to him in any manner in any speech that I had made, hence, without provocation. As soon as he sets his foot within the State he makes the direct charge that I was a party to a plot to force a constitution upon the people of Kansas against their will, and knowing that it would be denied, he talks about cramming the lie down the throat of any man who shall deny it, until he cries enough.

Why did he take it for granted that it would be denied unless he knew it to be false? Why did he deem it necessary to make a threat in advance that he would "cram the lie" down the throat of any man that should deny it? I have no doubt that the entire Abolition party consider it very polite for Mr. Trumbull to go round uttering calumnies of that kind, bullying and talking of cramming lies down men's throats; but if I deny any of his lies by calling him a liar, they are shocked at the indecency of the language; (laughter, and a voice, "but he is one,") hence, to-day, instead of calling him a liar I intend to prove that he is one. (Cries of "good," "that is the doctrine," "hit him hard," and three cheers for Douglas.)

I wish in the first place to refer to the evidence adduced by Trumbull, at Chicago, to sustain his charge. He there declared that Mr. Toombs, of Georgia, introduced a bill into Congress authorizing the people of Kansas to form a constitution and come into the Union, that when introduced it contained a clause requiring the constitution to be submitted to the people, and that I struck out the words of that clause. (A voice—"he made that charge here.")

Suppose it were true that there was such a clause in the bill and that I struck it out, is that proof of a plot to force a constitution upon a people against their will? Bear in mind, that from the days of Geo. Washington to the Administration of Franklin Pierce, there had never been passed by Congress, a bill requiring the submission of a constitution to the people. If Trumbull's charge, that I struck out that clause were true, it would only prove that I had reported the bill in the exact shape of every bill of like character that passed under Washington, Jefferson, Madison, Monroe, Jackson or any other President to the time of the then present Administration. I ask you would that be evidence of a design to force a constitution on a people against their will? (Loud cries of "no," and applause.) If it were so, it would be evidence against Washington, Jefferson, Madison, Jackson, Van Buren and every other President.

But upon examination, it turns out that the Toombs bill never did contain a clause requiring the constitution to be submitted. (Cries of "good," "that's so," and loud applause.) Hence no such clause was ever stricken out by me or by anybody else. (Cries of "give it to him," "turn him over," and applause.) It is true, however, that the Toombs bill and its authors all took it for granted that the constitution would be submitted. There had never been, in the history of this government, any attempt made to force a constitution upon an unwilling people, and no body dreamed that any such attempt would be made, or deemed it necessary to provide for such a contingency. If such a clause was necessary in Mr. Trumbull's opinion, why did he not offer an amendment to that effect?

In order to give more pertinency to that question, I will read an extract from Trumbull's speech in the Senate on the Toombs bill, made on the 2d July, 1856. He said:

> We are asked to amend this bill and make it perfect, and a liberal spirit seems to be manifested on the part of some Senators to have a fair bill. It is difficult, I admit, to frame a bill that will give satisfaction to all, but to approach it, or to come near it, I think two things must be done.

The first, then, he goes on to say, was the application of the Wilmot Proviso to the territories, and the second the repeal of all the laws passed by the Territorial Legislature. He did not then say that it was necessary to put in a clause requiring the submission of the constitution. Why, if he thought such a provision necessary, did he not introduce it? He says in his speech that he was invited to offer amendments! Why did he not do so? (A voice—"He wasn't smart enough" applause.) He cannot pretend that he had no chance to do this for he did offer some amendments, but none requiring the submission. (Applause.)

I now proceed to show that Mr. Trumbull knew at the time that the bill was silent as to the subject of submission and also that he, and every body else took it for granted that the constitution would be submitted. (Applause.) Now for the evidence. (A voice, "Don't leave a gimlet hole for him to get out of—he said he would not leave one for you.") In his second speech he says: "The bill in many of its features meets my approbation." So he did not think it so very bad. (Laughter and applause.)

Further on he says:

> In regard to the measure introduced by the Senator from Georgia, (Mr. Toombs) and recommended by the committee, I regard it, in many respects, as a most excellent bill; but we must look at it in the

light of surrounding circumstances. In the condition of things now existing in the country, I do not consider it as a safe measure, nor one which will give peace, and I will give my reasons. First, it affords no immediate relief. It provides for taking a census of the voters in the Territory, for an election in November, and the assembling of a convention in December, to form, if it thinks proper, a Constitution for Kansas, preparatory to its admission into the Union as a State. It is not until December, that the convention is to meet. It would take some time to form a constitution. *I suppose that constitution would have to be ratified by the people before it becomes valid.*

He there expressly declared that he supposed, under the bill, the constitution would have to be submitted to the people before it became valid. He went on to say:

No provision is made in this bill for such ratification. This is objectionable, to my mind. I do not think the people should be bound by a constitution, without passing upon it directly, themselves.

Why did he not offer an amendment providing for such a submission, if he thought it necessary? Notwithstanding the absence of such a clause, he took it for granted that the constitution would have to be ratified by the people, under the bill.

In another part of the same speech, he says:

There is nothing said in this bill, so far as I have discovered, about submitting the constitution which is to be framed, to the people, for their sanction or rejection. Perhaps the convention would have the right to submit it, if it should think proper; but it is certainly not compelled to do so, according to the provisions of the bill. If it is to be submitted to the people, it will take time, and it will not be until some time next year that this new Constitution, affirmed and ratified by the people, would be submitted here to Congress for its acceptance, and what is to be the condition of that people in the meantime?

You see that his argument then was that the Toombs bill would not get Kansas into the Union quick enough and was objectionable on that account. He had no fears about this submission, or why did he not introduce an amendment to meet the case? (Applause.)

A VOICE—Why didn't you? You were chairman of the committee.

MR. DOUGLAS—I will answer that question for you.

In the first place, no such provision had ever before been put in any similar act passed by Congress. I did not suppose that there was an honest man who would pretend that the omission of such a clause furnished evidence of a conspiracy or attempt to impose on the people. (Loud applause.) It could not be expected that such of us as did not think that omission was evidence of such a scheme, would offer such an amendment; but if Trumbull then believed what he now says, why did he not offer the amendment, and try to prevent it, when he was, as he says, invited to do so. (Tremendous applause.)

In this connection I will tell you what the main point of discussion was: There was a bill pending to admit Kansas whenever she should have a population of 93,420, that being the ratio required for a member of Congress. Under that bill Kansas could not have become a State for some years, because she would not have had the requisite population. Mr. Toombs took it into his head to bring in a bill to admit Kansas then, with only twenty five or thirty thousand people, and the question was whether we would allow Kansas to come in under his bill, or keep her out under mine until she had 93,420 people. The committee considered that question, and overruled me by deciding in favor of the immediate admission of Kansas, and I reported accordingly. I hold in my hand a copy of the report which I made at that time. I will read from it:

> The point upon which your committee have entertained the most serious and grave doubts in regard to the propriety of endorsing the proposition relates to the fact that in the absence of any census of the inhabitants, there is reason to apprehend that the Territory does not contain sufficient population to entitle them to demand admission under the treaty with France, if we take the ratio of representation for a member of Congress as the rule.

Thus you see that in the written report accompanying the bill, I said that the great difficulty with the committee was the question of population. In the same report I happened to refer to the question of submission. Now listen to what I said about that:

> In the opinion of your committee whenever a constitution shall be formed in any Territory preparatory to its admission into the Union as a State, justice, the genius of our institutions, the whole theory of our republican system, imperatively demands that the voice of the people shall be fairly expressed, and their will embodied in that fundamental law without fraud or violence, or intimidation, or any other improper or unlawful influence, and subject to no other restrictions than those imposed by the Constitution of the United States.

I read this from the report I made at the time, on the Toombs bill. (Loud applause.) I will read yet another passage from the same report, after setting out the features of the Toombs bill I contrast it with the proposition of Senator Seward, saying:

> "The revised proposition of the Senator from Georgia refers all matters in dispute to the decision of the present population, with guarantees of fairness and safeguards against frauds and violence, to which no reasonable man can find just grounds of exception," while the Senator from N.Y., if his proposition is designed to recognize and im-

part vitality to the Topeka Constitution, proposes to disfranchise not only all the emigrants who have arrived in the Territory this year, but all the law-abiding men who refused to join in the act of open rebellion against the constituted authorities of the Territory last year, by making the unauthorized and unlawful action of a political party, the fundamental law of the whole people.

Then, again, I repeat that under that bill the question is to be referred to the present population to decide for or against coming into the Union under the constitution they may adopt.

Mr. Trumbull, when at Chicago, rested his charge upon the allegation that the clause requiring submission was originally in the bill and was stricken out by me. When that falsehood was exposed by a publication of the record he went to Alton and made another speech, repeating the charge, and referring to other and different evidence to sustain it. (Laughter and applause.) He saw that he was caught in his first falsehood, so he changed the issue, and instead of resting upon the allegation of striking out he made it rest upon the declaration that I had introduced a clause into the bill prohibiting the people from voting upon the constitution. (A voice —"He said the same here.") I am told that he made the same charge here that he made at Alton, that I had actually introduced and incorporated into the bill, a clause which prohibited the people from voting upon their constitution. I hold his Alton speech in my hand, and will read the amendment which, he alleges, that I offered. It is in these words:

> And until the complete execution of this act no other election shall be held in said Territory.

Trumbull says that the object of that amendment was to prevent the Convention from submitting the Constitution to a vote of the people. I will read what he said at Alton on that subject:

> This clause put it out of the power of the Convention, had it been so disposed, to submit the Constitution to the people for adoption; for it absolutely prohibited the holding of any other election, than that for the election of delegates, till that act was completely executed, which would not have been till Kansas was admitted as a State, or at all events, till her Constitution was fully prepared and ready for submission to Congress for admission.

Now, do you suppose that Mr. Trumbull supposed that that clause prohibited the Convention from submitting the Constitution to the people, when in his speech in the Senate, he declared that the Convention had the right to submit it? (Great applause.) In his Alton speech, as will be seen by the extract which I have read, he declared that the clause put it out of the power of the Convention to submit the Constitution, and in his speech in the Senate he said:

> There is *nothing said in this bill*, so far as I have discovered, about submitting the Constitution which is to be formed, to the people, for their sanction or rejection. Perhaps the convention could have the right to submit it if it should think proper, but it is certainly not compelled to do so according to the provisions of the bill.

Thus, you see, that in Congress he declared the bill to be silent on the subject, and a few days since, at Alton, he made a speech, and said that there was a provision in the bill prohibiting submission. [Laughter.]

I have two answers to make to that. In the first place, the amendment which he quotes as depriving the people of an opportunity to vote upon the Constitution, *was stricken out on my motion*—[Cries of "good," and rapturous applause,] absolutely stricken out, and not voted on at all! [A voice, "Near enough for a blind man."] In the second place, in lieu of it, a provision was voted in authorizing the convention to order an election whenever it pleased. [Cheers.] I will read. After Trumbull had made his speech in the Senate declaring that the Constitution would probably be submitted to the people, although the bill was silent upon that subject, I made a few remarks, and offered two amendments, which you may find in the Appendix to the Congressional Globe, volume 33, first session XXXIVth Congress, page 795.

I quote:

> Mr. DOUGLAS—I have an amendment to offer from the Committee on Territories, on page 8, section 11, *strike out the words* "until the complete execution of this act, no other election shall be held in said Territory," and insert the amendment which I hold in my hand.

The amendment was as follows:

> That all persons who shall possess the other qualifications prescribed for voters under this act, and who shall have been *bona fide* inhabitants of said Territory since its organization, and who shall have absented themselves therefrom in consequence of the disturbances therein, and who shall return before the first day of October next, and become *bona fide* inhabitants of the Territory, with the intent of making it their permanent home, and shall present satisfactory evidence of these facts to the Board of Commissioners, shall be entitled to vote at said election, and shall have their names placed on said corrected list of voters for that purpose.

That amendment was adopted unanimously. After its adoption, the record shows the following:

Mr. DOUGLAS—I have another amendment to offer from the Committee to follow the amendment which has been adopted. The bill reads now, "and until the complete execution of this act, no other election shall be held in said Territory." It has been suggested that it should be modified in this way, "and to avoid all conflict in the complete execution of this act, all other elections in said Territory are hereby postponed until such time as said Convention shall appoint," so that they can appoint the day in the event that there should be a failure to come into the Union. (Tremendous applause.)

This amendment was also agreed to without dissent.

Thus you see that the amendment quoted by Trumbull at Alton as evidence against me, instead of being put into the bill by me was stricken out on my motion, and never became a part thereof at all. You also see that the substituted clause expressly authorized the convention to appoint such day of election as it should deem proper.

Mr. Trumbull when he made that speech knew these facts. He forged his evidence from beginning to end, and by falsifying the record he endeavors to bolster up his false charge. (Loud applause.) I ask you what you think of Trumbull thus going around the country falsifying and garbling the public records. I ask you whether you will sustain a man who will descend to the infamy of such conduct. (Cries of "Never," &c.)

Mr. Douglas proceeded to remark that he should not hereafter occupy his time in refuting such charges made by Trumbull, but that Lincoln having endorsed the character of Trumbull for veracity, he should hold him (Lincoln) responsible for the slanders.

The Judge, when his speech was concluded, was again conducted to the hotel by the vast procession. The guards went through their evolutions in his presence, and the band discoursed harmony during the evening. Later on in the night a ball was given in his honor, and at an early hour this morning the occasion was wound up by a serenade.

To Stephen A. Douglas[1]

[September 20, 1858]

Understanding that Judge Douglas would speak before dinner, I announced that I would address our friends at Freeland's Grove, at 2. P.M. As he does not begin till 1 o'clock, if he will announce the fact, so that I can understand it, I will postpone to 3. o'clock.

A LINCOLN

[1] ALS, owned by William H. Townsend, Lexington, Kentucky. Written in pencil, the document bears the following certification: "We certify that we saw Mr. George Lynn Jr. deliver this paper to Judge Douglas in his room at Sullivan House he stating at the time that he did so at the request of Mr. Lincoln & renewing the request verbally on behalf of Mr. Lincoln that Judge Douglas would make such announcement, to which request Mr. Douglas replied that he would make the announcement as desired, which we heard him do before he commenced his speech. Bushrod W. Henry/ John Gwin/ Cain Knight/ Jno [Z?] Hill/ A M [*sic*]" In spite of Lincoln's effort and the co-operation of Douglas in making the announcement, a mob conflict arose between the partisans at Sullivan when the Republican parade marching to the grove passed near the Democratic gathering before Douglas had concluded. Although there are ample reports of the brawl, no report of Lincoln's speech has been found.

To Norman B. Judd[1]

Hon. N. B. Judd: Danville, Ill., Sept. 23, 1858.

My Dear Sir: We had a fine and altogether satisfactory meeting here yesterday. Our friends here wish a German speaker, before the election. Can't you send one? Address Dr. W. Fithian, and set a time sufficiently distant to give full notice. I am behind in general news; and this is a bad point to get any. Still I believe we have got the gentleman, unless they overcome us by fraudulent voting. We must be especially prepared for this. It must be taken into anxious consideration at once. How can it be done? Men imported from other states and men not naturalized can be fought out; but if they should string out the qualified Irish voters of Chicago (for instance) into a doubtful district, having them to swear to an actual residence when they offer to vote, how can we prevent it? Is "Long John"[2] at hand? His genius should be employed on this question. Tell him so for me. I do not mean by this that the rest of us are to dismiss the question. It is a great danger, and we must all attend to it. Yours as ever, A. LINCOLN.

[1] *Illinois State Journal*, January 24, 1909, which cites the original letter in possession at that time of James P. Root of Springfield, Illinois.

[2] John Wentworth.

Statement Concerning Henry Chew[1]

September 25, 1858

My old friend, Henry Chew, the bearer of this, is in a stra[i]ght for some furniture to commence house-keeping. If any person will furnish him, Twenty-five dollars worth, and he does not pay for it by the first of January next, I will. A. LINCOLN

Sept. 25, 1858.

[1] ADS, DLC-RTL. At the bottom of the document appears the following: "Witness—/ C. M. Sherfy." Across the face, badly blotted, appears what seems to be as follows: "Paid by check, sent to A. Lincoln." On February 16, 1859, S. Little of Urbana, Illinois, wrote Lincoln, enclosing the document and requesting a draft to cover the amount (DLC-RTL). Lincoln sent a draft on H. A. Tucker, February 21, 1859. Henry Chew appears in the *Sangamo Journal*, March 7, 1844, as a member of the Springfield Whig Clay Club.

Response to a Serenade at Springfield, Illinois[1]

September 25, 1858

Mr. Lincoln returned to this city on Saturday night. His numerous friends will be glad to learn that he is in excellent health and spirits. The Republican Club, learning of his arrival, determined to serenade him, which they did immediately after the adjournment of their meeting. The Club were accompanied to his residence by their band, and a large concourse of citizens. After the band had played a few lively airs in front of his house, Mr. Lincoln appeared on the portico and thanked his friends for this renewed manifestation of their regard for the principles he defends, and after assuring them, wherever he has been the skies are bright and the prospects good for the triumph of those principles which are dear to us all, he excused himself and retired amid deafening cheers.

[1] *Illinois State Journal*, September 27, 1858.

Verses: To Rosa Haggard[1]

September 28, 1858

To Rosa—

You are young, and I am older;
You are hopeful, I am not—
Enjoy life, ere it grow colder—
Pluck the roses ere they rot.

Teach your beau to heed the lay—
That sunshine soon is lost in shade—
That *now's* as good as any day—
To take thee, Rosa, ere she fade.

Winchester, Sep. 28. 1858. A. LINCOLN—

[1] ADS, owned by E. G. Miner, Rochester, New York. Lincoln wrote the verses in the autograph album of Rosa Haggard, daughter of the proprietor of the hotel at Winchester, Illinois, where he stayed when speaking at that place on the same date. No report of the speech has been located. See also the verses to Linnie Haggard, *infra*.

Verses: To Linnie Haggard[1]

September 30, 1858

To Linnie—

A sweet plaintive song did I hear,
And I fancied that she was the singer—
May emotions as pure, as that song set a-stir
Be the worst that the future shall bring her.

Winchester Sep. 30– 1858– A. LINCOLN—

[1] ADS, owned by E. G. Miner, Rochester, New York. See also verses to Rosa Haggard and note, *supra.* Lincoln left Winchester on September 30 for Pittsfield, Illinois.

Fragment on Pro-slavery Theology[1]

[October 1, 1858?]

Suppose it is true, that the negro is inferior to the white, in the gifts of nature; is it not the exact reverse justice that the white should, for that reason, take from the negro, any part of the little which has been given him? "*Give* to him that is needy" is the christian rule of charity; but "Take from him that is needy" is the rule of slavery.

PRO-SLAVERY THEOLOGY.

The sum of pro-slavery theology seems to be this: "Slavery is not universally *right*, nor yet universally *wrong;* it is better for *some* people to be slaves; and, in such cases, it is the Will of God that they be such."

Certainly there is no contending against the Will of God; but still there is some difficulty in ascertaining, and applying it, to particular cases. For instance we will suppose the Rev. Dr. Ross[2] has a slave named Sambo, and the question is "Is it the Will of God that Sambo shall remain a slave, or be set free?" The Almighty gives no audable answer to the question, and his revelation —the Bible—gives none—or, at most, none but such as admits of a squabble, as to it's meaning. No one thinks of asking Sambo's opinion on it. So, at last, it comes to this, that *Dr. Ross* is to decide the question. And while he consider[s] it, he sits in the shade, with gloves on his hands, and subsists on the bread that Sambo is earning in the burning sun. If he decides that God Wills Sambo to continue a slave, he thereby retains his own comfortable position; but if he decides that God will's Sambo to be free, he thereby has to walk out of the shade, throw off his gloves, and delve for his own bread. Will Dr. Ross be actuated by that perfect impartiality, which has ever been considered most favorable to correct decisions?

But, slavery is good for some people!!! As a *good* thing, slavery is strikingly perculiar, in this, that it is the only good thing which no man ever seeks the good of, *for himself*.

Nonsense! Wolves devouring lambs, not because it is good for their own greedy maws, but because it [is] good for the lambs!!!

[1] AD, owned by Miss Elsie Logan, Springfield, Illinois. The date assigned by Nicolay and Hay has been retained in the absence of evidence to the contrary.

[2] Lincoln probably refers to the Reverend Frederick A. Ross, whose *Slavery Ordained of God* (Philadelphia, 1857) and numerous speeches on the subject placed him among the forefront of clergymen defending the peculiar institution.

Fragment: Notes for Speeches[1]

[October 1, 1858?]

But there is a larger issue than the mere question of whether the spread of negro slavery shall or shall not be prohibited by Congress. That larger issue is stated by the Richmond "Enquirer," a Buchanan paper in the South, in the language I now read. It is also stated by the New York "Day-book," a Buchanan paper in the North, in this language.—And in relation to indigent white children, the same Northern paper says.—In support of the Nebraska bill, on its first discussion in the Senate, Senator Pettit of Indiana declared the equality of men, as asserted in our Declaration of Independence, to be a "self-evident lie." In his numerous speeches now being made in Illinois, Senator Douglas regularly argues against the doctrine of the equality of men; and while he does not draw the conclusion that the superiors ought to enslave the inferiors, he evidently wishes his hearers to draw that conclusion. He shirks the responsibility of pulling the house down, but he digs under it that it may fall of its own weight. Now, it is impossible to not see that these newspapers and senators are laboring at a common object, and in so doing are truly representing the controlling sentiment of their party.

It is equally impossible to not see that that common object is to subvert, in the public mind, and in practical administration, our old and only standard of free government, that "all men are created equal," and to substitute for it some different standard. What that substitute is to be is not difficult to perceive. It is to deny the equality of men, and to assert the natural, moral, and religious right of one class to enslave another.

[1] NH, IV, 200-201. The date assigned by Nicolay and Hay has been retained for want of evidence to the contrary.

Speech at Pekin, Illinois[1]

October 5, 1858

Mr. Lincoln was welcomed to Tazewell county and introduced to the audience by Judge Bush[2] in a short and eloquently delivered speech, and when he came forward, was greeted with hearty applause. He commenced by alluding to the many years in which he had been intimately acquainted with most of the citizens of old Tazewell county, and expressed the pleasure which it gave him to see so many of them present. He then alluded to the fact that Judge Douglas, in a speech to them on Saturday, had, as he was credibly informed, made a variety of extraordinary statements concerning him. He had known Judge Douglas for twenty-five years, and was not now to be astonished by any statement which he might make, no matter what it might be. He was surprised, however, that his old political enemy but personal friend, Mr. John Haynes[3]—a gentleman whom he had always respected as a person of honor and veracity—should have made such statements about him as he was said to have made in a speech introducing Mr. Douglas to a Tazewell audience only three days before. He then rehearsed those statements, the substance of which was that Mr. Lincoln, while a member of Congress, helped starve his brothers and friends in the Mexican war by voting against the bills appropriating to them money, provisions and medical attendance. He was grieved and astonished that a man whom he had heretofore respected so highly, should have been guilty of such false statements, and he hoped Mr. Haynes was present that he might hear his denial of them. He was not a member of Congress he said, until after the return of Mr. Haynes' brothers and friends from the Mexican war to their Tazewell county homes—was not a member of Congress until after the war had practically closed. He then went into a detailed statement of his election to Congress, and of the votes he gave, while a member of that body, having any connection with the Mexican war. He showed that upon all occasions he voted for the supply bills for the army, and appealed to the official record for a confirmation of his statement.

Mr. Lincoln then proceeded to notice, successively, the charges made against him by Douglas in relation to the Illinois Central Railroad, in relation to an attempt to Abolitionize the Whig party and in relation to negro equality.

After finishing his allusions to the special charges brought against him by his antagonist, Mr. Lincoln branched out into one of the most powerful and telling speeches he has made during the campaign. It was the most forcible argument against Mr. Douglas' Democracy, and the best vindication of and eloquent plea for Republicanism, that we ever listened to from any man.

[1] Chicago *Press and Tribune*, October 7, 1858, copied from Peoria *Transcript*, October 6, 1858. [2] John M. Bush, probate judge at Pekin.

[3] John Haynes has not been identified. Possibly the name is the reporter's error for Jonathan Haines, Pekin banker. See Lincoln to Haines, November 24, 1856.

Fifth Debate with Stephen A. Douglas, at Galesburg, Illinois[1]

October 7, 1858

Fifth joint debate October 7. 1858, at Galesburg, Illinois Douglas, as reported in the Chicago Times. Lincoln, as reported in the Press & Tribune.[2]

MR. DOUGLAS' SPEECH.

When Senator Douglas appeared on the stand he was greeted with three tremendous cheers. He said:

Ladies and Gentlemen: Four years ago I appeared before the people of Knox county for the purpose of defending my political action upon the compromise measures of 1850 and the passage of the Kansas-Nebraska bill. Those of you before me, who were present then, will remember that I vindicated myself for supporting those two measures by the fact that they rested upon the great fundamental principle that the people of each State and each territory of this Union have the right, and ought to be permitted to exercise the right of regulating their own domestic concerns in their own way, subject to no other limitation or restriction than that which the Constitution of the United States imposes upon them. I then called upon the people of Illinois to decide whether that principle of self-government was right or wrong. If it was, and is right, then the compromise measures of 1850 were right, and, consequently, the Kansas and Nebraska bill, based upon the same principle, must necessarily have been right. (That's so, and cheers.)

The Kansas and Nebraska bill declared, in so many words, that

[1] Debates Scrapbook, ORB. As in the preceding debates, the editors have retained cheering and interruptions deleted by Lincoln. Lincoln's insertions and corrections are indicated in footnotes. Typographical errors not corrected in the scrapbook have been corrected by the editors. All bracketed passages in this debate are in the source.

[2] Lincoln's prefatory note in the debates scrapbook.

it was the true intent and meaning of the act not to legislate slavery into any State or territory, nor to exclude it therefrom, but to leave the people thereof perfectly free to form and regulate their domestic institutions in their own way, subject only to the Constitution of the United States. For the last four years I have devoted all my energies, in private and public, to commend that principle to the American people. Whatever else may be said in condemnation or support of my political course, I apprehend that no honest man will doubt the fidelity with which, under all circumstances, I have stood by it.

During the last year a question arose in the Congress of the United States whether or not that principle would be violated by the admission of Kansas into the Union under the Lecompton constitution. In my opinion, the attempt to force Kansas in under that constitution was a gross violation of the principle enunciated in the compromise measures of 1850, and Kansas and Nebraska bill of 1854, and therefore I led off in the fight against the Lecompton constitution and conducted it until the effort to carry that constitution through Congress was abandoned. And I can appeal to all men, friends and foes, Democrats and Republicans, Northern men, Southern men, that during the whole of that fight I carried the banner of Popular Sovereignty aloft, and never allowed it to trail in the dust, or lowered my flag until victory perched upon our arms. (Cheers!) When the Lecompton constitution was defeated, the question arose in the minds of those who had advocated it what they should next resort to in order to carry out their views. They devised a measure known as the English bill, and granted a general amnesty and political pardon to all men who had fought against the Lecompton constitution, provided they would support that bill. I for one did not choose to accept the pardon or to avail myself of the amnesty granted on that condition. The fact that the supporters of Lecompton were willing to forgive all differences of opinion at that time in the event those who opposed it favored the English bill, was an admission that they did not think that opposition to Lecompton impaired a man's standing in the Democratic party. Now the question arises, what was that English bill which certain men are now attempting to make a test of political orthodoxy in this country? It provided, in substance, that the Lecompton constitution should be sent back to the people of Kansas for their adoption or rejection, at an election which was held in August last, and in case they refused admission under it that Kansas should be kept out of the Union until she had 93,420 inhabitants. I was in favor of sending the constitution back in order to enable the people to say whether or not it was their act and deed, and embodied their will; but the other proposition, that if they refused to come into the Union under it, they should be kept out until they had double or treble the population they then had, I never would sanction by my vote. The reason why I could not sanction it is to be found in the fact that by the English bill, if the people of Kansas had only agreed to become a slaveholding State under the Lecompton constitution, they could have done so with 35,000 people, but if they insisted on being a free State, as they had a right to do, then they were to be punished by being kept out of the Union until they had nearly three times that population. I then said in my place in the Senate, as I now say to you, that whenever Kansas has population enough for a slave State she has population enough for a free State. (That's it, and cheers.) I have never yet given a vote, and I never intend to record one making an odious and unjust distinction between the different States of this Union. (Applause.) I hold it to be a fundamental principle in our republican form of government that all the States of this Union, old and new, free and slave, stand on an exact equality. Equality among the different States is a cardinal principle on which all our institutions rest. Wherever, therefore, you make a discrimination, saying to a slave State that it shall be admitted with 35,000 inhabitants, and to a free State that it shall not be admitted until it has 93,000 or 100,000 inhabitants, you are throwing the whole weight of the federal government into the scale in favor of one class of States against the other. Nor would I on the other hand any sooner sanction the doctrine that a free State could be admitted into the Union with 35,000 people, while a slave State was kept out until it had 93,000. I have always declared in the Senate my willingness, and I am willing now to adopt the rule, that no territory shall ever become a State until it has the requisite population for a member of Congress, according to the then existing ratio. But while I have always been, and am now willing to adopt that general rule, I was not willing and would not consent to make an exception of Kansas, as a punishment for her obstinacy, in demanding the right to do as she pleased in the formation of her constitution. It is proper that I should remark here, that my opposition to the Lecompton constitution did not rest upon the peculiar position taken by Kansas on the subject of slavery. I held then, and hold now, that if the people of Kansas want a slave State, it is their right to make one and be received into the Union under it; if, on the contrary, they want a free State, it is their right to have it, and no man should ever oppose their admission because they ask it under the one or the other. I hold to that great principle of self-government which asserts the right of every people to decide for themselves the nature and character of the domestic institutions and fundamental law under which they are to live.

The effort has been and is now being made in this State by certain postmasters and other federal office holders, to make a test of faith on the support of the English bill. These men are now making speeches all over the State against me and in favor of Lincoln, either directly or indirectly, because I would not sanction a discrimination between slave and free States by voting for the English bill. But while that bill is made a test in Illinois for the purpose of breaking up the Democratic organization in this State, how is it in the other States? Go to Indiana, and there you find English himself, the author of the English bill, who is a candidate for re-election to Congress, has been forced by public opinion to abandon his own darling project, and to give a promise that he will vote for the admission of Kansas at once, whenever she forms a constitution in pursuance of law, and ratifies it by a majority vote of her people. Not only is this the case with English himself, but I am informed that every Democratic candidate for Congress in Indiana takes that same ground. Pass to Ohio, and there you find that Groesbeck, and Pendleton, and Cox,[3] and all the other anti-Lecompton men who stood shoulder to shoulder with me against the Lecompton constitution, but voted for the English bill, now repudiate it and take the same ground that I do on that question. So it is with the Joneses[4] and others of Pennsylvania, and so it is with every other Lecompton Democrat in the free States. They now abandon even the English bill, and come back to the true platform which I proclaimed at the time in the Senate, and upon which the Democracy of Illinois now stand. And yet, notwithstanding the fact, that every Lecompton and anti-Lecompton Democrat in the free States has abandoned the English bill, you are told that it is to be made a test upon me, while the power and patronage of the government are all exerted to elect men to Congress in the other States who occupy the same position with reference to it that I do. It seems that my political offence consists in the fact that I first did not vote for the English bill, and thus pledge myself to keep Kansas out of the Union until she has a population of 93,420, and then return home, violate that pledge, repudiate the bill, and take the opposite ground. If I had done this, perhaps the administration would now be advocating my re-election, as it is that of the others who have pur-

[3] Representatives William S. Groesbeck, George H. Pendleton, and Samuel S. Cox.

[4] Representatives Jehu G. Jones and Owen Jones.

sued this course. I did not choose to give that pledge, for the reason that I did not intend to carry out that principle. I never will consent, for the sake of conciliating the frowns of power, to pledge myself to do that which I do not intend to perform. I now submit the question to you as my constituency, whether I was not right, first, in resisting the adoption of the Lecompton constitution; and secondly, in resisting the English bill. (An universal "Yes," from the crowd.) I repeat, that I opposed the Lecompton constitution because it was not the act and deed of the people of Kansas, and did not embody their will. I denied the right of any power on earth under our system of government to force a constitution on an unwilling people. (Hear, hear; that's the doctrine and cheers.) There was a time when some men could pretend to believe that the Lecompton constitution embodied the will of the people of Kansas, but that time has passed. The question was referred to the people of Kansas under the English bill last August, and then, at a fair election, they rejected the Lecompton constitution by a vote of from eight to ten against it to one in its favor. Since it has been voted down by so overwhelming a majority, no man can pretend that it was the act and deed of that people. (That's so; and cheers.) I submit the question to you whether or not if it had not been for me that constitution would have been crammed down the throats of the people of Kansas against their consent. (It would, it would. Hurra for Douglas; three cheers for Douglas, &c.) While at least ninety-nine out of every hundred people here present agree that I was right in defeating that project, yet my enemies use the fact that I did defeat it by doing right, to break me down and put another man in the U.S. Senate in my place. (No, no, you'll be returned; three cheers, &c.) The very men who acknowledge that I was right in defeating Lecompton, now form an alliance with federal office holders, professed Lecompton men, to defeat me, because I did right. (It can't be done.) My political opponent, Mr. Lincoln, has no hope on earth, and has never dreamed that he had a chance of success, were it not for the aid he is receiving from federal office holders, who are using their influence and the patronage of the government against me in revenge for my having defeated the Lecompton constitution. (Hear him; and applause.) What do you Republicans think of a political organization that will try to make an unholy and unnatural combination with its professed foes to beat a man merely because he has done right? (Shame on it.) You know such is the fact with regard to your own party. You know that the axe of decapitation is suspended over every man in office in Illinois, and the terror of proscription is threatened every Democrat by the present administration unless he supports the Republican ticket in preference to my Democratic associates and myself. (The people are with you. Let them threaten, &c.) I could find an instance in the postmaster of the city of Galesburg, and in every other postmaster in this vicinity, all of whom have been stricken down simply because they discharged the duties of their offices honestly, and supported the regular Democratic ticket in this State in the right. The Republican party is availing itself of every unworthy means in the present contest to carry the election, because its leaders know that if they let this chance slip they will never have another, and their hopes of making this a Republican State will be blasted forever.

Now, let me ask you whether the country has any interest in sustaining this organization known as the Republican party? That party is unlike all other political organizations in this country. All other parties have been national in their character—have avowed their principles alike in the slave and the free States, in Kentucky as well as in Illinois, in Louisiana as well as in Massachusetts. Such was the case with the old Whig party, and such was and is the case with the Democratic party. Whigs and Democrats could proclaim their principles boldly and fearlessly in the north and in the south, in the east and in the west, wherever the constitution ruled and the American flag waved over American soil.

But now you have a sectional organization, a party which appeals to the northern section of the Union against the southern, a party which appeals to northern passion, northern pride, northern ambition, and northern prejudices, against southern people, the southern States and southern institutions. The leaders of that party hope that they will be able to unite the northern States in one great sectional party, and inasmuch as the North is the strongest section, that they will thus be enabled to out vote, conquer, govern, and control the South. Hence you find that they now make speeches advocating principles and measures which cannot be defended in any slaveholding State of this Union. Is there a Republican residing in Galesburg who can travel into Kentucky and carry his principles with him across the Ohio? (No.) What Republican from Massachusetts can visit the Old Dominion without leaving his principles behind him when he crosses Mason and Dixon's line? Permit me to say to you in perfect good humor, but in all sincerity, that no political creed is sound which cannot be proclaimed fearlessly in every State of this Union where the Federal Constitution is not the supreme law of the land. ("That's so," and cheers.) Not only is this Republican party unable to proclaim its principles alike in the North and in the South, in the free States and in the slave States, but it cannot even proclaim them in the same forms and give them the same strength and meaning in all parts of the same State. My friend Lincoln finds its extremely difficult to manage a debate in the centre part of the State, where there is a mixture of men from the North and the South. In the extreme northern part of Illinois he can proclaim as bold and radical abolitionism as ever Giddings, Lovejoy, or Garrison enunciated, but when he gets down a little further South he claims that he is an old line Whig, (great laughter,) a disciple of Henry Clay, ("Singleton[5] says he defeated Clay's nomination for the Presidency," and cries of "that's so,") and declares that he still adheres to the old line Whig creed, and has nothing whatever to do with Abolitionism, or negro equality, or negro citizenship. ("Hurrah for Douglas.") I once before hinted this of Mr. Lincoln in a public speech, and at Charleston he defied me to show that there was any difference between his speeches in the North and in the South, and that they were not in strict harmony. I will now call your attention to two of them, and you can then say whether you would be apt to believe that the same man ever uttered both. (Laughter and cheers.) In a speech in reply to me at Chicago in July last, Mr. Lincoln, in speaking of the equality of the negro with the white man used the following language:

> I should like to know, if taking this old Declaration of Independence, which declares that all men are equal upon principle, and making exceptions to it, where will it stop? If one man says it does not mean a negro, why may not another man say it does not mean another man? (Laughter.) If the Declaration is not the truth, let us get the statute book in which we find it and tear it out. Who is so bold as to do it? If it is not true, let us tear it out.

You find that Mr. Lincoln there proposed that if the doctrine of the Declaration of Independence, declaring all men to be born equal, did not include the negro and put him on an equality with the white man, that we should take the statute book and tear it out. (Laughter and cheers.) He there took the ground that the negro race is included in the Declaration of Independence as the equal of the white race, and that there could be no such thing as a distinction in the races, making one superior and the other inferior. I read now from the same speech:

> My friends, [he says,] I have detained you about as long as I desire to do, and I have only to say let us discard all this quibbling about this man and the other man—this race and that race, and the other race being inferior and therefore they must be placed in an inferior position, discarding our standard that we have left us. Let us discard

[5] James W. Singleton of Brown County, Illinois, a Whig turned Democrat.

all these things, and unite as one people throughout this land, until we shall once more stand up declaring that all men are created equal.

("That's right," &c.)

Yes, I have no doubt that you think it is right, but the Lincoln men down in Coles, Tazewell and Sangamon counties *do not* think it is right. (Immense applause and laughter. Hit him again, &c.) In the conclusion of the same speech, talking to the Chicago Abolitionists, he said: "I leave you, hoping that the lamp of liberty will burn in your bosoms until there shall no longer be a doubt that all men are created free and equal." (Good, good, shame, &c.) Well, you say good to that, and you are going to vote for Lincoln because he holds that doctrine. ("That's so.") I will not blame you for supporting him on that ground, but I will show you in immediate contrast with that doctrine, what Mr. Lincoln said down in Egypt in order to get votes in that locality where they do not hold to such a doctrine. In a joint discussion between Mr. Lincoln and myself, at Charleston, I think, on the 18th of last month, Mr. Lincoln referring to this subject used the following language:

> I will say then, that I am not nor never have been in favor of bringing about in any way, the social and political equality of the white and black races; that I am not nor never have been in favor of making voters of the free negroes, or jurors, or qualifying them to hold office, or having them to marry with white people. I will say in addition, that there is a physical difference between the white and black races, which, I suppose, will forever forbid the two races living together upon terms of social and political equality, and inasmuch as they cannot so live, that while they do remain together, there must be the position of superior and inferior, that I as much as any other white man am in favor of the superior position being assigned to the white man.

(Good for Lincoln.)

Fellow-citizens, here you find men hurrahing for Lincoln and saying that he did right, when in one part of the State he stood up for negro equality, and in another part for political effect, discarded the doctrine and declared that there always must be a superior and inferior race. (They're not men. Put them out, &c.) Abolitionists up north are expected and required to vote for Lincoln because he goes for the equality of the races, holding that by the Declaration of Independence the white man and the negro were created equal and endowed by the Divine law with that equality, and down south he tells the old Whigs, the Kentuckians, Virginians, and Tennesseeans, that there is a physical difference in the races, making one superior and the other inferior, and that he is in favor of maintaining the superiority of the white race over the negro. Now, how can you reconcile those two positions of Mr.

Lincoln? He is to be voted for in the south as a pro-slavery man, and he is to be voted for in the north as an Abolitionist. ("Give it to him." "Hit him again.") Up here he thinks it is all nonsense to talk about a difference betweeen the races, and says that we must "discard all quibbling about this race and that race and the other race being inferior, and therefore they must be placed in an inferior position." Down south he makes this "quibble" about this race and that race and the other race being inferior as the creed of his party, and declares that the negro can never be elevated to the position of the white man. You find that his political meetings are called by different names in different counties in the State. Here they are called Republican meetings, but in old Tazewell, where Lincoln made a speech last Tuesday, he did not address a *Republican* meeting, but "a grand rally of the *Lincoln men*." (Great laughter.) There are very few Republicans there, because Tazewell county is filled with old Virginians and Kentuckians, all of whom are Whigs or Democrats, and if Mr. Lincoln had called an Abolition or Republican meeting there, he would not get many votes. (Laughter.) Go down into Egypt and you find that he and his party are operating under an alias there, which his friend Trumbull has given them, in order that they may cheat the people. When I was down in Monroe county a few weeks ago addressing the people, I saw handbills posted announcing that Mr. Trumbull was going to speak in behalf of Lincoln, and what do you think the name of his party was there? Why the "*Free Democracy*." (Great laughter.) Mr. Trumbull and Mr. Jehu Baker were announced to address the Free Democracy of Monroe county, and the bill was signed "Many Free Democrats." The reason that Lincoln and his party adopted the name of "Free Democracy" down there was because Monroe county has always been an old fashioned Democratic county, and hence it was necessary to make the people believe that they were Democrats, sympathized with them, and were fighting for Lincoln as Democrats. (That's it, &c.) Come up to Springfield, where Lincoln now lives and always has lived, and you find that the convention of his party which assembled to nominate candidates for legislature, who are expected to vote for him if elected, dare not adopt the name of Republican, but assembled under the title of "all opposed to the Democracy." (Laughter and cheers.) Thus you find that Mr. Lincoln's creed cannot travel through even one half of the counties of this State, but that it changes its hues and becomes lighter and lighter, as it travels from the extreme North, until it is nearly white, when it reaches the extreme south end of the State. (That's so, it's true, etc.) I ask you, my friends, why cannot Republicans avow their principles alike everywhere? I would despise myself if I thought that I was procuring your votes by concealing my opinions, and by avowing one set of principles in one part of the State, and a different set in another part. If I do not truly and honorably represent your feelings and principles, then I ought not to be your Senator; and I will never conceal my opinions, or modify or change them a hair's breadth in order to get votes. I tell you that this Chicago doctrine of Lincoln's—declaring that the negro and the white man are made equal by the Declaration of Independence and by Divine Providence—is a monstrous heresy. (That's so, and terrific applause.) The signers of the Declaration of Independence never dreamed of the negro when they were writing that document. They referred to white men, to men of European birth and European descent, when they declared the equality of all men. I see a gentleman there in the crowd shaking his head. Let me remind him that when Thomas Jefferson wrote that document he was the owner, and so continued until his death, of a large number of slaves. Did he intend to say in that Declaration that his negro slaves, which he held and treated as property, were created his equals by Divine law, and that he was violating the law of God every day of his life by holding them as slaves? ("No, no.") It must be borne in mind that when that Declaration was put forth every one of the thirteen colonies were slaveholding colonies, and every man who signed that instrument represented a slaveholding constituency. Recollect, also, that no one of them emancipated his slaves, much less put them on an equality with himself, after he signed the Declaration. On the contrary, they all continued to hold their negroes as slaves during the revolutionary war. Now, do you believe—are you willing to have it said—that every man who signed the Declaration of Independence declared the negro his equal, and then was hypocrite enough to continue to hold him as a slave, in violation of what he believed to be the divine law? ("No, no.") And yet when you say that the Declaration of Independence includes the negro, you charge the signers of it with hypocrisy.

I say to you, frankly, that in my opinion this government was made by our fathers on the white basis. It was made by white men for the benefit of white men and their posterity forever, and was intended to be administered by white men in all time to come. (That's so, and cheers.) But while I hold that under our constitution and political system the negro is not a citizen, cannot be a citizen, and ought not to be a citizen, it does not follow by any means that he should be a slave. On the contrary it does follow that the negro, as an inferior race, ought to possess every right, every privilege, every immunity which he can safely exercise consistent with the safety of the society in which he lives. (That's so, and cheers.) Humanity requires, and Christianity commands that you shall extend to every inferior being, and every dependent being, all the privileges, immunities and advantages which can be granted to them consistent with the safety of society. If you ask me the nature and extent of these privileges, I answer that that is a question which the people of each State must decide for themselves. (That's it.) Illinois has decided that question for herself. We have said that in this State the negro shall not be a slave, nor shall he be a citizen. Kentucky holds a different doctrine. New York holds one different from either, and Maine one different from all. Virginia, in her policy on this question, differs in many respects from the others, and so on, until there is hardly two States whose policy is exactly alike in regard to the relation of the white man and the negro. Nor can you reconcile them and make them alike. Each State must do as it pleases. Illinois had as much right to adopt the policy which we have on that subject as Kentucky had to adopt a different policy. The great principle of this government is that each State has the right to do as it pleases on all these questions, and no other State, or power on earth has the right to interfere with us, or complain of us merely because our system differs from theirs. In the compromise measures of 1850, Mr. Clay declared that this great principle ought to exist in the territories as well as in the States, and I reasserted his doctrine in the Kansas and Nebraska bill in 1854.

But Mr. Lincoln cannot be made to understand, and those who are determined to vote for him, no matter whether he is a pro-slavery man in the south and a negro equality advocate in the north, cannot be made to understand how it is that in a territory the people can do as they please on the slavery question under the Dred Scott decision. Let us see whether I cannot explain it to the satisfaction of all impartial men. Chief Justice Taney has said in his opinion in the Dred Scott case, that a negro slave being property, stands on an equal footing with other property, and that the owner may carry them into United States territory the same as he does other property. (That's so.) Suppose any two of you, neighbors, should conclude to go to Kansas, one carrying $100,000 worth of negro slaves and the other $100,000 worth of mixed merchandise, including quantities of liquors. You both agree that under that decision you may carry your property to Kansas, but when you get it there, the merchant who is possessed of the liquors is met by the Maine liquor law, which prohibits the sale or use of his property, and the owner of the slaves is met by equally unfriendly legislation, which makes his property worthless after he gets it there. What is the right to carry your property into the territory worth to either, when unfriendly legislation in the territory renders it worthless after you get it there? The slaveholder when he gets his slaves there finds that there is no local law to protect him in holding them, no slave code, no police regulation maintaining and supporting him in his right, and he discovers at once that the absence of such friendly legislation excludes his property from the territory, just as irresistibly as if there was a positive constitutional prohibition excluding it. Thus you find it is with any kind of property in a territory, it depends for its protection on the local and municipal law. If the people of a territory want slavery, they make friendly legislation to introduce it, but if they do not want it, they withhold all protection from it, and then it cannot exist there. Such was the view taken on the subject by different Southern men when the Nebraska bill passed. See the speech of Mr. Orr, of South Carolina, the present Speaker of the House of Representatives of Congress made at that time, and there you will find this whole doctrine argued out at full length. Read the speeches of other southern congressmen, Senators and Representatives, made in 1854, and you will find that they took the same view of the subject as Mr. Orr—that slavery could never be forced on a people who did not want it. I hold that in this country there is no power on the face of the globe that can force any institution on an unwilling people. The great fundamental principle of our government is that the people of each State and each territory shall be left perfectly free to decide for themselves what shall be the nature and character of their institutions. When this government was made, it was based on that principle. At the time of its formation there were twelve slaveholding States and one free State in this Union. Suppose this doctrine of Mr. Lincoln and the Republicans, of uniformity of the laws of all the States on the subject of slavery, had prevailed; suppose Mr. Lincoln himself had been a member of the convention which framed the constitution, and that he had risen in that august body, and addressing the father of his country, had said as he did at Springfield:

> A house divided against itself cannot stand. I believe this government cannot endure permanently half slave and half free. I do not expect the Union to be dissolved—I do not expect the house to fall, but I do expect it will cease to be divided. It will become all one thing or all the other.

What do you think would have been the result? (Hurrah for Douglas.) Suppose he had made that convention believe that doctrine and they had acted upon it, what do you think would have been the result? Do you believe that the one free State would have outvoted the twelve slaveholding States, and thus abolished slavery? (No! no! and cheers.) On the contrary, would not the twelve slaveholding States have outvoted the one free State, and under his doctrine have fastened slavery by an irrevocable constitutional provision upon every inch of the American Republic? Thus you see that the doctrine he now advocates, if proclaimed at the beginning of the government, would have established slavery everywhere throughout the American continent, and are you willing, now that we have the majority section, to exercise a power which we never would have submitted to when we were in the minority? ("No, no," and great applause.) If the Southern States had attempted to control our institutions, and make the States all slave when they had the power, I ask would you have submitted to it? If you would not, are you willing now that we have become the strongest under that great principle of self-government that allows each State to do as it pleases—to attempt to control the Southern institutions? ("No, no.") Then, my friends, I say to you that there is but one path of peace in this republic, and that is to administer this government as our fathers made it, divided into free and slave States, allowing each State to decide for itself whether it wants slavery or not. If Illinois will settle the slavery question for herself, mind her own business and let her neighbors alone, we will be at peace with Kentucky, and every other Southern State. If every other State in the Union will do the same there will be peace between the North and the South, and in the whole Union.

I am told that my time has expired. (Nine cheers for Douglas.)

MR. LINCOLN'S REPLY.

Mr. Lincoln was received as he came forward with three enthusiastic cheers, coming from every part of the vast assembly. After silence was restored, Mr. Lincoln said:

MY FELLOW CITIZENS—A very large portion of the speech which Judge Douglas has addressed to you has previously been delivered and put in print. [Laughter.] I do not mean that for a hit upon the Judge at all. [Renewed laughter.] If I had not been interrupted, I was going to say that such an answer as I was able to make to a very large portion of it, had already been more than once made and published. There has been an opportunity afforded to the public to see our respective views upon the topics discussed in a large portion of the speech which he has just delivered. I make these remarks for the purpose of excusing myself for not passing over the entire ground that the Judge has traversed. I however desire to take up some of the points that he has attended to, and ask your attention to them, and I shall follow him backwards upon some notes which I have taken, reversing the order by beginning where he concluded.

The Judge has alluded to the Declaration of Independence, and insisted that negroes are not included in that Declaration; and that it is a slander upon the framers of that instrument, to suppose that negroes were meant therein; and he asks you: Is it possible to believe that Mr. Jefferson, who penned the immortal paper, could have supposed himself applying the language of that instrument to the negro race, and yet held a portion of that race in slavery? Would he not at once have freed them? I only have to remark upon this part of the Judge's speech, (and that, too, very briefly, for I shall not detain myself, or you, upon that point for any great length of time,) that I believe the entire records of the world, from the date of the Declaration of Independence up to within three years ago, may be searched in vain for one single affirmation, from one single man, that the negro was not included in the Declaration of Independence. I think I may defy Judge Douglas to show that he ever said so, that Washington ever said so, that any President ever said so, that any member of Congress ever said so, or that any living man upon the whole earth ever said so, until the necessities of the present policy of the Democratic party, in regard to slavery, had to invent that affirmation. [Tremendous applause.] And I will remind Judge Douglas and this audience, that while Mr. Jefferson was the owner of slaves, as undoubtedly he was, in speaking upon this very subject, he used the strong language that "he trembled for his country when he remembered that God was just;" and I will offer the highest premium in my power to Judge Douglas if he will show that he, in all his life, ever uttered a sentiment at all akin to that of Jefferson. [Great applause and cries of "Hit him again," "good," "good."]

The next thing to which I will ask your attention is the Judge's comments upon the fact, as he assumes it to be, that we cannot call our public meetings as Republican meetings; and he instances Tazewell county as one of the places where the friends of Lincoln have called a public meeting and have not dared to name it a Republican meeting. He instances Monroe county as another where Judge Trumbull and Jehu Baker addressed the persons whom the Judge assumes to be the friends of Lincoln, calling them the "Free

Democracy." I have the honor to inform Judge Douglas that he spoke in that very county of Tazewell last Saturday, and I was there on Tuesday last, and when he spoke there he spoke under a call not venturing to use the word "Democrat." [Cheers and laughter.] (Turning to Judge Douglas.) What do you think of this? [Immense applause and roars of laughter.]

So again, there is another thing to which I would ask the Judge's attention upon this subject. In the contest of 1856 his party delighted to call themselves together as the "National Democracy," but now, if there should be a notice put up anywhere for a meeting of the "National Democracy," Judge Douglas and his friends would not come. [Laughter.] They would not suppose themselves invited. [Renewed laughter and cheers.] They would understand that it was a call for those hateful Postmasters whom he talks about. [Uproarious laughter.]

Now a few words in regard to these extracts from speeches of mine, which Judge Douglas has read to you, and which he supposes are in very great contrast to each other. Those speeches have been before the public for a considerable time, and if they have any inconsistency in them, if there is any conflict in them the public have been able to detect it. When the Judge says, in speaking on this subject, that I make speeches of one sort for the people of the Northern end of the State, and of a different sort for the Southern people, he assumes that I do not understand that my speeches will be put in print and read North and South. I knew all the while that the speech that I made at Chicago and the one I made at Jonesboro and the one at Charleston, would all be put in print and all the reading and intelligent men in the community would see them and know all about my opinions. And I have not supposed, and do not now suppose, that there is any conflict whatever between them. ["They are all good speeches!" "Hurrah for Lincoln!"] But the Judge will have it that if we do not confess that there is a sort of inequality between the white and black races, which justifies us in making them slaves, we must, then, insist that there is a degree of equality that requires us to make them our wives. [Loud applause, and cries, "Give it to him;" "Hit him again."] Now, I have all the while taken a broad distinction in regard to that matter; and that is all there is in these different speeches which he arrays here, and the entire reading of either of the speeches will show that that distinction was made. Perhaps by taking two parts of the same speech, he could have got up as much of a conflict as the one he has found. I have all the while maintained, that in so far as it should be insisted that there was an equality between the white and black races that should produce a perfect social and political equality, it was an impossibility. This you have seen in my printed speeches, and with it I have said, that in their right to "life, liberty and the pursuit of happiness," as proclaimed in that old Declaration, the inferior races are our equals. [Long-continued cheering.] And these declarations I have constantly made in reference to the abstract moral question, to contemplate and consider when we are legislating about any new country which is not already cursed with the actual presence of the evil—slavery. I have never manifested any impatience with the necessities that spring from the actual presence of black people amongst us, and the actual existence of slavery amongst us where it does already exist; but I have insisted that, in legislating for new countries, where it does not exist, there is no just rule other than that of moral and abstract right! With reference to those new countries, those maxims as to the right of a people to "life, liberty and the pursuit of happiness," were the just rules to be constantly referred to. There is no misunderstanding this, except by men interested to misunderstand it. [Applause.] I take it that I have to address an intelligent and reading community, who will peruse what I say, weigh it, and then judge whether I advance improper or unsound views, or whether I advance hypocritical, and deceptive, and contrary views in different portions of the country. I believe myself to be guilty of no such thing as the latter, though, of course, I cannot claim that I am entirely free from all error in the opinions I advance.

The Judge has also detained us a while in regard to the distinction between his party and our party. His he assumes to be a national party—ours, a sectional one. He does this in asking the question whether this country has any interest in the maintenance of the Republican party? He assumes that our party is altogether sectional—that the party to which he adheres is national; and the argument is, that no party can be a rightful party—can be based upon rightful principles—unless it can announce its principles everywhere. I presume that Judge Douglas could not go into Russia and announce the doctrine of our national democracy; he could not denounce the doctrine of kings, and emperors, and monarchies, in Russia; and it may be true of this country, that in some places we may not be able to proclaim a doctrine as clearly true as the truth of democracy, because there is a section so directly opposed to it that they will not tolerate us in doing so. Is it the true test of the soundness of a doctrine, that in some places people won't let you proclaim it? [No, no, no.] Is that the way to test the truth of any doctrine? [No, no, no.] Why, I understood that at one time the people of Chicago would not let Judge Douglas preach a certain favorite doctrine of his. [Laughter and cheers.] I commend to his consideration the question, whether he takes that as a test of the unsoundness of what he wanted to preach. [Loud cheers.]

There is another thing to which I wish to ask attention for a little while on this occasion. What has always been the evidence brought forward to prove that the Republican party is a sectional party? The main one was that in the southern portion of the Union the people did not let the Republicans proclaim their doctrine amongst them. That has been the main evidence brought forward—that they had no supporters, or substantially none, in the Slave States. The South have not taken hold of our principles as we announce them; nor does Judge Douglas now grapple with those principles. We have a Republican State Platform, laid down in Springfield in June last, stating our position all the way through the questions before the country. We are now far advanced in this canvass. Judge Douglas and I have made perhaps forty speeches apiece, and we have now for the fifth time met face to face in debate, and up to this day I have not found either Judge Douglas or any friend of his taking hold of the Republican platform or laying his finger upon anything in it that is wrong. [Cheers.] I ask you all to recollect that. Judge Douglas turns away from the platform of principles to the fact that he can find people somewhere who will not allow us to announce those principles. [Applause.] If he had great confidence that our principles were wrong, he would take hold of them and demonstrate them to be wrong. But he does not do so. The only evidence he has of their being wrong is in the fact that there are people who won't allow us to preach them. I ask again, is that the way to test the soundness of a doctrine? [Cries of "No," "No."]

I ask his attention also to the fact that by the rule of nationality he is himself fast becoming sectional. [Great cheers and laughter.] I ask his attention to the fact that his speeches would not go as current now south of the Ohio River as they have formerly gone there. [Loud cheers.] I ask his attention to the fact that he felicitates himself to-day that all the Democrats of the Free States are agreeing with him, [applause,] while he omits to tell us that the Democrats of any Slave State agree with him. If he has not thought of this, I commend to his consideration the evidence in his own declaration, on this day, of his becoming sectional too. [Immense cheering.] I see it rapidly approaching. Whatever may be the result of this ephemeral contest between Judge Douglas and myself, I see the day rapidly approaching when his pill of sectionalism, which he has been thrusting down the throats of Republicans for years past, will be crowded down his own throat. [Tremendous applause.]

Now in regard to what Judge Douglas said (in the beginning of his speech) about the Compromise of 1850, containing the principle of the Nebraska bill, although I have often presented my views upon that subject, yet as I have not done so in this canvass, I will, if you please, detain you a little with them. I have always maintained, so far as I was able, that there was nothing of the principle of the Nebraska bill in the compromise of 1850 at all—nothing whatever. Where can you find the principle of the Nebraska bill in that compromise? If anywhere, in the two pieces of the compromise organizing the Territories of New Mexico and Utah. It was expressly provided in these two acts, that, when they came to be admitted into the Union, they should be admitted with or without slavery, as they should choose, by their own constitutions. Nothing was said in either of those acts as to what was to be done in relation to slavery during the territorial existence of those territories, while Henry Clay constantly made the declaration, (Judge Douglas recognizing him as a leader) that, in his opinion, the old Mexican laws would control that question during the territorial existence, and that these old Mexican laws excluded slavery. How can that be used as a principle for declaring that during the territorial existence as well as at the time of framing the constitution, the people, if you please, might have slaves if they wanted them? I am not discussing the question whether it is right or wrong; but how are the New Mexican and Utah laws patterns for the Nebraska bill? I maintain that the organization of Utah and New Mexico *did not* establish a general principle at all. It had no feature of establishing a general principle. The acts to which I have referred were a part of a general system of Compromises. They did not lay down what was proposed as a regular policy for the Territories; only an agreement in this particular case to do in that way, because other things were done that were to be a compensation for it. They were allowed to come in in that shape, because in another way it was paid for—considering that as a part of that system of measures called the Compromise of 1850, which finally included half a dozen acts. It included the admission of California as a free State, which was kept out of the Union for half a year because it had formed a free Constitution. It included the settlement of the boundary of Texas, which had been undefined before, which was in itself a slavery question; for, if you pushed the line farther west, you made Texas larger, and made more slave territory; while, if you drew the line towards the east, you narrowed the boundary and diminished the domain of slavery, and by so much increased free territory. It included the abolition of the slave trade in the District of Columbia. It included the passage of a new Fugitive Slave Law. All these things were put together, and though passed in separate acts, were nevertheless in legislation, (as the speeches at the time will show,) made to depend upon each other. Each got votes, with the understanding that the other measures were to pass, and by this system of compromise, in that series of measures, those two bills—the New Mexico and Utah bills—were passed; and I say for that reason they could not be taken as models, framed upon their own intrinsic principle, for all future Territories. And I have the evidence of this in the fact that Judge Douglas, a year afterwards, or more than a year afterwards, perhaps, when he first introduced bills for the purpose of framing new Territories, did not attempt to follow these bills of New Mexico and Utah; and even when he introduced this Nebraska bill, I think you will discover that he did not exactly follow them. But I do not wish to dwell at great length upon this branch of the discussion. My own opinion is, that a thorough investigation will show most plainly that the New Mexico and Utah bills were part of a system of compromise, and not designed as patterns for future territorial legislation; and that this Nebraska bill did not follow them as a pattern at all.

The Judge tells, in proceeding, that he is opposed to making any odious distinctions between Free and Slave States. I am altogether unaware that the Republicans are in favor of making any odious distinctions between the Free and Slave States. But there still is a difference, I think, between Judge Douglas and the Republicans in this. I suppose that the real difference between Judge Douglas and his friends, and the Republicans on the contrary, is that the Judge is not in favor of making any difference between Slavery and Liberty—that he is in favor of eradicating, of pressing out of view, the questions of preference in this country for Free over Slave institutions; and consequently every sentiment he utters discards the idea that there is any wrong in Slavery. Everything that emanates from him or his coadjutors in their course of policy, carefully excludes the thought that there is anything wrong in Slavery. All their arguments, if you will consider them, will be seen to exclude the thought that there is anything whatever wrong in Slavery. If you will take the Judge's speeches, and select the short and pointed sentences expressed by him—as his declaration that he "don't care whether Slavery is voted up or down"—you will see at once that this is perfectly logical, if you do not admit that Slavery is wrong. If you do admit that it is wrong, Judge Douglas cannot logically say that he don't care whether a wrong is voted up or voted down. Judge Douglas declares that if any community want Slavery they have a right to have it. He can say that logically, if he says that there is no wrong in Slavery; but if you admit that there is a wrong in it, he cannot logically say that anybody has a right to do wrong. He insists that, upon the score of equality, the owners of slaves and owners of property—of horses and every other sort of property—should be alike and hold them alike in a new Territory. That is perfectly logical, if the two species of property are alike and are equally founded in right. But if you admit that one of them is wrong, you cannot institute any equality between right and wrong. And from this difference of sentiment—the belief on the part of one that the institution is wrong, and a policy springing from that belief which looks to the arrest of the enlargement of that wrong; and this other sentiment, that it is no wrong, and a policy sprung from that sentiment which will tolerate no idea of preventing that wrong from growing larger, and looks to there never being an end of it through all the existence of things,—arises the real difference between Judge Douglas and his friends, on the one hand, and the Republicans on the other. Now, I confess myself as belonging to that class in the country who contemplate slavery as a moral, social and political evil, having due regard for its actual existence amongst us and the difficulties of getting rid of it in any satisfactory way, and to all the constitutional obligations which have been thrown about it; but, nevertheless, desire a policy that looks to the prevention of it as a wrong, and looks hopefully to the time when as a wrong it may come to an end. [Great applause.]

Judge Douglas has again, for, I believe, the fifth time, if not the seventh, in my presence, reiterated his charge of a conspiracy or combination between the National Democrats and Republicans. What evidence Judge Douglas has upon this subject I know not, inasmuch as he never favors us with any. [Laughter and cheers.] I have said upon a former occasion, and I do not choose to suppress it now, that I have no objection to the division in the Judge's party. [Cheers.] He got it up himself. It was all his and their work. He had, I think, a great deal more to do with the steps that led to the Lecompton Constitution than Mr. Buchanan had [applause]; though at last, when they reached it, they quarrelled over it, and their friends divided upon it. [Applause.] I am very free to confess to Judge Douglas that I have no objection to the division, [loud applause and laughter]; but I defy the Judge to show any evidence that I have in any way promoted that division, unless he insists on being a witness himself in merely saying so. [Laughter.] I can give all fair friends of Judge Douglas here to understand exactly the view that Republicans take in regard to that division. Don't you remember how two years ago the opponents of the Democratic party were divided between Fremont and Fillmore? I guess you do. ["Yes, sir, we remember it mighty well."] Any Democrat who remembers that division, will remember also that he was at the time very glad of it, [laughter,] and then he will be able to see all there is between the National Democrats and the Republicans. What we now think of the two divisions of Democrats, you then thought of the Fremont and Fillmore divisions. [Great cheers.] That is all there is of it.

But, if the Judge continues to put forward the declaration that there is an unholy and unnatural alliance between the Republicans and the National Democrats, I now want to enter my protest against receiving him as an entirely competent witness upon that subject. [Loud cheers.] I want to call to the Judge's attention an attack he made upon me in the first one of these debates, at Ottawa, on the 21st of August. In order to fix extreme Abolitionism upon me, Judge Douglas read a set of resolutions which he declared had been passed by a Republican State Convention, in Oct., 1854, at Springfield, Illinois, and he declared I had taken part in that Convention. It turned out that although a few men calling themselves an Anti-Nebraska State Convention had sat at Springfield about that time, yet neither did I take any part in it, nor did it pass the resolutions or any such resolutions as Judge Douglas read. [Great applause.] So apparent had it become that the resolutions which he read had not been passed at Springfield at all, nor by a State Convention in which I had taken part, that seven days afterwards, at Freeport, Judge Douglas declared that he had been misled by Charles H. Lanphier, editor of the *State Register*, and Thomas L. Harris, member of Congress in that District, and he promised in that speech that when he went to Springfield he would investigate the matter. Since then Judge Douglas has been to Springfield, and I presume has made the investigation; but a month has passed since he has been there, and so far as I know, he has made no report of the result of his investigation. [Great applause.] I have waited as I think sufficient time for the report of that investigation, and I have some curiosity to see and hear it. [Applause.] A fraud—an absolute forgery was committed, and the perpetration of it was traced to the three—Lanphier, Harris and Douglas. [Applause and laughter.] Whether it can be narrowed in any way so as to exonerate any one of them, is what Judge Douglas' report would probably show. [Applause and laughter.]

It is true that the set of resolutions read by Judge Douglas were published in the Illinois *State Register* on the 16th Oct., 1854, as being the resolutions of an Anti-Nebraska Convention, which had sat in that same month of October, at Springfield. But it is also true that the publication in the *Register* was a forgery then, [cheers], and the question is still behind, which of the three, if not all of them, committed that forgery? [Great applause.] The idea that it was done by mistake, is absurd. The article in the Illinois *State Register* contains part of the real proceedings of that Springfield Convention, showing that the writer of the article had the real proceedings before him, and purposely threw out the genuine resolutions passed by the Convention, and fraudulently substituted the others. Lanphier then, as now, was the editor of the *Register*, so that there seems to be but little room for his escape. But then it is to be borne in mind that Lanphier had less interest in the object of that forgery than either of the other two. [Cheers.] The main object of that forgery at that time was to beat Yates and elect Harris to Congress, and that object was known to be exceedingly dear to Judge Douglas at that time. [Laughter.] Harris and Douglas were both in Springfield when the Convention was in session, and although they both left before the fraud appeared in the *Register*, subsequent events show that they have both had their eyes fixed upon that Convention.

The fraud having been apparently successful upon the occasion, both Harris and Douglas have more than once since then been attempting to put it to new uses. As the fisherman's wife, whose drowned husband was brought home with his body full of eels,[6] said when she was asked, "What was to be done with him?" "*Take the eels out and set him again.*" [great laughter;] so Harris and Douglas have shown a disposition to take the eels out of that stale fraud by which they gained Harris' election, and set the fraud again more than once. [Tremendous cheering and laughter.] On the 9th of July, 1856, Douglas attempted a repetition of it upon Trumbull on the floor of the Senate of the United States, as will appear from the appendix of the *Congressional Globe* of that date.

On the 9th of August Harris attempted it again upon Norton in

[6] Changed by Lincoln from "husband's body was brought home with the pockets full of eels" to "husband was brought home with his body full of eels."

the House of Representatives, as will appear by the same documents—the appendix to the *Congressional Globe* of that date. On the 21st of August last[7] all three—Lanphier, Douglas and Harris—re-attempted it upon me at Ottawa. [Tremendous applause.] It has been clung to and played out again and again as an exceedingly high trump by this blessed trio. [Roars of laughter and tumultuous applause, "Give it to him," &c.] And now that it has been discovered publicly to be a fraud, we find that Judge Douglas manifests no surprise at it at all. [Laughter, "That's it," "Hit him again."] He makes no complaint of Lanphier who must have known it to be a fraud from the beginning. He, Lanphier and Harris are just as cozy now,[8] and just as active in the concoction of new schemes as they were before the general discovery of this fraud. Now all this is very natural if they are all alike guilty in that fraud, [laughter and cheers,] and it is very unnatural if any one of them is innocent. [Great laughter, "Hit him again," "Hurrah for Lincoln."] Lanphier perhaps insists that the rule of honor among thieves does not quite require him to take all upon himself, [laughter,] and consequently my friend Judge Douglas finds it difficult to make a satisfactory report upon his investigation. [Laughter and applause.] But meanwhile the three are agreed that each is "*a most honorable man.*" [Cheers and explosions of laughter.]

Judge Douglas requires an indorsement of his truth and honor by a re-election to the United States Senate, and he makes and reports against me and against Judge Trumbull day after day charges which we know to be utterly untrue, without for a moment seeming to think that this one unexplained fraud, which he promised to investigate, will be the least drawback to his claim to belief. Harris ditto. He asks a re-election to the lower House of Congress without seeming to remember at all that he is involved in this dishonorable fraud! The Illinois *State Register*, edited by Lanphier, then, as now, the central organ of both Harris and Douglas, continues to din the public ear with this assertion without seeming to suspect that these assertions are at all lacking in title to belief.

After all, the question still recurs upon us, how did that fraud originally get into the *State Register*? Lanphier then as now was the editor of that paper. Lanphier knows. Lanphier cannot be ignorant of how and by whom it was originally concocted. Can he

7 "Last" inserted by Lincoln.

8 Changed by Lincoln from "Both Lanphier and Harris are just as crazy now" to "He, Lanphier and Harris are just as cozy now."

be induced to tell, or if he has told, can Judge Douglas be induced to tell how it originally was concocted? It may be true that Lanphier insists that the two men for whose benefit it was originally devised, shall at least bear their share of it! How that is, I do not know, and while it remains unexplained I hope to be pardoned if I insist that the mere fact of Judge Douglas making charges against Trumbull and myself is not quite sufficient evidence to establish them! [Great cheering. "Hit him again." "Give it to him," &c.]

While we were at Freeport, in one of these joint discussions, I answered certain interrogatories which Judge Douglas had propounded to me, and there in turn propounded some to him, which he in a sort of way answered. The third one of these interrogatories I have with me and wish now to make some comments upon it. It was in these words: "If the Supreme Court of the United States shall decide that the States cannot exclude slavery from their limits, are you in favor of acquiescing in, adhering to and following such decision, as a rule of political action?"

To this interrogatory Judge Douglas made no answer in any just sense of the word. He contented himself with sneering at the thought that it was possible for the Supreme Court ever to make such a decision. He sneered at me for propounding the interrogatory. I had not propounded it without some reflection, and I wish now to address to this audience some remarks upon it.

In the second clause of the sixth article, I believe it is of the Constitution of the United States, we find the following language: "This Constitution and the laws of the United States which shall be made in pursuance thereof; and all treaties made[9] or which shall be made under the authority of the United States, shall be the supreme law of the land; and the judges in every State shall be bound thereby anything in the Constitution or laws of any State to the contrary notwithstanding."

The essence of the Dred Scott case is compressed[10] into the sentence which I will now read: "Now, as we have already said in an earlier part of this opinion, upon a different point, the right of property in a slave is distinctly and expressly affirmed in the Constitution." I repeat it, "*The right of property in a slave is distinctly and expressly affirmed in the Constitution!*" What is it to be "*affirmed*" in the Constitution?[11] Made firm in the Constitution—so made that it cannot be separated from the Constitution without

[9] "The treaties" corrected by Lincoln to "treaties made."

[10] "Comprised" corrected by Lincoln to "compressed."

[11] "What is *affirmed* in the Constitution" corrected by Lincoln to "What is it to be '*affirmed*' in the Constitution?"

breaking the Constitution—durable as the Constitution, and part of the Constitution. Now, remembering the provision of the Constitution which I have read, affirming that that instrument is the supreme law of the land; that the Judges of every State shall be bound by it, any law or Constitution of any State to the contrary notwithstanding; that the right of property in a slave is affirmed in that Constitution, is made, formed into and cannot be separated from it without breaking it; durable as the instrument; part of the instrument;—what follows as a short and even syllogistic argument from it? I think it follows, and I submit to the consideration of men capable of arguing, whether as I state it in syllogistic form the argument has any fault in it:

Nothing in the Constitution or laws of any State can destroy a right distinctly and expressly affirmed in the Constitution of the United States.

The right of property in a slave is distinctly and expressly affirmed in the Constitution of the United States;

Therefore, nothing in the Constitution or laws of any State can destroy the right of property in a slave.

I believe that no fault can be pointed out in that argument; assuming the truth of the premises, the conclusion, so far as I have capacity at all to understand it, follows inevitably. There is a fault in it as I think, but the fault is not in the reasoning; but the falsehood in fact is a fault of the premises. I believe that the right of property in a slave *is not* distinctly and expressly affirmed in the Constitution, and Judge Douglas thinks it *is*. I believe that the Supreme Court and the advocates of that decision may search in vain for the place in the Constitution where the right of property in a slave is distinctly and expressly affirmed.[12] I say, therefore, that I think one of the premises is not true in fact. But it is true with Judge Douglas. It is true with the Supreme Court who pronounced it. They are estopped from denying it, and being estopped from denying it, the conclusion follows that the Constitution of the United States being the supreme law, no constitution or law can interfere with it. It being affirmed in the decision that the right of property in a slave is distinctly and expressly affirmed in the Constitution, the conclusion inevitably follows that no State law or constitution can destroy that right. I then say to Judge Douglas and to all others, that I think it will take a better answer than a sneer to show that those who have said that the right of property in a slave is distinctly and expressly affirmed in the Constitution, are not prepared to show that no constitution or law can destroy

12 "Affirmen" corrected by Lincoln to "affirmed."

that right. I say I believe it will take a far better argument than a mere sneer to show to the minds of intelligent men that whoever has so said, is not prepared, whenever public sentiment is so far advanced as to justify it, to say the other. ["That's so."] This is but an opinion, and the opinion of one very humble man; but it is my opinion that the Dred Scott decision, as it is, never would have been made in its present form if the party that made it had not been sustained previously by the elections. My own opinion is, that the new Dred Scott decision, deciding against the right of the people of the States to exclude slavery, will never be made, if that party is not sustained by the elections. [Cries of "Yes, yes."] I believe, further, that it is just as sure to be made as to-morrow is to come, if that party shall be sustained. ["We won't sustain it, never, never."] I have said, upon a former occasion, and I repeat it now, that the course of argument that Judge Douglas makes use of upon this subject, (I charge not his motives in this), is preparing the public mind for that new Dred Scott decision. I have asked him again to point out to me the reasons for his firm adherence to the Dred Scott decision as it is. I have turned his attention to the fact that General Jackson differed with him in regard to the political obligation of a Supreme Court decision. I have asked his attention to the fact that Jefferson differed with him in regard to the political obligation of a Supreme Court decision. Jefferson said, that "Judges are as honest as other men, and not more so." And he said, substantially, that "whenever a free people should give up in absolute submission to any department of government, retaining for themselves no appeal from it, their liberties were gone." I have asked his attention to the fact that the Cincinnati platform, upon which he says he stands, disregards a time-honored decision of the Supreme Court, in denying the power of Congress to establish a National Bank. I have asked his attention to the fact that he himself was one of the most active instruments at one time in breaking[13] down the Supreme Court of the State of Illinois, because it had made a decision distasteful to him—a struggle ending in the remarkable circumstance of his sitting down as one of the new Judges who were to overslaugh that decision—[loud applause]—getting his title of Judge in that very way. [Tremendous applause and laughter.]

So far in this controversy I can get no answer at all from Judge Douglas upon these subjects. Not one can I get from him, except that he swells himself up and says, "All of us who stand by the decision of the Supreme Court are the friends of the Constitution; all

13 "Backing" corrected by Lincoln to "breaking."

you fellows that dare question it in any way, are the enemies of the Constitution." [Continued laughter and cheers.] Now, in this very devoted adherence to this decision, in opposition to all the great political leaders whom he has recognized as leaders—in opposition to his former self and history, there is something very marked. And the manner in which he adheres to it—not as being right upon the merits, as he conceives (because he did not discuss that at all), but as being absolutely obligatory upon every one simply because of the source from whence it comes—as that which no man can gainsay, whatever it may be,—this is another marked feature of his adherence to that decision. It marks it in this respect, that it commits him to the next decision, whenever it comes, as being as obligatory as this one, since he does not investigate it, and won't inquire whether this opinion is right or wrong. So he takes the next one without inquiring whether *it* is right or wrong. [Applause.] He teaches men this doctrine, and in so doing prepares the public mind to take the next decision when it comes, without any inquiry. In this I think I argue fairly (without questioning motives at all) that Judge Douglas is most ingeniously and powerfully preparing the public mind to take that decision when it comes; and not only so, but he is doing it in various other ways. In these general maxims about liberty—in his assertions that he "don't care whether Slavery is voted up or voted down;" that "whoever wants Slavery has a right to have it;" that "upon principles of equality it should be allowed to go everywhere;" that "there is no inconsistency between free and slave institutions." In this he is also preparing (whether purposely or not), the way for making the institution of Slavery national! [Cries of "Yes," "Yes," "That's so."] I repeat again, for I wish no misunderstanding, that I do not charge that he means it so; but I call upon your minds to inquire, if you were going to get the best instrument you could, and then set it to work in the most ingenious way, to prepare the public mind for this movement, operating in the free States, where there is now an abhorrence of the institution of Slavery, could you find an instrument so capable of doing it as Judge Douglas? or one employed in so apt a way to do it? [Great cheering. Cries of "Hit him again," "That's the doctrine."]

I have said once before, and I will repeat it now, that Mr. Clay, when he was once answering an objection to the Colonization Society, that it had a tendency to the ultimate emancipation of the slaves, said that "those who would repress all tendencies to liberty and ultimate emancipation must do more than put down the benevolent efforts of the Colonization Society—they must go back to the era of our liberty and independence, and muzzle the cannon that thunders its annual joyous return—they must blot out the moral lights around us—they must penetrate the human soul, and eradicate the light of reason and the love of liberty!" And I do think—I repeat, though I said it on a former occasion—that Judge Douglas, and whoever like him teaches that the negro has no share, humble though it may be, in the Declaration of Independence, is going back to the era of our liberty and independence, and, so far as in him lies, muzzling the cannon that thunders its annual joyous return; ["That's so."] that he is blowing[14] out the moral lights around us, when he contends that whoever wants slaves has a right to hold them; that he is penetrating, so far as lies in his power, the human soul, and eradicating the light of reason and the love of liberty, when he is in every possible way preparing the public mind, by his vast influence, for making the institution of slavery perpetual and national. [Great applause, and cries of "Hurrah for Lincoln," "That's the true doctrine."]

There is, my friends, only one other point to which I will call your attention for the remaining time that I have left me, and perhaps I shall not occupy the entire time that I have, as that one point may not take me clear through it.

Among the interrogatories that Judge Douglas propounded to me at Freeport, there was one in about this language: "Are you opposed to the acquisition of any further territory to the United States, unless slavery shall first be prohibited therein?" I answered as I thought, in this way, that I am not generally opposed to the acquistion of additional territory, and that I would support a proposition for the acquisition of additional territory, according as my supporting it was or was not calculated to aggravate this slavery question amongst us. I then proposed to Judge Douglas another interrogatory, which was correlative to that: "Are you in favor of acquiring additional territory in disregard of how it may affect us upon the slavery question?" Judge Douglas answered, that is, in his own way he answered it. [Laughter.] I believe that, although he took a good many words to answer it, it was a little more fully answered than any other. The substance of his answer was, that this country would continue to expand—that it would need additional territory—that it was as absurd to suppose that we could continue upon our present territory, enlarging in population as we are, as it would be to hoop a boy twelve years of age, and expect him to grow to man's size without bursting the hoops. [Laughter.] I believe it was something like that. Consequently he

14 "Blotting" corrected by Lincoln to "blowing."

was in favor of the acquisition of further territory, as fast as we might need it, in disregard of how it might affect the slavery question. I do not say this as giving his exact language, but he said so substantially, and he would leave the question of slavery where the territory was acquired, to be settled by the people of the acquired territory. ["That's the doctrine."] May be it is; let us consider that for a while. This will probably, in the run of things, become one of the concrete manifestations of this slavery question. If Judge Douglas' policy upon this question succeeds, and gets fairly settled down, until all opposition is crushed out, the next thing will be a grab for the territory of poor Mexico, an invasion of the rich lands of South America, then the adjoining islands will follow, each one of which promises additional slave fields. And this question is to be left to the people of those countries for settlement. When we shall get Mexico, I don't know whether the Judge will be in favor of the Mexican people that we get with it settling that question for themselves and all others; because we know the Judge has a great horror for mongrels, [laughter,] and I understand that the people of Mexico are most decidedly a race of mongrels. [Renewed laughter.] I understand that there is not more than one person there out of eight who is pure white, and I suppose from the Judge's previous declaration that when we get Mexico or any considerable portion of it, that he will be in favor of these mongrels settling the question, which would bring him somewhat into collision with his horror of an inferior race.

It is to be remembered, though, that this power of acquiring additional territory is a power confided to the President and Senate of the United States. It is a power not under the control of the Representatives of the people any further than they, the President and the Senate can be considered the representatives of the people. Let me illustrate that by a case we have in our history. When we acquired the territory from Mexico in the Mexican war, the House of Representatives, composed of the immediate representatives of the people all the time insisted that the territory thus to be acquired should be brought in upon condition that slavery should be forever prohibited therein, upon the terms and in the language that slavery had been prohibited from coming into this country. That was insisted upon constantly, and never failed to call forth an assurance that any territory thus acquired should have that prohibition in it, so far as the House of Representatives was concerned. But at last the President and Senate acquired the territory without asking the House of Representatives anything about it, and took it without that prohibition. They have the power of acquiring territory without the immediate representatives of the people being called upon to say anything about it, and thus furnishing a very apt and powerful means of bringing new territory into the Union, and when it is once brought into the country, involving us anew in this slavery agitation. It is, therefore, as I think, a very important question for the consideration of the American people, whether the policy of bringing in additional territory, without considering at all how it will operate upon the safety of the Union in reference to this one great disturbing element in our national politics, shall be adopted as the policy of the country. You will bear in mind that it is to be acquired, according to the Judge's view, as fast as it is needed, and the indefinite part of this proposition is that we have only Judge Douglas and his class of men to decide how fast it is needed. We have no clear and certain way of determining or demonstrating how fast territory is needed by the necessities of the country. Whoever wants to go out filibustering, then, thinks that more territory is needed. Whoever wants wider slave fields, feels sure that some additional territory is needed as slave territory. Then it is as easy to show the necessity of additional slave territory as it is to assert anything that is incapable of absolute demonstration. Whatever motive a man or a set of men may have for making annexation of property or territory, it is very easy to assert, but much less easy to disprove, that it is necessary for the wants of the country.

And now it only remains for me to say that I think it is a very grave question for the people of this Union to consider whether, in view of the fact that this Slavery question has been the only one that has ever endangered our republican institutions—the only one that has ever threatened or menaced a dissolution of the Union—that has ever disturbed us in such a way as to make us fear for the perpetuity of our liberty—in view of these facts, I think it is an exceedingly interesting and important question for this people to consider, whether we shall engage in the policy of acquiring additional territory, discarding altogether from our consideration, while obtaining new territory, the question how it may affect us in regard to this the only endangering element to our liberties and national greatness. The Judge's view has been expressed. I, in my answer to his question, have expressed mine. I think it will become an important and practical question. Our views are before the public. I am willing and anxious that they should consider them fully—that they should turn it about and consider the importance of the question, and arrive at a just conclusion as to whether it is or is not wise in the people of this Union, in the acquisition of new territory, to consider whether it will add to the disturbance that is existing amongst us—whether it will add to the one only danger that has ever threatened the perpetuity of the Union or our own liberties. I think it is extremely important that they shall decide, and rightly decide that question before entering upon that policy.

And now, my friends, having said the little I wish to say upon this head, whether I have occupied the whole of the remnant of my time or not, I believe I could not enter upon any new topic so as to treat it fully without transcending my time, which I would not for a moment think of doing. I give way to Judge Douglas.

Three tremendous cheers for Lincoln from the whole vast audience were given with great enthusiasm, as their favorite retired.

MR. DOUGLAS' REPLY.

When Senator Douglas rose to reply to Mr. Lincoln, six cheers were called for in the crowd, and given with great spirit. He said, quieting the applause:

Gentlemen—The highest compliment you can pay me during the brief half hour that I have to conclude is by observing a strict silence. I desire to be heard rather than to be applauded. (Good.)

The first criticism that Mr. Lincoln makes on my speech was that it was in substance what I have said everywhere else in the State where I have addressed the people. I wish I could say the same of his speech. (Good; you have him, and applause.) Why, the reason I complain of him is because he makes one speech north and another south. (That's so.) Because he has one set of sentiments for the abolition counties and another set for the counties opposed to abolitionism. (Hit him over the knuckles.) My point of complaint against him is that I cannot induce him to hold up the same standard, to carry the same flag in all parts of the State. He does not pretend, and no other man will, that I have one set of principles for Galesburg and another for Charleston. (No, no.) He does not pretend that I hold to one doctrine in Chicago and to an opposite one in Jonesboro. I have proved that he has a different set of principles for each of these localities. All I asked of him was that he should deliver the speech that he has made here to-day in Coles county instead of in old Knox. It would have settled the question between us in that doubtful county. Here I understand him to reaffirm the doctrine of negro equality, and to assert that by the Declaration of Independence the negro is declared equal to the white man. He tells you to-day that the negro was included in the Declaration of Independence when it asserted that all men were created equal. ("We believe it.") Very well. (Here an uproar arose, persons in various parts of the crowd indulging in cat calls, groans, cheers, and other noises, preventing the speaker from proceeding.)

MR. DOUGLAS—Gentlemen, I ask you to remember that Mr. Lincoln was listened to respectfully, and I have the right to insist that I shall not be interrupted during my reply.

MR. LINCOLN—I hope that silence will be preserved.

MR. DOUGLAS—Mr. Lincoln asserts to-day as he did at Chicago, that the negro was included in that clause of the Declaration of Independence which says that all men were created equal and endowed by the Creator with certain inalienable rights, among which are life, liberty and the pursuit of happiness. (Ain't that so?) If the negro was made his equal and mine, if that equality was established by Divine law, and was the negro's inalienable right, how came he to say at Charleston to the Kentuckians residing in that section of our State, that the negro was physically inferior to the white man, belonged to an inferior race, and he was for keeping him always in that inferior condition? (Good.) I wish you to bear these things in mind. At Charleston he said that the negro belonged to an inferior race, and that he was for keeping him in that inferior condition. There he gave the people to understand that there was no moral question involved, because the inferiority being established, it was only a question of degree and not a question of right; here, to-day, instead of making it a question of degree, he makes it a moral question, says that it is a great crime to hold the negro in that inferior condition. (He's right.) Is he right now or was he right in Charleston? (Both.) He is right then, sir, in your estimation, not because he is consistent, but because he can trim his principles any way in any section, so as to secure votes. All I desire of him is that he will declare the same principles in the South that he does in the North.

But did you notice how he answered my position that a man should hold the same doctrines throughout the length and breadth of this republic? He said, "Would Judge Douglas go to Russia and proclaim the same principles he does here?" I would remind him that Russia is not under the American constitution. ("Good," and laughter.) If Russia was a part of the American republic, under our federal constitution, and I was sworn to support that constitution, I would maintain the same doctrine in Russia that I do in Illinois. (Cheers.) The slaveholding States are governed by the same federal constitution as ourselves, and hence a man's principles, in order to be in harmony with the constitution, must be the same in the South as they are in the North, the same in the free States as they are in the slave States. Whenever a man advocates one set of principles in one section, and another set in another section, his opinions are in violation of the spirit of the constitution which he has sworn to support. ("That's so.") When Mr. Lincoln went to Congress in 1847, and laying his hand upon the holy evangelists, made a solemn vow in the presence of high Heaven that he would be faithful to the constitution,—what did he mean? the constitution as he expounds it in Galesburg, or the constitution as he expounds it in Charleston? (Cheers.)

Mr. Lincoln has devoted considerable time to the circumstance that at Ottawa I read a series of resolutions as having been adopted at Springfield, in this State, on the 4th or 5th of October, 1854, which happened not to have been adopted there. He has used hard names; has dared to talk about fraud, (laughter), about forgery, and has insinuated that there was a conspiracy between Mr. Lanphier, Mr. Harris, and myself to perpetrate a forgery. (Renewed laughter.) Now, bear in mind that he does not deny that these resolutions were adopted in a majority of all the Republican counties of this State in that year; he does not deny that they were declared to be the platform of this Republican party in the first Congressional district, in the second, in the third, and in many counties of the fourth, and that they thus became the platform of his party in a majority of the counties upon which he now relies for support; he does not deny the truthfulness of the resolutions, but takes exception to the *spot* on which they were adopted. He takes to himself great merit because he thinks they were not adopted on the right spot for me to use them against him, just as he was very severe in Congress upon the government of his country when he thought that he had discovered that the Mexican war was not begun in the right *spot*, and was therefore unjust. (Renewed laughter.) He tries very hard to make out that there is something very extraordinary in the place where the thing was done, and not in the thing itself. I never believed before that Abraham Lincoln would be guilty of what he has done this day in regard to those resolutions. In the first place, the moment it was intimated to me that they had been adopted at Aurora and Rockford instead of Springfield, I did not wait for him to call my attention to the fact, but led off and explained in my first meeting after the Ottawa debate, what the mistake was, and how it had been made. (That's so.) I supposed that for an honest man, conscious of his own rectitude, that explanation would be sufficient. I did not wait for him, after the mistake was made, to call my attention to it, but frankly explained it at once as an honest man would.

(Cheers.) I also gave the authority on which I had stated that these resolutions were adopted by the Springfield Republican convention. That I had seen them quoted by Major Harris in a debate in Congress, as having been adopted by the first Republican State convention in Illinois, and that I had written to him and asked him for the authority as to the time and place of their adoption; that Major Harris being extremely ill, Charles H. Lanphier had written to me for him, that they were adopted at Springfield, on the 5th of October, 1854, and had sent me a copy of the Springfield paper containing them. I read them from the newspaper just as Mr. Lincoln reads the proceedings of meetings held years ago from the newspapers. After giving that explanation, I did not think there was an honest man in the State of Illinois who doubted that I had been led into the error, if it was such, innocently, in the way I detailed; and I will now say that I do not now believe that there is an honest man on the face of the globe who will not regard with abhorrence and disgust Mr. Lincoln's insinuations of my complicity in that forgery, if it was a forgery. (Cheers.) Does Mr. Lincoln wish to push these things to the point of personal difficulties here? I commenced this contest by treating him courteously and kindly; I always spoke of him in words of respect, and in return he has sought, and is now seeking, to divert public attention from the enormity of his revolutionary principles by impeaching men's sincerity and integrity, and inviting personal quarrels. (Give it to him, and cheers.)

I desired to conduct this contest with him like a gentleman, but I spurn the insinuation of complicity and fraud made upon the simple circumstance of an editor of a newspaper having made a mistake as to the place where a thing was done, but not as to the thing itself. These resolutions were the platform of this Republican party of Mr. Lincoln's of that year. They were adopted in a majority of the Republican counties in the State; and when I asked him at Ottawa whether they formed the platform upon which he stood, he did not answer, and I could not get an answer out of him. He then thought, as I thought, that those resolutions were adopted at the Springfield convention, but excused himself by saying that he was not there when they were adopted, but had gone to Tazewell court in order to avoid being present at the convention. He saw them published as having been adopted at Springfield, and so did I, and he knew that if there was a mistake in regard to them, that I had nothing under heaven to do with it. Besides, you find that in all these northern counties where the Republican candidates are running pledged to him, that the conventions which nominated them adopted that identical platform. One cardinal point in that platform which he shrinks from is this—that there shall be no more slave States admitted into the Union, even if the people want them. Lovejoy stands pledged against the admission of any more slave States. (Right, so do we.) So do you, you say. Farnsworth stands pledged against the admission of any more slave States. (Most right.) Washburne stands pledged the same way. (Good, good.) The candidate for the legislature who is running on Lincoln's ticket in Henderson and Warren, stands committed by his vote in the legislature to the same thing, and I am informed, but do not know of the fact, that your candidate here is also so pledged. (Hurrah for him, good.) Now, you Republicans all hurrah for him, and for the doctrine of "no more slave States," and yet Lincoln tells you that his conscience will not permit him to sanction that doctrine. (Immense applause.) And complains because the resolutions I read at Ottawa made him as a member of the party, responsible for sanctioning the doctrine of no more slave States. You are one way, you confess, and he is or pretends to be the other, and yet you are both governed by *principle* in supporting one another. If it be true, as I have shown it is, that the whole Republican party in the northern part of the State stands committed to the doctrine of no more slave States, and that this same doctrine is repudiated by the Republicans in the other part of the State, I wonder whether Mr. Lincoln and his party do not present the case which he cited from the Scriptures, of a house divided against itself which cannot stand! (Tremendous shouts of applause.) I desire to know what are Mr. Lincoln's principles and the principles of his party? I hold, and the party with which I am identified hold, that the people of each State, old and new, have the right to decide the slavery question for themselves, ("That's it," "Right," and immense applause,) and when I used the remark that I did not care whether slavery was voted up or down, I used it in the connection that I was for allowing Kansas to do just as she pleased on the slavery question. I said that I did not care whether they voted slavery up or down, because they had the right to do as they pleased on the question, and therefore my action would not be controlled by any such consideration. (That's the doctrine.) Why cannot Abraham Lincoln, and the party with which he acts, speak out their principles so that they may be understood? Why do they claim to be one thing in one part of the State and another in the other part? Whenever I allude to the abolition doctrines, which he considers a slander to be charged with being in favor of, you all endorse them, and hurrah for them, not knowing that your candidate is ashamed to acknowledge them. (You have them; and cheers.)

I have a few words to say upon the Dred Scott decision, which has troubled the brain of Mr. Lincoln so much. (Laughter.) He insists that that decision would carry slavery into the free States, notwithstanding that the decision says directly the opposite; and goes into a long argument to make you believe that I am in favor of, and would sanction the doctrine that would allow slaves to be brought here and held as slaves contrary to our constitution and laws. Mr. Lincoln knew better when he asserted this; he knew that one newspaper, and so far as is within my knowledge, but one ever asserted that doctrine, and that I was the first man in either House of Congress that read that article in debate, and denounced it on the floor of the Senate as revolutionary. When the Washington *Union*, on the 17th of last November published an article to that effect, I branded it at once, and denounced it, and hence the *Union* has been pursuing me ever since. Mr. Toombs, of Georgia, replied to me, and said that there was not a man in any of the slave States south of the Potomac river that held any such doctrine. Mr. Lincoln knows that there is not a member of the Supreme Court who holds that doctrine; he knows that every one of them, as shown by their opinions, holds the reverse. Why this attempt, then, to bring the Supreme Court into disrepute among the people? It looks as if there was an effort being made to destroy public confidence in the highest judicial tribunal on earth. Suppose he succeeds in destroying public confidence in the court, so that the people will not respect its decisions, but will feel at liberty to disregard them, and resist the laws of the land, what will he have gained? He will have changed the government from one of laws into that of a mob, in which the strong arm of violence will be substituted for the decisions of the courts of justice. ("That's so.") He complains because I did not go into an argument reviewing Chief Justice Taney's opinion, and the other opinions of the different judges, to determine whether their reasoning is right or wrong on the questions of law. What use would that be? He wants to take an appeal from the Supreme Court to this meeting to determine whether the questions of law were decided properly. He is going to appeal from the Supreme Court of the United States to every town meeting in the hope that he can excite a prejudice against that court, and on the wave of that prejudice ride into the Senate of the United States, when he could not get there on his own principles, or his own merits. (Laughter and cheers; "hit him again.") Suppose he should succeed in getting into the Senate of the United States, what then will he have to do with the decision of the Supreme Court in the Dred Scott case? Can he reverse that decision when he gets there? Can he act upon it? Has the Senate any right to reverse it or revise it? He will not pretend that it has. Then why drag the matter into this contest, unless for the purpose of making a false issue, by which he can direct public attention from the real issue?

He has cited General Jackson in justification of the war he is making on the decision of the court. Mr. Lincoln misunderstands the history of the country, if he believes there is any parallel in the two cases. It is true that the Supreme Court once decided that if a bank of the United States was a necessary fiscal agent of the government, it was constitutional, and if not, that it was unconstitutional, and also, that whether or not it was necessary for that purpose, was a political question for Congress and not a judicial one for the courts to determine. Hence the court would not determine the bank unconstitutional. Jackson respected the decision, obeyed the law, executed it and carried it into effect during its existence; (that's so,) but after the charter of the bank expired and a proposition was made to create a new bank, General Jackson said, "It is unnecessary, and improper, and therefore, I am against it on constitutional grounds as well as those of expediency." Is Congress bound to pass every act that is constitutional? Why, there are a thousand things that are constitutional, but yet are inexpedient and unnecessary, and you surely would not vote for them merely because you had the right to? And because General Jackson would not do a thing which he had a right to do, but did not deem expedient or proper, Mr. Lincoln is going to justify himself in doing that which he has no right to do. (Laughter.) I ask him, whether he is not bound to respect and obey the decisions of the Supreme Court as well as me? The Constitution has created that Court to decide all constitutional questions in the last resort, and when such decisions have been made, they become the law of the land, (that's so,) and you, and he, and myself, and every other good citizen are bound by them. Yet, he argues that I am bound by their decisions and he is not. He says that their decisions are binding on Democrats, but not on Republicans. (Laughter and applause.) Are not Republicans bound by the laws of the land, as well as Democrats? And when the court has fixed the construction of the constitution on the validity of a given law, is not their decision binding upon Republicans as well as upon Democrats? (It ought to be.) Is it possible that you Republicans have the right to raise your mobs and oppose the laws of the land and the constituted authorities, and yet hold us Democrats bound to obey them? My time is within half a minute of expiring, and all I have to say is, that I stand by the laws of the land. (That's it; hurrah for Douglas.) I stand by the constitution as our fathers made it, by the laws as they are enacted, and by the decisions of the court upon all points within their jurisdiction as they are pronounced by the highest tribunal on earth; and any man who resists these must resort to mob law and violence to overturn the government of laws.

Speech at Monmouth, Illinois[1]

October 11, 1858

. . . . Mr. Lincoln was then introduced to the audience by Philo E. Reed, Esq., President of the day. Of his speech I will only say that it lasted three hours, and that during all that time the whole audience seemed perfectly wrapt in attention, and that in power, pathos and eloquence, I have never heard it equalled. The Toombs bill was shown up, Dug's miserable attempt to lead off Old Clay Whigs was held up to the scorn and contempt of the crowd. Said Mr. Lincoln: "Judge Douglas is attempting to administer upon the political assets of Henry Clay. It is usual for the administrator to be a creditor or of kin to the deceased. Henry Clay did not owe anything politically to his old enemy, Douglas, and as to Douglas being of any kin to him, everybody knows they never had a single feeling in unison, and that Douglas was one of his most virulent abusers while living. And he is a pretty man to undertake to wrap the mantle of Clay around him, and strut about trying to palm himself off as his political administrator."

. . . . Mr. Lincoln lifted himself up and was about to reply, when Philo Reed, a very modest, unassuming young man, told him to sit down and wait till the glee band had a chance to spread themselves—which they did to the delight of the Republicans. Mr. Lincoln then proceeded. About the first hour of his speech was taken up with little *sharps* on Douglas, calculated to tickle the fancy of the Republicans. He referred to the speech made by Douglas last week, in which he was charged with being the attorney of the Illinois Central Railroad, at the time the charter was granted, to make a good bargain for the company against the State—and as having induced the legislature to change the per centage from fifteen to seven per cent. He didn't deny the charge that he was then or is now the attorney of the railroad, or that he is to-day receiving a big fee from that company as their attorney. He referred to the bargain between himself and Trumbull to Abolitionize the old line Whigs and Democrats, and said it was none of Douglas' business how he and Trumbull "managed their own domestic concerns." He referred to the Mexican war, while he was in congress giving aid and comfort to the enemy, and against his own country, pronouncing it unholy, unconstitutional, God abhorred, and not begun on the right "*spot.*" This portion of his speech he made as clear as mud. He then harped on the resolutions read at Ottawa by Douglas as a forgery because they were not adopted on the right "*spot,*" but never once said a word about the revolutionary heresies they contained. He harped over the conspiracy entered into by Douglas and the Supreme Court, the submission clause in the Toombs bill, &c., &c., all of which have been nailed and clinched as lies by Douglas time and again. His whole speech was a personal attack on Douglas and Democrats. He dodged the issues before the people, and failed entirely to discuss the principles dividing the two parties. It was not marked by the "abilities of a Statesman, or the dignity of a would be Senator," and was coldly received by the small crowd present.

[1] Chicago *Press and Tribune,* October 15, 1858; Monmouth *Review,* October 15, 1858.

Sixth Debate with Stephen A. Douglas, at Quincy, Illinois[1]

October 13, 1858

Sixth joint debate. October 13. 1858 at Quincy, Illinois. Lincoln as reported in the Press & Tribune Douglas as reported in the Chicago Times.[2]

MR. LINCOLN'S SPEECH.

At precisely half past two o'clock Mr. Lincoln was introduced to the audience, and having been received with three cheers, he proceeded:

LADIES AND GENTLEMEN:—I have had no immediate conference with Judge Douglas, but I will venture to say he and I will perfectly agree that your entire silence both when I speak and when he speaks will be most agreeable to us.

[1] Debates Scrapbook, ORB. As in the preceding debates, the editors have retained cheering and interruptions deleted by Lincoln. Insertions and corrections by Lincoln are indicated in footnotes. Typographical errors not corrected in the scrapbook have been corrected by the editors. Bracketed passages are in the source. [2] Lincoln's prefatory note in the debates scrapbook.

In the month of May, 1856, the elements in the State of Illinois, which have since been consolidated into the Republican party, assembled together in a State Convention at Bloomington. They adopted at that time what, in political language, is called a platform. In June of the same year, the elements of the Republican party in the nation assembled together in a National Convention at Philadelphia. They adopted what is called the National Platform. In June, 1858—the present year—the Republicans of Illinois re-assembled at Springfield, in State Convention, and adopted again their platform, as I suppose not differing in any essential particular from either of the former ones, but perhaps adding something in relation to the new developments of political progress in the country.

The Convention that assembled in June last did me the honor, if it be one, and I esteem it such, to nominate me as their candidate for the United States Senate. I have supposed that in entering upon this canvass I stood generally upon these platforms. We are now met together on the 13th of October of the same year, only four months from the adoption of the last platform, and I am unaware that in this canvass, from the beginning until to-day, any one of our adversaries has taken hold of our platforms or laid his finger upon anything that he calls wrong in them.

In the very first one of these joint discussions between Senator Douglas and myself, Senator Douglas, without alluding at all to these platforms, or any one of them, of which I have spoken, attempted to hold me responsible for a set of resolutions passed long before the meeting of either one of these Conventions of which I have spoken. And as a ground for holding me responsible for these resolutions, he assumed that they had been passed at a State Convention of the Republican party, and that I took part in that Convention. It was discovered afterwards that this was erroneous, that the resolutions which he endeavored to hold me responsible for, had not been passed by any State Convention anywhere —had not been passed at Springfield, where he supposed they had, or assumed that they had, and that they had been passed in no Convention in which I had taken part. The Judge, nevertheless, was not willing to give up the point that he was endeavoring to make upon me, and he therefore thought to still hold me to the point that he was endeavoring to make, by showing that the resolutions that he read, had been passed at a local Convention in the northern part of the State, although it was not a local Convention that embraced my residence at all, nor one that reached, as I suppose, nearer than 150 or 200 miles of where I was when it met, nor one in which I took any part at all. He also introduced other resolutions passed at other meetings, and by combining the whole, although they were all antecedent to the two State Conventions, and the one National Convention I have mentioned, still he insisted and now insists, as I understand, that I am in some way responsible for them.

At Jonesboro, on our third meeting, I insisted to the Judge that I was in no way rightfully held responsible for the proceedings of this local meeting or convention in which I had taken no part, and in which I was in no way embraced; but I insisted to him that if he thought I was responsible for every man or every set of men everywhere, who happen to be my friends, the rule ought to work both ways, and he ought to be responsible for the acts and resolutions of all men or sets of men who were or are now his supporters and friends, [good, good,] and gave him a pretty long string of resolutions, passed by men who are now his friends, and announcing doctrines for which he does not desire to be held responsible.

This still does not satisfy Judge Douglas. He still adheres to his proposition, that I am responsible for what some of my friends in different parts of the State have done; but that he is not responsible for what his have done. At least so I understand him. But in addition to that, the Judge at our meeting in Galesburg, last week, undertakes to establish that I am guilty of a species of double-dealing with the public—that I make speeches of a certain sort in the North, among the Abolitionists, which I would not make in the South, and that I make speeches of a certain sort in the South which I would not make in the North. I apprehend in the course I have marked out for myself that I shall not have to dwell at very great length upon this subject.

As this was done in the Judge's opening speech at Galesburg, I had an opportunity, as I had the middle speech then, of saying something in answer to it. He brought forward a quotation or two from a speech of mine delivered at Chicago, and then to contrast with it he brought forward an extract from a speech of mine at Charleston, in which he insisted that I was greatly inconsistent, and insisted that his conclusion followed that I was playing a double part, and speaking in one region one way and in another region another way. I have not time now to dwell on this as long as I would like, and I wish only now to re-quote that portion of my speech at Charleston which the Judge quoted, and then make some comments upon it. This he quotes from me as being delivered at Charleston, and I believe correctly: "I will say, then, that I am not, nor ever have been, in favor of bringing about in any way the social and political equality of the white and black races—that I am not nor ever have been in favor of making voters or jurors of negroes, nor of qualifying them to hold office, nor to intermarry[3] with white people; and I will say in addition to this that there is a physical difference between the white and black races which will ever forbid the two races living together on terms of social and political equality. And inasmuch as they cannot so live, while they do remain together, there must be the position of superior & inferior.[4] I am as much as any other man in favor of having the superior position assigned to the white race." ["Good," "Good," and loud cheers.] This, I believe, is the entire quotation from the Charleston speech as the Judge made it. His comments are as follows:

> Yes, here you find men who hurrah for Lincoln, and say he is right when he discards all distinction between races, or when he declares that he discards the doctrine that there is such a thing as a superior and inferior race; and Abolitionists are required and expected to vote for Mr. Lincoln because he goes for the equality of the races, holding that in the Declaration of Independence the white man and the negro were declared equal, and endowed by Divine law with equality. And down South with the Old Line Whigs, with the Kentuckians, the Virginians, and the Tennesseeans, he tells you that there is a physical difference between the races, making the one superior, the other inferior, and he is in favor of maintaining the superiority of the white race over the negro.

Those are the Judge's comments. Now I wish to show you, that a month, or only lacking three days of a month, before I made the speech at Charleston, which the Judge quotes from, he had himself heard me say substantially the same thing. It was in our first meeting, at Ottawa—and I will say a word about where it was and the atmosphere it was in, after a while—but, at our first meeting, at Ottawa, I read an extract from an old speech of mine, made nearly four years ago, not merely to show my sentiments, but to show that my sentiments were long entertained and openly expressed; in which extract I expressly declared that my own feelings would not admit a social and political equality between the white and black races, and that even if my own feelings would admit of it, I still knew that the public sentiment of the country would not, and that such a thing was an utter impossibility, or substantially that. That extract from my old speech the reporters, by some sort of accident, passed over, and it was not reported. I lay no blame upon anybody. I suppose they thought that I would hand

[3] "Intermingling" corrected by Lincoln to "intermarry."

[4] "& inferior" inserted by Lincoln.

it over to them, and dropped reporting while I was reading it, but afterwards went away without getting it from me. At the end of that quotation from my old speech, which I read at Ottawa, I made the comments which were reported at that time, and which I will now read, and ask you to notice how very nearly they are the same as Judge Douglas says were delivered by me down in Egypt. After reading I added these words: "Now, gentlemen, I don't want to read at any great length, but this is the true complexion[5] of all I have ever said in regard to the institution of slavery or the black race, and this is the whole of it; and anything that argues me into his idea of perfect social and political equality with the negro is but a specious and[6] fantastical arrangement of words by which a man can prove a horse-chestnut to be a chestnut horse. I will say here, while upon this subject, that I have no purpose directly or indirectly to interfere with the institution in the States where it exists. I believe I have no right to do so. I have no inclination to do so. I have no purpose to introduce political and social equality between the white and black races. There is a physical difference between the two, which, in my judgment, will probably forever forbid their living together on the footing of perfect equality, and inasmuch as it becomes a necessity that there must be a difference, I as well as Judge Douglas am in favor of the race to which I belong having the superior position." [Cheers, "That's the doctrine."] "I have never said anything to the contrary, but I hold that, notwithstanding all this, there is no reason in the world why the negro is not entitled to all the rights enumerated in the Declaration of Independence—the right of life, liberty and the pursuit of happiness. I hold that he is as much entitled to these as the white man. I agree with Judge Douglas that he is not my equal in many respects, certainly not in color—perhaps not in intellectual and moral endowments; but in the right to eat the bread without leave of anybody else which his own hand earns, he is my equal and the equal of Judge Douglas, and the equal of every[7] other man." [Loud cheers.]

I have chiefly introduced this for the purpose of meeting the Judge's charge that the quotation he took from my Charleston speech was what I would say down south among the Kentuckians, the Virginians, &c., but would not say in the regions in which was supposed to be more of the Abolition element. I now make this comment: That speech from which I have now read the quotation.

5 "Application" corrected by Lincoln to "complexion."

6 "Species of" corrected by Lincoln to "specious and."

7 "Any" corrected by Lincoln to "every."

and which is there given correctly, perhaps too much so for good taste, was made away up north in the Abolition district of this State *par excellence*—in the Lovejoy District—in the personal presence of Lovejoy, for he was on the stand with us when I made[8] it. It had been made and put in print in that region only three days less than a month before the speech made at Charleston, the like of which Judge Douglas thinks I would not make where there was any abolition element. I only refer to this matter to say that I am altogether unconscious of having attempted any double dealing anywhere—that upon one occasion I may say one thing and leave other things unsaid, and *vice versa;* but that I have said anything on one occasion that is inconsistent with what I have said elsewhere, I deny—at least I deny it so far as the intention is concerned. I find that I have devoted to this topic a larger portion of my time than I had intended. I wished to show, but I will pass it upon this occasion, that in the sentiment I have occasionally advanced upon the Declaration of Independence, I am entirely borne out by the sentiments advanced by our old Whig leader, Henry Clay, and I have the book here to show it from; but because I have already occupied more time than I intended to do on that topic, I pass over it.

At Galesburg, I tried to show that by the Dred Scott Decision, pushed to its legitimate consequences, slavery would be established in all the States as well as in the Territories. I did this because, upon a former occasion, I had asked Judge Douglas whether, if the Supreme Court should make a decision declaring that the States had not the power to exclude slavery from their limits, he would adopt and follow that decision as a rule of political action; and because he had not directly answered that question, but had merely contented himself with sneering at it, I again introduced it, and tried to show that the conclusion that I stated followed inevitably and logically from the proposition already decided by the court. Judge Douglas had the privilege of replying to me at Galesburg, and again he gave me no direct answer as to whether he would or would not sustain such a decision if made. I give[9] him this third chance to say yes or no. He is not obliged to do either—probably he will not do either—[laughter] but I give him the third chance. I tried to show then that this result—this conclusion inevitably followed from the point already decided by the court. The Judge, in his reply, again sneers at the thought of the court making any such decision, and in the course of his remarks upon this sub-

[8] "Read" corrected by Lincoln to "made."
[9] "Gave" corrected by Lincoln to "give."

ject, uses the language which I will now read. Speaking of me, the Judge says:

"He goes on and insists that the Dred Scott Decision would carry slavery into the Free States, notwithstanding the decision itself says the contrary." And he adds: "Mr. Lincoln knows that there is no member of the Supreme Court that holds that doctrine. He knows that every one of them in their opinions held the reverse."

I especially introduce this subject again for the purpose of saying that I have the Dred Scott Decision here, and I will thank Judge Douglas to lay his finger upon the place in the entire opinions of the court where any one of them "says the contrary." It is very hard to affirm a negative with entire confidence. I say, however, that I have examined that decision with a good deal of care, as a lawyer examines a decision, and so far as I have been able to do so, the Court has no where in its opinions said that the States have the power to exclude slavery, nor have they used other language substantially that. I also say, so far as I can find, not one of the concurring Judges has said that the States can exclude slavery, nor said anything that was substantially that. The nearest approach that any one of them has made to it, so far as I can find, was by Judge Nelson, and the approach he made to it was exactly, in substance, the Nebraska Bill—that the States had the exclusive power over the question of slavery, so far as they are not limited by the Constitution of the United States. I asked the question, therefore, if the non-concurring Judges, McLean or Curtis, had asked to get an express declaration that the States could absolutely exclude slavery from their limits, what reason have we to believe that it would not have been voted down by the majority of the Judges, just as Chase's amendment was voted down by Judge Douglas and his compeers when it was offered to the Nebraska Bill. [Cheers.]

Also at Galesburg, I said something in regard to those Springfield Resolutions that Judge Douglas had attempted to use upon me at Ottawa, and commented at some length upon the fact that they were, as presented, not genuine. Judge Douglas in his reply to me seemed to be somewhat exasperated. He said he would never have believed that Abraham Lincoln, as he kindly called me, would have attempted such a thing as I had attempted upon that occasion; and among other expressions which he used toward me, was that I dared to say forgery—that I had *dared* to say forgery [turning to Judge Douglas]. Yes, Judge, I did dare to say forgery. [Loud applause.] But in this political canvass, the Judge ought to remember that I was not the first who *dared* to say forgery. At Jacksonville Judge Douglas made a speech in answer to something said by Judge Trumbull, and at the close of what he said upon that subject, he *dared* to say that Trumbull had forged his evidence. He said, too, that he should not concern himself with Trumbull any more, but thereafter he should hold Lincoln responsible for the slanders upon him. [Laughter.] When I met him at Charleston after that, although I think that I should not have noticed the subject if he had not said he would hold me responsible for it, I spread out before him the statements of the evidence that Judge Trumbull had used, and I asked Judge Douglas, piece by piece, to put his finger upon one piece of all that evidence that he would say was a forgery! When I went through with each and every piece, Judge Douglas did not *dare* then to say that any piece of it was a forgery. [Laughter, and cries of "good, good."] So it seems that there are some things that Judge Douglas dares to do, and some that he dares not to do. [Great applause and laughter.]

A VOICE—It's the same thing with you.

MR. LINCOLN—Yes, sir, it's the same thing with me. I do dare to say forgery, when it's true, and I don't dare to say forgery when it's false. [Thunders of applause. Cries of "Hit him again," "Give it to him, Lincoln."] Now, I will say here to this audience and to Judge Douglas, I have not dared to say he committed a forgery, and I never shall until I know it; but I did dare to say—just to suggest to the Judge—that a forgery had been committed, which by his own showing had been traced to him and two of his friends. [Roars of laughter and loud cheers.] I dared to suggest to him that he had expressly promised in one of his public speeches to investigate that matter, and I dared to suggest to him that there was an implied promise that when he investigated it he would make known the result. I dared to suggest to the Judge that he could not expect to be quite clear of suspicion of that fraud, for since the time that promise was made he had been with those friends, and had not kept his promise in regard to the investigation and the report upon it. [Loud laughter. Cries of "Good, good," "Hit him hard."] I am not a very daring man, [laughter] but I dared that much, Judge, and I am not much scared about it yet. [Uproarious laughter and applause.] When the Judge says he wouldn't have believed of Abraham Lincoln that he would have made such an attempt as that, he reminds me of the fact that he entered upon this canvass with the purpose to treat me courteously; that touched me somewhat. [Great laughter.] It sets me to thinking. I was aware, when it was first agreed that Judge Douglas and I were to have these seven joint discussions, that they were the successive acts of a drama—perhaps I should say, to be enacted not merely in the face of audiences like this, but in the face of the nation, and to some extent, by my relation to him, and not from anything in myself, in the face of the world; and I am anxious that they should be conducted with dignity and in the good temper which would be befitting the vast audience before which it was conducted. But when Judge Douglas got home from Washington and made his first speech in Chicago, the evening afterwards I made some sort of a reply to it. His second speech was made at Bloomington, in which, he commented upon my speech at Chicago, and said that I had used language ingeniously contrived to conceal my intentions, or words to that effect. Now, I understand that this is an imputation upon my veracity and my candor. I do not know what the Judge understood by it; but in our first discussion at Ottawa, he led off by charging a bargain, somewhat corrupt in its character, upon Trumbull and myself—that we had entered into a bargain, one of the terms of which was that Trumbull was to abolitionize the old Democratic party, and I (Lincoln) was to abolitionize the old Whig party—I pretending to be as good an Old Line Whig as ever. Judge Douglas may not understand that he implicated my truthfulness and my honor, when he said I was doing one thing and pretending another; and I misunderstood him if he thought he was treating me in a dignified way, as a man of honor and truth, as he now claims he was disposed to treat me. Even after that time, at Galesburg, when he brings forward an extract from a speech made at Chicago, and an extract from a speech made at Charleston, to prove that I was trying to play a double part—that I was trying to cheat the public, and get votes upon one set of principles at one place and upon another set of principles at another place—I do not understand but what he impeaches my honor, my veracity and my candor, and because *he* does this, I do not understand that I am bound, if I see a truthful ground for it, to keep my hands off of him. As soon as I learned that Judge Douglas was disposed to treat me in this way, I signified in one of my speeches that I should be driven to draw upon whatever of humble resources I might have—to adopt a new course with him. I was not entirely sure that I should be able to hold my own with him, but I at least had the purpose made to do as well as I could upon him; and now I say that I will not be the first to cry "hold." I think it originated with the Judge, and when he quits, I probably will. [Roars of laughter.] But I shall not ask any favors at all. He asks me, or he asks the audience, if I wish to push this matter to the point of personal difficulty. I tell him, no. He did not make a mistake, in one of his early speeches, when he called me an "amiable" man, though perhaps he did when he called me an "intelligent" man. [Laughter.] It really hurts me very much to suppose that I have wronged anybody on earth. I again tell him, no! I very much prefer, when this canvass shall be over, however it may result, that we at least part without any bitter recollections of personal difficulties.

The Judge, in his concluding speech at Galesburg, says that I was pushing this matter to a personal difficulty, to avoid the responsibility for the enormity of my principles. I say to the Judge and to this audience now, that I will again state our principles as well as I hastily can in all their enormity, and if the Judge hereafter chooses to confine himself to a war upon these principles, he will probably not find me departing from the same course.[10]

We have in this nation this element of domestic slavery. It is a matter of absolute certainty that it is a disturbing element. It is the opinion of all the great men who have expressed an opinion upon it, that it is a dangerous element. We keep up a controversy in regard to it. That controversy necessarily springs from difference of opinion, and if we can learn exactly—can reduce to the lowest elements—what that difference of opinion is, we perhaps shall be better prepared for discussing the different systems of policy that we would propose in regard to that disturbing element. I suggest that the difference of opinion, reduced to its lowest terms, is no other than the difference between the men who think slavery a wrong and those who do not think it wrong. The Republican party think it wrong—we think it is a moral, a social and a political wrong. We think it is a wrong not confining itself merely to the persons or the States where it exists, but that it is a wrong in its tendency, to say the least, that extends itself to the existence of the whole nation. Because we think it wrong, we propose a course of policy that shall deal with it as a wrong. We deal with it as with any other wrong, in so far as we can prevent its growing any larger, and so deal with it that in the run of time there may be some promise of an end to it. We have a due regard to the actual presence of it amongst us and the difficulties of getting rid of it in any satisfactory way, and all the constitutional obligations thrown about it. I suppose that in reference both to its actual existence in the nation, and to our constitutional obligations, we have no right at all to disturb it in the States where it exists, and we profess that we have no more inclination to disturb it than we have the right to do it. We go further than that; we don't propose to disturb it where, in one instance, we think the Constitution

10 "It" corrected by Lincoln to "the same course."

would permit us. We think the Constitution would permit us to disturb it in the District of Columbia. Still we do not propose to do that, unless it should be in terms which I don't suppose the nation is very likely soon to agree to—the terms of making the emancipation gradual and compensating the unwilling owners. Where we suppose we have the constitutional right, we restrain ourselves in reference to the actual existence of the institution and the difficulties thrown about it. We also oppose it as an evil so far as it seeks to spread itself. We insist on the policy that shall restrict it to its present limits. We don't suppose that in doing this we violate anything due to the actual presence of the institution, or anything due to the constitutional guarantees thrown around it.

We oppose the Dred Scott decision in a certain way, upon which I ought perhaps to address you a few words. We do not propose that when Dred Scott has been decided to be a slave by the court, we, as a mob, will decide him to be free. We do not propose that, when any other one, or one thousand, shall be decided by that court to be slaves, we will in any violent way disturb the rights of property thus settled; but we nevertheless do oppose that decision as a political rule which shall be binding on the voter, to vote for nobody who thinks it wrong, which shall be binding on the members of Congress or the President to favor no measure that does not actually concur with the principles of that decision. We do not propose to be bound by it as a political rule in that way, because we think it lays the foundation not merely of enlarging and spreading out what we consider an evil, but it lays the foundation for spreading that evil into the States themselves. We propose so resisting it as to have it reversed if we can, and a new judicial rule established upon this subject.

I will add this, that if there be any man who does not believe that slavery is wrong in the three aspects which I have mentioned, or in any one of them, that man is misplaced, and ought to leave us. While, on the other hand, if there be any man in the Republican party who is impatient over the necessity springing from its actual presence, and is impatient of the constitutional guarantees thrown around it, and would act in disregard of these, he too is misplaced standing with us. He will find his place somewhere else; for we have a due regard, so far as we are capable of understanding them, for all these things.[11] This, gentlemen, as well as I can give it, is a plain statement of our principles in all their enormity.

I will say now that there is a sentiment in the country contrary

[11] "Thing" corrected by Lincoln to "things."

to me—a sentiment which holds that slavery is not wrong, and therefore it goes for policy that does not propose dealing with it as a wrong. That policy is the Democratic policy, and that sentiment is the Democratic sentiment. If there be a doubt in the mind of any one of this vast audience that this is really the central idea of the Democratic party, in relation to this subject, I ask him to bear with me while I state a few things tending, as I think, to prove that proposition. In the first place, the leading man—I think I may do my friend Judge Douglas the honor of calling him such—advocating the present Democratic policy, never himself says it is wrong. He has the high distinction, so far as I know, of never having said slavery is either right or wrong. [Laughter.] Almost everybody else says one or the other, but the Judge never does. If there be a man in the Democratic party who thinks it is wrong, and yet clings to that party, I suggest to him in the first place that his leader don't talk as he does, for he never says that it is wrong. In the second place, I suggest to him that if he will examine the policy proposed to be carried forward, he will find that he carefully excludes the idea that there is anything wrong in it. If you will examine the arguments that are made on[12] it, you will find that every one carefully excludes the idea that there is anything wrong in slavery. Perhaps that Democrat who says he is as much opposed to slavery as I am, will tell me that I am wrong about this. I wish him to examine his own course in regard to this matter a moment, and then see if his opinion will not be changed a little. You say it is wrong; but don't you constantly object to anybody else saying so? Do you not constantly argue that this is not the right place to oppose it? You say it must not be opposed in the free States, because slavery is not here; it must not be opposed in the slave States, because it is there; it must not be opposed in politics, because that will make a fuss; it must not be opposed in the pulpit, because it is not religion. [Loud cheers.] Then where is the place to oppose it? There is no suitable place to oppose it. There is no place in the country to oppose this evil overspreading the continent, which you say yourself is coming. Frank Blair and Gratz Brown tried to get up a system of gradual emancipation in Missouri, had an election in August and got beat, and you, Mr. Democrat, threw up your hat, and halloed "hurrah for Democracy." [Enthusiastic cheers.] So I say again that in regard to the arguments that are made, when Judge Douglas says he "don't care whether slavery is voted up or voted down," whether he means that as an individual expression of sentiment, or only as a sort of

[12] "In" corrected by Lincoln to "on."

statement of his views on national policy, it is alike true to say that he can thus argue logically if he don't see anything wrong in it; but he cannot say so logically if he admits that slavery is wrong. He cannot say that he would as soon see a wrong voted up as voted down. When Judge Douglas says that whoever, or whatever community, wants slaves, they have a right to have them, he is perfectly logical if there is nothing wrong in the institution; but if you admit that it is wrong, he cannot logically say that anybody has a right to do wrong. When he says that slave property and horse and hog property are alike to be allowed to go into the Territories, upon the principles of equality, he is reasoning truly, if there is no difference between them as property; but if the one is property, held rightfully, and the other is wrong, then there is no equality between the right and wrong; so that, turn it in any way you can, in all the arguments sustaining the Democratic policy, and in that policy itself, there is a careful, studied exclusion of the idea that there is anything wrong in slavery. Let us understand this. I am not, just here, trying[13] to prove that we are right and they are wrong. I have been stating where we and they stand, and trying to show what is the real difference between us; and I now say that whenever we can get the question distinctly stated—can get all these men who believe that slavery is in some of these respects wrong, to stand and act with us in treating it as a wrong—then, and not till then, I think we will in some way come to an end of this slavery agitation. [Prolonged cheers.]

SENATOR DOUGLAS' REPLY.

Senator Douglas, in taking the stand, was greeted with tremendous applause. He said:

Ladies and Gentlemen:—Permit me to say that unless silence is observed it will be impossible for me to be heard by this immense crowd, and my friends can confer no higher favor upon me than by omitting all expressions of applause or approbation. (We cannot help it, Douglas, &c.) I desire to be heard rather than to be applauded. I wish to address myself to your reason, your judgment, your sense of justice, and not to your passions.

I regret that Mr. Lincoln should have deemed it proper for him to again indulge in gross personalities and base insinuations in regard to the Springfield resolutions. It has imposed upon me the necessity of using some portion of my time for the purpose of calling your attention to the facts of the case, and it will then be for you to say what you think of a man who can predicate such a

[13] "Here" corrected by Lincoln to "not, just here, trying."

charge upon the circumstances he has this. I had seen the platform adopted by a Republican Congressional convention held in Aurora, the second Congressional district, in September, 1854, published as purporting to be the platform of the Republican party. That platform declared that the Republican party was pledged never to admit another slave State into the Union, and also that it pledged to prohibit slavery in all the territories of the United States, not only all that we then had, but all that we should thereafter acquire, and to repeal unconditionally the fugitive slave law, abolish slavery in the District of Columbia, and prohibit the slave trade between the different States. These and other articles against slavery were contained in this platform, and unanimously adopted by the Republican Congressional convention in that district. I had also seen that the Republican Congressional conventions at Rockford, in the first district, and at Bloomington, in the third, had adopted the same platform that year, nearly word for word, and had declared it to be the platform of the Republican party. I had noticed that Major Thomas L. Harris, a member of Congress from the Springfield district, had referred to that platform in a speech in Congress as having been adopted by the first Republican State Convention which assembled in Illinois. When I had occasion to use the fact in this canvass, I wrote to Major Harris to know on what day that convention was held, and to ask him to send me its proceedings. He being sick, Charles H. Lanphier answered my letter by sending me the published proceedings of the convention held at Springfield on the 5th of October, 1854, as they appeared in the report of the *State Register*. I read those resolutions from that newspaper the same as any of you would refer back and quote any fact from the files of a newspaper which had published it. Mr. Lincoln pretends that after I had so quoted those resolutions he discovered that they had never been adopted at Springfield. He does not deny their adoption by the Republican party at Aurora, at Bloomington, and at Rockford, and by nearly all the Republican county conventions in northern Illinois where his party is in a majority, but merely because they were not adopted on the "*spot*" on which I said they were, he chooses to quibble about the place rather than meet and discuss the merits of the resolutions themselves. I stated when I quoted them that I did so from the *State Register*. I gave my authority. Lincoln believed at the time, as he has since admitted, that they had been adopted at Springfield, as published. Does he believe now, that I did not tell the truth when I quoted those resolutions? He knows, in his heart, that I quoted them in good faith, believing, at the time, that they had been adopted at Springfield. I would consider myself an infamous wretch, if, under such circumstances, I could charge any man with being a party to a trick or a fraud. (Great applause.) And I will tell him, too, that it will not do to charge a forgery on Charles H. Lanphier or Thomas L. Harris. No man on earth, who knows them, and knows Lincoln, would take his oath against their word. (Cheers.) There are not two men in the State of Illinois, who have higher characters for truth, for integrity, for moral character, and for elevation of tone, as gentlemen, than Mr. Lanphier and Mr. Harris. Any man who attempts to make such charges as Mr. Lincoln has indulged in against them, only proclaims himself a slanderer. (Vociferous applause.)

I will now show you that I stated with entire fairness, as soon as it was made known to me, that there was a mistake about the spot where the resolutions had been adopted, although their truthfulness, as a declaration of the principles of the Republican party, had not, and could not be questioned. I did not wait for Lincoln to point out the mistake; but the moment I discovered it, I made a speech, and published it to the world, correcting the error. I corrected it myself, as a gentleman, and an honest man, and as I always feel proud to do when I have made a mistake. I wish Mr. Lincoln could show that he has acted with equal fairness, and truthfulness, when I have convinced him that he has been mistaken. (Hit him again, and cheers.) I will give you an illustration to show you how he acts in a similar case: In a speech at Springfield, he charged Chief Justice Taney, and his associates, President Pierce, President Buchanan, and myself, with having entered into a conspiracy at the time the Nebraska bill was introduced, by which the Dred Scott decision was to be made by the Supreme Court, in order to carry slavery everywhere under the constitution. I called his attention to the fact, that at the time alluded to, to wit: the introduction of the Nebraska bill, it was not possible that such a conspiracy could have been entered into, for the reason that the Dred Scott case had never been taken before the Supreme Court, and was not taken before it for a year after; and I asked him to take back that charge. Did he do it? (No.) I showed him that it was impossible that the charge could be true, I proved it by the record, and I then called upon him to retract his false charge. What was his answer? Instead of coming out like an honest man and doing so, he reiterated the charge, and said that if the case had not gone up to the Supreme Court from the courts of Missouri at the time he charged that the Judges of the Supreme Court entered into the conspiracy, yet, that there was an understanding with the Democratic owners of Dred Scott, that they would take it up. I have since asked him who the Democratic owners of Dred Scott were, but he could not tell, and why? Because there were no such Democratic owners in existence. Dred Scott at the time was owned by the Rev. Dr. Chaffee, an Abolition member of Congress, of Springfield, Massachusetts, in right of his wife. He was owned by one of Lincoln's friends, and not by Democrats at all; (immense cheers, "give it to him," &c.) his case was conducted in court by Abolition lawyers, so that both the prosecution and the defense were in the hands of the Abolition political friends of Mr. Lincoln. (Renewed cheering.) Notwithstanding I thus proved by the record that his charge against the Supreme Court was false, instead of taking it back, he resorted to another false charge to sustain the infamy of it. (Cheers.) He also charged President Buchanan with having been a party to the conspiracy. I directed his attention to the fact that the charge could not possibly be true, for the reason that at the time specified, Mr. Buchanan was not in America, but was three thousand miles off, representing the United States at the Court of St. James, and had been there for a year previous, and did not return until three years afterwards. Yet, I never could get Mr. Lincoln to take back his false charge, although I have called upon him over and over again. He refuses to do it, and either remains silent, or, resorts to other tricks to try and palm his slander off on the country. (Cheers.) Therein you will find the difference between Mr. Lincoln and myself. When I make a mistake, as an honest man, I correct it without being asked to do so, but when he makes a false charge he sticks to it, and never corrects it. ("Don't spare him," and cheers.) One word more in regard to these resolutions: I quoted them at Ottawa merely to ask Mr. Lincoln whether he stood on that platform. That was the purpose for which I quoted them. I did not think that I had a right to put idle questions to him, and I first laid a foundation for my questions by showing that the principles which I wished him either to affirm or deny had been adopted by some portion of his friends, at least, as their creed. Hence I read the resolutions, and put the questions to him, and he then refused to answer them. (Laughter, "he was afraid," &c.) Subsequently, one week afterwards, he did answer a part of them, but the others he has not answered up to this day. ("No, and never will," "never can," and cheers.) My friends, if you are my friends, you will be silent, instead of interrupting me by your applause. ("We can't help it.")

Now, let me call your attention for a moment to the answers which Mr. Lincoln made at Freeport to the questions which I propounded him at Ottawa, based upon the platform adopted by a majority of the Abolition counties of the State, which now as then supported him. In answer to my question whether he endorsed the Black Republican principle of "no more slave States," he answered that he was not pledged against the admission of any more slave States, but that he would be very sorry if he should ever be placed in a position where he would have to vote on the question; that he would rejoice to know that no more slave States would be admitted into the Union; "but," he added, "if slavery shall be kept out of the territories during the territorial existence of any one given territory, and then the people shall, having a fair chance and a clear field when they come to adopt the constitution, do such an extraordinary thing as to adopt a slave constitution, uninfluenced by the actual presence of the institution among them, I see no alternative, if we own the country, but to admit them into the Union." The point I wish him to answer is this: Suppose Congress should not prohibit slavery in the territory, and it applied for admission with a constitution recognizing slavery, then how would he vote? His answer at Freeport does not apply to any territory in America. I ask you, (turning to Lincoln,) will you vote to admit Kansas into the Union, with just such a constitution as her people want, with slavery or without as they shall determine? He will not answer. (He's afraid, and cheers.) I have put that question to him time and time again, and have not been able to get an answer out of him. I ask you again, Lincoln, will you vote to admit New Mexico when she has the requisite population with such a constitution as her people adopt, either recognizing slavery or not as they shall determine? He will not answer. I put the same question to him in reference to Oregon and the new States to be carved out of Texas, in pursuance of the contract between Texas and the United States, and he will not answer. He will not answer these questions in reference to any territory now in existence; but says, that if Congress should prohibit slavery in a territory, and when its people asked for admission as a State, they should adopt slavery as one of their institutions, that he supposes he would have to let it come in. (Laughter.) I submit to you whether that answer of his to my question does not justify me in saying that he has a fertile genius in devising language to conceal his thoughts. (Good for you, hurrah for Douglas, &c.) I ask you whether there is an intelligent man in America who does not believe, that that answer was made for the purpose of concealing what he intended to do. (No, no, and cheers.) He wished to make the old line Whigs believe that he would stand by the compromise measures of 1850, which declared that the States might come into the Union with slavery, or without as they pleased, while Lovejoy and his abolition allies up North, explained to the abolitionists, that in taking this ground he preached good abolition doctrine, because his proviso would not apply to any territory in America, and therefore there was no chance of his being governed by it. It would have been quite easy for him to have said, that he would let the people of a State do just as they pleased, if he desired to convey such an idea. Why did he not do it? (He was afraid to.) He would not answer my question directly, because up North, the abolition creed declares that there shall be no more slave States, while down south, in Adams county, in Coles, and in Sangamon, he and his friends are afraid to advance that doctrine. Therefore, he gives an evasive and equivocal answer, to be construed one way in the south and another way in the north, which, when analyzed, it is apparent is not an answer at all with reference to any territory now in existence. ("Hit him on the woolly side," "Hurrah for Douglas," &c.)

Mr. Lincoln complains that, in my speech the other day at Galesburg, I read an extract from a speech delivered by him at Chicago, and then another from his speech at Charleston, and compared them, thus showing the people that he had one set of principles in one part of the State and another in the other part. And how does he answer that charge? Why, he quotes from his Charleston speech as I quoted from it, and then quotes another extract from a speech which he made at another place, which he says is the same as the extract from his speech at Charleston; but he does not quote the extract from his Chicago speech, upon which I convicted him of double dealing. (Cheers.) I quoted from his Chicago speech to prove that he held one set of principles up north among the abolitionists, and from his Charleston speech to prove that he held another set down at Charleston and in southern Illinois. In his answer to this charge, he ignores entirely his Chicago speech, and merely argues that he said the same thing which he said at Charleston at another place. If he did, it follows that he has twice, instead of once, held one creed in one part of the State and a different creed in another part. (He can't get out of it, and cheers.) Up at Chicago, in the opening of the campaign, he reviewed my reception speech, and undertook to answer my argument attacking his favorite doctrine of negro equality. I had shown that it was a falsification of the Declaration of Independence to pretend that that instrument applied to and included negroes in the clause declaring that all men were created equal. What was Lincoln's reply? I will read from his Chicago speech, and the one which he did not quote, and dare not quote, in this part of the State. ("Good," "hear, hear," &c.) He said:

I should like to know, if taking this old Declaration of Independence, which declares that all men are equal upon principle, and making exceptions to it, where will it stop? If one man says it does not mean a negro, why may not another man say it does not mean another man? If that declaration is not the truth, let us get the statute book in which we find it and tear it out!

There you find that Mr. Lincoln told the abolitionists of Chicago that if the Declaration of Independence did not declare that the negro was created by the Almighty the equal of the white man, that you ought to take that instrument and tear out the clause which says that all men were created equal. ("Hurrah for Douglas.") But let me call your attention to another part of the same speech. You know that in his Charleston speech, an extract from which he has read, he declared that the negro belongs to an inferior race; is physically inferior to the white man, and should always be kept in an inferior position. I will now read to you what he said at Chicago on that point. In concluding his speech at that place, he remarked:

My friends, I have detained you about as long as I desire to do, and I have only to say let us discard all this quibbling about this man and the other man—this race and that race and the other race being inferior, and therefore they must be placed in an inferior position, discarding our standard that we have left us. Let us discard all these things, and unite as one people throughout this land until we shall once more stand up declaring that all men are created equal.

Thus you see, that when addressing the Chicago abolitionists he declared that all distinctions of race must be discarded and blotted out, because the negro stood on an equal footing with the white man; that if one man said the Declaration of Independence did not mean a negro when it declared all men are created equal, that another man would say that it did not mean another man; and hence we ought to discard all differences between the negro race and all other races, and declare them all created equal. Did old Giddings, when he came down among you four years ago, preach more radical abolitionism than that? ("No, never.") Did Lovejoy, or Lloyd Garrison, or Wendell Phillips, or Fred. Douglass, ever take higher abolition grounds than that? Lincoln told you that I had charged him with getting up these personal attacks to conceal the enormity of his principles, and then commenced talking about something else, omitting to quote this part of his Chicago speech which contained the enormity of his principles to which I alluded. He knew that I alluded to his negro-equality doctrines when I spoke of the enormity of his principles, yet he did not find it convenient to answer on that point. Having shown you what he said in his Chicago speech in reference to negroes being created equal to white men, and about discarding all distinctions between the two races, I will again read to you what he said at Charleston:

> I will say then, that I am not nor ever have been in favor of bringing about in any way, the social and political equality of the white and black races; that I am not nor ever have been in favor of making voters of the free negroes, or jurors, or qualifying them to hold office, or having them to marry with white people. I will say in addition, that there is a physical difference between the white and black races, which, I suppose, will forever forbid the two races living together upon terms of social and political equality, and inasmuch as they cannot so live, that while they do remain together, there must be the position of superior and inferior, that I as much as any other man am in favor of the superior position being assigned to the white man.

A VOICE—That's the doctrine.

MR. DOUGLAS—Yes, sir, that is good doctrine, but Mr. Lincoln is afraid to advocate it in the latitude of Chicago, where he hopes to get his votes. (Cheers.) It is good doctrine in the anti-abolition counties for him, and his Chicago speech is good doctrine in the abolition counties. I assert, on the authority of these two speeches of Mr. Lincoln, that he holds one set of principles in the abolition counties, and a different and contradictory set in the other counties. ("That's so," and cheers.) I do not question that he said at Ottawa what he quoted, but that only convicts him further, by proving that he has twice contradicted himself instead of once. ("Good," and applause.) Let me ask him why he cannot avow his principles the same in the North as in the South—the same in every county, if he has a conviction that they are just? But I forgot—he would not be a Republican if his principles would apply alike to every part of the country. The party to which he belongs is bounded and limited by geographical lines. With their principles they cannot even cross the Mississippi river on your ferry boats. (Immense applause.) They cannot cross over the Ohio into Kentucky. Lincoln himself cannot visit the land of his fathers, the scenes of his childhood, the graves of his ancestors, and carry his abolition principles, as he declared them at Chicago, with him. ("Hit him again," and cheers.)

This Republican organization appeals to the North against the South; it appeals to northern passion, northern prejudice, and northern ambition, against southern people, southern States, and southern institutions, and its only hope of success is by that appeal.

Mr. Lincoln goes on to justify himself in making a war upon slavery, upon the ground that Frank Blair and Gratz Brown did not succeed in their warfare upon the institution in Missouri. (Laughter.) Frank Blair was elected to Congress in 1856, from the State of Missouri as a Buchanan Democrat, and he turned Fremonter after the people elected him, thus belonging to one party before his election, and another afterwards. (Treachery never succeeds.) What right then had he to expect, after having thus cheated his constituency, that they would support him at another election? ("None." "Hurrah for Douglas," &c.) Mr. Lincoln thinks that it is his duty to preach a crusade in the free States, against slavery, because it is a crime, as he believes, and ought to be extinguished; and because the people of the slave States will never abolish it. How is he going to abolish it? Down in the southern part of the State he takes the ground openly that he will not interfere with slavery where it exists, and says that he is not now and never was in favor of interfering with slavery where it exists in the States. Well, if he is not in favor of that, how does he expect to bring slavery in a course of ultimate extinction? ("Hit him again.") How can he extinguish it in Kentucky, in Virginia, in all the slave States by his policy, if he will not pursue a policy which will interfere with it in the States where it exists? ("That's so.") In his speech at Springfield before the Abolition or Republican convention, he declared his hostility to any more slave States in this language:

> Under the operation of that policy the agitation has not only not ceased, but has constantly augmented. In my opinion it will not cease until a crisis shall have been reached and passed. "A house divided against itself cannot stand." I believe this Government cannot endure permanently half slave and half free. I do not expect the Union to be dissolved—I do not expect the house to fall—but I do expect it will cease to be divided. It will become all one thing or all the other. Either the opponents of slavery will arrest the further spread of it, and place it where the public mind shall rest in the belief that it is in the course of ultimate extinction; or, its advocates will push it forward until it shall become alike lawful in all the States—old as well as new, North as well as South.

Mr. Lincoln there told his Abolition friends that this government could not endure permanently, divided into free and slave States as our fathers made it, and that it must become all free or all slave, otherwise, that the government could not exist. How then does Lincoln propose to save the Union, unless by compelling all the States to become free, so that the house shall not be divided against itself? He intends making them all free; he will preserve the Union in that way, and yet, he is not going to interfere with slavery anywhere it now exists. How is he going to bring it about? Why, he will agitate, he will induce the North to agitate until the South shall be worried out, and forced to abolish slavery. Let us examine the policy by which that is to be done. He first tells you that he would prohibit slavery everywhere in the territories. He would thus confine slavery within its present limits. When he thus gets it confined, and surrounded, so that it cannot spread, the natural laws of increase will go on until the negroes will be so plenty that they cannot live on the soil. He will hem them in until starvation seizes them, and by starving them to death, he will put slavery in the course of ultimate extinction. If he is not going to interfere with slavery in the States, but intends to interfere and prohibit it in the territories, and thus smother slavery out, it naturally follows, that he can extinguish it only by extinguishing the negro race, for his policy would drive them to starvation. This is the humane and Christian remedy that he proposes for the great crime of slavery.

He tells you that I will not argue the question whether slavery is right or wrong. I tell you why I will not do it. I hold that under the Constitution of the United States, each State of this Union has a right to do as it pleases on the subject of slavery. In Illinois we have exercised that sovereign right by prohibiting slavery within our own limits. I approve of that line of policy. We have performed our whole duty in Illinois. We have gone as far as we have a right to go under the constitution of our common country. It is none of our business whether slavery exists in Missouri or not. Missouri is a sovereign State of this Union, and has the same right to decide the slavery question for herself that Illinois has to decide it for herself. (Good.) Hence I do not choose to occupy the time allotted to me in discussing a question that we have no right to act upon. (Right.) I thought that you desired to hear us upon those questions coming within our constitutional power of action. Lincoln will not discuss these. What one question has he discussed that comes within the power or calls for the action or interference of an United States Senator? He is going to discuss the rightfulness of slavery when Congress cannot act upon it either way. He wishes to discuss the merits of the Dred Scott decision when under the constitution, a Senator has no right to interfere with the decision of judicial tribunals. He wants your exclusive attention to two questions that he has no power to act upon; to two questions that he could not vote upon if he was in Congress, to two questions that are not practical, in order to conceal your attention from other questions which he might be required to vote upon should he ever become a member of Congress. He tells you that he does not like the Dred Scott decision. Suppose he does not, how is he going to help himself? He says that he will reverse it. How will he reverse it? I know of but one mode of reversing judicial decisions, and that is by appealing from the inferior to the superior court. But I have never yet learned how or where an appeal could be taken from the Supreme Court of the United States! The Dred Scott decision was pronounced by the highest tribunal on earth. From that decision there is no appeal this side of Heaven. Yet, Mr. Lincoln says he is going to reverse that decision. By what tribunal will he reverse it? Will he appeal to a mob? Does he intend to appeal to violence, to Lynch law? Will he stir up strife and rebellion in the land and overthrow the court by violence? He does not deign to tell you how he will reverse the Dred Scott decision, but keeps appealing each day from the Supreme Court of the United States to political meetings in the country. (Laughter.) He wants me to argue with you the merits of each point of that decision before this political meeting. I say to you, with all due respect, that I choose to abide by the decisions of the Supreme Court as they are pronounced. It is not for me to inquire after a decision is made whether I like it in all the points or not. When I used to practice law with Lincoln, I never knew him to be beat in a case that he did not get mad at the judge and talk about appealing; (laughter,) and when I got beat I generally thought the court was wrong, but I never dreamed of going out of the court house and making a stump speech to the people against the judge, merely because I had found out that I did not know the law as well as he did. (Great laughter.) If the decision did not suit me, I appealed until I got to the Supreme Court, and then if that court, the highest tribunal in the world, decided against me, I was satisfied, because it is the duty of every law-abiding man to obey the constitutions, the laws, and the constituted authorities. He who attempts to stir up odium and rebellion in the country against the constituted authorities, is stimulating the passions of men to resort to violence and to mobs instead of to the law. Hence, I tell you that I take the decisions of the Supreme Court as the law of the land, and I intend to obey them as such.

But, Mr. Lincoln says that I will not answer his question as to what I would do in the event of the court making so ridiculous a decision as he imagines they would by deciding that the free State of Illinois could not prohibit slavery within her own limits. I told him at Freeport why I would not answer such a question. I told him that there was not a man possessing any brains in America, lawyer or not, who ever dreamed that such a thing could be done. (Right.) I told him then, as I say now, that by all the principles set forth in the Dred Scott decision, it is impossible. I told him then, as I do now, that it is an insult to men's understanding, and a gross calumny on the court, to presume in advance that it was going to degrade itself so low as to make a decision known to be in direct violation of the constitution.

A Voice.—The same thing was said about the Dred Scott decision before it passed.

Mr. Douglas—Perhaps you think that the Court did the same thing in reference to the Dred Scott decision: I have heard a man talk that way before. The principles contained in the Dred Scott decision had been affirmed previously in various other decisions. What court or judge ever held that a negro was a citizen? (Laughter.) The State courts had decided that question over and over again, and the Dred Scott decision on that point only affirmed what every court in the land knew to be the law.

But, I will not be drawn off into an argument upon the merits of the Dred Scott decision. It is enough for me to know that the Constitution of the United States created the Supreme Court for the purpose of deciding all disputed questions touching the true construction of that instrument, and when such decisions are pronounced, they are the law of the land, binding on every good citizen. Mr. Lincoln has a very convenient mode of arguing upon the subject. He holds that because he is a Republican that he is not bound by the decisions of the Court, but that I being a Democrat am so bound. (Laughter and cheers.) It may be that Republicans do not hold themselves bound by the laws of the land and the Constitution of the country as expounded by the courts; it may be an article in the Republican creed that men who do not like a decision, have a right to rebel against it; but when Mr. Lincoln preaches that doctrine, I think he will find some honest Republican—some law-abiding man in that party—who will repudiate such a monstrous doctrine. The decision in the Dred Scott case is binding on every American citizen alike; and yet Mr. Lincoln argues that the Republicans are not bound by it, because they are opposed to it, (laughter,) whilst Democrats are bound by it, because we will not resist it. A Democrat cannot resist the constituted authorities of this country. (Good.) A Democrat is a law-abiding man, a Democrat stands by the Constitution and the laws, and relies upon liberty as protected by law, and not upon mob or political violence.

I have never yet been able to make Mr. Lincoln understand, or can I make any man who is determined to support him, right or wrong, understand how it is that under the Dred Scott decision the people of a Territory, as well as a State, can have slavery or not, just as they please. I believe that I can explain that proposition to all constitution-loving, law-abiding men in a way that they cannot fail to understand it. Chief Justice Taney, in his opinion in the Dred Scott case, said that slaves being property, the owner of them has a right to take them into a territory the same as he would any other property; in other words, that slave property, so far as the right to enter a territory is concerned, stands on the same footing with other property. Suppose we grant that proposition. Then any man has a right to go to Kansas and take his property with him, but when he gets there he must rely upon the local law to protect his property, whatever it may be. (That's so.) In order to illustrate this, imagine that three of you conclude to go to Kansas. One takes $10,000 worth of slaves, another $10,000 worth of liquors, and the third $10,000 worth of dry goods. When the man who owns the dry goods arrives out there and commences selling them, he finds that he is stopped and prohibited from selling until he gets a license, which will destroy all the profits he can make on his goods to pay for. When the man with the liquors gets there and tries to sell he finds a Maine liquor law in force which prevents him. Now, of what use is his right to go there with his property unless he is protected in the enjoyment of that right after he gets there? (That's it.) The man who goes there with his slaves finds that there is no law to protect him when he arrives there. He has no remedy if his slaves run away to another country: there is no slave code or police regulations, and the absence of them excludes his slaves from the territory just as effectually and as positively as a constitutional prohibition could.

Such was the understanding when the Kansas and Nebraska bill was pending in Congress. Read the speech of Speaker Orr, of South Carolina, in the House of Representatives, in 1856, on the Kansas question, and you will find that he takes the ground that while the owner of a slave has a right to go into a territory, and carry his slaves with him, that he cannot hold them one day or hour unless there is a slave code to protect him. He tells you that slavery would not exist a day in South Carolina, or any other State, unless there was a friendly people and friendly legislation. Read the speeches of that giant in intellect, Alexander H. Stephens, of Georgia, and you will find them to the same effect. Read the speeches of Sam Smith, of Tennessee, and of all Southern men, and you will find that they all understood this doctrine then as we understand it now. Mr. Lincoln cannot be made to understand it, however. Down at Jonesboro, he went on to argue that if it be the law that a man has a right to take his slaves into territory of the United States under the constitution, that then a member of Congress was perjured if he did not vote for a slave code. I ask him whether the decision of the Supreme Court is not binding upon him as well as on me? If so, and he holds that he would be perjured if he did not vote for a slave code under it, I ask him whether, if elected to Congress, he will so vote? I have a right to his answer, and I will tell you why. He put that question to me down in Egypt, and did it with an air of triumph. This was about the form of it: "In the event of a slaveholding citizen of one of the territories should need and demand a slave code to protect his slaves, will you vote for it?" I answered him that a fundamental article in the Democratic creed, as put forth in the Nebraska bill and the Cincinnati platform, was non-intervention by Congress with slavery in the States and territories, ("Good," "That's the doctrine," and cheers,) and hence, that I would not vote in Congress for any code of laws either for or against slavery in any territory. I will leave the people perfectly free to decide that question for themselves. (Cheers.)

Mr. Lincoln and the Washington *Union* both think this a monstrous bad doctrine. Neither Mr. Lincoln or the Washington *Union* like my Freeport speech on that subject. The *Union*, in a late number, has been reading me out of the Democratic party because I hold that the people of a territory, like those of a State, have the right to have slavery or not, as they please. It has devoted three and a half columns to prove certain propositions, one of which I will read. It says:

> We propose to show that Judge Douglas' action in 1850 and 1854 was taken with especial reference to the announcement of doctrine and programme which was made at Freeport. The declaration at Freeport was, that "in his opinion the people can, by lawful means, exclude slavery from a territory before it comes in as a State;" and he declared that his competitor had "heard him argue the Nebraska bill on that principle all over Illinois in 1854, 1855, and 1856, and had no excuse to pretend to have any doubt upon that subject."

The Washington *Union* there charges me with the monstrous crime of now proclaiming on the stump the same doctrine that I carried out in 1850, by supporting Clay's compromise measures. The *Union* also charges that I am now proclaiming the same doctrine that I did in 1854 in support of the Kansas and Nebraska bill. It is shocked that I should now stand where I stood in 1850, when I was supported by Clay, Webster, Cass and the great men of that day, and where I stood in 1854, and in 1856, when Mr. Buchanan was elected President. It goes on to prove and succeeds in proving from my speeches in Congress on Clay's compromise measures, that

I held the same doctrines at that time that I do now, and then proves that by the Kansas and Nebraska bill I advanced the same doctrine that I now advance. It remarks:

So much for the course taken by Judge Douglas on the compromises of 1850. The record shows, beyond the possibility of cavil or dispute, that he expressly intended in those bills to give the territorial legislatures power to exclude slavery. How stands his record in the memorable session of 1854 with reference to the Kansas-Nebraska bill itself? We shall not overhaul the votes that were given on that notable measure. Our space will not afford it. We have his own words, however, delivered in his speech closing the great debate on that bill on the night of March 3, 1854, to show that *he meant* to do in 1854 precisely what *he had meant* to do in 1850. The Kansas-Nebraska bill being upon its passage, he said:

It then quotes my remarks upon the passage of the bill as follows:

The principle which we propose to carry into effect by this bill is this: That Congress shall neither legislate slavery into any Territory or State nor out of the same; but the people shall be left free to regulate their domestic concerns in their own way, subject only to the Constitution of the United States. In order to carry this principle into practical operation, it becomes necessary to remove whatever legal obstacles might be found in the way of its free exercise. It is only for the purpose of carrying out this great fundamental principle of self-government that the bill renders the eighth section of the Missouri act inoperative and void.

Now, let me ask, will those Senators who have arraigned me, or any one of them, have the assurance to rise in his place and declare that this great principle was never thought of or advocated as applicable to territorial bills, in 1850; that, from that session until the present, nobody ever thought of incorporating this principle in all new territorial organizations, &c., &c. I will begin with the compromises of 1850. Any Senator who will take the trouble to examine our journals will find that on the 25th of March of that year I reported from the committee on territories two bills, including the following measures: the admission of California, a territorial government for Utah, a territorial government for New Mexico and the adjustment of the Texas boundary. These bills proposed to leave the people of Utah and New Mexico free to decide the slavery question for themselves, *in the precise language of the Nebraska bill* now under discussion. A few weeks afterwards the committee of thirteen took those bills and put a wafer between them and reported them back to the Senate as one bill, with some slight amendments. *One of these amendments was, that the territorial legislatures should not legislate upon the subject of African slavery. I objected to this provision,* upon the ground that it subverted the great principle of self-government, *upon which the bill had been originally framed by the territorial committee.* On the first trial the Senate refused to strike it out, but subsequently did so, upon full debate, in order to establish that principle as the rule of action in territorial organizations.

The *Union* comments thus upon my speech on that occasion:

Thus it is seen that, in framing the Nebraska-Kansas bill, Judge Douglas framed it in the terms and upon the model of those of Utah and New Mexico, and that in the debate he took pains expressly to revive the recollection of the voting which had taken place upon amendments affecting the powers of the territorial legislatures over the subject of slavery in the bills of 1850, in order to give the same meaning, force, and effect to the Nebraska-Kansas bill on this subject as had been given to those of Utah and New Mexico.

The *Union* proves the following propositions: First, that I sustained Clay's compromise measures on the ground that they established the principle of self-government in the territories. Secondly, that I brought in the Kansas and Nebraska bill founded upon the same principles as Clay's compromise measures of 1850; and thirdly, that my Freeport speech is in exact accordance with those principles. And what do you think is the imputation that the *Union* casts upon me for all this? It says that my Freeport speech is not Democratic, and that I was not a Democrat in 1854 or in 1850! Now, is not that funny? (Great laughter and cheers.) Think that the author of the Kansas and Nebraska bill was not a Democrat when he introduced it. The *Union* says I was not a sound Democrat in 1850, nor in 1854, nor in 1856, nor am I in 1858 because I have always taken and now occupy the ground that the people of a territory, like those of a State, have the right to decide for themselves whether slavery shall or shall not exist in a territory. I wish to cite for the benefit of the Washington *Union* and the followers of that sheet, one authority on that point, and I hope the authority will be deemed satisfactory to that class of politicians. I will read from Mr. Buchanan's letter accepting the nomination of the Democratic Convention for the Presidency. You know that Mr. Buchanan, after he was nominated, declared to the Keystone Club, in a public speech, that he was no longer James Buchanan, but the embodiment of the Democratic platform. In his letter to the committee which informed him of his nomination, accepting it he defined the meaning of the Kansas and Nebraska bill and the Cincinnati platform in these words:

The recent legislation of Congress respecting domestic slavery, derived as it has been from the original and pure fountain of legitimate political power, the will of the majority, promises ere long to allay the dangerous excitement. This legislation is founded upon principles as ancient as free government itself, and in accordance with them has simply declared that the people of a territory like those of a State shall decide for themselves whether slavery shall or shall not exist within their limits.

Thus you see that James Buchanan accepted the nomination at Cincinnati, on the condition that the people of a territory, like those of a State, should be left to decide for themselves whether slavery should, or should not exist within their limits. I sustained James Buchanan for the Presidency on that platform, as adopted at Cincinnati, and expounded by himself. He was elected President on that platform, and now we are told by the Washington *Union* that no man is a true Democrat who stands on the platform on which Mr. Buchanan was nominated, and which he has explained and expounded himself. (Laughter.) We are told that a man is not a Democrat who stands by Clay, Webster, and Cass, and the Compromise measures of 1850, and the Kansas and Nebraska bill of 1854. Whether a man be a Democrat or not on that platform, I intend to stand there as long as I have life. (Stick to it, and cheers.) I intend to cling firmly to that great principle which declares the right of each State and each territory to settle the question of slavery, and every other domestic question for themselves. I hold that if they want a slave State they have a right under the Constitution of the United States to make it so, and if they want a free State, it is their right to have it. But the *Union*, in advocating the claims of Lincoln over me to the Senate, lays down two unpardonable heresies which it says I advocate. The first, is the right of the people of a territory, the same as a State, to decide for themselves the question whether slavery shall exist within their limits, in the language of Mr. Buchanan; and the second is, that a constitution shall be submitted to the people of a territory for its adoption or rejection before their admission as a State under it. It so happens that Mr. Buchanan is pledged to both these heresies, for supporting which the Washington *Union* has read me out of the Democratic church. In his annual message he said that he trusted that the example of the Minnesota case would be followed in all future cases, requiring a submission of the constitution; and in his letter of acceptance, he said that the people of a territory, the same as a State, had the right to decide for themselves whether slavery should exist within their limits. Thus you find that this little corrupt gang who control the *Union*, and wish to elect Lincoln in preference to me—because, as they say, of these two heresies which I support—denounce President Buchanan when they denounce me, if he stands now by the principles upon which he was elected. Will they pretend that he does not now stand by the principles on which he was elected? Do they hold that he has abandoned the Kansas-Nebraska bill, the Cincinnati platform, and his own letter accepting his nomination, all of which declare the right of the people of a territory, the same as a State, to decide the slavery question for themselves? I will not believe that he has betrayed or intends to betray the platform which elected him ("good"); but if he does, I will not follow him. ("Good again.") I will stand by that great principle, no matter who may desert it. I intend to stand by it for the purpose of preserving peace between the North and the South, the free and the slave States. ("Hurrah for Douglas.") If each State will only agree to mind its own business, and let its neighbors alone, there will be peace forever between us. We in Illinois tried slavery when a territory, and found it was not good for us in this climate and with our surroundings, and hence we abolished it. We then adopted a free State constitution, as we had a right to do. In this State we have declared that a negro shall not be a citizen ("all right"), and we have also declared that he shall not be a slave. We had a right to adopt that policy. Missouri has just as good a right to adopt the other policy. (That's it.) I am now speaking of rights under the constitution, and not of moral or religious rights. I do not discuss the morals of the people of Missouri, but let them settle that matter for themselves. I hold that the people of the slaveholding States are civilized men as well as ourselves, that they bear consciences as well as we, and that they are accountable to God and their posterity and not to us. It is for them to decide therefore the moral and religious right of the slavery question for themselves within their own limits. I assert that they had as much right under the constitution to adopt the system of policy which they have as we had to adopt ours. So it is with every other State in this Union. Let each State stand firmly by that great constitutional right, let each State mind its own business and let its neighbors alone, and there will be no trouble on this question. If we will stand by that principle, then Mr. Lincoln will find that this republic can exist forever divided into free and slave States, as our fathers made it and the people of each State have decided. Stand by that great principle and we can go on as we have done, increasing in wealth, in population, in power, and in all the elements of greatness, until we shall be the admiration and terror of the world. We can go on and enlarge as our population increases, and we require more room, until we make this continent one ocean-bound republic. Under that principle the United States can perform that great mission, that destiny which Providence has marked out for us. Under that principle we can receive with entire safety that stream of intelligence which is constantly flowing from the Old World to the New, filling up our prairies, clearing our wildernesses and building cities, towns, railroads and other internal improvements, and thus make this the asylum of the oppressed of the whole earth. We have this great mission to perform, and it can only be performed by adhering faithfully to that principle of self-government on which our institutions were all established. I repeat that the principle is the right of each State, each territory, to decide this slavery question for itself, to have slavery or not, as it chooses, and it does not become Mr. Lincoln, or anybody else, to tell the people of Kentucky that they have no consciences, that they are living in a state of iniquity, and that they are cherishing an institution to their bosoms in violation of the law of God. Better for him to adopt the doctrine of "judge not lest ye be judged." (Good, and applause.) Let him perform his own duty at home, and he will have a better fate in the future. I think there are objects of charity enough in the free States to excite the sympathies and open the pockets of all the benevolence we have amongst us, without going abroad in search of negroes, of whose condition we know nothing. We have enough objects of charity at home, and it is our duty to take care of our own poor, and our own suffering, before we go abroad to intermeddle with other people's business.

My friends, I am told that my time is within two minutes of expiring. I have omitted many topics that I would like to have discussed before you at length. There were many points touched by Mr. Lincoln that I have not been able to take up for the want of time. I have hurried over each subject that I have discussed as rapidly as possible so as to omit but few, but one hour and a half is not time sufficient for a man to discuss at length one half of the great questions which are now dividing the public mind.

In conclusion, I desire to return to you my grateful acknowledgements for the kindness and the courtesy with which you have listened to me. It is something remarkable that in an audience as vast as this, composed of men of opposite politics and views, with their passions highly excited, there should be so much courtesy, kindness and respect exhibited not only towards one another, but towards the speakers, and I feel that it is due to you that I should thus express my gratitude for the kindness with which you have treated me. (Nine cheers were here given for Douglas.)

MR. LINCOLN'S REJOINDER.

On taking the stand, Mr. Lincoln was received with a tremendous cheer. He said:

MY FRIENDS:—Since Judge Douglas has said to you in his conclusion that he had not time in an hour and a half to answer all I had said in an hour, it follows of course that I will not be able to answer in half an hour all that he said in an hour and a half. [Cheers and laughter.]

I wish to return Judge Douglas my profound thanks for his public annunciation here to-day, to be put on record, that his system of policy in regard to the institution of slavery *contemplates that it shall last forever*. [Great cheers, and cries of "Hit him again."] We are getting a little nearer the true issue of this controversy, and I am profoundly grateful for this one sentence. Judge Douglas asks you "why cannot the institution of slavery, or rather, why cannot the nation, part slave and part free, continue as our fathers made it *forever*?" In the first place, I insist that our fathers *did not* make this nation half slave and half free, or part slave and part free. [Applause, and "That's so."] I insist that they found the institution of slavery existing here. They did not make it so, but they left it so because they knew of no way to get rid of it at that time. ["Good," "Good," "That's true."] When Judge Douglas undertakes to say that as a matter of choice the fathers of the government made this nation part slave and part free, *he assumes what is historically a falsehood*. [Long continued applause.] More than that; when the fathers of the government cut off the source of slavery by the abolition of the slave trade, and adopted a system of restricting it from the new Territories where it had not existed, I maintain that they placed it where they understood, and all sensible men understood, it was in the course of ultimate extinction ["that's so"]; and when Judge Douglas asks me why it cannot continue as our fathers made it, I ask him why he and his friends could not let it remain as our fathers made it? [Tremendous cheering.]

It is precisely all I ask of him in relation to the institution of slavery, that it shall be placed upon the basis that our fathers placed it upon. Mr. Brooks, of South Carolina, once said, and truly said, that when this government was established, no one expected the institution of slavery to last until this day; and that the men who formed this government were wiser and better men than the men of these days; but the men of these days had experience which the fathers had not, and that experience had taught them the invention of the cotton gin, and this had made the perpetuation of the institution of slavery a necessity in this country. Judge Douglas could not let it stand upon the basis upon which our fathers placed it, but removed it and *put it upon the cotton gin basis*. [Roars of laughter and enthusiastic applause.] It is a question, therefore, for him and his friends to answer—why they could not let it remain where the fathers of the Government originally placed it. [Cheers, and cries of "Hurrah for Lincoln!" "Good!" "Good!"]

I hope nobody has understood me as trying to sustain the doctrine that we have a right to quarrel with Kentucky, or Virginia, or any of the slave States, about the institution of slavery—thus giving the Judge an opportunity to make himself eloquent and valiant against us in fighting for their rights. I expressly declared in my opening speech, that I had neither the inclination to exercise, nor the belief in the existence of the right to interfere with the States of Kentucky or Virginia in doing as they pleased with slavery or any other existing institution. [Loud applause.] Then what becomes of all his eloquence in behalf of the rights of States, which are assailed by no living man? [Applause. "He knows it's all humbuggery."]

But I have to hurry on, for I have but a half hour. The Judge has informed me, or informed this audience, that the Washington *Union* is laboring for my election to the United States Senate. [Cheers and laughter.] That is news to me—not very ungrateful news either. [Turning to Mr. W. H. Carlin, who was on the stand] —I hope that Carlin will be elected to the State Senate and will vote for me.[14] [Mr. Carlin shook his head.] Carlin don't fall in, I perceive, and I suppose he will not do much for me [laughter], but I am glad of all the support I can get anywhere, if I can get it without practicing any deception to obtain it. In respect to this large portion of Judge Douglas' speech, in which he tries to show that in the controversy between himself and the Administration party he is in the right, I do not feel myself at all competent or inclined to answer him. I say to him, "Give it to them [laughter]—give it to them just all you can" [renewed laughter and cheers]—and, on the other hand, I say to Carlin, and Jake Davis,[15] and to this man Wagley[16] up here in Hancock, "Give it to Douglas [roars of laughter] —just pour it into him." [Cheers and laughter—"Good for you," "Hurrah for Lincoln!"]

Now in regard to this matter of the Dred Scott decision, I wish to say a word or two. After all, the Judge will not say whether, if a decision is made holding that the people of the *States* cannot exclude slavery, he will support it or not. He obstinately refuses to say what he will do in that case. The Judges of the Supreme Court as obstinately refused to say what they would do on this subject. Before this I reminded him that at Galesburg he had said the Judges had expressly declared the contrary, and you remember

[14] State Senator William H. Carlin of Adams County was not re-elected.

[15] Jacob C. Davis, in the state senate 1844-1848, 1850-1856.

[16] William C. Wagley of Warsaw, Illinois, a Buchanan Democrat, candidate for state senator.

that in my opening speech I told him I had the book containing that decision here, and I would thank him to lay his finger on the place where any such thing was said. He has occupied his hour and a half, and he has not ventured to try to sustain his assertion. [Loud cheers.] *He never will.* [Renewed cheers.] But he is desirous of knowing how we are going to reverse the Dred Scott decision. Judge Douglas ought to know how. Did not he and his political friends find a way to reverse the decision of that same Court in favor of the constitutionality of the National Bank? [Cheers and laughter.] Didn't they find a way to do it so effectually that they have reversed it as completely as any decision ever was reversed—so far as its practical operation is concerned? [Cheers, and cries of "good," "good."] And let me ask you, didn't Judge Douglas find a way to reverse the decision of our Supreme Court, when it decided that Carlin's father—old Governor Carlin—had not the constitutional power to remove a Secretary of State? [Great cheering and laughter.] Did he not appeal to the "MOBS" as he calls them? Did he not make speeches in the lobby to show how villainous that decision was, and how it ought to be overthrown? Did he not succeed too in getting an act passed by the Legislature to have it overthrown? And didn't he himself sit down on that bench as one of the five added judges, who were to overslaugh the four old ones—getting his name of "Judge" in that way and no other? [Thundering cheers and laughter.] If there is a villainy in using disrespect or making opposition to Supreme Court decisions, I commend it to Judge Douglas' earnest consideration. [Cheers and laughter.] I know of no man in the State of Illinois who ought to know so well about *how much* villainy it takes to oppose a decision of the Supreme Court, as our honorable friend, Stephen A. Douglas. [Long continued applause.]

Judge Douglas also makes the declaration that I say the Democrats are bound by the Dred Scott decision while the Republicans are not. In the sense in which he argues, I never said it; but I will tell you what I have said and what I do not hesitate to repeat to-day. I have said that as the Democrats believe that decision to be correct and that the extension of slavery is affirmed in the National Constitution, they are bound to support it as such; and I will tell you here that General Jackson once said each man was bound to support the Constitution "as he understood it." Now, Judge Douglas understands the Constitution according to the Dred Scott decision, and he is bound to support it as he understands it. [Cheers.] I understand it another way, and therefore I am bound to support it in the way in which I understand it. [Prolonged applause.] And as Judge Douglas believes that decision to be correct, I will remake that argument if I have time to do so. Let me talk to some gentleman down there among you who looks me in the face. We will say you are a member of the Territorial Legislature, and like Judge Douglas, you believe that the right to take and hold slaves there is a constitutional right. The first thing you do is to *swear you will support the Constitution* and all rights guaranteed therein; that you will, whenever your neighbor needs your legislation to support his constitutional rights, not withhold that legislation. If you withhold that necessary legislation for the support of the Constitution and constitutional rights, do you not commit perjury? [Cries of "Yes."] I ask every sensible man, if that is not so? ["Yes, yes"—"That's a fact."] That is undoubtedly just so, say what you please. Now that is precisely what Judge Douglas says, that this is a constitutional right. Does the Judge mean to say that the Territorial Legislature in legislating may by withholding necessary laws, or by passing unfriendly laws, *nullify that constitutional right*? Does he mean to say that? Does he mean to ignore the proposition so long known and well established in the law, that what you cannot do directly, you cannot do indirectly? Does he mean that? The truth about the matter is this: Judge Douglas has sung paeans to his "Popular Sovereignty" doctrine until his Supreme Court co-operating with him has *squatted* his Squatter Sovereignty out. [Uproarious laughter and applause.] But he will keep up this species of humbuggery about Squatter Sovereignty. He has at last invented this sort of *do nothing Sovereignty*—[renewed laughter]—that the people may exclude slavery by a sort of "Sovereignty" that is exercised by doing nothing at all. [Continued laughter.] Is not that running his Popular Sovereignty down awfully? [Laughter.] Has it not got down as thin as the homoeopathic soup that was made by boiling the shadow of a pigeon that had starved to death? [Roars of laughter and cheering.] But at last, when it is brought to the test of close reasoning, there is not even that thin decoction of it left. It is a presumption impossible in the domain of thought. It is precisely no other than the putting of that most unphilosophical proposition, that two bodies may occupy the same space at the same time. The Dred Scott decision covers the whole ground, and while it occupies it, there is no room even for the shadow of a starved pigeon to occupy the same ground. [Great cheering and laughter.]

A Voice, on the platform—"Your time is almost out." [Loud cries of "Go on, go on"—"We'll listen all day."]

Well, I'll talk to you a little longer. Judge Douglas, in reply to what I have said about having upon a previous occasion made the speech at Ottawa as the one he took an extract from, at Charleston, says it only shows that I practiced the deception twice. Now, my friends, are any of you obtuse enough to swallow that? ["No, no, we're not such fools."] Judge Douglas had said I had made a speech at Charleston that I would not make up north, and I turned around and answered him by showing I *had* made that same speech up north—had made it at Ottawa—made it in his hearing—made it in *the* Abolition District—in Lovejoy's District—in the personal presence of Lovejoy himself—in the same atmosphere exactly in which I had made my Chicago speech of which he complains so much.

Now, in relation to my not having said anything about the quotation from the Chicago speech: He thinks that is a terrible subject for me to handle. Why, gentlemen, I can show you that the substance of the Chicago speech I delivered two years ago in "Egypt," as he calls it. It was down at Springfield. That speech is here in this book, and I could turn to it and read it to you but for the lack of time. I have not now the time to read it. ["Read it, read it, read it."] No, gentlemen, I am obliged to use discretion in disposing most advantageously of my brief time. The Judge has taken great exception to my adopting the heretical statement in the Declaration of Independence, that "all men are created equal," and he has a great deal to say about negro equality. I want to say that in sometimes alluding to the Declaration of Independence, I have only uttered the sentiments that Henry Clay used to hold. Allow me to occupy your time a moment with what he said. Mr. Clay was at one time called upon in Indiana, and in a way that I suppose was very insulting, to liberate his slaves, and he made a written reply to that application, and one portion of it is in these words:

> What is the *foundation* of this appeal to me in Indiana, to liberate the slaves under my care in Kentucky? It is a general declaration in the act announcing to the world the independence of the thirteen American colonies, that "*men are created equal.*" Now, as an abstract principle, *there is no doubt of the truth of that declaration*, and it is desirable in the *original construction* of society, and in organized societies, to keep it in view as a great fundamental principle.

[Loud cheers. "Hurrah for Clay."] When I sometimes, in relation to the organization of new societies in new countries, where the soil is clean and clear, insisted that we should keep that principle in view, Judge Douglas will have it that I want a negro wife. [Great laughter.] He never can be brought to understand that there is any middle ground on this subject. I have lived until my fiftieth year, and have never had a negro woman either for a slave or a wife, [cheers] and I think I can live fifty centuries, for that matter, without having had one for either. [Cheers and laughter.] I maintain that you may take Judge Douglas' quotations from my Chicago speech, and from my Charleston speech, and the Galesburg speech,—in his speech of to-day, and compare them over, and I am willing to trust them with you upon his proposition that they show rascality or double dealing. I deny that they do. [Great applause.]

The Judge does not seem at all disposed to have peace, but I find he is disposed to have a personal warfare with me. He says that my oath would not be taken against the bare word of Charles H. Lanphier or Thomas L. Harris. Well, that is altogether a matter of opinion. [Laughter.] It is certainly not for me to vaunt my word against oaths of these gentlemen, but I will tell Judge Douglas again the facts upon which I "*dared*" to say they proved a forgery. I pointed out at Galesburg that the publication of these resolutions in the Illinois *State Register* could not have been the result of accident, as the proceedings of that meeting bore unmistakable evidence of being done by a man who *knew* it was a forgery; that it was a publication partly taken from the real proceedings of the convention, and partly from the proceedings of a convention at another place; which showed that he had the real proceedings before him, and taking one part of the resolutions, he threw out another part and substituted false and fraudulent ones in their stead. I pointed that out to him, and also that his friend Lanphier, who was editor of the *Register* at that time and now is, must have known how it was done. Now whether *he* did it or got some friend to do it for him, I could not tell, but he certainly knew all about it. I pointed out to Judge Douglas that in his Freeport speech he had promised to *investigate* that matter. Does he now say he did not make that promise? ["No," "No."] I have a right to ask *why he did not keep it*? [Tremendous applause.] I call upon him to tell here to-day why he did not keep that promise. That fraud has been traced up so that it lies between him, Harris and Lanphier. There is little room for escape for Lanphier. [Laughter.] Lanphier is doing the Judge good service, and Douglas desires his word to be taken for the truth. He desires Lanphier to be taken as authority in what he states in his newspaper. He desires Harris to be taken as a man of vast credibility, and when this thing lies among them, they will not press it to show where the guilt really belongs. Now, as he has said that he would investigate it, and implied that he would tell us the result of his investigation, I demand of him to tell why he did not investigate it, if he did not; and if he did, *why he won't tell the result.* [Great cheers.] I call upon him for that.

This is the third time that Judge Douglas has assumed that he learned about these resolutions by Harris' attempting to use them against Norton[17] on the floor of Congress. I tell Judge Douglas the public records of the country show that *he* himself attempted it upon Trumbull a month before Harris tried them on Norton [great applause]—that Harris had the opportunity of *learning it from him,* rather than he from Harris. I now ask his attention to that part of the record on the case. My friends, I am not disposed to detain you longer in regard to that matter.

I am told that I still have five minutes left. There is another matter I wish to call attention to. He says, when he discovered there was a mistake in that case, he came forward magnanimously, without my calling his attention to it, and explained it. I will tell you how he became so magnanimous. When the newspapers of our side had discovered and published it, and put it beyond his power to deny it, then he came forward and made a virtue of necessity by acknowledging it. [Great applause.] Now he argues that all the point there was in those resolutions, although never passed at Springfield, is retained by their being passed at other localities. Is that true? He said I had a hand in passing them, in his opening speech—that I was in the Convention and helped to pass them. Do the resolutions touch me at all? It strikes me there is some difference between holding a man responsible for an act which he *has not* done, and holding him responsible for an act that he *has* done. You will judge whether there is any difference in the "*spots.*" [Laughter and cheers.] And he has taken credit for great magnanimity in coming forward and acknowledging what is proved on him beyond even the capacity of Judge Douglas to deny, and he has more capacity in that way than any other living man. [Laughter and cheers.]

Then he wants to know why I won't withdraw the charge in regard to a conspiracy to make slavery national, as he has withdrawn the one he made. May it please his worship, I will withdraw it *when it is proven false*[18] *on me as that was proved false*[19] *on him.* [Shouts of applause and laughter.] I will add a little more than that. I will withdraw it whenever a reasonable man shall be brought to believe that the charge is not true. [Renewed applause.] I have asked Judge Douglas' attention to certain matters of fact tending to prove the charge of a conspiracy to nationalize slavery, and he says he convinces me that this is all untrue because Buchanan was not in the country at that time, and because the Dred Scott case had not then got into the Supreme Court; and he

[17] U.S. Representative Jesse O. Norton, Joliet, Illinois.

[18] "False" inserted by Lincoln. [19] "False" inserted by Lincoln.

says that I say the *Democratic* owners of Dred Scott got up the case. I never did say that. [Applause.] I defy Judge Douglas to show that I ever said so *for I never uttered it.* [One of Mr. Douglas' reporters gesticulated affirmatively at Mr. Lincoln.] I don't care if your hireling does say I did, I tell you myself that *I never said the "Democratic" owners of Dred Scott got up the case.* [Tremendous enthusiasm.] I have never pretended to know whether Dred Scott's owners were Democrats or Abolitionists, or Free Soilers or Border Ruffians. I have said that there is evidence about the case tending to show that it was a made up case, for the purpose of getting that decision. I have said that that evidence was very strong in the fact that when Dred Scott was declared to be a slave, the owner of him made him free, showing that he had had the case tried and the question settled for such[20] use as could be made of that decision; he cared nothing about the property thus declared to be his by that decision. [Enthusiastic applause.] But my time is out and I can say no more.

[20] "As much" corrected by Lincoln to "such."

Seventh and Last Debate with Stephen A. Douglas at Alton, Illinois[1]

October 15, 1858

Seventh, and last joint debate. October 15. 1858. Douglas as reported in the Chicago Times. Lincoln as reported in the Press & Tribune.[2]

SENATOR DOUGLAS' SPEECH.

Long and loud bursts of applause greeted Senator Douglas when he appeared on the stand. As he was about to commence speaking, he was interrupted by Dr. Hope, one of the Danite faction.[3]

DR. HOPE.—Judge, before you commence speaking, allow me to ask you a question.

SENATOR DOUGLAS.—If you will not occupy too much of my time.

DR. HOPE.—Only an instant.

[1] Debates Scrapbook, ORB. As in the other debates, the editors have retained cheering and interruptions deleted by Lincoln. Insertions and corrections made by Lincoln are indicated in footnotes. Typographical errors not corrected in the scrapbook have been corrected by the editors. Bracketed passages are in the source unless otherwise noted.

[2] Lincoln's prefatory note in the debates scrapbook.

[3] Thomas M. Hope. "Danite" was the popular designation for Buchanan Democrats.

SENATOR DOUGLAS.—What is your question?

MR. HOPE.—Do you believe that the Territorial legislatures ought to pass laws to protect slavery in the territories?

SENATOR DOUGLAS.—You will get an answer in the course of my remarks. (Applause.)

LADIES AND GENTLEMEN: It is now nearly four months since the canvass between Mr. Lincoln and myself commenced. On the 16th of June the Republican Convention assembled at Springfield and nominated Mr. Lincoln as their candidate for the U.S. Senate, and he, on that occasion, delivered a speech in which he laid down what he understood to be the Republican creed and the platform on which he proposed to stand during the contest. The principal points in that speech of Mr. Lincoln's were: First, that this government could not endure permanently divided into free and slave States, as our fathers made it; that they must all become free or all become slave; all become one thing or all become the other, otherwise this Union could not continue to exist. I give you his opinions almost in the identical language he used. His second proposition was a crusade against the Supreme Court of the United States because of the Dred Scott decision; urging as an especial reason for his opposition to that decision that it deprived the negroes of the rights and benefits of that clause in the Constitution of the United States which guarantees to the citizens of each State, all the rights, privileges, and immunities of the citizens of the several States. On the 10th of July I returned home, and delivered a speech to the people of Chicago, in which I announced it to be my purpose to appeal to the people of Illinois to sustain the course I had pursued in Congress. In that speech I joined issue with Mr. Lincoln on the points which he had presented. Thus there was an issue clear and distinct made up between us on these two propositions laid down in the speech of Mr. Lincoln at Springfield, and controverted by me in my reply to him at Chicago. On the next day, the 11th of July, Mr. Lincoln replied to me at Chicago, explaining at some length, and re-affirming the positions which he had taken in his Springfield speech. In that Chicago speech he even went further than he had before, and uttered sentiments in regard to the negro being on an equality with the white man. (That's so.) He adopted in support of this position the argument which Lovejoy and Codding, and other Abolition lecturers had made familiar in the northern and central portions of the State, to wit: that the Declaration of Independence having[4] declared all men free and equal, by Divine law, also that negro equality was

[4] Probably the reporter's error for "had."

an inalienable right, of which they could not be deprived. He insisted, in that speech, that the Declaration of Independence included the negro in the clause asserting that all men were created equal, and went so far as to say that if one man was allowed to take the position, that it did not include the negro, others might take the position that it did not include other men. He said that all these distinctions between this man and that man, this race and the other race, must be discarded, and we must all stand by the Declaration of Independence, declaring that all men were created equal.

The issue thus being made up between Mr. Lincoln and myself on three points, we went before the people of the State. During the following seven weeks, between the Chicago speeches and our first meeting at Ottawa, he and I addressed large assemblages of the people in many of the central counties. In my speeches I confined myself closely to those three positions which he had taken controverting his proposition that this Union could not exist as our fathers made it, divided into free and slave States, controverting his proposition of a crusade against the Supreme Court because of the Dred Scott decision, and controverting his proposition that the Declaration of Independence included and meant the negroes as well as the white men, when it declared all men to be created equal. (Cheers for Douglas.) I supposed at that time that these propositions constituted a distinct issue between us, and that the opposite positions we had taken upon them we would be willing to be held to in every part of the State. I never intended to waver one hair's breadth from that issue either in the north or the south, or wherever I should address the people of Illinois. I hold that when the time arrives that I cannot proclaim my political creed in the same terms not only in the northern but the southern part of Illinois, not only in the northern but the southern States, and wherever the American flag waves over American soil, that then there must be something wrong in that creed. ("Good, good," and cheers.) So long as we live under a common constitution, so long as we live in a confederacy of sovereign and equal States, joined together as one for certain purposes, that any political creed is radically wrong which cannot be proclaimed in every State, and every section of that Union alike. I took up Mr. Lincoln's three propositions in my several speeches, analyzed them, and pointed out what I believed to be the radical errors contained in them. First, in regard to his doctrine that this government was in violation of the law of God which says, that a house divided against itself cannot stand, I repudiated it as a slander upon the immortal framers of our constitution. I then said, have often repeated, and now again assert, that in my opinion this government can endure forever, (good) divided into free and slave States as our fathers made it,—each State having the right to prohibit, abolish or sustain slavery just as it pleases. ("Good," "right," and cheers.) This government was made upon the great basis of the sovereignty of the States, the right of each State to regulate its own domestic institutions to suit itself, and that right was conferred with understanding and expectation that inasmuch as each locality had separate interests, each locality must have different and distinct local and domestic institutions, corresponding to its wants and interests. Our fathers knew when they made the government, that the laws and institutions which were well adapted to the green mountains of Vermont, were unsuited to the rice plantations of South Carolina. They knew then, as well as we know now, that the laws and institutions which would be well adapted to the beautiful prairies of Illinois would not be suited to the mining regions of California. They knew that in a Republic as broad as this, having such a variety of soil, climate and interest, there must necessarily be a corresponding variety of local laws—the policy and institutions of each State adapted to its condition and wants. For this reason this Union was established on the right of each State to do as it pleased on the question of slavery, and every other question; and the various States were not allowed to complain of, much less interfere, with the policy of their neighbors. ("That's good doctrine," "that's the doctrine," and cheers.)

Suppose the doctrine advocated by Mr. Lincoln and the abolitionists of this day had prevailed when the Constitution was made, what would have been the result? Imagine for a moment that Mr. Lincoln had been a member of the convention that framed the Constitution of the United States, and that when its members were about to sign that wonderful document, he had arisen in that convention as he did at Springfield this summer, and addressing himself to the President, had said "a house divided against itself cannot stand; (laughter) this government divided into free and slave States cannot endure, they must all be free or all be slave, they must all be one thing or all be the other, otherwise, it is a violation of the law of God, and cannot continue to exist;"—suppose Mr. Lincoln had convinced that body of sages, that that doctrine was sound, what would have been the result? Remember that the Union was then composed of thirteen States, twelve of which were slaveholding and one free. Do you think that the one free State would have outvoted the twelve slaveholding States, and thus have secured the abolition of slavery? (No, no.) On the other hand, would not the twelve slaveholding States have outvoted the one free State, and thus have fastened slavery, by a Constitutional provision, on every foot of the American Republic forever? You see that if this abolition doctrine of Mr. Lincoln had prevailed when the government was made, it would have established slavery as a permanent institution, in all the States whether they wanted it or not, and the question for us to determine in Illinois now as one of the free States is, whether or not we are willing, having become the majority section, to enforce a doctrine on the minority, which we would have resisted with our heart's blood had it been attempted on us when we were in a minority. ("We never will," "good, good," and cheers.) How has the South lost her power as the majority section in this Union, and how have the free States gained it, except under the operation of that principle which declares the right of the people of each State and each territory to form and regulate their domestic institutions in their own way. It was under that principle that slavery was abolished in New Hampshire, Rhode Island, Connecticut, New York, New Jersey, and Pennsylvania; it was under that principle that one half of the slaveholding States became free; it was under that principle that the number of free States increased until from being one out of twelve States, we have grown to be the majority of States of the whole Union, with the power to control the House of Representatives and Senate, and the power, consequently, to elect a President by Northern votes without the aid of a Southern State. Having obtained this power under the operation of that great principle, are you now prepared to abandon the principle and declare that merely because we have the power you will wage a war against the Southern States and their institutions until you force them to abolish slavery everywhere. (No, never, and great applause.)

After having pressed these arguments home on Mr. Lincoln for seven weeks, publishing a number of my speeches, we met at Ottawa in joint discussion, and he then began to crawfish a little, and let himself down. (Immense applause.) I there propounded certain questions to him. Amongst others, I asked him whether he would vote for the admission of any more slave States in the event the people wanted them. He would not answer. (Applause and laughter.) I then told him that if he did not answer the question there I would renew it at Freeport, and would then trot him down into Egypt and again put it to him. (Cheers.) Well, at Freeport, knowing that the next joint discussion took place in Egypt, and being in dread of it, he did answer my question in regard to no more slave States in a mode which he hoped would be satisfactory to me, and accomplish the object he had in view. I will show you what his answer was. After saying that he was not pledged to the Republican doctrine of "no more slave States," he declared

> I state to you freely, frankly, that I should be exceedingly sorry to ever be put in the position of having to pass upon that question. I should be exceedingly glad to know that there never would be another slave State admitted into this Union.

Here, permit me to remark, that I do not think the people will ever force him into a position against his will. (Great laughter and applause.) He went on to say:

> But I must add in regard to this, that if slavery shall be kept out of the territory during the territorial existence of any one given territory and then the people should, having a fair chance and clear field when they come to adopt a constitution, if they should do the extraordinary thing of adopting a slave constitution, uninfluenced by the actual presence of the institution among them, I see no alternative if we own the country, but we must admit it into the Union.

That answer Mr. Lincoln supposed would satisfy the old-line Whigs, composed of Kentuckians and Virginians, down in the southern part of the State. Now, what does it amount to? I desired to know whether he would vote to allow Kansas to come into the Union with slavery or not as her people desired. He would not answer; but in a round about way said that if slavery should be kept out of a territory during the whole of its territorial existence, and then the people, when they adopted a State constitution, asked admission as a slave State, he supposed he would have to let the State come in. The case I put to him was an entirely different one. I desired to know whether he would vote to admit a State if Congress had not prohibited slavery in it during its territorial existence, as Congress never pretended to do under Clay's compromise measures of 1850. He would not answer, and I have not yet been able to get an answer from him. (Laughter, "he'll answer this time," "he's afraid to answer," etc.) I have asked him whether he would vote to admit Nebraska if her people asked to come in as a State with a constitution recognizing slavery, and he refused to answer. ("Put him through," "give it to him," and cheers.) I have put the question to him with reference to New Mexico, and he has not uttered a word in answer. I have enumerated the territories, one after another, putting the same question to him with reference to each, and he has not said, and will not say, whether, if elected to Congress, he will vote to admit any territory now in existence with such a constitution as her people may adopt. He invents a case which does not exist, and cannot exist under this government, and answers it; but he will not answer the question I put to him in connection with any of the territories now in existence. ("Hurrah for Douglas," "three cheers for Douglas.") The contract we entered into with Texas when she entered the Union obliges us to allow four States to be formed out of the old State, and admitted with or without slavery as the respective inhabitants of each may determine. I have asked Mr. Lincoln three times in our joint discussions whether he would vote to redeem that pledge, and he has never yet answered. He is as silent as the grave on the subject. (Laughter, "Lincoln must answer," "he will," &c.) He would rather answer as to a state of the case which will never arise than commit himself by telling what he would do in a case which would come up for his action soon after his election to Congress. ("He'll never have to act on any question," and laughter.) Why can he not say whether he is willing to allow the people of each State to have slavery or not as they please, and to come into the Union when they have the requisite population as a slave or a free State as they decide? I have no trouble in answering the question. I have said everywhere, and now repeat it to you, that if the people of Kansas want a slave State they have a right, under the constitution of the United States, to form such a State, and I will let them come into the Union with slavery or without, as they determine. ("That's right," "good," "hurrah for Douglas all the time," and cheers.) If the people of any other territory desire slavery let them have it. If they do not want it let them prohibit it. It is their business not mine. ("That's the doctrine.") It is none of your business in Missouri whether Kansas shall adopt slavery or reject it. It is the business of her people and none of yours. The people of Kansas has as much right to decide that question for themselves as you have in Missouri to decide it for yourselves, or we in Illinois to decide it for ourselves. ("That's what we believe," "We stand by that," and cheers.)

And here I may repeat what I have said in every speech I have made in Illinois, that I fought the Lecompton constitution to its death, not because of the slavery clause in it, but because it was not the act and deed of the people of Kansas. I said then in Congress, and I say now, that if the people of Kansas want a slave State, they have a right to have it. If they wanted the Lecompton constitution, they had a right to have it. I was opposed to that constitution because I did not believe that it was the act and deed of the people, but on the contrary, the act of a small, pitiful minority acting in the name of the majority. When at last it was determined to send that constitution back to the people, and accordingly, in August last, the question of admission under it was submitted to a popular vote, the citizens rejected it by nearly ten to one, thus showing conclusively, that I was right when I said that the Lecompton constitution was not the act and deed of the people of Kansas, and did not embody their will. (Cheers.)

I hold that there is no power on earth, under our system of government, which has the right to force a constitution upon an unwilling people. (That's so.) Suppose there had been a majority of ten to one in favor of slavery in Kansas, and suppose there had been an abolition President, and an abolition administration, and by some means the abolitionists succeeded in forcing an abolition constitution on those slaveholding people, would the people of the South have submitted to that act for one instant. (No, no.) Well, if you of the South would not have submitted to it a day, how can you, as fair, honorable and honest men insist on putting a slave constitution on a people who desire a free State. ("That's so," and cheers.) Your safety and ours depend upon both of us acting in good faith, and living up to that great principle which asserts the right of every people to form and regulate their domestic institutions to suit themselves, subject only to the Constitution of the United States. ("That's the doctrine," and immense applause.)

Most of the men who denounced my course on the Lecompton question, objected to it not because I was not right, but because they thought it expedient at that time, for the sake of keeping the party together, to do wrong. (Cheers.) I never knew the Democratic party to violate any one of its principles out of policy or expediency, that it did not pay the debt with sorrow. There is no safety or success for our party unless we always do right, and trust the consequences to God and the people. I chose not to depart from principle for the sake of expediency in the Lecompton question, and I never intend to do it on that or any other question. (Good.)

But I am told that I would have been all right if I had only voted for the English bill after Lecompton was killed. (Laughter and cheers.) You know a general pardon was granted to all political offenders on the Lecompton question, provided they would only vote for the English bill. I did not accept the benefits of that pardon, for the reason that I had been right in the course I had pursued, and hence did not require any forgiveness. Let us see how the result has been worked out. English brought in his bill referring the Lecompton Constitution back to the people, with the provision that if it was rejected Kansas should be kept out of the Union until she had the full ratio of population required for a member of Congress, thus in effect declaring that if the people of Kansas would only consent to come into the Union under the Lecompton Constitution, and have a slave State when they did not want it, they should be admitted with a population of 35,000, but that if they were so obstinate as to insist upon having just such a constitution as they thought best, and to desire admission as a free State, then they should be kept out until they had 93,420 inhabitants. I then said, and I now repeat to you, that whenever Kansas has people enough for a slave State she has people enough for a free State. ("That's the doctrine all over," "Hurrah for Douglas.") I was and am willing to adopt the rule that no State shall ever come into the Union until she has the full ratio of population for a member of Congress, provided that rule is made uniform. I made that proposition in the Senate last winter, but a majority of the Senators would not agree to it; and I then said to them if you will not adopt the general rule I will not consent to make an exception of Kansas.

I hold that it is a violation of the fundamental principles of this government to throw the weight of federal power into the scale, either in favor of the free or the slave States. Equality among all the States of this Union is a fundamental principle in our political system. We have no more right to throw the weight of the federal government into the scale in favor of the slaveholding than the free States, and last of all should our friends in the South consent for a moment that Congress should withhold its powers either way when they know that there is a majority against them in both Houses of Congress.

Fellow citizens, how have the supporters of the English bill stood up to their pledges not to admit Kansas until she obtained a population of 93,420 in the event she rejected the Lecompton constitution? How? The newspapers inform us that English himself, whilst conducting his canvass for re-election, and in order to secure it, pledged himself to his constituents that if returned he would disregard his own bill and vote to admit Kansas into the Union with such population as she might have when she made application. (Laughter and applause.) We are informed that every Democratic candidate for Congress in all the States where elections have recently been held, was pledged against the English bill, with perhaps one or two exceptions. Now, if I had only done as these Anti-Lecompton men who voted for the English bill in Congress, pledging themselves to refuse to admit Kansas if she refused to become a slave State until she had a population of 93,420, and then returned to their people, forfeited their pledge, and made a new pledge to admit Kansas at any time she applied, without regard to population, I would have had no trouble. You saw the whole power and patronage of the federal government wielded in Indiana, Ohio, and Pennsylvania to re-elect Anti-Lecompton men to Congress who voted against Lecompton, then voted for the English bill, and then denounced the English bill, and pledged themselves to their people to disregard it. (Good.) My sin consists in not having given a pledge, and then in not having afterwards forfeited it. For that reason, in this State, every postmaster, every route agent, every collector of the ports, and every federal office holder, forfeits his head the moment he expresses a preference for the Democratic candidates against Lincoln and his abolition associates. (That's so, and cheers.) A Democratic Administration which we helped to bring into power, deems it consistent with its fidelity to principle and its regard to duty, to wield its power in this State in behalf of the Republican abolition candidates in every county and every Congressional district against the Democratic party. All I have to say in reference to the matter is, that if that administration have not regard enough for principle, if they are not sufficiently attached to the creed of the Democratic party to bury forever their personal hostilities in order to succeed in carrying out our glorious principles, I have. (Good, good, and cheers.) I have no personal difficulties with Mr. Buchanan or his cabinet. He chose to make certain recommendations to Congress as he had a right to do on the Lecompton question. I could not vote in favor of them. I had as much right to judge for myself how I should vote as he had how he should recommend. He undertook to say to me, if you do not vote as I tell you, I will take off the heads of your friends. (Laughter.) I replied to him, "you did not elect me, I represent Illinois and I am accountable to Illinois, as my constituency, and to God, but not to the President or to any other power on earth." (Good, good, and vociferous applause.)

And now this warfare is made on me because I would not surrender my connections of duty, because I would not abandon my constituency, and receive the orders of the executive authorities how I should vote in the Senate of the United States. ("Never do it," "three cheers," &c.) I hold that an attempt to control the Senate on the part of the Executive is subversive of the principles of our constitution. ("That's right.") The Executive department is independent of the Senate, and the Senate is independent of the President. In matters of legislation the President has a veto on the action of the Senate, and in appointments and treaties the Senate has a veto on the President. He has no more right to tell me how

I shall vote on his appointments than I have to tell him whether he shall veto or approve a bill that the Senate has passed. Whenever you recognize the right of the Executive to say to a Senator, "do this, or I will take off the heads of your friends," you convert this government from a republic into a despotism. (Hear, hear, and cheers.) Whenever you recognize the right of a President to say to a member of Congress, "vote as I tell you, or I will bring a power to bear against you at home which will crush you," you destroy the independence of the representative, and convert him into a tool of Executive power. ("That's so," and applause.) I resisted this invasion of the constitutional rights of a Senator, and I intend to resist it as long as I have a voice to speak, or a vote to give. Yet, Mr. Buchanan cannot provoke me to abandon one iota of Democratic principles out of revenge or hostility to his course. ("Good, good, three cheers for Douglas.") I stand by the platform of the Democratic party, and by its organization, and support its nominees. If there are any who choose to bolt, the fact only shows that they are not as good Democrats as I am. ("That's so," "good," and applause.)

My friends, there never was a time when it was as important for the Democratic party, for all national men, to rally and stand together as it is to-day. We find all sectional men giving up past differences and continuing the one question of slavery, and when we find sectional men thus uniting, we should unite to resist them and their treasonable designs. Such was the case in 1850, when Clay left the quiet and peace of his home, and again entered upon public life to quell agitation and restore peace to a distracted Union. Then we Democrats, with Cass at our head, welcomed Henry Clay, whom the whole nation regarded as having been preserved by God for the times. He became our leader in that great fight, and we rallied around him the same as the Whigs rallied around old Hickory in 1832, to put down nullification. (Cheers.) Thus you see that whilst Whigs and Democrats fought fearlessly in old times about banks, the tariff, distribution, the specie circular, and the sub-treasury, all united as a band of brothers when the peace, harmony, or integrity of the Union was imperiled. (Tremendous applause.) It was so in 1850, when abolitionism had even so far divided this country, North and South, as to endanger the peace of the Union; Whigs and Democrats united in establishing the compromise measures of that year, and restoring tranquillity and good feeling. These measures passed on the joint action of the two parties. They rested on the great principle that the people of each State and each territory should be left perfectly free to form and regulate their domestic institutions to suit themselves. You Whigs and we Democrats justified them in that principle. In 1854, when it became necessary to organize the territories of Kansas and Nebraska, I brought forward the bill on the same principle. In the Kansas-Nebraska bill you find it declared to be the true intent and meaning of the act not to legislate slavery into any State or territory, nor to exclude it therefrom, but to leave the people thereof perfectly free to form and regulate their domestic institutions in their own way. ("That's so," and cheers.) I stand on that same platform in 1858 that I did in 1850, 1854, and 1856. The Washington *Union*, pretending to be the organ of the Administration, in the number of the 5th of this month, devotes three columns and a half to establish these propositions: First, that Douglas, in his Freeport speech, held the same doctrine that he did in his Nebraska bill in 1854; second, that in 1854 Douglas justified the Nebraska bill upon the ground that it was based upon the same principle as Clay's compromise measures of 1850. The *Union* thus proved that Douglas was the same in 1858 that he was in 1856, 1854, and 1850, and consequently argued that he was never a Democrat. (Great laughter.) Is it not funny that I was never a Democrat? (Renewed laughter.) There is no pretence that I have changed a hair's breadth. The *Union* proves by my speeches that I explained the compromise measures of 1850 just as I do now, and that I explained the Kansas and Nebraska bill in 1854 just as I did in my Freeport speech, and yet says that I am not a Democrat, and cannot be trusted, because I have not changed during the whole of that time. It has occurred to me that in 1854 the author of the Kansas and Nebraska bill was considered a pretty good Democrat. (Cheers.) It has occurred to me that in 1856, when I was exerting every nerve and every energy for James Buchanan, standing on the same platform then that I do now, that I was a pretty good Democrat. (Renewed applause.) They now tell me that I am not a Democrat, because I assert that the people of a territory, as well as those of a State, have the right to decide for themselves whether slavery can or can not exist in such territory. Let me read what James Buchanan said on that point when he accepted the Democratic nomination for the Presidency in 1856. In his letter of acceptance, he used the following language:

> The recent legislation of Congress respecting domestic slavery, derived as it has been from the original and pure fountain of legitimate political power, the will of the majority, promises ere long to allay the dangerous excitement. This legislation is founded upon principles as ancient as free government itself, and in accordance with them has

simply declared that the people of a territory like those of a state, shall decide for themselves WHETHER SLAVERY SHALL OR SHALL NOT EXIST WITHIN THEIR LIMITS.

Dr. Hope will there find my answer to the question he propounded to me before I commenced speaking. (Vociferous shouts of applause.) Of course no man will consider it an answer, who is outside of the Democratic organization, bolts Democratic nominations, and indirectly aids to put abolitionists into power over Democrats. But whether Dr. Hope considers it an answer or not, every fair minded man will see that James Buchanan has answered the question, and has asserted that the people of a territory, like those of a State, shall decide for themselves whether slavery shall or shall not exist within their limits. I answer specifically if you want a further answer, and say that while under the decision of the Supreme Court, as recorded in the opinion of Chief Justice Taney, slaves are property like all other property and can be carried into territory of the United States the same as any other description of property, yet when you get them there they are subject to the local law of the territory just like all other property. You will find in a recent speech delivered by that able and eloquent statesman, Hon. Jefferson Davis, at Bangor, Maine, that he took the same view of this subject that I did in my Freeport speech. He there said:

> If the inhabitants of any territory should refuse to enact such laws and police regulations as would give security to their property or to his, it would be rendered more or less valueless in proportion to the difficulties of holding it without such protection. In the case of property in the labor of man, or what is usually called slave property, the insecurity would be so great that the owner could not ordinarily retain it. Therefore, though the right would remain, the remedy being withheld, it would follow that the owner would be practically debarred, by the circumstances of the case, from taking slave property into a territory where the sense of the inhabitants was opposed to its introduction. So much for the oft repeated fallacy of forcing slavery upon any community.

You will also find that the distinguished Speaker of the present House of Representatives, Hon. Jas. L. Orr, construed the Kansas and Nebraska bill in this same way in 1856, and also that great intellect of the South, Alex. H. Stephens, put the same construction upon it in Congress that I did in my Freeport speech. The whole South are rallying to the support of the doctrine that if the people of a Territory want slavery they have a right to have it, and if they do not want it that no power on earth can force it upon them. I hold that there is no principle on earth more sacred to all the friends of freedom than that which says that no institution, no law, no constitution, should be forced on an unwilling people contrary to their wishes; and I assert that the Kansas and Nebraska bill contains that principle. It is the great principle contained in that bill. It is the principle on which James Buchanan was made President. Without that principle he never would have been made President of the United States. I will never violate or abandon that doctrine if I have to stand alone. (Hurrah for Douglas.) I have resisted the blandishments and threats of power on the one side, and seduction on the other, and have stood immovably for that principle, fighting for it when assailed by Northern mobs, or threatened by Southern hostility. ("That's the truth," and cheers.) I have defended it against the North and the South, and I will defend it against whoever assails it, and I will follow it wherever its logical conclusions lead me. ("So will we all," "hurrah for Douglas.") I say to you that there is but one hope, one safety for this country, and that is to stand immovably by that principle which declares the right of each State and each territory to decide these questions for themselves. (Hear him, hear him.) This government was founded on that principle, and must be administered in the same sense in which it was founded.

But the Abolition party really think that under the Declaration of Independence the negro is equal to the white man, and that negro equality is an inalienable right conferred by the Almighty, and hence, that all human laws in violation of it are null and void. With such men it is no use for me to argue. I hold that the signers of the Declaration of Independence had no reference to negroes at all when they declared all men to be created equal. They did not mean negro, nor the savage Indians, nor the Fejee Islanders, nor any other barbarous race. They were speaking of white men. ("It's so," "it's so," and cheers.) They alluded to men of European birth and European descent—to white men, and to none others, when they declared that doctrine. ("That's the truth.") I hold that this government was established on the white basis. It was established by white men for the benefit of white men and their posterity forever, and should be administered by white men, and none others. But it does not follow, by any means, that merely because the negro is not a citizen, and merely because he is not our equal, that, therefore, he should be a slave. On the contrary, it does follow, that we ought to extend to the negro race, and to all other dependent races all the rights, all the privileges, and all the immunities which they can exercise consistently with the safety of society. Humanity requires that we should give them all these privileges; christianity commands that we should extend those privileges to them. The question then arises what are those privileges, and what is the nature and extent of them. My answer is that that is a question which each State must answer for itself. We in Illinois have decided it for ourselves. We tried slavery, kept it up for twelve years, and finding that it was not profitable we abolished it for that reason, and became a free State. We adopted in its stead the policy that a negro in this State shall not be a slave and shall not be a citizen. We have a right to adopt that policy. For my part I think it is a wise and sound policy for us. You in Missouri must judge for yourselves whether it is a wise policy for you. If you choose to follow our example, very good; if you reject it, still well, it is your business, not ours. So with Kentucky. Let Kentucky adopt a policy to suit herself. If we do not like it we will keep away from it, and if she does not like ours let her stay at home, mind her own business and let us alone. If the people of all the States will act on that great principle, and each State mind its own business, attend to its own affairs, take care of its own negroes and not meddle with its neighbors, then there will be peace between the North and the South, the East and the West, throughout the whole Union. (Cheers.) Why can we not thus have peace? Why should we thus allow a sectional party to agitate this country, to array the North against the South, and convert us into enemies instead of friends, merely that a few ambitious men may ride into power on a sectional hobby? How long is it since these ambitious Northern men wished for a sectional organization? Did any one of them dream of a sectional party as long as the North was the weaker section and the South the stronger? Then all were opposed to sectional parties; but the moment the North obtained the majority in the House and Senate by the admission of California, and could elect a President without the aid of Southern votes, that moment ambitious Northern men formed a scheme to excite the North against the South, and make the people be governed in their votes by geographical lines, thinking that the North, being the stronger section, would outvote the South, and consequently they, the leaders, would ride into office on a sectional hobby. I am told that my hour is out. It was very short.

MR. LINCOLN'S REPLY.

On being introduced to the audience, after the cheering had subsided Mr. Lincoln said:

LADIES AND GENTLEMEN:—I have been somewhat, in my own mind, complimented by a large portion of Judge Douglas' speech

—I mean that portion which he devotes to the controversy between himself and the present Administration. [Cheers and laughter.] This is the seventh time Judge Douglas and myself have met in these joint discussions, and he has been gradually improving in regard to his war with the Administration. [Laughter, "That's so."] At Quincy, day before yesterday, he was a little more severe upon the Administration than I had heard him upon any former occasion, and I took pains to compliment him for it. I then told him to "Give it to them with all the power he had;" and as some of them were present I told them I would be very much obliged if they would *give it to him* in about the same way. [Uproarious laughter and cheers.] I take it he has now vastly improved upon the attack he made then upon the Administration. I flatter myself he has really taken my advice on this subject. All I can say now is to recommend to him and to them what I then commended—to prosecute the war against one another in the most vigorous manner. I say to them again—"Go it, husband!—Go it, bear!" [Great laughter.]

There is one other thing I will mention before I leave this branch of the discussion—although I do not consider it much of my business, any way. I refer to that part of the Judge's remarks where he undertakes to involve Mr. Buchanan in an inconsistency. He reads something from Mr. Buchanan, from which he undertakes to involve him in an inconsistency; and he gets something of a cheer for having done so. I would only remind the Judge that while he is very valiantly fighting for the Nebraska bill and the repeal of the Missouri Compromise, it has been but a little while since he was the *valiant advocate of* the Missouri Compromise. [Cheers.] I want to know if Buchanan has not as much right to be inconsistent as Douglas has? [Loud applause and laughter; "Good, good!" "Hurrah for Lincoln!"] Has Douglas the *exclusive right*, in this country, of being *on all sides of all questions?* Is nobody allowed that high privilege but himself? Is he to have an entire *monopoly* on that subject? [Great laughter.]

So far as Judge Douglas addressed his speech to me, or so far as it was about me, it is my business to pay some attention to it. I have heard the Judge state two or three times what he has stated to day—that in a speech which I made at Springfield, Illinois, I had in a very especial manner, complained that the Supreme Court in the Dred Scott case had decided that a negro could never be a citizen of the United States. I have omitted by some accident heretofore to analyze this statement, and it is required of me to notice it now. In point of fact it is *untrue*. I never have complained *espe-*

cially of the Dred Scott decision because it held that a negro could not be a citizen, and the Judge is always wrong when he says I ever did so complain of it. I have the speech here, and I will thank him or any of his friends to show where I said that a negro should be a citizen, and complained especially of the Dred Scott decision because it declared he could not be one. I have done no such thing, and Judge Douglas' so persistently insisting that I have done so, has strongly impressed me with the belief of a pre-determination on his part to misrepresent me. He could not get his foundation for insisting that I was in favor of this negro equality anywhere else as well as he could by assuming that untrue proposition. Let me tell this audience what is true in regard to that matter; and the means by which they may correct me if I do not tell them truly is by a recurrence to the speech itself. I spoke of the Dred Scott decision in my Springfield speech, and I was then endeavoring to prove that the Dred Scott decision was a portion of a system or scheme to make slavery national in this country. I pointed out what things had been decided by the court. I mentioned as a fact that they had decided that a negro could not be a citizen—that they had done so, as I supposed, to deprive the negro, under all circumstances, of the remotest possibility of ever becoming a citizen and claiming the rights of a citizen of the United States under a certain clause of the Constitution. I stated that, without making any complaint of it at all. I then went on and stated the other points decided in the case, namely: that the bringing of a negro into the State of Illinois and holding him in slavery for two years here was a matter in regard to which they would not decide whether it made him free or not; that they decided the further point that taking him into a United States Territory where slavery was prohibited by act of Congress, did not make him free because that act of Congress as they held was unconstitutional. I mentioned these three things as making up the points decided in that case. I mentioned them in a lump taken in connection with the introduction of the Nebraska bill, and the amendment of Chase, offered at the time, declaratory of the right of the people of the Territories to *exclude slavery*, which was voted down by the friends of the bill. I mentioned all these things together, as evidence tending to prove a combination and conspiracy to make the institution of slavery national. In that connection and in that way I mentioned the decision on the point that a negro could not be a citizen, and in no other connection.

Out of this, Judge Douglas builds up his beautiful fabrication—of my purpose to introduce a perfect, social, and political equality between the white and black races. His assertion that I made an "especial objection" (that is his exact language) to the decision on this account, is untrue in point of fact.

Now, while I am upon this subject, and as Henry Clay has been alluded to, I desire to place myself, in connection with Mr. Clay, as nearly right before this people as may be. I am quite aware what the Judge's object is here by all these allusions. He knows that we are before an audience, having strong sympathies southward by relationship, place of birth, and so on. He desires to place me in an extremely Abolition attitude. He read upon a former occasion, and alludes without reading to-day, to a portion of a speech which I delivered in Chicago. In his quotations from that speech as he has made them upon former occasions, the extracts were taken in such a way, as I suppose, brings them within the definition of what is called *garbling*—taking portions of a speech which, when taken by themselves, do not present the entire sense of the speaker as expressed at the time. I propose, therefore, out of that same speech, to show how one portion of it which he skipped over (taking an extract before and an extract after) will give a different idea and the true idea I intended to convey. It will take me some little time to read it, but I believe I will occupy the time in that way.

You have heard him frequently allude to my controversy with him in regard to the Declaration of Independence. I confess that I have had a struggle with Judge Douglas on that matter, and I will try briefly to place myself right in regard to it on this occasion. I said—and it is between the extracts Judge Douglas has taken from this speech, and put in his published speeches—:

> It may be argued that there are certain conditions that make necessities and impose them upon us, and to the extent that a necessity is imposed upon a man he must submit to it. I think that was the condition in which we found ourselves when we established this government. We had slaves among us, we could not get our Constitution unless we permitted them to remain in slavery, we could not secure the good we did secure if we grasped for more; and having by necessity submitted to that much, it does not destroy the principle that is the charter of our liberties. Let that charter remain as our standard.

Now I have upon all occasions declared as strongly as Judge Douglas against the disposition to interfere with the existing institution of slavery. You hear me read it from the same speech from which he takes garbled extracts for the purpose of proving upon me a disposition to interfere with the institution of slavery, and establish a perfect social and political equality between negroes and white people.

Allow me while upon this subject briefly to present one other extract from a speech of mine, more than a year ago, at Springfield, in discussing this very same question, soon after Judge Douglas took his ground that negroes were not included in the Declaration of Independence:

> I think the authors of that notable instrument intended to include *all* men, but they did not mean to declare all men equal *in all respects*. They did not mean to say all men were equal in color, size, intellect, moral development or social capacity. They defined with tolerable distinctness in what they did consider all men created equal—equal in certain inalienable rights, among which are life, liberty and the pursuit of happiness. This they said, and this they meant. They did not mean to assert the obvious untruth, that all were then actually enjoying that equality, nor yet, that they were about to confer it immediately upon them. In fact they had no power to confer such a boon. They meant simply to declare the *right* so that the *enforcement* of it might follow as fast as circumstances should permit.
>
> They meant to set up a standard maxim for free society which should be familiar to all: constantly looked to, constantly labored for, and even though never perfectly attained, constantly approximated and thereby constantly spreading and deepening its influence and augmenting the happiness and value of life to all people, of all colors, everywhere.

There again are the sentiments I have expressed in regard to the Declaration of Independence upon a former occasion—sentiments which have been put in print and read wherever anybody cared to know what so humble an individual as myself chose to say in regard to it.

At Galesburg the other day, I said in answer to Judge Douglas, that three years ago there never had been a man, so far as I knew or believed, in the whole world, who had said that the Declaration of Independence did not include negroes in the term "all men." I re-assert it to-day. I assert that Judge Douglas and all his friends may search the whole records of the country, and it will be a matter of great astonishment to me if they shall be able to find that one human being three years ago had ever uttered the astounding sentiment that the term "all men" in the Declaration did not include the negro. Do not let me be misunderstood. I know that more than three years ago there were men who, finding this assertion constantly in the way of their schemes to bring about the ascendancy and perpetuation of slavery, *denied the truth of it*. I know that Mr. Calhoun and all the politicians of his school denied the truth of the Declaration. I know that it ran along in the mouths of some Southern men for a period of years, ending at last in that shameful though rather forcible declaration of Pettit of Indiana, upon the floor of the United States Senate, that the Declaration of Independence was in that respect "a self-evident lie," rather than a self-evident truth. But I say, with a perfect knowledge of all this hawking at the Declaration without directly attacking it, that three years ago there never had lived a man who had ventured to assail it in the sneaking way of pretending to believe it and then asserting it did not include the negro. [Cheers.] I believe the first man who ever said it was Chief Justice Taney in the Dred Scott case, and the next to him was our friend Stephen A. Douglas. [Cheers and laughter.] And now it has become the catch-word of the entire party. I would like to call upon his friends everywhere to consider how they have come in so short a time to view this matter in a way so entirely different from their former belief? to ask whether they are not being borne along by an irresistible current—whither, they know not? [Great applause.]

In answer to my proposition at Galesburg last week, I see that some man in Chicago has got up a letter addressed to the Chicago *Times*, to show as he professes that somebody *had* said so before; and he signs himself "An Old Line Whig," if I remember correctly. In the first place I would say he *was not* an Old Line Whig. I am somewhat acquainted with Old Line Whigs. I was with the Old Line Whigs from the origin to the end of that party; I became pretty well acquainted with them, and I know they always had some sense, whatever else you could ascribe to them. [Great laughter.] I know there never was one who had not more sense than to try to show by the evidence he produces[5] that some man had, prior to the time I named, said that negroes were not included in the term "all men" in the Declaration of Independence. What is the evidence he produces? I will bring forward *his* evidence and let you see what *he* offers by way of showing that somebody more than three years ago had said negroes were not included in the Declaration. He brings forward part of a speech from Henry Clay—*the* part of *the* speech of Henry Clay which I used to bring forward to prove precisely the contrary. [Laughter.] I guess we are surrounded to some extent to-day, by the old friends of Mr. Clay, and they will be glad to hear anything from that authority. While he was in Indiana a man presented him a petition to liberate his negroes, and he, (Mr. Clay) made a speech in answer to it, which I suppose he carefully wrote out himself and caused to be published. I have before me an extract from that speech which constitutes the evidence this pretended "Old Line Whig" at Chicago brought forward to show that Mr. Clay didn't suppose the negro

5 "By the evidence he produces" inserted by Lincoln.

was included in the Declaration of Independence. Hear what Mr. Clay said:

And what is the foundation of this appeal to me in Indiana, to liberate the slaves under my care in Kentucky? It is a general declaration in the act announcing to the world the independence of the thirteen American colonies, that all men are created equal. Now, as an abstract principle, *there is no doubt of the truth of that declaration;* and it is desirable *in the original construction of society, and in organized societies,* to keep it in view as a great fundamental principle. But, then, I apprehend that in no society that ever did exist, or ever shall be formed, was or can the equality asserted among the members of the human race be practically enforced and carried out. There are portions, large portions, women, minors, insane, culprits, transient sojourners, that will always probably remain subject to the government of another portion of the community.

That declaration whatever may be the extent of its import, was made by the delegations of the thirteen States. In most of them slavery existed, and had long existed, and was established by law. It was introduced and forced upon the colonies by the paramount law of England. Do you believe, that in making that Declaration the States that concurred in it intended that it should be tortured into a virtual emancipation of all the slaves within their respective limits? Would Virginia and other Southern States have ever united in a declaration which was to be interpreted into an abolition of slavery among them? Did any one of the thirteen colonies entertain such a design or expectation? To impute such a secret and unavowed purpose would be to charge a political fraud upon the noblest band of patriots that ever assembled in council; a fraud upon the confederacy of the Revolution; a fraud upon the union of those States whose constitution not only recognized the lawfulness of slavery, but permitted the importation of slaves from Africa until the year 1808.

This is the entire quotation brought forward to prove that somebody previous to three years ago had said the negro was not included in the term "all men" in the Declaration. How does it do so? In what way has it a tendency to prove that? Mr. Clay says *it is true as an abstract principle* that all men are created equal, but that we cannot practically apply it in all cases. He illustrates this by bringing forward the cases of females, minors and insane persons with whom it cannot be enforced; but he says it is true as an abstract principle in the organization of society as well as in organized society, and it should be kept in view as a fundamental principle. Let me read a few words more before I add some comments of my own. Mr. Clay says a little further on:

I desire no concealment of my opinions in regard to the institution of slavery. I look upon it as a great evil; and deeply lament that we have derived it from the parental government; and from our ancestors. But here they are and the question is, how can they be best dealt with?

If a state of nature existed and we were about to lay the foundations of society, *no man would be more strongly opposed than I should be, to incorporating the institution of slavery among its elements.*

Now here in this same book—in this same speech—is this same extract brought forward to prove that Mr. Clay held that the negro was not included in the Declaration of Independence—no such statement on his part, but the declaration *that it is a great fundamental truth*, which should be constantly kept in view in the organization of society and in societies already organized. But if I say a word about it—if I attempt, as Mr. Clay said all good men ought to do, to keep it in view—if, in this "organized society," I ask to have the public eye turned upon it—if I ask, in relation to the organization of new Territories that the public eye should be turned upon it—forthwith I am villified as you hear me to-day. What have I done, that I have not the license of Henry Clay's illustrious example here in doing? Have I done aught that I have not his authority for, while maintaining that in organizing new Territories and societies this fundamental principle should be regarded, and in organized society holding it up to the public view and recognizing what *he* recognized as the great principle of free government? [Great applause, and cries of "Hurrah for Lincoln."]

And when this new principle—this new proposition that no human being ever thought of three years ago,—is brought forward, *I combat it* as having an evil tendency, if not an evil design; I combat it as having a tendency to dehumanize the negro—to take away from him the right of ever striving to be a man. I combat it as being one of the thousand things constantly done in these days to prepare the public mind to make property, and nothing but property of the *negro in all the States of this Union.* [Tremendous applause. "Hurrah for Lincoln." "Hurrah for Trumbull."]

But there is a point that I wish before leaving this part of the discussion to ask attention to. I have read, and I repeat the words of Henry Clay:

> I desire no concealment of my opinions in regard to the institution of slavery. I look upon it as a great evil and deeply lament that we have derived it from the parental government, and from our ancestors. I wish every slave in the United States was in the country of his ancestors. But here they are; the question is how they can best be dealt with? If a state of nature existed and we were about to lay the foundation of society, no man would be more strongly opposed than I should be to incorporate the institution of slavery among its elements.

The principle upon which I have insisted in this canvass, is in relation to laying the foundations of new societies. I have never sought to apply these principles to the old States for the purpose of abolishing slavery in those States. It is nothing but a miserable perversion of what I *have* said, to assume that I have declared Missouri, or any other slave State shall emancipate her slaves. I have proposed no such thing. But when Mr. Clay says that in laying the foundations of societies in our Territories where it does not exist he would be opposed to the introduction of slavery as an element, I insist that we have *his warrant*—his license for insisting upon the exclusion of that element, which he declared in such strong and emphatic language *was most hateful to him.* [Loud applause.]

Judge Douglas has again referred to a Springfield speech in which I said "a house divided against itself cannot stand." The Judge has so often made the entire quotation from that speech that I can make it from memory. I used this language:

> We are now far into the fifth year since a policy was initiated with the avowed object and confident promise of putting an end to the slavery agitation. Under the operation of this policy, that agitation has not only not ceased but has constantly augmented. In my opinion it will not cease until a crisis shall have been reached and passed. "A house divided against itself cannot stand." I believe this government cannot endure permanently half Slave and half Free. I do not expect the house to fall—but I do expect it will cease to be divided. It will become all one thing, or all the other. Either the opponents of Slavery will arrest the further spread of it, and place it where the public mind shall rest in the belief that it is in the course of ultimate extinction, or its advocates will push it forward till it shall become alike lawful in all the States—old as well as new, North as well as South.

That extract and the sentiments expressed in it, have been extremely offensive to Judge Douglas. He has warred upon them as Satan does upon the Bible. [Laughter.] His perversions upon it are endless. Here now are my views upon it in brief.

I said we were now far into the fifth year since a policy was initiated with the avowed object and confident promise of putting an end to the slavery agitation. Is it not so? When that Nebraska bill was brought forward four years ago last January, was it not for the "avowed object" of putting an end to the slavery agitation? We were to have no more agitation in Congress; it was all to be banished to the Territories. By the way, I will remark here that, as Judge Douglas is very fond of complimenting Mr. Crittenden in these days, Mr. Crittenden has said there was a falsehood in that whole business, for there was *no slavery agitation at that time to allay*. We were for a little while *quiet* on the troublesome thing and that very allaying plaster of Judge Douglas', stirred it up again. [Applause and laughter.] But was it not understood or intimated with the "confident promise" of putting an end to the slavery agitation. Surely it was. In every speech you heard Judge Douglas make, until he got into this "imbroglio," as they call it, with the Administration about the Lecompton Constitution, every speech on that Nebraska bill was full of his felicitations that we were *just at the end* of the slavery agitation. The last tip of the last joint of the old serpent's tail was just drawing out of view. [Cheers and laughter.] But has it proved so? I have asserted that under that policy that agitation "has not only not[6] ceased, but has constantly augmented." When was there ever a greater agitation in Congress than last winter? When was it as great in the country as to-day?

There was a collateral object in the introduction of that Nebraska policy which was to clothe the people of the Territories with a superior degree of self-government, beyond what they had ever had before. The first object and the main one of conferring upon the people a higher degree of "self government," is a question of fact to be determined by you in answer to a single question. Have you ever heard or known of a people any where on earth who had as little to do, as, in the first instance of its use, the people of Kansas had with this same right of "self-government"? [Loud applause.] In its main policy, and in its collateral object, *it has been nothing but a living, creeping lie from the time of its introduction, till to-day.* [Loud cheers.]

I have intimated that I thought the agitation would not cease until a crisis should have been reached and passed. I have stated in what way I thought it would be reached and passed. I have said that it might go one way or the other. We might, by arresting the further spread of it and placing it where the fathers originally placed it, put it where the public mind should rest in the belief that it was in the course of ultimate extinction. Thus the agitation may cease. It may be pushed forward until it shall become alike lawful in all the States, old as well as new, North as well as South. I have said, and I repeat, my wish is that the further spread of it may be arrested, and that it may be placed where the public mind shall rest in the belief that it is in the course of ultimate extinction. [Great applause.] I have expressed that as my wish. I entertain the opinion upon evidence sufficient to my mind, that the fathers of this Government placed that institution where the public mind *did* rest in the belief that it was in the course of ultimate extinction. Let me ask why they made provision that the source of slavery—the African slave trade—should be cut off at the end of twenty years? Why did they make provision that in all the new territory

6 "Not" inserted by Lincoln.

we owned at that time slavery should be forever inhibited? Why stop its spread in one direction and cut off its source in another, if they did not look to its being placed in the course of ultimate extinction?

Again; the institution of slavery is only mentioned in the Constitution of the United States two or three times, and in neither of these cases does the word "slavery" or "negro race" occur; but covert language is used each time, and for a purpose full of significance. What is the language in regard to the prohibition of the African slave trade? It runs in about this way: "The migration or importation of such persons as any of the States now existing shall think proper to admit, shall not be prohibited by the Congress prior to the year one thousand eight hundred and eight."

The next allusion in the Constitution to the question of slavery and the black race, is on the subject of the basis of representation, and there the language used is, "Representatives and direct taxes shall be apportioned among the several States which may be included within this Union, according to their respective numbers, which shall be determined by adding to the whole number of free persons, including those bound to service for a term of years, and excluding Indians not taxed—three-fifths of all other persons."

It says "persons," not slaves, not negroes; but this "three-fifths" can be applied to no other class among us than the negroes.

Lastly, in the provision for the reclamation of fugitive slaves it is said: "No person held to service or labor in one State under the laws thereof escaping into another, shall in consequence of any law or regulation therein, be discharged from such service or labor, but shall be delivered up, on claim of the party to whom such service or labor may be due." There again there is no mention of the word "negro" or of slavery. In all three of these places, being the only allusions to slavery in the instrument, covert language is used. Language is used not suggesting that slavery existed or that the black race were among us. And I understand the contemporaneous history of those times to be that covert language was used with a purpose, and that purpose was that in our Constitution, which it was hoped and is still hoped will endure forever—when it should be read by intelligent and patriotic men, after the institution of slavery had passed from among us—there should be nothing on the face of the great charter of liberty suggesting that such a thing as negro slavery had ever existed among us. [Enthusiastic applause.] This is part of the evidence that the fathers of the Government expected and intended the institution of slavery to come to an end. They expected and intended that it should be in the course of ultimate extinction. And when I say that I desire to see the further spread of it arrested I only say I desire to see that done which the fathers have first done. When I say I desire to see it placed where the public mind will rest in the belief that it is in the course of ultimate extinction, I only say I desire to see it placed where they placed it. It is not true that our fathers, as Judge Douglas assumes, made this government part slave and part free. Understand the sense in which he puts it. He assumes that slavery is a rightful thing within itself,—was introduced by the framers of the Constitution. The exact truth is, that they found the institution existing among us, and they left it as they found it. But in making the government they left this institution with many clear marks of disapprobation upon it. They found slavery among them and they left it among them because of the difficulty—the absolute impossibility of its immediate removal. And when Judge Douglas asks me why we cannot let it remain part slave and part free as the fathers of the government made, he asks a question based upon an assumption which is itself a falsehood; and I turn upon him and ask him the question, when the policy that the fathers of the government had adopted in relation to this element among us was the best policy in the world—the only wise policy—the only policy that we can ever safely continue upon—that will ever give us peace unless this dangerous element masters us all and becomes a national institution—*I turn upon him and ask him why he could not let it alone?* [Great and prolonged cheering.] I turn and ask him why he was driven to the necessity of introducing a *new policy* in regard to it? He has himself said he introduced a new policy. He said so in his speech on the 22d of March of the present year, 1858. I ask him why he could not let it remain where our fathers placed it? I ask too of Judge Douglas and his friends why we shall not again place this institution upon the basis on which the fathers left it? I ask you when he infers that I am in favor of setting the free and slave States at war, when the institution was placed in that attitude by those who made the constitution, *did they make any war?* ["No;" "no;" and cheers.] If we had no war out of it when thus placed, wherein is the ground of belief that we shall have war out of it if we return to that policy? Have we had any peace upon this matter springing from any other basis? ["No, no."] I maintain that we have not. I have proposed nothing more than a return to the policy of the fathers.

I confess, when I propose a certain measure of policy, it is not enough for me that I do not intend[7] anything evil in the result, but

[7] "Perceive" corrected by Lincoln to "intend."

it is incumbent on me to show that it has not a *tendency* to that result. I have met Judge Douglas in that point of view. I have not only made the declaration that I do not *mean* to produce a conflict between the States, but I have tried to show by fair reasoning, and I think I have shown to the minds of fair men, that I propose nothing but what has a most peaceful tendency. The quotation that I happened to make in that Springfield speech, that "a house divided against itself cannot stand," and which has proved so offensive to the Judge, was part and parcel of the same thing. He tries to show that variety in the domestic institutions of the different States is necessary and indispensable. I do not dispute it. I have no controversy with Judge Douglas about that. I shall very readily agree with him that it would be foolish for us to insist upon having a cranberry law here, in Illinois, where we have no cranberries, because they have a cranberry law in Indiana, where they have cranberries. [Laughter, "good, good."] I should insist that it would be exceedingly wrong in us to deny to Virginia the right to enact oyster laws where they have oysters, because we want no such laws here. [Renewed laughter.] I understand, I hope, quite as well as Judge Douglas or anybody else, that the variety in the soil and climate and face of the country, and consequent variety in the industrial pursuits and productions of a country, require systems of law conforming to this variety in the natural features of the country. I understand quite as well as Judge Douglas, that if we here raise a barrel of flour more than we want, and the Louisianians raise a barrel of sugar more than they want, it is of mutual advantage to exchange. That produces commerce, brings us together, and makes us better friends. We like one another the more for it. And I understand as well as Judge Douglas, or anybody else, that these mutual accommodations are the cements which bind together the different parts of this Union—that instead of being a thing to "divide the house"—figuratively expressing the Union,—they tend to sustain it; they are the props of the house tending always to hold it up.

But when I have admitted all this, I ask if there is any parallel between these things and this institution of slavery? I do not see that there is any parallel at all between them. Consider it. When have we had any difficulty or quarrel amongst ourselves about the cranberry laws of Indiana, or the oyster laws of Virginia, or the pine lumber laws of Maine, or the fact that Louisiana produces sugar, and Illinois flour? When have we had any quarrels over these things? When have we had perfect peace in regard to this thing which I say is an element of discord in this Union? We have sometimes had peace, but when was it? It was when the institution of slavery remained quiet where it was. We have had difficulty and turmoil whenever it has made a struggle to spread itself where it was not. I ask then, if experience does not speak in thunder tones, telling us that the policy which has given peace to the country heretofore, being returned to, gives the greatest promise of peace again. ["Yes;" "yes;" "yes."] You may say and Judge Douglas has intimated the same thing, that all this difficulty in regard to the institution of slavery is the mere agitation of office seekers and ambitious Northern politicians. He thinks we want to get "his place," I suppose. [Cheers and laughter.] I agree that there are office seekers amongst us. The Bible says somewhere that we are desperately selfish. I think we would have discovered that fact without the Bible. I do not claim that I am any less so than the average of men, but I do claim that I am not more selfish than Judge Douglas. [Roars of laughter and applause.]

But is it true that all the difficulty and agitation we have in regard to this institution of slavery springs from office seeking—from the mere ambition of politicians? Is that the truth? How many times have we had danger from this question? Go back to the day of the Missouri Compromise. Go back to the Nullification question, at the bottom of which lay this same slavery question. Go back to the time of the Annexation of Texas. Go back to the troubles that led to the Compromise of 1850. You will find that every time, with the single exception of the Nullification question, they sprung from an endeavor to spread this institution. There never was a party in the history of this country, and there probably never will be of sufficient strength to disturb the general peace of the country. Parties themselves may be divided and quarrel on minor questions, yet it extends not beyond the parties themselves. But does *not* this question make a disturbance outside of political circles? Does it not enter into the churches and rend them asunder? What divided the great Methodist Church into two parts, North and South? What has raised this constant disturbance in every Presbyterian General Assembly that meets? What disturbed the Unitarian Church in this very city two years ago? What has jarred and shaken the great American Tract Society recently, not yet splitting it, but sure to divide it in the end. Is it not this same mighty, deep seated power that somehow operates on the minds of men, exciting and stirring them up in every avenue of society—in politics, in religion, in literature, in morals, in all the manifold relations of life? [Applause.] Is this the work of politicians? Is that irresistible power which for fifty years has shaken the government and agitated the people to be stilled and subdued by pretending that it is an exceedingly simple thing, and we ought not to talk about it? [Great cheers and laughter.] If you will get everybody else to stop talking about it, I assure I will quit before they have half done so. [Renewed laughter.] But where is the philosophy or statesmanship which assumes that you can quiet that disturbing element in our society which has disturbed us for more than half a century, which has been the only serious danger that has threatened our institutions —I say, where is the philosophy or the statesmanship based on the assumption that we are to quit talking about it [applause], and that the public mind is all at once to cease being agitated by it? Yet this is the policy here in the North that Douglas is advocating —that we are to care nothing about it! I ask you if it is not a false philosophy? Is it not a false statesmanship that undertakes to build up a system of policy upon the basis of caring nothing about *the very thing that every body does care the most about?* ["Yes, yes," and applause]—a thing which all experience has shown we care a very great deal about? [Laughter and applause.]

The Judge alludes very often in the course of his remarks to the exclusive right which the States have to decide the whole thing for themselves. I agree with him very readily that the different States have that right. He is but fighting a man of straw when he assumes that I am contending against the[8] right of the States to do as they please about it. Our controversy with him is in regard to the new Territories. We agree that when the States come in as States they have the right and the power to do as they please. We have no power as citizens of the free States or in our federal capacity as members of the Federal Union through the general government, to disturb slavery in the States where it exists. We profess constantly that we have no more inclination than belief in the power of the Government to disturb it; yet we are driven constantly to defend ourselves from the assumption that we are warring upon the rights of the *States*. What I insist upon is, that the new Territories shall be kept free from it while in the Territorial condition. Judge Douglas assumes that we have no interest in them—that we have no right whatever to interfere. I think we have some interest. I think that as white men we have. Do we not wish for an outlet for our surplus population, if I may so express myself? Do we not feel an interest in getting to that outlet with such institutions as we would like to have prevail there? If *you* go to the Territory opposed to slavery and another man comes upon the same ground with his slave, upon the assumption that the things are equal, it turns out

8 "The" inserted by Lincoln.

that he has the equal right all his way and you have no part of it your way. If he goes in and makes it a slave Territory, and by consequence a slave State, is it not time that those who desire to have it a free State were on equal ground. Let me suggest it in a different way. How many Democrats are there about here ["a thousand"] who have left slave States and come into the free State of Illinois to get rid of the institution of slavery. [Another voice—"a thousand and one."] I reckon there are a thousand and one. [Laughter.] I will ask you, if the policy you are now advocating had prevailed when this country was in a Territorial condition, where would you have gone to get rid of it? [Applause.] Where would you have found your free State or Territory to go to? And when hereafter, for any cause, the people in this place shall desire to find new homes, if they wish to be rid of the institution, where will they find the place to go to? [Loud cheers.]

Now irrespective of the moral aspect of this question as to whether there is a right or wrong in enslaving a negro, I am still in favor of our new Territories being in such a condition that white men may find a home—may find some spot where they can better their condition—where they can settle upon new soil and better their condition in life. [Great and continued cheering.] I am in favor of this not merely, (I must say it here as I have elsewhere,) for our own people who are born amongst us, but as an outlet for *free white people everywhere*, the world over—in which Hans and Baptiste and Patrick, and all other men from all the world, may find new homes and better their conditions in life. [Loud and long continued applause.]

I have stated upon former occasions, and I may as well state again, what I understand to be the real issue in this controversy between Judge Douglas and myself. On the point of my wanting to make war between the free and the slave States, there has been no issue between us. So, too, when he assumes that I am in favor of introducing a perfect social and political equality between the white and black races. These are false issues, upon which Judge Douglas has tried to force the controversy. There is no foundation in truth for the charge that I maintain either of these propositions. The real issue in this controversy—the one pressing upon every mind—is the sentiment on the part of one class that looks upon the institution of slavery *as a wrong*, and of another class that *does not* look upon it as a wrong. The sentiment that contemplates the institution of slavery in this country as a wrong is the sentiment of the Republican party. It is the sentiment around which all their actions—all their arguments circle—from which all their propositions radiate. They look upon it as being a moral, social and political wrong; and while they contemplate it as such, they nevertheless have due regard for its actual existence among us, and the difficulties of getting rid of it in any satisfactory way and to all the constitutional obligations thrown about it. Yet having a due regard for these, they desire a policy in regard to it that looks to its not creating any more danger. They insist that it should as far as may be, *be treated* as a wrong, and one of the methods of treating it as a wrong is to *make provision that it shall grow no larger*. [Loud applause.] They also desire a policy that looks to a peaceful end of slavery at sometime, as being wrong. These are the views they entertain in regard to it as I undertand them; and all their sentiments—all their arguments and propositions are brought within this range. I have said and I repeat it here, that if there be a man amongst us who does not think that the institution of slavery is wrong in any one of the aspects of which I have spoken, he is misplaced and ought not to be with us. And if there be a man amongst us who is so impatient of it as a wrong as to disregard its actual presence among us and the difficulty of getting rid of it suddenly in a satisfactory way, and to disregard the constitutional obligations thrown about it, that man is misplaced if he is on our platform. We disclaim sympathy with him in practical action. He is not placed properly with us.

On this subject of treating it as a wrong, and limiting its spread, let me say a word. Has any thing ever threatened the existence of this Union save and except this very institution of Slavery? What is it that we hold most dear amongst us? Our own liberty and prosperity. What has ever threatened our liberty and prosperity save and except this institution of Slavery? If this is true, how do you propose to improve the condition of things by enlarging Slavery—by spreading it out and making it bigger? You may have a wen or a cancer upon your person and not be able to cut it out lest you bleed to death; but surely it is no way to cure it, to engraft it and spread it over your whole body. That is no proper way of treating what you regard a wrong. You see this peaceful way of dealing with it as a wrong—restricting the spread of it, and not allowing it to go into new countries where it has not already existed. That is the peaceful way, the old-fashioned way, the way in which the fathers themselves set us the example.

On the other hand, I have said there is a sentiment which treats it as *not* being wrong. That is the Democratic sentiment of this day. I do not mean to say that every man who stands within that range positively asserts that it is right. That class will include all who positively assert that it is right, and all who like Judge Douglas treat it as indifferent and do not say it is either right or wrong. These two classes of men fall within the general class of those who do not look upon it as a wrong. And if there be among you anybody who supposes that he as a Democrat, can consider himself "as much opposed to slavery as anybody," I would like to reason with him. You never treat it as a wrong. What other thing that you consider as a wrong, do you deal with as you deal with that? Perhaps you *say* it is wrong, *but your leader never does, and you quarrel with anybody who says it is wrong.* Although you pretend to say so yourself you can find no fit place to deal with it as a wrong. You must not say anything about it in the free States, *because it is not here.* You must not say anything about it in the slave States, *because it is there.* You must not say anything about it in the pulpit, because that is religion and has nothing to do with it. You must not say anything about it in politics, *because that will disturb the security of "my place."* [Shouts of laughter and cheers.] There is no place to talk about [it][9] as being a wrong, although you say yourself it *is* a wrong. But finally you will screw yourself up to the belief that if the people of the slave States should adopt a system of gradual emancipation on the slavery question, you would be in favor of it. You would be in favor of it. You say that is getting it in the right place, and you would be glad to see it succeed. But you are deceiving yourself. You all know that Frank Blair and Gratz Brown, down there in St. Louis, undertook to introduce that system in Missouri. They fought as valiantly as they could for the system of gradual emancipation which you pretend you would be glad to see succeed. Now I will bring you to the test. After a hard fight they were beaten, and when the news came over here you threw up your hats and *hurrahed for Democracy.* [Great applause and laughter.] More than that, take all the argument made in favor of the system you have proposed, and it carefully excludes the idea that there is anything wrong in the institution of slavery. The arguments to sustain that policy carefully excluded it. Even here to-day you heard Judge Douglas quarrel with me because I uttered a wish that it might sometime come to an end. Although Henry Clay could say he wished every slave in the United States was in the country of his ancestors, I am denounced by those pretending to respect Henry Clay for uttering a wish that it might sometime, in some peaceful way, come to an end. The Democratic policy in regard to that institution will not tolerate the merest breath, the slightest hint, of the least degree of wrong about it.

[9] Inserted by the editors.

Try it by some of Judge Douglas' arguments. He says he "don't care whether it is voted up or voted down" in the Territories. I do not care myself in dealing with that expression, whether it is intended to be expressive of his individual sentiments on the subject, or only of the national policy he desires to have established. It is alike valuable for my purpose. Any man can say that who does not see anything wrong in slavery, but no man can logically say it who does see a wrong in it; because no man can logically say he don't care whether a wrong is voted up or voted down. He may say he don't care whether an indifferent thing is voted up or down, but he must logically have a choice between a right thing and a wrong thing. He contends that whatever community wants slaves has a right to have them. So they have if it is not a wrong. But if it is a wrong, he cannot say people have a right to do wrong. He says that upon the score of equality, slaves should be allowed to go in a new Territory, like other property. This is strictly logical if there is no difference between it and other property. If it and other property are equal, his argument is entirely logical. But if you insist that one is wrong and the other right, there is no use to institute a comparison between right and wrong. You may turn over everything in the Democratic policy from beginning to end, whether in the shape it takes on the statute book, in the shape it takes in the Dred Scott decision, in the shape it takes in conversation or the shape it takes in short maxim-like arguments—it everywhere carefully excludes the idea that there is anything wrong in it.

That is the real issue. That is the issue that will continue in this country when these poor tongues of Judge Douglas and myself shall be silent. It is the eternal struggle between these two principles—right and wrong—throughout the world. They are the two principles that have stood face to face from the beginning of time; and will ever continue to struggle. The one is the common right of humanity and the other the divine right of kings. It is the same principle in whatever shape it develops itself. It is the same spirit that says, "You work and toil and earn bread, and I'll eat it." [Loud applause.] No matter in what shape it comes, whether from the mouth of a king who seeks to bestride the people of his own nation and live by the fruit of their labor, or from one race of men as an apology for enslaving another race, it is the same tyrannical principle. I was glad to express my gratitude at Quincy, and I re-express it here to Judge Douglas—*that he looks to no end of the institution of slavery*. That will help the people to see where the struggle really is. It will hereafter place with us all men who really do wish the wrong may have an end. And whenever we can get rid of the fog which obscures the real question—when we can get Judge Douglas and his friends to avow a policy looking to its perpetuation—we can get out from among them that class of men and bring them to the side of those who treat it as a wrong. Then there will soon be an end of it, and that end will be its "ultimate extinction." Whenever the issue can be distinctly made, and all extraneous matter thrown out so that men can fairly see the real difference between the parties, this controversy will soon be settled, and it will be done peaceably too. There will be no war, no violence. It will be placed again where the wisest and best men of the world, placed it. Brooks of South Carolina once declared that when this Constitution was framed, its framers did not look to the institution existing until this day. When he said this, I think he stated a fact that is fully borne out by the history of the times. But he also said they were better and wiser men than the men of these days; yet the men of these days had experience which they had not, and by the invention of the cotton gin it became a necessity in this country that slavery should be perpetual. I now say that willingly or unwillingly, purposely or without purpose, Judge Douglas has been the most prominent instrument in changing the position of the institution of slavery which the fathers of the government expected to come to an end ere this—*and putting it upon Brooks' cotton gin basis,* [Great applause,]—placing it where he openly confesses he has no desire there shall ever be an end of it. [Renewed applause.]

I understand I have ten minutes yet. I will employ it in saying something about this argument Judge Douglas uses, while he sustains the Dred Scot decision, that the people of the Territories can still somehow exclude slavery. The first thing I ask attention to is the fact that Judge Douglas constantly said, before the decision, that whether they could or not, *was a question for the Supreme Court.* [Cheers.] But after the Court has made the decision he virtually says it is *not* a question for the Supreme Court, but for the people. [Renewed applause.] And how is it he tells us they can exclude it? He says it needs "police regulations," and that admits of "unfriendly legislation." Although it is a right established by the constitution of the United States to take a slave into a Territory of the United States and hold him as property, yet unless the Territorial Legislature will give friendly legislation, and, more especially, if they adopt unfriendly legislation, they can practically exclude him. Now, without meeting this proposition as a matter of fact, I pass to consider the real constitutional obligation. Let me take the gentleman who looks me in the face before me, and let us suppose that he is a member of the Territorial Legislature. The first thing he will do will be to swear that he will support the Constitution of the United States. His neighbor by his side in the Territory has slaves and needs Territorial legislation to enable him to enjoy that constitutional right. Can he withhold the legislation which his neighbor needs for the enjoyment of a right which is fixed in his favor in the Constitution of the United States which he has sworn to support? Can he withhold it without violating his oath? And more especially, can he pass unfriendly legislation to violate his oath? Why this is a *monstrous* sort of talk about the Constitution of the United States! [Great applause.] *There has never been as outlandish or lawless a doctrine from the mouth of any respectable man on earth.* [Tremendous cheers.] I do not believe it is a constitutional right to hold slaves in a Territory of the United States. I believe the decision was improperly made and I go for reversing it. Judge Douglas is furious against those who go for reversing a decision. But he is for legislating it out of all force while the law itself stands. I repeat that there has never been so monstrous a doctrine uttered from the mouth of a respectable man. [Loud cheers.]

I suppose most of us, (I know it of myself,) believe that the people of the Southern States are entitled to a Congressional fugitive slave law—that it is a right fixed in the Constitution. But it cannot be made available to them without Congressional legislation. In the Judge's language, it is a "barren right" which needs legislation before it can become efficient and valuable to the persons to whom it is guaranteed. And as the right is constitutional I agree that the legislation shall be granted to it—and that not that we like the institution of slavery. We profess to have no taste for running and catching niggers—at least I profess no taste for that job at all. Why then do I yield support to a fugitive slave law? Because I do not understand that the Constitution, which guarantees that right, can be supported without it. And if I believed that the right to hold a slave in a Territory was equally fixed in the Constitution with the right to reclaim fugitives, I should be bound to give it the legislation necessary to support it. I say that no man can deny his obligation to give the necessary legislation to support slavery in a Territory, who believes it is a constitutional right to have it there. No man can, who does not give the Abolitionist an argument to deny the obligation enjoined by the constitution to enact a fugitive slave law. Try it now. It is the strongest abolition argument ever made. I say if that Dred Scott decision is correct then the right to hold slaves in a Territory is equally a constitutional right with the right of a slaveholder to have his runaway returned. No one can show the distinction between them. The one is express, so that we cannot deny it. The other is construed to be in the constitution, so that he who believes the decision to be correct believes in the right. And the man who argues that by unfriendly legislation, in spite of that constitutional right, slavery may be driven from the Territories, cannot avoid furnishing an argument by which Abolitionists may deny the obligation to return fugitives, and claim the power to pass laws unfriendly to the right of the slaveholder to reclaim his fugitive. I do not know how such an argument may strike a popular assembly like this, but I defy anybody to go before a body of men whose minds are educated to estimating evidence and reasoning, and show that there is an iota of difference between the constitutional right to reclaim a fugitive, and the constitutional right to hold a slave, in a Territory, provided this Dred Scott decision is correct. [Cheers.] I defy any man to make an argument that will justify unfriendly legislation to deprive a slaveholder of his right to hold his slave in a Territory, that will not equally, in all its length, breadth and thickness furnish an argument for nullifying the fugitive slave law. Why there is not such an Abolitionist in the nation as Douglas, after all. [Loud and enthusiastic applause.]

MR. DOUGLAS' REPLY.

Mr. Lincoln has concluded his remarks by saying that there is not such an Abolitionist as I am in all America. (Laughter.) If he could make the Abolitionists of Illinois believe that, he would not have much show for the Senate. (Great laughter and applause.) Let him make the Abolitionists believe the truth of that statement and his political back is broken. (Renewed laughter.)

His first criticism upon me is the expression of his hope that the war of the administration will be prosecuted against me and the Democratic party of his State with vigor. He wants that war prosecuted with vigor; I have no doubt of it. His hopes of success, and the hopes of his party depend solely upon it. They have no chance of destroying the Democracy of this State except by the aid of federal patronage. ("That's a fact," "good," and cheers.) He has all the federal office-holders here as his allies, ("That's so,") running separate tickets against the Democracy to divide the party although the leaders all intend to vote directly the Abolition ticket, and only leave the green-horns to vote this separate ticket who refuse to go into the Abolition camp. (Laughter and cheers.) There is something really refreshing in the thought that Mr. Lincoln is in favor of prosecuting one war vigorously. (Roars of laughter.) It is the first war I ever knew him to be in favor of prosecuting. (Renewed laughter.) It is the first war that I ever knew him to believe to be just or constitutional. (Laughter and cheers.) When the Mexican war [was][10] being waged, and the American army was surrounded by the enemy in Mexico, he thought that war was unconstitutional, unnecessary and unjust. ("That's so," "you've got him," "he voted against it," &c.) He thought it was not commenced on the right *spot*. (Laughter.)

When I made an incidental allusion of that kind in the joint discussion over at Charleston some weeks ago, Lincoln, in replying, said that I, Douglas, had charged him with voting against supplies for the Mexican war, and then he reared up, full length, and swore that he never voted against the supplies—that it was a slander—and caught hold of Ficklin, who sat on the stand, and said, "Here, Ficklin, tell the people that it is a lie." (Laughter and cheers.) Well, Ficklin, who had served in Congress with him, stood up and told them all that he recollected about it. It was that when George Ashmun, of Massachusetts, brought forward a resolution declaring the war unconstitutional, unnecessary, and unjust, that Lincoln had voted for it. "Yes," said Lincoln, "I did." Thus he confessed that he voted that the war was wrong, that our country was in the wrong, and consequently that the Mexicans were in the right; but charged that I had slandered him by saying that he voted against the supplies. I never charged him with voting against the supplies in my life, because I knew that he was not in Congress when they were voted. (Tremendous shouts of laughter.) The war was commenced on the 13th day of May, 1846, and on that day we appropriated in Congress ten millions of dollars and fifty thousand men to prosecute it. During the same session we voted more men and more money, and at the next session we voted more men and more money, so that by the time Mr. Lincoln entered Congress we had enough men and enough money to carry on the war, and had no occasion to vote any more. (Laughter and cheers.) When he got into the House, being opposed to the war, and not being able to stop the supplies, because they had all gone forward, all he could do was to follow the lead of Corwin, and prove that the war was not begun on the right spot, and that it was unconstitutional, unnecessary, and wrong. Remember, too, that this he did after the war had been begun. It is one thing to be opposed to the declaration of a war, another and very different thing to take sides with the enemy against your own country after the war has been com-

10 Inserted by the editors.

menced. ("Good," and cheers.) Our army was in Mexico at the time, many battles had been fought; our citizens, who were defending the honor of their country's flag, were surrounded by the daggers, the guns and the poison of the enemy. Then it was that Corwin made his speech in which he declared that the American soldiers ought to be welcomed by the Mexicans with bloody hands and hospitable graves; then it was that Ashmun and Lincoln voted in the House of Representatives that the war was unconstitutional and unjust; and Ashmun's resolution, Corwin's speech, and Lincoln's vote were sent to Mexico and read at the head of the Mexican army, to prove to them that there was a Mexican party in the Congress of the United States who were doing all in their power to aid them. ("That's the truth," "Lincoln's a traitor," etc.) That a man who takes sides with the common enemy against his own country in time of war should rejoice in a war being made on me now, is very natural. (Immense applause.) And in my opinion, no other kind of a man would rejoice in it. ("That's true," "hurrah for Douglas," and cheers.)

Mr. Lincoln has told you a great deal to-day about his being an old line Clay Whig. ("He never was.") Bear in mind that there are a great many old Clay Whigs down in this region. It is more agreeable, therefore, for him to talk about the old Clay Whig party than it is for him to talk Abolitionism. We did not hear much about the old Clay Whig party up in the Abolition districts. How much of an old line Henry Clay Whig was he? Have you read Gen. Singleton's speech at Jacksonville? (Yes, yes, and cheers.) You know that Gen. Singleton was, for twenty-five years, the confidential friend of Henry Clay in Illinois, and he testified that in 1847, when the constitutional convention of this State was in session, the Whig members were invited to a Whig caucus at the house of Mr. Lincoln's brother-in-law, where Mr. Lincoln proposed to throw Henry Clay overboard and take up Gen. Taylor in his place, giving, as his reason, that if the Whigs did not take up Gen. Taylor the Democrats would. (Cheers and laughter.) Singleton testifies that Lincoln, in that speech, urged, as another reason for throwing Henry Clay overboard, that the Whigs had fought long enough for principle and ought to begin to fight for success. Singleton also testifies that Lincoln's speech did have the effect of cutting Clay's throat, and that he, Singleton, and others withdrew from the caucus in indignation. He further states that when they got to Philadelphia to attend the national convention of the Whig party, that Lincoln was there, the bitter and deadly enemy of Clay, and that he tried to keep him (Singleton) out of the convention because he insisted on voting for Clay, and Lincoln was determined to have Taylor. (Laughter and applause.) Singleton says that Lincoln rejoiced with very great joy when he found the mangled remains of the murdered Whig statesman lying cold before him. Now, Mr. Lincoln tells you that he is an old line Clay Whig! (Laughter and cheers.) Gen. Singleton testifies to the facts I have narrated in a public speech which has been printed and circulated broadcast over the State for weeks, yet not a lisp have we heard from Mr. Lincoln on the subject, except that he is an old Clay Whig.

What part of Henry Clay's policy did Lincoln ever advocate? He was in Congress in 1848-9 when the Wilmot proviso warfare disturbed the peace and harmony of the country until it shook the foundation of the republic from its centre to its circumference. It was that agitation that brought Clay forth from his retirement at Ashland again to occupy his seat in the Senate of the United States, to see if he could not, by his great wisdom and experience, and the renown of his name, do something to restore peace and quiet to a disturbed country. Who got up that sectional strife that Clay had to be called upon to quell? I have heard Lincoln boast that he voted forty-two times for the Wilmot proviso, and that he would have voted as many times more if he could. (Laughter.) Lincoln is the man, in connection with Seward, Chase, Giddings, and other Abolitionists, who got up that strife that I helped Clay to put down. (Tremendous applause.) Henry Clay came back to the Senate in 1849, and saw that he must do something to restore peace to the country. The Union Whigs and the Union Democrats welcomed him the moment he arrived, as the man for the occasion. We believed that he, of all men on earth, had been preserved by Divine Providence to guide us out of our difficulties, and we Democrats rallied under Clay then, as you Whigs in nullification time rallied under the banner of old Jackson, forgetting party when the country was in danger, in order that we might have a country first, and parties afterwards. ("Three cheers for Douglas.")

And this reminds me that Mr. Lincoln told you that the slavery question was the only thing that ever disturbed the peace and harmony of the Union. Did not nullification once raise its head and disturb the peace of this Union in 1832? Was that the slavery question, Mr. Lincoln? Did not disunion raise its monster head during the last war with Great Britain? Was that the slavery question, Mr. Lincoln? The peace of this country has been disturbed three times, once during the war with Great Britain, once on the tariff question, and once on the slavery question. ("Three cheers for

Douglas.") His argument, therefore, that slavery is the only question that has ever created dissension in the Union falls to the ground. It is true that agitators are enabled now to use this slavery question for the purpose of sectional strife. ("That's so.") He admits that in regard to all things else, the principle that I advocate, making each State and territory free to decide for itself ought to prevail. He instances the cranberry laws, and the oyster laws, and he might have gone through the whole list with the same effect. I say that all these laws are local and domestic, and that local and domestic concerns should be left to each State and each territory to manage for itself. If agitators would acquiesce in that principle, there never would be any danger to the peace and harmony of this Union. ("That's so," and cheers.)

Mr. Lincoln tries to avoid the main issue by attacking the truth of my proposition, that our fathers made this government divided into free and slave States, recognizing the right of each to decide all its local questions for itself. Did they not thus make it? It is true that they did not establish slavery in any of the States, or abolish it in any of them; but finding thirteen States twelve of which were slave and one free, they agreed to form a government uniting them together, as they stood divided into free and slave States, and to guarantee forever to each State the right to do as it pleased on the slavery question. (Cheers.) Having thus made the government, and conferred this right upon each State forever, I assert that this government can exist as they made it, divided into free and slave States, if any one State chooses to retain slavery. (Cheers.) He says that he looks forward to a time when slavery shall be abolished everywhere. I look forward to a time when each State shall be allowed to do as it pleases. If it chooses to keep slavery forever, it is not my business, but its own; if it chooses to abolish slavery, it is its own business—not mine. I care more for the great principle of self-government, the right of the people to rule, than I do for all the negroes in Christendom. (Cheers.) I would not endanger the perpetuity of this Union. I would not blot out the great inalienable rights of the white men for all the negroes that ever existed. (Renewed applause.) Hence, I say, let us maintain this government on the principles that our fathers made it, recognizing the right of each State to keep slavery as long as its people determine, or to abolish it when they please. (Cheers.) But Mr. Lincoln says that when our fathers made this government they did not look forward to the state of things now existing; and therefore he thinks the doctrine was wrong; and he quotes Brooks, of South Carolina, to prove that our fathers then thought that probably slavery would be abolished, by each State acting for itself before this time. Suppose they did; suppose they did not foresee what has occurred,—does that change the principles of our government? They did not probably foresee the telegraph that transmits intelligence by lightning, nor did they foresee the railroads that now form the bonds of union between the different States, or the thousand mechanical inventions that have elevated mankind. But do these things change the principles of the government? Our fathers, I say, made this government on the principle of the right of each State to do as it pleases in its own domestic affairs, subject to the constitution, and allowed the people of each to apply to every new change of circumstance such remedy as they may see fit to improve their condition. This right they have for all time to come. (Cheers.)

Mr. Lincoln went on to tell you that he does not at all desire to interfere with slavery in the States where it exists, nor does his party. I expected him to say that down here. (Laughter.) Let me ask him then how he is going to put slavery in the course of ultimate extinction everywhere, if he does not intend to interfere with it in the States where it exists? (Renewed laughter.) He says that he will prohibit it in all territories, and the inference is then that unless they make free States out of them he will keep them out of the Union; for, mark you, he did not say whether or not he would vote to admit Kansas with slavery or not, as her people might apply; (he forgot that as usual, &c;) he did not say whether or not he was in favor of bringing the territories now in existence into the Union on the principle of Clay's compromise measures on the slavery question. I told you that he would not. (Give it to him, he deserves it, &c.) His idea is that he will prohibit slavery in all the territories, and thus force them all to become free States, surrounding the slave States with a cordon of free States, and hemming them in, keeping the slaves confined to their present limits whilst they go on multiplying until the soil on which they live will no longer feed them, and he will thus be able to put slavery in a course of ultimate extinction by starvation. (Cheers.) He will extinguish slavery in the Southern States as the French general exterminated the Algerines when he smoked them out. He is going to extinguish slavery by surrounding the slave States, hemming in the slaves, and starving them out of existence as you smoke a fox out of his hole. And he intends to do that in the name of humanity and Christianity, in order that we may get rid of the terrible crime and sin entailed upon our fathers of holding slaves. (Laughter and cheers.) Mr. Lincoln makes out that line of policy, and appeals to the moral sense of justice, and to the Christian feeling of the community to sustain him. He says that any man who holds to the contrary doctrine is in the position of the king who claimed to govern by divine right. Let us examine for a moment and see what principle it was that overthrew the divine right of George the Third to govern us. Did not these colonies rebel because the British parliament had no right to pass laws concerning our property and domestic and private institutions without our consent? We demanded that the British government should not pass such laws unless they gave us representation in the body passing them,—and this the British government insisting on doing,—we went to war, on the principle that the home government should not control and govern distant colonies without giving them a representation. Now, Mr. Lincoln proposes to govern the territories without giving the people a representation, and calls on Congress to pass laws controlling their property and domestic concerns without their consent and against their will. Thus, he asserts for his party the identical principle asserted by George III. and the tories of the Revolution. (Cheers.)

I ask you to look into these things, and then to tell me whether the democracy or the abolitionists are right. I hold that the people of a territory, like those of a State, (I use the language of Mr. Buchanan in his letter of acceptance,) have the right to decide for themselves whether slavery shall or shall not exist within their limits. ("That's the idea," "Hurrah for Douglas.") The point upon which Chief Justice Taney expresses his opinion is simply this, that slaves being property, stand on an equal footing with other property, and consequently that the owner has the same right to carry that property into a territory that he has any other, subject to the same conditions. Suppose that one of your merchants was to take fifty or one hundred thousand dollars worth of liquors to Kansas. He has a right to go there under that decision, but when he gets there he finds the Maine liquor law in force, and what can he do with his property after he gets it there? He cannot sell it, he cannot use it, it is subject to the local law, and that law is against him, and the best thing he can do with it is to bring it back into Missouri or Illinois and sell it. If you take negroes to Kansas, as Col. Jeff. Davis said in his Bangor speech, from which I have quoted to-day, you must take them there subject to the local law. If the people want the institution of slavery they will protect and encourage it; but if they do not want it they will withhold that protection, and the absence of local legislation protecting slavery excludes it as completely as a positive prohibition. ("That's so," and cheers.) You slaveholders of Missouri might as well understand what you know practically, that you cannot carry slavery where the people do not want it. ("That's so.") All you have a right to ask is that the people shall do as they please; if they want slavery let them have it; if they do not want it, allow them to refuse to encourage it.

My friends, if, as I have said before, we will only live up to this great fundamental principle there will be peace between the North and the South. Mr. Lincoln admits that under the constitution on all domestic questions, except slavery, we ought not to interfere with the people of each State. What right have we to interfere with slavery any more than we have to interfere with any other question. He says that this slavery question is now the bone of contention. Why? Simply because agitators have combined in all the free States to make war upon it. Suppose the agitators in the States should combine in one-half of the Union to make war upon the railroad system of the other half? They would thus be driven to the same sectional strife. Suppose one section makes war upon any other peculiar institution of the opposite section, and the same strife is produced. The only remedy and safety is that we shall stand by the constitution as our fathers made it, obey the laws as they are passed, while they stand the proper test and sustain the decisions of the Supreme Court and the constituted authorities.

Fragment: Opinion on Election Laws of Illinois[1]

[October 15?] 1858

It is made a question whether, under our laws, a person offering to vote, and being challenged, and having taken the oath prescribed by the act of 1849, is then *absolutely* entitled to vote, or whether his oath may be disproved, and his vote thereon lawfully rejected.

In Purple's Statutes, Vol. 1, all our existing election laws are brought together commencing on page 514 and extending to page 532. They consist of acts and parts of acts passed at different times.

The true way of reading so much of the law as applies to the above question, is to first read (64) Sec. X–, including the form of the oath, on page 528. Then turn back and read (19) Sec. XIX on page 518.

If it be said that the Section last mentioned is not now in force, turn forward to (75) Sec. XXI, on page 530, where it is expressly declared to be in force.

The result is that when a person has taken the oath, his oath may still be proved to be false, and his vote thereupon rejected. It may be proved to be false by cross-examining the prop[os]ed voter himself, or by any other person, or competent testimony, known to the general law of Evidence

On page 532 is an extract of a Supreme Court decision on the very Sec. 19– on page 518, in which, among other things, the Court say:

"If such person takes the oath prescribed by law, the Judges must receive his vote, *unless the oath be proved false.*["] Something of a definition of residence is also therein given.

[1] AD, DLC-RTL. Probably written in October prior to the election on November 2, this fragment bears the date given it in the *Complete Works*. Lincoln may have written the opinion as a guide for the editors of the *Illinois State Journal*. On November 1, the *Journal* carried an extended editorial "To the Judges and Clerks of Election," in which the references to Norman H. Purple's *Statutes* (1856) cited by Lincoln are quoted at length.

Extracts from Speeches on Slavery[1]

October 18, 1858

The following extracts are taken from various speeches of mine delivered at various times and places; and I believe the[y] contain the substance of all I have ever said about "negro equality" The first three are from my answer to Judge Douglas, Oct. 16, 1854– at Peoria.

[The extracts are as follows: seven paragraphs beginning, "This is the *repeal* of the Missouri Compromise. . . ."; five paragraphs beginning, "Judge Douglas frequently, with bitter irony and sarcasm. . . ."; paragraph beginning, "In the course of his reply, Senator Douglas remarked. . . ."]

The fourth extract is from a speech delivered June 26– 1857, at Springfield.

[Two paragraphs beginning, "I think the authors of that notable instrument. . . ."]

The following marked 5– is from my speech at Chicago, July 10. 1858. Because garbled extracts are often taken from this speech, I have given the whole which touches "negro equality."

[Concluding paragraphs of the speech beginning, "We were often—more than once, at least—in the course of Judge Douglas' speech last night. . . ."]

The following marked 6, was brought in immediately, after reading the first extract in this scrap-book, in the first joint meeting with Judge Douglas, Aug. 21. 1858 at Ottawa.

[Paragraph beginning, "Now gentlemen, I don't want to read. . . ."]

The following, marked 7 is from my speech in the fourth joint meeting, Sep. 18. 1858 at Charleston.

[Paragraph beginning, "While I was at the hotel. . . ."]

[1] AD, CSmH. The letter to James N. Brown, *infra,* is written in a little notebook on the pages immediately following the newspaper clippings from Lincoln's speeches dealing with slavery. In lieu of repeating so many lengthy passages from speeches appearing elsewhere, the editors have substituted for each clipping a bracketed identification of the passages represented.

To James N. Brown[1]

Hon. J. N. Brown | Springfield,
My dear Sir | Oct. 18. 1858

I do not perceive how I can express myself, more plainly, than I have done in the foregoing extracts. In four of them I have expressly disclaimed all intention to bring about social and political equality between the white and black races, and, in all the rest, I have done the same thing by clear implication

I have made it equally plain that I think the negro is included in the word "men" used in the Declaration of Independence.

I believe the declara[tion] that "all men are created equal" is the great fundamental principle upon which our free institutions rest; that negro slavery is violative of that principle; but that, by our frame of government, that principle has not been made one of legal obligation; that by our frame of government, the States which have slavery are to retain it, or surrender it at their own pleasure; and that all others—individuals, free-states and national government—are constitutionally bound to leave them alone about it.

I believe our government was thus framed because of the *necessity* springing from the actual presence of slavery, when it was framed.

That such necessity does not exist in the teritories, where slavery is not present.

In his Mendenhall speech Mr. Clay says

"Now, as an abstract principle, there is no doubt of the truth of that declaration (all men created equal) and it is desireable, in the original construction of society, and in organized societies, to keep it in view, as a great fundamental principle"

Again, in the same speech Mr. Clay says:

"If a state of nature existed, and we were about to lay the foundations of society, no man would be more strongly opposed than

I should to incorporate the institution of slavery among it's elements;

Exactly so. In our new free teritories, a state of nature *does* exist. In them Congress lays the foundations of society; and, in laying those foundations, I say, with Mr. Clay, it is desireable that the declaration of the equality of all men shall be kept in view, as a great fundamental principle; and that Congress, which lays the foundations of society, should, like Mr. Clay, be strongly opposed to the incorporation of slavery among it's elements.

But it does not follow that social and political equality between whites and blacks, *must* be incorporated, because slavery must *not*. The declaration does not so require. Yours as ever

A. LINCOLN

[1] ALS, CSmH and ADf, DLC-RTL. Before leaving Springfield on October 18 for his speaking engagement at Meredosia, Lincoln wrote this letter to James N. Brown of Island Grove (Sangamon County representative 1840-1844, 1846-1848, 1852-1854) in a small notebook following clippings from his speeches dealing with slavery (*vide supra*), which he had presumably carried with him during the debates. Nicolay and Hay print part of the draft or copy of the letter which Lincoln preserved under the title "Fragment: Notes for Speeches [September 16?] 1858" (NH, IV, 88).

Speech at Meredosia, Illinois[1]

October 18, 1858

On Monday night last he addressed a small meeting at Meredosia. His object was to convert two or three Germans at that place to the republican faith. To effect this object, we are informed he took for his text the Declaration of Independence and labored for an hour to prove by that instrument that the negro was born with rights equal with the whites; thus by implication assailing the Constitution of the United States, which protects the institution of negro servitude in the slave states.

In the course of his speech he remarked that, while at Naples on the preceding[2] day he had noticed about a dozen Irishmen on the levee, and it had occurred to him that those Irishmen had been imported expressly to vote him down.

Doubtless Mr. Lincoln entertains a holy horror of all Irishmen and other adopted citizens who have sufficient self-respect to believe themselves superior to the negro. What right have adopted citizens to vote Mr. Lincoln and his negro equality doctrines down? He would doubtless disfranchise every one of them if he had the power. His reference to the danger of his being voted down by foreigners, was a cue to his followers, similar in character to the intimation of the Chicago Press a few days since, that the republicans of the interior counties should protect their rights; in other words, that under the pretext of protecting their rights, they should keep adopted citizens from the polls. We hope no adopted citizen will attempt to put in an illegal vote; yet every adopted citizen, be a democrat or republican, should have his vote. And every foreigner in old Morgan who is a legal voter, *will have his vote* in spite of Mr. Lincoln.

The effect produced by Mr. Lincoln's significant reference to the danger he apprehended from the foreign vote, was manifested before the close of the meeting. Dr. Wackly,[3] a highly respectable merchant of Meredosia, who is an influential German, and also a German speaker of considerable talent, a few evenings before, in a speech had expressed the opinion that Mr. Lincoln was a know-nothing. Mr. Lincoln referred to this charge, and retorted on to the Dr. in severe, personal manner.

[1] Jacksonville *Sentinel*, October 22, 1858.
[2] Lincoln stopped at Naples on the way to Meredosia on the same day.
[3] Probably an error for Dr. W. J. Wackerle of Meredosia.

Speech at Rushville, Illinois[1]

October 20, 1858

He devoted the opening of his speech to the opinions and policy of Henry Clay on the slavery question, showing that his ideas and Clay's coincided, exactly, namely: That in the States where it already exists, it should not be interfered with, but in laying the foundation of societies, in our new Territories, where slavery does not exist, it should not be introduced as an element.

Mr. Lincoln next took up that portion of his Springfield speech, about which so much has been said. As we find about the same ideas involved in his late Alton speech, that he introduced here, we take the liberty to transfer them to our columns as being more satisfactory to our readers.

[There follows nearly two columns from Lincoln's reply to Douglas at Alton, October 15, *supra.*]

[1] *Schuyler Citizen,* October 27, 1858.

To Norman B. Judd[1]

Hon. N. B. Judd Rushville, Oct. 20, 1858

My dear Sir: I now have a high degree of confidence that we shall succeed, if we are not over-run with fraudulent votes to a greater extent than usual. On alighting from the cars and walking three squares at Naples on Monday, I met about fifteen Celtic gentlemen, with black carpet-sacks in their hands.

I learned that they had crossed over from the Rail-road in Brown county, but where they were going no one could tell. They dropped in about the doggeries, and were still hanging about when I left. At Brown County yesterday I was told that about four hundred of the same sort were to be brought into Schuyler, before the election, to work on some new Railroad; but on reaching here I find Bagby[2] thinks that is not so.

What I most dread is that they will introduce into the doubtful districts numbers of men who are legal voters in all respects except *residence* and who will swear to residence and thus put it beyond our power to exclude them. They can & I fear will swear falsely on that point, because they know it is next to impossible to convict them of Perjury upon it.

Now the great remaining part of the campaign, is finding a way to head this thing off. Can it be done at all?

I have a bare suggestion. When there is a known body of these voters, could not a true man, of the "*detective*" class, be introduced among them in disguise, who could, at the nick of time, control their votes? Think this over. It would be a great thing, when this trick is attempted upon us, to have the saddle come up on the other horse.

I have talked, more fully than I can write, to Mr. Scripps,[3] and he will talk to you.

If we can head off the fraudulent votes we shall carry the day.

Yours as ever A. LINCOLN

[1] ALS-P, ISLA. [2] John C. Bagby. [3] John L. Scripps.

Speech at Carthage, Illinois[1]

October 22, 1858

At Carthage, Hancock County, Oct. 22, Mr. Lincoln discussed the following topics, not included in any of the joint debates with Judge Douglas:

On the 4th of October, at Woodford County, I learned that Judge Douglas had been imputing to me and my friends a purpose to release the Central Railroad Company from paying into the State Treasury the seven per cent, upon their gross earnings, which, by law, they are now bound to do. I learn he repeated the same imputation at Pekin, Oquawka, Monmouth and this place, though he has never mentioned it at any of our joint meetings, or elsewhere in my presence. I mention it now to correct any false impression that may have been made. I understand the Judge states, among other things, that I once received a fee of $5,000 from that Company. My partner and I did receive such fee under the following circumstances: By their charter, the Company are bound to make periodical payments into the State Treasury, in exemption of all other taxes. This exempts them from county and city taxes. The Legislature intended, as I understand, in consideration of the large land grant, to make the Company pay about as much as they could bear; and to make them pay it into the State Treasury, so that the *whole* people could share the benefit, instead of paying any to the counties through which the road passes, to the exclusion of those through which it does not pass. This was a fair way of dealing with the whole people, as was thought. The county of McLean, one of the counties through which the road passes, claimed that the exemption was unconstitutional, and that the Company was bound to pay county taxes on their property within the limits of the county; and the parties went to Court to try the question. The Railroad Company employed me as one of their lawyers in the case, the county having declined to employ me. I was not upon a salary, and no agreement was made as to the amount of fee. The Railroad Company finally gained the case. The decision, I thought, and still think, was worth half a million dollars to them. I wanted them to pay me $5,000, and they wanted to pay me about $500. I sued them and got the $5,000. This is the whole truth about the fee; and what tendency it has to prove that I received any of the people's money, or that I am on very cozy terms with the Railroad Company, I do not comprehend.

It is a matter of interest to you that the Company shall not be released from their obligations to pay money into the State Treasury. Every dollar they so pay relieves the whole people of just so much in the way of taxation. I am a candidate for no office wherein I could release them, if elected. The State Legislature alone can release them. Therefore, all you need to do is to know your candidates for the Legislature, how they will vote on the question of release, if elected. I doubt not every candidate who is a friend of mine is ready to show his hand; and perhaps it would be well to have Judge Douglas' friends show their hands also. See to your members of the Legislature, and you are beyond the power of all others as to releasing the Central Railroad from its obligations. This is your perfect security.

[1] Chicago *Press and Tribune*, October 27, 1858.

To Norman B. Judd[1]

Hon. N. B. Judd: Blandonville [Blandinsville],
My dear Sir Oct. 24. 1858

Just out of Hancock. Spoke three times in that county. *Tight*, with chances slightly in our favor. Think Henderson will ballance Schuyler, so that if we carry Hancock, we elect Bagby.[2]

Heared nothing new about fraudulent voters since I wrote by Mr. Scripps.[3]

I shall reach Springfield on Thursday, 28th. when & where I wish to find a letter from you telling how the whole field looks from your point of view. Yours as ever A. LINCOLN

[1] ALS, IHi. [2] John C. Bagby.

[3] John L. Scripps of the Chicago *Press and Tribune* had formerly been a resident of Rushville in Schuyler County.

To John Moses[1]

Hon. John Moses Blandonville [Blandinsville]
My Dear Sir: Oct. 24. 1858

Throw on all your weight. Some things I have heard make me think your case is not so desperate as you thought when I was in Winchester. Put in your best licks. Yours in haste

A. LINCOLN—

[1] Copy, DLC-HW. John Moses sent Herndon this copy written at bottom of his letter to Herndon, September 19, 1866, in which he explains that at the time he [Moses] was "candidate for the state senate in the counties of Scott, Pike & Calhoun."

To Alexander Sympson[1]

A. Sympson, Esq Blandonville [Blandinsville],
Dear Sir Oct. 24. 1858

Since parting with you this morning I heared some things which make me believe that Edmunds and Morrill,[2] will spend this week among the National democrats trying to induce them to content themselves by voting for Jake Davis,[3] and then to vote for the Douglas candidates for Senator and Representative. Have this headed off, if you can. Call Wagley's[4] attention to it, & have him and the National democrat for Rep. to counteract it as far as they can. Yours as ever A. LINCOLN

[1] ALS-P, ISLA. Nicolay and Hay misdate this letter October 26, 1858 (NH, V, 89), repeating date given in Tarbell (Appendix), p. 335.

[2] George Edmunds of Carthage, Illinois, and Milton M. Morrill of Nauvoo, Illinois. [3] Jacob C. Davis. [4] William C. Wagley.

Speech at Macomb, Illinois[1]

October 25, 1858

It is impossible for us to give its various points, but we may mention among them, the successful vindication of the wisdom and conservatism of the Republican platform—the complete demonstration that he gave of its consistency with the action and views of the fathers of the government—and with those of Henry Clay—and a scorching exposition of the inconsistencies—sophistries—and misrepresentations of the Douglas faction.

[1] Quincy *Whig*, October 27, 1858.

Speech at Petersburg, Illinois[1]

October 29, 1858

His speech was a clear logical demonstration of the identity of his position with the doctrines of the Fathers of the Republic, in which he showed that all the great statesmen of the nation whom we loved while living, and reverence now that they are dead, held the same doctrines that he now advocates, to be true. He dwelt more particularly on the grounds held by H. Clay on the question of slavery, leaving no doubt in the minds of any candid man who heard him, that his own position was the same as Clay's.

He touched upon the most important of the many slanders and misrepresentations which have been urged against him, all of which vanished before the ethereal like touch of truth.

[1] *Menard Index,* November 4, 1858.

To Edward Lusk[1]

Edward Lusk, Esq — Springfield,
Dear Sir — Oct. 30, 1858

I understand the story is still being told, and insisted upon, that I have been a Know-Nothing. I repeat, what I stated in a public speech at Meredosia, that I am not, nor ever have been, connected with the party called the Know-Nothing party, or party calling themselves the American party. *Certainly* no man of truth, and I *believe,* no man [of] good character for truth can be found to say on his own knowledge that I ever was connected with that party.

Yours very truly — A. LINCOLN

[1] ALS, IHi. Edward Lusk was an ex-steamboat operator and farmer at Meredosia, Illinois. On the same page below Lincoln's letter appears a letter of the same date from Ozias M. Hatch addressed to S. P. Thompson in corroboration of Lincoln's letter. Thompson has not been identified, but the inference is that he was a friend of Lusk's.

Fragment: Last Speech of the Campaign at Springfield, Illinois[1]

October 30, 1858

My friends, to-day closes the discussions of this canvass. The planting and the culture are over; and there remains but the preparation, and the harvest.

I stand here surrounded by friends—some *political, all personal* friends, I trust. May I be indulged, in this closing scene, to say a few words of myself. I have borne a laborious, and, in some respects to myself, a painful part in the contest. Through all, I have neither assailed, nor wrestled with any part of the constitution. The legal right of the Southern people to reclaim their fugitives I have constantly admitted. The legal right of Congress to interfere with their institution in the states, I have constantly denied. In resisting the spread of slavery to new teritory, and with that, what appears to me to be a tendency to subvert the first principle of free government itself my whole effort has consisted. To the best of my judgment I have labored *for*, and not *against* the Union. As I have not felt, so I have not expressed any harsh sentiment towards our Southern bretheren. I have constantly declared, as I really believed, the only difference between them and us, is the difference of circumstances.

I have meant to assail the motives of no party, or individual; and if I have, in any instance (of which I am not conscious) departed from my purpose, I regret it.

I have said that in some respects the contest has been painful to me. Myself, and those with whom I act have been constantly accused of a purpose to destroy the union; and bespattered with every immaginable odious epithet; and some who were friends, as it were but yesterday have made themselves most active in this. I have cultivated patience, and made no attempt at a retort.

Ambition has been ascribed to me. God knows how sincerely I prayed from the first that this field of ambition might not be opened. I claim no insensibility to political honors; but today could the Missouri restriction be restored, and the whole slavery question replaced on the old ground of "toleration["] by *necessity* where it exists, with unyielding hostility to the spread of it, on principle, I would, in consideration, gladly agree, that Judge Douglas should never be *out*, and I never *in*, an office, so long as we both or either, live.

[1] AD, ORB. Lincoln delivered a speech of some length, but only this two-page manuscript is extant. The *Illinois State Journal* (November 1, 1858) commented on the speech as follows: "We have neither time nor room to give even a sketch

of his remarks to-day. Suffice it to say, the speech was one of his very best efforts, distinguished for its clearness and force, and for the satisfactory manner in which he exposed the roorbacks and misrepresentations of the enemy. The conclusion of this speech was one of the most eloquent appeals ever addressed to the American people. It was received with spontaneous bursts of enthusiasm unequalled by any thing ever before enacted in this city." From this account it may be inferred that the fragment is the conclusion of the speech, perhaps the only portion which Lincoln committed to paper.

To William H. Bissell[1]

November 3, 1858

I was at the Champaign Circuit Court at the time of the conviction of Jones,[2] but was not engaged in the case. From what I heard there as well as from the above statement of the Judge and Prossecuting Attorney, I concur in the recommendation that he be pardoned. Your Obt. Servt. A LINCOLN

Novr. 3. 1858.

[1] AES, I-Ar. Lincoln's communication is written at bottom of the second page of Judge David Davis' letter to Governor Bissell. Ward H. Lamon, prosecuting attorney, joined in Davis' plea for clemency.

[2] Orin B. Jones, convicted of larceny.

To John J. Crittenden[1]

Hon: J. J. Crittenden Springfield, Novr. 4– 1858

My dear Sir Yours of the 27th. ult. was taken from the Post-Office by my law-partner, and, in the confusion consequent upon the recent election, was handed to me only this moment. I am sorry the allusion made in the Mo. Republican, to the private correspondence between yourself and me, has given you any pain. It gave me scarcely a thought, perhaps for the reason that, being away from home, I did not see it till only two days before the election. It never occurred to me to cast any blame upon you. I have been told that the correspondence has been alluded to in the Mo. Rep. several times, but I only saw one, of the allusions, and in which it was stated, as I remember that a gentleman of St. Louis had seen a copy of your letter to me. As I had given no copy, nor ever showed the original, of course I infered he had seen it in your hands, but it did not occur to me to blame you for showing what you had written yourself. It was not said that the gentleman had seen a copy or the original of my letter to you.

The emotions of defeat, at the close of a struggle in which I felt more than a merely selfish interest, and to which defeat the use of your name contributed largely, are fresh upon me; but, even in this mood, I can not for a moment suspect you of anything dishonorable. Your Obt. Servt. A. LINCOLN—

1 ALS, owned by William H. Townsend, Lexington, Kentucky. Crittenden wrote from Frankfort, Kentucky, that the reference in the *Republican* was wholly unauthorized and that he hoped Lincoln would not permit publication of their correspondence.

To Horace Greeley[1]

Hon: H. Greely. Springfield, Ills.

Dear Sir Novr. 8. 1858

This will introduce our mutual friend John G. Nicolay, who resides here. He wishes an arrangement to correspond for your paper. He is entirely trust-worthy; and, so far as I am capable of judging, altogether competent for such a situation. I hope you will conceive it your interest to engage him. Yours truly

A. LINCOLN.

1 ALS, DLC-RTL. Entirely in Lincoln's hand, this document may be the original preserved by Nicolay, or a copy preserved by Lincoln.

Testimonial Written for Isaac Larrance[1]

Springfield, Ills. Novr. 10. 1858

Having hastily examined "Larrance's Post-office Chart" and considered the principle upon which it is arranged, I think it will prove a great convenience to Post-Masters and others whose business lead them to search out particular localities upon maps.

A LINCOLN

1 ADS, owned by R. E. Burdick, New York City. Larrance's *Post Office Key* . . . was published at Plainville, Ohio, in 1881. Presumably Lincoln examined a forerunner of the later publication. According to a signed statement accompanying Lincoln's testimonial, Larrance's children, Ellis Lawrence and Phebe Lawrence Wardan, maintain that the name is properly spelled "Lawrence."

To Norman B. Judd[1]

Hon N B Judd Springfield Nov 15 1858

My dear Sir I have the pleasure to inform you that I am convalescent and hoping these lines may find you in the same improving state of health. Doubtless you have suspected for some time that I entertain a personal wish for a term in the US Senate; and had the suspicion taken the shape of a direct charge, I think I could not have truthfully denied it. But let the past as nothing be.

For the future my view is that the fight must go on. The returns here are not yet completed, but it is believed that Doughertys vote will be slightly greater than Millers majority over Foncy [Fondey].[2] We have some hundred and twenty thousand clear Republican votes. That pile is worth keeping together. It will elect a state trustee [treasurer?] two years hence.

In that day I shall fight in the ranks, but I shall be in no ones way for any of the places. I am especially for Trumbulls reelection; and by the way this brings me to the principal object of this letter. Can you not take your draft of an apportionment law, and carefully revise it till it shall be strictly & obviously just in all particulars, & then by an early & persistent effort get enough of the enemies men to enable you to pass it. I believe if you & Peck[3] make a job of it begin early & work earnestly & quietly, you can succeed in it. Unless something be done Trumbull is eventually beaten two years hence. Take this into serious consideration. Yours as ever A LINCOLN

[1] Copy, DLC-RTL, enclosed by Mrs. Norman B. Judd to John Hay, June 24, 1882. The copy seems none too accurate, but no trace of the original has been found.

[2] The name "Foncy" in the source is obviously an error for "Fondey." The vote for state treasurer was as follows: John Dougherty (Buchanan candidate) 5,071; William B. Fondey (Douglas candidate) 121,607; James Miller (Republican candidate) 125,430.

[3] Ebenezer Peck.

To Norman B. Judd[1]

Hon: N. B. Judd Springfield, Nov. 16. 1858

My dear Sir Yours of the 15th. is just received. I wrote *you* the same day. As to the pecuniary matter, I am willing to pay according to my ability; but I am the poorest hand living to get others to pay. I have been on expences so long without earning any thing that I am absolutely without money now for even household purposes. Still, if you can put in two hundred and fifty dollars for me towards discharging the debt of the Committee, I will allow it when you and I settle the private matter between us. This, with what I have already paid, and with an outstanding note of mine, will exceed my subscription of five hundred dollars. This too, is exclusive of my ordinary expences during the campaign, all which being added to my loss of time and business, bears pretty heavily upon one no better off in world's goods than I; but as I had the post of honor, it is not for me to be over-nice.

You are feeling badly. "*And this too shall pass away.*" Never fear. Yours as ever A. LINCOLN

[1] ALS, owned by Norman J. Gould, Seneca Falls, New York.

To Samuel C. Davis and Company[1]

Messrs S. C. Davis & Co Springfield,
Gentlemen Novr. 17. 1858

You perhaps need not to be reminded how I have been personally engaged the last three or four months. Your letter to Lincoln & Herndon, of Oct. 1st. complaining that the lands of those against whom we obtained judgments last winter for you, have not been sold on execution has just been handed to me to-day. I will try to "explain how our" (your) "interests have been so much neglected" as you choose to express it. After these judgments were obtained we wrote you that under our law, the selling of land on execution is a delicate and dangerous, matter; that it could not be done safely, without a careful examination of titles; and also of the *value* of the property. Our letters to you will show this. To do this would require a canvass of half the State. We were puzzled, & you sent no definite instructions. At length we employed a young man to visit all the localities, and make as accurate a report on titles and values as he could. He did this, expending three or four weeks time, and as he said, over a hundred dollars of his own money in doing so. When this was done we wrote you, asking if we should sell and bid in for you in accordance with this information. This letter you never answered.

My mind is made up. I will have no more to do with this class of business. I can do business in Court, but I can not, and will not follow executions all over the world. The young man who collected the information for us is an active young lawyer living at Carrollton, Greene County I think. We promised him a share of the compensation we should ultimately receive. He must be somehow paid; and I believe you would do well to turn the whole business over to him. I believe we have had, of legal fees, which you are to recover back from the defendants, one hundred dollars. I would not go through the same labor and vexation again for five hundred; still, if you will clear us of Mr. William Fishback[2] (such is his name) we will be most happy to surrender to him, or to any other person you may name. Yours &c A. LINCOLN

1 ALS-F, ISLA. The facsimile shows at the beginning a notation "Never to be published—Herndon" and at the end another "This shall never be published. Herndon."

2 William M. Fishback had moved to Arkansas, where he became active in politics as a Unionist in 1864 and was later elected governor of the state (1893-1895).

To Henry Asbury[1]

Henry Asbury, Esq Springfield,
My dear Sir Novr. 19, 1858

Yours of the 13th. was received some days ago. The fight must go on. The cause of civil liberty must not be surrendered at the end of *one*, or even, one *hundred* defeats. Douglas had the ingenuity to be supported in the late contest both as the best means to *break down*, and to *uphold* the Slave interest. No ingenuity can keep those antagonistic elements in harmony long. Another explosion will soon come. Yours truly A. LINCOLN—

1 ALS, ORB.

To Anson G. Henry[1]

Dr. A. G. Henry Springfield, Ills. Nov: 19, 1858

My dear Sir Yours of the 27th. of Sept. was received two days ago. I was at Oquawka, Henderson county, on the 9th. of October; and I may then have seen Majr. A. N. Armstrong;[2] but having nothing then to fix my attention, I do not remember such a man. I have concluded, as the best way of serving you, to inclose your letter to E. A. Paine, Esq,[3] of Monmouth, Ills, a reliable lawyer, asking him to do what you ask of me. If a suit is to be brought, he will correspond directly with you.

You doubtless have seen, ere this, the result of the election here. Of course I *wished*, but I did not much *expect* a better result. The popular vote [of the St]ate is with us; so that the seat in the

[*Lower portion of page cut off*.]

whole canvass. On the contrary, John and George Weber,[4] and several such old democrats were furiously for me. As a general rule, out of Sangamon, as well as in it, much of the plain old democracy is with us, while nearly all the old exclusive silk-stocking whiggery is against us. I do not mean nearly all the old whig party; but nearly all of the nice exclusive sort. And why not? There has been nothing in politics since the Revolution so congenial to their nature, as the present position of the great democratic party.

I am glad I made the late race. It gave me a hearing on the great and durable question of the age, which I could have had in no other way; and though I now sink out of view, and shall be forgotten, I believe I have made some marks which will tell for the cause of civil liberty long after I am gone.

Mary joins me in sending our best wishes to Mrs. Henry and others of your family; . . . .

[1] AL, owned by Mrs. Frances H. Foster, Los Gatos, California.

[2] A. N. Armstrong, surveyor and engineer at Oquawka, Illinois.

[3] Eleazar A. Paine. See Lincoln to Paine, *infra.*

[4] John B. Weber and George R. Weber, brothers who were early settlers in Sangamon County and prominent citizens of Springfield.

To Anson S. Miller[1]

Anson Miller, Esq Springfield,
My dear Sir Nov. 19, 1858.

Your very kind and complimentary letter of the 15th. was received yesterday; and for which I sincerely thank you. In the last canvass I strove to do my whole duty both to our cause, and to the kind friends who had assigned me the post of honor; and now if those friends find no cause to regret that they did not assign that post to other hands, I have none for having made the effort, even though it has ended in personal defeat. I hope and believe seed has been sown that will yet produce fruit. The fight must go on. Douglas managed to be supported both as the best means to *break down*, and to *uphold* the slave power. No ingenuity can long keep those opposing elements in harmony. Another explosion will come before a great while. Yours very truly A. LINCOLN.

[1] ALS, owned by Miss Alvera Miller, Oakland, California. Anson S. Mil[illegible] was representative in the Illinois legislature from Winnebago County 18[illegible] 1845 and state senator 1846-1847.

To Eleazar A. Paine[1]

E. A. Paine, Esq Springfield,
My dear Sir Novr. 19. 1858

Inclosed you find a letter and inclosure from my old friend Dr. A. G. Henry[2]—now of Lafayette, Oregon Teritory. Please look after the matter, and write him or me.

Well, the election is over; and, in the main point, we are beaten. Still, my view is that the fight must go on. Let no one falter. The *question* is not half settled. New splits and divisions will soon be upon our adversaries; and we shall [have] fun again. Yours in haste A. LINCOLN

[1] ALS, owned by Thomas Evans, Philadelphia, Pennsylvania.

[2] See Lincoln to Henry, *supra.*

To Newton Bateman[1]

Newton Bateman Esq. Springfield
Dr Sir. Nov 20. 1858.

Our State Central Committee find itself considerably in debt, *and there is a necessity*, for meeting it promptly. We have been taxing ourselves, pretty freely, and are compelled, reluctantly, to call upon some of our friends for assistance. If you can without great inconvenience assist in liquidating this debt, please do so. N. B. Judd, Chicago, is the Chairman as you know. He writes that the committee owe about twenty five hundred dollars. Yours very truly

O. M. HATCH
A. LINCOLN—
JESSE K DUBOIS

[1] LS, owned by Mrs. W. Ross Lloyd, Decatur, Illinois. On November 2, Bateman had been elected state superintendent of education.

To M. M. Inman[1]

M. M. Inman, Esq Springfield,
My dear Sir Nov. 20. 1858

Your very kind letter of the 9th. was duly received. I shall duly consider it's contents. The fight must go on. We are right, and can not finally fail. There will be another blow-up in the so-called democratic party before long.

In the mean time, let all Republicans stand fast by their guns. Your truly A. LINCOLN

[1] ALS-P, ISLA. Inman wrote from Annan [Anna?], Illinois, suggesting that "if Douglas can spend from fifty to a hundred thousand dollars to get men elected to the Legislator [*sic*] to vote for him, why can not the whole Republican party rais [*sic*] 50 or 60 thousand dollars to get them out. . . ." (DLC-RTL).

To Charles H. Ray[1]

Dr. C. H. Ray Springfield,
My dear Sir Novr. 20, 1858

I wish to preserve a Set of the late debates (if they may be called so) between Douglas and myself. To enable me to do so, please get two copies of each number of your paper containing the whole, and send them to me by Express; and I will pay you for the papers & for your trouble. I wish the two sets, in order to lay one away in the raw, and to put the other in a Scrap-book. Remember, if part of any debate is on *both* sides of one sheet, it will take two sets to make one scrap-book.

I believe, according to a letter of yours to Hatch you are "feeling like h—ll yet." Quit that. You will soon feel better. Another "blow-up" is coming; and we shall have fun again. Douglas managed to be supported both as the best instrument to *put down* and to *uphold* the slave power; but no ingenuity can long keep these antagonisms in harmony. Yours as ever A. LINCOLN

[1] ALS, ORB.

To Joel A. Matteson[1]

Hon: J. A. Matteson Springfield, Nov. 25. 1858

Dear Sir Last summer when a movement was made in court against your Road,[2] you engaged us to be on your side. It has so happened that, so far, we have performed no service in the case; but we lost a cash fee offered us on the other side. Now, being hard run, we propose a little compromise. We will claim nothing for the matter just mentioned, if you will relieve us at once from the old matter at the Marine & Fire Insurance Co. and be greatly obliged to boot. Can you not do it? Yours truly A. LINCOLN

[1] ALS (copy?), DLC-RTL. There is no reply from Matteson in the Lincoln Papers, and hence it may be wondered whether Lincoln's letter was ever sent.
[2] The Chicago and Alton Railroad.

To B. Clarke Lundy[1]

Dr. B. C. Lundy: Springfield,
My dear Sir Novr. 26 1858

Your kind letter, with enclosure, is received, and for which I thank you. It being my own judgment that the fight must go on, it affords me great pleasure to learn that our friends are nowhere dispirited. There will be another "blow up" in the democracy. Douglas managed to be supported both as the best instrument to *break down,* and to *uphold* the slave power. No ingenuity can keep this deception—this double position—up a great while. Yours very truly A. LINCOLN—

[1] ALS, owned by Perc S. Brown, Newark, New Jersey.

To Samuel C. Davis and Company[1]

Messrs. S. C. Davis & Co. Springfield,
Gentlemen: Nov. 30, 1858.

Yours of the 27th returning letter of Mr. Fishback[2] is just received. What amount will have to be paid Mr. Fishback, we can not tell until we hear further from him.

We await your direction about making sales. The first Monday of January will be the third day, so that judgment can be obtained at the January Term if process be served as early as the 24th of Decr. being ten days. If suits be commenced as early as the 15th, the Marshal will have from then till the 24th to find the parties, and serve the process—reasonable time but not quite so safe as if it were a little greater. Yours &c, LINCOLN & HERNDON

[1] Copy, ISLA. See Lincoln to Davis and Company, November 17, *supra.*
[2] William Fishback.

To William McNeely[1]

Wm. McNeely, Esq Springfield,
Dear Sir Novr. 30. 1858

Your letter requesting me to attend to a certain case for you when it shall reach the Supreme Court is received. I will attend to it. Yours truly A. LINCOLN—

[1] ALS, owned by H. T. Morgan, Peoria, Illinois. McNeely wrote from Petersburg, Illinois, November 6, 1858, that his claim as administrator of an estate against the Tonica and Petersburg Railroad, allowed by the probate court, had been reversed by the circuit court (DLC-RTL). Lincoln is not named as attorney in the Supreme Court report of Tonica & Petersburg Railroad *v.* William McNeely.

To Henry C. Whitney[1]

H. C. Whitney, Esq Springfield
My dear Sir: Nov. 30. 1858

Being desirous of preserving in some permanent form, the late joint discussions between Douglas and myself, ten days ago I wrote to Dr. Ray, requesting him to forward to me, by express, two sets of the Nos. of the Tribune, which contain the reports of those discussions. Up to date I have no word from him on the subject. Will you, if in your power procure them and forward them to me by Express? If you will, I will pay all charges, and be greatly obliged to boot.

Hoping to meet you before long I remain As ever your friend
A. LINCOLN

[1] ALS-P, ISLA. Whitney replied on December 8 that he had called on Ray, who said that he had never received Lincoln's letter (*vide supra,* November 20) but that no papers were available except for the file. Whitney offered his own set and promised to try to get another (DLC-RTL). See Lincoln to Whitney, December 25, *infra.*

To James T. Thornton[1]

James T. Thornton, Esq Springfield,
Dear Sir Decr. 2. 1858

Yours of the 29th. written in behalf of Mr. John H. Widmer,[2] is received. I am absent altogether too much to be a suitable instructer for a law-student. When a man has reached the age that Mr. Widner has, and has already been doing for himself, my judgment is, that he reads the books for himself without an instructer. That is precisely the way I came to the law. Let Mr. Widner read Blackstone's Commentaries, Chitty's Pleading's—Greenleaf's Evidence, Story's Equity, and Story's Equity Pleading's, get a license, and go to the practice, and still keep reading. That is my judgment of the cheapest, quickest, and best way for Mr. Widner to make a lawyer of himself. Yours truly

A. LINCOLN.

[1] ALS-P, ISLA. James T. Thornton, a native of Kentucky who moved to Sangamon County in 1833 and later to Putnam County, Illinois.

[2] John H. Widmer, whose name Lincoln also spells "Widner," was admitted to the bar at LaSalle, Illinois, in 1860.

To H. D. Sharpe[1]

H. D. Sharpe, Esq Springfield, Dec. 8. 1858

Dear Sir Your very kind letter of Novr. 9th. was duly received. I do not know that you expected or desired an answer; but glancing over the contents of yours again, I am prompted to say that while I desired the result of the late canvass to have been different, I still regard it as an exceeding small matter. I think we have fairly entered upon a durable struggle as to whether this nation is to ultimately become all slave or all free, and though I fall early in the contest, it is nothing if I shall have contributed, in the least degree, to the final rightful result. Respectfully yours

A. LINCOLN.

[1] ALS, NN. Sharpe was author of a plan of emancipation published in 1849 and again in 1859. Writing from New York City, he expressed his interest in the Lincoln-Douglas debates and thanked Lincoln for his advocacy of the rights of man (DLC-RTL).

To Lyman Trumbull[1]

Hon. L. Trumbull: Springfield,
My dear Sir Decr. 11. 1858

Your letter of the 7th. inclosing one from Mr. Underwood,[2] is received. I have not the slightest thought of being a candidate for

Congress in this District. I am not spoken of in that connection; and I can scarcely conceive what has misled Mr. Underwood in regard to the matter.

As to what we shall do, the Republicans are a little divided. The Danites say if we will stand out of the way, they will run a man, and divide the democratic forces with the Douglasites; and some of our friends are in favor of this course. Others think such a course would demoralize us, and hurt us in the future; and they, of course, are in favor of running a man of our own at all events. This latter view will probably prevail.

Since you left, Douglas has gone South, making characteristic speeches, and seeking to re-instate himself in that section. The majority of the democratic politicians of the nation mean to kill him; but I doubt whether they will adopt the aptest way to do it. Their true way is to present him with no new test, let him into the Charleston Convention, and then outvote him, and nominate another. In that case, he will have no pretext for bolting the nomination, and will be as powerless as they can wish. On the other hand, if they push a Slave code upon him, as a test, he will bolt at once, turn upon us, as in the case of Lecompton, and claim that all Northern men shall make common cause in electing him President as the best means of breaking down the Slave power. In that case, the democratic party go into a minority inevitably; and the struggle in the whole North will be, as it was in Illinois last summer and fall, whether the Republican party can maintain it's identity, or be broken up to form the tail of Douglas' new kite. Some of our great Republican doctors will then have a splendid chance to swallow the pills they so eagerly prescribed for us last Spring. Still I hope they will not swallow them; and although I do not feel that I owe the said doctors much, I will help them, to the best of my ability, to reject the said pills. The truth is, the Republican principle can, in no wise live with Douglas; and it is arrant folly now, as it was last Spring, to waste time, and scatter labor already performed, in dallying with him. Your friend as ever

A. LINCOLN—

[1] ALS, CSmH.

[2] John C. Underwood of the Emigrant Aid and Homestead Company in New York City had been driven out of Virginia for attending the Frémont convention in 1856. His letter to Trumbull, December 6, expressed his belief in the importance of Lincoln's election to Congress to fill the vacancy caused by the death of Thomas L. Harris after the November election (DLC-RTL).

To Alexander Sympson[1]

Alexander Sympson, Esq. Springfield, Dec. 12, 1858.

My dear Sir: I expect the result of the election went hard with you. So it did with me, too, perhaps not quite so hard as you may have supposed. I have an abiding faith that we shall beat them in the long run. Step by step the objects of the leaders will become too plain for the people to stand them. I write merely to let you know that I am neither dead nor dying. Please give my respects to your good family, and all inquiring friends. Yours as ever,

A. LINCOLN.

[1] Tarbell (Appendix), p. 335.

To William M. Fishback[1]

Wm. Fishback, Esq Springfield,
My dear Sir: Dec. 19. 1858

Yours of the 1st. to C. M. Smith, has been handed me to answer. Soon after the political campaign closed here Messrs. S. C. Davis & Co wrote us rather complaining that lands had not been sold upon their executions. I answered them, saying it was their own fault, as they never answered after we informed them of the work you had done. I also informed them that in the future we would not follow executions, and requested them to pay you for what you have already done, and transfer all the business in our hands to you. They replied they would do so; but by that time we had learned that you were gone. Very reluctantly I had to write them that you were gone, and that we must renew our effort to collect the money on their executions. And so we have pitched into it again. To my regret I find that I have either lost one of your letters, or your researches did not go so far as I thought. I find nothing about the case at Browning in Schuyler County.

We drew on S. C. Davis & Co for $100 and send you the proceeds.

Unless your prospects are flattering where you are, or your health will not permit, I wish you would return and take charge of this business. With the general chances of a young man, and additional business of the same sort which we could from time [to time] put in your hands, I feel confident you could make a living. Yours very truly A. LINCOLN

[1] ALS, IHi. See Lincoln to Samuel C. Davis and Company, November 17, *supra.*

Inscription in Autograph Album of George P. Davis[1]

December 21, 1858

My young friend George Perrin Davis, has allowed me the honor of being the first to write his name in this book.

Bloomington, Dec. 21. 1858— A. LINCOLN—

[1] ADS-F, ISLA. George Perrin Davis was the son of Judge David Davis.

To Henry C. Whitney[1]

H. C. Whitney Esq Springfield,
My dear Sir: Dec. 25. 1858

I have just received yours of the 23, inquiring whether I received the newspapers you sent me by Express. I did receive them, and am very much obliged. There is some probability that my Scrap-book will be reprinted; and if it shall, I will save you a copy. Your friend as ever A. LINCOLN—

[1] ALS-P, ISLA.

Opinion Concerning the Will of John Franklin[1]

December 30, 1858

In the case of the Will of John Franklin, sr. two points of difficulty have arisen.

One is that eighty acres of land is bequeathed to Nelson N. Franklin, upon condition that he pay in one year after the decease of the Testator, eight dollars per acre. It turns out that forty acres of the land had previously been deeded to Nelson. I think he is entitled to have the forty acres not previously deeded, on paying eight dollars per acre for it, without paying anything for the forty previously deeded.

The next difficulty is, that certain lands are bequeathed to the widow during her life, and the same lands, and one hundred & ten acres additional, are bequeathed to Wesley P. Franklin, at the widows death, he paying the other heirs eight dollars per acre. At what *time* does he get the one hundred and ten acres? I think he is to have it at once, upon paying the eight dollars per acre for it.

There is also a question outside of the Will, which is that some of the minor children have, while living with the Testator, their father, and by his consent and permission, accumulated some personal property, as their own. The question is, do these children keep their respective parts of this property, independent of the estate, or does it fall back into the estate? I think they are to keep it independent of the estate.

I see nothing upon which I think the Will can be broken.

Bloomington Dec. 30. 1858. A. LINCOLN—

[1] ADS-F, ISLA.

To Maria Bullock[1]

Dear Aunt Springfield, Ills, Jan. 3. 1859

I have recently had two letters from our cousin Charles Carr,[2] in relation to your business. It annoys me to have to say that I can not collect money now. I now believe the quickest way I can get your money is for me to buy the debts of you, as soon as I can get in any money of my own to do it with. I keep some money loaned at ten per cent; and when I can get hold of some, it would be a ready investment for me to just take these debts off your hands; and I shall try to do so. I think it will be better all round than to resort to the law. This does not apply to the small debt of eighty odd dollars, upon which I shall sue and foreclose the mortgage next court.

All well. Yours as ever, A. LINCOLN

[1] ALS, IHi.

[2] Charles D. Carr, an attorney at Lexington, Kentucky, was Mrs. Bullock's nephew. Carr's letters are not extant, and there is no record of Lincoln's purchasing the mortgages.

Opinion Concerning Land Surveys[1]

January 6, 1859

The 11th. Section of the act of Congress, approved Feb. 11, 1805, prescribing rules for the subdivision of Sections of land within the United States system of Surveys, standing unrepealed, in my opinion, is binding on the respective purchasers of different parts of the same Section, and furnishes the true rule for Surveyors in establishing lines between them. That law, being in force at the time each became a purchaser, becomes a condition of the purchase.

And, by that law, I think the true rule for dividing into quarters, any interior Section, or Section which is not fractional, is to run straight lines through the Section from the opposite quarter section corners, fixing the point where such straight lines cross, or interesect each other, as the middle, or center of the Section.

Nearly, perhaps quite, all the original surveys are to some extent, erroneous, and, in some of the Sections, greatly so. In each of the latter, it is obvious that a more equitable mode of division than the above, might be adopted; but as error is infinitely various, perhaps no better single rules can be prescribed.

At all events I think the above has been prescribed by the competent authority. A. LINCOLN—

Springfield, Jany. 6, 1859—

[1] ALS-F, ISLA.

To W. H. Wells[1]

W. H. Wells, Esq. Springfield, Ills.
My dear Sir: Jany. 8, 1859.

Yours of the 3rd. Inst. is just received. I regret to say that the joint discussions between Judge Douglas and myself have been published in no shape except in the first newspaper reports; and that I have no copy of them, or even of the single one at Freeport, which I could send you. By dint of great labor since the election, I have got together a nearly, (not quite) complete single set to preserve myself. I shall preserve your address, and if I can, in a reasonable time, lay my hand on an old paper containing the Freeport discussion, I will send it to you.

All dallying with Douglas by Republicans, who are such at heart, is, at the very least, time, and labor lost; and all such, who so dally with him, will yet bite their lips in vexation for their own folly. His policy, which rigourously excludes all idea of there being any *wrong* in slavery, does lead inevitably to the nationalization of the Institution; and all who deprecate that consummation, and yet are seduced into his support, do but cut their own throats. True, Douglas *has* opposed the administration on one measure, and yet *may* on some other; but while he upholds the Dred Scott decision, declares that he cares not whether slavery be voted down or voted up; that it is simply a question of dollars and cents, and that the Almighty has drawn a line on one side of which labor *must* be performed by slaves; to support him or Buchanan, is simply to reach the same goal by only slightly different roads. Very Respectfully A. LINCOLN—

[1] ALS, The Rosenbach Company, Philadelphia and New York. W. H. Wells, "a young man and a 'jour printer,'" wrote from Waynesburg, Pennsylvania, for a copy of the debates, particularly the debate at Freeport, to use in answering the editor of the county paper, a Republican turned anti-Lecompton Democrat (DLC-RTL).

To Mrs. J. M. Mozart[1]

Madam: [January 10?] 1859

The undersigned, wishing to testify their appreciation of your merits as an artist, and their most perfect satisfaction with the concert given by you on last Saturday evening, respectfully request you to give another entertainment, similar in character, on your return from Jacksonville.

Your most excellent treatment of those sterling songs and ballads, has left a deep and lasting impression on those who had the pleasure of listening to you, and created an earnest desire to hear you once more before you leave the West. Trusting that your engagements will permit you to accede to our request, we are, dear Madam, your most obedient servants,

[1] *Illinois State Journal*, January 11, 1859. Lincoln's name appears as one of fifty-two signers, omitted for reasons of space. Mrs. Mozart's letter of January 10 acceding to the request to give another performance before returning to New York, is also printed in the *Journal*. Her first concert scheduled for January 6, was postponed because of inclement weather until Saturday, January 8, and in response to the above letter she sang again on the night of Tuesday, January 11 at Cook's Hall.

To Messrs. Cole and Wall[1]

Messrs Cole & Wall Springfield,
Gentlemen Jany. 21, 1859

Judge Emerson[2] is here, and his lawyer, Edwards[3] wanted me this morning, to consent to a continuance of your case, saying that if I did not they would have to dismiss it, and sue again. I said I could not continue it without your direction; and I promised Edwards to write you, which I now do. I suppose it is for you now to say whether case shall be continued, or dismissed. Write me at once which shall be done. Yours truly A. LINCOLN—

[1] ALS, IHi. Messrs. Cole and Wall have not been identified, and no record of the case in question is available.

[2] Charles Emerson, or *Emmerson*, judge of the Seventeenth Circuit.

[3] Since the case has not been found, it has not been determined whether Ninian W. Edwards or Benjamin S. Edwards served as Emerson's attorney.

Testimonial Letter for Samuel M. Hitt[1]

Whom it may concern. Springfield, Illinois, Jany. 25. 1859.

My friend, Mr. Samuel M Hitt, the bearer of this, visits the Eastern States, with some pecuniary objects. Mr. Hitt and myself reside more than a hundred miles apart; so that I am but little acquainted with his private affairs. I know him to have the possession, and apparant ownership, of a large, and well stocked, and improved landed estate. Besides this, his long established, and well sustained character for honor and integrity, does not permit me to doubt that any representation of his own, will be strictly correct, and may be safely relied upon. ABRAHAM LINCOLN.

[1] ALS, owned by Wright Hitt, Kansas City, Missouri, great-grandson of Samuel M. Hitt, an uncle of Robert Hitt who reported the Lincoln-Douglas Debates.

To Lyman Trumbull[1]

Hon: L. Trumbull Springfield, Jany. 29. 1859

Dear Sir I have just received your late speech,[2] in pamphlet form, sent me by yourself. I had seen, and read it, before, in a newspaper; and I really think it is a capital one.

When you can find leisure, write me your present impressions of Douglas' movements.

Our friends here from different parts of the State, in and out of the Legislature, are united, resolute, and determined; and I think it is almost certain that we shall be far better organized for 1860 than ever before.

We shall get no just apportionment; and the best we can do, (if we can even do that) is to prevent one being made, worse than the present. Yours as ever A. LINCOLN—

[1] ALS, CSmH.

[2] Trumbull's speech of January 7, replying to Senator Alfred Iverson of Georgia, who had threatened secession and charged Republicans with being a disunion party pledged to abolish slavery.

To Elihu B. Washburne[1]

Hon. E. B. Washburne. Springfield

My dear Sir Jany. 29. 1859

I have just received your brother's speech[2] sent me by yourself. I had read it before; and you will oblige me by presenting him with my respects, and telling him I doubly thank him for making it—first, because the points are so just and well put; and next, because it is so well timed. We needed, from some one who can get the public attention, just such a speech just at this time. His objection to the Oregon constitution because it excludes free negroes, is the only thing I wish he had omitted. Your friend as ever

A. LINCOLN

[1] ALS, owned by Douglas S. Brown, Elm Grove, Wisconsin.

[2] Representative Israel Washburn, Jr., of Maine, who in common with other members of the family, excepting his brother Elihu, spelled his name without an *e*, delivered a speech on the Republican party in the House of Representatives on January 10.

Certificate of Examination for Henry I. Atkins[1]

Springfield, Ill., Jan. 31, 1859.

The undersigned, having in pursuance of the within appointment, examined the said applicant, Henry I. Atkins, touching his qualifications to practice law, respectfully report that having performed the said duty, they find the applicant qualified to practice law, and recommend that he be licensed.

M. HAY,
A. LINCOLN,
B. S. EDWARDS.

[1] Howard F. Dyson, "Lincoln in Rushville," *Transactions of the Illinois State Historical Society*, Publication No. 8, 1903 (Springfield, 1904), pp. 224-25. Milton H. Hay and Benjamin S. Edwards, co-signers with Lincoln, were attorneys at Springfield.

Opinion Concerning Swamp Lands in Bureau County, Illinois[1]

January 31, 1859

September 28. 1850, by an act of that date, Congress granted the whole of the "swamp and overflowed lands, made unfit thereby for cultivation" which remained unsold at that date, to the several States in which they were situated. By that act, upon the assumption that the data for doing so were in the Department of the Interior, the Secretary of that department was directed to make lists of those lands, and cause a patent to be issued for them to each State; and it was provided that the proceeds of said lands should be exclusively applied, so far as necessary, to the reclaiming of those lands by levees and drains.

June 22– 1852, by an act of that date, the Illinois Legislature adopted a system for the man[a]gement of the Swamp lands, so granted, within the state. By this act the lands were granted to the counties respectively, and placed under their control with power

[1] ADS, Bureau County Files. Accompanying the document are true copies of the Resolutions of the Bureau County Board of Supervisors, April 28, 1856, marked (A), Promissory note form marked (B), Certificate of purchase form marked (C).

to sell upon certain terms and limitations. Also by this act the Surveyors of the several counties were to select and designate the swamp lands in their respective counties, which they did, generally taking all the unentered lands. Meanwhile, the United States Land Offices remaining open, and having nothing to guide them, individuals continued to purchase lands within them, in many instances the same tracts which had been selected by the Surveyors as Swamp lands.

The deficiency of *data* in the Department of the Interior by which to designate the Swamp-lands from other lands; the very liberal designations made by the County Surveyors, and the numerous purchases made, and sought to be made, by individuals from the United States, of tracts claimed by the State as Swamp-land, led to much difficulty, confusion and embarrassment; even to the taking proof in the local Land Offices, whether particular tracts were or were not, in fact, Swamp land.

March 2, 1855 another act of Congress was passed intended to mitigate, if not entirely overcome this difficulty

No single patent, as seemed to be contemplated by the first named act of Congress, ever issued; but on the 20th. day of October 1856, a Patent issued to the Governor of Illinois, for the Swamp lands in the Dixon Land District, which District includes the county of *Bureau.*

April 28, 1856, the Board of Supervisors of Bureau county passed, and entered of record a set of resolutions for the sale of the swamp-lands within that county, of which resolutions the paper hereto attached, marked (A) contains true copies.

In pursuance of those resolutions the "Drainage Commissioner["] of that county, made sale of those lands to various purchasers, taking notes, and giving certificates to said purchasers, of which notes and certificates, the papers attached, marked respectively (B) and (C) are blank forms. Some of the purchasers *did*, and some did *not* present their certificates and receive bonds as indicated. The paper attached, marked (D) is a blank form of the bonds given, and ready to be given.

February 18, 1857, some question having been made as to the validity of this sale, the Illinois Legislature passed an act ratifying and confirming it.

March 3, 1857, Congress passed another act, confirming a certain selection of Swamp lands, and directing the same to be patented; which "selection" so confirmed, was in fact the same, for part of the lands included in which, the Patent aforesaid had then already been issued.

The notes, as shown by the blank attached, are in common form, containing unconditional promises to pay.

Upon this state of facts, my legal opinion is asked upon the question, following:

"Can the sale of the Swamp Land, by the county, be inforced by the Courts?"

I should state the question, thus:

"Can the makers of the notes successfully defend suits brought upon them?"

Unquestionably they can not, unless they can allege and prove want, or failure of consideration. Neither of these can they do. No deception was practiced upon them. At the time they purchased, and made the notes, they had both constructive and actual notice of everything concerning the title, which really exists. Nothing new has come to light. The certificate received by each purchaser, refers to the resolutions of the Board; and those resolutions show upon what condition, and what alone, the purchaser can be relieved from his note. The condition is "if the title of the County to any such tract, so contested, shall fail, suitable effort to sustain the same having been made by the purchaser, to the satisfaction of the "Drainage Commissioner" at the time of such contest, the County will repay to such purchaser the money, and cancel or release the note received therefor &c" I understand no such contest has been made in any case; and until this shall be done, no successful defence to a suit upon any of these notes can be made.

If, by any means, any tract was sold, by the county, which was not granted to the State by the United States, the title to such tract would fail, but such case would be an exception. With such, or similar exceptions, if there be any such, the title to the lands sold by the county has not failed, and quite certainly, never will fail. Test it, by supposing practical cases. Suppose the purchaser takes *possession—how*, and *by whom* can he be got out? Will the United States undertake to put him out? Will the United States re-assume ownership, and sell, and give a Patent to some individual? Will the State do either of these things? Manifestly not. The idea of such possession ever being so disturbed is absurd. Suppose, then, a stranger squats upon the land, and the purchaser thus loses it, unless he can dispossess the squatter. He brings his Ejectment; shows the acts of Congress, and the Patent of the United States to the State; the acts of the Legislature transfering the title to the county, authorizing a sale by the county, and afterwards confirming the sale actually made by the county, together with the conveyance by the county to himself; and his case is made out. Suppose the squatter shall then offer to say, that by the acts of Congress, the proceeds of the lands were to be appropriated to the draining of the lands, and that this has not been done. Can a naked wrongdoer be allowed to alledge this? And if alledged, could it, at law, overturn the United States Patent? Was the Patent good, so long as the proceeds remained unappropriated, and bad after they were misapplied? A Bill in Equity, could not be for a moment maintained against the Patent, by a mere wrongdoer.

My opinion is, that the purchasers from the County, will never lose the land, unless it be by some fault of their own; and that they can not successfully defend suits brought upon the notes.

Springfield, Jany. 31, 1859— A. LINCOLN—

To Mark W. Delahay[1]

M. W. Delahay, Esq Springfield, Ills. Feb. 1. 1859

My dear Sir: Yours of the 22nd. of January is received. I do expect to visit Council Bluffs some time between this, and next summer; and I should be pleased if I could arrange it so as to meet a Republican mass convention at your city. Until the Legislature shall adjourn, no one can tell what will be the time of holding court in any county—a thing I must keep my eye on this year, as I lost pretty nearly all of the last. When I can speak more definitely I will write again. Let me say now, however, that I think the latter in May the better, unless you could defer until the last half of June, which would be the very best for me. I am obliged to be here the first half of June. Yours very truly A. LINCOLN

[1] ALS, DLC-HW.

To Lyman Trumbull[1]

Hon: L. Trumbull Springfield, Feb. 3. 1859

My dear Sir Yours of the 29th. is received. The article mentioned by you, prepared for the Chicago Journal,[2] I have not seen; nor do I wish to see it, though I heard of it a month, or more, ago. Any effort to put enmity between you and me, is as idle as the wind. I do not for a moment doubt that you, Judd, Cook, Palmer,[3] and the republicans generally, coming from the old democratic ranks, were as sincerely anxious for my success in the late contest, as I myself, and the old whig republicans were. And I beg to assure you, beyond all possible cavil, that you can scarcely be more anxious to be sustained two years hence than I am that you shall be so sustained. I can not conceive it possible for me to be a rival of yours, or to take sides against you in favor of any rival. Nor do I think there is much danger of the old democratic and whig elements of our party breaking into opposing factions. They certainly shall not, if I can prevent it.

I do not perceive that there is any feeling here about Cuba; and so I think, you can safely venture to act upon your own judgment upon any phase of it which may be presented.

The H.R. passed an apportionment bill yesterday—slightly better for [us] than the present in the Senate districts; but perfectly outrageous in the H.R. districts. It can be defeated without any revolutionary movement, unless the session be prolonged. Yours as ever A. LINCOLN

[1] ALS, CSmH.

[2] The article is described in Trumbull's letter as being said to be the work of John Wentworth, designed to stir up bad feeling between ex-Whig and ex-Democrat in the party, but professing to be a justification by Charles L. Wilson, editor of the *Journal*, for having nominated Lincoln in the Republican convention (DLC-RTL).

[3] Norman B. Judd, Burton C. Cook, and John M. Palmer were like Trumbull, ex-Democrats.

Second Lecture on Discoveries and Inventions[1]

[February 11, 1859]

We have all heard of Young America. He is the most *current* youth of the age. Some think him conceited, and arrogant; but has he not reason to entertain a rather extensive opinion of himself? Is he not the inventor and owner of the *present*, and sole hope of the *future?* Men, and things, everywhere, are ministering unto him. Look at his apparel, and you shall see cotten fabrics from Manchester and Lowell; flax-linen from Ireland; wool-cloth from [Spain;][2] silk from France; furs from the Arctic regions, with a

[1] AD, ORB. Lincoln's first lecture on Discoveries and Inventions was written at least by April 6, 1858 (*vide supra*), on which date he delivered it before the Young Men's Association of Bloomington, Illinois. Completely rewritten for delivery before the Phi Alpha Society of Illinois College at Jacksonville on February 11, 1859 (*Illinois State Journal*, February 14, 1859), the lecture was repeated a few days later in Decatur, and again in Springfield on February 21, before the Springfield Library Association at Concert Hall (*ibid.*, February 21). Further invitations to lecture were turned down because of pressure of business (letters to W.M. Morris, March 28, and T.J. Pickett, April 16, *infra*). The second manuscript, like the first, was preserved in the satchel of documents which Lincoln left with Elizabeth Todd Grimsley a few days before leaving for Washington in 1861. It later passed into the Gunther Collection and then into the Barrett Collection.

[2] Lincoln left a blank space in which "Spain" has been pencilled by another hand.

buffalo-robe from the Rocky Mountains, as a general out-sider. At his table, besides plain bread and meat made at home, are sugar from Louisiana; coffee and fruits from the tropics; salt from Turk's Island; fish from New-foundland; tea from China, and spices from the Indies. The whale of the Pacific furnishes his candle-light; he has a diamond-ring from Brazil; a gold-watch from California, and a spanish cigar from Havanna. He not only has a present supply of all these, and much more; but thousands of hands are engaged in producing fresh supplies, and other thousands, in bringing them to him. The iron horse is panting, and impatient, to carry him everywhere, in no time; and the lightening stands ready harnessed to take and bring his tidings in a trifle less than no time. He owns a large part of the world, by right of possessing it; and all the rest by right of *wanting* it, and *intending* to have it. As Plato had for the immortality of the soul, so Young America has "a pleasing hope—a fond desire—a longing after" teritory. He has a great passion—a perfect rage—for the "*new*"; particularly new men for office, and the new earth mentioned in the revelations, in which, being no more sea, there must be about three times as much land as in the present. He is a great friend of humanity; and his desire for land is not selfish, but merely an impulse to extend the area of freedom. He is very anxious to fight for the liberation of enslaved nations and colonies, provided, always, they *have* land, and have *not* any liking for his interference. As to those who have no land, and would be glad of help from any quarter, he considers *they* can afford to wait a few hundred years longer. In knowledge he is particularly rich. He knows all that can possibly be known; inclines to believe in spiritual rappings, and is the unquestioned inventor of "*Manifest Destiny*." His horror is for all that is old, particularly "Old Fogy"; and if there be any thing old which he can endure, it is only old whiskey and old tobacco.

If the said Young America really is, as he claims to be, the owner of all present, it must be admitted that he has considerable advantage of Old Fogy. Take, for instance, the first of all fogies, father Adam. There he stood, a very perfect physical man, as poets and painters inform us; but he must have been very ignorant, and simple in his habits. He had had no sufficient time to learn much by observation; and he had no near neighbors to teach him anything. No part of his breakfast had been brought from the other side of the world; and it is quite probable, he had no conception of the world having any other side. In all of these things, it is very plain, he was no equal of Young America; the most that can be said is, that *according to his chance* he may have been quite as much of a man as his very self-complaisant descendant. Little as was what he knew, let the Youngster discard all he has learned from others, and then show, if he can, any advantage on his side. In the way of *land*, and *live stock*, Adam was quite in the ascendant. He had dominion over all the earth, and all the living things upon, and round about it. The land has been sadly divided out since; but never fret, Young America will *re-annex* it.

The great difference between Young America and Old Fogy, is the result of *Discoveries*, *Inventions*, and *Improvements*. These, in turn, are the result of *observation*, *reflection* and *experiment*. For instance, it is quite certain that ever since water has been boiled in covered vessels, men have seen the lids of the vessels rise and fall a little, with a sort of fluttering motion, by force of the steam; but so long as this was not specially observed, and reflected and experimented upon, it came to nothing. At length however, after many thousand years, some man observes this long-known effect of hot water lifting a pot-lid, and begins a train of reflection upon it. He says "Why, to be sure, the force that lifts the pot-lid, will lift any thing else, which is no heavier than the pot-lid." "And, as man has much hard lifting to do, can not this hot-water power be made to help him?" He has become a little excited on the subject, and he fancies he hears a voice answering "Try me" He does try it; and the *observation*, *reflection*, and *trial* gives to the world the control of that tremendous, and now well known agent, called steam-power. This is not the actual history in detail, but the general principle.

But was this first inventor of the application of steam, wiser or more ingenious than those who had gone before him? Not at all. Had he not learned much of them, he never would have succeeded —probably, never would have thought of making the attempt. To be fruitful in invention, it is indispensable to have a *habit* of observation and reflection; and this *habit*, our steam friend acquired, no doubt, from those who, to him, were old fogies. But for the difference in *habit* of observation, why did yankees, almost instantly, discover gold in California, which had been trodden upon, and over-looked by indians and Mexican greasers, for centuries? Gold-mines are not the only mines overlooked in the same way. There are more mines above the Earth's surface than below it. All nature—the whole world, material, moral, and intellectual,—is a mine; and, in Adam's day, it was a wholly unexplored mine. Now, it was the destined work of Adam's race to develope, by discoveries, inventions, and improvements, the hidden treasures of this mine. But Adam had nothing to turn his attention to the work. If he should do anything in the way of invention, he had first to invent the art of invention—the *instance* at least, if not the *habit* of observation and reflection. As might be expected he seems not to have been a very observing man at first; for it appears he went about naked a considerable length of time, before he even noticed that obvious fact. But when he did observe it, the observation was not lost upon him; for it immediately led to the first of all inventions, of which we have any direct account—*the fig-leaf apron.*

The inclination to exchange thoughts with one another is probably an original impulse of our nature. If I be in pain I wish to let you know it, and to ask your sympathy and assistance; and my pleasurable emotions also, I wish to communicate to, and share with you. But to carry on such communication, some *instrumentality* is indispensable. Accordingly speech—articulate sounds rattled off from the tongue—was used by our first parents, and even by Adam, before the creation of Eve. He gave names to the animals while she was still a bone in his side; and he broke out quite volubly when she first stood before him, the best present of his maker. From this it would appear that speech was not an invention of man, but rather the direct gift of his Creator. But whether Divine gift, or invention, it is still plain that if a mode of communication had been left to invention, *speech* must have been the first, from the superior adaptation to the end, of the organs of speech, over every other means within the whole range of nature. Of the organs of speech the tongue is the principal; and if we shall test it, we shall find the capacities of the tongue, in the utterance of articulate sounds, absolutely wonderful. You can count from one to one hundred, quite distinctly in about forty seconds. In doing this two hundred and eighty three distinct sounds or syllables are uttered, being seven to each second; and yet there shall be enough difference between every two, to be easily recognized by the ear of the hearer. What other *signs* to represent *things* could possibly be produced so rapidly? or, even, if ready made, could be *arranged* so rapidly to express the sense? *Motions* with the hands, are no adequate substitute. *Marks* for the recognition of the eye—*writing*—although a wonderful auxiliary for speech, is no worthy substitute for it. In addition to the more slow and laborious process of getting up a communication in writing, the materials—pen, ink, and paper—are not always at hand. But one always has his tongue with him, and the breath of his life is the ever-ready material with which it works. Speech, then, by enabling different individuals to interchange thoughts, and thereby to combine their powers of observation and reflection, greatly facilitates useful discoveries and inventions. What one observes, and would himself infer nothing from, he tells to another, and that other at once sees a valuable hint in it. A result is thus reached which neither *alone* would have arrived at.

And this reminds me of what I passed unnoticed before, that the very first invention was a joint operation, Eve having shared with Adam in the getting up of the apron. And, indeed, judging from the fact that sewing has come down to our times as "woman's work" it is very probable she took the leading part; he, perhaps, doing no more than to stand by and thread the needle. That proceeding may be reckoned as the mother of all "Sewing societies"; and the first and most perfect "world's fair" all inventions and all inventors then in the world, being on the spot.

But speech alone, valuable as it ever has been, and is, has not advanced the condition of the world much. This is abundantly evident when we look at the degraded condition of all those tribes of human creatures who have no considerable additional means of communicating thoughts. *Writing*—the art of communicating thoughts to the mind, through the eye—is the great invention of the world. Great in the astonishing range of analysis and combination which necessarily underlies the most crude and general conception of it—great, very great in enabling us to converse with the dead, the absent, and the unborn, at all distances of time and of space; and great, not only in its direct benefits, but greatest help, to all other inventions. Suppose the art, with all conception of it, were this day lost to the world, how long, think you, would it be, before even Young America could get up the letter A. with any adequate notion of using it to advantage? The precise period at which writing was invented, is not known; but it certainly was as early as the time of Moses; from which we may safely infer that it's inventors were very old fogies.

Webster, at the time of writing his Dictionary, speaks of the English Language as then consisting of seventy or eighty thousand words. If so, the language in which the five books of Moses were written must, at that time, now thirtythree or four hundred years ago, have consisted of at least one quarter as many, or, twenty thousand. When we remember that words are *sounds* merely, we shall conclude that the idea of representing those sounds by *marks,* so that whoever should at any time after see the marks, would understand what sounds they meant, was a bold and ingenius conception, not likely to occur to one man of a million, in the run of a thousand years. And, when it did occur, a distinct mark for each word, giving twenty thousand different marks first to be learned, and afterwards remembered, would follow as the second thought, and would present such a difficulty as would lead to the conclusion that the whole thing was impracticable. But the *necessity* still would exist; and we may readily suppose that the idea was conceived, and lost, and reproduced, and dropped, and taken up again and again, until at last, the thought of dividing sounds into parts, and making a mark, not to represent a whole sound, but only a part of one, and then of combining these marks, not very many in number, upon the principles of permutation, so as to represent any and all of the whole twenty thousand words, and even any additional number was somehow conceived and pushed into practice. This was the invention of *phoenetic* writing, as distinguished from the clumsy picture writing of some of the nations. That it was difficult of conception and execution, is apparant, as well by the foregoing reflections, as by the fact that so many tribes of men have come down from Adam's time to ours without ever having possessed it. It's utility may be conceived, by the reflection that, to *it* we owe everything which distinguishes us from savages. Take it from us, and the Bible, all history, all science, all government, all commerce, and nearly all social intercourse go with it.

The great activity of the tongue, in articulating sounds, has already been mentioned; and it may be of some passing interest to notice the wonderful powers of the *eye*, in conveying ideas to the mind from writing. Take the same example of the numbers from *one* to *one hundred*, written down, and you can run your eye over the list, and be assured that every number is in it, in about one half the time it would require to pronounce the words with the voice; and not only so, but you can, in the same short time, determine whether every word is spelled correctly, by which it is evident that every separate letter, amounting to eight hundred and sixty four, has been recognized, and reported to the mind, within the incredibly short space of twenty seconds, or one third of a minute.

I have already intimated my opinion that in the world's history, certain inventions and discoveries occurred, of peculiar value, on account of their great efficiency in facilitating all other inventions and discoveries. Of these were the arts of writing and of printing—the discovery of America, and the introduction of Patent-laws. The date of the first, as already stated, is unknown; but it certainly was as much as fifteen hundred years before the Christian era; the second—printing—came in 1436, or nearly three thousand years after the first. The others followed more rapidly—the discovery of

America in 1492, and the first patent laws in 1624. Though not apposite to my present purpose, it is but justice to the fruitfulness of that period, to mention two other important events—the Lutheran Reformation in 1517, and, still earlier, the invention of negroes, or, of the present mode of using them, in 1434. But, to return to the consideration of printing, it is plain that it is but the *other* half —and in real utility, the *better* half—of writing; and that both together are but the assistants of speech in the communication of thoughts between man and man. When man was possessed of speech alone, the chances of invention, discovery, and improvement, were very limited; but by the introduction of each of these, they were greatly multiplied. When writing was invented, any important observation, likely to lead to a discovery, had at least a chance of being written down, and consequently, a better chance of never being forgotten; and of being seen, and reflected upon, by a much greater number of persons; and thereby the chances of a valuable hint being caught, proportionably augmented. By this means the observation of a single individual might lead to an important invention, years, and even centuries after he was dead. In one word, by means of writing, the seeds of invention were more permanently preserved, and more widely sown. And yet, for the three thousand years during which printing remained undiscovered after writing was in use, it was only a small portion of the people who could write, or read writing; and consequently the field of invention, though much extended, still continued very limited. At length printing came. It gave ten thousand copies of any written matter, quite as cheaply as ten were given before; and consequently a thousand minds were brought into the field where there was but one before. This was a great *gain;* and history shows a great *change* corresponding to it, in point of time. I will venture to consider *it,* the true termination of that period called "the dark ages." Discoveries, inventions, and improvements followed rapidly, and have been increasing their rapidity ever since. The effects could not come, all at once. It required time to bring them out; and they are still coming. The *capacity* to read, could not be multiplied as fast as the *means* of reading. Spelling-books just began to go into the hands of the children; but the teachers were not very numerous, or very competent; so that it is safe to infer they did not advance so speedily as they do now-a-days. It is very probable—almost certain—that the great mass of men, at that time, were utterly unconscious, that their *conditions,* or their *minds* were capable of improvement. They not only looked upon the educated few as superior beings; but they supposed themselves to be naturally incapable of rising to equality To immancipate the mind from this false and under estimate of itself, is the great task which printing came into the world to perform. It is difficult for us, *now* and *here*, to conceive how strong this slavery of the mind was; and how long it did, of necessity, take, to break it's shackles, and to get a habit of freedom of thought, established. It is, in this connection, a curious fact that a new country is most favorable—almost necessary—to the immancipation of thought, and the consequent advancement of civilization and the arts. The human family originated as is thought, somewhere in Asia, and have worked their way princip[al]ly Westward. Just now, in civilization, and the arts, the people of Asia are entirely behind those of Europe; those of the East of Europe behind those of the West of it; while we, here in America, *think* we discover, and invent, and improve, faster than any of them. *They* may think this is arrogance; but they can not deny that Russia has called on us to show her how to build steam-boats and railroads—while in the older parts of Asia, they scarcely know that such things as S.Bs & RR.s. exist. In anciently inhabited countries, the dust of ages—a real downright old-fogyism—seems to settle upon, and smother the intellects and energies of man. It is in this view that I have mentioned the discovery of America as an event greatly favoring and facilitating useful discoveries and inventions.

Next came the Patent laws. These began in England in 1624; and, in this country, with the adoption of our constitution. Before then [these?], any man might instantly use what another had invented; so that the inventor had no special advantage from his own invention. The patent system changed this; secured to the inventor, for a limited time, the exclusive use of his invention; and thereby added the fuel of *interest* to the *fire* of genius, in the discovery and production of new and useful things.

Endorsement: Alonzo Lyons to Lincoln[1]

The document above described was this day mailed back to Alonzo Lyons, Tolono, Champaign County, Illinois.

Feby. 16. 1859. R. T. LINCOLN

[1] AE, DLC-RTL. The envelope carries an additional notation in Lincoln's hand "A Lyons, Save as receipt." The signature is Robert Todd Lincoln's. Alonzo Lyons had written Lincoln on February 15, enclosing for collection a draft on the Fund Commissioners of the State of Illinois. Presumably it could not be collected at the time.

Veto Message of Apportionment Bill Written for Governor William H. Bissell[1]

February 22, 1859

Gentlemen of the House of Representatives.

I herewith return to your Honorable body, in which the same originated, the bill entitled "A bill for an act to create Senatorial and Representative Districts, and apportion the representation in the General Assembly of this State."

I object to said bill becoming a law, because it's effect, as a law, would be to continue the control of of [*sic*] the General Assembly in the hands of a minority of the people. This being substantially the very objection urged against the Lecompton Constitution, by the authors of the bill, in common with others, it is but fair to presume that it found it's way into this bill, by mere over-sight; and that it's authors will be glad of the oppertunity, now afforded, to expel it, and to give the bill such shape as to fairly represent the people.

I also object to said bill becoming a law, because, by it, the new county of Ford is placed wholly within the ninth Senatorial District, and also wholly within the eighteenth Senatorial District.

I also object to said bill becoming a law because, by it, in the matter of giving excesses, the provision of the tenth Section of the third article of the constitution is disregarded. I insist that, by this bill, the spirit of the constitution is violated in the *unnecessary* departures from the principle of single districts. A glaring instance is the thirty-second representative district, composed of the counties of Champaign, Piatt, DeWitt, Macon, Moultrie, Shelby and Effingham, and to which three representatives are given. The map, and census tables show that these seven counties divide neatly into three separate districts, each entitled to a representative, the smallest in population being greater, and the largest much smaller, than several other single districts established by the bill.

For these reasons, I object to said bill becoming a law, and herewith return it to the House in which it originated.

Springfield Feby 22d 1859 WM. H. BISSELL

[1] AD, DLC-RTL. All but the date and signature are in Lincoln's handwriting. The Democratic Speaker of the House refused to accept the governor's message on the ground that a quorum was not present. An altercation ensued in which the message and the bill were placed on the speaker's table, brushed by him onto the floor, and rescued by Representative William H. Green of Massac County. Republican members entered a protest against the speaker's action, but the speaker refused to receive the protest. On the next day the House, without a quorum being present, adopted a joint resolution to adjourn *sine die*, February

24. Before adjournment, a Republican protest was allowed to be entered on the *House Journal*, and the governor's message was ordered to be printed (*Illinois State Journal*, February 24, 1859).

Speech at Chicago, Illinois[1]

March 1, 1859

I understand that you have to-day rallied around your principles and they have again triumphed in the city of Chicago. I am exceedingly happy to meet you under such cheering auspices on this occasion—the first on which I have appeared before an audience since the campaign of last year. It is unsuitable to enter into a lengthy discourse, as is quite apparent, at a moment like this. I shall therefore detain you only a very short while.

It gives me peculiar pleasure to find an opportunity under such favorable circumstances to return my thanks for the gallant support that you of the city of Chicago and of Cook County gave to the cause in which we were all engaged in the late momentous struggle in Illinois. And while I am at it, I will through you thank all the Republicans of the State for the earnest devotion and glorious support they gave to the cause.

I am resolved not to deprive myself of the pleasure of believing, now, and so long as I live, that all those who, while we were in that contest, professed to be the friends of the cause, were really and truly so—that we are all really brothers in the work, with no false hearts among us.

For myself I am also gratified that during that canvass and since, however disappointing its termination, there was among my party friends so little fault found in me as to the manner in which I bore my part. I hardly dared hope to give as high a degree of satisfaction

[1] *The North American Review*, July, 1893, pp. 120-24. Although taken down in shorthand by Robert Hitt, reporter for the Chicago *Press and Tribune*, this speech was not printed until 1893. Hitt's prefatory note in *The North American Review* relates that in 1860 he read the speech to Lincoln from the shorthand notes, with a view toward getting Lincoln's sanction for its publication, but that Lincoln objected on the grounds that the comments on "the course of Mr. Greeley . . . would tend to awaken a discussion now past and closed, and as Greeley in the *Tribune* was then doing magnificent work for the cause, it would be better to let the speech go" (*ibid.*, p. 121). The occasion of the speech was a Republican rally on the night of the Chicago municipal election. The similarity of some of Lincoln's remarks and some of his points in the Cincinnati speech, September 17, *infra*, and more particularly between the Chicago speech and the manuscript notes for the Ohio speeches, September 16, 17, *infra*, suggest that the manuscript notes were in part prepared in February or March, at the time when Lincoln contemplated a trip to the Kansas state Republican convention (see letters to Delahay, February 1, *supra*, March 4 and May 14, *infra*). It is even likely that Lincoln may have used portions of these same notes in making the present speech.

as it has since been my pleasure to believe I did in the part I bore in the contest.

I remember in that canvass but one instance of dissatisfaction with my course, and I allude to that, not for the purpose of reviving any matter of dispute or producing any unpleasant feeling, but in order to help get rid of the point upon which that matter of disagreement or dissatisfaction arose. I understand that in some speeches I made I said something, or was supposed to have said something, that some very good people, as I really believe them to be, commented upon unfavorably, and said that rather than support one holding such sentiments as I had expressed, the real friends of liberty could afford to wait awhile. I don't want to say anything that shall excite unkind feeling, and I mention this simply to suggest that I am afraid of the effect of that sort of argument. I do not doubt that it comes from good men, but I am afraid of the result upon organized action where great results are in view, if any of us allow ourselves to seek out minor or separate points on which there may be difference of views as to policy and right, and let them keep us from uniting in action upon a great principle in a cause on which we all agree; or are deluded into the belief that all can be brought to consider alike and agree upon every minor point before we unite and press forward in organization, asking the coöperation of all good men in that resistance to the extension of slavery upon which we all agree. I am afraid that such methods would result in keeping the friends of liberty waiting longer than we ought to. I say this for the purpose of suggesting that we consider whether it would not be better and wiser, so long as we all agree that this matter of slavery is a moral, political and social wrong, and ought to be treated as a wrong, not to let anything minor or subsidiary to that main principle and purpose make us fail to coöperate.

One other thing, and that again I say in no spirit of unkindness. There was a question amongst Republicans all the time of the canvass of last year, and it has not quite ceased yet, whether it was not the true and better policy for the Republicans to make it their chief object to reëlect Judge Douglas to the Senate of the United States. Now, I differed with those who thought that the true policy, but I have never said an unkind word of any one entertaining that opinion. I believe most of them were as sincerely the friends of our cause as I claim to be myself; yet I thought they were mistaken, and I speak of this now for the purpose of justifying the course that I took and the course of those who supported me. In what I say now there is no unkindness even towards Judge Douglas. I have believed, that in the Republican situation in Illinois, if we, the Republicans of this State, had made Judge Douglas our candidate for the Senate of the United States last year and had elected him, there would to-day be no Republican party in this Union. I believed that the principles around which we have rallied and organized that party would live; they will live under all circumstances, while we will die. They would reproduce another party in the future. But in the meantime all the labor that has been done to build up the present Republican party would be entirely lost, and perhaps twenty years of time, before we would again have formed around that principle as solid, extensive, and formidable an organization as we have, standing shoulder to shoulder to-night in harmony and strength around the Republican banner.

It militates not at all against this view to tell us that the Republicans could make something in the State of New York by electing to Congress John B. Haskin, who occupied a position similar to Judge Douglas, or that they could make something by electing Hickman,[2] of Pennsylvania, or Davis,[3] of Indiana. I think it likely that they could and do make something by it; but it is false logic to assume that for that reason anything could be gained by us in electing Judge Douglas in Illinois. And for this reason: It is no disparagement to these men, Hickman and Davis, to say that individually they were comparatively small men, and the Republican party could take hold of them, use them, elect them, absorb them, expel them, or do whatever it pleased with them, and the Republican organization be in no wise shaken. But it is not so with Judge Douglas. Let the Republican party of Illinois dally with Judge Douglas; let them fall in behind him and make him their candidate, and they do not absorb him; he absorbs them. They would come out at the end all Douglas men, all claimed by him as having indorsed every one of his doctrines upon the great subject with which the whole nation is engaged at this hour—that the question of negro slavery is simply a question of dollars and cents; that the Almighty has drawn a line across the continent, on one side of which labor—the cultivation of the soil—must always be performed by slaves. It would be claimed that we, like him, do not care whether slavery is voted up or voted down. Had we made him our candidate and given him a great majority, we should have never heard an end of declarations by him that we had indorsed all these dogmas. Try it by an example.

You all remember that at the last session of Congress there was a measure introduced in the Senate by Mr. Crittenden, which pro-

[2] John Hickman. [3] John G. Davis.

posed that the pro-slavery Lecompton constitution should be left to a vote to be taken in Kansas, and if it and slavery were adopted Kansas should be at once admitted as a slave State. That same measure was introduced into the House by Mr. Montgomery, and therefore got the name of the Crittenden-Montgomery bill; and in the House of Representatives the Republicans all voted for it under the peculiar circumstances in which they found themselves placed. You may remember also that the New York *Tribune*, which was so much in favor of our electing Judge Douglas to the Senate of the United States, has not yet got through the task of defending the Republican party, after that one vote in the House of Representatives, from the charge of having gone over to the doctrine of popular sovereignty. Now, just how long would the New York *Tribune* have been in getting rid of the charge that the Republicans had abandoned their principles, if we had taken up Judge Douglas, adopted all his doctrines and elected him to the Senate, when the single vote upon that one point so confused and embarrassed the position of the Republicans that it has kept the *Tribune* one entire year arguing against the effect of it?

This much being said on that point, I wish now to add a word that has a bearing on the future. The Republican principle, the profound central truth that slavery is wrong and ought to be dealt with as a wrong, though we are always to remember the fact of its actual existence amongst us and faithfully observe all the constitutional guarantees—the unalterable principle never for a moment to be lost sight of that it is a wrong and ought to be dealt with as such, cannot advance at all upon Judge Douglas' ground—that there is a portion of the country in which slavery must always exist; that he does not care whether it is voted up or voted down, as it is simply a question of dollars and cents. Whenever, in any compromise or arrangement or combination that may promise some temporary advantage, we are led upon that ground, then and there the great living principle upon which we have organized as a party is surrendered. The proposition now in our minds that this thing is wrong being once driven out and surrendered, then the institution of slavery necessarily becomes national.

One or two words more of what I did not think of when I arose. Suppose it is true that the Almighty has drawn a line across this continent, on the south side of which part of the people will hold the rest as slaves; that the Almighty ordered this; that it is right, unchangeably right, that men ought there to be held as slaves, and that their fellow men will always have the right to hold them as slaves. I ask you, this once admitted, how can you believe that it is not right for us, or for them coming here, to hold slaves on this other side of the line? Once we come to acknowledge that it is right, that it is the law of the Eternal Being, for slavery to exist on one side of that line, have we any sure ground to object to slaves being held on the other side? Once admit the position that a man rightfully holds another man as property on one side of the line, and you must, when it suits his convenience to come to the other side, admit that he has the same right to hold his property there. Once admit Judge Douglas's proposition and we must all finally give way. Although we may not bring ourselves to the idea that it is to our interest to have slaves in this Northern country, we shall soon bring ourselves to admit that, while we may not want them, if any one else does he has the moral right to have them. Step by step —south of the Judge's moral climate line in the States, then in the Territories everywhere, and then in all the States—it is thus that Judge Douglas would lead us inevitably to the nationalization of slavery. Whether by his doctrine of squatter sovereignty, or by the ground taken by him in his recent speeches in Memphis and through the South,[4]—that wherever the climate makes it the interest of the inhabitants to encourage slave property, they will pass a slave code—whether it is covertly nationalized, by Congressional legislation, or by the Dred Scott decision, or by the sophistical and misleading doctrine he has last advanced, the same goal is inevitably reached by the one or the other device. It is only travelling to the same place by different roads.

In this direction lies all the danger that now exists to the Republican cause. I take it that so far as concerns forcibly establishing slavery in the Territories by Congressional legislation, or by virtue of the Dred Scott decision, that day has passed. Our only serious danger is that we shall be led upon this ground of Judge Douglas, on the delusive assumption that it is a good way of whipping our opponents, when in fact, it is a way that leads straight to final surrender. The Republican party should not dally with Judge Douglas when it knows where his proposition and his leadership would take us, nor be disposed to listen to it because it was best somewhere else to support somebody occupying his ground. That is no just reason why we ought to go over to Judge Douglas, as we were called upon to do last year. Never forget that we have before us this whole matter of the right or wrong of slavery in this Union, though the immediate question is as to its spreading out into new Territories and States.

[4] Douglas spoke in Memphis on November 29, in New Orleans on December 6, 1858, and in Baltimore on January 5, 1859.

I do not wish to be misunderstood upon this subject of slavery in this country. I suppose it may long exist, and perhaps the best way for it to come to an end peaceably is for it to exist for a length of time. But I say that the spread and strengthening and perpetuation of it is an entirely different proposition. There we should in every way resist it as a wrong, treating it as a wrong, with the fixed idea that it must and will come to an end. If we do not allow ourselves to be allured from the strict path of our duty by such a device as shifting our ground and throwing ourselves into the rear of a leader who denies our first principle, denies that there is an absolute wrong in the institution of slavery, then the future of the Republican cause is safe and victory is assured. You Republicans of Illinois have deliberately taken your ground; you have heard the whole subject discussed again and again; you have stated your faith, in platforms laid down in a State Convention, and in a National Convention; you have heard and talked over and considered it until you are now all of opinion that you are on a ground of unquestionable right. All you have to do is to keep the faith, to remain steadfast to the right, to stand by your banner. Nothing should lead you to leave your guns. Stand together, ready, with match in hand. Allow nothing to turn you to the right or to the left. Remember how long you have been in setting out on the true course; how long you have been in getting your neighbors to understand and believe as you now do. Stand by your principles; stand by your guns; and victory complete and permanent is sure at the last.

To Peter H. Watson[1]

P. H. Watson, Esq., Chicago,
My dear Sir: March 2, 1859.

At last I am here to give some attention to the suit of Haines and Haines vs. Talcott[2] and others. I write chiefly now to get up a correspondence with you by which, if possible, the labor may be lightened, and the time shortened, in getting the case ready for trial. I have looked over your answer, and filed a Replication. By the Answer you lay a foundation to take, and, I suppose, intend to take a great deal of proof, all which must be by depositions. We will have to take some on our part to begin with, besides rebutting yours as well as we may be able. In all this it is desirable that we agree upon times and places, without the labor and delay of formal notices.

Besides this, it occurs to me that we might manage to get the opinion of the Court on our branch of the law, even if that be for you, it would save all the labor as to the other. I mean for us, with the consent of the Court, to first make the question of infringement, if our right be as it apparently is, on the face of the patent, have you infringed it? If this be decided for you, it is an end of the case. If for us, we can then enter upon the larger and more laborious plan of trying whether our apparent right is or is not a real one —whether it is substantially the same as are now on older things.

Consider this and write me, at Springfield, as soon as you conveniently can. Make any suggestions of your own with the same frankness as I have done. Yours truly, A. LINCOLN.

[1] Tracy, pp. 101-102. See Lincoln's letters to Watson, July 23, 1855, and to Jonathan Haines, November 24, 1856, November 25, 1857, March 27, 1858, *supra*, and June 9, *infra*.

[2] Alfred Haines and Jonathan Haines of Pekin, Illinois, *v*. Wait Talcott, John H. Manny, *et al.*, a suit over patent infringements. Haines' letters to Lincoln contain data concerning the suit (see particularly, July 26, August 15, and September 7, 1858, DLC-RTL).

To Hayden Keeling[1]

Haden Keeling Esq Springfield March 3, 1859

Dear Sir Yours of Feb. 28th. 1859 is received. I do not think there is the least use of doing any more with the law suit. I not only do not think you are sure to gain it, but I do think you are sure to lose it. Therefore the sooner it ends the better. Yours truly

A. LINCOLN

[1] Copy, DLC-HW. The copy was enclosed to Herndon by H. L. Wright of Canton, Illinois, November 28, 1866. Hayden Keeling, formerly of Springfield, was a resident of Canton, but his lawsuit has not been identified.

To Mark W. Delahay[1]

M. W. Delahay, Esq Springfield,
My dear Sir March 4, 1859.

Your second letter in relation to my being with you at your Republican convention, was duly received. It is not at hand just now, but I had the impression from it that the convention was to be at *Leavenworth;* but day before yesterday a friend handed me a letter from Judge M. F. Conway,[2] in which he also expresses a wish for me to come; and he fixes the place at *Ossawatomie*. This I believe is off of the river, and will require more time and labor to get to it.

It will push me hard to get there without injury to my own business; but I shall *try* to do it, though I am not yet quite certain I shall succeed.

I should like to know before coming, that while some of you wish me to come, there may not be others, who would quite as lief I would stay away. Write me again. Yours as ever

A. LINCOLN

[1] ALS, ORB. Delahay replied, March 15, that "the Democrats perhaps would rather you would not be with us. . . . You have more friends in Kansas and better friends than any living man." (DLC-RTL)

[2] Martin F. Conway of Lawrence, Kansas, first U.S. representative from Kansas, who did not take his seat in Congress until the admission of Kansas in 1861. Lincoln also wrote to Conway on March 4, letter not extant, and Conway replied on March 16 that "no one whose favor is of any value, amongst us, will feel otherwise than pleased with your presence at our Convention." (DLC-RTL)

Call for Springfield Republican Convention[1]

March 14, 1859

A mass Convention of the Republicans of Springfield will be held

ON MONDAY, THE 21ST INST., AT 7 P.M.

At Cook's Hall for the purpose of nominating candidates for municipal officers at the approaching City Election. A full and punctual attendance is requested.

H. G. Fitzhugh,	J. M. Allen,
A. Johnston,	E. B. Hawley,
F. Springer,	W. H. Herndon,
M. Hay,	Z. A. Enos,
J. Armstrong,	D. Morse,
T. S. Mather,	A. Lincoln,

I. A. Hawley,—*Executive Committee.*

[1] *Illinois State Journal*, March 14, 1859. Signers of the call not previously identified are: Harrison G. Fitzhugh, carpenter; Adam Johnston, proprietor of a marble works; Reverend Francis Springer, superintendent of schools; Daniel Morse, proprietor of a meat market.

To William A. Ross[1]

Wm. A. Ross, Esq: Lincoln, Logan Co. Ills.

My dear Sir: March 26– 1859–

Yours of the 18th. was received a week ago. I would really be pleased with a publication substantially as you propose. But I would suggest a few variations from your plan. I would not include the Republican platform; because that would give the work a one-sided & party cast, unless the democratic platform was also included.

I would not take *all* the speeches from the Press & Tribune; but

I would take mine from that paper; and those of Judge Douglas from the Chicago Times. This would represent each of us, as reported by his own friends, and thus be mutual, and fair. I would take the speeches alone; rigidly excluding all comments of the newspapers.

I would include the correspondence between Judge Douglas and myself which led to the joint discussions.

I would call the thing "Illinois political canvass of 1858"; and, as falling within the title, I would select and include half a dozen of the National Democratic speeches.

Last autumn and winter I got up a Scrap-book precisely on the plan I have stated. The parts stand in the order following—

My speech at Springfield, at the Republican convention, June 16, 1858.

Douglas' speech at Chicago, July 9, 1858

My speech at Chicago July 10, 1858–

Douglas' speech at Bloomington July 16, 1858

Douglas' speech at Springfield, July 17, 1858.

My speech at Springfield, July 17, 1858–

The correspondence which led to the joint discussions.

The joint discussions, in the order in which they occurred.

The National Democratic speeches, to come in after the others, in the order among themselves in which they were delivered.

In my own speeches I have corrected only a few small typographical errors. The other speeches I have not touched; but merely pasted them in from the papers in which they were reported.

Judge Douglas would have the right to correct typographical errors in his, if he desired; but I think the necessity, in his case, would be less than in mine; because he had two hired reporters travelling with him, and probably revised their manuscripts before they went to press; while I had no reporter of my own, but depended on a very excellent one sent by the Press & Tribune; but who never waited to show me his notes or manuscripts; so that the first I saw of my speeches, after delivering them, was in the Press & Tribune precisely as they now stand.

My Scrap-book would be the best thing to print from; still, as it cost me a good deal of labor to get it up, and as I am very desirous to preserve the substance of it permanently, I would not let it go out of my own control. If an arrangement could be made to print it in Springfield, under my own supervision, I would allow the Scrap-book to be used, and would claim no share in any profit that could be made out of the publication.

I am here now, attending court; and seize a moment to answer yours, which I ought to have done sooner. Let me hear from you again. Yours with respect A. LINCOLN—

[1] ALS, IHi. William A. Ross wrote from Washington, Illinois. Replying to Lincoln's letter on April 2, Ross proposed to go ahead with publication (DLC-RTL), but there is no record of further negotiations.

To William M. Morris[1]

W M Morris Esq Springfield March 28. 1859.

Dear Sir, Your kind note inviting me to deliver a lecture at Galesburg, is received. I regret to say I can not do so now; I must stick to the courts awhile. I read a sort of lecture to three different audiences during the last month and this;[2] but I did so under circumstances which made it a waste of no time whatever. Yours very truly, A. LINCOLN.

[1] Copy, DLC-HW. Morris enclosed the copy to Herndon, September 21, 1866, relating that in 1859 while a student at Knox College and secretary of a student literary society he had invited Lincoln to lecture at Galesburg.

[2] *Vide supra*, February 11.

To William H. Bissell[1]

Hon William H Bissell Bloomington Ills

Sir April 4th 1859

Charles J Beattie of Livingston County is about to apply to your excellency to be appointed Pros Atty for the 20th Judicial Circuit in the Place of Samson DeWitt deceased. If it is the wish of the Bar of that Circuit I should be glad to see him appointed to that office Respectfully JNO M SCOTT

W H HANNA

A. LINCOLN

[1] LS, I-Ar. The letter was written by Scott and signed by Hanna and Lincoln—the latter in pencil. The letter bears Bissell's endorsement suggesting that Ozias M. Hatch, secretary of state, issue the commission. John M. Scott and William H. Hanna were attorneys at Bloomington, Illinois.

To Henry L. Pierce and Others[1]

Messrs. Henry L. Pierce, & others. Springfield, Ills.

Gentlemen April 6. 1859

Your kind note inviting me to attend a Festival in Boston, on the 13th. Inst. in honor of the birth-day of Thomas Jefferson, was duly received. My engagements are such that I can not attend.

Bearing in mind that about seventy years ago, two great political parties were first formed in this country, that Thomas Jefferson was the head of one of them, and Boston the head-quarters of the other, it is both curious and interesting that those supposed to descend politically from the party opposed to Jefferson, should now be celebrating his birth-day in their own original seat of empire, while those claiming political descent from him have nearly ceased to breathe his name everywhere.

Remembering too, that the Jefferson party were formed upon their supposed superior devotion to the *personal* rights of men, holding the rights of *property* to be secondary only, and greatly inferior, and then assuming that the so-called democracy of to-day, are the Jefferson, and their opponents, the anti-Jefferson parties, it will be equally interesting to note how completely the two have changed hands as to the principle upon which they were originally supposed to be divided.

The democracy of to-day hold the *liberty* of one man to be absolutely nothing, when in conflict with another man's right of *property*. Republicans, on the contrary, are for both the *man* and the *dollar;* but in cases of conflict, the man *before* the dollar.

I remember once being much amused at seeing two partially intoxicated men engage in a fight with their great-coats on, which fight, after a long, and rather harmless contest, ended in each having fought himself *out* of his own coat, and *into* that of the other. If the two leading parties of this day are really identical with the two in the days of Jefferson and Adams, they have performed about the same feat as the two drunken men.

But soberly, it is now no child's play to save the principles of Jefferson from total overthrow in this nation.

One would start with great confidence that he could convince any sane child that the simpler propositions of Euclid are true; but, nevertheless, he would fail, utterly, with one who should deny the definitions and axioms. The principles of Jefferson are the definitions and axioms of free society. And yet they are denied, and evaded, with no small show of success. One dashingly calls them "glittering generalities"; another bluntly calls them "self evident lies"; and still others insidiously argue that they apply only to "superior races."

These expressions, differing in form, are identical in object and effect—the supplanting the principles of free government, and restoring those of classification, caste, and legitimacy. They would delight a convocation of crowned heads, plotting against the people. They are the van-guard—the miners, and sappers—of returning despotism. We must repulse them, or they will subjugate us.

This is a world of compensations; and he who would *be* no slave, must consent to *have* no slave. Those who deny freedom to others, deserve it not for themselves; and, under a just God, can not long retain it.

All honor to Jefferson—to the man who, in the concrete pressure of a struggle for national independence by a single people, had the coolness, forecast, and capacity to introduce into a merely revolutionary document, an abstract truth, applicable to all men and all times, and so to embalm it there, that to-day, and in all coming days, it shall be a rebuke and a stumbling-block to the very harbingers of re-appearing tyrany and oppression. Your obedient Servant A. LINCOLN—

[1] ALS, RPB. The form letter of invitation dated March 19 bears the signatures of Henry L. Pierce, Boston manufacturer, later state representative (1860-1862) and mayor of Boston (1873, 1878), and a committee of five Republicans in charge of the festival (DLC-RTL). Lincoln's reply was given wide circulation by the Republican press.

To Gustave P. Koerner[1]

Hon. G. Koerner Springfield, April 11, 1859

My dear Sir Reaching home last night, I found your letter of the 4th. The meeting of the Central committee was at Bloomington, and not here. I was there attending court; and, in common with several other outsiders, one of whom was Judge Trumbull, was in conference with the committee, to some extent. Judd privately mentioned the subject, of which you write, to me, and requested me to prepare a resolution, which I did. When I brought in the resolution and read it to the committee, and others present, in an informal way, Judge Trumbull suggested that it would be better to select some act of our adversaries, rather than of our own friends, upon which to base a protest against any distinction between native and naturalized citizens, as to the right of suffrage. This led to a little parley, I was called from the room, the thing passed from my mind, and I do not now know whether any thing was done about it by the committee. Judge Trumbull will be in Belleville when this reaches you, and he probably can tell you all about it. Whether any thing was done or not, something must be, the next time the committee meets, which I presume will be before long.

I am right glad the Committee put in operation, our plan of organization which we started here last winter. They appointed Mr. Fell of Bloomington, as Secretary. Yours as ever

A. LINCOLN.

[1] ALS, MoSHi. Koerner wrote asking that the state central committee pass a strong resolution disavowing the act of the Republican legislature of Massachusetts in requiring naturalized citizens to wait two years before voting. German papers were threatening to leave the Republican party, and the loss of the German vote would be injurious to the cause (DLC-RTL).

Call for Republican Meeting[1]

April 11, 1859

REPUBLICAN MEETING—Fourth Ward.

A Mass Meeting of the Republicans of the Fourth Ward will be held at the factory of R. B. Bell, on Wednesday evening, the 13th instant, at 7 o'clock, for the purpose of nominating a candidate for Alderman.

J. M. ALLEN,
ISAAC A. HAWLEY,
A. LINCOLN,
Executive Com., 4th Ward.

[1] *Illinois State Journal*, April 11, 1859.

To Thomas J. Pickett[1]

T. J. Pickett, Esq — Springfield,
My dear Sir. — April 16. 1859.

Yours of the 13th. is just received. My engagements are such that I can not, at any very early day, visit Rock-Island, to deliver a lecture, or for any other object.

As to the other matter you kindly mention, I must, in candor, say I do not think myself fit for the Presidency. I certainly am flattered, and gratified, that some partial friends think of me in that connection; but I really think it best for our cause that no concerted effort, such as you suggest, should be made.

Let this be considered confidential. Yours very truly

A. LINCOLN—

[1] ALS, ORB; ALS copy, DLC-RTL. In addition to the authentic originals, there is a spurious copy in the Chicago Historical Society, and at least one other spurious copy bearing the date April 30, 1859, has been sold at auction. Curiously enough, the copy which Pickett enclosed to William H. Herndon, on November 29, 1866, is also spurious and grossly inaccurate, even to being dated March 5, 1859 (DLC-HW). The inference may be that Pickett lost or parted with the original and attempted to copy the letter from memory. Thomas J. Pickett had edited newspapers at Pekin, Illinois, and in 1859 was editor of the Rock Island *Register*. His letter to Lincoln suggested that he would like to promote the simultaneous announcement of Lincoln for the presidency in the Republican papers of the state (DLC-RTL).

To Robert E. Williams and Major W. Packard[1]

Messrs. Williams & Packard: Springfield,
Gentlemen: April 16, 1859.

I filed your plea this morning and on inquiry find that Messrs. Moffett & Son[2] are the lawyers who brought the suit. They reside here. Yours truly, A. LINCOLN.

[1] Bloomington *Pantagraph*, February 6, 1909. Williams and Packard were law partners at Bloomington, Illinois.

[2] Thomas and James W. Moffett.

To Salmon P. Chase[1]

Hon: S. P. Chase Springfield, Ills. April 30. 1859.

Dear Sir Reaching home yesterday I found your kind note of the 14th. informing me that you have given Mr. Whitney the appointment he desired;[2] and also mentioning the present encouraging aspects of the Republican cause—and our Illinois canvass of last year. I thank you for the appointment. Allow me also to thank you as being one of the very few distinguished men, whose sympathy we in Illinois did receive last year, of all those whose sympathy we thought we had reason to expect.

Of course I would have preferred success; but failing in that, I have no regrets for having rejected all advice to the contrary, and resolutely made the struggle. Had we thrown ourselves into the arms of Douglas, as re-electing him by our votes would have done, the Republican cause would have been anihilated in Illinois, and, as I think, demoralized, and prostrated everywhere for years, if not forever. As it is, in the language of Benton "we are clean" and the Republican star gradually rises higher everywhere. Yours truly.

A. LINCOLN

[1] ALS, PHi.

[2] Probably an appointment as commissioner of deeds of Ohio for Illinois. Whitney to Nathaniel P. Banks, June 1, 1859 (Banks MSS., IHi), requests a similar appointment for Massachusetts and encloses a letter of recommendation from Lincoln which has not been located.

To Mark W. Delahay[1]

M. W. Delahay, Esq Springfield Ills
My Dear Sir May 14 1859

I find it impossible for me to attend your Republican convention at Ossawatan [Ossawatomie] on the 18th. It would have afforded me much personal gratification to see your fine new country, and to meet the good people who have cast their lot there; and still more, if I could thereby contribute any thing to the Republican cause. You probably will adopt resolutions in the nature of a platform; and, as I think, the only danger will be the temptation to lower the Republican Standard in order to gather recruits. In my judgement such a step would be a serious mistake —would open a gap through which more would pass *out* than pass *in*. And this would be the same, whether the letting down should be in deference to Douglasism, or to the southern opposition element. Either would surrender the *o[b]ject* of the Republican organization—the preventing the *spread* and *nationalization* of Slavery. This object surrendered, the organization would go to pieces. I do not mean by this, that no southern man must be placed upon our Republican National ticket for 1860. There are many men in the slave states for any one of whom I would cheerfully vote to be either President or Vice President provided he would enable[2] me to do so with *safety* to the Republican cause—without lowering the Republican Standard. This is the indispensable condition of a union with us. It is idle to think of any other. Any other would be as fruitless to the South, as distasteful to the North, the whole ending in common defeat. Let a union be attempted on the basis of ignoring the Slavery question, and magnifying other questions which the people just now are really caring nothing about, and it will result in gaining no single electorial vote in the *South* and losing ev[e]ry one in the North. Yours very truly

A. LINCOLN

[1] LS, ORB. Delahay's name and the close and signature are in Lincoln's handwriting.

[2] "Allow" deleted and "enable" inserted in Lincoln's handwriting.

Enclosure to Mark W. Delahay[1]

[May 14, 1859]

I send letters like this to J. L. Dugger & M. F. Conway. I still think I will speak in your teritory before the election. Yours &c

A.L.

[1] ADS, The Rosenbach Company, Philadelphia and New York. This note was originally enclosed with the copy of the form letter addressed to Delahay on this date. The copies mailed to Jefferson L. Dugger of Leavenworth and Martin F. Conway of Lawrence, Kansas, are presumably not extant. Conway to Lincoln, March 16, 1859 (DLC-RTL) replies to Lincoln to Conway, March 4, 1859, presumably not extant. See also Lincoln to Delahay, March 4, *supra*.

To Peter H. Watson[1]

P. H. Watson, Esq., [May 14, 1859]

My dear Sir: Reaching here the 14th, I found yours of the 7th. I have not heard from Haines for some time, and until I do hear from him I can say nothing definite about taking evidence. When I hear from him I will write you. Yours truly, A. LINCOLN.

[1] Tracy, p. 105. This letter is undated in the source, but Peter H. Watson's letter of May 7, 1859, asking when and where Lincoln will commence taking depositions, establishes the date (DLC-RTL). See also Lincoln to Watson, March 2, *supra.*

To Theodore Canisius[1]

Dr. Theodore Canisius Springfield, May 17, 1859

Dear Sir: Your note asking, in behalf of yourself and other german citizens, whether I am for or against the constitutional provision in regard to naturalized citizens, lately adopted by Massachusetts; and whether I am for or against a fusion of the republicans, and other opposition elements, for the canvass of 1860, is received.

Massachusetts is a sovereign and independent state; and it is no privilege of mine to scold her for what she does. Still, if from what she *has done*, an inference is sought to be drawn as to what I *would do*, I may, without impropriety, speak out. I say then, that, as I understand the Massachusetts provision, I am against it's adoption in Illinois, or in any other place, where I have a right to oppose it. Understanding the spirit of our institutions to aim at the *elevation* of men, I am opposed to whatever tends to *degrade* them. I have some little notoriety for commiserating the oppressed condition of the negro; and I should be strangely inconsistent if I could favor any project for curtailing the existing rights of *white men*, even though born in different lands, and speaking different languages from myself.

As to the matter of fusion, I am for it, if it can be had on republican grounds; and I am not for it on any other terms. A fusion on any other terms, would be as foolish as unprincipled. It would lose the whole North, while the common enemy would still carry the whole South. The question of *men* is a different one. There are good patriotic men, and able statesmen, in the South whom I would cheerfully support, if they would now place themselves on republican ground. But I am against letting down the republican standard a hair's breadth.

I have written this hastily, but I believe it answers your questions substantially. Yours truly A. LINCOLN

[1] ALS, ICHi. Canisius published this letter in his *Illinois Staats-Anzeiger* and also in the *Illinois State Journal*, May 18, 1859, whence it was widely copied by other papers.

Call for Old Settlers Convention[1]

May 25, 1859

The undersigned, desirous of preserving the early history of the City of Springfield and Sangamon county, now known in a great degree only to a few "Pioneers," would suggest a meeting at the Court House on the 1st of June, of all surviving settlers who became residents of the county previous to the "winter of the deep snow," (1830-31,) for the purpose of organizing a permanent society in furtherance of this object.

Springfield, May 25th, 1859.

[1] *Illinois State Journal*, May 26, 1859. Lincoln's name appears among the sixty-one signers.

To Samuel W. Fuller[1]

Hon. S. W. Fuller
Springfield,
Dear Sir
May 27. 1859

In thinking over the Farni case[2] it seems to me the push by the plaintiffs will be to prove that the bond sued on was, in fact, accepted; and that the injunction was dissolved, not for want of a sufficient bond, but for want of Equity in the Bill. That, I think, is the point for us to guard. Yours truly A. LINCOLN

[1] ALS-P, ISLA. Samuel W. Fuller, formerly an attorney at Pekin, Illinois, had moved to Chicago in 1857 and formed a partnership with Jonathan Y. Scammon.

[2] Farni *v.* Tesson involved a bond made by Christian and Peter Farni of Woodford County, Illinois. Originating in the Peoria County Circuit Court, the case was carried ultimately to the U.S. Supreme Court. On November 3, 1859, Fuller wrote to Lincoln asking whether he would handle the case before the Supreme Court, judgment having been against Farni. There is no record of Lincoln's reply.

To William H. Bissell, Jesse K. Dubois and James Miller[1]

May 28, 1859

To the Governor Auditor and Treasurer of the State of Illinois
Gentlemen

In reply to your inquiry, requesting our written opinion as to what your duty requires you to do in executing the latter clause of the Seventh Section of "An Act in relation to the payment of the principal and interest of the State debt" Approved Feby 22 1859 we reply that said last clause of said section is certainly indefinite general and ambiguous in its description of the Bonds to be issued by you; giving no time at which the Bonds are to be made payable, no place at which either principal or interest are to be paid, and no rate of interest which the Bonds are to bear; nor any other description except that they are to be *Coupon Bonds* which in Commercial usage means interest paying Bonds with obligations or orders attached to them for the payment of annual or semiannual interest; there is we suppose no difficulty in ascertaining, if this Act stood alone what ought to be the construction of the terms "Coupon Bonds" and that it would mean Bonds bearing interest from the time of issuing the same[.] And under this act considered by itself the Creditors would have a right to require such Bonds—but your inquiry in regard to a class of Bonds on which no interest is to be paid or shall begin to run until January 1. 1860, is whether the Act of February 18, 1857 would not authorise you to refuse to give Bonds with any Coupons attached payable before the first day of July 1860

We have very maturely considered this question and have arrived at the conclusion that you have a right to use such measures as will secure the state against the loss of six months interest on these Bonds by the indefiniteness of the Act of 1859. Whilst it cannot be denied that the *letter* of the Laws favour the construction claimed by some of the creditors that interest bearing Bonds were required to be issued to them inasmuch as the restriction that no interest is to run on said Bonds until 1st January 1860 relates solely to the Bonds issued under the Act of 1857—and the Act of 1859 directing you to issue new Bonds does not contain this restriction, But directs you to issue Coupon Bonds. Nevertheless the very indefiniteness and generality of the Act of 1859 giving no rate of interest no time due no place of payment no postponement of the time when interest commences necessarily implies that the Legislature intended to invest you with a discretion to impose such terms and restrictions as would protect the interest of the State and we think you have a right and that it is your duty to see that the State Bonds are so issued that the State shall not lose six months interest. Two plans present themselves either of which will secure the state.

1st. If in litteral compliance with the law you issue Bonds bearing interest from 1st. July 1859, you may deduct from the Bonds presented three thousand from every $100,000 of Bonds and issue $97,000 of Coupon Bonds by this plan $3,000 out of $100,000 of principal would be extinguished in consideration of paying $2910 interest on the first of January 1860—and the interest on the $3,000 would forever cease—this would be no doubt most advantageous to the State

But if the Auditor will not consent to this then

2nd. Cut off of each Bond all the Coupons payable before 1st. July 1860

One of these plans would undoubtedly have been prescribed by the Legislature if its attention had been directed to this question

May 28 1859 STEPHEN T. LOGAN
A. LINCOLN

[1] LS, ORB.

Contract with Theodore Canisius[1]

May [30?] 1859

This instrument witnesseth that the Printing-press, german types &c. purchased of John Burkhardt,[2] belong to Abraham Lincoln; that Theodore Canissius is to have immediate possession of them, and is to commence publishing in Springfield, Illinois, a Republican newspaper, to be chiefly in the german language, with occasional translations into English at his option; the first number to issue in the ensuing month of June, and to continue thenceforward issuing weekly or oftener, at the option of said Cannissius, he, said Cannissius, bearing all expences, and charges, and taking all incomes and profits; said paper, in political sentiment, not to depart from the Philadelphia and Illinois Republican platforms; and for a material departure in that respect, or a failure of said paper to issue as often as weekly, or any attempt to remove said press, types &c, from Springfield, or to print with them any thing opposed to, or designed to injure the Republican party, said Lincoln may, at his option, at once take possession of said press, types &c, and deal with them as his own. On the contrary, if said Canissius shall issue a newspaper, in all things conformable hereto, until after the Presidential election of 1860, then said press, types &c are to be his property absolutely, not, however, to be used against the Republican party; nor to be removed from Springfield without the consent of said Lincoln. A. LINCOLN

May 1859 TH CANISIUS

May 30. 1859. Jacob Bunn, bought the press, types &c. of John Burkhardt, for me, and with my money A. LINCOLN

[1] ADS, RPB.

[2] Probably John M. Burkhardt, an early German settler who became a prominent merchant at Springfield.

Endorsement: John S. Wolfe to Lincoln[1]

[June 1, 1859]

Yes, use my name by way of reference, if J. M. Palmer says so. I put it on this condition because my personal acquaintance with you is not sufficient for me to act on my own knowledge Yours &c.

A. LINCOLN

[1] AES, IHi. Wolfe wrote from Carlinville on June 1, 1859, that he was about to enter a law partnership with "Jarvis Wilkinson, a member of the N. Y. Bar," and wished to use Lincoln's name as a reference.

To Salmon P. Chase[1]

Hon: S. P. Chase: Springfield, Ills.
Dear Sir June 9. 1859

Please pardon the liberty I take in addressing you, as I now do. It appears by the papers that the late Republican State convention of Ohio adopted a Platform, of which the following is one plank, "A repeal of the atrocious Fugitive Slave Law."

This is already damaging us here. I have no doubt that if that plank be even *introduced* into the next Republican National convention, it will explode it. Once introduced, its supporters and it's opponents will quarrel irreconcilably. The latter believe the U.S. constitution declares that a fugitive slave "*shall be delivered up*"; and they look upon the above plank as dictated by the spirit which declares a fugitive slave "*shall not be delivered up*"

I enter upon no argument one way or the other; but I assure you the cause of Republicanism is hopeless in Illinois, if it be in any way made responsible for that plank. I hope you can, and will, contribute something to relieve us from it. Your Obt. Servt.

A. LINCOLN

[1] ALS, PHi. See Lincoln to Chase, June 20, and note, *infra*.

To Jonathan Haines[1]

Jonathan Haines, Esq Springfield,
Dear Sir: June 9 1859

I have just come home and found your letter of May 30th. I have done nothing further with the Rugg[2] case. How Dickey[3] keeps that matter hanging along I do not comprehend. I do believe it would be better all round to let me surrender both your cases to some lawyer at Chicago. I really can not give them proper attention.

There is no such thing as the Rugg suit being dead. It lingers along because I never find Dickey at Chicago, and I hate to press the thing without him. As to my entering on a campaign of taking proof in the pending suit, I think I must say that is impossible.

I have received of Fox[4] one hundred dollars—being fifty at each of two different times—and credited it on one of your notes. Yours truly A. LINCOLN.

[1] ALS, IHi.

[2] George H. Rugg. See Lincoln to Haines, November 24, 1856, *supra.*

[3] Hugh T. Dickey.

[4] Benjamin F. Fox, Springfield hardware merchant, who was instructed to pay over to Lincoln money he owed Haines (Haines to Lincoln, December 4, 1858, DLC-RTL).

To the Chicago *Press and Tribune* Company[1]

Press & Tribune Co Springfield

Gentlemen June 15. 1859

Herewith is a little draft to pay for your Daily another year from to-day. I suppose I shall take the Press & Tribune so long as it, and I both live, unless I become unable to pay for it. In it's devotion to our cause always, and to me personally last year I owe it a debt of gratitude, which I fear I shall never be able to pay. Yours very truly A. LINCOLN—

[1] ALS, The Chicago *Tribune,* Chicago, Illinois.

To Henry A. Clark[1]

Henry A. Clark, Esq Springfield,

Dear Sir June 15– 1859

The cases of Cochran & Hall against Camp & others & against J. L. D. Morrison, are already continued.[2]

I have never had any definite arrangement with any one about a fee on these cases; and the consequence is I am bothered with them every court, without understanding any thing about them. I blame no one for this; but it would be better all round for me to either get out of the cases, or get in deep enough to understand and prepare them. Yours truly A. LINCOLN

[1] ALS-P, ISLA. Henry A. Clark was an attorney at Chicago, Illinois.

[2] The U.S. District Court cases referred to involved lands entered along the right-of-way of the Ohio and Illinois Railroad by Irwin Camp of Erie, Pennsylvania, the contractor who built the Illinois division of the road. James L. D. Morrison had acted as agent for Camp and his associates in entering the lands (Camp to Lincoln, November 2, 1859, DLC-RTL).

To Salmon P. Chase[1]

Hon. S. P. Chase Springfield, Ills.
My dear Sir June 20. 1859

Yours of the 13th. Inst. is received. You say you would be glad to have my views. Although I think congress has constitutional authority to enact a Fugitive Slave law, I have never elaborated an opinion upon the subject. My view has been, and is, simply this: The U.S. constitution says the fugitive slave "*shall be delivered up*" but it does not expressly say *who* shall deliver him up. Whatever the constitution says "*shall be done*" and has omitted saying who shall do it, the government established by that constitution, *ex vi termini*, is vested with the power of doing; and congress is, by the constitution, expressly empowered to make all laws which shall be necessary and proper for carrying into execution all powers vested by the constitution in the government of the United States. This would be my view, on a simple reading of the constitution; and it is greatly strengthened by the historical fact that the constitution was adopted, in great part, in order to get a government which could execute it's own behests, in contradistinction to that under the Articles of confederation, which depended, in many respects, upon the States, for its' execution; and the other fact that one of the earliest congresses, under the constitution, did enact a Fugitive Slave law.

But I did not write you on this subject, with any view of discussing the constitutional question. My only object was to impress you with what I believe is true, that the introduction of a proposition for repeal of the Fugitive Slave law, into the next Republican National convention, will explode the convention and the party. Having turned your attention to the point, I wish to do no more.

Yours very truly A. LINCOLN.

[1] ALS, PHi. In answer to Lincoln's letter of June 9, *supra*, Chase expressed gratification at Lincoln's reliance on him to avoid extremes, but expressed his view that repeal of the Fugitive Slave Act was indispensable and his hope that the party in Illinois would accept repeal. Pointing out his reasons for believing the act unconstitutional, he asked Lincoln's views (DLC-RTL).

To Charles Ambos[1]

Chas. Ambos, Esq. Springfield, Ills,
Dear Sir June 21, 1859

I have had two or three letters from you recently in regard to the claim of your Company against J. A. Barret. Mr. Barret has been telling me for three months past that there is some money at Christian Co, of the claim assigned to your Co as security, which can be had when he and I can go there together to release a portion of the land involved; but I have been unable to get off at any time when I could [get] Barret to go with me. I now think I will get off in a few days. It is so very much better to get the debt reduced by actual payments, than to push forward in sole reliance upon the law, that I am loth to lose any oppertunity of the sort.

I would now very gladly surrender the charge of the case to any-one you would designate, without charging anything for the much trouble I have already had. Yours &c A. LINCOLN

[1] ALS, CSmH. On December 9, 1858, Lincoln filed praecipe and declaration in Ambos *v.* Barrett *et al.*, and a bill to foreclose a mortgage in Ambos *v.* Barrett. Both cases in the U.S. Circuit Court involved James A. Barrett's indebtedness to the Columbus Machine Manufacturing Company of Columbus, Ohio. On February 14, 1859, Lincoln collected $1,000 as part payment, but Ambos was dissatisfied with Lincoln's handling of the suits. See Lincoln to Samuel Galloway, July 27, *infra.*

To Nathan Sargent[1]

Hon. Nathan Sargent. Springfield, Ills.
My dear Sir June 23, 1859

Your very acceptable letter of the 13th. was duly received. Of course I would be pleased to see all the elements of opposition united for the approaching contest of 1860; but I confess I have not much hope of seeing it. You state a platform for such union in these words "*Opposition to the opening of the Slave-trade; & eternal hostility to the rotten democracy.*" You add, by way of comment "I say, if the republicans would be content with this, there will be no obstacle to a union of the *opposition.* But this should be distinctly understood, before Southern men are asked to join them in a National convention" Well, I say such a platform, unanamously adopted by a National convention, with two of the best men living placed upon it as candidates, would probably carry Maryland, and would certainly not carry a single other state. It would gain nothing in the South, and lose every thing in the North. Mr. Goggin[2] has just been beaten in Virginia on just such a platform. Last year the Republicans of Illinois cast 125-000 votes; on such a platform as yours they can not cast as many by 50.000. You could not help perceiving this, if you would but reflect that the republican party is utterly pow[er]less everywhere, if it will, by any means, drive from it all those who came to it from the democracy for the sole object of preventing the spread, and nationalization of slavery. Whenever this object is waived by the organization, they will drop the organization; and the organization itself will dissolve into thin air. Your platform proposes to allow the spread, and nationalization of slavery to proceed without let or hindrance, save only that it shall not receive supplies directly from Africa. Surely you do not seriously believe the Republicans can come to any such terms.

From the passage of the Nebraska-bill up to date, the Southern opposition have constantly sought to gain an advantage over the rotten democcracy, by running ahead of them in extreme opposition to, and vilifacation and misrepresentation of black republicans. It will be a good deal, if we fail to remember this in malice, (as I hope we shall fail to remember it;) but it is altogether too much to ask us to try to stand with them on the platform which has proved altogether insufficient to sustain them alone.

If the rotten democracy shall be beaten in 1860, it has to be done by the North; no human invention can deprive them of the South. I do not deny that there are as good men in the South as the North; and I guess we will elect one of them if he will allow us to do so on Republican ground. I think there can be no other ground of Union. For my single self I would be willing to risk some Southern men without a platform; but I am satisfied that is not the case with the Republican party generally. Yours very truly

A. LINCOLN

[1] ALS-F, ISLA. Nathan Sargent was an old Whig at Washington, D.C., who had served as sergeant at arms of the House of Representatives during Lincoln's term in Congress.

[2] William L. Goggin, Whig candidate for governor of Virginia.

To Dave Walker[1]

D. Walker, &c., Springfield,
My Dear Sir: June 24th, 1859.

Your kind invitation to me to be with you on the 4th is duly received and for which I thank you. It is out of my power to accept. I am compelled to economise time this year, and have already agreed to attend one celebration on that day, at a place near enough here to take only the single day. Yours very truly,

A. LINCOLN.

[1] Ottawa *Republican*, July 9, 1859. Lincoln's letter appears along with letters of regret from William H. Bissell, James Shields, Lyman Trumbull, and others, invited to join in the Ottawa celebration of the Fourth of July. Dave Walker was a druggist at Ottawa.

To the Editor of the *Central Transcript*[1]

Editor of the Central Transcript. Springfield,
Dear Sir: July 3, 1859

Your paper of the 1st. which I presume you sent me is received. Put me on your subscription list, and I will pay at fall court.

I cut a slip from this number and return it with a word of comment. I shall heartily support for Governor whoever shall be nominated by a Republican State convention; and no one more heartily than any one of the five you name. But is not the fling you make at our Northern bretheren both unjust to them, and dangerous to our cause? You open by saying, "A strong controversy is going on between the Chicago papers as to who shall be the next Republican nominee for Governor." I was unaware of this. I have not seen in any Chicago paper, a man named, or pointed to, whom such paper declares for as it's candidate for Governor. Have you? Again, ought you to say, as you do that "the matter will be entirely controlled by the Central and Southern portions of the state"? Surely, on reflection, you will agree that the matter must be controlled, in due proportions, by all parts of the State. Again, you say "The defeat of Mr. Lincoln may be attributed to the course pursued by these Northerners in putting none but the most ultra men on the track, as candidates for the most important state and Federal offices &c." This statement is, indeed, strange. The Republican party, since its organization in Illinois, has gone through two general elections—in 1856 and 1858; and "these Northerners" have not even had a single candidate for a State office, or a Federal office, commensurate with the state, either residing within their section, or holding their supposed ultra views. In 1856 they put on the track, Bissell, of Bellville, for Governor; Hatch of Pike Co, for Secretary of State; Dubois, of Lawrence Co, for Auditor; Miller, of Bloomington, for Treasurer; Powell of Peoria for School Superintendant; and Wood of Quincy, for Lieutenant Governor; and they elected all of them. In 1858, all these, but two, held over; and one of them, Mr. Miller was again put upon the track; and in lieu of Mr. [Powell,][2] Mr. Bateman,[3] still further South, was put on the track; and again, both elected. Now, can you, on reflection, say either of these men is an ultra man? or that "these Northerners" could have had any peculiarly selfish reason for supporting them? Another very marked fact is that "these Northerners" in the two past elections, gave nearly all the votes which carried them; and that the next election will be lost, unless "these Northerners" do the same thing again. Your fling about men entangled with the

"Matteson Robbery" as you express it; and men indicted for stealing niggers and mail-bags,[4] I think is unjust and impolitic. Why manufacture slang to be used against us by our enemies? The world knows who are alluded to by the mention of stealing niggers and mail-bags; and as to the Canal script fraud, the charge of being entangled with it, would be as just, if made against you, as against any other Republican in the State.

Finally, can articles such as the inclosed, fail to weaken our party, and our cause?

I beg your pardon for writing thus freely, without a better acquaintance with you; and I plead in excuse, my great anxiety that we shall have harmony and not discord; have candidates by agreement, and not by force;—*help* one another instead of trying to *hurt* one another.

I do not write this for publication; and would not have written at all, had I expected a chance to see and talk with you soon. Yours very truly A. LINCOLN

[1] ALS, RPB. Isaac N. Coltrin was editor of the *Central Transcript*, published at Clinton, Illinois. [2] Manuscript is torn.

[3] Newton Bateman of Morgan County, elected superintendent of public instruction in 1858 and re-elected in 1860.

[4] The allusions in the editorial, "men who boast of stealing Negroes," and "We want a man . . . who has never been indicted for stealing niggers or mail bags," probably refer on the one hand to abolitionist Republicans and on the other, to the then current Chicago post office investigation involving Isaac Cook, postmaster at Chicago who was a Buchanan Democrat purported to be in secret alliance with the Republicans against Douglas.

To Schuyler Colfax[1]

Hon: Schuyler Colfax: Springfield, Ills, July 6, 1859.

My dear Sir: I much regret not seeing you while you were here among us. Before learning that you were to be at Jacksonville on the 4th. I had given my word to be at another place. Besides a strong desire to make your personal acquaintance, I was anxious to speak with you on politics, a little more fully than I can well do in a letter. My main object in such conversation would be to hedge against divisions in the Republican ranks generally, and particularly for the contest of 1860. The point of danger is the temptation in different localities to "*platform*" for something which will be popular just there, but which, nevertheless, will be a firebrand elsewhere, and especially in a National convention. As instances, the movement against foreigners in Massachusetts; in New-Hampshire, to make obedience to the Fugitive Slave law, punishable as a crime; in Ohio, to repeal the Fugitive Slave law; and squatter sovereignty in Kansas. In these things there is explosive matter enough to blow up half a dozen national conventions, if it gets into them; and what gets very rife outside of conventions is very likely to find it's way into them. What is desirable, if possible, is that in every local convocation of Republicans, a point should be made to avoid everything which will distract republicans elsewhere. Massachusetts republicans should have looked beyond their noses; and then they could not have failed to see that tilting against foreigners would ruin us in the whole North-West. New-Hampshire and Ohio should forbear tilting against the Fugitive Slave law in such way as [to] utterly overwhelm us in Illinois with the charge of enmity to the constitution itself. Kansas, in her confidence that she can be saved to freedom on "squatter sovereignty"—ought not to forget that to prevent the spread and nationalization of slavery is a national concern, and must be attended to by the nation. In a word, in every locality we should look beyond our noses; and at least say *nothing* on points where it is probable we shall disagree.

I write this for your eye only; hoping however that if you see danger as I think I do, you will do what you can to avert it. Could not suggestions be made to the leading men in the State and congressional conventions; and so avoid, to some extent at least, these apples of discord? Yours very truly A. LINCOLN

[1] ALS-P, ISLA. In general agreement with Lincoln, Colfax, U.S. representative from Indiana, replied on July 14 that the great problem was to consolidate the conflicting elements in the anti-slavery ranks and opined that "he who could accomplish it, is worthier than Napoleon or [Victor] Emanuel [*sic*]." (DLC-RTL).

To Frederick C. W. Koehnle[1]

My dear Sir Springfield, July 11. 1859

By this mail I send you a specimen copy of the new german paper started here. I think you could not do a more efficient service than to get it a few subscribers, if possible. I have sent a copy to Capps at Pulaski.[2] Yours as ever A. LINCOLN

[1] ALS, CSmH. Koehnle was a German who came to the United States in 1853. At the time this letter was written, he was an assistant in the circuit clerk's office at Lincoln, Illinois. The newspaper which Lincoln enclosed was the *Illinois Staats-Anzeiger*, edited by Theodore Canisius. See Lincoln's contract with Canisius, May 30, *supra*.

[2] Lincoln probably refers to John Capps, a merchant at Mount Pulaski in Logan County. No "Capps" has been located at Pulaski, Pulaski County, Illinois, of this date.

To James Miller[1]

Hon: James Miller: Springfield, Ills. July 11– 1859

Dear Sir We suppose you are persistently urged to pay something upon the new McCallister and Stebbins bonds.[2] As friends of yours, and of the people, we advise you to pay nothing upon them under any possible circumstances. The holders of them did a great wrong, and are now persisting in it, in a way which deserves severe punishment. They know the Legislature has again and again refused to fully recognize the old bonds. Seizing upon an act never intended to apply to them, they besieged Gov. Bissell more than a year ago to fund the old bonds; he refused. They sought a mandamus upon him from the Supreme court; the court refused.[3] Again they besieged the Governor last winter; he sought to have them go before the Legislature; they refused. Still they persisted, and dogged him in his afflicted condition till they got from him what the agent in New-York acted upon, and issued the new bonds. Now they refuse to surrender them, hoping to force an acquiescence, for Gov. Bissell's sake. "That cock wont fight," and they may as well so understand at once. If the news of the surrender of the new bonds does not reach here in ten days from this date, we shall do what we can to have them repudiated *in toto*, finally and forever. If they were less than demons they would at once relieve Gov. Bissell from the painful position they have dogged him into; and if they still persist, they shall never see even the twentysix cents to the dollar, if we can prevent it. Yours very truly,

A. LINCOLN
S. T. LOGAN
O. M. HATCH

P. S. Dubois is not at home. H.[4]

[1] ADfS or ALS copy, DLC-RTL. Lincoln's authorship of this letter is not certain. The fact that the postscript bearing Hatch's initial is in Lincoln's hand, initial included, suggests that the document may be only a copy made by Lincoln for his file. The financial tangle in which the state treasurer, James Miller, found himself led to his resignation on September 3, 1859.

[2] The McCallister and Stebbins [Charles Macallister and Henry Stebbins of New York] bonds were hypothecated in 1841 as a guarantee of a loan of $321,600, to be applied on the interest on the state debt. Upon failure of the state financial system in 1842, the bonds dropped to thirty cents on the dollar. In 1859, under a misapprehension of the law for refunding old indebtedness, Governor Bissell gave instructions which resulted in the issuance of new bonds for the old. [3] February 3, 1858.

[4] Jesse K. Dubois, state auditor, whose signature might have been expected by Miller.

To Daniel T. Jewett[1]

D. T. Jewett, Esq — Springfield,
Dear Sir: — July 23. 1859

After an absence of nine days I reached home last evening and found yours of the 20th. I find Judge Treat has decided in your favor,[2] rendering judgment for $517.00. & costs. You will have to advance the cost before execution will issue. So says the clerk. Yours truly A. LINCOLN.

1 ALS, CtY. Jewett was an attorney at St. Louis, Missouri, who represented the plaintiff in Elbridge Whiting *v.* Solomon H. Mudge in the U.S. Circuit Court.

2 Judge Samuel H. Treat handed down the judgment on July 11, while Lincoln was on a trip with a party of state officials assessing the Illinois Central's property.

To Samuel Galloway[1]

Hon. Samuel Galloway — Springfield, Ill.,
My dear Sir: — July 27, 1859.

Your letter in relation to the claim of Mr. Ambos[2] for the Columbus Machine Manufacturing Company against Barret[3] and others is received. This has been a somewhat disagreeable matter to me. As I remember, you first wrote me on the general subject, Barret having then had a credit of four or five hundred dollars, and there was some question about his taking the machinery. I think you inquired as to Barret's responsibility; and that I answered I considered him an honest and honorable man, having a great deal of property, owing a good many debts, and hard pressed for ready cash. I was a little surprised soon after to learn that they had enlarged the credit to near ten thousand dollars, more or less. They wrote me to take notes and a mortgage, and to hold on to the notes awhile to fix amounts. I inferred the notes and mortgage were both to be held up for a time, and did so; Barret gave a second mortgage on part of the premises, which was first recorded, and then I was blamed some for not having recorded the other mortgage when first executed. My chief annoyance with the case now is that the parties at Columbus seem to think it is by my neglect that they do not get their money. There is an older mortgage on the real estate mortgaged, though not on the machinery. I got a decree of foreclosure in this present month; but I consented to delay advertising for sale till September, on a reasonable prospect that something will then be paid on a collateral Barret has put in my hands. When we come to sell on the decree, what will we do about the older mortgage? Barret has offered one or two other good notes—that is, notes on good men—if we would take them, *pro tanto*, as payment, but I notified Mr. Ambos, and he declined. My impression is that the whole of the money cannot be got very soon, anyway, but that it all will be ultimately collected, and that it could be got faster by turning in every little parcel we can, than by trying to force it through by the law in a lump. There are no special personal relations between Barret and myself. We are personal friends in a general way—no business transactions between us—not akin, and opposed on politics. Yours truly,

A. LINCOLN.

[1] NH (1894 edition), I, 536-37. The text of this letter is reproduced from the early two-volume edition because of omissions in the text as given in the Tandy edition of 1905, (V, 134-36). Samuel Galloway was an attorney at Columbus, Ohio. [2] Charles Ambos. See Lincoln's letter, June 21, *supra*.
[3] James A. Barrett.

To Samuel Galloway[1]

Hon. Samuel Galloway Springfield, Ills.
My dear Sir: July 28. 1859

Your very complimentary, not to say flattering letter of the 23rd. Inst. is received. Dr. Reynolds[2] had induced me to expect you here; and I was disappointed, not a little, by your failure to come. And yet I fear you have formed an estimate of me which can scarcely be sustained on a personal acquaintance.

Two things done by the Ohio Republican convention—the repudiation of Judge Swan,[3] and the "plank" for a repeal of the Fugitive Slave law—I very much regretted. These two things are of a piece; and they are viewed by many good men, sincerely opposed to slavery, as a struggle against, and in disregard of, the constitution itself. And it is the very thing that will greatly endanger our cause, if it be not be [*sic*] kept out of our national convention. There is another thing our friends are doing which gives me some uneasiness. It is their leaning towards "*popular sovereignty*." There are three substantial objections to this. First, no party can command respect which sustains this year, what it opposed last. Secondly, Douglas, (who is the most dangerous enemy of liberty, because the most insidious one) would have little support in the North, and by consequence, no capital to trade on in the South, if it were not for our friends thus magnifying him and his humbug. But lastly, and chiefly, Douglas' popular sovereignty, accepted by the public mind, as a just principle, nationalizes slavery, and revives the African Slave-trade, inevitably. Taking slaves into new teritories, and buying slaves in Africa, are identical things—identical *rights* or identical *wrongs*—and the argument which establishes one will establish the other. Try a thousand years for a sound reason why congress shall not hinder the people of Kansas from having slaves, and when you have found it, it will be an equally good one why congress should not hinder the people of Georgia from importing slaves from Africa.

As to Gov. Chase, I have a kind side for him. He was one of the few distinguished men of the nation who gave us, in Illinois, their sympathy last year. I never saw him, suppose him to be able, and right-minded; but still he may not be the most suitable as a candidate for the Presidency.

I must say I do not think myself fit for the Presidency. As you propose a correspondence with me, I shall look for your letters anxiously.

I have not met Dr. Reynolds since receiving your letter; but when I shall, I will present your respects, as requested. Yours very truly A. LINCOLN

1 ALS, owned by Mrs. Yeatman Anderson, Cincinnati, Ohio. Presumably Lincoln received Galloway's letter after he had written the business letter to Galloway on July 27, *supra.*

2 Reverend William M. Reynolds, D.D., president of Illinois University and pastor of the English Lutheran Church at Springfield. Galloway wrote of visiting "my relatives Dr. Reynolds family" (DLC-RTL).

3 Chief Justice Joseph R. Swan of the Ohio Supreme Court, who handed down the verdict upholding the fugitive slave law in a *habeas corpus* case.

To Thomas H. Cory[1]

Thomas H. Cory, Esq Springfield,
My dear Sir July 29 1859

Your letter of the 2nd. came to hand in due course. If you have reliable assurances that you can be elected to congress in this District, you unquestionably are the man for us to run. Still I do not think any Republican committee is authorized to decide who shall be the candidate. A convention, or common consent, are the only legitimate party tribunals to decide such questions. I have no doubt that if you can satisfy the Republican party of the District that you can carry the election,——you can have the chance of trying. Yours very truly A. LINCOLN—

1 ALS, owned by J. Barrett, Albany, California. Cory was a farmer residing near Hillsboro, Illinois. His letter requested that Lincoln lay his position before the state central committee (DLC-RTL).

To Nathan B. Dodson[1]

N. B. Dodson, Secretary &c. Springfield,
My dear Sir July 29, 1859

Your kind invitation to me to deliver an agricultural address at Morris on the 3rd. of September next is received. I regret the necessity of declining. This year I must devote to my private business.

Our own Sangamon circuit court will be in session at that time.

Yours very truly A. LINCOLN

[1] ALS, ORB. Nathan B. Dodson, hardware dealer at Morris, Illinois, and secretary of the Grundy County Agricultural Society, wrote Lincoln on July 28, asking him to speak at the Grundy County Fair (DLC-RTL).

Speech at Council Bluffs, Iowa[1]

August 13, 1859

Abe Lincoln on the Slope.

The people of this city were edified, last Saturday evening, by a speech from Hon. ABE LINCOLN, of Illinois. He apologized very handsomely for appearing before an Iowa audience during a Campaign in which he was not interested. He then, with many excuses and a lengthy explanation, as if conscious of the nauseous nature of that Black Republican nostrum, announced his intention to speak about the "eternal Negro," to use his own language, and entered into a lengthy and ingenious analysis of the Nigger question, impressing upon his hearers that it was the only question to be agitated until finally settled. He carefully avoided coming directly to the extreme ground occupied by him in his canvass against Douglas, yet the doctrines which he preached, carried out to their legitimate results, amount to precisely the same thing. He was decidedly opposed to any fusion or coalition of the Republican party with the opposition of the South, and clearly proved the correctness of his ground, in point of policy. They must retain their sectional organization and sectional character, and continue to wage their sectional warfare by slavery agitation; but if the opposition South would accede to their views and adopt their doctrines, he was willing to run for president in 1860, a Southern man with Northern principles, or in other words, with Abolition proclivities. His speech was in the character of an exhortation to the Republican party, but was in reality as good a speech as could have been made for the interest of the Democracy. He was listened to with much attention, for his Waterloo defeat by Douglas has magnified him into quite a lion here.

[1] Council Bluffs *Bugle*, August 17, 1859. Although from a Democratic paper, this is the most complete report available. Accompanied by Ozias M. Hatch, Lincoln made the trip to Council Bluffs to examine land owned by Norman B. Judd, which Judd deeded to Lincoln November 11, 1859, as security for a $3,000 debt. After his arrival in the city, Lincoln accepted an invitation to speak.

To D. J. Powers[1]

D. J. Powers, Esq
Dear Sir

Springfield, Ills.
Aug. 18. 1859

Reaching home after an absence [of] nine days I find yours of the 12th. I had also received that of July 27; and, to be plain, I disliked to decline the honor you tendered me. Two difficulties were in the way—first, I could not well spare the time, from the courts; and secondly, I had no address of the sort prepared; and could scarcely spare the time to prepare one; and I was waiting, before answering you, to determine whether these difficulties could be surmounted. I will write you definitely on the 1st. day of September, if you can safely delay so long. Yours very truly

A. LINCOLN

[1] ALS, CSmH. D. J. Powers, co-editor of the *Wisconsin Farmer and Northwestern Cultivator* and chairman of the executive committee for the Wisconsin Agricultural Fair had invited Lincoln to address the Agricultural Society at the Milwaukee fair on September 30.

To Daniel Rohrer[1]

Daniel Rohrer, Esq
Dear Sir

Springfield,
Aug. 19. 1859

Your letter inviting me "to visit your state during the fall, and participate in the coming canvass" was duly received; and I have neglected to answer it so long because I disliked to decline the invitation. But on full consideration, I feel constrained to decline; from the necessity, (made very stringent by having lost nearly the whole of last year,) of my attending our fall courts. I regret this; but it is no less than a necessity with me. Yours very truly

A. LINCOLN

[1] ALS, OMC. Rohrer was chairman of the Republican central committee of Minnesota, and an attorney at St. Paul.

Fragments: Notes for Speeches[1]

[c. September, 1859?]

[I]

What will Douglas do now? He does not quite know himself. Like a skilful gambler he will play for all the chances. His first wish is to be the nominee of the Charleston convention, without any new test. The democratic party proper do not wish to let it go just that way. They are thinking of getting up a Slave code test for him. They better not. Their true policy is to let him into the convention, beat him then, and give him no plausable excuse to bolt the nomination. But if they press the Slave code test upon him, he will not take it; but, as in the case of Lecompton, will appeal to the North on his bravery in opposing it. True the logic of his position, as an indorser of the Dred Scott decision imperatively requires him to go the Slave code. Honestly believing in that decision, he can not, without perjury, refuse to go the Slave code. But he will refuse. He never lets the logic of principle, displace the logic of success. And then, when he thus turns again to the North, we shall have the Lecompton phase of politics reproduced on a larger scale. It will then be a question whether the Republican party of the Nation shall make him President, in magnanamous gratitude for having opposed a Slave code, just as it was, last year, a question whether the Illinois Republicans should re-elect him Senator, in magnanamous gratitude for having opposed Lecompton. Some larger gentlemen will then have a chance of swallowing the same pill which they somewhat persistently prescribed for us little fellows last year. I hope they will not swallow it. For the sake of the *cause*, rather than the *men*, I hope they will not swallow it. The Republican cause can not live by Douglas' position. His position, whether for or against a slave code, for or against Lecompton, leads inevitably to the nationalizing and perpetuity of slavery, and the Republican cause can not live by it. Dallying with Douglas is, at best, for Republicans, only loss of labor, and loss of time. Wander with him however long, at last they must turn back and strike for a policy, which shall deal with slavery as a wrong, restrain it's enlargement, and look to its termination.

[II]

The effort to prove that our fathers who framed the government under which we live, understood that a proper division of local from federal authority, and some provision of the constitution, both forbid the federal government to control slavery in the federal teritories, is as if, when a man stands before you, so that you see him, and lay your hand upon him, you should go about examining his tracks, and insisting therefrom, that he is not present, but somewhere else. They *did*, through the federal government, control slavery in the federal teritories. They did the identical thing, which D. insists they understood they ought not to do.

[III]

Negro equality! Fudge!! How long, in the government of a God, great enough to make and maintain this Universe, shall there continue knaves to vend, and fools to gulp, so low a piece of demagougeism as this.

[1] AD, owned by Norman B. Frost, Washington, D.C. Mr. Frost writes (letter to the editor, April 19, 1948) as follows: "At the time he gave the notes to me, they were in an envelope bearing on the outside the following in Mr. Robert Lincoln's handwriting: 'A. L. Douglas Speech Notes.'" Unable to find any particular speech in which the fragments occur verbatim, the editors have supplied a probable date based on the contents of the first and second fragments. The earliest similar reference to the contents of the first fragment is in Lincoln's letter to Lyman Trumbull, December 11, 1858, *supra*, and Lincoln may well have used this fragment at any time during 1859 or the early months of 1860. The second fragment with its reference to Douglas' article in *Harper's* for September, 1859, at the earliest would seem to be contemporary with the speech at Columbus, Ohio, September 16, 1859, in which Lincoln makes much the same point concerning Douglas' phrase about the "fathers who framed the government under which we live." But Lincoln continued to refer to Douglas' article and Columbus speech in the speeches in Kansas in December, 1859, and made of the argument a major theme in his address at Cooper Institute, February 27, 1860. The third fragment might well have been jotted down at any time between December, 1858, and March, 1860.

Agreement with John Hutchinson[1]

September 3, 1859

We, the undersigned, proprietors of lots in Hutchinsons Cemetery, in the City of Springfield, Illinois, constitute and appoint John Hutchinson our agent to take charge, and general superintendence of said Cemetery, until February 1st. 1861—which agent is assured any expenses which he, in his discretion, may incur, in such superintendence, we bind ourselves to pay. Sept. 3, 1859

A. Lincoln
Thos. Moffett
E. B. Hawley
Asahel Stone
J. H. Kent
Isaac Lindsay

Absalom Kalb
George Leggott
Isaac A. Hawley
Phinias H. Conant
Willard & Zimmerman
J. Bunn
Francis Springer

J. G. Loose
D. Sherman
James C Conkling
Sanford Bell
J. A. Hough
D. Wickersham

[1] ADS-P, ISLA.

To Hawkins Taylor[1]

Hawkins Taylor, Esq
My dear Sir:

Springfield, Ills,
Sep. 6. 1859.

Yours of the 3rd. is just received. There is some mistake about my expected attendance of the U.S. Court in your city on the 3rd.

Tuesday of this month. I have had no thought of being there. It is bad to be poor. I shall go to the wall for bread and meat, if I neglect my business this year as well as last. It would please me much to see the City, and good people, of Keokuck, but for this year it is little less than an impossibility. I am constantly receiving invitations which I am compelled to decline. I was pressingly urged to go to Minnesota; and I now have two invitations to go to Ohio. These last are prompted by Douglas' going there; and I am really tempted to make a flying trip to Columbus & Cincinnati.

I do hope you will have no serious trouble in Iowa. What thinks Grimes[2] about it? I have not known him to be mistaken about an election in Iowa. Present my respects to Col. Curtis,[3] & any other friends; and believe me Yours truly A. LINCOLN

[1] ALS, IaHA. Hawkins Taylor of Keokuk, Iowa, was a prominent Republican who had served in the Iowa House of Representatives. [2] James W. Grimes.

[3] Samuel R. Curtis, former mayor of Keokuk and Republican U.S. representative from Iowa, 1857-1861.

To Peter Zinn[1]

Peter Zinn, Esq Springfield, Ills.
Dear Sir Sep. 6. 1859

Yours of the 2nd. in relation to my appearing at Cincinnati in behalf of the Opposition is received. I already had a similar letter from Mr. W. T. Bascom, Secretary of the Republican State central committee at Columbus, which I answer to-day.[2] You are in correspondence with him, and will learn all from him. I shall try to speak at Columbus and Cincinnati; but can not do more. Yours truly A. LINCOLN

[1] ALS, owned by William P. Zinn, Columbus, Ohio. Peter Zinn was an attorney at Delhi, Ohio, and a member of the Republican state central committee.

[2] Lincoln's letter to William T. Bascom is presumably not extant, but Bascom's letter to Lincoln, September 9, 1859 (DLC-RTL), mentions receiving it. Also a member of the Republican state central committee of Ohio, Bascom was an editor of the *Ohio State Journal*.

Speech at Columbus, Ohio[1]

Fellow-citizens of the State of Ohio: September 16, 1859

I cannot fail to remember that I appear for the first time before an audience in this now great State—an audience that is accus-

[1] *Illinois State Journal*, September 24, 1859. Typographical errors have been corrected. Other editorial suggestions with question mark are enclosed in brackets. Brackets not questioned appear in the source.

tomed to hear such speakers as Corwin, and Chase, and Wade,[2] and many other renowned men; and, remembering this, I feel that it will be well for you, as for me, that you should not raise your expectations to that standard to which you would have been justified in raising them had one of these distinguished men appeared before you. You would perhaps be only preparing a disappointment for yourselves, and, as a consequence of your disappointment, mortification to me. I hope, therefore, you will commence with very moderate expectations; and perhaps, if you will give me your attention, I shall be able to interest you to a moderate degree.

Appearing here for the first time in my life, I have been somewhat embarrassed for a topic by way of introduction to my speech; but I have been relieved from that embarrassment by an introduction which the Ohio *Statesman* newspaper gave me this morning. In this paper I have read an article, in which, among other statements, I find the following:

In debating with Senator Douglas during the memorable contest of last fall, Mr. Lincoln declared in favor of negro suffrage, and attempted to defend that vile conception against the Little Giant.

I mention this now, at the opening of my remarks, for the purpose of making three comments upon it. The first I have already announced—it furnishes me an introductory topic; the second is to show that the gentleman is mistaken; thirdly, to give him an opportunity to correct it.[3] (A voice—"That he won't do.")

In the first place, in regard to this matter being a mistake. I have found that it is not entirely safe, when one is misrepresented under his very nose, to allow the misrepresentation to go uncontradicted. I therefore purpose, here at the outset, not only to say that this is a misrepresentation, but to show conclusively that it is so; and you will bear with me while I read a couple of extracts from that very "memorable" debate with Judge Douglas, last year, to which this newspaper refers. In the first pitched battle which Senator Douglas and myself had, at the town of Ottawa, I used the language which I will now read. Having been previously reading an extract, I continued as follows:

Now gentlemen, I don't want to read at any greater length, but this is the true complexion of all I have ever said in regard to the institution of slavery and the black race. This is the whole of it, and anything that argues me into his idea of perfect social and political equal-

[2] Thomas Corwin, Salmon P. Chase, and Senator Benjamin F. Wade.

[3] Editor George W. Manypenny's reply appeared in the *Ohio Statesman* for September 22, 1859. "We give Mr. Lincoln the benefit of this denial, and yet we are not satisfied but that he did in some parts of Illinois preach that doctrine in the campaign of 1858."

ity with the negro, is but a specious and fantastic arrangement of words, by which a man can prove a horse chestnut to be a chestnut horse. I will say here, while upon this subject, that I have no purpose directly or indirectly to interfere with the institution of slavery in the States where it exists. I believe I have no lawful right to do so and I have no inclination to do so. I have no purpose to introduce political and social equality between the white and the black races. There is a physical difference between the two which in my judgment will probably forever forbid their living together upon the footing of perfect equality, and inasmuch as it becomes a necessity that there must be a difference, I, as well as Judge Douglas, am in favor of the race to which I belong, having the superior position. I have never said anything to the contrary, but I hold that notwithstanding all this, there is no reason in the world why the negro is not entitled to all the natural rights enumerated in the Declaration of Independence, the right to life, liberty, and the pursuit of happiness. I hold that he is as much entitled to these as the white man. I agree with Judge Douglas, he is not my equal in many respects—certainly not in color, perhaps not in moral or intellectual endowments. But in the right to eat the bread, without leave of anybody else, which his own hand earns, *he is my equal and the equal of Judge Douglas and the equal of every living man.*

Upon a subsequent occasion, when the reason for making a statement like this recurred, I said:

While I was at the hotel to-day an elderly gentleman called upon me to know whether I was really in favor of producing perfect equality between the negroes and white people. While I had not proposed to myself on this occasion to say much on that subject, yet as the question was asked me I thought I would occupy perhaps five minutes in saying something in regard to it. I will say then that I am not, nor ever have been in favor of bringing about in any way the social and political equality of the white and black races—that I am not, nor ever have been in favor of making voters or jurors of negroes, nor of qualifying them to hold office, or intermarry with white people; and I will say in addition to this that there is a physical difference between the white and black races which I believe will forever forbid the two races living together on terms of social and political equality. And inasmuch as they cannot so live, while they do remain together there must be the position of superior and inferior, and I as much as any other man am in favor of having the superior position assigned to the white race. I say upon this occasion I do not perceive that because the white man is to have the superior position, the negro should be denied everything. I do not understand that because I do not want a negro woman for a slave, I must necessarily want her for a wife. My understanding is that I can just let her alone. I am now in my fiftieth year, and I certainly never have had a black woman for either a slave or a wife. So it seems to me quite possible for us to get along without making either slaves or wives of negroes. I will add to this that I have never seen to my knowledge a man, woman or child, who was in favor of producing a perfect equality, social and political, between negroes and white men.

I recollect of but one distinguished instance that I ever heard of so frequently as to be satisfied of its correctness—and that is the case of Judge Douglas' old friend Col. Richard M. Johnson. I will also add to the remarks I have made, (for I am not going to enter at large upon this subject,) that I have never had the least apprehension that I or my friends would marry negroes, if there was no law to keep them from it; but as Judge Douglas and his friends seem to be in great apprehension that they might, if there were no law to keep them from it, I give him the most solemn pledge that I will to the very last stand by the law of the State, which forbids the marrying of white people with negroes.

There, my friends, you have briefly what I have, upon former occasions, said upon the subject to which this newspaper, to the extent of its ability, [laughter] has drawn the public attention. In it you not only perceive as a probability that in that contest I did not at any time say I was in favor of negro suffrage; but the absolute proof that twice—once substantially and once expressly—I declared against it. Having shown you this, there remains but a word of comment on that newspaper article. It is this: that I presume the editor of that paper is an honest and truth-loving man, [a voice—"that's a great mistake,"] and that he will be very greatly obliged to me for furnishing him thus early an opportunity to correct the misrepresentation he has made, before it has run so long that malicious people can call him a liar. [Laughter and applause.]

The Giant himself has been here recently. [Laughter.] I have seen a brief report of his speech. If it were otherwise unpleasant to me to introduce the subject of the negro as a topic for discussion, I might be somewhat relieved by the fact that he dealt exclusively in that subject while he was here. I shall, therefore, without much hesitation or diffidence, enter upon this subject.

The American people, on the first day of January, 1854, found the African slave trade prohibited by a law of Congress. In a majority of the States of this Union, they found African slavery, or any other sort of slavery, prohibited by State constitutions. They also found a law existing, supposed to be valid, by which slavery was excluded from almost all the territory the United States then owned. This was the condition of the country, with reference to the instituiton of slavery, on the 1st of January, 1854. A few days after that, a bill was introduced into Congress, which ran through its regular course in the two branches of the National Legislature, and finally passed into a law in the month of May, by which the act of Congress prohibiting slavery from going into the territories of the United States was repealed. In connection with the law itself, and, in fact, in the terms of the law, the then existing prohibition was not only repealed, but there was a declaration of a purpose on the part of Congress never thereafter to exercise any power that they might have, real or supposed, to prohibit the extension or spread of slavery. This was a very great change; for the law thus repealed was of more than thirty years' standing. Following rapidly upon the heels of this action of Congress, a decision of the Supreme Court is made, by which it is declared that Congress, if it desires to prohibit the spread of slavery into the territories, has no constitutional power to do so. Not only so, but that decision lays down principles, which, if pushed to their logical conclusion—I say pushed to their logical conclusion—would decide that the constitutions of the Free States, forbidding slavery, are themselves unconstitutional. Mark me, I do not say the judge[s?] said this, and let no man say that I affirm the judge[s?] used these words; but I only say it is my opinion that what they did say, if pressed to its logical conclusion, will inevitably result thus. [Cries of "Good! good!"]

Looking at these things, the Republican party, as I understand its principles and policy, believe that there is great danger of the institution of slavery being spread out and extended, until it is ultimately made alike lawful in all the States of this Union; so believing, to prevent that incidental and ultimate consummation, is the original and chief purpose of the Republican organization. I say "chief purpose" of the Republican organization; for it is certainly true that if the national House shall fall into the hands of the Republicans, they will have to attend to all the other matters of national house-keeping, as well as this. This chief and real purpose of the Republican party is eminently conservative. It proposes nothing save and except to restore this government to its original tone in regard to this element of slavery, and there to maintain it, looking for no further change, in reference to it, than that which the original framers of the government themselves expected and looked forward to.

The chief danger to this purpose of the Republican party is not just now the revival of the African slave trade, or the passage of a Congressional slave code, or the declaring of a second Dred Scott decision, making slavery lawful in all the States. These are not pressing us just now. They are not quite ready yet. The authors of these measures know that we are too strong for them; but they will be upon us in due time, and we will be grappling with them hand to hand, if they are not now headed off. They are not now the chief danger to the purpose of the Republican organization;

but the most imminent danger that now threatens that purpose is that insidious Douglas Popular Sovereignty. This is the miner and sapper. While it does not propose to revive the African slave trade, nor to pass a slave code, nor to make a second Dred Scott decision, it is preparing us for the onslaught and charge of these ultimate enemies when they shall be ready to come on and the word of command for them to advance shall be given. I say this Douglas Popular Sovereignty—for there is a broad distinction, as I now understand it, between that article and a genuine popular sovereignty.

I believe there is a genuine popular sovereignty. I think a definition of genuine popular sovereignty, in the abstract, would be about this: That each man shall do precisely as he pleases with himself, and with all those things which exclusively concern him. Applied to government, this principle would be, that a general government shall do all those things which pertain to it, and all the local governments shall do precisely as they please in respect to those matters which exclusively concern them. I understand that this government of the United States, under which we live, is based upon this principle; and I am misunderstood if it is supposed that I have any war to make upon that principle.

Now, what is Judge Douglas' Popular Sovereignty? It is, as a principle, no other than that, if one man chooses to make a slave of another man, neither that other man nor anybody else has a right to object. [Cheers and laughter.] Applied in government, as he seeks to apply it, it is this: If, in a new territory into which a few people are beginning to enter for the purpose of making their homes, they choose to either exclude slavery from their limits, or to establish it there, however one or the other may affect the persons to be enslaved, or the infinitely greater number of persons who are afterward to inhabit that territory, or the other members of the families of communities, of which they are but an incipient member, or the general head of the family of States as parent of all—however their action may affect one or the other of these, there is no power or right to interfere. That is Douglas' popular sovereignty applied.

He has a good deal of trouble with his popular sovereignty. His explanations explanatory of explanations explained are interminable. [Laughter.] The most lengthy, and, as I suppose, the most maturely considered of his long series of explanations, is his great essay in Harper's Magazine.[4] [Laughter.] I will not attempt to enter upon any very thorough investigation of his argument, as

[4] September issue, 1859.

there made and presented. I will nevertheless occupy a good portion of your time here in drawing your attention to certain points in it. Such of you as may have read this document will have perceived that the Judge, early in the document, quotes from two persons as belonging to the Republican party, without naming them, but who can readily be recognized as being Gov. Seward of New York and myself. It is true, that exactly fifteen months ago this day, I believe, I for the first time expressed a sentiment upon this subject, and in such a manner that it should get into print, that the public might see it beyond the circle of my hearers; and my expression of it at that time is the quotation that Judge Douglas makes. He has not made the quotation with accuracy, but justice to him requires me to say that it is sufficiently accurate not to change its sense.

The sense of that quotation condensed is this—that this slavery element is a durable element of discord among us, and that we shall probably not have perfect peace in this country with it until it either masters the free principle in our government, or is so far mastered by the free principle as for the public mind to rest in the belief that it is going to its end. This sentiment, which I now express in this way, was, at no great distance of time, perhaps in different language, and in connection with some collateral ideas, expressed by Gov. Seward. Judge Douglas has been so much annoyed by the expression of that sentiment that he has constantly, I believe, in almost all his speeches since it was uttered, been referring to it. I find he alluded to it in his speech here, as well as in the copy-right essay. [Laughter.] I do not now enter upon this for the purpose of making an elaborate argument to show that we were right in the expression of that sentiment. In other words, I shall not stop to say all that might properly be said upon this point; but I only ask your attention to it for the purpose of making one or two points upon it.

If you will read the copy-right essay, you will discover that Judge Douglas himself says a controversy between the American Colonies and the government of Great Britain began on the slavery question in 1699, and continued from that time until the Revolution; and, while he did not say so, we all know that it has continued with more or less violence ever since the Revolution.

Then we need not appeal to history, to the declarations of the framers of the government, but we know from Judge Douglas himself that slavery began to be an element of discord among the white people of this country as far back as 1699, or one hundred and sixty years ago, or five generations of men—counting thirty years to a generation. Now it would seem to me that it might have occurred to Judge Douglas, or anybody who had turned his attention to these facts, that there was something in the nature of that thing, Slavery, somewhat durable for mischief and discord. [Laughter.]

There is another point I desire to make in regard to this matter, before I leave it. From the adoption of the constitution down to 1820 is the precise period of our history when we had comparative peace upon this question—the precise period of time when we came nearer to having peace about it than any other time of that entire one hundred and sixty years, in which he says it began, or of the eighty years of our own constitution. Then it would be worth our while to stop and examine into the probable reason of our coming nearer to having peace then than at any other time. This was the precise period of time in which our fathers adopted, and during which they followed a policy restricting the spread of slavery, and the whole Union was acquiescing in it. The whole country looked forward to the ultimate extinction of the institution. It was when a policy had been adopted and was prevailing, which led all just and right-minded men to suppose that slavery was gradually coming to an end, and that they might be quiet about it, watching it as it expired. I think Judge Douglas might have perceived that too, and whether he did or not, it is worth the attention of fair-minded men, here and else where, to consider whether that is not the truth of the case. If he had looked at these two facts, that this matter has been an element of discord for one hundred and sixty years among this people, and that the only comparative peace we have had about it was when that policy prevailed in this government, which he now wars upon, he might then, perhaps, have been brought to a more just appreciation of what I said fifteen months ago—that "a house divided against itself cannot stand. I believe that this government cannot endure permanently half slave and half free. I do not expect the house to fall. I do not expect the Union to dissolve; but I do expect it will cease to be divided. It will become all one thing or all the other. Either the opponents of slavery will arrest the further spread of it, and place it where the public mind will rest in the belief that it is in the course of ultimate extinction; or its advocates will push it forward, until it shall become alike lawful in all the States, old as well as new, north as well as south." That was my sentiment at that time. In connection with it, I said, "we are now, far into the fifth year since a policy was inaugurated with the avowed object and confident promise of putting an end to slavery agitation. Under the operation of the policy, that agitation has not only not ceased, but has constantly augmented." I now say to you here that we are advanced still farther into the sixth year since that policy of Judge Douglas—that Popular Sovereignty of his, for quieting the Slavery question—was made the national policy. Fifteen months more have been added since I uttered that sentiment, and I call upon you, and all other right-minded men to say whether that fifteen months have belied or corroborated my words. ["Good, good! that's the truth!"]

While I am here upon this subject, I cannot but express gratitude that this true view of this element of discord among us—as I believe it is—is attracting more and more attention. I do not believe that Gov. Seward uttered that sentiment because I had done so before, but because he reflected upon this subject and saw the truth of it. Nor do I believe, because Gov. Seward or I uttered it, that Mr. Hickman[5] of Pennsylvania, in different language, since that time, has declared his belief in the utter antagonism which exists between the principles of liberty and slavery. You see we are multiplying. [Applause and laughter.] Now, while I am speaking of Hickman, let me say, I know but little about him. I have never seen him, and know scarcely anything about the man; but I will say this much of him: Of all the Anti-Lecompton Democracy that have been brought to my notice, he alone has the true, genuine ring of the metal. And now, without endorsing anything else he has said, I will ask this audience to give three cheers for Hickman. [The audience responded with three rousing cheers for Hickman.]

Another point in the copy-right essay to which I would ask your attention, is rather a feature to be extracted from the whole thing, than from any express declaration of it at any point. It is a general feature of that document, and, indeed, of all of Judge Douglas' discussions of this question, that the territories of the United States and the States of this Union are exactly alike—that there is no difference between them at all—that the constitution applies to the territories precisely as it does to the States—and that the United States Government, under the constitution, may not do in a State what it may not do in a territory, and what it must do in a State, it must do in a territory. Gentlemen, is that a true view of the case? It is necessary for this squatter sovereignty; but is it true?

Let us consider. What does it depend upon? It depends altogether upon the proposition that the States must, without the interference of the general government, do all those things that pertain

5 Representative John Hickman, a Douglas Democrat who turned Republican.

exclusively to themselves—that are local in their nature, that have no connection with the general government. After Judge Douglas has established this proposition, which nobody disputes or ever has disputed, he proceeds to assume, without proving it, that slavery is one of those little, unimportant, trivial matters which are of just about as much consequence as the question would be to me, whether my neighbor should raise horned cattle or plant tobacco (laughter); that there is no moral question about it, but that it is altogether a matter of dollars and cents; that when a new territory is opened for settlement, the first man who goes into it may plant there a thing which, like the Canada thistle, or some other of those pests of the soil, cannot be dug out by the millions of men who will come thereafter; that it is one of those little things that is so trivial in its nature that it has no effect upon anybody save the few men who first plant upon the soil; that it is not a thing which in any way affects the family of communities composing these States, nor any way endangers the general government. Judge Douglas ignores altogether the very well known fact, that we have never had a serious menace to our political existence, except it sprang from this thing which he chooses to regard as only upon a par with onions and potatoes. [Laughter.]

Turn it, and contemplate it in another view. He says, that according to his Popular Sovereignty, the general government may give to the territories governors, judges, marshals, secretaries, and all the other chief men to govern them, but they must not touch upon this other question. Why? The question of who shall be governor of a territory for a year or two, and pass away, without his track being left upon the soil, or an act which he did for good or for evil being left behind, is a question of vast national magnitude. It is so much opposed in its nature to locality, that the nation itself must decide it; while this other matter of planting slavery upon a soil—a thing which once planted cannot be eradicated by the succeeding millions who have as much right there as the first comers or if eradicated, not without infinite difficulty and a long struggle —he considers the power to prohibit it, as one of these little, local, trivial things that the nation ought not to say a word about; that it affects nobody save the few men who are there.

Take these two things and consider them together, present the question of planting a State with the Institution of slavery by the side of a question of who shall be Governor of Kansas for a year or two, and is there a man here,—is there a man on earth, who would not say that the Governor question is the little one, and the slavery question is the great one? I ask any honest Democrat if the small, the local, and the trivial and temporary question is not, who shall be Governor? While the durable, the important and the mischievous one is, shall this soil be planted with slavery?

This is an idea, I suppose, which has arisen in Judge Douglas' mind from his peculiar structure. I suppose the institution of slavery really looks small to him. He is so put up by nature that a lash upon his back would hurt him, but a lash upon anybody else's back does not hurt him. [Laughter.] That is the build of the man, and consequently he looks upon the matter of slavery in this unimportant light.

Judge Douglas ought to remember when he is endeavoring to force this policy upon the American people that while he is put up in that way a good many are not. He ought to remember that there was once in this country a man by the name of Thomas Jefferson, supposed to be a Democrat—a man whose principles and policy are not very prevalent amongst Democrats to-day, it is true; but that man did not take exactly this view of the insignificance of the element of slavery which our friend Judge Douglas does. In contemplation of this thing, we all know he was led to exclaim, "I tremble for my country when I remember that God is just!" We know how he looked upon it when he thus expressed himself. There was danger to this country—danger of the avenging justice of God in that little unimportant popular sovereignty question of Judge Douglas. He supposed there was a question of God's eternal justice wrapped up in the enslaving of any race of men, or any man, and that those who did so braved the arm of Jehovah—that when a nation thus dared the Almighty every friend of that nation had cause to dread His wrath. Choose ye between Jefferson and Douglas as to what is the true view of this element among us. [Applause.]

There is another little difficulty about this matter of treating the Territories and States alike in all things, to which I ask your attention, and I shall leave this branch of the case. If there is no difference between them, why not make the Territories States at once? What is the reason that Kansas was not fit to come into the Union when it was organized into a Territory, in Judge Douglas' view? Can any of you tell any reason why it should not have come into the Union at once? They are fit, as he thinks, to decide upon the slavery question—the largest and most important with which they could possibly deal—what could they do by coming into the Union that they are not fit to do, according to his view, by staying out of it? Oh, they are not fit to sit in Congress and decide upon the rates of postage, or questions of *ad valorem* or specific duties on foreign goods, or live oak timber contracts (laughter); they are not fit to decide these vastly important matters, which are national in their import, but they are fit, "from the jump," to decide this little negro question. But, gentlemen, the case is too plain; I occupy too much time on this head, and I pass on.

Near the close of the copyright essay, the Judge, I think, comes very near kicking his own fat into the fire (laughter). I did not think, when I commenced these remarks, that I would read from that article, but I now believe I will:

> This exposition of the history of these measures, shows conclusively that the authors of the Compromise Measures of 1850 and of the Kansas-Nebraska act of 1854, as well as the members of the Continental Congress of 1774, and the founders of our system of government subsequent to the Revolution, regarded the people of the Territories and Colonies as political communities which were entitled to a free and exclusive power of legislation in their provisional [provincial?] legislatures, where their representation could alone be preserved, in all cases of taxation and internal polity.

When the Judge saw that putting in the word "slavery" would contradict his own history, he put in what he knew would pass as synonymous with it: "internal polity." Whenever we find *that* in one of his speeches, the substitute is used in this manner; and I can tell you the reason. It would be too bald a contradiction to say slavery, but "internal polity" is a general phrase, which would pass in some quarters, and which he hopes will pass with the reading community for the same thing.

> This right pertains to the people collectively, as a law-abiding and peaceful community, and not in the isolated individuals who may wander upon the public domain in violation of the law. It can only be exercised where there are inhabitants sufficient to constitute a government, and capable of performing its various functions and duties, a fact to be ascertained and determined by—

Who do you think? Judge Douglas says "By Congress!" [Laughter.]

> Whether the number shall be fixed at ten, fifteen or twenty thousand inhabitants does not affect the principle.

Now I have only a few comments to make. Popular Sovereignty, by his own words, does not pertain to the few persons who wander upon the public domain in violation of law. We have his words for that. When it does pertain to them, is when they are sufficient to be formed into an organized political community, and he fixes the minimum for that at 10,000, and the maximum at 20,000. Now I would like to know what is to be done with the 9,000? Are they all to be treated, until they are large enough to be organized into a political community, as wanderers upon the public land in violation of law? And if so treated and driven out at what point of time would there ever be ten thousand? (Great laughter.) If they were not driven out, but remained there as trespassers upon the public land in violation of the law, can they establish slavery there? No,—the Judge says Popular Sovereignty don't pertain to them then. Can they exclude it then? No, Popular Sovereignty don't pertain to them then. I would like to know, in the case covered by the Essay, what condition the people of the Territory are in before they reach the number of ten thousand?

But the main point I wish to ask attention to is, that the question as to when they shall have reached a sufficient number to be formed into a regular organized community, is to be decided "by Congress." Judge Douglas says so. Well, gentlemen, that is about all we want. [Here some one in the crowd made a remark inaudible to the reporter, whereupon Mr. Lincoln continued.] No, that is all the Southerners want. That is what all those who are for slavery want. They do not want Congress to prohibit slavery from coming into the new territories, and they do not want Popular Sovereignty to hinder it; and as Congress is to say when they are ready to be organized, all that the south has to do is to get Congress to hold off. Let Congress hold off until they are ready to be admitted as a State, and the south has all it wants in taking slavery into and planting it in all the territories that we now have, or hereafter may have. In a word, the whole thing, at a dash of the pen, is at last put in the power of Congress; for if they do not have this Popular Sovereignty until Congress organizes them, I ask if it at last does not come from Congress? If, at last, it amounts to anything at all, Congress gives it to them. I submit this rather for your reflection than for comment. After all that is said, at last by a dash of the pen, everything that has gone before is undone, and he puts the whole question under the control of Congress. After fighting through more than three hours, if you undertake to read it, he at last places the whole matter under the control of that power which he had been contending against, and arrives at a result directly contrary to what he had been laboring to do. He at last leaves the whole matter to the control of Congress.

There are two main objects, as I understand it, of this Harper's Magazine essay. One was to show, if possible, that the men of our revolutionary times were in favor of his popular sovereignty; and the other was to show that the Dred Scott Decision had not entirely squelched out this popular sovereignty. I do not propose, in regard to this argument drawn from the history of former times, to enter into a detailed examination of the historical statements he has made. I have the impression that they are inaccurate in a great many instances. Sometimes in positive statement but very much more inaccurate by the suppression of statements that really belong to the history. But I do not propose to affirm that this is so to any very great extent; or to enter into a very minute examination of his historical statements. I avoid doing so upon this principle—that if it were important for me to pass out of this lot in the least period of time possible and I came to that fence and saw by a calculation of my known [own?] strength and agility that I could clear it at a bound, it would be folly for me to stop and consider whether I could or [could?] not crawl through a crack. [Laughter.] So I say of the whole history, contained in his essay, where he endeavored to link the men of the revolution to popular sovereignty. It only requires an effort to leap out of it—a single bound to be entirely successful. If you read it over you will find that he quotes here and there from documents of the revolutionary times, tending to show that the people of the colonies were desirous of regulating their own concerns in their own way, that the British Government should not interfere; that at one time they struggled with the British Government to be permitted to exclude the African slave trade; if not directly, to be permitted to exclude it indirectly by taxation sufficient to discourage and destroy it. From these and many things of this sort, Judge Douglas argues that they were in favor of the people of our own territories excluding slavery if they wanted to, or planting it there if they wanted to, doing just as they pleased from the time they settled upon the territory. Now, however his history may apply, and whatever of his argument there may be that is sound and accurate or unsound and inaccurate, if we can find out what these men did themselves do upon this very question of slavery in the territories, does it not end the whole thing? If, after all this labor and effort to show that the men of the revolution were in favor of his popular sovereignty and his mode of dealing with slavery in the territories, we can show that these very men took hold of that subject, and dealt with it, we can see for ourselves *how* they dealt with it. It is not a matter of argument or inference, but we know what they thought about it.

It is precisely upon that part of the history of the country, that one important omission is made by Judge Douglas. He selects parts of the history of the United States upon the subject of slavery, and treats it as the whole; omitting from his historical sketch the legislation of Congress in regard to the admission of Missouri, by which the Missouri Compromise was established, and slavery excluded from a country half as large as the present United States. All this is left out of his history, and in no wise alluded to by him, so far as I remember, save once, when he makes a remark, that upon his principle the Supreme Court were authorized to pronounce a decision that the act called the Missouri Compromise was unconstitutional. All that history has been left out. But this part of the history of the country was not made by the men of the Revolution.

There was another part of our political history made by the very men who were the actors in the Revolution, which has taken the name of the ordinance of '87. Let me bring that history to your attention. In 1784, I believe, this same Mr. Jefferson drew up an ordinance for the government of the country upon which we now stand; or rather a frame or draft of an ordinance for the government of this country, here in Ohio; our neighbors in Indiana; us who live in Illinois; our neighbors in Wisconsin and Michigan. In that ordinance, drawn up not only for the government of that territory, but for the territories south of the Ohio River, Mr. Jefferson expressly provided for the prohibition of slavery. Judge Douglas says, and perhaps is right, that that provision was lost from that ordinance. I believe that is true. When the vote was taken upon it, a majority of all present in the Congress of the Confederation voted for it; but there was [were?] so many absentees that those voting for it did not make the clear majority necessary, and it was lost. But three years after that the Congress of the Confederation were together again, and they adopted a new ordinance for the government of this north-west territory, not contemplating territory south of the river, for the States owning that territory had hitherto refrained from giving it to the general Government; hence they made the ordinance to apply only to what the Government owned. In that, the provision excluding slavery *was inserted and passed unanimously*, or at any rate it passed and became a part of the law of the land. Under that ordinance we live. First here in Ohio you were a territory, then an enabling act was passed authorizing you to form a constitution and State government, provided it was republican and not in conflict with the ordinance of '87. When you framed your constitution and presented it for admission, I think you will find the legislation upon the subject, it will show that, "whereas you had formed a constitution that was republican and not in conflict with the ordinance of '87," therefore you were admitted upon equal footing with the original States. The same process in a few years was gone through with in Indiana, and so with Illinois, and the same substantially with Michigan and Wisconsin.

Not only did that ordinance prevail, but it was constantly looked to whenever a step was taken by a new Territory to become a State. Congress always turned their attention to it, and in all their movements upon this subject, they traced their course by that ordinance of '87. When they admitted new States they advertised them of this ordinance as a part of the legislation of the country. They did so because they had traced the ordinance of '87 throughout the history of this country. Begin with the men of the Revolution, and go down for sixty entire years, and until the last scrap of that territory comes into the Union in the form of the State of Wisconsin—everything was made to conform with the ordinance of '87 excluding slavery from that vast extent of country.

I omitted to mention in the right place that the Constitution of the United States was in process of being framed when that ordinance was made by the Congress of the Confederation; and one of the first acts of Congress itself under the new Constitution itself was to give force to that ordinance by putting power to carry it out into the hands of the new officers under the Constitution, in place of the old ones who had been legislated out of existence by the change in the government from the Confederation to the Constitution. Not only so, but I believe Indiana once or twice, if not Ohio, petitioned the general government for the privilege of suspending that provision and allowing them to have slaves. A report made by Mr. Randolph[6] of Virginia, himself a slaveholder, was directly against it, and the action was to refuse them the privilege of violating the ordinance of '87.

This period of history which I have run over briefly is, I presume, as familiar to most of this assembly as any other part of the history of our country. I suppose that few of my hearers are not as familiar with that part of history as I am, and I only mention it to recall your attention to it at this time. And hence I ask how extraordinary a thing it is that a man who has occupied a position upon the floor of the Senate of the United States, who is now in his third term, and who looks to see the government of this whole country fall into his own hands, pretending to give a truthful and accurate history of the slavery question in this country, should so

[6] Edmund J. Randolph.

entirely ignore the whole of that portion of our history—the most important of all. Is it not a most extraordinary spectacle that a man should stand up and ask for any confidence in his statements, who sets out as he does with portions of history calling upon the people to believe that it is a true and fair representation, when the leading part, and controlling feature of the whole history, is carefully suppressed.

But the mere leaving out is not the most remarkable feature of this most remarkable essay. His proposition is to establish that the leading men of the revolution were for his great principle of non-intervention by the government in the question of slavery in the territories; while history shows that they decided in the cases actually brought before them, in exactly the contrary way, and he knows it. Not only did they so decide at that time, but they stuck to it during sixty years, through thick and thin, as long as there was one of the revolutionary heroes upon the stage of political action. Through their whole course, from first to last, they clung to freedom. And now he asks the community to believe that the men of the revolution were in favor of his great principle, when we have the naked history that they themselves dealt with this very subject matter of his principle, and utterly repudiated his principle, acting upon a precisely contrary ground. It is as impudent and absurd as if a prosecuting attorney should stand up before a jury, and ask them to convict A as the murderer of B, while B was walking alive before them. [Cheers and laughter.]

I say again, if Judge Douglas asserts that the men of the Revolution acted upon principles by which, to be consistent with themselves, they ought to have adopted his popular sovereignty, then, upon a consideration of his own argument, he had a right to make you believe that they understood the principles of government, but misapplied them—that he has arisen to enlighten the world as to the just application of this principle. He has a right to try to persuade you that he understands their principles better than they did, and therefore he will apply them now, not as they did, but as they ought to have done. He has a right to go before the community, and try to convince them of this; but he has no right to attempt to impose upon any one the belief that these men themselves approved of his great principle. There are two ways of establishing a proposition. One is by trying to demonstrate it upon reason; and the other is, to show that great men in former times have thought so and so, and thus to pass it by the weight of pure authority. Now, if Judge Douglas will demonstrate somehow that this is popular sovereignty—the right of one man to make a slave of another, without any right in that other, or any one else, to object—demonstrate it as Euclid demonstrated propositions—there is no objection. But when he comes forward, seeking to carry a principle by bringing to it the authority of men who themselves utterly repudiate that principle, I ask that he shall not be permitted to do it. [Applause.]

I see, in the Judge's speech here, a short sentence in these words, "Our fathers, when they formed this government under which we live, understood this question just as well and even better than we do now." That is true; I stick to that. (Great cheers and laughter.) I will stand by Judge Douglas in that to the bitter end. (Renewed laughter.) And now, Judge Douglas, come and stand by me, and truthfully show how they acted, understanding it better than we do. All I ask of you, Judge Douglas, is to stick to the proposition that the men of the revolution understood this proposition, that the men of the revolution understood this subject better than we do now, *and with that better understanding they acted better than you are trying to act now.* [Applause and laughter.]

I wish to say something now in regard to the Dred Scott decision, as dealt with by Judge Douglas. In that "memorable debate," between Judge Douglas and myself last year, the Judge thought fit to commence a process of catechising me, and at Freeport I answered his questions, and propounded some to him. Among others propounded to him was one that I have here now. The substance, as I remember it, is, "Can the people of a United States territory, under the Dred Scott decision, in any lawful way, against the wish of any citizen of the United States, exclude slavery from its limits, prior to the formation of a State Constitution?" He answered that they could lawfully exclude slavery from the United States territories, notwithstanding the Dred Scott decision. There was something about that answer that has probably been a trouble to the Judge ever since. [Laughter.]

The Dred Scott decision expressly gives every citizen of the United States a right to carry his slaves into the United States' Territories. And now there was some inconsistency in saying that the decision was right, and saying too, that the people of the Territory could lawfully drive slavery out again. When all the trash, the words, the collateral matter was cleared away from it; all the chaff was fanned out of it, it was a bare absurdity—*no less than a thing may be lawfully driven away from where it has a lawful right to be.* [Cheers and laughter.] Clear it of all the verbiage, and that is the naked truth of his proposition—that a thing may be lawfully driven from the place where it has a lawful right to stay. Well, it was because the Judge couldn't help seeing this, that he has had so much trouble with it; and what I want to ask your especial attention to, just now, is to remind you, if you have not noticed the fact, that the Judge does not any longer say that the people cannot [can?] exclude slavery. He does not say so in the copyright essay; he did not say so in the speech that he made here, and so far as I know, since his re-election to the Senate, he has never said as he did at Freeport, that the people of the Territories can exclude slavery. He desires that you, who wish the Territories to remain free, should believe that he stands by that position, but he does not say it himself. He escapes to some extent the absurd position I have stated by changing his language entirely. What he says now is something different in language, and we will consider whether it is not different in sense too. It is now that the Dred Scott decision, or rather the Constitution under that decision, does not carry slavery into the Territories beyond the power of the people of the Territories *to control it as other property*. He does not say the people can drive it out, but they can control it as other property. The language is different, we should consider whether the sense is different. Driving a horse out of this lot, is too plain a proposition to be mistaken about; it is putting him on the other side of the fence. [Laughter.] Or it might be a sort of exclusion of him from the lot if you were to kill him and let the worms devour him; but neither of these things is the same as "controlling him as other property." That would be to feed him, to pamper him, to ride him, to use and abuse him, to make the most money out of him "as other property"; but, please you, what do the men who are in favor of slavery want more than this? [Laughter and applause.] What do they really want, other than that slavery being in the Territories, shall be controlled as other property. [Renewed applause.]

If they want anything else, I do not comprehend it. I ask your attention to this, first for the purpose of pointing out the change of ground the Judge has made; and, in the second place, the importance of the change—that that change is not such as to give you gentlemen who want his popular sovereignty the power to exclude the institution or drive it out at all. I know the Judge sometimes squints at the argument that in controlling it as other property by unfriendly legislation they may control it to death, as you might in the case of a horse, perhaps, feed him so lightly and ride him so much that he would die. [Cheers and laughter.] But when you come to legislative control, there is something more to be attended to. I have no doubt, myself, that if the people of the territories should undertake to control slave property as other property—that is, control it in such a way that it would be the most valuable as property, and make it bear its just proportion in the way of burdens as property—really deal with it as property—the Supreme Court of the United States will say, "God speed you and amen." But I undertake to give the opinion, at least, that if the territories attempt by any direct legislation to drive the man with his slave out of the territory, or to decide that his slave is free because of his being taken in there, or to tax him to such an extent that he cannot keep him there, the Supreme Court will unhesitatingly decide all such legislation unconstitutional, as long as that Supreme Court is constructed as the Dred Scott Supreme Court is. The first two things they have already decided, except that there is a little quibble among lawyers between the words *dicta* and decision. They have already decided a negro cannot be made free by territorial legislation.

What is that Dred Scott decision? Judge Douglas labors to show that it is one thing, while I think it is altogether different. It is a long opinion, but it is all embodied in this short statement: "The Constitution of the United States forbids Congress to deprive a man of his property, without due process of law; the right of property in slaves is distinctly and expressly affirmed in that Constitution; therefore, if Congress shall undertake to say that a man's slave is no longer his slave, when he crosses a certain line into a territory, that is depriving him of his property without due process of law, and is unconstitutional." There is the whole Dred Scott decision. They add that if Congress cannot do so itself, Congress cannot confer any power to do so, and hence any effort by the Territorial Legislature to do either of these things is absolutely decided against. It is a foregone conclusion by that court.

Now, as to this indirect mode by "unfriendly legislation," all lawyers here will readily understand that such a proposition cannot be tolerated for a moment, because a legislature cannot indirectly do that which it cannot accomplish directly. Then I say any legislation to control this property, as property, for its benefit as property, would be hailed by this Dred Scott Supreme Court, and fully sustained; but any legislation driving slave property out, or destroying it as property, directly or indirectly, will most assuredly, by that court, be held unconstitutional.

Judge Douglas says if the Constitution carries slavery into the territories, beyond the power of the people of the territories to control it as other property, then it follows logically that every one who swears to support the Constitution of the United States, must give that support to that property which it needs. And if the Constitution carries slavery into the territories, beyond the power of the people to control it as other property, then it also carries it into the States, because the Constitution is the supreme law of the land. Now, gentlemen, if it were not for my excessive modesty, I would say that I told that very thing to Judge Douglas quite a year ago. This argument is here in print, and if it were not for my modesty, as I said, I might call your attention to it. If you read it, you will find that I not only made that argument, but made it better than he has made it since. [Laughter.]

There is, however, this difference. I say now, and said then, there is no sort of question that the Supreme Court *has* decided that it is the right of the slaveholder to take his slave and hold him in the territory; and saying this, Judge Douglas himself admits the conclusion. He says if that is so, this consequence will follow; and because this consequence would follow, his argument is, the decision cannot, therefore, be that way—"that would spoil my popular sovereignty, and it cannot be possible that this great principle has been squelched out in the [this?] extraordinary way. It might be, if it were not for the extraordinary consequence of spoiling my humbug." [Cheers and laughter.]

Another feature of the Judge's argument about the Dred Scott case is, an effort to show that that decision deals altogether in declarations of negatives; that the constitution does not affirm anything as expounded by the Dred Scott decision, but it only declares a want of power—a total absence of power, in reference to the territories. It seems to be his purpose to make the whole of that decision to result in a mere negative declaration of a want of power in Congress to do anything in relation to this matter in the territories. I know the opinion of the Judges states that there is a total absence of power; but that is, unfortunately, not all it states; for the Judges add that the right of property in a slave is distinctly and expressly affirmed in the constitution. It does not stop at saying that the right of property in a slave is recognized in the constitution, is declared to exist somewhere in the constitution, but says it is *affirmed* in the constitution. Its language [is?] equivalent to saying that it is embodied and so woven into that instrument that it cannot be detached without breaking the constitution itself. In a word, it is part of the constitution.

Douglas is singularly unfortunate in his effort to make out that decision to be altogether negative, when the express language at the vital part is that this is distinctly affirmed in the Constitution. I think myself, and I repeat it here, that this decision does not merely carry slavery into the Territories, but by its logical conclusion it carries it into the States in which we live. One provision of that Constitution is, that it shall be the supreme law of the land—I do not quote the language—any Constitution or law of any State to the contrary notwithstanding. This Dred Scott decision says that the right of property in a slave is affirmed in that Constitution, which is the supreme law of the land, any State Constitution or law notwithstanding. Then I say that to destroy a thing which is distinctly affirmed and supported by the supreme law of the land, even by a State Constitution or law, is a violation of that supreme law and there is no escape from it. In my judgment there is no avoiding that result, save that the American people shall see that Constitutions are better construed than our Constitution is construed in that decision. They must take care that it is more faithfully and truly carried out than it is there expounded.

I must hasten to a conclusion. Near the beginning of my remarks, I said that this insidious Douglas popular sovereignty is the measure that now threatens the purpose of the Republican party, to prevent slavery from being nationalized in the United States. I propose to ask your attention for a little while to some propositions in affirmance of that statement. Take it just as it stands, and apply it as a principle; extend and apply that principle elsewhere and consider where it will lead you. I now put this proposition that Judge Douglas' popular sovereignty applied will re-open the African slave trade; and I will demonstrate it by any variety of ways in which you can turn the subject or look at it.

The Judge says that the people of the territories have the right, by his principle, to have slaves, if they want them. Then I say that the people of Georgia have the right to buy slaves in Africa, if they want them, and I defy any man on earth to show any distinction between the two things—to show that the one is either more wicked or more unlawful; to show, on original principles, that one is better or worse than the other; or to show by the constitution, that one differs a whit from the other. He will tell me, doubtless, that there is no constitutional provision against people taking slaves into the new territories, and I tell him that there is equally no constitutional provision against buying slaves in Africa. He will tell you that a people, in the exercise of popular sovereignty, ought to do as they please about that thing, and have slaves if they want them; and I tell you that the people of Georgia are as much entitled to popular sovereignty and to buy slaves in Africa, if they want them, as the people of the territory are to have slaves if they want them.

I ask any man, dealing honestly with himself, to point out a distinction.

I have recently seen a letter of Judge Douglas', in which without stating that to be the object, he doubtless endeavors, to make a distinction between the two. He says he is unalterably opposed to the repeal of the laws against the African Slave trade. And why? He then seeks to give a reason that would not apply to his popular sovereignty in the territories. What is that reason? "The abolition of the African slave trade is a compromise of the constitution." I deny it. There is no truth in the proposition that the abolition of the African slave trade is a compromise of the constitution. No man can put his finger on anything in the constitution, or on the line of history which shows it. It is a mere barren assertion, made simply for the purpose of getting up a distinction between the revival of the African slave trade and his "great principle."

At the time the constitution of the United States was adopted it was expected that the slave trade would be abolished. I should assert, and insist upon that, if Judge Douglas denied it. But I know that it was equally expected that slavery would be excluded from the territories and I can show by history, that in regard to these two things, public opinion was exactly alike, while in regard to positive action, there was more done in the Ordinance of '87, to resist the spread of slavery than was ever done to abolish the foreign slave trade. Lest I be misunderstood, I say again that at the time of the formation of the constitution, public expectation was that the slave trade would be abolished, but no more so than the spread of slavery in the territories should be restrained. They stand alike, except that in the Ordinance of '87 there was a mark left by public opinion showing that it was more committed against the spread of slavery in the territories than against the foreign slave trade.

Compromise! What word of compromise was there about it. Why the public sense was then in favor of the abolition of the slave trade; but there was at the time a very great commercial interest involved in it and extensive capital in that branch of trade. There were doubtless the incipient stages of improvement in the South in the way of farming, dependent on the slave trade, and they made a proposition to the Congress to abolish the trade after allowing it twenty years, a sufficient time for the capital and commerce engaged in it to be transferred to other channels. They made no provision that it should be abolished [in?] twenty years; I do not doubt that they expected it would be; but they made no bargain about it. The public sentiment left no doubt in the minds of any that it would be done away. I repeat there is nothing in the history of those times, in favor of that matter being a *compromise* of the Constitution. It was the public expectation at the time, manifested in a thousand ways, that the spread of slavery should also be restricted.

Then I say if this principle is established, that there is no wrong in slavery, and whoever wants it has a right to have it, is a matter of dollars and cents, a sort of question as to how they shall deal with brutes, that between us and the negro here there is no sort of question, but that at the South the question is between the negro and the crocodile. That is all. It is a mere matter of policy; there is a perfect right according to interest to do just as you please—when this is done, where this doctrine prevails, the miners and sappers will have formed public opinion for the slave trade. They will be ready for Jeff. Davis and Stephens and other leaders of that company, to sound the bugle for the revival of the slave trade, for the second Dred Scott decision, for the flood of slavery to be poured over the free States, while we shall be here tied down and helpless and run over like sheep.

It is to be a part and parcel of this same idea, to say to men who want to adhere to the Democratic party, who have always belonged to that party, and are only looking about for some excuse to stick to it, but nevertheless hate slavery, that Douglas' Popular Sovereignty is as good a way as any to oppose slavery. They allow themselves to be persuaded easily in accordance with their previous dispositions, into this belief, that it is about as good a way of opposing slavery as any, and we can do that without straining our old party ties or breaking up old political associations. We can do so without being called negro worshippers. We can do that without being subjected to the jibes and sneers that are so readily thrown out in place of argument where no argument can be found; so let us stick to this Popular Sovereignty—this insidious Popular Sovereignty. Now let me call your attention to one thing that has really happened, which shows this gradual and steady debauching of public opinion, this course of preparation for the revival of the slave trade, for the territorial slave code, and the new Dred Scott decision that is to carry slavery into the free States. Did you ever five years ago, hear of anybody in the world saying that the negro had no share in the Declaration of National Independence; that it did not mean negroes at all; and when "all men" were spoken of negroes were not included?

I am satisfied that five years ago that proposition was not put upon paper by any living being anywhere. I have been unable at any time to find a man in an audience who would declare that he had ever known any body saying so five years ago. But last year there was not a Douglas popular sovereign in Illinois who did not say it. Is there one in Ohio but declares his firm belief that the Declaration of Independence did not mean negroes at all? I do not know how this is; I have not been here much; but I presume you are very much alike everywhere. Then I suppose that all now express the belief that the Declaration of Independence never did mean negroes. I call upon one of them to say that he said it five years ago.

If you think that now, and did not think it then, the next thing that strikes me is to remark that there has been a *change* wrought in you (laughter and applause), and a very significant change it is, being no less than changing the negro, in your estimation, from the rank of a man to that of a brute. They are taking him down, and placing him, when spoken of, among reptiles and crocodiles, as Judge Douglas himself expresses it.

Is not this change wrought in your minds a very important change? Public opinion in this country is everything. In a nation like ours this popular sovereignty and squatter sovereignty have already wrought a change in the public mind to the extent I have stated. There is no man in this crowd who can contradict it.

Now, if you are opposed to slavery honestly, as much as anybody I ask you to note that fact, and the like of which is to follow, to be plastered on, layer after layer, until very soon you are prepared to deal with the negro everywhere as with the brute. If public sentiment has not been debauched already to this point, a new turn of the screw in that direction is all that is wanting; and this is constantly being done by the teachers of this insidious popular sovereignty. You need but one or two turns further until your minds, now ripening under these teachings will be ready for all these things, and you will receive and support, or submit to, the slave trade; revived with all its horrors; a slave code enforced in our territories, and a new Dred Scott decision to bring slavery up into the very heart of the free North. This, I must say, is but carrying out those words prophetically spoken by Mr. Clay, many, many years ago. I believe more than thirty years when he told an audience that if they would repress all tendencies to liberty and ultimate emancipation, they must go back to the era of our independence and muzzle the cannon which thundered its annual joyous return on the Fourth of July; they must blow out the moral lights around us; they must penetrate the human soul and eradicate the love of liberty; but until they did these things, and others eloquently enumerated by him, they could not repress all tendencies to ultimate emancipation.

I ask attention to the fact that in a pre-eminent degree these popular sovereigns are at this work; blowing out the moral lights around us; teaching that the negro is no longer a man but a brute; that the Declaration has nothing to do with him; that he ranks with the crocodile and the reptile; that man, with body and soul, is a matter of dollars and cents. I suggest to this portion of the Ohio Republicans, or Democrats if there be any present, the serious consideration of this fact, that there is now going on among you a steady process of debauching public opinion on this subject. With this my friends, I bid you adieu.

Notes for Speeches at Columbus and Cincinnati, Ohio[1]

[September 16, 17, 1859]

Introduction.

Purpose of the Republican organization.

The Republican party believe there is danger that slavery will be further extended, and ultimately made national in the United States; and to prevent this incidental, and final consummation, is the *purpose* of their organization.

Chief danger to that purpose

A congressional slave code, for the territories, and the revival of the African trade and a second Dred Scott decision, are not, just

[1] AD, DLC-RTL. This manuscript comprising pages 1893-1915 in the Lincoln Papers, under date of September 16, 1859, caused Nicolay and Hay some trouble. In the *Complete Works,* V, 260-81, it is dated December 1-5, 1859, and given the title "Speeches in Kansas." In a footnote Nicolay and Hay explain that "Mr. Lincoln made a visit to Kansas in December, 1859, and made speeches at Elwood, . . . Troy, Doniphan, Atchison, and Leavenworth, Kansas. Among his papers were a number of disconnected sheets of autograph manuscript, which contained internal evidence that they were portions of the addresses made by him on these occasions." Newspaper reports of the speeches made in December (*vide infra*) hardly corroborate the use of these notes at the times indicated, and the speeches made in Ohio in September, on the other hand, do make use of portions of the argument which Nicolay and Hay were correct in identifying as having been prepared for use in Kansas. The obvious solution seems to be that Lincoln prepared a manuscript in February or March, 1859, when he contemplated accepting the invitations extended by Kansas Republicans to speak before their state convention (see letters to Delahay, February 1, March 4, and May 14, *supra*), and finding it impossible to make the trip, preserved the manuscript until September, when he incorporated a few paragraphs in the notes prepared for his speeches at Columbus, September 16, Dayton and Cincinnati, September 17. Upon going to Kansas in December and having used up his earlier Kansas material in Ohio, he prepared new speeches on somewhat different topics for delivery at the places designated (*vide infra*). The several portions of the manuscript have been identified in footnotes, according to the opinion of the editors. The first portion represents notes for the speech at Columbus, September 16.

now, the chief danger to our purpose. These will press us in due time, but they are not quite ready yet—they know that, as yet, we are too strong for them. The insidious Douglas popular sovereignty, which prepares the way for this ultimate danger, it is, which just now constitutes our chief danger.

Popular Sovereignty.

I say Douglas popular sovereignty; for there is a broad distinction between *real* popular Sovereignty and Douglas popular sovereignty. That the nation shall control what concerns it; that a state, or any minor political community, shall control what exclusively concerns it; and that an individual shall control what exclusively concerns him, is a *real* popular sovereignty, which no republican opposes.

But this is not Douglas popular sovereignty. Douglas popular sovereignty, as a matter of principle, simply is "If one man would enslave another, neither that other, nor any third man, has a right to object."

Douglas popular sovereignty, as he practically applies it, is "If any organized political community, however new and small, would enslave men, or forbid their being enslaved within its own teritorial limits; however the doing the one or the other, may affect the men sought to be enslaved, or the vastly superior number of men who are afterwards to come within those limits; or the family of communities of which it is but a member, or the head of that family, as the parent, and common guardian of the whole—however any, or all, these are to be effected, neither any nor all may interfere"

This is Douglas popular sovereignty.

He has great difficulty with it. His speeches and letters, and essays, and explanations, explanatory of explanations explained, upon it, are legion. The most lengthy, and, as I suppose, the most maturely considered, is that recently published in Harper's Magazine. It has too [*sic*] leading objects—the first, to appropriate the authority and reverence, due the great and good men of the revolution, to his popular sovereignty; and secondly, to show that the Dred Scott decision has not entirely squelched his popular sovereignty.

Before considering these main objects, I wish to consider a few minor points of the copy-right essay.

Last year Gov. Seward and myself, at different times and occasions, expressed the opinion that slavery is a durable element of discord, and that we shall not have peace with it, until it either masters, or is mastered by, the free principle. This gave great offence to Judge Douglas; and his denunciations of it, and absurd inferences from it have never ceased. Almost at the very beginning of the copy-right essay he quotes the language respectively of Seward and myself (not quite accurately, but substantially in my case) upon this point, and repeats his absurd and extravagant inference. For lack of time I omit much which I might say here with propriety; and content myself with two remarks only upon this point. The first is that, in asmuch as Douglas, in this very essay, tells us slavery agitation began in this country, in 1699, and has not yet ceased—has lasted through a hundred and sixty years—through ten entire generations of men—it might have occurred to even him that slavery, in its tendency to agitation and discord, has something slightly durable about it. The second remark is that Judge Douglas might have noted, if he would while he was diving so deeply into history—the historical fact that the only comparative peace we have had with slavery during that hundred and sixty years, was in the period from the Revolution to 1820—precisely the period through which we were closing out the African slave-trade, abolishing slavery in several of the states, and restraining the spread of it into new ones, by the ordinance of '87—precisely the period in which the public mind had reason to rest, and did rest, in the belief that slavery was in course of ultimate extinction.

Another point, which for the present I shall touch only hastily, is Judge Douglas' assumption that the states and terrtories differ only in the fact that the States are *in* the Union, and the terrtories are not in it. But if this be the only difference, why not instantly bring the terrtories in? Why keep them out? Do you say they are unfitted for it? What unfits them? Especially what unfits them for any duty in the Union, after they are fit, if they choose, to plant the soil they sparsely inhabit, with slavery, beyond the power of their millions of successors to eradicate it; and to the durable discord of the Union? What function of sovereignty, out of the Union or in it, is so portentous as this? What function of government requires such perfect maturity; in numbers, and everything else, among those who exercise it? It is a concealed assumption of Douglas' popular sovereignty that slavery is a little, harmless, indifferent thing, having no wrong in it, and no power for mischief about it. If all men looked upon it as he does, his policy in regard to it might do. But neither all, nor half the world, so look upon it.

Near the close of the essay Douglas tells us that his popular sovereignty pertains to a people only after they are regularly organized into a political community; and that congress, in it's discretion, must decide when they are fit, in point of numbers, to be so organized. Now I should like for him to point out, in the constitution any clause conferring that discretion upon congress, which, when pointed out, will not be equally a power in congress to govern them, in it's discretion, till they are admitted as a State. Will he try? He intimates that before the exercise of that discretion, their number must be ten, fifteen, or twenty thousand. Well, what is to be done for them, or with them, or by them, before they number ten thousand? If any one of them desires to have slaves, is any other one bound to help him, or at liberty to hinder him? Is it his plan that any time before they reach the required, number, those who are on hand shall be driven out as trespassers? If so, it will probably be a good while before a sufficient number to organize, will get in.

But plainly enough this conceding to congress the discretion as to *when* a community shall be organized, is a total surrender of his popular sovereignty. He says himself it does not pertain to a people until they are organized; and that *when* they shall be organized is in the discretion of congress. Suppose congress shall choose to not organize them, until they are numerous enough to come into the Union as a State. By his own rule, his popular sovereignty is derived from congress, and can not be exercised by the people till congress chooses to confer it. After toiling through nineteen mortal pages of Harper, to show that congress can not keep the people of a new country from excluding slavery, in a single closing paragraph he makes the whole thing depend on congress at last. And should congress refuse to organize, how will that affect the question of planting slavery in a new country? If individuals choose to plant it, the people can not prevent them, for they are not yet clothed with popular sovereignty. If it be said that it can not be planted, in fact, without protective law, that is already falsified by history; for it was originally planted on this continent without protective law.

And, by the way, it is probable that no act of teritorial organization could be passed by the present Senate; and almost certainly not by both the Senate and House of Representatives. If an act declared the right of congress to exclude slavery, the Republicans would vote for it, and both wings of the democracy against it. If it denied the power to either exclude or protect it, the Douglasites would vote for it, and both the Republicans and slave-coders against it. If it denied the power to exclude, and asserted the power to protect, the slave-coders would vote for it, and the Republicans and Douglasites against it.

You are now a part of a people of a teritory,[2] but that teritory is soon to be a state of the Union. Both in your individual, and collective capacities, you have the same interest in the past, the present, and the future, of the United States, as any other portion of the people. Most of you came from the states, and all of you soon will be citizens of the common Union. What I shall now address to you will have neither greater nor less application to you, than to any other people of the nation.

You are gathered, to-day, as a Republican convention—republican, in the party sense, and, as we hope, in the true, original, sense of the word republican.

I assume that Republicans, throughout the nation, believe they are right, and are earnest, and determined in their cause.

Let them, then, keep constantly in view that the chief object of their organization is to prevent the *spread* and *Nationalization*, of Slavery. With this ever distinctly before us we can always better see at what point our cause is most in danger.

We are, as I think, in the present temper, or state of public sentiment, in no danger from the open advocates of a congressional slave-code for the teritories, and of the revival of the African slave-trade. As yet we are strong enough to meet, and master any combination openly formed on those grounds. It is only the insidious position of Douglas, that endangers our cause. That position is simply an ambuscade. By entering into contest with our open enemies, we are to be lured into his train; and then, having lost our own organization, and arms, we are to be turned over to those same open enemies.

Douglas' position leads to the *nationalization* of Slavery as surely as does that of Jeff. Davis and Mason of Virginia. The two positions are but slightly different roads to the same place—with this difference, that the nationalization of slavery *can* be reached by Douglas' route, and never can by the other.

I have said that in our present moral tone and temper, we are strong enough for our open enemies; and so we are. But the chief effect of Douglasism, is to change that tone and temper. Men who support the measures of a political leader do, almost of necessity, adopt the reasoning and sentiments the leader advances in support of them. The reasoning and sentiments advanced by Douglas in support of his policy as to slavery, all spring from the view that

[2] This portion of the manuscript, bearing Lincoln's numbering "2-1, 2-2, 2-3," etc., seems to have been incorporated from an earlier manuscript, probably prepared in February or March, 1859, for the Kansas state Republican convention, and used in part at Chicago, March 1, and Cincinnati, September 17.

slavery is not *wrong*. In the first place he never says it is *wrong*. He says he does not care whether it shall be voted *down* or voted *up*. He says whoever wants slavery has a right to have it. He says the question whether people will have it or not is simply a question of dollars and cents. He says the Almighty has drawn a line across the continent, on *one side* of which the soil *must* be cultivated by slave labor.

Now, let the people of the free-states adopt these sentiments, and they will be unable to see a single reason for maintaining their prohibitions of slavery in their own states. "What! Do you mean to say that anything in these sentiments requires us to believe it will be the *interest* of the Northern states to have slavery?" No. I do mean to say, that although it is not the interest of the Northern states to grow *cotten*, none of them have, or need, any law against it; and it would be tyrany to deprive any *one* man of the previlege to grow cotten in Illinois. There are many individual men in all the free-states who desire to have slaves; and if you admit that slavery is not wrong, it is absolute tyrany to deny them the previlege. It is no just function of government to prohibit what is *not wrong*.

Again, if slavery is right—ordained by the Almighty—on *one side* of a line, dividing sister states of a common Union, then it is positively wrong to harrass, and bedevil the owners of it, with constitutions, and laws, and prohibitions of it, on the other side of the line.

In short, there is no justification for prohibiting slavery anywhere, save only in the assumption that slavery is *wrong*. And whenever the sentiment, that slavery is wrong, shall give way in the North, all legal prohibitions of it will also give way.

If it be insisted that men may support Douglas' measures, without adopting his sentiments, let it be tested by what is actually passing before us. You can, even now, find no Douglas man who will disavow any one of these sentiments; and none but will actually indorse them, if pressed to the point.

Five years ago no living man had placed on record, nor, as I believe, verbally expressed, a denial that negroes have, a share in the Declaration of Independence. Two or three years since Douglas began to deny it; and now every Douglas man in the nation denies it.

To the same effect is the absurdity compounded of *support* to the Dred Scott decision, and *unfriendly* legislation, to Slavery, by the teritories—the absurdity which asserts that a thing may be *lawfully* driven from a place, at which place it has a *lawful* right to remain. That absurd position will not be long maintained by any one. The Dred Scott half of it, will soon master the other half. The process will probably be about this: some terrtorial legislature will adopt *unfriendly legislation;* the Supreme court will decide that legislation to be unconstitutional, and then the advocates of the present "compound[")] absurdity, will acquiesce in the decision. The only effect of that position now is, to prepare it's advocates for such acquiesence when the time comes. Like wood for ox-bows, they are merely being *soaked* in it, preparatory to the bending. The advocates of a slave code are not now strong enough to master us; and they never will be, unless recruits enough to make them so, be tolled in through the gap of Douglasism. Douglas, on the sly, is affecting more for them, than all their open advocates. He has reason to be provoked, that they will not understand him, and recognize him as their best friend. He can not be *more* plain, without being *so* plain, as to lure no one into their trap—so plain, as to lose his power to serve them profitably. Take[3] other instances. Last year *both* Gov. Seward and myself expressed the belief that this government can not endure permanently half-slave and half-free. This gave great offence to Douglas, and after the fall election in Illinois, he became quite rampant upon it. At Chicago, St. Louis, Memphis and New-Orleans, he denounced it as a "*fatal heresy.*" With great pride he claimed that he had crushed it in Illinois, and modestly regretted that he could not have been in New-York to crush it there too. *How* the *heresy* is fatal to any thing, or *what* the *thing* is to which it is fatal, he has never paused to tell us. At all events, it is a fatal heresy in his view *when expressed* by Northern men. Not so, when expressed by men of the South. In 1856, Roger A. Pryor, editor of the Richmond Enquirer, expressed the same belief in that paper—quite two years before it was expressed by either Seward or me. But Douglas perceived no "heresy" in it then—talked not of going to Virginia to crush it out. Nay, more,—he now has that same Mr. Pryor at Washington, editing the "States" newspaper as his especial organ.

This brings us to see that in Douglas' view this opinion is a "fatal heresy" when expressed by men wishing to have the nation all *free;* and is no heresy at all, when expressed by men wishing to have it all *slave.* Douglas has cause to complain that the South will not note this and give him credit for it.

At Memphis Douglas told his audience that he was for the negro against the crocodile, but for the white man against the negro. This

[3] Beginning here, the manuscript is in pencil, the rest of the page having been cut off and another page pasted on the preceding.

was not a sudden thought spontaneously thrown off at Memphis. He said the same thing many times in Illinois last summer and autumn, though I am not sure it was reported then. It is a carefully framed illustration of the estimate he places upon the negro and the manner he would have him dealt with. It is a sort of proposition in proportion. "*As* the negro is to the crocodile, *so* the white man is to the negro." As the negro ought to treat the crocodile as a beast, so the white man ought to treat the negro as a beast. Gentlemen of the South, is not that satisfactory? Will you give Douglas no credit for impressing that sentiment on the Northern mind for your benefit? Why, you should magnify him to the utmost, in order that he may impress it the more deeply, broadly, and surely.[4]

A hope is often expressed that all the elements of opposition to the so-called democracy may unite in the next presidential election; and to favor this, it is suggested that at least *one* candidate on the opposition national ticket, must be resident in the slave states. I strongly sympathize with this hope; and the particular suggestion presents no difficulty with me. There are very many men in the slave states who, *as* men, and statesmen, and patriots, are quite acceptable to me for either President or Vice-President. But there is a difficulty of another sort; and I think it most prudent for us to face that difficulty at once. *Will* those good men of the South occupy any ground upon which we of the free-states *can* vote for them? There's the rub. They seem to labor under a huge mistake in regard to us. They say they are *tired* of slavery *agitation*. We think the slaves, and free white laboring men too, have more reason to be tired of *slavery*, than masters have to be tired of *agitation* about it. In Kentucky a democratic candidate for congress takes ground *against* a congressional slave code for the territories; whereupon his opponent, in full hope to unite with Republicans in 1860, takes ground *in favor* of such slave code. Such hope, under such circumstances, is delusion gross as insanity itself. Rational men can only entertain it, in the strange belief that Republicans are not in earnest for their principles—that they are really devoted to no principle of their own, but are ready for, and anxious to jump to, any position not occupied by the democracy. This mistake must be dispelled. For the sake of their principles, in forming their party, they broke and sacraficed, the strongest mere

[4] The end of section "2." The next portion bears Lincoln's numbering "3-1, 3-2," etc., and was used, together with the remainder of the manuscript at Chicago, March 1, and again at Cincinnati. Although the phraseology is not identical, the several topics may be readily found in the Chicago and Cincinnati speeches.

party ties and advantages which can exist. Republicans believe that slavery is wrong; and they insist, and will continue to insist upon a national policy which recognizes it, and deals with it, *as a wrong*. There *can* be no letting down about this. Simultaneously with such letting down, the republican organization itself would go to pieces, and half it's elements go in a different direction, leaving an easy victory to the common ene[my.] No ingenuity of political trading could possibly hold it together. About this there is no joke, and can be no trifling. Understanding this, that Republicanism can never mix with terrtorial slave-codes, becomes self evident.[5]

In this contest, mere men are nothing. We could come down to Douglas, quite as well, as to any other man standing *with* him; and better than to any other standing below, or beyond him. The simple problem is, will any good and capable man of the South, allow the Republicans to elect him, on their own platform? If such man can be found, I believe the thing can be done. It can be done, in no other way.

But what do *we* gain, say you, by such a union? Certainly not everything; but still *something*, and quite *all* that we, for our lives, can possibly give. In yielding a share of the high honors and offices to you, you gain the assurance that ours is not a mere struggle to secure those honors and offices for one section. You gain the assurance that we mean no *more* than we say in our platforms; else we would not entrust you to execute them. You gain the assurance that we intend no invasion of your rights or your honor, else we would not make one of you the executor of the laws, and commander of the Army and Navy.

As a matter of mere partizan policy, there is no reason *for*, and much *against*, any letting down of the Republican platform in order to form a union with the Southern opposition. By no possibility can a union ticket secure a simple electoral vote in the South, unless the Republican platform be so far let down as to lose every electoral vote in the North; and, even at that, not a single vote would be secured in the South, unless, by bare possibility, those of Maryland.

There is no successful basis of union, but for some good Southern man to allow us of the North to elect him square on *our* platform. Plainly, it is that, or nothing.

The St. Louis Intellig[enc]er is out in favor of a *good man* for

[5] The end of section "3." The next portion is unnumbered and is written in pencil.

President, to be run *without* a platform. Well, I am not wedded to the formal written platform system; but a thousand to one, the editor is not himself in favor of his plan, except with the qualification, that he and his sort, are to select and name the "*good man.*" To bring him to the test, is he willing to take *Seward* without a platform? O, no; Seward's antecedents exclude him, say you. Well, is your *good man,* without antecedents? If he is, how shall the nation know that he is a good man? The sum of the matter is that, in the absence of formal written platforms, the antecedents of candidates become their platforms. On just such platforms, all our earlier and better Presidents were elected; but this by no means facilitates a union of men who differ in principles.

Nor [do I believe][6] we can ever *advance* our *principles,* by supporting *men* who *oppose* our principles. Last year, as you know, we republicans in Illinois, were advised by numerous, and respectable outsiders to re-elect Douglas to the Senate by our votes. I never questioned the motives of such advisers; nor the devotion to the republican cause of such as professed to be republicans. But I never, for a moment, thought of following the advice; and have never yet regretted that we did not follow it. True, Douglas is back in the Senate in spite of us; but we are *clear* of *him,* and *his* principles; and, we are uncrippled and ready to fight both him and them straight along till they shall be finally "closed out." Had we followed the advice, there would now be no Republican party in Illinois, and none, to speak of, anywhere else. The whole thing would now be floundering along after Douglas, upon the Dred Scott and crocodile theory. It would have been the grandest "*haul*" for slavery, ever yet made. Our principles [would][7] still live, and ere long would produce a party; but we should have lost all our past *labor,* and twenty years of *time,* by the folly.

Take an illustration. About a year ago, all the republicans in congress voted for what was called the Crittenden-Montgomery-bill; and forthwith Douglas claimed, and still claims, that they were all committed to his "gur-reat pur-rinciple." And republicans have been so far embarrassed by the claim, that they have ever since been protesting that they were not so committed, and trying to explain why. Some of the very newspapers which advised Douglas' return to the Senate by republican votes, have been largely and continuously engaged in these protests, and explanations. For such, let us state a question in the Rule of Three. If voting for the Crittenden-Montgomery bill, entangle the republicans with Doug-

[6] Manuscript torn; restorations taken from the *Complete Works.*

[7] Restoration taken from the *Complete Works.*

las' dogmas for one year, how long would voting for Douglas himself, so entangle, them?

It is nothing to the contrary, that republicanism gained something by electing Haskin, Hickman, and Davis.[8] They were comparatively *small* men. I mean no disrespect; they may have large merit; but Republicans can dally with them, and absorb, or expel them, at pleasure. If they dally with Douglas, he absorbs them.

We[9] want, and must have, a national policy, as to slavery, which deals with it as being a wrong. Whoever would prevent slavery becoming national and perpetual, yields all when he yields to a policy which treats it either as being *right*, or as being a matter of indifference.

We admit that the U.S. general government is not charged with the duty of redressing, or preventing, all the wrongs in the world. But that government rightfully may, and, subject to the constitution, ought to, redress and prevent, all wrongs, which are wrongs to the nation itself. It is expressly charged with the duty of providing for the general welfare. We think slavery impairs, and endangers the general welfare. Those who do not think this are not of us, and we can not argue with them. We must shape our own course by our own judgment.

We must not disturb slavery in the states where it exists, because the constitution, and the peace of the country, both forbid us. We must not withhold an efficient fugitive slave law, because the constitution demands it.

But we must, by a national policy, prevent the spread of slavery into new territories, or free states, because the constitution does not forbid us, and the general welfare does demand such prevention. We must prevent the revival of the African slave trade, because the constitution does not forbid us, and the general welfare does require the prevention. We must prevent these things being done by either *congresses* or *courts*. The people—the people—are the rightful masters of both congresses, and courts—not to overthrow the constitution, but to overthrow the *men* who pervert it.

To effect our main object, we have to employ auxiliary means. We must hold conventions, adopt platforms, select candidates, and

[8] Representatives John B. Haskin of New York, John Hickman of Pennsylvania, and John G. Davis of Indiana, anti-Lecompton Democrats.

[9] The last portion of the manuscript begins here. In addition to the draft of this portion which furnishes the text (pp. 1913-15 in the Lincoln Papers), there is a first draft of this portion (pp. 1894-95) with numerous revisions, which in common with section "2" seems to be part of the earlier manuscript prepared in February or March for use in Kansas, and here revised for use at Cincinnati.

carry elections. At every step we must be true to the main purpose. If we adopt a platform, falling short of our principle, or elect a man rejecting our principle, we not only take nothing affirmative by our success; but we draw upon us the positive embarrassment of seeming ourselves to have abandoned our principle.

That our principle, however baffled, or delayed, will finally triumph, I do not permit myself to doubt. Men will pass away—die—die, politically, and naturaly; but the principle will live, and live forever. Organizations, rallied around that principle, may, by their own dereliction, go to pieces, thereby losing all their time and labor. But the principle will remain, and will reproduce another, and another, till the final triumph will come.

But to bring it *soon*, we must save our labor already performed—our organization, which has cost so much time and toil to create. We must keep our principle constantly in view, and never be false to it.

And as to men, for leaders, we must remember that "He that is not *for* us, is against us; and he that gathereth not with us scattereth."

Speech at Dayton, Ohio[1]

September 17, 1859

Mr. Lincoln directed the greater part of his speech to demonstrate the falsity of the assumption contained in the question in Senator Douglas' Magazine essay, by which he seeks to make the framers of this government consider slavery a desirable feature in the material out of which the Union was formed.

Mr. Lincoln met this assumption by a condensed statement of the facts in the history of the government, going to show that the framers of the government found slavery existing when the constitution was formed, and got along with it as well as they could in accomplishing the Union of the States, contemplating and expecting the advent of the period when slavery in the United States should no longer exist.

He referred to the limitation of the time for the continuance of the slave trade, by which the supply of slaves should be cut off—to the fact that the word slave does not occur in the constitution, for the reason given at the period of its formation, that when, in after times, slavery should cease to exist, no one should know from the language of the constitution itself, that slavery had ever existed in the United States. We cannot attempt to follow Mr. Lincoln in his statement of facts and arguments in exposing the false assumption of Senator Douglas, but Mr. L. showed conclusively that instead of *desiring* that we should have a Union made up of free and slave States, as a sort of happy admixture of political elements, the framers of our government regarded the removal of slavery as only a question of time, and that at some day, not far distant, the people among whom it existed would get rid of it.

Mr. Lincoln referred to the assertion of Mr. Douglas that the ordinance of 1787 had never made a free State, and that Ohio had been made free *solely* by the action of its own people. Mr. Lincoln spoke of the difficulty of getting rid of slavery wherever it gained a foothold. He spoke of the trouble which encompassed the formation of a free constitution in a territory where there were slaves held as property, and attributed the untrammelled action of the Convention which framed the constitution of Ohio in 1802 to the fact, that the Ordinance of 1787 had prohibited the ingress of slaves, and so had relieved the question of a free constitution of all embarrassment.

In connection with the action of the people of Ohio, Mr. Lincoln referred to what is said of the influence of climate and soil in inviting slave labor to agricultural pursuits. He contended that the soil and climate of Ohio were just as favorable to the employment of slave labor as were the soil and climate of Kentucky. And yet without the Ordinance of 1787 Kentucky was made a slave State, and with the Ordinance Ohio was made a free State.

Mr. Lincoln closed with an eloquent defence of the rights of free labor.[2] The free white men had a right to claim that the new territories into which they and their children might go to seek a livelihood should be preserved free and clear of the incumbrance of slavery, and that no laboring white man should be placed in a position where, by the introduction of slavery into the territories, he would be compelled to toil by the side of a slave.

[1] Dayton *Journal*, September 19, 1859. This is the most complete report available. The summary in the Dayton *Empire*, September 19, 1859, agrees essentially with the *Journal* report, and both indicate that Lincoln covered much of the same ground as in the preceding speech at Columbus and added a conclusion which he also used at Cincinnati. Lincoln also spoke briefly at Hamilton, Ohio, on his way from Dayton to Cincinnati (Daniel G. Ryan, *Lincoln and Ohio*, 1923), but no contemporary newspaper report is available.

[2] This portion of the Dayton speech was repeated at Cincinnati, *infra*

Speech at Cincinnati, Ohio[1]

September 17, 1859

My fellow-citizens of the State of Ohio: This is the first time in my life that I have appeared before an audience in so great a city as this. I therefore—though I am no longer a young man—make this appearance under some degree of embarrassment. But, I have found that when one is embarrassed, usually the shortest way to get through with it is to quit talking or thinking about it, and go at something else. (Applause.)

WHAT DID DOUGLAS SAY?

I understand that you have had recently with you, my very distinguished friend, Judge Douglas, of Illinois, (laughter) and I understand, without having had an opportunity, (not greatly sought to be sure,) of seeing a report of the speech, that he made here, that he did me the honor to mention my humble name. I suppose that he did so for the purpose of making some objection to some sentiment at some time expressed by me. I should expect, it is true, that Judge Douglas had reminded you, or informed you, if you had never before heard it, that I had once in my life declared it as my opinion that this government cannot "endure permanently half slave and half free; that a house divided against itself cannot stand," and, as I had expressed it, I did not expect the house to fall; that I did not expect the Union to be dissolved; but, that I did expect that it would cease to be divided; that it would become all one thing or all the other, that either the opponents of Slavery would arrest the further spread of it, and place it where the public mind would rest in the belief that it was in the course of ultimate extinction; or the friends of Slavery will push it forward until it becomes alike lawful in all the States, old or new, Free as well as Slave. I did, fifteen months ago, express that opinion, and upon many occasions Judge Douglas has denounced it, and has greatly, intentionally or unintentionally, misrepresented my purpose in the expression of that opinion.

I presume, without having seen a report of his speech, that he did so here. I presume that he alluded also to that opinion in dif-

[1] *Illinois State Journal*, October 7, 1859. On October 6 the *Journal* announced that Lincoln had corrected his Cincinnati speech and that it would appear the next day. Presumably Lincoln used the text of the Cincinnati *Gazette*, September 19, 1859, since the *Journal* follows the *Gazette* closely except for the extensive revisions. There are, however, a number of errors of omission in the *Journal* which have been corrected with reference to the *Gazette*, and all typographical errors have been corrected by the editors. Brackets are in the source unless otherwise noted.

ferent language, having been expressed at a subsequent time by Governor Seward of New York, and that he took the two in a lump and denounced them; that he tried to point out that there was something couched in this opinion which led to the making of an entire uniformity of the local institutions of the various States of the Union, in utter disregard of the different States, which in their nature would seem to require a variety of institutions, and a variety of laws, conforming to the differences in the nature of the different States.

Not only so; I presume he insisted that this was a declaration of war between the Free and Slave States—that it was the sounding to the onset of continual war between the different States, the Slave and Free States.

This charge, in this form, was made by Judge Douglas on, I believe, the 9th of July, 1858, in Chicago, in my hearing. On the next evening, I made some reply to it. I informed him that many of the inferences he drew from that expression of mine were altogether foreign to any purpose entertained by me, and in so far as he should ascribe those inferences to me, as my purpose, he was entirely mistaken; and in so far as he might argue that whatever might be my purpose, actions, conforming to my views, would lead to these results, he might argue and establish if he could; but, so far as purposes were concerned, he was totally mistaken as to me.

When I made that reply to him—when I told him, on the question of declaring war between the different States of the Union, that I had not said I did not expect any peace upon this question until Slavery was exterminated; that I had only said I expected peace when that institution was put where the public mind should rest in the belief that it was in course of ultimate extinction; that I believed from the organization of our government, until a very recent period of time, the institution had been placed and continued upon such a basis; that we had had comparative peace upon that question through a portion of that period of time, only because the public mind rested in that belief in regard to it, and that when we returned to that position in relation to that matter, I supposed we should again have peace as we previously had. I assured him, as I now assure you, that I neither then had, nor have, or ever had, any purpose in any way of interfering with the institution of Slavery, where it exists. [Long continued applause.] I believe we have no power, under the Constitution of the United States; or rather under the form of government under which we live, to interfere with the institution of Slavery, or any other of the institutions of our sister States, be they Free or Slave States. [Cries of "Good," and applause.] I declared then and I now re-declare, that I have as little inclination to so interfere with the institution of Slavery where it now exists, through the instrumentality of the general Government, or any other instrumentality, as I believe we have no power to do so. [A voice—"You're right."] I accidentally used this expression: I had no purpose of entering into the Slave States to disturb the institution of Slavery! So, upon the first occasion that Judge Douglas got an opportunity to reply to me, he passed by the whole body of what I had said upon that subject, and seized upon the particular expression of mine, that I had no purpose of entering into the Slave States to disturb the institution of Slavery! "Oh, no," said he, "he (Lincoln) won't enter into the Slave States to disturb the institution of Slavery; he is too prudent a man to do such a thing as that; he only means that he will go on to the line between the Free and Slave States, and shoot over at them. [Laughter.] This is all he means to do. He means to do them all the harm he can, to disturb them all he can, in such a way as to keep his own hide in perfect safety." [Laughter.]

OPPORTUNITY TO SHOOT ACROSS THE LINE.

Well, now, I did not think, at that time, that that was either a very dignified or very logical argument; but so it was, I had to get along with it as well as I could.

It has occurred to me here to-night, that if I ever do shoot over the line at the people on the other side of the line into a Slave State, and purpose to do so, keeping my skin safe, that I have now about the best chance I shall ever have. [Laughter and applause.] I should not wonder that there are some Kentuckians about this audience; we are close to Kentucky; and whether that be so or not, we are on elevated ground, and by speaking distinctly, I should not wonder if some of the Kentuckians would hear me on the other side of the river. [Laughter.] For that reason I propose to address a portion of what I have to say to the Kentuckians.

INTRODUCING HIMSELF TO KENTUCKIANS.

I say, then, in the first place, to the Kentuckians, that I am what they call, as I understand it, a "Black Republican." (Applause and laughter.) I think Slavery is wrong, morally, and politically. I desire that it should be no further spread in these United States, and I should not object if it should gradually terminate in the whole Union. (Applause.) While I say this for myself, I say to you, Kentuckians, that I understand you differ radically with me upon this proposition; that you believe Slavery is a good thing; that Slavery is right; that it ought to be extended and perpetuated in this Union. Now, there being this broad difference between us, I do not pretend in addressing myself to you, Kentuckians, to attempt proselyting you; that would be a vain effort. I do not enter upon it. I only propose to try to show you that you ought to nominate for the next Presidency, at Charleston, my distinguished friend Judge Douglas. [Applause.] In all that there is a difference between you and him, I understand he is as sincerely for you, and more wisely for you, than you are for yourselves. [Applause.] I will try to demonstrate that proposition. Understand now, I say that I believe he is as sincerely for you, and more wisely for you, than you are for yourselves.

ADVOCATES THE "GIANT'S CLAIMS."

What do you want more than anything else to make successful your views of Slavery,—to advance the outspread of it, and to secure and perpetuate the nationality of it? What do you want more than anything else? What is needed absolutely? What is indispensable to you? Why! if I may be allowed to answer the question, it is to retain a hold upon the North—it is to retain support and strength from the Free States. If you can get this support and strength from the Free States, you can succeed. If you do not get this support and this strength from the Free States, you are in the minority, and you are beaten at once.

If that proposition be admitted,—and it is undeniable, then the next thing I say to you, is that Douglas of all the men in this nation is the only man that affords you any hold upon the Free States; that no other man can give you any strength in the Free States. This being so, if you doubt the other branch of the proposition, whether he is for you—whether he is really for you as I have expressed it, I propose asking your attention for awhile to a few facts.

The issue between you and me, understand, is that I think Slavery is wrong, and ought not to be outspread, and you think it is right and ought to be extended and perpetuated. (A voice, "oh, Lord.") That is my Kentuckian I am talking to now. (Applause.)

I now proceed to try to show you that Douglas is as sincerely for you and more wisely for you than you are for yourselves.

DOUGLAS AT THE WORK OF THE SOUTH.

In the first place we know that in a Government like this, in a Government of the people, where the voice of all the men of the country, substantially enter into the execution,—or administration rather—of the Government—in such a Government, what lies at the bottom of all of it, is public opinion. I lay down the proposition, that Douglas is not only the man that promises you in advance a hold upon the North, and support in the North, but that he constantly moulds public opinion to your ends; that in every possible way he can, he constantly moulds the public opinion of the North to your ends; and if there are a few things in which he seems to be against you—a few things which he says that appear to be against you, and a few that he forbears to say which you would like to have him say—you ought to remember that the saying of the one, or the forbearing to say the other, would loose his hold upon the North, and, by consequence, would lose his capacity to serve you. (A Voice, "That is so.")

Upon this subject of moulding public opinion, I call your attention to the fact—for a well-established fact it is—that the Judge never says your institution of Slavery is wrong; he never says it is right, to be sure, but he never says it is wrong. [Laughter.] There is not a public man in the United States, I believe, with the exception of Senator Douglas, who has not, at some time in his life, declared his opinion whether the thing is right or wrong; but, Senator Douglas never declares it is wrong. He leaves himself at perfect liberty to do all in your favor which he would be hindered from doing if he were to declare the thing to be wrong. On the contrary, he takes all the chances that he has for inveigling the sentiment of the North, opposed to Slavery, into your support, by never saying it is right. [Laughter.] This you ought to set down to his credit. [Laughter.] You ought to give him full credit for this much, little though it be, in comparison to the whole which he does for you.

SEE-SAW.

Some other things I will ask your attention to. He said upon the floor of the United States Senate, and he has repeated it as I understand, a great many times, that he does not care whether Slavery is "voted up or voted down." This again shows you, or ought to show you, if you would reason upon it, that he does not believe it to be wrong, for a man may say, when he sees nothing wrong in a thing, that he does not care whether it be voted up or voted down, but no man can logically say that he cares not whether a thing goes up or goes down, which to him appears to be wrong. You therefore have a demonstration in this, that to Douglas' mind your favorite institution which you would have spread out, and made perpetual, is no wrong.

THE ALMIGHTY'S DIVIDING LINE.

Another thing he tells you, in a speech made at Memphis in Tennessee, shortly after the canvass in Illinois, last year. He there distinctly told the people, that there was a "line drawn by the Almighty across this continent, on the one side of which the soil must always be cultivated by slaves," that he did not pretend to know exactly where that line was, [laughter and applause,] but that there was such a line. I want to ask your attention to that proposition again; that there is one portion of this continent where the Almighty has designed the soil shall always be cultivated by slaves; that its being cultivated by slaves at that place is right; that it has the direct sympathy and authority of the Almighty. Whenever you can get these Northern audiences to adopt the opinion that Slavery is right on the other side of the Ohio; whenever you can get them, in pursuance of Douglas' views, to adopt that sentiment, they will very readily make the other argument, which is perfectly logical, that that which is right on that side of the Ohio, cannot be wrong on this, [laughter;] and that if you have that property on that side of the Ohio, under the seal and stamp of the Almighty, when by any means it escapes over here, it is wrong to have constitutions and laws, "to devil" you about it. So Douglas is moulding the public opinion of the North, first to say that the thing is right in your State over the Ohio river, and hence to say that that which is right there is not wrong here, [at this moment the cannon was fired; to the great injury of sundry panes of glass in the vicinity,] and that all laws and constitutions here, recognizing it as being wrong, are themselves wrong, and ought to be repealed and abrogated. He will tell you, men of Ohio, that if you choose here to have laws against Slavery it is in conformity to the idea that your climate is not suited to it, that your climate is not suited to slave labor, and therefore you have constitutions and laws against it.

Let us attend to that argument for a little while and see if it be sound. You do not raise sugar cane—[except the new fashioned sugar cane, and you won't raise that long] but they do raise it in Louisiana. You don't raise it in Ohio because you can't raise it profitably, because the climate don't suit it. [Here again the cannon interrupted. Its report was followed by another fall of window glass.] They do raise it in Louisiana because there it is profitable. Now, Douglas will tell you that is precisely the Slavery question. That they do have slaves there because they are profitable, and you don't have them here because they are not profitable. If that is so, then it leads to dealing with the one precisely as with the other. Is there then anything in the Constitution or laws of Ohio against raising sugar cane? Have you found it necessary to put any such provision in your law? Surely not! No man desires to raise sugar cane in Ohio; but, if any man did desire to do so, you would say it was a tyrannical law that forbid his doing so, and whenever you shall agree with Douglas, whenever your minds are brought to adopt his argument, as surely you will have reached the conclusion, that although Slavery is not profitable in Ohio, if any man wants it, it is wrong to him not to let him have it.

In this matter Judge Douglas is preparing the public mind for you of Kentucky, to make perpetual that good thing in your estimation, about which you and I differ.

THE CHANGES IN FIVE YEARS.

In this connection let me ask your attention to another thing. I believe it is safe to assert that five years ago, no living man had expressed the opinion that the negro had no share in the Declaration of Independence. Let me state that again: five years ago no living man had expressed the opinion that the negro had no share in the Declaration of Independence. If there is in this large audience any man who ever knew of that opinion being put upon paper as much as five years ago, I will be obliged to him now or at a subsequent time to show it.

If that be true I wish you then to note the next fact; that within the space of five years Senator Douglas, in the argument of this question, has got his entire party, so far as I know, without exception, to join in saying that the negro has no share in the Declaration of Independence. If there be now in all these United States, one Douglas man that does not say this, I have been unable upon any occasion to scare him up. Now if none of you said this five years ago, and all of you say it now, that is a matter that you Kentuckians ought to note. That is a vast change in the Northern public sentiment upon that question.

Of what tendency is that change? The tendency of that change is to bring the public mind to the conclusion that when men are spoken of, the negro is not meant; that when negroes are spoken of, brutes alone are contemplated. That change in public sentiment has already degraded the black man in the estimation of Douglas and his followers from the condition of a man of some sort, and assigned him to the condition of a brute. Now, you Kentuckians ought to give Douglas credit for this. That is the largest possible stride that can be made in regard to the perpetuation of your thing of Slavery.

A VOICE—"Speak to Ohio men, and not to Kentuckians!"

MR. LINCOLN—I beg permission to speak as I please. (Laughter.)

THE BIBLE THEORY.

In Kentucky, perhaps, in many of the Slave States certainly, you are trying to establish the rightfulness of Slavery by reference to the Bible. You are trying to show that slavery existed in the Bible times by Divine ordinance. Now Douglas is wiser than you, for your own benefit, upon that subject. Douglas knows that whenever you establish that Slavery was right by the Bible, it will occur that that Slavery was the Slavery of the *white* man—of men without reference to color—and he knows very well that you may entertain that idea in Kentucky as much as you please, but you will never win any Northern support upon it. He makes a wiser argument for you; he makes the argument that the slavery of the *black* man, the slavery of the man who has a skin of a different color from your own, is right. He thereby brings to your support Northern voters who could not for a moment be brought by your own argument of the Bible-right of slavery. Will you not give him credit for that? Will you not say that in this matter he is more wisely for you than you are for yourselves.

Now having established with his entire party this doctrine—having been entirely successful in that branch of his efforts in your behalf; he is ready for another.

A SUM IN THE RULE OF THREE.

At this same meeting at Memphis, he declared that while in all contests between the negro and the white man, he was for the white man, but that in all questions between the negro and the crocodile he was for the negro. (Laughter.) He did not make that declaration accidentally at Memphis. He made it a great many times in the canvass in Illinois last year, (though I don't know that it was reported in any of his speeches there,) but he frequently made it. I believe he repeated it at Columbus, and I should not wonder if he repeated it here. It is, then, a deliberate way of expressing himself upon that subject. It is a matter of mature deliberation with him thus to express himself upon that point of his case. It therefore requires some deliberate attention.

The first inference seems to be that if you do not enslave the negro you are wronging the white man in some way or other, and that whoever is opposed to the negro being enslaved is in some way or other against the white man. Is not that a falsehood? If there was a necessary conflict between the white man and the negro, I should be for the white man as much as Judge Douglas; but I say there is no such necessary conflict. I say that there is room enough for us all to be free, (loud manifestations of applause,) and that it not only does not wrong the white man that the negro should be free, but it positively wrongs the mass of the white men that the negro should be enslaved; that the mass of white men are really injured by the effect of slave labor in the vicinity of the fields of their own labor. (Applause.)

But I do not desire to dwell upon this branch of the question more than to say that this assumption of his is false, and I do hope that that fallacy will not long prevail in the minds of intelligent white men. At all events, you Kentuckians ought to thank Judge Douglas for it. It is for your benefit it is made.

The other branch of it is, that in a struggle between the negro and the crocodile, he is for the negro. Well, I don't know that there is any struggle between the negro and the crocodile, either. (Laughter.) I suppose that if a crocodile (or as we old Ohio river boatmen used to call them, alligators) should come across a white man, he would kill him if he could, and so he would a negro. But what, at last, is this proposition? I believe it is a sort of proposition in proportion, which may be stated thus: As the negro is to the white man, so is the crocodile to the negro, and as the negro may rightfully treat the crocodile as a beast or reptile, so the white man may rightfully treat the negro as a beast or a reptile. (Applause.) That is really the "knip" of all that argument of his.

Now, my brother Kentuckians, who believe in this, you ought to thank Judge Douglas for having put that in a much more taking way than any of yourselves have done. (Applause.)

THE "GREAT PRINCIPLE."

Again, Douglas' *great principle*, "Popular Sovereignty," as he calls it, gives you, by natural consequence, the revival of the Slave-trade whenever you want it. If you question this, listen a while, consider a while, what I shall advance in support of that proposition.

He says that it is the sacred right of the man who goes into the Territories, to have Slavery if he wants it. Grant that for argument's sake. Is it not the sacred right of the man that don't go there equally to buy slaves in Africa, if he wants them? Can you point out the difference? The man who goes into the Territories of Kansas and Nebraska, or any other new Territory, with the sacred right of taking a slave there which belongs to him, would certainly have no more right to take one there than I would who own no slave, but who would desire to buy one and take him there. You will not say—you, the friends of Douglas—but that the man who does not own a slave, has an equal right to buy one and take him to the Territory, as the other does?

A VOICE. "I want to ask a question. Don't foreign nations interfere with the Slave-trade?"

MR. LINCOLN. Well! I understand it to be a principle of Democracy to whip foreign nations whenever they interfere with us. (Laughter and applause.)

VOICE. "I only asked for information. I am a Republican myself."

MR. LINCOLN. You and I will be on the best terms in the world, but I do not wish to be diverted from the point I was trying to press.

I say that Douglas' Popular Sovereignty, establishing a sacred right in the people, if you please, if carried to its logical conclusion, gives equally the sacred right to the people of the States or the Territories themselves to buy slaves, wherever they can buy them cheapest; and if any man can show a distinction, I should like to hear him try it. If any man can show how the people of Kansas have a better right to slaves because they want them, than the people of Georgia have to buy them in Africa, I want him to do it. I think it cannot be done. If it is "Popular Sovereignty" for the people to have slaves because they want them, it is Popular Sovereignty for them to buy them in Africa, because they desire to do so.

A CHAPTER ON COMPROMISES.

I know that Douglas has recently made a little effort—not seeming to notice that he had a different theory—has made an effort to get rid of that. He has written a letter addressed to somebody, I believe, who resides in Iowa, declaring his opposition to the repeal of the laws that prohibit the African Slave Trade. He bases his opposition to such repeal upon the ground that these laws are themselves one of the compromises of the Constitution of the United States. Now it would be very interesting to see Judge Douglas or any of his friends turn to the Constitution of the United States and point out that compromise, to show where there is any compromise in the Constitution or provision in the Constitution, express or implied, by which the Administrators of that Constitution are under any obligation to repeal the African Slave-trade. I know, or at least I think I know, that the framers of that Constitution did expect that the African Slave-trade would be abolished at the end of twenty years, to which time their prohibition against its being abolished extended. I think there is abundant contemporaneous history to show that the framers of the Constitution expected it to be abolished. But while they so expected, they gave nothing for that expectation, and they put no provision in the Constitution requiring it should be so abolished. The migration or importation of such persons as the States shall see fit to admit shall not be prohibited, but a certain tax might be levied upon such importation. But what was to be done after that time? The Constitution is as silent about that, as it is silent personally about myself. There is absolutely nothing in it about that subject—there is only the expectation of the framers of the Constitution that the Slave-trade would be abolished at the end of that time and they expected it would be abolished, owing to public sentiment, before that time, and they put that provision in, in order that it should not be abolished before that time, for reasons which I suppose they thought to be sound ones, but which I will not now try to enumerate before you.

But while they expected the Slave-trade would be abolished at that time, they expected that the spread of Slavery into the new Territories should also be restricted. It is as easy to prove that the framers of the Constitution of the United States, expected that Slavery should be prohibited from extending into the new Territories, as it is to prove that it was expected that the Slave-trade should be abolished. Both these things were expected. One was no more expected than the other, and one was no more a compromise of the Constitution than the other. There was nothing said in the Constitution in regard to the spread of Slavery into the Territory. I grant that, but there was something very important said about it by the same generation of men in the adoption of the old Ordinance of '87, through the influence of which you here in Ohio, our neighbors in Indiana, we in Illinois, our neighbors in Michigan and Wisconsin are happy, prosperous, teeming millions of free men. (Continued applause.) That generation of men, though not to the full extent members of the Convention that framed the Constitution, were to some extent members of that Convention, holding seats, at the same time in one body and the other, so that if there was any compromise on either of these subjects, the strong evidence is that that compromise was in favor of the restriction of Slavery from the new territories.

But Douglas says that he is unalterably opposed to the repeal of those laws; because, in his view, it is a compromise of the Constitution. You Kentuckians, no doubt, are somewhat offended with that! You ought not to be! You ought to be patient! You ought to know that if he said less than that, he would lose the power of "lugging" the Northern States to your support. Really, what you would push him to do would take from him his entire power to serve you. And you ought to remember how long, by precedent, Judge Douglas holds himself obliged to stick by compromises. You ought to remember that by the time you yourselves think you are ready to inaugurate measures for the revival of the African Slave-trade that sufficient time will have arrived by precedent, for Judge Douglas to break through that compromise. He says now nothing more strong than he said in 1849 when he declared in favor of the Missouri Compromise—that precisely four years and a quarter after he declared that compromise to be a sacred thing, which "no ruthless hand would ever dare to touch," he, himself, brought forward the measure, ruthlessly to destroy it. (A voice—"hit him again!" Applause.) By a mere calculation of time it will only be four years more until he is ready to take back his profession about the sacredness of the Compromise abolishing the slave trade. Precisely as soon as you are ready to have his services in that direction, by fair calculation you may be sure of having them. (Applause and laughter.)

UNFRIENDLY LEGISLATION.

But you remember and set down to Judge Douglas' debit, or discredit, that he, last year, said the people of the Territories can, in spite of the Dred Scott decision, exclude your slaves from those territories; that he declared by "unfriendly legislation," the extension of your property into the new Territories may be cut off in the teeth of the decision of the Supreme Court of the United States.

He assumed that position at Freeport on the 27th of August, 1858. He said that the people of the Territories can exclude Slavery in so many words. You ought, however, to bear in mind that he has never said it since. (Laughter.) You may hunt in every speech that he has since made, and he has never used that expression once. He has never seemed to notice that he is stating his views differently from what he did then; but, by some sort of accident, he has always really stated it differently. He has always since then declared that "the Constitution does not carry Slavery into the Territories of the United States beyond the power of the people legally to control it, as other property." Now, there is a difference in the language used upon that former occasion and in this latter day. There may or may not be a difference in the meaning, but it is worth while considering whether there is not also a difference in meaning.

What is it to exclude? Why, it is to drive it out. It is in some way to put it out of the Territory. It is to force it across the line, or change its character, so that as property it is out of existence. But what is the controlling of it "as other property?" Is controlling it as other property the same thing [as][2] destroying it, or driving it away? I should think not. I should think the controlling of it as other property would be just about what you in Kentucky should want. I understand the controlling of property means the controlling of it for the benefit of the owner of it. While I have no doubt the Supreme Court of the United States would say "God speed" to any of the Territorial legislatures that should thus control slave property, they would sing quite a different tune if by the pretense of controlling it they were to undertake to pass laws which virtually excluded it, and that upon a very well known principle to all lawyers, that what a legislature cannot directly do, it cannot do by indirection; that as, the legislature has not the power to drive slaves out, they have no power by indirection, by tax or by imposing burdens in any way on that property, to effect the same end, and that any attempt to do so would be held by the Dred Scott Court unconstitutional.

Douglas is not willing to stand by his first proposition that they can exclude it, because we have seen that that proposition amounts to nothing more nor less than the naked absurdity, that you may lawfully drive out that which has a lawful right to remain. He admitted at first that the slave might be lawfully taken into the Territories under the Constitution of the United States, and yet asserted that he might be lawfully driven out. That being the proposition, it is the absurdity I have stated. He is not willing to stand in the face of that direct, naked and impudent absurdity; he has, therefore, modified his language into that of being "*controlled as other property*."

SWEARING BY THE COURTS.

The Kentuckians don't like this in Douglas! I will tell you where it will go. He now swears by the Court. He was once a leading man in Illinois to break down a Court, because it had made a decision he did not like. But he now not only swears by the Court, the

[2] This passage was considerably revised by Lincoln, and an "as" became lost in the process.

courts having got to working for you, but he denounces all men that do not swear by the Courts, as unpatriotic, as bad citizens. When one of these acts of unfriendly legislation shall impose such heavy burdens as to, in effect, destroy property in slaves in a Territory and show plainly enough that there can be no mistake in the purpose of the Legislature to make them so burdensome, this same Supreme Court will decide that law to be unconstitutional, and he will be ready to say for your benefit, "I swear by the Court; I give it up;" and while that is going on he has been getting all his men to swear by the Courts, and to give it up with him. In this again he serves you faithfully, and as I say, more wisely than you serve yourselves.

A WORD ABOUT PATRIOTIC SPEECHES.

Again! I have alluded in the beginning of these remarks to the fact, that Judge Douglas has made great complaint of my having expressed the opinion that this Government "cannot endure permanently half slave and half free." He has complained of Seward for using different language, and declaring that there is an "irrepressible conflict" between the principles of free and slave labor.

(A voice—"He says it is not original with Seward. That is original with Lincoln.")

I will attend to that immediately, sir. Since that time, Hickman,[3] of Pennsylvania expressed the same sentiment. He has never denounced Mr. Hickman: why? There is a little chance, notwithstanding, that opinion in the mouth of Hickman, that he may yet be a Douglas man. That is the difference! It is not unpatriotic to hold that opinion, if a man is a Douglas man.

But neither I nor Seward, nor Hickman, is entitled to the enviable or unenviable distinction of having first expressed that idea. That same idea was expressed by the Richmond *Enquirer* in Virginia, in 1856; quite two years before it was expressed by the first of us. And while Douglas was pluming himself, that in his conflict with my humble self, last year, he had "squelched out" that fatal heresy, as he delighted to call it, and had suggested that if he only had had a chance to be in New York and meet Seward he would have "squelched" it there also, it never occurred [to him?][4] to breathe a word against Pryor.[5] I don't think that you can discover that Douglas ever talked of going to Virginia to "squelch" out that idea there. No. More than that. That same Roger A. Pryor

[3] Representative John Hickman.

[4] Another passage considerably revised by Lincoln which seems to have lost a phrase.

[5] Roger A. Pryor was editor of the Richmond *Enquirer*.

was brought to Washington City and made the editor of the *par excellence* Douglas paper, after making use of that expression, which, in us, is so unpatriotic and heretical. From all this, my Kentucky friends may see that this opinion is heretical in his view only when it is expressed by men suspected of a desire that the country shall all become free and not when expressed by those fairly known to entertain the desire that the whole country shall become slave. When expressed by that class of men, it is in no wise offensive to him. In this again, my friends of Kentucky, you have Judge Douglas with you.

ON GIGANTIC CAPACITY.

There is another reason why you Southern people ought to nominate Douglas at your convention at Charleston. That reason is the wonderful capacity of the man; [laughter] the power he has of doing what would seem to be impossible. Let me call your attention to one of these apparently impossible things.

Douglas had three or four very distinguished men of the most extreme anti-slavery views of any men in the Republican party, expressing their desire for his re-election to the Senate last year. That would, of itself, have seemed to be a little wonderful, but that wonder is heightened when we see that Wise[6] of Virginia, a man exactly opposed to them, a man who believes in the Divine right of slavery, was also expressing his desire that Douglas should be re-elected, that another man that may be said to be kindred to Wise, Mr. Breckinridge,[7] the Vice President, and of your own State, was also agreeing with the anti-slavery men in the North; that Douglas ought to be re-elected. Still, to heighten the wonder, a Senator from Kentucky, whom I have always loved with an affection as tender and endearing as I have ever loved any man; who was opposed to the anti-slavery men for reasons which seemed sufficient to him, and equally opposed to Wise and Breckinridge, was writing letters into Illinois to secure the re-election of Douglas. Now that all these conflicting elements should be brought, while at dagger's points, with one another, to support him, is a feat that is worthy for you to note and consider. It is quite probable, that each of these classes of men thought by the re-election of Douglas, their peculiar views would gain something, it is probable that the antislavery men thought their views would gain something that Wise and Breckinridge thought so too, as regards their opinions, that Mr. Crittenden thought that his views would gain something, although he was opposed to both these other men. It

[6] Governor Henry A. Wise. [7] John C. Breckinridge.

is probable that each and all of them thought that they were using Douglas, and it is yet an unsolved problem whether he was not using them all. If he was, then it is for you to consider whether that power to perform wonders, is one for you lightly to throw away.

AN ALTERNATIVE PROPOSED.

There is one other thing that I will say to you in this relation. It is but my opinion, I give it to you without a fee. It is my opinion that it is for you to take him or be defeated; and that if you do take him you may be beaten. You will surely be beaten if you do not take him. We, the Republicans and others forming the Opposition of the country, intend to "stand by our guns," to be patient and firm, and in the long run to beat you whether you take him or not. [Applause.] We know that before we fairly beat you, we have to beat you both together. We know that you are "all of a feather," [loud applause,] and that we have to beat you altogether, and we expect to do it. [Applause] We don't intend to be very impatient about it. We mean to be as deliberate and calm about it as it is possible to be, but as firm and resolved, as it is possible for men to be. When we do as we say, beat you, you perhaps want to know what we will do with you. [Laughter]

I will tell you, so far as I am authorized to speak for the Opposition, what we mean to do with you. We mean to treat you as near as we possibly can, like Washington, Jefferson and Madison treated you. [Cheers] We mean to leave you alone, and in no way to interfere with your institution; to abide by all and every compromise of the constitution, and, in a word, coming back to the original proposition, to treat you, so far as degenerated men (if we have degenerated) may, according to the examples of those noble fathers—Washington, Jefferson and Madison. [Applause] We mean to remember that you are as good as we; that there is no difference between us other than the difference of circumstances. We mean to recognise and bear in mind always that you have as good hearts in your bosoms as other people, or as we claim to have, and treat you accordingly. We mean to marry your girls when we have a chance—the white ones I mean—[laughter] and I have the honor to inform you that I once did have a chance in that way. [A voice, "Good for you," and applause]

I have told you what we mean to do. I want to know, now, when that thing takes place, what you mean to do. I often hear it intimated that you mean to divide the Union whenever a Republican, or anything like it, is elected President of the United States.

[A voice, "That is so."] "That is so," one of them says. I wonder if he is a Kentuckian? [A voice, "He is a Douglas man."] Well, then, I want to know what you are going to do with your half of it? [Applause and laughter] Are you going to split the Ohio down through, and push your half off a piece? Or are you going to keep it right alongside of us outrageous fellows? Or are you going to build up a wall some way between your country and ours, by which that moveable property of yours can't come over here any more, to the danger of your losing it? Do you think you can better yourselves on that subject, by leaving us here under no obligation whatever to return those specimens of your moveable property that come hither? You have divided the Union because we would not do right with you as you think, upon that subject; when we cease to be under obligations to do anything for you, how much better off do you think you will be? Will you make war upon us and kill us all? Why, gentlemen, I think you are as gallant and as brave men as live; that you can fight as bravely in a good cause, man for man, as any other people living; that you have shown yourselves capable of this upon various occasions; but, man for man, you are not better than we are, and there are not so many of you as there are of us. [Loud cheering.] You will never make much of a hand at whipping us. If we were fewer in numbers than you, I think that you could whip us; if we were equal it would likely be a drawn battle; but being inferior in numbers, you will make nothing by attempting to master us.

THE ORDINANCE OF '87.

But perhaps I have addressed myself as long, or longer, to the Kentuckians than I ought to have done inasmuch as I have said that whatever course you take we intend in the end to beat you. I propose to address a few remarks to our friends by way of discussing with them the best means of keeping that promise, that I have in good faith made. [Long continued applause.]

It may appear a little episodical for me to mention the topic of which I shall speak now. It is a favorite proposition of Douglas' that the interference of the General Government, through the Ordinance of '87, or through any other act of the General Government, never has made or ever can make a Free State; that the Ordinance of '87 did not make Free States of Ohio, Indiana or Illinois. That these States are free upon his "great principle" of Popular Sovereignty, because the people of those several States have chosen to make them so. At Columbus, and probably here, he undertook to compliment the people that they themselves have made the State of Ohio free and that the Ordinance of '87 was not entitled in any degree to divide the honor with them. I have no doubt that the people of the State of Ohio did make her free according to their own will and judgment, but let the facts be remembered.

In 1802, I believe, it was you who made your first constitution, with the clause prohibiting slavery, and you did it I suppose very nearly unanimously, but you should bear in mind that you—speaking of you as one people—that you did so unembarrassed by the actual presence of the institution amongst you; that you made it a Free State, not with the embarrassment upon you of already having among you many slaves, which if they had been here, and you had sought to make a Free State, you would not know what to do with. If they had been among you, embarrassing difficulties, most probably, would have induced you to tolerate a slave constitution instead of a free one, as indeed these very difficulties have constrained every people on this continent who have adopted slavery.

Pray what was it that made you free? What kept you free? Did you not find your country free when you came to decide that Ohio should be a Free State? It is important to enquire by what reason you found it so? Let us take an illustration between the States of Ohio and Kentucky. Kentucky is separated by this river Ohio, not a mile wide. A portion of Kentucky, by reason of the course of the Ohio, is further north than this portion of Ohio in which we now stand. Kentucky is entirely covered with slavery—Ohio is entirely free from it. What made that difference? Was it climate? No! A portion of Kentucky was further north than this portion of Ohio. Was it soil? No! There is nothing in the soil of the one more favorable to slave labor than the other. It was not climate or soil that caused one side of the line to be entirely covered with slavery and the other side free of it. What was it? Study over it. Tell us, if you can, in all the range of conjecture, if there be anything you can conceive of that made that difference, other than that there was no law of any sort keeping it out of Kentucky? while the Ordinance of '87 kept it out of Ohio. If there is any other reason than this, I confess that it is wholly beyond my power to conceive of it. This, then, I offer to combat the idea that that ordinance has never made any State free.

I don't stop at this illustration. I come to the State of Indiana; and what I have said as between Kentucky and Ohio I repeat as between Indiana and Kentucky; it is equally applicable. One additional argument is applicable also to Indiana. In her Territorial condition she more than once petitioned Congress to abrogate the ordinance entirely, or at least so far as to suspend its operation for a time, in order that they should exercise the "Popular Sovereignty" of having slaves if they wanted them. The men then controlling the General Government, imitating the men of the Revolution, refused Indiana that privilege. And so we have the evidence that Indiana supposed she could have slaves, if it were not for that ordinance that she besought Congress to put that barrier out of the way; that Congress refused to do so, and it all ended at last in Indiana being a Free State. Tell me not, then, that the Ordinance of '87 had nothing to do with making Indiana a free state, when we find some men chafing against and only restrained by that barrier.

Come down again to our State of Illinois. The great Northwest Territory including Ohio, Indiana, Illinois, Michigan and Wisconsin, was acquired, first I believe by the British Government, in part at least, from the French. Before the establishment of our independence, it became a part of Virginia, enabling Virginia afterwards to transfer it to the general government. There were French settlements in what is now Illinois, and at the same time there were French settlements in what is now Missouri—in the tract of country that was not purchased till about 1803. In these French settlements negro slavery had existed for many years—perhaps more than a hundred, if not as much as two hundred years—at Kaskaskia in Illinois, and at St. Genevieve, or Cape Girardeau, perhaps, in Missouri. The number of slaves was not very great, but there was about the same number in each place. They were there when we acquired the Territory. There was no effort made to break up the relation of master and slave and even the Ordinance of 1787 was not so enforced as to destroy that slavery in Illinois; nor did the Ordinance apply to Missouri at all.

What I want to ask your attention to, at this point, is that Illinois and Missouri came into the Union about the same time, Illinois in the latter part of 1818, and Missouri, after a struggle, I believe some time in 1820. They had been filling up with American people about the same period of time; their progress enabling them to come into the Union [at] about the same [time].[8] At the end of that ten years, in which they had been so preparing, (for it was about that period of time) the number of slaves in Illinois had actually decreased; while in Missouri, beginning with very few, at the end of that ten years, there were about ten thousand. This being so, and it being remembered that Missouri and Illinois are, to

[8] Omissions supplied from the *Gazette.*

a certain extent, in the same parallel of latitude—that the Northern half of Missouri and the Southern half of Illinois are in the same parallel of latitude—so that climate would have the same effect upon one as upon the other, and that in the soil there is no material difference so far as bears upon the question of slavery being settled upon one or the other—there being none of those natural causes to produce a difference in filling them, and yet there being a broad difference in their filling up, we are led again to inquire what was the cause of that difference.

It is most natural to say that in Missouri there was no law to keep that country from filling up with slaves, while in Illinois there was the Ordinance of '87. The Ordinance being there, slavery decreased during that ten years—the Ordinance not being in the other, it increased from a few to ten thousand. Can anybody doubt the reason of the difference?

I think all these facts most abundantly prove that my friend Judge Douglas' proposition, that the Ordinance of '87 or the national restriction of slavery, never had a tendency to make a Free State, is a fallacy—a proposition without the shadow or substance of truth about it.

POPULAR SOVEREIGNTY CAUSING FREEDOM.

Douglas sometimes says that all the States (and it is part of this same proposition I have been discussing) that have become free, have become so upon his "great principle"—that the State of Illinois itself came into the Union as a slave State, and that the people upon the "great principle" of Popular Sovereignty have since made it a Free State. Allow me but a little while to state to you what facts there are to justify him in saying that Illinois came into the Union as a Slave State.

I have mentioned to you that there were a few old French slaves there. They numbered, I think, one or two hundred. Besides that there had been a Territorial law for indenturing black persons. Under that law, in violation of the Ordinance of '87, but without any enforcement of the Ordinance to overthrow the system, there had been a small number of slaves introduced as indentured persons. Owing to this the clause for the prohibition of slavery, was slightly modified. Instead of running like yours, that neither slavery nor involuntary servitude, except for crime of which the party shall have been duly convicted, should exist in the State, they said that neither slavery nor involuntary servitude should thereafter be introduced, and that the children of indentured servants should be born free; and nothing was said about the few old French slaves.

Out of this fact, that the clause for prohibiting slavery was modified because of the actual presence of it, Douglas asserts again and again that Illinois came into the Union as a Slave State. How far the facts sustain the conclusion that he draws, it is for intelligent and impartial men to decide. I leave it with you with these remarks, worthy of being remembered, that that little thing, those few indentured servants being there, was of itself sufficient to modify a Constitution made by a people ardently desiring to have a free Constitution; showing the power of the actual presence of the institution of slavery to prevent any people, however anxious to make a Free State, from making it perfectly so.

I have been detaining you longer perhaps than I ought to do. [Long and repeated cries of "go on."]

COMPARISONS.

I am in some doubt whether to introduce another topic upon which I could talk awhile. [Cries of "Go on," and "Give us it."] It is this then. Douglas' Popular Sovereignty as a principle, is simply this: If one man chooses to make a slave of another man, neither that other man or anybody else has a right to object. [Cheers and laughter.] Apply it to government, as he seeks to apply it and it is this—if, in a new Territory, into which a few people are beginning to enter for the purpose of making their homes, they choose to either exclude slavery from their limits, or to establish it there, however one or the other may affect the persons to be enslaved, or the infinitely greater number of persons who are afterwards to inhabit that Territory, or the other members of the family of communities, of which they are but an incipient member, or the general head of the family of states as parent of all—however their action may affect one or the other of these, there is no power or right to interfere. That is Douglas' Popular sovereignty applied. Now I think that there is a real popular sovereignty in the world. I think a definition of popular sovereignty, in the abstract, would be about this—that each man shall do precisely as he pleases with himself, and with all those things which exclusively concern him. Applied in government, this principle would be, that a general government shall do all those things which pertain to it, and all the local governments shall do precisely as they please in respect to those matters which exclusively concern them.

Douglas looks upon slavery as so insignificant that the people must decide that question for themselves, and yet they are not fit to decide who shall be their Governor, Judge or secretary, or who shall be any of their officers. These are vast national matters in his estimation but the little matter in his estimation, is that of planting slavery there. That is purely of local interest, which nobody should be allowed to say a word about. [Applause.]

Labor is the great source from which nearly all, if not all, human comforts and necessities are drawn. There is a difference in opinion about the elements of labor in society. Some men assume that there is a necessary connection between capital and labor, and that connection draws within it the whole of the labor of the community. They assume that nobody works unless capital excites them to work. They begin next to consider what is the best way. They say that there are but two ways; one is to hire men and to allure them to labor by their consent; the other is to buy the men and drive them to it, and that is slavery. Having assumed that, they proceed to discuss the question of whether the laborers themselves are better off in the condition of slaves or of hired laborers, and they usually decide that they are better off in the condition of slaves.

In the first place, I say, that the whole thing is a mistake. That there is a certain relation between capital and labor, I admit. That it does exist, and rightfully exists, I think is true. That men who are industrious, and sober, and honest in the pursuit of their own interests should after a while accumulate capital, and after that should be allowed to enjoy it in peace, and also if they should choose when they have accumulated it to use it to save themselves from actual labor and hire other people to labor for them is right. In doing so they do not wrong the man they employ, for they find men who have not of their own land to work upon, or shops to work in, and who are benefited by working for others, hired laborers, receiving their capital for it. Thus a few men that own capital, hire a few others, and these establish the relation of capital and labor rightfully. A relation of which I make no complaint. But I insist that that relation after all does not embrace more than one-eighth of the labor of the country.

The speaker proceeded to argue that the hired laborer with his ability to become an employer, must have every precedence over him who labors under the inducement of force.[9] He continued:

[9] This strange omission seems all the more unaccountable when an apparently identical fragment of autograph manuscript fits precisely into the niche in the newspaper report (see Fragment on Free Labor, *infra*). That Lincoln had a prepared manuscript at Cincinnati is not probable, but it is possible that the omitted paragraphs on free labor were among the notes for the Cincinnati speech (*supra*, September 16, 17). The fact that such an important passage was omitted by the reporter becomes all the more mysterious when it is considered that Lincoln made no effort to supply the omission when making his extensive revision and correction for the *Journal*.

HOW TO WIN THE FIGHT.

I have taken upon myself in the name of some of you to say, that we expect upon these principles to ultimately beat them. In order to do so, I think we want and must have a national policy in regard to the institution of slavery, that acknowledges and deals with that institution as being wrong. (Loud cheering) Whoever desires the prevention of the spread of slavery and the nationalization of that institution, yields all, when he yields to any policy that either recognizes slavery as being right, or as being an indifferent thing. Nothing will make you successful but setting up a policy which shall treat the thing as being wrong. When I say this, I do not mean to say that this general government is charged with the duty of redressing or preventing all the wrongs in the world; but I do think that it is charged with the duty of preventing and redressing all wrongs which are wrongs to itself. This government is expressly charged with the duty of providing for the general welfare. We believe that the spreading out and perpetuity of the institution of slavery impairs the general welfare. We believe—nay, we know, that that is the only thing that has ever threatened the perpetuity of the Union itself. The only thing which has ever menaced the destruction of the government under which we live, is this very thing. To repress this thing, we think is providing for the general welfare. Our friends in Kentucky differ from us. We need not make our argument for them, but we who think it is wrong in all its relations, or in some of them at least, must decide as to our own actions, and our own course, upon our own judgment.

I say that we must not interfere with the institution of slavery in the states where it exists, because the constitution forbids it, and the general welfare does not require us to do so. We must not withhold an efficient fugitive slave law because the constitution requires us, as I understand it, not to withhold such a law. But we must prevent the outspreading of the institution, because neither the constitution nor general welfare requires us to extend it. We must prevent the revival of the African slave trade and the enacting by Congress of a territorial slave code. We must prevent each of these things being done by either Congresses or courts. The people of these United States are the rightful masters of both Congresses and courts (Applause) not to overthrow the constitution, but to overthrow the men who pervert that constitution. (Applause.)

To do these things we must employ instrumentalities. We must hold conventions; we must adopt platforms if we conform to ordinary custom; we must nominate candidates, and we must carry elections. In all these things, I think that we ought to keep in view our real purpose, and in none do anything that stands adverse to our purpose. If we shall adopt a platform that fails to recognize or express our purpose, or elect a man that declares himself inimical to our purpose, we not only take nothing by our success, but we tacitly admit that we act upon no [other][10] principle than a desire to have "the loaves and fishes," by which, in the end our apparent success is really an injury to us.

I know that it is very desirable with me, as with everybody else, that all the elements of the Opposition shall unite in the next Presidential election and in all future time. I am anxious that that should be, but there are things seriously to be considered in relation to that matter. If the terms can be arranged, I am in favor of the Union. But suppose we shall take up some man and put him upon one end or the other of the ticket, who declares himself against us in regard to the prevention of the spread of slavery—who turns up his nose and says he is tired of hearing anything about it, who is more against us than against the enemy, what will be the issue? Why he will get no slave states after all—he has tried that already until being beat is the rule for him. If we nominate him upon that ground, he will not carry a slave state; and not only so, but that portion of our men who are high strung upon the principle we really fight for, will not go for him, and he won't get a single electoral vote anywhere except, perhaps, in the state of Maryland. There is no use in saying to us that we are stubborn and obstinate, because we won't do some such thing as this. We cannot do it. We cannot get our men to vote it. I speak by the card, that we cannot give the state of Illinois in such case by fifty thousand. We would be flatter down than the "Negro Democracy" themselves have the heart to wish to see us.

After saying this much, let me say a little on the other side. There are plenty of men in the slave states that are altogether good enough for me to be either President or Vice President, provided they will profess their sympathy with our purpose, and will place themselves on the ground that our men, upon principle, can vote for them. There are scores of them, good men in their character for intelligence and talent and integrity. If such a one will place himself upon the right ground I am for his occupying one place upon the next Republican or Opposition ticket. [Applause] I will heartily go for him. But, unless he does so place himself, I think it a

10 Omission supplied from the *Gazette*.

matter of perfect nonsense to attempt to bring about a union upon any other basis; that if a union be made, the elements will scatter so that there can be no success for such a ticket, nor anything like success. The good old maxims of the Bible are applicable, and truly applicable to human affairs, and in this as in other things, we may say here that he who is not for us is against us; he who gathereth not with us scattereth. [Applause] I should be glad to have some of the many good, and able, and noble men of the south to place themselves where we can confer upon them the high honor of an election upon one or the other end of our ticket. It would do my soul good to do that thing. It would enable us to teach them that inasmuch as we select one of their own number to carry out our principles, we are free from the charge that we mean more than we say.

But, my friends I have detained you much longer than I expected to do. I believe I may do myself the compliment to say that you have stayed and heard me with great patience, for which I return you my most sincere thanks.

Fragment on Free Labor[1]

[September 17, 1859?]

change conditions with either Canada or South Carolina? *Equality*, in society, alike beats *inequality*, whether the lat[t]er be of the British aristocratic sort, or of the domestic slavery sort.

We know, Southern men declare that their slaves are better off than hired laborers amongst us. How little they *know*, whereof they *speak*! There is no permanent class of hired laborers amongst us. Twentyfive years ago, I was a hired laborer. The hired laborer of yesterday, labors on his own account to-day; and will hire others to labor for him to-morrow. Advancement—improvement in condition—is the order of things in a society of equals. As Labor is the common *burthen* of our race, so the effort of *some* to shift their share of the burthen on to the shoulders of *others*, is the great, durable, curse of the race. Originally a curse for transgression upon the whole race, when, as by slavery, it is concentrated on a part only, it becomes the double-refined curse of God upon his creatures.

Free labor has the inspiration of hope; pure slavery has no hope. The power of hope upon human exertion, and happiness, is wonderful. The slave-master himself has a conception of it; and hence the system of *tasks* among slaves. The slave whom you can not drive with the lash to break seventy-five pounds of hemp in a day, if you will task him to break a hundred, and promise him pay for all he does over, he will break you a hundred and fifty. You have substituted *hope*, for the *rod*. And yet perhaps it does not occur to you, that to the extent of your gain in the case, you have given up the slave system, and adopted the free system of labor.

[1] AD-P, ISLA. In all probability this fragment represents part of the missing passage on free labor in the speech at Cincinnati (*q.v.*, note 9, *supra*). Nicolay and Hay print this fragment under title of "Fragment. On Slavery [July 1, 1854?]" (*Complete Works*, II, 184), but there is no evidence to support this supplied date. The fact that both the Dayton and Cincinnati speeches contained a discussion of free labor and that Lincoln prepared his most extensive discussion of labor and capital for his address before the Wisconsin State Agricultural Society on September 30 point to the probability that this fragment is contemporary with these speeches.

Speech at Indianapolis, Indiana[1]

September 19, 1859

Mr. Lincoln addressed the people as "Fellow citizens of the State of Indiana," and said:

He now, for the first time in his life, appeared before a large audience in Indiana. Appearing at the capital of this now great State, and traveling through a good portion of it in coming from Cincinnati, had combined to revive his recollection of the earlier years of his life. Away back in the fall of 1816, when he was in his eighth year, his father brought him over from the neighboring State of Kentucky, and settled in the State of Indiana, and he grew up to his present enormous height on our own good soil of Indiana. [Laughter.] The scenes he passed through to-day are wonderfully different from the first scenes he witnessed in the State of Indiana, where he was raised, in Spencer county, on the Ohio river. There was an unbroken wilderness there then, and an axe was put in his hand; and with the trees and logs and grubs he fought until he reached his twentieth year.

He expected the people came to hear something about politics. It was almost impossible for him to speak of politics without associating Judge Douglas with it. He hoped he would be permitted to take, among the range of political topics, the same that Judge Douglas took, if he spoke here while stopping on his way to Chicago, or the one he would have chosen. He knew his Democratic friends thought a Republican speaker could not speak of anything but the negro. He would ask if they ever heard their leader talk of anything else in the past few years of his political career. He did not hesitate to enter upon this subject. There were so many points arising out of

[1] Indianapolis *Atlas*, September 19, 1859. According to the *Illinois State Journal*, September 22, 1859, Lincoln made two speeches in Indiana on his Ohio-Indiana trip. Efforts to find the other speech, or even a reference to the time and place of delivery, have been unsuccessful.

that single topic, in the range that it has taken, that he could give but a very small portion of it.

Some time during the last canvass, he had expressed the opinion that this government of ours cannot "endure permanently, half slave and half free; that a house divided against itself cannot stand;" that some time after, Governor Seward, of New York, in a speech of his, expressed the same opinion in different language. These expressions of opinion had given very great offense to Judge Douglas. He had denounced them as heresy, a fatal heresy. How it is fatal, or in what way fatality is to come out of it, the Judge had not said. Still he had denounced it as a heresy, and rung a great many changes on it. Among other things, he asked, "why cannot this government endure forever, part free, part slave, as the original framers of the constitution made it?" He would take this as one of the topics on which to speak to his audience.

There was no falsehood absolutely in that question. Perhaps it was hardly to be said that a man can very well utter a falsehood in putting an interrogatory. But he insisted in the first place, that there was couched in that interrogatory the *assumption* of a falsehood. It was true that our fathers made this government, and that when it was made it was part slave and part free. But the assumption of the interrogatory is, that our fathers made the government part free and part slave from choice—that they had chosen to make it so because they thought a government thus made, was the best that could be made. Of choice they made it part free and part slave. That was the assumption of the interrogatory, and he would try to prove it untrue. It was not the judgment of the framers of the Constitution, that it was best that the States should be part free and part slave. There was no provision made for peopling one portion of the States with slaves. There was no place spoken of where slaves could be got. There was no provision made in the Constitution, that the African slave trade should ever be suppressed—that it should be repealed. There was a total silence on that question. There is a misunderstanding with some people on this subject.

It was his opinion that our fathers did expect Congress to prohibit the slave trade in 20 years. They made a provision in the constitution by which they prohibited them from doing so prior to the expiration of twenty years. The language is the migration or importation of such persons as the States shall see fit to admit shall not be prohibited, but a certain tax might be levied on such importation. None of the States then existing should be prohibited for twenty years. But what was to be done after that time? The Constitution is silent about that. There is absolutely nothing said about it—the framers of the Constitution expected that the slave trade would be abolished before that time, owing to public sentiment—nothing was said about new States—it had reference to the then existing States. All the States had slavery, with one exception—some, so small an amount as not to feel it, and others quite a large amount. All the States of the South had a considerable amount of slavery in them. The trade of importing slaves was carried on by the commerce of those States where the small amount of slavery existed. It was so carried on that the whole government had an interest invested in some way or other. The Southern people were cultivating their soil with slaves, and it was in deference to that state of things that the framers of the Constitution put in the provision, that Congress should not prohibit that trade until after the expiration of twenty years.

The ordinance of 1787 was passed simultaneously with the making of the Constitution of the United States. It prohibited the taking of slavery into the North-western Territory, consisting of Ohio, Indiana, Illinois, Michigan and Wisconsin. There was nothing said in the Constitution relative to the spread of slavery in the Territories, but the same generation of men said something about it in this ordinance of '87, through the influence of which you of Indiana, and your neighbors in Ohio, Illinois, Wisconsin and Michigan, are prosperous, free men. That generation of men, though not to the full extent members of the Convention that framed the Constitution, were to some extent members of that Convention, holding seats, at the same time in one body and the other, so that if there was any compromise in either of these subjects, the strong evidence is, that that compromise was in favor of the restriction of slavery from the new Territories. Our fathers who made the government, made the ordinance of 1787.

Under the control of this same generation of men, in 1802, the first portion of this North-Western Territory sought admission into the Union. An enabling act was passed by Congress to enable Ohio to make a Constitution and come into the Union in accordance with the ordinance of 1787. Congress composed of the same generation of men that framed the Constitution, enabled Ohio to make a State Constitution, provided it was not repugnant to this ordinance. The same process was gone through when Indiana applied for admission. Then followed Illinois and Wisconsin. In the case of Michigan there was no enabling act. Indiana, in her territorial condition, more than once petitioned Congress to abrogate the ordinance entirely, or at least to so far suspend its operation for a time, in order that they should exercise the "popular sovereignty" of having slaves if they wanted them. The men then controlling the government refused Indiana that privilege—so, had it not been for the ordinance of '87, Indiana would have been a slave State, and all the other States included in the North-Western Territory. Thus, down through a period of sixty years, until the last inch of that Territory came into the Union, the prohibition of slavery was religiously adhered to.

That the fathers of this government did not make it part slave and part free to remain permanently so, he would bring forward a few facts tending to show a reasonable and unbiassed mind, that it was expected at that time that the institution of slavery would gradually come to an end. If they intended it to endure forever, why did they hedge it into its then existent limits. There is nothing said about it in the Constitution. The word slave or slavery is not mentioned in it. This was very singular if it was the intention that slavery should become a permanent institution. It was his opinion that the whole subject was left out by design—it was not done by accident but by design—as every one could see the framers of the Constitution expected that the institution would die. Some of them declared it as their desire that it should. Nothing should be left on the face of the Constitution to tell that there had ever been slavery in the land. If this were so, then we had the fact established, that our fathers made the government contrary to the manner in which Judge Douglas said it was done. The assumption of his interrogatory was false in truth and in fact.

No one of Judge Douglas's propositions was with the ordinance of '87. He had repeatedly asserted that Congressional interference never did make any State a free State, and that if Ohio was a free State, it was made free on his *great principle* of "Popular Sovereignty." While a Territory, a portion of the people of Indiana asked Congress to suspend the ordinance of 1787, but Congress refused to do so. The people wanted to exercise the principle of popular sovereignty, and chafed at the barrier of the ordinance of '87, but that ordinance kept slavery out of their limits and made Indiana a free State. There was no difficulty in introducing slaves into Kentucky if the people wished, but it is a hard job to get them out of it. When the Kentuckians came to form the Constitution, they had the embarrassing circumstances of slavery among them—they were not a free people to make their Constitution. The people of Indiana had no such embarrassment, but would have had, had not slavery been kept away by the ordinance of '87.

The general course of the river Ohio, from the eastern boundary of the State of Ohio, was very nearly south-west—perhaps a little more west than south. The north-eastern part of Kentucky, and the western part of Virginia, are considered north of that portion of Ohio where Cincinnati is, and still farther north of the southern portions of this State and Illinois. Now, it so happens that the country south of the Ohio is slave, and the country north, free. What caused this? Judge Douglas says that the ordinance of '87 did not do it. If not, what did? There is no difference in soil nor in climate. He never heard that the left bank of the Ohio was more favorable to slavery than the right. It could not be because the people had worse hearts. They were as good as we of the North—the same people. There was some other reason. You could light upon nothing in the whole range of conjecture, save and except that the ordinance of '87, in the incipient stages, kept it out of the country north of the Ohio, and no law kept it out of Kentucky and the South. It was not the great principle of popular sovereignty.

In 1810 there was a little slavery in Illinois and a little in Missouri. The two States ran along together, getting ready to form a State Constitution until 1820. Each one of them had a few slaves. When they were ready to come into the Union, they had not kept parallel on the subject of slavery. In Illinois it had decreased, while in Missouri the number of slaves had increased to 10,000. Missouri came in as a slave State and Illinois as a free State. The two States are to a certain extent in the same parallel of latitude, at least the northern half of Missouri and the southern half of Illinois are in the same latitude, so that the climate would have the same effect on one as the other, and in the soil there is no material difference as far as bears upon the question of slavery being settled upon one or the other. There were no natural causes to make a difference in the filling up of the two States, yet there was—what was the cause of that difference?

It is most natural to say, that in Missouri there was no law to keep that country from filling up with slaves, while in Illinois there was the ordinance of 1787. The ordinance being there, slavery decreased during that ten years—not being in the other, it increased from a few to ten thousand. The proposition of Judge Douglas, that the ordinance of '87, or the national restriction of slavery never had a tendency to make a Free State, was not true—it had not the semblance of truth about it. Douglas had sometimes said, that all the States that have become free, have become so on his great principle. There was not a single free State in the Union but what had a national prohibition of slavery in it when it came into the Union. He wanted to know where the "great principle of popular sovereignty" had made a free State? Several free States had come into the Union since the original thirteen—and they had all come in with the national prohibition of slavery over them during their existence as Territories. All the States south of the Ohio and the Missouri compromise had come into the Union as slave States. The ordinance of '87 did not apply to them. They could make use of the "great principle of popular sovereignty." Kansas will come in as a free State, not because of popular sovereignty, but because the people of the North are making a strong effort in her behalf. But Kansas is not in yet. Popular sovereignty has not made a single free State in a run of seventy or eighty years.

He said it was agreed, on every hand, that labor was the great source from whence all our comforts and necessaries were derived. There is a difference of opinion among political economists, about the elements of labor in society. Some men say that there is a necessary connection between labor and capital, and this connection draws within it the whole of the labor of the community. They assume that nobody works unless capital excites them to work. They say there are but two ways: the one is to hire men, and to allow them to labor by their own consent; the other is to buy the men and drive them to it, and that is slavery. Assuming that, they proceed to discuss the question of whether the laborers themselves are better off in the condition of slaves or of hired laborers. They generally decide that they are better off as slaves. They have no responsibility on them then, and when they get old, they are taken care of. In the State of Indiana, of all that is produced, seven-eighths of it is produced by the hands of men who work upon their own ground; and no more than one-eighth is produced by hired men. The condition of the hired man was not worse than that of the slave.

The speaker himself had been a hired man twenty-eight years ago. He didn't think he was worse off than a slave. He might not be doing as much good as he could, but he was now working for himself. He thought the whole thing was a mistake. There was a certain relation between capital and labor, and it was proper that it existed. Men who were industrious and sober, and honest in the pursuit of their own interests, should after a while accumulate capital, and after that should be allowed to enjoy it in peace, and if they chose, when they had accumulated capital, to use it to save themselves from actual labor and hire other people to labor for them, it was right. They did not wrong the man they employed, for they found men who have not their own land to work upon or shops to work in, and who were benefitted by working for them as hired laborers, receiving their capital for it.

If a hired laborer worked as a true man, he saved means to buy land of his own, a shop of his own, and to increase his property. For a new beginner, this was the true, genuine principle of free labor. A few men that own capital, hire others, and thus establish the relation of capital and labor rightfully. The hired laborer, with his ability to become an employer, must have every precedence over him who labors under the inducement of force.

Judge Douglas's popular sovereignty, as a principle, was simply this: If one man choose to make a slave of another man, neither that other man or anybody else has a right to object. Applied in government, as he seeks to apply it, and it was this—if, in a new Territory, into which a few people are beginning to enter, they choose to either exclude or to establish it there, however one or the other may affect the persons to be enslaved, or the greater number of persons who are to inhabit that Territory, there is no power or right to interfere. This is the application of Douglas's popular sovereignty. Douglas thinks slavery so insignificant that the people must decide that question for themselves, though they are not fit to decide who shall be their officers. Planting slavery is a small matter, in his estimation, and nobody ought to be allowed to say anything about it.

He thought that there was a feature in connection with Judge Douglas's Popular Sovereignty, that was more dangerous than anything else, that was not generally observed. That was the debauching of public sentiment. The maxims he taught in regard to the institution of slavery, and by relative operation upon the principle of liberty itself, were more pernicious than anything else. The Judge said he did not care whether slavery was voted up or voted down. That was as much as to say, that he does not believe it to be wrong. This was not the opinion held by the good men of the Revolution of it. It was not the expressed opinion of Mr. Jefferson. Douglas don't care whether slavery goes up or down. He tells us that the Declaration of Independence never meant negroes, and not only does he tell us so, but every follower joins in and says that the Declaration does not apply to negroes. The speaker asked any Democrat present, if he would have the boldness to say that the Declaration did not include negroes as well as whites? [Here Mr. Lincoln looked hard at Gov. Willard, who was sitting in front of him.] He never heard any one say so, and he had asked thousands. No President had ever said so—no head of any department, nor a member of Congress.

And yet you allow this man to debauch public sentiment among you. You have taken the negro out of the catalogue of man, when you had not thought of such a thing five years ago. Five years ago no living man expressed the opinion that the negro had no share in the Declaration of Independence. But within that space Douglas had got his entire party, almost without exception, to join in saying that the negro has no share in the Declaration. The tendency of that change, that debauchery in public sentiment is to bring the public mind to the conclusion that when white men are spoken of, the negro is not meant, and when negroes are spoken of, brutes alone are contemplated. That change had already depressed the black man in the estimation of Douglas himself, and the negro was thus being debased from the condition of a man of some sort to that of a brute.

Douglas had declared that in all contests between the negro and the white man, he was for the white man, but that in all contests between the negro and the crocodile, he was for the negro [laughter.] He (Douglas) had made the remark a great many times in the canvass in Illinois. It was a deliberate way of expressing himself on that subject. The first inference from this remark, seemed to the speaker to be that you are wronging the white man in some way or other, and that whoever is opposed to the negro being enslaved is in some way opposed to the white man. That was not true. If there were any conflict between the white man and negro, he [the speaker] would be for the white man as much as Douglas. There was no such conflict. The mass of white men were injured by the effect of slave labor in the neighborhood of their own labor.

The next inference is, that there is a conflict between the negro and the crocodile. The speaker did not think there was any such struggle. He supposed that if a crocodile (or alligator, as the broad horn men on the Ohio river used to term it), came across a white man, he would kill him if he could! And so he would a negro. The proposition amounted to something like this—as the negro is to the white man, so is the crocodile to the negro, and as the negro may treat the crocodile as a beast or reptile, so the white man may treat the negro as a beast or reptile. [Laughter and applause.] That was what it amounted to.

To Salmon P. Chase[1]

Hon. S. P. Chase:— Springfield, Ill. Sept. 21, 1859.

My dear Sir—This is my first opportunity to express to you my great regret at not meeting you personally while in Ohio. However, you were at work in the cause, and that, after all, was better.

It is useless for me to say to you (and yet I cannot refrain from saying it) that you must not let your approaching election in Ohio so result as to give encouragement to Douglasism. That ism is all which now stands in the way of an early and complete success of Republicanism; and nothing would help it or hurt us so much as for Ohio to go over or falter just now. You must, one and all, put yours souls into the effort. Your obedient servant

A. LINCOLN.

[1] Hertz, p. 758. Governor Chase had been visiting Ohio counties where his presence was needed before the election (Chase to Lincoln, September 29, 1859, DLC-RTL).

Address before the Wisconsin State Agricultural Society, Milwaukee, Wisconsin[1]

September 30, 1859

Members of the Agricultural Society and Citizens of Wisconsin:

Agricultural Fairs are becoming an institution of the country; they are useful in more ways than one; they bring us together, and thereby make us better acquainted, and better friends than we otherwise would be. From the first appearance of man upon the earth, down to very recent times, the words "*stranger*" and "*enemy*" were *quite* or *almost*, synonymous. Long after civilized nations had defined robbery and murder as high crimes, and had affixed severe punishments to them, when practiced among and upon their own people respectively, it was deemed no offence, but even meritorious, to rob, and murder, and enslave *strangers*, whether as nations or as individuals. Even yet, this has not totally disappeared. The man of the highest moral cultivation, in spite of all which abstract principle can do, likes him whom he *does* know, much better than him whom he does *not* know. To correct the evils,

[1] Milwaukee *Sentinel*, October 1, 1859; Chicago *Press and Tribune*, October 1, 1859. The original manuscript of the address was supposed to have been handed to Henry W. Bleyer of the *Sentinel* for printing, and the two pages of manuscript which are extant generally support the supposition that the *Sentinel* text is superior to that of the *Press and Tribune*. The *Press and Tribune*, however, may also have had access to the manuscript in printing the address, and both newspaper texts seem to be superior to the text preserved in the official proceedings of the Wisconsin State Agricultural Society (see *Lincoln on Agriculture*, Lincoln Fellowship of Wisconsin, 1943, Historical Bulletin No. 1). In any event, the manuscript has been dispersed, and except for two pages is not known to be extant. The *Sentinel* text is followed, with the exception of the two pages corrected from the manuscript as indicated in footnotes, and with significant variations in the *Press and Tribune* indicated in footnotes. The *Sentinel* punctuation is followed except where the *Press and Tribune* is obviously better.

great and small, which spring from want of sympathy, and from positive enmity, among *strangers,* as nations, or as individuals, is one of the highest functions of civilization. To this end our Agricultural Fairs contribute in no small degree. They make more pleasant, and more strong, and more durable, the bond of social and political union among us. Again, if, as Pope declares, "happiness is our being's end and aim," our Fairs contribute much to that end and aim, as occasions of recreation—as holidays. Constituted as man is, he has positive need of occasional recreation; and whatever can give him this, associated with virtue and advantage, and free from vice and disadvantage, is a positive good. Such recreation our Fairs afford. They are a present pleasure, to be followed by no pain, as a consequence; they are a present pleasure, making the future more pleasant.

But the chief use of agricultural fairs is to aid in improving the great calling of *agriculture,* in all it's departments, and minute divisions—to make mutual exchange of agricultural discovery, information, and knowledge; so that, at the end, *all* may know every thing, which may have been known to but *one*, or to but a *few,* at the beginning—to bring together especially all which is supposed to not be generally known, because of recent discovery, or invention.[2]

And not only to bring together, and to impart all which has been *accidentally* discovered or invented upon ordinary motive; but, by exciting emulation, for premiums, and for the pride and honor of success—of triumph, in some sort—to stimulate that[3] discovery and invention into extraordinary activity. In this, these Fairs are kindred to the patent clause in the Constitution of the United States; and to the department, and practical system, based upon that clause.

One feature, I believe, of every fair, is a regular *address.* The Agricultural Society of the young, prosperous, and soon to be, great State of Wisconsin, has done me the high honor of selecting me to make that address upon this occasion—an honor for which I make my profound, and grateful acknowledgement.

I presume I am not expected to employ the time assigned me, in the mere flattery of the farmers, as a class. My opinion of them is that, in proportion to numbers, they are neither better nor worse than other people. In the nature of things they are more numerous than any other class; and I believe there really are more attempts at flattering them than any other; the reason of which I

[2] This paragraph is corrected from the original manuscript page (AD, THaroL). [3] *P&T* omits "that."

cannot perceive, unless it be that they can cast more votes than any other. On reflection, I am not quite sure that[4] there is not cause of suspicion against you, in selecting me, in some sort a politician, and in no sort a farmer, to address you.

But farmers, being the most numerous class, it follows that their interest is the largest interest. It also follows that that interest is most worthy of all to be cherished and cultivated—that if there be inevitable conflict between that interest and any other, that other should yield.

Again, I suppose it is not expected of me to impart to you much specific information on Agriculture. You have no reason to believe, and do not believe, that I possess it—if that were what you seek in this address, any one of your own number, or class, would be more able to furnish it.

You, perhaps, do expect me to give some general interest to the occasion; and to make some general suggestions, on practical matters. I shall attempt nothing more. And in such suggestions by me, quite likely very little will be new to you, and a large part of the rest possibly already known to be erroneous.

My first suggestion is an inquiry as to the effect of greater *thoroughness* in all the departments of Agriculture than now prevails in the North-West—perhaps I might say in America. To speak entirely within bounds, it is known that fifty bushels of wheat, or one hundred bushels of Indian corn can be produced from an acre. Less than a year ago I saw it stated that a man, by extraordinary care and labor, had produced of wheat, what was equal to two hundred bushels from an acre. But take fifty of wheat, and one hundred of corn, to be the *possibility*,[5] and compare with it the actual crops of the country. Many years ago I saw it stated in a Patent Office Report that eighteen bushels[6] was the average crop throughout the wheat growing region of the United States; and this year an intelligent farmer of Illinois, assured me that he did not believe the land harvested in that State this season, had yielded more than an average of eight bushels to the acre. The brag crop I heard of in our vicinity was two thousand bushels from ninety acres. Many crops were thrashed, producing no more than three bushels to the acre; much was cut, and then abandoned as not worth threshing; and much was abandoned as[7] not worth cutting. As to Indian corn, and, indeed, most other crops, the case has not been much better. For the last four years I do not believe the ground planted with corn in Illinois, has produced an average

[4] *P&T* omits "that." [5] *P&T* has "*probability*."
[6] *P&T* has "bushels to the acre." [7] *P&T* has "without cutting."

of twenty bushels to the acre. It is true, that heretofore we have had better crops, with no better cultivators; but I believe it is also true that the soil has never been pushed up to one-half of its capacity.

What would be the effect upon the farming interest, to push the soil up to something near its full capacity? Unquestionably it will take more labor to produce *fifty* bushels from an acre, than it will to produce *ten* bushels from the same acre. But will it take more labor to produce fifty bushels from *one* acre, than from *five*? Unquestionably, thorough cultivation will require more labor to the *acre;* but will it require more to the *bushel*? If it should require just as *much* to the bushel, there are some *probable*, and several *certain*, advantages in favor of the thorough practice. It is probable it would develope those unknown causes, or develope unknown cures for those causes, which of late years have cut down our crops below their former average. It is almost certain, I think, that in the deeper plowing, analysis of soils, experiments with manures, and varieties of seeds, observance of seasons, and the like, these cases [causes?][8] would be found. It is certain that thorough cultivation would spare half or more than half, the cost of land, simply because the same product would be got from half, or from less than half the quantity of land. This proposition is self-evident, and can be made no plainer by repetitions or[9] illustrations. The cost of land is a great item, even in new countries; and constantly grows greater and greater, in comparison with other items, as the country grows older.

It also would spare[10] a large proportion of the making and maintaining of inclosures—the same, whether these inclosures should be hedges, ditches, or fences. This again, is a heavy item—heavy at first, and heavy in its continual demand for repairs. I remember once being greatly astonished by an apparently authentic exhibition of the proportion the cost of inclosures bears to all the other expenses of the farmer; though I can not remember exactly what that proportion was. Any farmer, if he will, can ascertain it in his own case, for himself.

Again, a great amount of "locomotion" is spared by thorough cultivation. Take fifty bushels of wheat, ready for the harvest, standing upon a *single* acre, and it can be harvested in any of the known ways, with less than half the labor which would be required if it were spread over *five* acres. This would be true, if cut by the

8 *P&T* has "cures." 9 *P&T* has "and."

10 *Sentinel* has "span," undoubtedly a typographical error for "spare," which is the *P&T* reading.

old hand sickle; true, to a greater extent if by the scythe and cradle; and to a still greater extent, if by the machines[11] now in use. These machines are chiefly valuable, as a means of substituting animal power for the power of men in this branch of farm work. In the highest degree of perfection yet reached in applying the[12] horse power to harvesting, fully nine-tenths of the power is expended by the animal in carrying himself and dragging the machine over the field, leaving certainly not more than one-tenth to be applied directly to the only end of the whole operation—the gathering in the grain, and clipping of the straw. When grain is very thin on the ground, it is always more or less intermingled with weeds, chess and the like, and a large part of the power is expended in cutting these. It is plain that when the crop is very thick upon the ground, the larger[13] proportion of the power is directly applied to gathering in and cutting it; and the smaller, to that which is totally useless as an end. And what I have said of harvesting is true, in a greater or less degree of mowing, plowing, gathering in of crops generally, and, indeed, of almost all farm work.

The effect of thorough cultivation upon the farmer's own mind, and, in reaction through his mind, back upon his business, is perhaps quite equal to any other of its effects. Every man is proud of what he does *well;* and no man is proud of what he does *not* do well. With the former, his heart is in his work; and he will do twice as much of it with less fatigue. The latter performs a little imperfectly, looks at it in disgust, turns from it, and imagines himself exceedingly tired. The little he has done,[14] comes to nothing, for want of finishing.

The man who produces a good full crop will scarcely ever let any part of it go to waste. He will keep up the enclosure about it, and allow neither man nor beast to trespass upon it. He will gather it in due season and store it in perfect security. Thus he labors with satisfaction, and saves[15] himself the whole fruit of his labor. The other, starting with no purpose for a full crop, labors less, and with less satisfaction; allows his fences to fall, and cattle to trespass; gathers not in due season, or not at all. Thus the labor he has performed, is wasted away, little by little, till in the end, he derives scarcely anything from it.

The ambition for broad acres leads to poor farming, even with men of energy. I scarcely ever knew a mammoth farm to sustain itself; much less to return a profit upon the outlay. I have more

11 *P&T* has "machinery."
12 *P&T* omits "the."
13 *P&T* has "the largest."
14 *P&T* has "he does."
15 *P&T* has "saves to himself."

than once known a man to spend a respectable fortune upon one; fail and leave it; and then some man of more modest aims,[16] get a small fraction of the ground, and make a good living upon it. Mammoth farms are like tools or weapons, which are too heavy to be handled. Ere long they are thrown aside, at a great loss.

The successful application of *steam power*, to farm work is a *desideratum*—especially a Steam Plow. It is not enough, that a machine operated by steam, will really plow. To be successful, it must, all things considered, plow *better* than can be done with animal power. It must do all the work as well, and *cheaper;* or more *rapidly*, so as to get through more perfectly *in season;* or in some way afford an advantage over plowing with animals, else it is no success. I have never seen a machine intended for a Steam Plow. Much praise, and admiration, are bestowed upon some of them; and they may be, for aught I know, already successful; but I have not perceived the demonstration of it. I have thought a good deal, in an abstract way, about a Steam Plow. That one which shall be so contrived as to apply the larger[17] proportion of its power to the cutting and turning[18] the soil, and the smallest, to the moving itself over the field, will be the best one. A very small stationary engine would draw a large gang of plows through the ground from a short distance to itself; but when it is not stationary, but has to move along like a horse, dragging the plows after it, it must have additional power to carry itself; and the difficulty grows by what is intended to overcome it; for what adds power also adds size, and weight to the machine, thus increasing again, the demand for power. Suppose you should construct the machine so as to cut a succession of short furrows, say a rod in length, transversely to the course the machine is locomoting, something like the shuttle in weaving. In such case the whole machine would move North only the width of a furrow, while in length, the furrow would be a rod from East to West. In such case, a very large proportion of the power, would be applied to the actual plowing. But in this, too, there would be a difficulty, which would be the getting of the plow *into*, and *out of*, the ground, at the ends of all these short furrows.

I believe, however, ingenious men will, if they have not already, overcome the difficulty[19] I have suggested. But there is still another, about which I am less sanguine. It is the supply of *fuel*, and especially of *water*, to make steam. Such supply is clearly practicable, but can the expense of it be borne? Steamboats live upon the water, and find their fuel at stated places. Steam mills, and

16 *P&T* has "more moderate aims." 17 *P&T* has "largest."
18 *P&T* has "turning of." 19 *P&T* has "difficulties."

other stationary steam machinery, have their stationary supplies of fuel and water. Railroad locomotives have their regular wood and water station.[20] But the steam plow is less fortunate. It does not live upon the water; and[21] if it be once at a water station, it will work away from it, and when it gets away[22] can not return, without leaving its work, at a great expense of its time and strength. It will occur that a wagon and horse team might be employed to supply it with fuel and water; but this, too, is expensive; and the question recurs, "can the expense be borne?" When this is added to all other expenses, will not the plowing cost more than in the old way?

It is to be hoped that the steam plow will be finally[23] successful, and if it[24] shall be, "*thorough cultivation*"—putting the soil to the top of its capacity—producing the largest crop possible from a given quantity of ground—will be most favorable to it. Doing a large amount of work upon a small quantity of ground, it will be, as nearly as possible, stationary while working, and as free as possible from locomotion; thus expending its strength as much as possible upon its work, and as little as possible in travelling. Our thanks, and something more substantial than thanks, are due to every man engaged in the effort to produce a successful steam plow. Even the unsuccessful will bring something to light, which, in the hands of others, will contribute to the final success. I have not pointed out difficulties, in order to discourage, but in order that being seen, they may be the more readily overcome.

The world is agreed that *labor* is the source from which human wants are mainly supplied. There is no dispute upon this point. From this point, however, men immediately diverge. Much disputation is maintained as to the best way of applying and controlling the labor element. By some it is[25] assumed that labor is available only in connection with capital—that nobody labors, unless somebody else, owning capital, somehow, by the use of that capital,[26] induces him to do it. Having assumed this, they proceed to consider whether it is best that capital shall *hire* laborers, and thus induce them to work by their own consent; or *buy* them, and drive them to it without their consent. Having proceeded so far they naturally conclude that all laborers are necessarily either *hired*

20 *P&T* has "stations." 21 *P&T* has "even." 22 *P&T* has "dry."

23 *P&T* has "will finally be." 24 *P&T* has "it ever shall."

25 The facsimile of the manuscript page (Julius E. Olson, "Lincoln in Wisconsin," *Wisconsin Magazine of History*, IV, 1, September, 1920) containing this paragraph does not clearly show the "is," which was apparently inserted above the line, but the newspaper texts are certainly correct.

26 *P&T* has "use of it."

laborers, or *slaves*. They further assume that whoever is once a *hired* laborer, is fatally fixed in that condition for life; and thence again that his condition is as bad as, or worse than that of a slave. This is the "*mud-sill*" theory.

But[27] another class of reasoners hold the opinion that there is no *such* relation between capital and labor, as assumed; and that there is no such thing as a freeman being fatally fixed for life, in the condition of a hired laborer, that both these assumptions are false, and all inferences from them groundless. They hold that labor is prior to, and independent of, capital; that, in fact, capital is the fruit of labor, and could never have existed if labor had not *first* existed—that labor can exist without capital, but that capital could never have existed[28] without labor. Hence they hold that labor is the superior—greatly the superior—of capital.

They do not deny that there is, and probably always will be, *a* relation between labor and capital. The error, as they hold, is in assuming that the *whole* labor of the world exists within that relation. A few men own capital; and that few avoid labor themselves, and with their capital, hire, or buy, another few to labor for them. A large majority belong to neither class—neither work for others, nor have others working[29] for them. Even in all our slave States, except South Carolina, a majority of the whole people of all colors, are neither slaves nor masters. In these Free States, a large majority are neither *hirers* nor *hired*. Men, with their families—wives, sons and daughters—work for themselves, on their farms, in their houses and in their shops, taking the whole product to themselves, and asking no favors of capital on the one hand, nor of hirelings or slaves on the other. It is not forgotten that a considerable number of persons mingle their own labor with capital; that is, labor with their own hands, and also buy slaves or hire freemen to labor for them; but this is only a *mixed*, and not a *distinct* class. No principle stated is disturbed by the existence of this mixed class. Again, as has already been said, the opponents of the "*mud-sill*" theory insist that there is not, of necessity, any such thing as the free hired laborer being fixed to that condition for life. There is demonstration for saying this. Many independent men, in this assembly, doubtless a few years ago were hired laborers. And their case is almost if not quite the general rule.

The prudent, penniless beginner in the world, labors for wages

[27] The last line of the manuscript page shows a paragraph as in the *Press and Tribune*, but not in the *Sentinel*. [28] *P&T* has "existence."

[29] *P&T* has "work."

awhile, saves a surplus with which to buy tools or land, for himself; then labors on his own account another while, and at length hires another new beginner to help him. This, say its advocates, is *free* labor—the just and generous, and prosperous system, which opens the way for all—gives hope to all, and energy, and progress, and improvement of condition to all. If any continue through life in the condition of the hired laborer, it is not the fault of the system, but because of either a dependent nature which prefers it, or[30] improvidence, folly, or singular misfortune. I have said this much about the elements of labor generally, as introductory to the consideration of a new phase which that element is in process of assuming. The old general rule was that *educated* people did not perform manual labor. They managed to eat their bread, leaving the toil of producing it to the uneducated. This was not an insupportable evil to the working bees, so long as the class of drones remained very small. But *now*, especially in these free States, nearly all are educated—quite too nearly all, to leave the labor of the uneducated, in any wise[31] adequate to the support of the whole. It follows from this that henceforth educated people[32] must labor. Otherwise, education itself would become a positive and intolerable evil. No country[33] can sustain, in idleness, more than a small per centage of its numbers. The great majority must labor at something[34] productive. From these premises the problem springs, "How can *labor* and *education* be the most satisfactorily combined?"

By the "*mud-sill*" theory it is assumed that labor and education are incompatible; and any practical combination of them impossible. According to that theory, a blind horse upon a tread-mill, is a perfect illustration of what a laborer should be—all the better for being blind, that he could[35] not tread out of place, or kick understandingly. According to that theory, the education[36] of laborers, is not only useless, but pernicious, and dangerous. In fact, it is, in some sort, deemed a misfortune that laborers should have heads at all. Those same heads are regarded as explosive materials, only to be safely kept in damp places, as far as possible from that peculiar sort of fire which ignites them. A Yankee who could invent a strong *handed* man without a head would receive[37] the everlasting gratitude of the "mud-sill" advocates.

But Free Labor says "no!" Free Labor argues that, as the Author

[30] *P&T* has "or of." [31] *P&T* has "anyway adequate."
[32] *P&T* has "people too." [33] *P&T* has "community."
[34] *P&T* has "something useful—something productive."
[35] *P&T* has "can." [36] *P&T* has "educating." [37] *P&T* has "secure."

of man makes every individual with one head and one pair of hands, it was probably intended that heads and hands should co-operate as friends; and that that particular head, should direct and control that particular pair of hands. As each man has one mouth to be fed, and one pair of hands to furnish food, it was probably intended that that particular pair of hands should feed that particular mouth—that each head is the natural guardian, director, and protector of the hands and mouth inseparably connected with it; and that being so, every head should be cultivated, and improved, by whatever will add to its capacity for performing its charge. In one word Free Labor insists on universal education.

I have so far stated the opposite theories of "*Mud-Sill*" and "Free Labor" without declaring any preference of my own between them. On an occasion like this I ought not to declare any. I suppose, however, I shall not be mistaken, in assuming as a fact, that the people of Wisconsin prefer free labor, with its natural companion, education.

This leads to the further reflection, that no other human occupation opens so wide a field for the profitable and agreeable combination of labor with cultivated thought, as agriculture. I know of nothing so pleasant to the mind, as the discovery of anything which is at once *new* and *valuable*—nothing which so lightens and sweetens toil, as the hopeful pursuit of such discovery. And how vast, and how varied a field is agriculture, for such discovery. The mind, already trained to thought, in the country school, or higher school, cannot fail to find there[38] an exhaustless source of profitable enjoyment. Every blade of grass is a study; and to produce two, where there was but one, is both a profit and a pleasure. And not grass alone; but soils, seeds, and seasons—hedges, ditches, and fences, draining, droughts, and irrigation—plowing, hoeing, and harrowing—reaping, mowing, and threshing—saving crops, pests of crops, diseases of crops, and what will prevent or cure them—implements, utensils, and machines, their relative merits, and [how][39] to improve them—hogs, horses, and cattle—sheep, goats, and poultry—trees, shrubs, fruits, plants,[40] and flowers—the thousand things of which these are specimens—each a world of study within itself.

In all this, book-learning is available. A capacity, and taste, for reading, gives access to whatever has already been discovered by others. It is the key, or one of the keys, to the already solved prob-

[38] *P&T* has "it."
[39] "How" is in the *Press and Tribune*, not in the *Sentinel*.
[40] *P&T* omits "plants."

lems. And not only so. It gives a relish, and facility, for successfully pursuing the [yet][41] unsolved ones. The rudiments of science, are available, and highly valuable. Some knowledge of Botany assists in dealing with the vegetable world—with all growing crops. Chemistry assists in the analysis of soils, selection, and application of manures, and in numerous other ways. The mechanical branches of Natural Philosophy, are ready help in almost everything; but especially in reference to implements and machinery.

The thought recurs[42] that education—cultivated thought—can best be combined with agricultural labor, or any labor, on the principle of *thorough* work—that careless, half performed, slovenly work, makes no place for such combination. And thorough work, again, renders sufficient, the smallest quantity of ground to each man. And this again, conforms to what must occur in a world less inclined to wars, and more devoted to the arts of peace, than heretofore. Population must increase rapidly—more rapidly than in former times—and ere long the most valuable of all arts, will be the art of deriving a comfortable subsistence from the smallest area of soil. No community whose every member possesses this art, can ever be the victim of oppression in any of its forms. Such community will be alike independent of crowned-kings, money-kings, and land-kings.

But, according to your programme, the awarding of premiums awaits the closing of this address. Considering the deep interest necessarily pertaining to that performance, it would be no wonder if I am already heard with some impatience. I will detain you but a moment longer. Some of you will be successful, and such will need but little philosophy to take them home in cheerful spirits; others will be disappointed, and will be in a less happy mood. To such, let it be said,[43] "Lay it not too much to heart." Let them adopt the maxim, "Better luck next time;" and then, by renewed exertion, make that better luck for themselves.

And by the successful, and the unsuccessful, let it be remembered, that while occasions like the present, bring their sober and durable benefits, the exultations and mortifications of them, are but temporary; that the victor shall soon be the vanquished, if he relax in his exertion; and that the vanquished this year, may be victor the next, in spite of all competition.

It is said an Eastern monarch once charged his wise men to invent him a sentence,[44] to be ever in view, and which should be

[41] "Yet" is in the *Press and Tribune*, not in the *Sentinel.*

[42] *P&T* has "occurs."

[43] *P&T* has "let me say."

[44] *P&T* has "sentiment."

true and appropriate in all times and situations. They presented him the words: "*And this, too, shall pass away*." How much it expresses! How chastening in the hour of pride!—how consoling in the depths of affliction! "And this, too, shall pass away." And yet let us hope it is not *quite* true. Let us hope, rather, that by the best cultivation of the physical world, beneath and around us; and the intellectual and moral world within us, we shall secure an individual, social, and political prosperity and happiness, whose course shall be onward and upward, and which, while the earth endures, shall not pass away.

Speech at Beloit, Wisconsin[1]

October 1, 1859

He opened with a statement of the different positions taken by the different political parties of the country. He named 4 existing dem. parties, or, rather, sub-divisions of the great Democratic party. These were united on one point, viz: their opposition to the Republican organization and to Republican principles. At the South, the hostility to organization proceeded, in a great measure, from ignorance and misapprehension of the principles and aims of that organization. The Democratic leaders there sedulously strive, by misrepresentation and falsehood, to produce the impression that the Republicans desire to meddle with their existing institutions.

Mr. Lincoln then went on to state the real position of the Republican party. Its underlying principle is hatred to the institution of Slavery; hatred to it in all its aspects, moral, social, and political. This is the foundation of the Republican party—its active, life-giving principle. The expression, by words and deeds, of this hatred to Slavery, is the policy of the party; and this expression, is, and should be, made in every *legitimate*, *Constitutional* way. With Slavery in the States they had nothing to do; but when it attempts to overleap its present limits, and fasten itself upon free territory, they would resist and force it back. This, he said, was what the Republican party was now trying to do. On this point he clashed with the popular sovereignty doctrine, and accordingly, he proceeded to pay his respects to the author of that stupendous humbug. This he did in a way that must have convinced every

[1] Beloit *Journal*, October 5, 1859. On the night of September 30, following his address at the Milwaukee Fair, Lincoln gave a political speech at the Newhall House in Milwaukee. No report has been located. At two o'clock the next afternoon, however, he delivered the speech at Beloit which is reported in the Beloit *Journal*.

candid man in the audience of the emptiness of his arguments, and of the baneful results of the adoption of Douglas' policy by the National government. First, as to the working of the popular sovereignty principle. In no single case had it, when left free to work out its own legitimate results, brought into the Union a Free State. Every Free State which has been carved out of territory belonging to the United States, and has been received into the Union since the compact was formed between the original thirteen, had been, at some time during its territorial existence, subject to a prohibition of slavery. In the states formed out of the Northwestern territory, it was prohibited by the Ordinance of '87; in the Free states formed out of the Louisiana purchase by the Missouri compromise, and in California, by the Missouri compromise, and by Mexican laws. In every territory where slavery had, in accordance with popular sovereignty, obtained a foothold, it had maintained its position after the state organization. Kansas would probably be the first instance of a free state's being formed under the auspices of popular sovereignty. In this case, freedom was secured at the expense of a civil war.

The cause of this uniform result is this: Suppose that one-fifth of the inhabitants of a territory are slaves, and it is proposed to form a State Constitution. The question of course arises of Slavery or no Slavery? Before a prohibition is decided upon, several other questions are to be settled relative to the disposition of the slaves already in the territory. One man thinks that it is unjust to deprive a man of his lawful property at all, and all differ as to the means by which the difficulty shall be removed. The result of their disagreement will be, that the institution is permitted to remain undisturbed.

Slavery may thus be introduced into and retained upon territory where a large majority of the population are decidedly opposed to it. The practical difficulty in the way of removing the curse overbalances their aversion to it in principle, and in its practical effects upon the prosperity of the country. Mr. Lincoln proceeded to speak of the demoralizing tendency of a general prevalence of Douglas' doctrines in the country. Mr. Douglas takes it for granted that slavery is not a moral wrong. To him it is a matter of indifference whether it is "voted up or voted down." Of course, then, if he makes any pretence to morality, he considers that no moral question is involved. It is right and necessary at the south, he says, and he sneers at the idea of an "irrepressible conflict" between negro bondage and human freedom. "They are an inferior race." "Between the white man and the negro, he goes for the white man; but between the negro and the crocodile, he goes for the negro." These are Douglas' sentiments. The man who expresses such sentiments as these can see no moral wrong in slavery. But if it is morally right below the line of 36 30, it must be above. Questions of abstract right and wrong cannot be questions of locality. But slavery is unprofitable at the north, Mr. Douglas says; but this is no reason for its prohibition. Cotton cannot be profitably grown at the north; but who ever thought of State enactments forbidding the raising of Cotton for such a reason?

The natural result of a general belief in such doctrines would be the ultimate establishment of slavery in every State of the Union.

The orator then went on to prove the identity of the Republican principles with those of the Fathers of the Republic. This he did most satisfactorily, citing in proof the passage of the Ordinance of '87, and the refusal three several [separate?] times of the Federal Legislature to grant the petition of a majority of the inhabitants of the territory of Indiana for liberty to hold slaves in that territory. Innumerable other cases might be cited to prove the same point. If twelve good sound democrats could be found in the county of Rock, he would put them on oath as a jury. He would bring his evidence in form of depositions in a court, and wring from them the verdict that the Republicans hold to the same principles which Washington, Jefferson, Adams, Madison and their compeers held.

Mr. Lincoln closed with an eloquent passage from Mr. Clay, pointing out, with prophetic voice, the ruin which the adoption by the people of such principles as Douglas advocates would bring upon the country, and denouncing, in terrible language, the authors of such a change of public policy.

Speech at Janesville, Wisconsin[1]

October 1, 1859

He enquired why slavery existed on one side of the Ohio river and not on the other? Why did we find that institution in Kentucky, and not in Ohio? There was very little difference in the soil or the climate, and the people on one side of the line loved liberty as well as on the other. The northern portion of Kentucky was opposite free territory, while the southern portions of Ohio,

[1] Janesville *Morning Gazette,* October 4, 1859. Lincoln spoke in Janesville at night, traveling by carriage from Beloit after his speech in the afternoon. In reporting the speech the *Gazette* explained that "Of the several points made we select only one, and this we cannot give in the author's own words, as we took no notes."

Indiana and Illinois, had for neighbors states in which slavery existed. Indiana while a territory had petitioned congress three times to allow them to introduce slavery; while slavery actually existed in Illinois when she was admitted as a free state. It was apparent that some of the people wanted slavery. Mr. Lincoln said that there could be no other reason than that it was prohibited by congress. If it had been left to the people, as proposed by Mr. Douglas, a few slaves would have found a place there—if ten thousand had been admitted into Ohio while she was a territory, many questions would have been presented that would have been embarrassing, which would not have perplexed the people if slavery had been prohibited by congress—the question would have come up, what shall we do with these ten thousand slaves? Shall we make them free and destroy property which people supposed they possessed? If they abolished slavery what would they do with the negroes? &c. These questions would be troublesome and difficult to decide. The power of this amount of property in the hands of wealthy and educated men, who would most likely own the slaves, would in the end prevail and slavery would be established; whereas if congress had prohibited it until the state constitution was about to be formed, slavery and freedom would start upon an equal platform, and without the embarrassing questions named—freedom in this case would prevail and slavery would be prohibited. Slavery comes gradually into territory where it is not prohibited without notice, and without alarming the people, until having obtained a foothold, it cannot be driven out.

Thus we see that in all the new states where slavery was not prohibited, it was established. In Kentucky, Tennessee, Mississippi, Alabama, Louisiana, Arkansas and Missouri, the principle of popular sovereignty prevailed—congress permitted the people to establish the institution of slavery if they pleased. In all these instances, where they had their choice, slavery had been introduced; but, on the contrary, in all the new states, where slavery had been prohibited, and where popular sovereignty had no choice until state constitutions were formed, the states have prohibited slavery in their constitutions; such was the case in Ohio, Indiana, Illinois, Michigan, Wisconsin, Iowa, California and Minnesota. In California it had been prohibited by the old Mexican law, which was not abrogated before California became a state. Minnesota was a territory five years after the Missouri compromise was repealed, but commenced its settlement with a congressional restriction against slavery.

It is therefore, evident, if the principle of popular sovereignty becomes the settled policy of the country, that slavery will have a great advantage over freedom, and the history of the country proves this to be true.

Mr. Lincoln said that he had failed to find a man who five years ago had expressed it his belief that the declaration of independence did not embrace the colored man. But the public mind had become debauched by the popular sovereignty dogma of Judge Douglas. The first step down the hill is the denial of the negro's rights as a human being. The rest comes easy. Classing the colored race with brutes frees from all embarrassment the idea that slavery is right if it only has the endorsement of the popular will. Douglas has said that in a conflict between the white and the negro, he is for the white man; but in a conflict between the negro and the crocodile, he is for the negro. Or the matter might be put in this shape: As the white man is to the negro, so is the negro to the crocodile! (Applause and laughter.) But the idea that there was a conflict between the two races, or that the freedom of the white man was insecure unless the negro was reduced to a state of abject slavery, was false and that as long as his tongue could utter a word he would combat that infamous idea. There was room for all races and as there was no conflict so there was no necessity of getting up an excitement in relation to it.

To Jesse K. Dubois[1]

Hon Jesse K. Dubois October 10, 1859

Auditor of Public Accounts in and for the State of Illinois

Sir You are hereby notified that the Illinois Central Railroad Company appeals, and the said Company does hereby appeal, from the decision made by you in the "list and valuation" of which the annexed paper, is your notice to said Company, of the making out by you, of said "list and valuation" October 10. 1859

A LINCOLN for the Illinois
Central Railroad Company

[1] Copy, Illinois Central Railroad Volume, State Auditor's Office, Springfield, Illinois. State Auditor Dubois' "list and valuation" of the property of the Illinois Central totaled $13,000,000.

To Edward Wallace[1]

Dr. Edward Wallace: Clinton,

My dear Sir: Oct. 11th. 1859

I am here, just now, attending court. Yesterday, before I left Springfield, your brother, Dr. William S. Wallace, showed me a letter of yours, in which you kindly mention my name, inquire for my tariff views; and suggest the propriety of my writing a letter upon the subject. I was an old Henry Clay tariff whig. In old times I made more speeches on that subject, than on any other. I have not since changed my views. I believe yet, if we could have a moderate, carefully adjusted, protective tariff, so far acquiesed in, as to not be a perpetual subject of political strife, squabbles, charges, and uncertainties, it would be better for us. Still, it is my opinion that, just now, the revival of that question, will not advance the cause itself, or the man who revives it. I have not thought much upon the subject recently; but my general impression is, that the necessity for a protective tariff will, ere long, force it's old opponents to take it up; and then it's old friends can join in, and establish it on a more firm and durable basis. We, the old whigs, have been entirely beaten out on the tariff question; and we shall not be able to re-establish the policy, until the absence of it, shall have demonstrated the necessity for it, in the minds of men heretofore opposed to it.

With this view, I should prefer, to not now, write a public letter upon the subject. I therefo[re] wish this to be considered confidential.

I shall be very glad to receive a letter from you. Yours truly

A. LINCOLN—

[1] ALS, owned by Mrs. H. A. Reninger, Allentown, Pennsylvania. Dr. Edward Wallace was a physician at Reading, Pennsylvania. His reply concurs with Lincoln's views and expresses the opinion that a Western presidential candidate with protective views would be most acceptable to Pennsylvania (October 17, 1859, DLC-RTL).

Speech at Clinton, Illinois[1]

October 14, 1859

Lincoln was loudly called for and he promptly mounted the stand and responded to the call. He spoke of the purpose for which the meeting was called—the Republican triumphs lately obtained in the East and West—that many such demonstrations were being made in many places—that, perhaps, the victories would be celebrated in St. Louis, the chief mart and emporium of the South-Western Slave States, and which was thoroughly Republican in sentiment. He then spoke of the evils and disasters attending the repeal of the Missouri Compromise, by which the barriers protecting freedom and free labor were broken down and the Territories transformed into asylums for slavery and niggers, and clearly showed that, by this breach of a sacred compact a scope of Territory half as large as the whole United States was thrown open to the blighting influences of slavery. He pitched into the Dred Scott decision and "my great principle" in a truly refreshing manner, and held up to the gaze of his hearers in a way that could not fail to be visible that the Dred Scott decision and Squatter Sovereignty would not mix or affiliate—that either one principle virtually killed the other. The state and condition of political parties next occupied his attention—he reminded his hearers that in '56 a middle party (the American) was in existence, but now that organization was absorbed into both the other great parties, and that *now*, and only *now*, we could rejoice over a true and genuine Republican triumph. He then traced the beginning of the Republican party in 1854 to its present altitude of power and greatness, and in an able and masterly manner reviewed the momentous questions which now agitate the minds of our people. He alluded to the fact[2] that Judge Douglas and himself fully agreed upon one point as set forth in Douglas' Columbus Speech, viz: that the fathers of this Government understood its powers over the institution of slavery better than we do now; and he proceeded to show that the Democratic party had departed from the old landmarks; had set up a new theory and a different policy, and at their present rate of progress, would speedily make slavery a national institution, over which even the States should exercise no control. In this the Democracy were resisted and must be resisted by the Republicans; that their position was identical, so far as the slavery question is concerned, with that occupied by the founders of the Government; and referred to the recent glorious Republican victories as indicative that the good old doctrines of the fathers of the Republic would yet again prevail, and become the rule of action of the Government. "Our position," says Mr. L., "is right—our principles are good and just, but I would desire to impress on every Republican present to have patience and steadiness under all circumstances—whether defeated or successful. But I do hope that as there is a just and righteous God in Heaven, our principles will and shall prevail sooner or later."

He closed his eloquent and masterly exposition of the true intent of our cherished and time-honored principles and the sophistries and delusions of our enemies, amid the loud, prolonged and stentorian cheering of the vast audience, that made the rafters of the court-house ring again.

[1] Clinton *Weekly Central Transcript*, October 20, 1859. Lincoln was attending court at Clinton when a rally was called to celebrate the Republican vic-

tories in Ohio, Pennsylvania, Iowa, and Minnesota. Following Lincoln, Leonard Swett and Lawrence Weldon spoke.

[2] The remainder of this sentence and the next is identical with the report of the speech at Springfield, October 15, *infra*, a fact which would arouse no curiosity were it not that both sources contain the same typographical errors, which have been corrected by the editors in the present text. Possibly the *Transcript*, published two days later than the *Journal*, copied a portion of the report in the *Journal*, but Lincoln certainly made much the same speech at both places.

Speech at Springfield, Illinois[1]

October 15, 1859

We have not space, of course, to give anything like a report of Mr. Lincoln's speech. Although entirely unpremeditated, it was in every respect, one of the ablest we have ever heard him deliver. He set out by alluding to the fact that Judge Douglas and himself fully agreed upon one point as set forth in Douglas' Columbus speech, viz: that the fathers of this Government understood its powers over the institution of slavery better than we do now; and he proceeded to show that the Democratic party had departed from the old land marks; and set up a new theory and a different policy, and at their present rate of progress, would speedily make slavery a national institution, over which even the states should exercise no control. In this the Democracy were resisted and must be resisted by the Republicans; that their position was identical, so far as the slavery question is concerned, with that occupied by the founders of the Government; and referred to the recent glorious victories achieved by the Republicans in Ohio and other States as clearly indicative that the good old doctrines of the fathers of the Republic would yet again prevail, and become the rule of action of the Government. He continued his remarks at considerable length, and made many strong points, which again and again brought down the crowd.

[1] *Illinois State Journal*, October 18, 1859. Upon Lincoln's return to Springfield from Clinton, on Saturday night a Republican victory parade marched to the Lincoln home. Following a tribute by Dr. William Jayne, Lincoln was invited to proceed to the state house and address the assembled citizens in the Capitol's rotunda. The brief summary of the speech given by the *Journal* is the most complete report available.

To Mark W. Delahay[1]

PRIVATE

Dear Delahay. Springfield, Oct. 17. 1859

Your letter requesting me to drop a line in your favor to Gen: Lane[2] was duly received. I have thought it over, and concluded that that is not the best way. Any open attempt on my part would injure you; and if the object merely be to assure Gen: Lane of my friendship for you, show him the letter herewith enclosed. I never saw him, or corresponded with him; so that a letter directly from me to him, would run a great hazzard of doing harm to both you and me.

As to the pecuniary matter, about which you formerly wrote me, I again appealed to our friend Turner,[3] by letter; but he never answered. I can but repeat to you that I am so pressed myself, as to be unable to assist you, unless I could get it from him. Yours as ever A LINCOLN

[1] ALS, DLC-HW.

[2] James H. Lane, commander of the free state troops and leader of the free state party, who was elected in 1856 to the United States Senate but did not take his seat until he was re-elected in 1861 after the admission of Kansas to the Union.

[3] Probably Thomas J. Turner, who on July 16, 1858, had given Lincoln a note for $400 at 10 per cent, which was not collected until 1866, by David Davis, administrator of Lincoln's estate.

To Mark W. Delahay[1]

M. W. Delahay, Esq. Springfield,

My dear Sir Oct. 17. 1859

I hear your name mentioned for one of the seats in the U.S. Senate from your new state. I certainly would be gratified with your success; and if there was any proper way for me to give you a lift, I would do it. But, as it is, I can only wish you well. It would be improper for me to interfere; and if I were to attempt it, it probably would do you harm. Your friend, as ever

A. LINCOLN

P.S. Is not the election news glorious?

[1] ALS, DLC-HW.

To William M. Dickson[1]

Hon: W. M. Dickson Springfield,

My dear Sir Oct. 17. 1859

Well, the election in Ohio is over; and there is nothing to regret but the loss of Cincinnati & Hamilton county. Pecuniarily, I suppose it is better for you to be remitted to the bar. The general result in the state—and in the other states—is, indeed, glorious. Now, let our friends bear, and forbear, and not quarrel over the spoils.

We were very glad to learn by your letter that your children were through the danger of Scarlet fever. Tell cousin Annie[2] that her cousin Ann,[3] here, now has it among her children. Otherwise the relations here are well. Give our love [to] Uncle Dr. Parker,[4] and particularly to our Republican Aunt.[5] Yours very truly

A. LINCOLN

[1] ALS-P, ISLA. William M. Dickson, prominent Cincinnati Republican attorney who had been appointed by Governor Salmon P. Chase to fill an unexpired term as judge of the Common Pleas Court of Hamilton County, Ohio, had retired on November 7, 1859. Lincoln had made his acquaintance on the occasion of the speech at Cincinnati, September 17, and together with Mrs. Lincoln had visited in the Dickson home the next day.

[2] Dickson's wife, Annie M. (Parker) Dickson.

[3] Ann (Todd) Smith, wife of Clark M. Smith and younger sister of Mrs. Lincoln.

[4] Dickson's father-in-law and Mrs. Lincoln's uncle, Dr. John Todd Parker of Lexington, Kentucky.

[5] Possibly Dickson's mother-in-law, Jane L. (Allen) Parker, but evidence of her Republican political preferences is lacking.

To William E. Frazer[1]

W. E. Frazer, Esq   Springfield, Ills.
Dear Sir: Nov. 1. 1859

Yours of the 24th. ult. was forwarded to me from Chicago. It certainly is important to secure Pennsylvania for the Republicans, in the next Presidential contest; and not unimportant to, also, secure Illinois. As to the ticket you name, I shall be heartily for it, *after* it shall have been fairly nominated by a Republican national convention; and I can not be committed to it *before*. For my single self, I have enlisted for the permanent success of the Republican cause; and, for this object, I shall labor faithfully in the ranks, unless, as I think not probable, the judgment of the party shall assign me a different position. If the Republicans of the great State of Pennsylvania, shall present Mr. Cameron as their candidate for the Presidency, such an indorsement of his fitness for the place, could scarcely be deemed insufficient. Still, as I would not like the *public* to know, so I would not like *myself* to know I had entered a combination with any man, to the prejudice of all others whose friends respectively may consider them preferable Yours truly

A. LINCOLN

[1] ALS copy, DLC-RTL. Frazer was a resident of Cookstown, Pennsylvania, and a supporter of Senator Simon Cameron. His letter of October 24 is not in the Lincoln Papers, but his acknowledgment of November 9 is.

To Doctor ———[1]

Dear Doctor: Springfield, Nov. 2. 1859

Your business makes it convenient for you to do a good deal in the way of getting all our friends to the polls next Tuesday. Please do it. We begin to hope we can elect Palmer.[2] He is a good man, and deserves to be elected, both for his own, and the cause's sake.

Yours truly A. LINCOLN

[1] ALS, RPB. The editors have been unable to identify the doctor whose business in the sixth congressional district would have justified Lincoln's request.

[2] John M. Palmer was defeated by Democrat John A. McClernand.

To William Dungy[1]

William Dungy, Esq Springfield, Nov. 2. 1859

Dear Sir Yours of Oct. 27. is received. When a mortgage is given to secure two notes, and one of the notes is sold and assigned, if the mortgaged premises are only sufficient to pay one note, the one assigned will take all.

Also, an execution, from a judgment on the assigned note, may take it all; it being the same thing in substance. There is redemption on execution sales from the U.S. court, just as from any other court.

You did not mention the name[2] of the plaintiff or defendant in the suit; and so I can tell nothing about it, as to sales, bids &c.

Write again. Yours &c A. LINCOLN

[1] ALS, OCHP. William Dungy was a resident of Franklin County, Illinois. See further, letter of November 21, *infra*.

[2] "S" has been added by someone other than Lincoln to read "names."

To P. Quinn Harrison[1]

P. Quinn, Harrison. Springfield,

Dear Sir: Nov. 3. 1859

I have reason to doubt that our friends are doing the best they can about the election. Still, you can do some more, if you will. A young man, before the enemy has learned to watch him, can do more than any other. Pitch in and try. Palmer is good and true, and deserves the best vote we can give him. If you can make your precinct 20 votes better than it was last we probably shall redeem the county. Try. Yours truly A. LINCOLN

[1] ALS-F, *The Bulletin of the California State Society Sons of the Revolution*, XVI, 4 (October-December, 1937). Peachy Quinn Harrison, son of Lincoln's friend Peyton Harrison and grandson of Peter Cartwright, had been defended by Lincoln a few weeks earlier in a famous murder case, being acquitted on September 3 in the Sangamon County Circuit Court of the murder of Greek Crafton.

Harrison had stabbed his brother-in-law Crafton in an altercation over politics, and Crafton died a few days later. Peter Cartwright's testimony concerning Crafton's deathbed forgiveness of his slayer was perhaps largely responsible for the jury's verdict.

To Jesse A. Pickrell[1]

Dear Jesse— Springfield, Nov. 3. 1859

I am never done asking for favors. I shall be much obliged if you and William,[2] and your sons will do what you can to get as good a vote for Palmer as possible. He is a good and true man; and we possibly may elect him. Get all our voters out that you can. Yours as ever A. LINCOLN

[1] ALS, owned by Harry E. Pickrell, Lanesville, Illinois.

[2] Jesse A. and William S. Pickrell were farmers living near Mechanicsburg in Sangamon County; all of Jesse's five sons, and two of William's six, were of voting age.

Speech at Mechanicsburg, Illinois[1]

November 4, 1859

On Friday night Mr. Lincoln addressed the people of Mechanicsburg in a most able and eloquent speech. He arraigned the Democratic party for the agitation which now exists throughout the country showing that they and they alone, were responsible for it all, and urged that sectionalism and wrangling on the slavery question would never be brought to an end until the power of the so-called Democratic party was broken in the nation. Douglas, the prime mover in the conspiracy must be rebuked, and in his own home.

[1] *Illinois State Journal*, November 7, 1859.

To Michael G. Dale[1]

Hon: M. G. Dale Springfield,
Dear Sir Nov. 8. 1859

Yours of the 4th. is just received. My expectation is to be at the Mount-Vernon Supreme Court, reaching there the 21st. of the month. Can then attend to your case if it be not disposed of before. I am just leaving home to be absent several days; so that it may not be convenient for me to get the copy of the Articles of Association. I think Jo. Gillespie has such copy. Yours truly

A. LINCOLN

[1] ALS, IHi. Michael G. Dale, an attorney at Edwardsville, Illinois, wrote that he wished to take Salmon A. Phelps *v.* Curtiss Blakeman, involving the Missis-

sippi and Atlantic Railroad, to the state Supreme Court before further hearings could be held before Federal Judge Samuel H. Treat, who had decided all points against the railroad (DLC-RTL).

To James A. Briggs[1]

James A. Briggs, Esq Danville, Ills., Nov. 13, 1859

Dear Sir Yours of the 1st. closing with my proposition for compromise, was duly received. I will be on hand; and in due time, will notify you of the exact day. I believe, after all, I shall make a political speech of it. You have no objection?

I would like to know, in advance, whether I am also to speak, or lecture, in New-York.

Very—very—glad your election went right. Yours truly,

A. LINCOLN

P.S. I am here at court, but my address is still at Springfield, Ills.

A. L.

[1] ALS, OClWHi. The letter is written on stationery of the M'Cormack House. An earlier letter to Briggs is presumably not extant, but is mentioned in Briggs to Lincoln, November 1, 1859 (DLC-Nicolay Papers), James A. Briggs was a member of a committee arranging a lecture in Plymouth Church, Brooklyn, New York. Lincoln's earlier letter had agreed to the lecture provided the committee would accept a February date and a "political" speech. Briggs' reply for the committee accepted Lincoln's "compromise" and promised $200, adding "I think they will arrange for a Lecture in N. Y. also, and will pay you $200 for that, with your consent." As the arrangements developed, however, a new committee of the Young Men's Central Republican Union, New York City, took charge, and only one speech was arranged for, at Cooper Institute on February 27, 1860. Lincoln remained under the impression that he was to speak in Brooklyn until he had reached New York to fill the engagement.

To William Dungy[1]

William Dungy, Esq United States Marshal's Office,
Dear Sir: Springfield, Ill., Nov. 21. 1859

I now find the suit is Shaw Buel & Barber against Hill & Hill. The Marshal says the execution has been levied on land, but that there has not, as yet been a sale of it.

Once more I tell you, the land can be so sold, as to leave you liable on the other note & you better watch it. Yours &c A. LINCOLN

[1] ALS, ORB. See Lincoln to Dungy, November 2, *supra*. Dungy's letter of November 11, specified that "the land was mortgaged to secure both notes, one was due last Christmas and the other next Christmas the one that is due was sued on . . . and judgement obtained against Jas. Hill and others . . . now I want to know whether the land is sold or not . . . and whether the last named note will have any chance at the land. . . . Hill gave the land that was mortgaged up to Satisfy the execution now I want to know whether that Sale will keep out the last note. . . ." (DLC-RTL).

To Lyman Trumbull[1]

Hon. L. Trumbull. Springfield, Nov. 28. 1859

My dear Sir: Yours of the 23rd. is received. I agree with you entirely about the contemplated election of Forney.[2] Nothing could be more short-sighted than to place so strong a man as Forney in position to keep Douglas on foot. I know nothing of Forney personally; but I would put no man in position to help our enemies in the point of our hardest strain.

There is nothing new here. I have written merely to give my view about this Forney business. Yours as ever A. LINCOLN

[1] ALS, CSmH.

[2] John W. Forney, anti-Lecompton editor of the Democratic Philadelphia *Press*, who had served as clerk of the House 1851-1855. Trumbull wrote that he had learned in New York of a move to make Forney clerk of the House, without any assurance from him that he would act with the Republicans, the idea being that he would bring enough anti-Lecompton Democrats with him to give the Republicans the speakership (DLC-RTL). Forney was elected clerk, and William Pennington, New Jersey Whig, was elected to the speakership on the forty-fourth *viva voce* vote.

Speech at Elwood, Kansas[1]

December 1 [November 30?], 1859

Mr. Lincoln was received with great enthusiasm. He stated the reasons why he was unable to make a speech this evening. He could only say a few words to us who had come out to meet him the first time he had placed his foot upon the soil of Kansas. Mr. Lincoln said that it was possible that we had local questions in regard to Railroads, Land Grants and internal improvements which were matters of deeper interest to us than the questions arising out of national politics, but of these local interests he knew nothing and should say nothing. We had, however, just adopted a State Constitution, and it was probable, that, under that Constitution, we should soon cease our Territorial existence, and come forward to take our place in the brotherhood of States, and act our parts as a member of the confederation. Kansas would be Free, but the same questions we had had here in regard to Freedom or Slavery would arise in regard to other Territories and we should have to take our part in deciding them. People often ask, "why make such a fuss about a few *niggers*?" I answer the question by asking what will you do to dispose of this question? The Slaves constitute one seventh of our entire population. Wherever there is an element of this magnitude in a government it will be talked about. The general feeling in regard to Slavery had changed entirely since the early days of the Republic. You may examine the debates under the Confederation, in the Convention that framed the Constitution and in the first session of Congress and you will not find a single man saying that Slavery is a good thing. They all believed it was an evil. They made the Northwest Territory—the only Territory then belonging to the government—forever *free*. They prohibited the African Slave trade. Having thus prevented its extension and cut off the supply, the Fathers of the Republic believed Slavery must soon disappear. There are only three clauses in the Constitution which refer to Slavery, and in neither of them is the word Slave or Slavery mentioned. The word is not used in the clause prohibiting the African Slave trade; it is not used in the clause which makes Slaves a basis of representation; it is not used in the clause requiring the return of fugitive Slaves. And yet in all the debates in the Convention the question was discussed and Slaves and Slavery talked about. Now *why* was this word kept out of that instrument and so carefully kept out that a European, be he ever so intelligent, if not familiar with our institutions, might read the Constitution over and over again and never learn that Slavery existed in the United States. The reason is this. The Framers of the Organic Law believed that the Constitution would *outlast* Slavery and they did not want a word there to tell future generations that Slavery had ever been legalized in America.

Your Territory has had a marked history—no other Territory has ever had such a history. There had been strife and bloodshed here, both parties had been guilty of outrages; he had his opinions as to the relative guilt of the parties, but he would not say who had been most to blame. One fact was certain—there had been loss of life, destruction of property; our material interests had been retarded. Was this desirable? There is a peaceful way of settling these questions—the way adopted by government until a recent period. The bloody code has grown out of the new policy in regard to the government of Territories.

Mr. Lincoln in conclusion adverted briefly to the Harper's Ferry Affair.[2] He believed the attack of Brown wrong for two reasons. It was a violation of law and it was, as all such attacks must be, futile as far as any effect it might have on the extinction of a great evil.

We have a means provided for the expression of our belief in regard to Slavery—it is through the ballot box—the peaceful method provided by the Constitution. John Brown has shown great courage, rare unselfishness, as even Gov. Wise[3] testifies. But no man, North or South, can approve of violence or crime. Mr. Lincoln closed his brief speech by wishing all to go out to the election on Tuesday and to vote as became the Freemen of Kansas.

[1] Elwood *Free Press*, December 3, 1859. Although the *Free Press* reported Lincoln's arrival and speech at Elwood "on Thursday," December 1, there has been considerable question of the date. Fred W. Brinkerhoff ("The Kansas Tour of Lincoln the Candidate," *Kansas Historical Quarterly*, XIII, 294-307) critically examines contemporary sources and arrives at the conclusion that Lincoln spoke at Elwood on the night of November 30, at Troy in the afternoon and at Doniphan on the night of December 1. If Lincoln spoke at all three places on December 1, his schedule of travel seems all but impossible.

[2] October 16-18, 1859. This is apparently Lincoln's first reference to John Brown, whose execution scheduled for December 2, 1859, undoubtedly placed him in the forefront of conversational topics among his former friends and enemies in Kansas. [3] Henry A. Wise of Virginia.

Remarks upon Arriving at Leavenworth, Kansas[1]

December 3, 1859

Mr. Lincoln was called for with loud cheers and made a few remarks, alluding briefly to political matters, giving a short sketch of the progress of the Republican party; of the trials of the Free State men in making this beautiful country the home of the free. He said their battles would never have to be fought over again. (Loud cries of "that's so," and "no! no!") and after returning his sincere thanks for so flattering a reception, and remarking that he should address them in the evening, he retired amid the cheers of the crowd.

[1] Leavenworth *Times*, December 5, 1859. Lincoln's remarks were made in reply to a speech of welcome by Colonel John C. Vaughan on the balcony of the Mansion House.

Speech at Leavenworth, Kansas[1]

December 3, 1859

"LADIES AND GENTLEMEN: You are, as yet, the people of a Territory; but you probably soon will be the people of a State of the

[1] *Illinois State Journal*, December 12, 1859. In an editorial comment the *Journal* specifies that the speech was delivered "in Leavenworth city on the 4th inst. as we find it in the Leavenworth *Register*." The date is doubtless an error. Other sources confirm the fact that Lincoln spoke twice at Leavenworth on Saturday, December 3. Upon his arrival he replied briefly to Colonel John C. Vaughan's speech of welcome at the Mansion House, *supra*. That night he delivered his prepared speech in Stockton Hall, which was reported in Jefferson L. Dugger's *Register*, formerly published by Mark W. Delahay. On Monday, December 5, the day before the Kansas election, he spoke again, by request, in Stockton Hall (*vide infra*).

Union. Then you will be in possession of new privileges, and new duties will be upon you. You will have to bear a part in all that pertains to the administration of the National Government. That government, from the beginning, has had, has now, and must continue to have a policy in relation to domestic slavery. It cannot, if it would, be without a policy upon that subject. And that policy must, of necessity, take one of two directions. It must deal with the institution as being *wrong* or as *not* being wrong."

Mr. Lincoln then stated, somewhat in detail, the early action of the General Government upon the question—in relation to the foreign slave trade, the basis of Federal representation, and the prohibition of slavery in the Federal territories; the Fugitive Slave clause in the Constitution, and insisted that, plainly that early policy, was based on the idea of slavery being wrong; and tolerating it so far, and only so far, as the necessity of its actual presence required.

He then took up the policy of the Kansas-Nebraska act, which he argued was based on opposite ideas—that is, the idea that slavery is *not* wrong. He said: "You, the people of Kansas, furnish the example of the first application of this new policy. At the end of about five years, after having almost continual struggles, fire and bloodshed, over this very question, and after having framed several State Constitutions, you have, at last, secured a Free State Constitution, under which you will probably be admitted into the Union. You have, at last, at the end of all this difficulty, attained what we, in the old North-western Territory, attained without any difficulty at all. Compare, or rather contrast, the actual working of this new policy with that of the old, and say whether, after all, the old way—the way adopted by Washington and his compeers—was not the better way."

Mr. Lincoln argued that the new policy had proven false to all its promises—that its promise to the Nation was to speedily end the slavery agitation, which it had not done, but directly the contrary—that its promises to the people of the Territories was to give them greater control of their own affairs than the people of former Territories had had; while, by the actual experiment, they had had less control of their own affairs, and had been more bedeviled by outside interference than the people of any other Territory ever had.

He insisted that it was deceitful in its expressed wish to confer additional privileges upon the people; else it would have conferred upon them the privilege of choosing their own officers. That if there be any just reason why all the privileges of a State should not be conferred on the people of a Territory at once, it only could be the smallness of numbers; and that if while their number was small, they were fit to do some things, and unfit to do others, it could only be because those they were unfit to do, were the larger and more important things—that, in this case, the allowing the people of Kansas to plant their soil with slavery, and not allowing them to choose their own Governor, could only be justified on the idea that the planting a new State with slavery was a very small matter, and the election of Governor a very much greater matter. "Now," said he, "compare these two matters and decide which is really the greater. You have already had, I think, five Governors, and yet, although their doings, in their respective days, were of some little interest to you, it is doubtful whether you now, even remember the names of half of them. They are gone (all but the last) without leaving a trace upon your soil, or having done a single act which can, in the least degree, help or hurt you, in all the indefinite future before you. This is the size of the Governor question. Now, how is it with the slavery question? If your first settlers had so far decided in favor of slavery, as to have got five thousand slaves planted on your soil, you could, by no moral possibility, have adopted a Free State Constitution. Their owners would be influential voters among you as good men as the rest of you, and, by their greater wealth, and consequent, greater capacity, to assist the more needy, perhaps the most influential among you. You could not wish to destroy, or injuriously interfere with their property. You would not know what to do with the slaves after you had made them free. You would not wish to keep them as underlings; nor yet to elevate them to social and political equality. You could not send them away. The slave States would not let you send them there; and the free States would not let you *send* them there. All the rest of your property would not pay for sending them to Liberia. In one word, you could not have made a free State, if the first half of your own numbers had got five thousand slaves fixed upon the soil. You could have disposed of, not merely five, but five hundred Governors easier. There they would have stuck, in spite of you, to plague you and your children, and your children's children, indefinitely. Which is the greater, this, or the Governor question? Which could the more safely be intrusted to the first few people who settle a Territory? Is it that which, at most, can be but temporary and brief in its effects? or that which being done by the first few, can scarcely ever be undone by the succeeding many?"

He insisted that, little as was Popular Sovereignty at first, the

Dred Scott decision, which is indorsed by the author of Popular Sovereignty, has reduced it to still smaller proportions, if it has not entirely crushed it out. That, in fact, all it lacks of being crushed out entirely by that decision, is the lawyer's technical distinction between *decision* and *dictum*. That the Court has already *said* a Territorial government cannot exclude slavery; but because they did not say it in a case where a Territorial government had tried to exclude slavery, the lawyers hold that saying of the Court to be *dictum* and not *decision*. "But," said Mr. Lincoln, "is it not certain that the Court will make a *decision* of it, the first time a Territorial government tries to exclude slavery?"

Mr. Lincoln argued that the doctrine of Popular Sovereignty, carried out, renews the African Slave Trade. Said he: "Who can show that one people have a better right to carry slaves to where they have never been, than another people have to buy slaves wherever they please, even in Africa?"

He also argued that the advocates of Popular Sovereignty, by their efforts to brutalize the negro in the public mind—denying him any share in the Declaration of Independence, and comparing him to the crocodile—were beyond what avowed pro-slavery men ever do, and really did as much, or more than they, toward making the institution national and perpetual.

He said many of the Popular Sovereignty advocates were "as much opposed to slavery as any one;" but that they could never find any proper time or place to oppose it. In their view, it must not be opposed in politics, because that is agitation; nor in the pulpit, because it is not religion; nor in the Free States, because it is not there; nor in the Slave States, because it is there. These gentlemen, however, are never offended by hearing Slavery supported in any of these places. Still, they are "as much opposed to Slavery as anybody." One would suppose that it would exactly suit them if the people of the Slave States would themselves adopt emancipation; but when Frank Blair tried this last year, in Missouri, and was beaten, every one of them threw up his hat and shouted "Hurrah for the Democracy!"

Mr. Lincoln argued that those who thought Slavery right ought to unite on a policy which should deal with it as being right; that they should go for a revival of the Slave Trade; for carrying the institution everywhere, into Free States as well as Territories; and for a surrender of fugitive slaves in Canada, or war with Great Britain. Said he, "all shades of Democracy, popular sovereign as well as the rest, are fully agreed that slaves are property, and only property. If Canada now had as many horses as she has slaves belonging to Americans, I should think it just cause of war if she did not surrender them on demand.

"On the other hand, all those who believe slavery is wrong should unite on a policy, dealing with it as a wrong. They should be deluded into no deceitful contrivances, pretending indifference, but really working for that to which they are opposed." He urged this at considerable length.

He then took up some of the objections to Republicans. They were accused of being sectional. He denied it. What was the proof? "Why, that they have no existence, get no votes in the South. But that depends on the South, and not on us. It is their volition, not ours; and if there be fault in it, it is primarily theirs, and remains so, unless they show that we repel them by some wrong principle. If they attempt this, they will find us holding no principle, other than those held and acted upon by the men who gave us the government under which we live. They will find that the charge of sectionalism will not stop at us, but will extend to the very men who gave us the liberty we enjoy. But if the mere fact that we get no votes in the slave states makes us sectional, whenever we shall get votes in those states, we shall cease to be sectional; and we are sure to get votes, and a good many of them too, in these states next year.

"You claim that you are conservative; and we are not. We deny it. What is conservatism? Preserving the old against the new. And yet you are conservative in struggling for the new, and we are destructive in trying to maintain the old. Possibly you mean you are conservative in trying to maintain the existing institution of slavery. Very well; we are not trying to destroy it. The peace of society, and the structure of our government both require that we should let it alone, and we insist on letting it alone. If I might advise my Republican friends here, I would say to them, leave your Missouri neighbors alone. Have nothing whatever to do with their slaves. Have nothing whatever to do with the white people, save in a friendly way. Drop past differences, and so conduct yourselves that if you cannot be at peace with them, the fault shall be wholly theirs.

"You say we have made the question more prominent than heretofore. We deny it. It is more prominent; but we did not make it so. Despite of us, you would have a change of policy; we resist the change, and in the struggle, the greater prominence is given to the question. Who is responsible for that, you or we? If you would have the question reduced to its old proportions go back to the old policy. That will effect it.

"But you are for the Union; and you greatly fear the success of the Republicans would destroy the Union. Why? Do the Republicans declare against the Union? Nothing like it. Your own statement of it is, that if the Black Republicans elect a President, you won't stand it. You will break up the Union. That will be your act, not ours. To justify it, you must show that our policy gives you just cause for such desperate action. Can you do that? When you attempt it, you will find that our policy is exactly the policy of the men who made the Union. Nothing more and nothing less. Do you really think you are justified to break up the government rather than have it administered by Washington, and other good and great men who made it, and first administered it? If you do you are very unreasonable; and more reasonable men cannot and will not submit to you. While you elect [the] President, we submit, neither breaking nor attempting to break up the Union. If we shall constitutionally elect a President, it will be our duty to see that you submit. Old John Brown has just been executed for treason against a state. We cannot object, even though he agreed with us in thinking slavery wrong. That cannot excuse violence, bloodshed, and treason. It could avail him nothing that he might think himself right. So, if constitutionally we elect a President, and therefore you undertake to destroy the Union, it will be our duty to deal with you as old John Brown has been dealt with. We shall try to do our duty. We hope and believe that in no section will a majority so act as to render such extreme measures necessary."

Mr. Lincoln closed by an appeal to all—opponents as well as friends—to think soberly and maturely, and never fail to cast their vote, insisting that it was not a privilege only, but a duty to do so.

Second Speech at Leavenworth, Kansas[1]

December 5, 1859

Mr. Lincoln opened by reviewing the Territorial policy of our Government at the start, proving conclusively that it was in favor of liberty and was ever so exerted except in some of the Southern States where slavery existed by municipal law or was made a distinctive feature of the articles of cession. But where these causes were not there was freedom proclaimed.

The Fathers did not seek to interfere with slavery where it existed but to prevent its extension. This was the policy of the Republican party of to-day.

[1] Leavenworth *Times*, December 6, 1859.

The divisions of sentiment in the Democratic party in regard to slavery were flimsy and immaterial. The most advanced element could boast of no higher sentiment than an indifference to the peculiar institution. No part of the Democracy ever declared slavery wrong in itself; and they reached a sublime height when they said they didn't care whether it was voted up or voted down.

This indifference was all the slave-power could ask. It was a virtual recognition of the right of slavery to universal extension.

If a house was on fire there could be but two parties. One in favor of putting out the fire. Another in favor of the house burning. But these popular sovereignty fellows would stand aloof and argue against interfering. The house must take care of itself subject only to the constitution and the conditions of fire and wood.

The speaker alluded, with much force and wit, to the great line (which we are assured by Senator Douglas was ordained of God) on one side of which slave-labor alone could be employed—on the other free-labor. Thought the Missouri River might be the line referred to. If the line was ordained of God it ought to be plain and palpable, but he had never been able to put his finger upon it.

The attempt to identify the Republican party with the John Brown business was an electioneering dodge. Was glad to know that the Democracy underrated the good sense of the people as the great Republican victories in New York, New Jersey, Minnesota and Iowa—where the argument was brought out with extraordinary emphasis—clearly demonstrated. In Brown's hatred of slavery the speaker sympathized with him. But Brown's insurrectionary attempt he emphatically denounced. He believed the old man insane, and had yet to find the first Republican who endorsed the proposed insurrection. If there was one he would advise him to step out of the ranks and correct his politics. But slavery was responsible for their uprisings. They were fostered by the institution. In 1830-31, the slaves themselves arose and killed fifty-eight whites in a single night. These servile upheavings must be continually occurring where slavery exists.

The democracy was constituted of two great elements. First. The original and unadulterated Democrats. Second. The Old line and *eminently* conservative Whigs. This incongruous party was ever charging the Republicans with favoring negro suffrage, sustaining this charge by instancing the two Republican States of Massachusetts and New Hampshire where negroes are allowed to vote. But it so happens that the law conferring this franchise was enacted by the Old Whigs in Massachusetts and the Democrats in New Hampshire. Kansas was the only State where the Republicans had the framing of the organic law and here they confined the elective franchise to the white man alone.

Mr. Lincoln said that, *in political arguments*, the Democracy turned up their noses at "amalgamation." But while there were only one hundred and seventy-nine mulattoes in the Republican State of New Hampshire, there were *seventy-nine thousand* in the good old Democratic State of Virginia—and the only notable instance of the amalgamation that occurred to him was in the case of a Democratic Vice President.

Mr. Lincoln wanted the races kept distinct. Because he did not wish to hold a negro woman as a slave it did not follow that he wanted her for a wife. Such flimsy diatribes were perpetrated by the Democracy to divert the public mind from the real issue—the extension or the non-extension of slavery—its localization or its nationalization.

Mr. Lincoln closed by a clear and forcible definition of the aims and the principles of the Republican party. He showed how they harmonized with the teachings of those by whom the Government was founded and how their predominance was "essential to the proper development of our country—its progress and its glory—to the salvation of the Union and the perpetuity of Free Institutions."

Inscription in the Autograph Album of Mary Delahay[1]

Dear Mary December 7, 1859

With pleasure I write my name in your Album. Ere long some younger man will be more happy to confer *his* name upon *you.*

Dont allow it, Mary, until fully assured that he is worthy of the happiness. Dec. 7– 1859 Your friend A. LINCOLN

[1] ADS, ORB. Mary was the daughter of Lincoln's old friend Mark W. Delahay, in whose home he had been a guest during his stay at Leavenworth, Kansas. The inscription was written on the day of his departure for Springfield.

To Levant L. Jones[1]

L. L. Jones, Esq Springfield, Ills.

My dear Sir: Dec. 9. 1859

Your kind invitation to me to visit Lawrence, was handed me at Leavenworth on Saturday the 3rd. Inst. I was advertised to speak there that evening and also on Monday the 5th; so that it was not possible for me to be at Lawrence before, or at, the election. I supposed there was not sufficient object for me to go *after* the election, through the excessive cold.

Please present my respects, and make my acknowledgments, to the other gentlemen, who joined you in the inv[it]ation, and accept the same for yourself. Very truly yours A. LINCOLN

[1] ALS-F, Kansas City, Missouri, *Times*, February 9, 1929. Jones was a young lawyer from Connecticut who had gone with the Free-Staters to settle in Olathe, Kansas. His letter dated November 29 bears thirteen signatures in addition to his own (DLC-RTL).

To Norman B. Judd[1]

Hon. N. B. Judd Springfield Dec. 9. 1859.

My dear Sir: I have just reached home from Kansas and found your long letter of the 1st. inst. It has a tone of blame towards myself which I think is not quite just; but I will not stand upon that, but will consider a day or two, and put something in the best shape I can, and send it to you. A great difficulty is that they make no distinct charge against you, which I can contradict. You did vote for Trumbull against me; and, although I think, and have said a thousand times, that was no injustice to me, I cannot change the fact, nor compel people to cease speaking of it. Ever since that matter occurred, I have constantly labored, as I believe you know, to have all recollection of it dropped.

The vague charge that you played me false last year, I believe to be false and outrageous; but, it seems, I can make no impression by expressing that belief. I made a special job of trying to impress that upon Baker, Bridges and Wilson,[2] here last winter. They all well know that I believe no such charge against you. But they choose to insist that they know better about it than I do.

As to the charge of your intriguing for Trumbull against me, I believe as little of that as any other charge. If Trumbull and I were candidates for the same office, you would have a right to prefer him, and I should not blame you for it; but all my acquaintance with you induces me to believe you would not *pretend* to be for me while really for him. But I do not understand Trumbull & myself to be rivals. You know I am pledged to not enter a struggle with him for the seat in the Senate now occupied by him; and yet I would rather have a full term in the Senate than in the Presidency.

I have made this letter longer than I expected when I began. Your friend as ever A. LINCOLN

P.S. I omitted to say that I have, in no single instance, permitted a charge against [*sic*][3] such as above alluded to, to go uncontradicted, when made in my presence. A.L.

[1] Copy, DLC-RTL. Copy is in John Hay's handwriting on stationery of "Room 1, Cushing's Block, Cleveland, O. . . . . . 188–."

[2] Hay has copied "Baker, Budger and Wilson," but in a note at bottom of the page he confesses, "I am not sure about this name. It might be Badger, Bridges, or Budger." Judd's letter to Lincoln, however, names the men in the following sentence: "There is only one mode of replacing the harmony of the party—and that is John Wentworth is to be driven out or silenced and Charley Wilson, S. L. Baker, E. T. Bridges and their lying associates kicked into the kennell with the other curs." (DLC-RTL). Edwin T. Bridges, not previously identified, was connected with the Chicago *Evening Journal* and was an active Republican.

[3] The *sic* is John Hay's.

To Daniel W. Wilder[1]

D. W. Wilder, Esq Springfield, Ills.
My dear Sir: Dec. 9, 1859

While at Elwood I promised the editor of the Free-soil paper at St. Joseph (Dr. Benjamin,[2] as I remember) to try to be at St. Jo– Tuesday evening on my return home. As things went, I could not get there; and when I reached [there] on Wednesday evening, I did not get to see him. When you meet him please make my appology. The reason I trouble you is that I am not quite sure of his name, or the name of paper. Yours very truly

A. LINCOLN—

[1] ALS-P, ISLA. Daniel W. Wilder was editor of the Elwood, Kansas, *Free Press.* [2] O. A. Benjamin, editor of the St. Joseph, Missouri, *Free Democrat.*

To William Kellogg[1]

Hon: William Kellogg. Springfield, Ills.
My dear Sir: Dec. 11. 1859

I have been a good deal relieved this morning by a sight of Greeley's letter to you, published in the Tribune.[2] Before seeing it, I much feared you had, in charging interviews between Douglas & Greely, stated what you *believed*, but did not certainly *know* to be true; and that it might be untrue, and our enemies would get an advantage of you. However, as G. admits the interviews, I think it will not hurt you that he denies conversing with D. about his re-[e]lection to the Senate. G. I think, will not tell a falsehood; and I think he will scarcely deny that he had the interviews with D. in order to assure himself from D's own lips, better than he could from his public acts & declarations, whether to try to bring the Republican party to his support generally, including his re-election to the Senate. What else could the interviews be for? Why immediately followed in the Tribune the advice that all anti-Lecompton democrats should be re-elected? The world will not consider it any thing that D's reelection to the Senate was not specifically talked of by him & G.

Now, mark, I do not charge that G. was corrupt in this. I do not think he was, or is. It was his judgment that the course he took was the best way of serving the Republican cause. For this reason, and for the further reason, that he is now pulling straight with us, I think, if I were you, I would not pursue him further than necessary to my own justification. If I were you I would however be greatly tempted [to] ask him if he really thinks D.s advice to his friends to vote for a Lecompton & Slave code man, is very "*plucky*"

Please excuse what I have said, in the way of unsolicited a[d]-vice. I believe you will not doubt the sincerity of my friendship for you. Yours very truly A. LINCOLN

1 ALS, ORB.

2 Lincoln refers to Greeley's signed editorial, "A Word with a Congressman," in the New York *Tribune*, December 8, 1859, in which Greeley replied to Kellogg's charge, made in the U.S. House of Representatives, December 5, 1859, that Greeley and others "met in the parlor of Senator Douglas [in 1858], plotting and planning to sell Illinois and Missouri too. . . ." Greeley admitted that he had visited Douglas, but maintained that "Mr. Douglas's reelection to the Senate, or his future election to any post whatever, was not even mentioned."

To George W. Dole, Gurdon S. Hubbard, and William H. Brown[1]

Messrs. Dole, Hubbard & Brown— Springfield,
Gent. Dec. 14, 1859

Your favor of the 12th. is at hand, and it gives me pleasure to be able to answer it. It is not my intention to take part in any of the rivalries for the Gubernatorial nomination; but the fear of being misunderstood upon that subject, ought not to deter me from doing justice to Mr. Judd, and preventing a wrong being done to him by the use of my name in connection with alledged wrongs to me.

In answer to your first question as to whether Mr. Judd was guilty of any unfairness to me at the time of Senator Trumbull's election, I answer unhesitatingly in the negative. Mr. Judd owed no political allegiance to any party whose candidate I was. He was in the Senate, holding over, having been elected by a democratic constituency. He never was in any caucus of the friends who sought to make me U.S. Senator—never gave me any promises or pledges to support me—and subsequent events have greatly tended to prove the wisdom, politically, of Mr. Judd's course. The election of Judge Trumbull strongly tended to sustain and preserve the position of that portion of the Democrats who condemned the repeal of the

Missouri compromise, and left them in a position of joining with us in forming the Republican party, as was done at the Bloomington convention in 1856

During the canvass of 1858 for the Senatorship my belief was, and still is, that I had no more sincere and faithful friend than Mr. Judd—certainly none whom I trusted more. His position as Chairman of the State Central committee, led to my greater intercourse with him, and to my giving him a larger share of my confidence, than with, or, to almost any other friend; and I have never suspected that that confidence was, to any degree, misplaced.

My relations with Mr. Judd, since the organization of the Republican party, in our State, in 1856, and, especially since the adjournment of the Legislature in Feb. 1857, have been so very intimate, that I deem it an impossibility that he could have been dealing treacherously with me. He has also, at all times, appeared equally true and faithful to the party. In his position, as Chairman of the Committee, I believe he did all that any man could have done. The best of us are liable to commit errors, which become apparant, by subsequent developement; but I do not now know of a single error, even, committed by Mr. Judd, since he and I have acted together politically.

I had occasionally heard these insinuations against Mr. Judd, before the receipt of your letter; and in no instance have I hesitated to pronounce them wholly unjust, to the full extent of my knowledge and belief. I have been, and still am, very anxious to take no part between the many friends, all good and true, who are mentioned as candidates for a Republican Gubernatorial nomination; but I can not feel that my own honor is quite clear, if I remain silent, when I hear any one of them assailed about matters of which I believe I know more than his assailants.

I take pleasure in adding that of all the avowed friends I had in the canvass of last year, I do not suspect any of having acted treacherously to me, or to our cause; and that there is not one of them in whose honesty, honor, and integrity I, to-day, have greater confidence than I have in those of Mr. Judd.

I dislike to appear before the public, in this matter; but you are at liberty to make such use of this letter as you may think justice requires. Yours very truly A. LINCOLN

[Enclosure] You can use your discretion as to whether you make this public.[2]

[1] ALS, ICHi; ADfS (1st. and 2nd.), DLC-RTL. The text follows the letter sent, both drafts being considerably revised. Dole, Hubbard, and Brown were prominent businessmen and Republicans of Chicago. Brown, not previously iden-

tified, was a banker and a lawyer, and first president of the Chicago Historical Society. A copy of their letter, December 12, 1859, made by Lincoln, is also in the Lincoln Papers. See Lincoln to Judd, December 9, *supra*, and December 14, *infra*. The letter sent seems to have gone to Judd in care of Lyman Trumbull, rather than to the persons addressed (see Lincoln to Trumbull, December 25, *infra*) and was published together with the letter from Dole, Hubbard, and Brown, in the Republican papers of the state.

[2] This is a slip pasted on the first draft and copied on the second draft with Lincoln's additional notation "Slip sent with original." The enclosure is no longer with the letter sent, however, and the text is taken from the draft and copy in the Lincoln Papers.

To Norman B. Judd[1]

Springfield, Decr. 14, 1859

Dear Judd: Herewith is the letter of our old whig friends,[2] and my answer, sent as you requested. I showed both to Dubois,[3] and he feared the clause about leave to publish, in the answer, would not be quite satisfactory to you. I hope it will be satisfactory; as I would rather not seem to come before the public as a volunteer; still if, after considering this, you still deem it important, you may, substitute the inclosed slip, by pasting it down over the original clause.[4]

I find some of our friends here, attach more consequence to getting the National convention into our State than I did, or do. Some of them made me promise to say so to you. As to the *time*, it must certainly be after the Charleston fandango; and I think, within bounds of reason, the later the better.

As to that matter about the Committee, in relation to appointing delegates by general convention, or by Districts, I shall attend to it as well as I know how, which, G–d knows, will not be very well.

Write me, if you can find any thing to write. Yours as ever

A. LINCOLN

[1] ALS copy, DLC-RTL. [2] See letter to Dole, Hubbard, and Brown, *supra*.
[3] Jesse K. Dubois. [4] See enclosure with letter, *supra*.

To Jackson Grimshaw[1]

Jackson Grimshaw, Esq Springfield,
My dear Sir: Dec. 15. 1859

Herewith I return your business letter, with a note upon it which explains itself.

Judd has started East to attend the sitting of the National committee, at N. Y. the 21st. Previous to going he wrote that soon after his return he would call the State Committee together; and he wished me to see some of the members, including yourself, upon a matter which I can tell you better when I see you, than I can write about it. In a general way I may say it was relative to whether Delegates to the National convention shall be appointed, by general convention, or by districts. Perhaps it would be as well to make no committal on this, till we have a conference. Yours very truly A. LINCOLN.

We will consent to a renewal of all the stipulations of the last trial, for this ensuing one, with the understanding that either party offers any additional competent evidence which he may choose.

A. LINCOLN

P.S. Bring this over with you.

[1] ALS and AES, IHi. The endorsement appears on the letter which Lincoln returned. Grimshaw had written concerning the case of Powell *v.* Ament asking whether stipulations made for the first trial will be renewed "or shall we be required to prove them."

To George M. Parsons and Others[1]

Springfield, Ills., Dec. 19, 1859.

Messrs. Geo. M. Parsons and Others, Cent. Ex. Com., &c.

Gentlemen: Your letter of the 7th inst., accompanied by a similar one from the Governor elect, the Republican State officers, and the Republican members of the State Board of Equalization of Ohio, both requesting of me, for publication in permanent form, copies of the political debates between Senator Douglas and myself, last year, has been received. With my grateful acknowledgments to both you and them, for the very flattering terms in which the request is communicated, I transmit you the copies.[2] The copies I send you are reported and printed, by the respective friends of Senator Douglas and myself, at the time—that is, his by his friends, and mine by mine. It would be an unwarrantable liberty for us to change a word or a letter in his, and the changes I have made in mine, you perceive, are verbal only, and very few in number. I wish the reprint to be precisely as the copies I send, without any comment whatever. Yours very truly, A. LINCOLN.

[1] *Illinois State Journal*, January 30, 1860, and *Political Debates* (Follett, Foster and Company, 1860), p. 5.

[2] This was the scrapbook with clippings of the debates corrected by Lincoln, referred to as the "Debates Scrapbook," which was used for the Follett, Foster and Company edition of the *Debates*, and which provides the text of the debates in the present edition of Lincoln's writings.

To Jesse W. Fell, Enclosing Autobiography[1]

J. W. Fell, Esq Springfield,
My dear Sir: Dec. 20. 1859

Herewith is a little sketch, as you requested. There is not much of it, for the reason, I suppose, that there is not much of me.

If any thing be made out of it, I wish it to be modest, and not to go beyond the material. If it were thought necessary to incorporate any thing from any of my speeches, I suppose there would be no objection. Of course it must not appear to have been written by myself. Yours very truly A. LINCOLN

I was born Feb. 12, 1809, in Hardin County, Kentucky. My parents were both born in Virginia, of undistinguished families—second families, perhaps I should say. My mother, who died in my tenth year, was of a family of the name of Hanks, some of whom now reside in Adams, and others in Macon counties, Illinois. My paternal grandfather, Abraham Lincoln, emigrated from Rockingham County, Virginia, to Kentucky, about 1781 or 2, where, a year or two later, he was killed by indians, not in battle, but by stealth, when [where?] he was laboring to open a farm in the forest. His ancestors, who were quakers, went to Virginia from Berks County, Pennsylvania. An effort to identify them with the New-England family of the same name ended in nothing more definite, than a similarity of Christian names in both families, such as Enoch, Levi, Mordecai, Solomon, Abraham, and the like.

My father, at the death of his father, was but six years of age; and he grew up, litterally without education. He removed from Kentucky to what is now Spencer county, Indiana, in my eighth year. We reached our new home about the time the State came into the Union. It was a wild region, with many bears and other wild animals still in the woods. There I grew up. There were some schools, so called; but no qualification was ever required of a teacher, beyond "*readin, writin, and cipherin,*"[2] to the Rule of Three. If a straggler supposed to understand latin, happened to sojourn in the neighborhood, he was looked upon as a wizzard. There was absolutely nothing to excite ambition for education. Of course when I came of age I did not know much. Still somehow, I could read, write, and cipher to the Rule of Three; but that was all. I have not been to school since. The little advance I now have upon this store of education, I have picked up from time to time under the pressure of necessity.

I was raised to farm work, which I continued till I was twenty two. At twenty one I came to Illinois, and passed the first year in Illinois—Macon county. Then I got to New-Salem, (at that time[3] in Sangamon, now in Menard county, where I remained a year as a sort of Clerk in a store. Then came the Black-Hawk war; and I was elected a Captain of Volunteers—a success which gave me more pleasure than any I have had since. I went the campaign, was elated, ran for the Legislature the same year (1832) and was beaten—the only time I have been beaten by the people. The next, and three succeeding biennial elections, I was elected to the Legislature. I was not a candidate afterwards. During this Legislative period I had studied law, and removed to Springfield to practice it. In 1846 I was once elected to the lower House of Congress. Was not a candidate for re-election. From 1849 to 1854, both inclusive, practiced law more assiduously than ever before. Always a whig in politics, and generally on the whig electoral tickets, making active canvasses. I was losing interest in politics, when the repeal of the Missouri Compromise aroused me again. What I have done since then is pretty well known.

If any personal description of me is thought desirable, it may be said, I am, in height, six feet, four inches, nearly; lean in flesh, weighing, on an average, one hundred and eighty pounds; dark complexion, with coarse black hair, and grey eyes—no other marks or brands recollected. Yours very truly A. LINCOLN

Hon. J. W. Fell.[4]

[1] ALS, ORB; AD, DLC. The one-page letter and the two-and-one-half page sketch have become separated in the course of years and now rest in the places indicated. Fell requested the sketch on behalf of Joseph J. Lewis of West Chester, Pennsylvania, who used it in preparing an article on Lincoln, published in the *Chester County Times*, February 11, 1860, and widely copied in Republican papers.

[2] Lincoln deleted "reading, writing, and Arithmetic" and substituted this phrase. [3] "Then" deleted; "at that time" inserted.

[4] "Hon. J. W. Fell" and "Yours very truly/A. Lincoln," clipped from Lincoln's letter to Fell, October 5, 1860, *infra*, have been pasted on the document, presumably at the time the sketch was first reproduced in facsimile.

To Lyman Trumbull[1]

Hon. Lyman Trumbull Springfield, Dec. 25, 1859

Dear Sir: About the 15th. by direction of Mr. Judd, I sent a letter and inclosures to him, addressed to your care; and I have not yet learned whether he received it.[2]

I have carefully read your speech;[3] and I judge that, by the interruptions it came out a much better speech than you expected to make when you began. It really is an excellent one, many of the points being most admirably made.

I was in the inside of the Post-Office last evening when a mail came bringing a considerable number of your documents; and the Post-Master said to me "These will be put in the boxes, and half will never be called for. If Trumbull would send them to me I would distribute a hundred to where he will get ten distributed this way." I said, shall I write this to Trumbull. He replied "If you choose you may." I believe he was sincere; but you will judge of that for yourself. Yours as ever A. LINCOLN

[1] ALS, CSmH.

[2] See letters to Judd and to Dole, Hubbard and Brown, December 14, *supra*.

[3] Trumbull's speech in the Senate, December 8, 1859, dealt with the principles of the Republican Party.

To Zophar Case[1]

Zopher Case, Esq Springfield Ills Dec 29 1859

Mr. A Sanders Piatt of Ohio, has engaged us to bring some ejectment suits in the U.S. Court. Some of the land lies in your County & he has refered us to you for what has to be done on the Spot. Herewith is a declaration

The blanks in which you will fill properly, and also fill the blanks in the Notice with a day distant enough—then make a copy of declaration and Notice; Serve it on the Defendant make affidavit of the Sirvice on the declaration and return it by mail to us Yours &c LINCOLN & HERNDON.

[1] LS, OClCS. Only the salutation and close are in Lincoln's handwriting. Zophar Case was clerk of the U.S. Circuit Court and newspaper editor at Carlyle, Illinois. The declaration carrying Case's affidavit was filed January 16, 1860, in the U.S. Circuit Court for Southern Illinois.

To Leonard Swett[1]

Hon. L. Swett Springfield,
Dear Sir Jan. 9, 1860

This introduces Mr. William Yates, who visits Bloomington on some business matter. He is pecuniarily responsible for anything he will say; and, in fact, for anything he will say on any subject. Yours very truly A. LINCOLN

[1] ALS, owned by David Davis, IV, Bloomington, Illinois. Tracy, p. 175, misdates this letter January 9, 1861. William Yates was a partner of Clark M. Smith in the general merchandise business at Springfield.

To Alonzo J. Grover[1]

A. J. Grover, Esq Springfield, Ills.
My dear Sir: Jany. 15. 1860

Yours of the 9th. was duly received. In my joint debate with Douglas, at Freeport, Aug. 27. 1858, I said about all I have ever publicly said concerning the Fugitive slave law of 1850, and you can find it in print in the report of that debate. I said then in substance, and have often said, I think Congress has constitutional power to enact *a* Fugitive slave law; that the law of 1850 appears to me objectionable in some of its provisions; but whether it is unconstitutional in any of it's provisions, I do not remember that I have ever undertaken to decide. I should be glad to see you, and to talk with you more fully than I can write. Yours truly

A. Lincoln

[1] ALS, IHi. Alonzo J. Grover, lawyer and abolitionist of Earlville, Illinois, a member of the Republican committee of LaSalle County, wrote on January 9, 1860, asking Lincoln's views on the constitutionality of the Fugitive Slave Law (DLC-RTL).

To Fernando Jones[1]

Fernando Jones, Esq Springfield,
My dear Sir: Jany. 15. 1860

Yours of the 10th. was received two or three days ago; and, being much engaged, I have postponed attending to it until now. Our republican friend, J. W. Fell, of Bloomington, Illinois, can furnish you the materials for a brief sketch of my history, if it be desired.

I shall be happy to receive a letter from you at any time. Yours truly A. Lincoln

[1] ALS, ICHi. Fernando Jones was a real estate operator and an alderman of Chicago.

To Gustave P. Koerner[1]

Hon: G. Koerner— Springfield, Jany. 20. 1860

My dear Sir Yesterday the Judge decided the demurrer against us on all the points. On looking over your memorandum[2] left with me, I find you desire me to "have the case set for trial as late as I can"—but really I find I have no power [to] set a time for the trial. The opposite party is not here, in person, or by counsel; and the Judge, properly enough, refuses to make a stipulation for the absent party. He says he understands, however that the case is not to come up before the 24th. I have Telegraphed you to-day; but if this reaches you before you leave, you might see Jewett[3] at St. Louis, and make an arrangement. Yours truly A. LINCOLN

[1] ALS, MoSHi.

[2] Koerner's memorandum (DLC-RTL) of January 14 gives the client's name and address as "Salomon Kepfli, Highland, Madison Cy Ills." Directories give the name as "Koepfli." [3] Daniel T. Jewett.

To James W. Sheahan[1]

Jas. W. Sheahan, Esq Springfield, Jan. 24. 1860

Dear Sir Yours of the 21st., requesting copies of my speeches now in progress of publication in Ohio, is received. I have no such copies now at my control; having sent the only sett I ever had, to Ohio. Mr. Geo. M. Parsons has taken an active part among those who have the matter in charge, in Ohio; and I understand Messrs. Follett, Foster & Co are to be the publishers. I make no objection to any satisfactory arrangement you may make with Mr. Parsons and the publishers; and, if it will facilitate you, you are at liberty to show them this note.

You labor under a mistake, somewhat injurious to me, if you suppose I have *revised* the speeches, in any just sense of the word. I only made some small verbal corrections, mostly such as an inteligent reader would make for himself; not feeling justified to do more, when republishing the speeches along with those of Senator Douglas—his and mine being mutually answers and replies to one another. Yours truly A. LINCOLN.

[1] ALS, ICHi; ALS copy, DLC-RTL. James W. Sheahan was editor of the Chicago *Times*.

Recommendation for Henry S. Greene[1]

Springfield, Ill., Jan. 28, 1860.

We, the undersigned, report that we have examined Mr. Henry S. Greene and find him well qualified to practice as an attorney and counselor at law. We therefore recommend that he be licensed as such.

A. LINCOLN,
L. W. ROSS,
O. H. BROWNING.

[1] Howard F. Dyson, "Lincoln in Rushville," *Transactions of the Illinois State Historical Society, 1903*, No. 8, p. 225.

To Abraham Jonas[1]

Hon: A. Jonas Springfield, Feb. 4 1860

My dear Sir: Yours of the 3rd. inquiring how you can get a copy of the debates now being published in Ohio, is received. As you are one of my most valued friends, and have complimented me by the expression of a wish for the book, I propose doing myself the honor of presenting you with one, so soon as I can. By the arrangement our Ohio friends have made with the publishers, I am to have one hundred copies gratis. When I shall receive them I will send you one by Express. I understand they will not be out before March; and I probably shall be absent about that time, so that you must not be disappointed if you do not receive yours before about the middle of that month. Yours very truly A. LINCOLN

1 ALS, IHi.

To Norman B. Judd[1]

Hon. N. B. Judd: Springfield, Feb. 5, 1860

My dear Sir: Your two letters were duly received. Whether Mr. Storrs[2] shall come to Illinois, and assist in our approaching campaign, is a question of dollars & cents. Can we pay him? If we can, that is the sole question. I consider his services very valuable.

A day or so before you wrote about Mr. Herndon,[3] Dubois told me that he, H, had been talking to William Jayne in the way you indicate. At first sight afterwards, I mentioned it to him; he rather denied the charge, and I did not press him about the past; but got his solemn pledge to say nothing of the sort in the future. I had done this before I received your letter. I impressed upon him as well as I could, first that such, was untrue, and unjust to you, and second, that *I* would be held responsible for what he said. Let this be private.

Some folks are pretty bitter towards me about the Dole, Hubbard, & Brown letter. Yours as ever A. LINCOLN

1 ALS, owned by Norman J. Gould, Seneca Falls, New York.

2 A copy of C. Storrs, Jr., to Joseph Medill, January 9, 1860, written from Gardner, Kansas, offering to return to Chicago if he can serve the Republican cause as he did in 1856, is enclosed by Judd to Lincoln, January 27, 1860 (DLC-RTL). Judd expressed a wish to employ Storrs "if we had the means." Storrs was supervisor of county commissioners in Johnson County, Kansas.

3 Judd wrote, January 31, "I am advised that Herndon is a believer in [Samuel L.] Baker and is talking about misapplication of funds by me &cc. This ought not to be and is not true. Can not you set him right. . . ." (DLC-RTL). See also Lincoln to David L. Phillips, February 17, *infra*.

To Henry E. Dummer[1]

Hon: H. E. Dummer— Springfield
My dear Sir: Feb. 8, 1860

I have examined and considered the question propounded in your letter accompanying copy of contract in relation Lard Tanks, apparatus &c, and my opinion is that Messrs H. C. Chadsey & Co,[2] would, as a general proposition, have the right to continue to use the Tanks, apparatus &c, which they have on hand.

The reason why I say "*as a general proposition*" is that I fear the particular phraseology of their contract, deprives them of it. The language of the contract is so explicit, and so oft repeated, that the right to use, "shall be until the expiration of said patent" that I fear it will be held that by their contract, they can not have the benefit of the extension.

Much may be said on the other side; and I only mean to say that in my mind the question, on the phraseology of the contract is doubtful, and perhaps is worth trying Yours as ever

A. LINCOLN

[1] ALS, IHi.
[2] Henry C. Chadsey & Co. were meat packers at Beardstown, Illinois.

To Norman B. Judd[1]

Hon. N. B. Judd, Springfield Feb. 9. 1860

Dear Sir: I am not in a position where it would hurt much for me to not be nominated on the national ticket; but I am where it would hurt some for me to not get the Illinois delegates. What I expected when I wrote the letter to Messrs Dole and others is now happening. Your discomfitted assailants are most bitter against me; and they will, for revenge upon me, lay to the Bates egg in the South, and to the Seward egg in the North, and go far towards squeezing me out in the middle with nothing. Can you not help me a little in this matter, in your end of the vineyard?

I mean this to be private. Yours as ever A. LINCOLN

[1] Copy, DLC-RTL. The copy is in the handwriting of John Hay on stationery of "Room 1, Cushing's Block, Cleveland, O. . . . . 188–."

To Josiah M. Lucas[1]

Springfield, February 9, 1860.

My dear Sir: Your late letter, suggesting, among other things, that I might aid your election as postmaster, by writing to Mr.

Burlingame,[2] was duly received the day the Speaker was elected; so that I had no hope a letter of mine could reach Mr. B. before your case would be decided, as it turned out in fact it could not. We are all much gratified here to see you are elected. We consider you our peculiar friend at court.

I shall be glad to receive a letter from you at any time you can find leisure to write one. Yours very truly, A. LINCOLN.

[1] NH, V, 291. Lincoln's old friend Josiah M. Lucas was elected to the postmastership of the U.S. House of Representatives.

[2] Anson Burlingame, representative from Massachusetts.

To Major W. Packard[1]

M. W. Packard, Esq Springfield,
Dear Sir: Feb 10– 1860.

William Florville, a colored barber here, owns four lots in Bloomington, on which I have been paying the taxes for him several years, but which I forgot [to] do, though under promise, when I was at Bloomington last. Will you please collect the ten dollars fee we spoke of, add enough of your own money, pay all taxes due, and send me the receipt, or receipts? If you will I shall be greatly obliged; and besides, will return you the money you advance by the first mail.

William Thomas, Larrimore,[2] and others there know about these lots. Yours truly A. LINCOLN

[1] ALS, IHi.

[2] William Thomas was county treasurer at Bloomington, and John N. Larrimore was a real estate dealer.

To John C. Henshaw[1]

Major John C. Henshaw. Springfield Ills.
My dear Sir: Feb. 13. 1860

Your letter of the 2nd. Inst. notifying me that you had forwarded to me by the hand of Mr. Blinn,[2] a certain book on Labor & Capital, was duly received. I have not yet received the book; but I presume I shall, so soon as I shall visit Bloomington. I am much gratified by this mark of your kind remembrance.[3] I expect to be in New-York about the 27th. Inst. when & where I shall be truly happy to meet you. Yours very truly A. LINCOLN.

[1] ALS, RPB. John C. Henshaw of New York City had sent Lincoln a copy of a book by his father-in-law, Edward Kellogg, *Labor and Other Capital: the Rights*

of *Each Secured and the Wrongs of Both Eradicated*, New York, 1849 (DLC-RTL).

[2] Blinn is identified in Henshaw's letter as "of McLean County Bank," Bloomington, Illinois.

[3] Henshaw had met Lincoln at Clinton, Illinois, in the fall of 1859.

To Horace White[1]

Friend White Springfield, Feb. 13. 1860.

Your kind note, inclosing the letter of Mr. Billinghurst is just received. It so happens that I am engaged to be at Brooklyn,[2] on the evening of the 27th. so that, of course, I can not be in Wisconsin, on the 28th. and I have so written Mr. B.[3]

Thank you for your anticipations of the future for me, as well as for your many past kindnesses. Your friend as ever

A LINCOLN

[1] ALS, RPB. Horace White of the Chicago *Press and Tribune* wrote February 10, enclosing a letter from Charles Billinghurst, Republican ex-congressman from Wisconsin (1855-1859) who was in ignorance concerning Lincoln's address (DLC-RTL).

[2] Lincoln did not know that he was to speak at Cooper Institute until he arrived in New York.

[3] The letter to Billinghurst is presumably not extant.

To Oliver P. Hall, Jacob N. Fullinwider, and William F. Correll[1]

Messrs. O. P. Hall Springfield,
J. R. Fullinwider & W. F. Correll. Feb. 14. 1860

Gentlemen. Your letter, in which among other things, you ask "what I meant when I said this Union could not stand half slave and half free—and also what I meant when I said a house divided against itself could not stand" is received, and I very cheerfully answer it as plainly as I may be able. You misquote, to some material extent, what I did say; which induces me to think you have not, very carefully read the speech in which the expressions occur which to [*sic*] puzzle you to understand. For this reason and because the language I used is as plain as I can make it, I now quote at length the whole paragraph in which the expressions which puzzle you occur. It is as follows: "We are now far into the fifth year since a policy was initiated with the avowed object, and confident promise of putting an end to slavery agitation. Under the operation of that policy that agitation has not only not ceased but constantly augmented. I believe it will not cease until a crisis shall have been reached, and passed. A house divided against itself can not stand. I believe this government can not endure *permanently*, half slave, and half free. I do not expect the Union to be dissolved; I do not expect the house to fall; but I do expect it will cease to be divided. It will become all one thing, or all the other. Either the opponents of slavery will arrest the further spread of it, and place it where the public mind shall rest in the belief that it is in course of ultimate extinction; or it's advocates will push it forward till it will become alike lawful in all the states, old as well as new, North, as well as South."

That is the whole paragraph; and it puzzles me to make my meaning plainer. Look over it carefully, and conclude I meant all I said and did not mean anything I did not say, and you will have my meaning. Douglas attacked me upon this, saying it was a declaration of war between the slave and the free states. You will perceive I said no such thing, and I assure you I thought of no such thing.

If I had said "I believe this government can not *last always*, half slave and half free" would you understand it any better than you do? "Endure permanently" and "last always" have exactly the same meaning.

If you, or any of you, will state to me some meaning which you suppose I had, I can, and will instantly tell you whether that was my meaning. Yours very truly A. LINCOLN

[1] ALS, ICU. Oliver P. Hall, Jacob N. Fullinwider, whose middle initial Lincoln misread, and William F. Correll were Sangamon County farmers who wrote on January 9, asking for an explanation of Lincoln's famous phrase (DLC-RTL).

To Eunice E. Howell[1]

Eunice E. Howell: Springfield, Ills. Feb. 17. 1860

I now find it impossible that I should lecture for you this winter. Several things conspire, forcing me to this conclusion. Yours &c

A. LINCOLN

[1] ALS, owned by C. Norton Owen, Glencoe, Illinois. The envelope accompanying the letter is addressed to "Alfred Center, New-York."

To David L. Phillips[1]

D. L. Philips, Esq Springfield,
My dear Sir: Feb. 17, 1860.

Yours of the 13th. was received a day or two since, and I have been so busy that I could not attend to it till now. There are four judgments, all against Bennett & Scott. The plaintiffs are—

White & Wright — date Jan. 20, 1858 — $179.97 — Cost	23.65
Cawfield & Moffett " " " " " 94.98 — "	23.65
Fisher & Bennett " " " " "114.25 — "	23.65
Marcus Fechhemmer " " " " "364.44 "	23.65

I have not yet mentioned the matter of the "paper" to Dubois,[2] but will so soon as I see him. Yours very truly A. LINCOLN.

[1] ALS, IHi. David L. Phillips, Republican committeeman and partner of Benjamin L. Wiley and Nathan Dresser in a land office and collecting agency at Anna, Illinois, wrote February 13 for a record of judgments recorded on the docket of the U.S. District Court against W. W. Bennett and S. E. Scott, or William Bennett, or W. W. Bennett & Co. (DLC-RTL).

[2] Phillips had written "I recd. a dispatch from Dubois on Friday saying 'The Baker papers are in my possession.' I hoped to get them on Saturday. If he has not sent them have him mail them to Judd, as I shall be in Chicago tuesday night." The reference undoubtedly is to papers detrimental to Norman B. Judd which Samuel L. Baker was passing around. See Lincoln to Judd, February 5, *supra*.

To John Olney[1]

John Olney, Esq Springfield,
My dear Sir: Feb. 21. 1860.

Your excellent letter of the 14th. is just received. It puts some propositions so admirably that I am tempted to publish them—without names, of course. Yours very truly A. LINCOLN.

[1] ALS, CSmH. Olney's letter is not in the Lincoln Papers, and the editors are tempted to think Lincoln may have had it published, without identification. Olney, a Shawneetown attorney, was a Republican presidential elector in the 1860 campaign.

To Simon Cameron[1]

Hon: Simon Cameron: New-York.
Dear Sir Feb. 26. 1860

I write this to say the card of yourself, and Hon. David Wilmot, was handed me yesterday at Philadelphia, just as I was leaving for this city. I barely had time to step over to the Girard, where I learned that you and he were not at your rooms. I regret that being so near, we did not meet; but hope we may yet meet before a great while.

Will you please forward the inclosed to Mr. Wilmot, as I do not remember his address?[2] Yours truly A. LINCOLN.

[1] ALS, DLC-Cameron Papers.

[2] Apparently Lincoln's enclosed letter to his old acquaintance in the House of Representatives is not extant.

Address at Cooper Institute, New York City[1]

February 27, 1860

MR. PRESIDENT AND FELLOW-CITIZENS OF NEW-YORK:—The facts with which I shall deal this evening are mainly old and familiar; nor is there anything new in the general use I shall make of them. If there shall be any novelty, it will be in the mode of presenting the facts, and the inferences and observations following that presentation.

In his speech last autumn, at Columbus, Ohio, as reported in "The New-York Times," Senator Douglas said:

"Our fathers, when they framed the Government under which we live, understood this question just as well, and even better, than we do now."

I fully indorse this, and I adopt it as a text for this discourse. I so adopt it because it furnishes a precise and an agreed starting point for a discussion between Republicans and that wing of the Democracy headed by Senator Douglas. It simply leaves the inquiry: *"What was the understanding those fathers had of the question mentioned?"*

What is the frame of Government under which we live?

The answer must be: "The Constitution of the United States." That Constitution consists of the original, framed in 1787, (and under which the present government first went into operation,) and twelve subsequently framed amendments, the first ten of which were framed in 1789.[2]

[1] *The Address of the Hon. Abraham Lincoln, in [V]indication of the Policy of the Framers of the Constitution and the Principles of the Republican Party, Delivered at Cooper Institute, February 27th, 1860,* Issued by the Young Men's Republican Union, (659 Broadway, New-York,) with Notes by Charles C. Nott & Cephas Brainerd, Members of the Board of Control. New-York: George F. Nesbitt & Co., Printers and Stationers, 1860. The manuscript of the address is not extant, but of the several texts available, the Nott and Brainerd pamphlet issued in September, 1860, has strong claim as a definitive text. Lincoln supervised its preparation, as he did not the printing of the speech from his manuscript in the New York *Tribune,* February 28, 1860, or the issues of the *Tribune Tracts* No. 4 which followed. His letters to Nott (May 31, September 6, and September 22, *infra*) are concerned with its preparation and indicate that Lincoln carefully corrected the copy of *Tribune Tracts* No. 4 which Nott had revised, and that he later corrected the proof sheets of the new pamphlet. The extensive annotation prepared by Nott and Brainerd, which Lincoln thought "exceedingly valuable," has also been reproduced from the source in the succeeding footnotes.

[2] The Constitution is attested September 17, 1787. It was ratified by all of the States, excepting North Carolina and Rhode Island, in 1788, and went into operation on the first Wednesday in January, 1789. The first Congress proposed, in 1789, ten articles of amendments, all of which were ratified. Article XI. of the amendments was prepared by the Third Congress, in 1794, and Article XII. by the Eighth Congress, in 1803. Another Article was proposed by the Eleventh Congress, prohibiting *citizens* from receiving titles of nobility, presents or offices,

Who were our fathers that framed the Constitution? I suppose the "thirty-nine" who signed the original instrument may be fairly called our fathers who framed that part of the present Government. It is almost exactly true to say they framed it, and it is altogether true to say they fairly represented the opinion and sentiment of the whole nation at that time. Their names, being familiar to nearly all, and accessible to quite all, need not now be repeated.[3]

I take these "thirty-nine" for the present, as being "our fathers who framed the Government under which we live."

What is the question which, according to the text, those fathers understood "just as well, and even better than we do now?"

It is this: Does the proper division of local from federal authority, or anything in the Constitution, forbid *our Federal Government* to control as to slavery in *our Federal Territories?*

Upon this, Senator Douglas holds the affirmative, and Republicans the negative. This affirmation and denial form an issue; and this issue—this question—is precisely what the text declares our fathers understood "better than we."

Let us now inquire whether the "thirty-nine," or any of them, ever acted upon this question; and if they did, how they acted upon it—how they expressed that better understanding?

In 1784, three years before the Constitution—the United States then owning the Northwestern Territory, and no other,[4] the Con-

from foreign nations. Although this has been printed as one of the amendments, it was in fact never ratified, being approved by but twelve States. *Vide* Message of President Monroe, Feb. 4, 1818.

[3] The Convention consisted of *sixty-five* members. Of these, *ten* did not attend the Convention, and *sixteen* did not sign the Constitution. Of these sixteen, six refused to sign, and published their reasons for so refusing, *viz:* Robert Yates and John Lansing, of New-York; Edmund Randolph and George Mason, of Virginia; Luther Martin, of Maryland, and Elbridge Gerry, of Mass. Alexander Hamilton alone subscribed for New-York, and Rhode Island was not represented in the Convention. The names of the "thirty-nine," and the States which they represented are subsequently given.

[4] The cession of territory was authorized by New-York, Feb. 19, 1780; by Virginia, January 2, 1781, and again, (without certain conditions at first imposed,) "at their sessions, begun on the 20th day of October, 1783;" by Mass., Nov. 13, 1784; by Conn., May —, 1786; by S. Carolina, March 8, 1787; by N. Carolina, Dec. —, 1789; and by Georgia at some time prior to April, 1802.

The deeds of cession were executed by New-York, March 1, 1781; by Virginia, March 1, 1784; by Mass., April 19, 1785; by Conn., Sept. 13, 1786; by S. Carolina, August 9, 1787; by N. Carolina, Feb. 25, 1790; and by Georgia, April 24, 1802. Five of these grants were therefore made before the adoption of the Constitution, and one afterward; while the sixth (North Carolina) was authorized before, and consummated afterward. The cession of this State contains the express proviso "that no regulations made, or to be made by Congress, shall tend to emancipate slaves." The cession of Georgia conveys the Territory subject to the Ordinance of '87, except the provision prohibiting slavery.

These dates are also interesting in connection with the extraordinary assertions

gress of the Confederation had before them the question of prohibiting slavery in that Territory; and four of the "thirty-nine," who afterward framed the Constitution, were in that Congress, and voted on that question. Of these, Roger Sherman, Thomas Mifflin, and Hugh Williamson voted for the prohibition,[5] thus showing that, in their understanding, no line dividing local from federal authority, nor anything else, properly forbade the Federal Government to control as to slavery in federal territory. The other of the four—James M'Henry—voted against the prohibition, showing that, for some cause, he thought it improper to vote for it.[6]

In 1787, still before the Constitution, but while the Convention was in session framing it, and while the Northwestern Territory still was the only territory owned by the United States, the same question of prohibiting slavery in the territory again came before the Congress of the Confederation; and two more of the "thirty-nine" who afterward signed the Constitution, were in that Congress, and voted on the question. They were William Blount and William Few;[7] and they both voted for the prohibition—thus show-

of Chief Justice Taney, (19 How, page 434,) that "the example of Virginia was soon afterwards followed by other States," and that (p. 436) the power in the Constitution "to dispose of and make all needful rules and regulations respecting the Territory or other property belonging to the United States," was intended only "to transfer to the new Government the property then held in common," "and has no reference whatever to any Territory or other property, which the new sovereignty might afterwards itself acquire." On this subject, *vide* Federalist, No. 43, sub. 4 and 5.

[5] Sherman was from Connecticut; Mifflin from Penn.; Williamson from North Carolina, and M'Henry from Maryland.

[6] What Mr. M'Henry's views were, it seems impossible to ascertain. When the Ordinance of '87 was passed he was sitting in the Convention. He was afterward appointed Secretary of War; yet no record has thus far been discovered of his opinion. Mr. M'Henry also wrote a biography of La Fayette, which, however, cannot be found in any of the public libraries, among which may be mentioned the State Library at Albany, and the Astor, Society, and Historical Society Libraries, at New-York.

Hamilton says of him, in a letter to Washington, (*Works*, vol. 6, p. 65): "M'Henry you know. He would give no strength to the Administration, but he would not disgrace the office; his views are good."

[7] William Blount was from North Carolina, and William Few, from Georgia—the two States which afterward ceded their territory to the United States. In addition to these facts the following extract from the speech of Rufus King in the Senate, on the Missouri Bill, shows the entire unanimity with which the Southern States approved the prohibition:—

"The State of Virginia, which ceded to the United States her claims to this Territory, consented, by her delegates in the old Congress, to this Ordinance. Not only Virginia, but North Carolina, South Carolina and Georgia, by the unanimous votes of their delegates in the Old Congress, approved of the Ordinance of 1787, by which Slavery is forever abolished in the Territory northwest of the river Ohio. Without the votes of these States the Ordinance could not have been passed; and there is no recollection of an opposition from any of these States to the act of confirmation passed under the actual Constitution."

ing that, in their understanding, no line dividing local from federal authority, nor anything else, properly forbade the Federal Government to control as to slavery in federal territory. This time the prohibition became a law, being part of what is now well known as the Ordinance of '87.[8]

The question of federal control of slavery in the territories, seems not to have been directly before the Convention which framed the original Constitution; and hence it is not recorded that the "thirty-

[8] "The famous ordinance of Congress of the 13th July, 1787, which has ever since constituted, in most respects, the model of all our territorial governments, and is equally remarkable for the brevity and exactness of its text, and for its masterly display of the fundamental principles of civil and religious liberty."—*Justice Story, 1 Commentaries*, § 1312.

"It is well known that the Ordinance of 1787 was drawn by the Hon. Nathan Dane, of Massachusetts, and adopted with scarcely a verbal alteration by Congress. It is a noble and imperishable monument to his fame." —*Id.* note.

The ordinance was reported by a committee, of which Wm. S. Johnson and Charles Pinckney were members. It recites that, "for extending the fundamental principles of civil and religious liberty, which form the basis whereon these republics, their laws and constitutions, are erected; to fix and establish those principles as the basis of all laws, constitutions and governments which forever hereafter shall be formed in the said Territory; to provide also for the establishment of States and permanent government, and for their admission to a share in the federal councils, on an equal footing with the original States, at as early periods as may be consistent with the general interest—

"It is hereby ordained and declared, by the authority aforesaid, that the following articles shall be considered as articles of compact between the original States and the people and States in the said Territory, and forever remain unalterable, unless by common consent, to wit:" * * * *

"*Art.* 6. There shall be neither slavery nor involuntary servitude in the said Territory otherwise than in the punishment of crimes whereof the party shall have been duly convicted; provided always that any person escaping into the same, from whom labor or service is lawfully claimed in any one of the original States, such fugitive may be lawfully reclaimed, and conveyed to the person claiming his or her labor or service."

On passing the ordinance, the ayes and nays were required by Judge Yates, of New-York, when it appeared *that his was the only vote in the negative.*

The ordinance of April 23, 1784, was a brief outline of that of '87. It was reported by a Committee, of which Mr. Jefferson was chairman, and the report contained a slavery prohibition intended to take effect in 1800. This was stricken out of the report, six States voting to retain it—three voting to strike out—one being divided (N. C.,) and the others not being represented. (The assent of nine States was necessary to retain any provision.) And this is the vote alluded to by Mr. Lincoln. But subsequently, March 16, 1785, a motion was made by Rufus King to commit a proposition "that there be neither slavery nor involuntary servitude" in any of the Territories; which was carried by the vote of eight States, including Maryland.—*Journal Am. Congress*, vol. 4, pp. 373, 380, 481, 752.

When, therefore, the ordinance of '87 came before Congress, on its final passage, the subject of slavery prohibition had been "*agitated*" for nearly three years; and the deliberate and almost unanimous vote of that body upon that question leaves no room to doubt what the fathers believed, and how, in that belief, they acted.

nine," or any of them, while engaged on that instrument, expressed any opinion of that precise question.[9]

[9] It singularly and fortunately happens that one of the "thirty-nine," "while engaged on that instrument," viz., while advocating its ratification before the Pennsylvania Convention, did express an opinion upon this "precise question," which opinion was *never* disputed or doubted, in that or any other Convention, and was accepted by the opponents of the Constitution, as an indisputable fact. This was the celebrated James Wilson, of Pennsylvania. The opinion is as follows:—

MONDAY, *Dec.* 3, 1787.

"With respect to the clause restricting Congress from prohibiting the migration or importation of such persons as any of the States now existing shall think proper to admit, prior to the year 1808: The Hon. gentleman says that this clause is not only dark, but intended to grant to Congress, for that time, the power to admit the importation of slaves. No such thing was intended; but I will tell you what was done, and it gives me high pleasure that so much was done. Under the present Confederation, the States may admit the importation of slaves as long as they please; but by this article, after the year 1808, the Congress will have power to prohibit such importation, notwithstanding the disposition of any State to the contrary. I consider this as laying the foundation for banishing slavery out of this country; and though the period is more distant than I could wish, yet it will produce the same kind, gradual change which was pursued in Pennsylvania. It is with much satisfaction that I view this power in the general government, whereby they may lay an interdiction on this reproachful trade. But an immediate advantage is also obtained; for a tax or duty may be imposed on such importation, not exceeding $10 for each person; and this, sir, operates as a partial prohibition; it was all that could be obtained. I am sorry it was no more; but from this I think there is reason to hope that yet a few years, and it will be prohibited altogether. *And in the meantime, the new States which are to be formed will be under the control of Congress in this particular, and slaves will never be introduced amongst them.*"—2 *Elliott's Debates*, 423.

It was argued by Patrick Henry in the Convention in Virginia, as follows:

"May not Congress enact that every black man must fight? Did we not see a little of this in the last war? We were not so hard pushed as to make emancipation general. But acts of Assembly passed, that every slave who would go to the army should be free. Another thing will contribute to bring this event about. Slavery is detested. We feel its fatal effects. We deplore it with all the pity of humanity. Let all these considerations press with full force on the minds of Congress. Let that urbanity which, I trust, will distinguish America, and the necessity of national defence—let all these things operate on their minds, they will search that paper, and see if they have power of manumission. And have they not, sir? Have they not power to provide for the general defence and welfare? May they not think that these call for the abolition of slavery? May they not pronounce all slaves free, and will they not be warranted by that power? There is no ambiguous implication, no logical deduction. The paper speaks to the point; they have the power in clear, unequivocal terms, and will clearly and certainly exercise it."—3 *Elliott's Debates*, 534.

Edmund Randolph, one of the framers of the Constitution, replied to Mr. Henry, admitting the general force of the argument, but claiming that, because of other provisions, it had no application to the *States* where slavery *then* existed; thus conceding that power to exist in Congress as to all territory belonging to the United States.

Dr. Ramsay, a member of the Convention of South Carolina, in his history of the United States, vol. 3, pages 36, 37, says: "Under these liberal principles, Congress, in organizing *colonies*, bound themselves to impart to their inhabitants all the privileges of coequal States, as soon as they were capable of enjoying them.

In 1789, by the first Congress which sat under the Constitution, an act was passed to enforce the Ordinance of '87, including the prohibition of slavery in the Northwestern Territory. The bill for this act was reported by one of the "thirty-nine," Thomas Fitzsimmons, then a member of the House of Representatives from Pennsylvania. It went through all its stages without a word of opposition, and finally passed both branches without yeas and nays, which is equivalent to an unanimous passage.[10] In this Congress there were sixteen of the thirty-nine fathers who framed the original Constitution. They were John Langdon, Nicholas Gilman, Wm. S. Johnson, Roger Sherman, Robert Morris, Thos. Fitzsimmons, William Few, Abraham Baldwin, Rufus King, William Paterson, George Clymer, Richard Bassett, George Read, Pierce Butler, Daniel Carroll, James Madison.[11]

This shows that, in their understanding, no line dividing local from federal authority, nor anything in the Constitution, properly forbade Congress to prohibit slavery in the federal territory; else both their fidelity to correct principle, and their oath to support the Constitution, would have constrained them to oppose the prohibition.

Again, George Washington, another of the "thirty-nine," was then President of the United States, and, as such, approved and signed the bill; thus completing its validity as a law, and thus showing that, in his understanding, no line dividing local from federal authority, nor anything in the Constitution, forbade the Federal Government, to control as to slavery in federal territory.

In their infancy, *government was administered for them* without any expense. As soon as they should have 60,000 inhabitants, they were authorized to call a convention, and, by common consent, to form their own constitution. This being done, they were entitled to representation in Congress, and every right attached to the original States. These privileges are not confined to any particular country or *complexion*. They are communicable to the emancipated slave, (for in the new State of Ohio, slavery is altogether prohibited), to the copper-colored native, and all other human beings who, after a competent residence and degree of civilization, are capable of enjoying the blessings of regular government."

[10] The Act of 1789, as reported by the Committee, was received and read Thursday, July 16th. The second reading was on Friday, the 17th, when it was committed to the Committee of the whole house, "on Monday next." On Monday, July 20th, it was considered in Committee of the whole, and ordered to a third reading on the following day; on the 21st, it passed the House, and was sent to the Senate. In the Senate it had its first reading on the same day, and was ordered to a second reading on the following day, (July 22d,) and on the 4th August it passed, and on the 7th was approved by the President.

[11] The "sixteen" represented these States:—Langdon and Gilman, New Hampshire; Sherman and Johnson, Connecticut; Morris, Fitzsimmons and Clymer, Pennsylvania; King, Massachusetts; Paterson, New Jersey; Few and Baldwin, Georgia; Bassett and Read, Delaware; Butler, South Carolina; Carroll, Maryland; and Madison, Virginia.

No great while after the adoption of the original Constitution, North Carolina ceded to the Federal Government the country now constituting the State of Tennessee; and a few years later Georgia ceded that which now constitutes the States of Mississippi and Alabama. In both deeds of cession it was made a condition by the ceding States that the Federal Government should not prohibit slavery in the ceded country.[12] Besides this, slavery was then actually in the ceded country. Under these circumstances, Congress, on taking charge of these countries, did not absolutely prohibit slavery within them. But they did interfere with it—take control of it—even there, to a certain extent. In 1798, Congress organized the Territory of Mississippi. In the act of organization, they prohibited the bringing of slaves into the Territory, from any place without the United States, by fine, and giving freedom to slaves so brought.[13] This act passed both branches of Congress without yeas and nays. In that Congress were three of the "thirty-nine" who framed the original Constitution. They were John Langdon, George Read and Abraham Baldwin.[14] They all, probably, voted for it. Certainly they would have placed their opposition to it upon record, if, in their understanding, any line dividing local from federal authority, or anything in the Constitution, properly forbade the Federal Government to control as to slavery in federal territory.

In 1803, the Federal Government purchased the Louisiana country. Our former territorial acquisitions came from certain of our own States; but this Louisiana country was acquired from a foreign nation. In 1804, Congress gave a territorial organization to that part of it which now constitutes the State of Louisiana. New Orleans, lying within that part, was an old and comparatively large city. There were other considerable towns and settlements, and slavery was extensively and thoroughly intermingled with the people. Congress did not, in the Territorial Act, prohibit slavery; but they did interfere with it—take control of it—in a more marked and extensive way than they did in the case of Mississippi. The substance of the provision therein made, in relation to slaves, was:

First. That no slave should be imported into the territory from foreign parts.

Second. That no slave should be carried into it who had been imported into the United States since the first day of May, 1798.

Third. That no slave should be carried into it, except by the

[12] *Vide* note 4, *ante*.

[13] Chap. 28, § 7, U.S. Statutes, 5th Congress, 2d Session.

[14] Langdon was from New Hampshire, Read from Delaware, and Baldwin from Georgia.

owner, and for his own use as a settler; the penalty in all the cases being a fine upon the violator of the law, and freedom to the slave.[15]

This act also was passed without yeas and nays. In the Congress which passed it, there were two of the "thirty-nine." They were Abraham Baldwin and Jonathan Dayton.[16] As stated in the case of Mississippi, it is probable they both voted for it. They would not have allowed it to pass without recording their opposition to it, if, in their understanding, it violated either the line properly dividing local from federal authority, or any provision of the Constitution.

In 1819-20, came and passed the Missouri question. Many votes were taken, by yeas and nays, in both branches of Congress, upon the various phases of the general question. Two of the "thirty-nine" —Rufus King and Charles Pinckney—were members of that Congress.[17] Mr. King steadily voted for slavery prohibition and against all compromises, while Mr. Pinckney as steadily voted against slavery prohibition and against all compromises. By this, Mr. King showed that, in his understanding, no line dividing local from federal authority, nor anything in the Constitution, was violated by Congress prohibiting slavery in federal territory; while Mr. Pinckney, by his votes, showed that, in his understanding, there was some sufficient reason for opposing such prohibition in that case.[18]

[15] Chap. 38, § 10, U.S. Statutes, 8th Congress, 1st Session.

[16] Baldwin was from Georgia, and Dayton from New Jersey.

[17] Rufus King, who sat in the old Congress, and also in the Convention, as the representative of Massachusetts, removed to New-York and was sent by that State to the U.S. Senate of the first Congress. Charles Pinckney was in the House, as a representative of South Carolina.

[18] Although Mr. Pinckney opposed "slavery prohibition" in 1820, yet his views, with regard to the *powers* of the general government, may be better judged by his actions in the Convention:

FRIDAY, *June 8th*, 1787.—"Mr. Pinckney moved 'that the National Legislature shall have the power of negativing all laws to be passed by the State Legislatures, which they may judge improper,' in the room of the clause as it stood reported.

"He grounds his motion on the necessity of one supreme controlling power, and he considers this as the *corner-stone* of the present system; and hence, the necessity of retrenching the State authorities, in order to preserve the good government of the national council."—P. 400, *Elliott's Debates*.

And again, THURSDAY, *August 23d*, 1787, Mr. Pinckney renewed the motion with some modifications.—P. 1409, *Madison Papers*.

And although Mr. Pinckney, as correctly stated by Mr. Lincoln, "steadily voted against slavery prohibition, and against all compromises," he still regarded the passage of the Missouri Compromise as a great triumph of the South, which is apparent from the following letter.

CONGRESS HALL, *March 2d*, 1820, 3 *o'clock at night*.

DEAR SIR:—I hasten to inform you, that this moment WE have carried the question to admit Missouri, and all Louisiana to the southward of 36°30′, free from the restriction of slavery, and give the South, in a short time, an addition

The cases I have mentioned are the only acts of the "thirty-nine," or of any of them, upon the direct issue, which I have been able to discover.

To enumerate the persons who thus acted, as being four in 1784, two in 1787, seventeen in 1789, three in 1798, two in 1804, and two in 1819-20—there would be thirty of them. But this would be counting John Langdon, Roger Sherman, William Few, Rufus King, and George Read, each twice, and Abraham Baldwin, three times. The true number of those of the "thirty-nine" whom I have shown to have acted upon the question, which, by the text, they understood better than we, is twenty-three, leaving sixteen not shown to have acted upon it in any way.[19]

Here, then, we have twenty-three out of our thirty-nine fathers "who framed the Government under which we live," who have, upon their official responsibility and their corporal oaths, acted upon the very question which the text affirms they "understood just as well, and even better than we do now;" and twenty-one of them—a clear majority of the whole "thirty-nine"—so acting upon it as to make them guilty of gross political impropriety and wilful perjury, if, in their understanding, any proper division between local and federal authority, or anything in the Constitution they had made themselves, and sworn to support, forbade the Federal Government to control as to slavery in the federal territories. Thus the twenty-one acted; and, as actions speak louder than words, so actions, under such responsibility, speak still louder.

Two of the twenty-three voted against Congressional prohibition

---

of six, perhaps eight, members to the Senate of the United States. It is considered here by the slaveholding States, as a great triumph.

The votes were close—ninety to eighty-six—produced by the seceding and absence of a few moderate men from the North. To the north of 36°30′, there is to be, by the present law, restriction; which you will see by the votes, I voted against. But it is at present of no moment; it is a vast tract, uninhabited, only by savages and wild beasts, in which not a foot of the Indian claims to soil is extinguished, and in which, according to the ideas prevalent, no land office will be opened for a great length of time. With respect, your obedient servant,

CHARLES PINCKNEY.

But conclusive evidence of Mr. Pinckney's views is furnished in the fact, that *he was himself a member of the Committee which reported the Ordinance of* '87, and that *on every occasion, when it was under the consideration of Congress, he voted against all amendments.*—Jour. Am. Congress, *Sept. 29th,* 1786. *Oct. 4th.* When the ordinance came up for its final passage, Mr. Pinckney was sitting in the Convention, and did not take part in the proceedings of Congress.

[19] By reference to notes 5, 7, 11, 14, 16, and 17, it will be seen that, of the twenty-three who acted upon the question of prohibition, twelve were from the present slaveholding States.

of slavery in the federal territories, in the instances in which they acted upon the question. But for what reasons they so voted is not known. They may have done so because they thought a proper division of local from federal authority, or some provision or principle of the Constitution, stood in the way; or they may, without any such question, have voted against the prohibition, on what appeared to them to be sufficient grounds of expediency. No one who has sworn to support the Constitution, can conscientiously vote for what he understands to be an unconstitutional measure, however expedient he may think it; but one may and ought to vote against a measure which he deems constitutional, if, at the same time, he deems it inexpedient. It, therefore, would be unsafe to set down even the two who voted against the prohibition, as having done so because, in their understanding, any proper division of local from federal authority, or anything in the Constitution, forbade the Federal Government to control as to slavery in federal territory.[20]

The remaining sixteen of the "thirty-nine," so far as I have discovered, have left no record of their understanding upon the direct question of federal control of slavery in the federal territories. But there is much reason to believe that their understanding upon that question would not have appeared different from that of their twenty-three compeers, had it been manifested at all.[21]

For the purpose of adhering rigidly to the text, I have purposely omitted whatever understanding may have been manifested by any person, however distinguished, other than the thirty-nine fathers who framed the original Constitution; and, for the same reason, I have also omitted whatever understanding may have been manifested by any of the "thirty-nine" even, on any other phase of the general question of slavery. If we should look into their acts and declarations on those other phases, as the foreign slave trade, and the morality and policy of slavery generally, it would appear to us that on the direct question of federal control of slavery in federal territories, the sixteen, if they had acted at all, would probably have acted just as the twenty-three did. Among that sixteen were several of the most noted anti-slavery men of those times—as Dr. Franklin, Alexander Hamilton and Gouverneur Morris—while

[20] *Vide* notes 6 and 18, *ante*.

[21] "The remaining sixteen" were Nathaniel Gorham, Mass.; Alex. Hamilton, New-York; William Livingston and David Brearly, New Jersey; Benjamin Franklin, Jared Ingersoll, James Wilson and Gouverneur Morris, Penn.; Gunning Bedford, John Dickinson and Jacob Broom, Delaware; Daniel, of St. Thomas, Jenifer, Maryland; John Blair, Virginia; Richard Dobbs Spaight, North Carolina; and John Rutledge and Charles Cotesworth Pinckney, South Carolina.

there was not one now known to have been otherwise, unless it may be John Rutledge, of South Carolina.[22]

The sum of the whole is, that of our thirty-nine fathers who framed the original Constitution, twenty-one—a clear majority of the whole—certainly understood that no proper division of local from federal authority, nor any part of the Constitution, forbade the Federal Government to control slavery in the federal territories; while all the rest probably had the same understanding. Such, unquestionably, was the understanding of our fathers who framed the original Constitution; and the text affirms that they understood the question "better than we."

But, so far, I have been considering the understanding of the question manifested by the framers of the original Constitution. In and by the original instrument, a mode was provided for amending it; and, as I have already stated, the present frame of "the Government under which we live" consists of that original, and

[22] "The only distinction between freedom and slavery consists in this: in the former state, a man is governed by the laws to which he has given his consent, either in person or by his representative; in the latter, he is governed by the will of another. In the one case, his life and property are his own; in the other, they depend upon the pleasure of a master. It is easy to discern which of the two states is preferable. No man in his senses can hesitate in choosing to be free rather than slave. * Were not the disadvantages of slavery too obvious to stand in need of it, I might enumerate and describe the tedious train of calamities inseparable from it. I might show that it is fatal to religion and morality; that it tends to debase the mind, and corrupt its noblest springs of action. I might show that it relaxes the sinews of industry and clips the wings of commerce, and works misery and indigence in every shape."—*Hamilton, Works*, vol. 2, pp. 3, 9.

"That you will be pleased to countenance the restoration of *liberty* to those unhappy *men*, who alone in this land of freedom, are degraded into perpetual bondage, and who, amidst the general joy of surrounding freemen, are groaning in servile subjection; that you will devise means for removing this inconsistency from the character of the American people; that you will promote mercy and *justice* toward this distressed race; and that you will step to the *very verge* of the power vested in you for discouraging every species of traffic in the persons of our fellow-men."—*Philadelphia, Feb. 3d*, 1790. *Franklin's Petition to Congress for the Abolition of Slavery.*

Mr. Gouverneur Morris said:—"He never would concur in upholding domestic slavery. It was a nefarious institution. It was the curse of heaven on the States where it prevailed. * * * The admission of slavery into the representation, when fairly explained, comes to this—that the inhabitant of South Carolina or Georgia, who goes to the coast of Africa, and, in defiance of the most sacred laws of humanity, tears away his fellow-creatures from their dearest connections, and damns them to the most cruel bondage, shall have more votes, in a government instituted for the protection of the rights of mankind, than the citizen of Pennsylvania or New Jersey, who views, with a laudable horror, so nefarious a practice. * * * * * * * * He would sooner submit himself to a tax for paying for all the negroes in the United States than saddle posterity with such a constitution."—*Debate on Slave Representation in the Convention.—Madison Papers.*

twelve amendatory articles framed and adopted since. Those who now insist that federal control of slavery in federal territories violates the Constitution, point us to the provisions which they suppose it thus violates; and, as I understand, they all fix upon provisions in these amendatory articles, and not in the original instrument. The Supreme Court, in the Dred Scott case, plant themselves upon the fifth amendment, which provides that no person shall be deprived of "life, liberty or property without due process of law;" while Senator Douglas and his peculiar adherents plant themselves upon the tenth amendment, providing that "the powers not delegated to the United States by the Constitution," "are reserved to the States respectively, or to the people."[23]

Now, it so happens that these amendments were framed by the first Congress which sat under the Constitution—the identical Congress which passed the act already mentioned, enforcing the prohibition of slavery in the Northwestern Territory. Not only was it the same Congress, but they were the identical, same individual men who, at the same session, and at the same time within the session, had under consideration, and in progress toward maturity, these Constitutional amendments, and this act prohibiting slavery in all the territory the nation then owned. The Constitutional amendments were introduced before, and passed after the act enforcing the Ordinance of '87; so that, during the whole pendency of the act to enforce the Ordinance, the Constitutional amendments were also pending.[24]

[23] An eminent jurist (Chancellor Walworth) has said that "The preamble which was prefixed to these amendments, as adopted by Congress, is important to show in what light that body considered them." (8 *Wend. R.*, p. 100.) It declares that a number of the State Conventions "having at the time of their adopting the Constitution *expressed a desire*, in order to prevent *misconstruction or abuse of its powers*, that further *declaratory* and restrictive clauses should be added," resolved, &c.

This preamble is in substance the preamble affixed to the "Conciliatory Resolutions" of Massachusetts, which were drawn by Chief Justice Parsons, and offered in the Convention as a compromise by John Hancock. (*Life Ch. J. Parsons*, p. 67.) They were afterward copied and adopted with some additions by New Hampshire.

The fifth amendment, on which the Supreme Court relies, is taken almost literally from the declaration of rights put forth by the convention of New-York, and the clause referred to forms the ninth paragraph of the declaration. The tenth amendment, on which Senator Douglas relies, is taken from the Conciliatory Resolutions, and is the first of those resolutions somewhat modified. Thus, these two amendments sought to be used for slavery, originated in the two great anti-slavery States, New-York and Massachusetts.

[24] The amendments were proposed by Mr. Madison in the House of Representatives, June 8, 1789. They were adopted by the House, August 24, and some further amendments seem to have been transmitted by the Senate, September 9. The printed journals of the Senate do not state the time of the final passage, and

The seventy-six members of that Congress, including sixteen of the framers of the original Constitution, as before stated, were preeminently our fathers who framed that part of "the Government under which we live," which is now claimed as forbidding the Federal Government to control slavery in the federal territories.

Is it not a little presumptuous in any one at this day to affirm that the two things which that Congress deliberately framed, and carried to maturity at the same time, are absolutely inconsistent with each other? And does not such affirmation become impudently absurd when coupled with the other affirmation from the same mouth, that those who did the two things, alleged to be inconsistent, understood whether they really were inconsistent better than we—better than he who affirms that they are inconsistent?

It is surely safe to assume that the thirty-nine framers of the original Constitution, and the seventy-six members of the Congress which framed the amendments thereto, taken together, do certainly include those who may be fairly called "our fathers who framed the Government under which we live."[25] And so assuming, I defy any man to show that any one of them ever, in his whole life, declared that, in his understanding, any proper division of local from federal authority, or any part of the Constitution, forbade the Federal Government to control as to slavery in the federal territories. I go a step further. I defy any one to show that any living man in the whole world ever did, prior to the beginning of the present century, (and I might almost say prior to the beginning of the last half of the present century,) declare that, in his understanding, any proper division of local from federal authority, or any part of the Constitution, forbade the Federal Government to control as to slavery in the federal territories. To those who now so declare, I give, not only "our fathers who framed the Government under which we live," but with them all other living men within the century in which it was framed, among whom to search, and they shall not be able to find the evidence of a single man agreeing with them.

Now, and here, let me guard a little against being misunderstood. I do not mean to say we are bound to follow implicitly in

---

the message transmitting them to the State Legislatures speaks of them as adopted at the first session, begun on the fourth day of March, 1789. The date of the introduction and passage of the act enforcing the ordinance of '87, will be found at note 10, *ante*.

[25] It is singular that while two of the "thirty-nine" were in that Congress of 1819, there was but one (besides Mr. King) of the "seventy-six." The one was William Smith, of South Carolina. He was then a Senator, and, like Mr. Pinckney, occupied extreme Southern ground.

whatever our fathers did. To do so, would be to discard all the lights of current experience—to reject all progress—all improvement. What I do say is, that if we would supplant the opinions and policy of our fathers in any case, we should do so upon evidence so conclusive, and argument so clear, that even their great authority, fairly considered and weighed, cannot stand; and most surely not in a case whereof we ourselves declare they understood the question better than we.

If any man at this day sincerely believes that a proper division of local from federal authority, or any part of the Constitution, forbids the Federal Government to control as to slavery in the federal territories, he is right to say so, and to enforce his position by all truthful evidence and fair argument which he can. But he has no right to mislead others, who have less access to history, and less leisure to study it, into the false belief that "our fathers, who framed the Government under which we live," were of the same opinion—thus substituting falsehood and deception for truthful evidence and fair argument. If any man at this day sincerely believes "our fathers who framed the Government under which we live," used and applied principles, in other cases, which ought to have led them to understand that a proper division of local from federal authority or some part of the Constitution, forbids the Federal Government to control as to slavery in the federal territories, he is right to say so. But he should, at the same time, brave the responsibility of declaring that, in his opinion, he understands their principles better than they did themselves; and especially should he not shirk that responsibility by asserting that they "understood the question just as well, and even better, than we do now."

But enough! *Let all who believe that "our fathers, who framed the Government under which we live, understood this question just as well, and even better, than we do now," speak as they spoke, and act as they acted upon it. This is all Republicans ask—all Republicans desire—in relation to slavery. As those fathers marked it, so let it be again marked, as an evil not to be extended, but to be tolerated and protected only because of and so far as its actual presence among us makes that toleration and protection a necessity. Let all the guaranties those fathers gave it, be, not grudgingly, but fully and fairly maintained.* For this Republicans contend, and with this, so far as I know or believe, they will be content.

And now, if they would listen—as I suppose they will not—I would address a few words to the Southern people.

I would say to them:—You consider yourselves a reasonable and a just people; and I consider that in the general qualities of reason and justice you are not inferior to any other people. Still, when you speak of us Republicans, you do so only to denounce us as reptiles, or, at the best, as no better than outlaws. You will grant a hearing to pirates or murderers, but nothing like it to "Black Republicans." In all your contentions with one another, each of you deems an unconditional condemnation of "Black Republicanism" as the first thing to be attended to. Indeed, such condemnation of us seems to be an indispensable prerequisite—license, so to speak—among you to be admitted or permitted to speak at all. Now, can you, or not, be prevailed upon to pause and to consider whether this is quite just to us, or even to yourselves? Bring forward your charges and specifications, and then be patient long enough to hear us deny or justify.

You say we are sectional. We deny it. That makes an issue; and the burden of proof is upon you. You produce your proof; and what is it? Why, that our party has no existence in your section—gets no votes in your section. The fact is substantially true; but does it prove the issue? If it does, then in case we should, without change of principle, begin to get votes in your section, we should thereby cease to be sectional. You cannot escape this conclusion; and yet, are you willing to abide by it? If you are, you will probably soon find that we have ceased to be sectional, for we shall get votes in your section this very year. You will then begin to discover, as the truth plainly is, that your proof does not touch the issue. The fact that we get no votes in your section, is a fact of your making, and not of ours. And if there be fault in that fact, that fault is primarily yours, and remains so until you show that we repel you by some wrong principle or practice. If we do repel you by any wrong principle or practice, the fault is ours; but this brings you to where you ought to have started—to a discussion of the right or wrong of our principle. If our principle, put in practice, would wrong your section for the benefit of ours, or for any other object, then our principle, and we with it, are sectional, and are justly opposed and denounced as such. Meet us, then, on the question of whether our principle, put in practice, would wrong your section; and so meet us as if it were possible that something may be said on our side. Do you accept the challenge? No! Then you really believe that the principle which "our fathers who framed the Government under which we live" thought so clearly right as to adopt it, and indorse it again and again, upon their official oaths, is in fact so clearly wrong as to demand your condemnation without a moment's consideration.

Some of you delight to flaunt in our faces the warning against sectional parties given by Washington in his Farewell Address. Less than eight years before Washington gave that warning, he had, as President of the United States, approved and signed an act of Congress, enforcing the prohibition of slavery in the Northwestern Territory, which act embodied the policy of the Government upon that subject up to and at the very moment he penned that warning; and about one year after he penned it, he wrote La Fayette that he considered that prohibition a wise measure, expressing in the same connection his hope that we should at some time have a confederacy of free States.[26]

Bearing this in mind, and seeing that sectionalism has since arisen upon this same subject, is that warning a weapon in your hands against us, or in our hands against you? Could Washington himself speak, would he cast the blame of that sectionalism upon us, who sustain his policy, or upon you who repudiate it? We respect that warning of Washington, and we commend it to you, together with his example pointing to the right application of it.

But you say you are conservative—eminently conservative—while we are revolutionary, destructive, or something of the sort. What is conservatism? Is it not adherence to the old and tried, against the new and untried? We stick to, contend for, the identical old policy on the point in controversy which was adopted by "our fathers who framed the Government under which we live;" while you with one accord reject, and scout, and spit upon that old policy, and insist upon substituting something new. True, you disagree among yourselves as to what that substitute shall be. You are divided on new propositions and plans, but you are unanimous in rejecting and denouncing the old policy of the fathers. Some of you are for reviving the foreign slave trade; some for a Congres-

[26] The following is an extract from the letter referred to:—

"I agree with you cordially in your views in regard to negro slavery. I have long considered it a most serious evil, both socially and politically, and I should rejoice in any feasible scheme to rid our States of such a burden. The Congress of 1787 adopted an ordinance which prohibits the existence of involuntary servitude in our Northwestern Territory forever. I consider it a wise measure. It meets with the approval and assent of nearly every member from the States more immediately interested in Slave labor. The prevailing opinion in Virginia is against the spread of slavery in our new territories, and I trust we shall have a confederation of free States."

The following extract from a letter of Washington to Robert Morris, April 12th, 1786, shows how strong were his views, and how clearly he deemed emancipation a subject for legislative enactment:—"I can only say that there is no man living who wishes more sincerely than I do to see a plan adopted for the abolition of it; but there is but one proper and effective mode by which it can be accomplished, and that is, BY LEGISLATIVE AUTHORITY, and that, as far as *my suffrage will go, shall never be wanting.*"

sional Slave-Code for the Territories; some for Congress forbidding the Territories to prohibit Slavery within their limits; some for maintaining Slavery in the Territories through the judiciary; some for the "gur-reat pur-rinciple" that "if one man would enslave another, no third man should object," fantastically called "Popular Sovereignty;" but never a man among you in favor of federal prohibition of slavery in federal territories, according to the practice of "our fathers who framed the Government under which we live." Not one of all your various plans can show a precedent or an advocate in the century within which our Government originated. Consider, then, whether your claim of conservatism for yourselves, and your charge of destructiveness against us, are based on the most clear and stable foundations.

Again, you say we have made the slavery question more prominent than it formerly was. We deny it. We admit that it is more prominent, but we deny that we made it so. It was not we, but you, who discarded the old policy of the fathers. We resisted, and still resist, your innovation; and thence comes the greater prominence of the question. Would you have that question reduced to its former proportions? Go back to that old policy. What has been will be again, under the same conditions. If you would have the peace of the old times, readopt the precepts and policy of the old times.

You charge that we stir up insurrections among your slaves. We deny it; and what is your proof? Harper's Ferry! John Brown!! John Brown was no Republican; and you have failed to implicate a single Republican in his Harper's Ferry enterprise. If any member of our party is guilty in that matter, you know it or you do not know it. If you do know it, you are inexcusable for not designating the man and proving the fact. If you do not know it, you are inexcusable for asserting it, and especially for persisting in the assertion after you have tried and failed to make the proof. You need not be told that persisting in a charge which one does not know to be true, is simply malicious slander.[27]

[27] A Committee of five, consisting of Messrs. Mason, Davis and Fitch, (Democrats,) and Collamer and Doolittle, (Republicans,) was appointed Dec. 14, 1859, by the U.S. Senate, to investigate the Harper's Ferry affair. That Committee was directed, among other things, to inquire: (1.) "Whether such invasion and seizure was made under color of any organization intended to subvert the government of any of the States of the Union." (2.) "What was the character and extent of such organization." (3.) "And whether any citizen of the United States, not present, were implicated therein, or accessory thereto, by contributions of money, arms, munitions, or otherwise."

The majority of the Committee, Messrs. Mason, Davis, and Fitch, reply to the inquiries as follows:

1. "There will be found in the Appendix, a copy of the proceedings of a Convention held at Chatham, Canada, of the Provisional Form of Government there

Some of you admit that no Republican designedly aided or encouraged the Harper's Ferry affair; but still insist that our doctrines and declarations necessarily lead to such results. We do not believe it. We know we hold to no doctrine, and make no declaration, which were not held to and made by "our fathers who framed the Government under which we live." You never dealt fairly by us in relation to this affair. When it occurred, some important State elections were near at hand, and you were in evident glee with the belief that, by charging the blame upon us, you could get an advantage of us in those elections. The elections came, and your expectations were not quite fulfilled. Every Republican man knew that, as to himself at least, your charge was a slander, and he was not much inclined by it to cast his vote in your favor. Republican doctrines and declarations are accompanied with a continual protest against any interference whatever with your slaves, or with you about your slaves. Surely, this does not encourage them to revolt. True, we do, in common with "our fathers, who framed the Government under which we live," declare our belief that slavery is wrong; but the slaves do not hear us declare even this. For anything we say or do, the slaves would scarcely know there is a Republican party. I believe they would not, in fact, generally know it but for your misrepresentations of us, in their hearing. In your political contests among yourselves, each faction charges the other with sympathy with Black Republicanism; and then, to give point

---

pretended to have been instituted, the object of which clearly was to subvert the government of one or more States, and of course, to that extent, the government of the United States." By reference to the copy of Proceedings it appears that *nineteen* persons were present at that Convention, *eight* of whom were either killed or executed at Charlestown, and one examined before the Committee.

2. "The character of the military organization appears, by the commissions issued to certain of the armed party as captains, lieutenants, &c., a specimen of which will be found in the Appendix."

(These Commissions are signed by John Brown as Commander-in-Chief, under the Provisional Government, and by J. H. Kagi as Secretary.)

"It clearly appeared that the scheme of Brown was to take with him comparatively but few men; but those had been carefully trained by military instruction previously, and were to act as officers. For his military force he relied, very clearly, on inciting insurrection amongst the Slaves."

3. "It does not appear that the contributions were made with actual knowledge of the use for which they were designed by Brown, although it does appear that money was freely contributed by those styling themselves the friends of this man Brown, and friends alike of what they styled the cause of freedom, (of which they claimed him to be an especial apostle,) without inquiring as to the way in which the money would be used by him to advance such pretended cause."

In concluding the report the majority of the Committee thus characterize the "invasion:" "It was simply the act of lawless ruffians, under the sanction of no public or political authority—distinguishable only from ordinary felonies by the ulterior ends in contemplation by them," &c.

to the charge, defines Black Republicanism to simply be insurrection, blood and thunder among the slaves.

Slave insurrections are no more common now than they were before the Republican party was organized. What induced the Southampton insurrection, twenty-eight years ago, in which, at least, three times as many lives were lost as at Harper's Ferry?[28] You can scarcely stretch your very elastic fancy to the conclusion that Southampton was "got up by Black Republicanism." In the present state of things in the United States, I do not think a general, or even a very extensive slave insurrection, is possible. The indispensable concert of action cannot be attained. The slaves have no means of rapid communication; nor can incendiary freemen, black or white, supply it. The explosive materials are everywhere in parcels; but there neither are, nor can be supplied, the indispensable connecting trains.

Much is said by Southern people about the affection of slaves for their masters and mistresses; and a part of it, at least, is true. A plot for an uprising could scarcely be devised and communicated to twenty individuals before some one of them, to save the life of a favorite master or mistress, would divulge it. This is the rule; and the slave revolution in Hayti was not an exception to it, but a case occurring under peculiar circumstances.[29] The gunpowder plot of

[28] The Southampton insurrection, August, 1831, was induced by the remarkable ability of a slave calling himself General Nat Turner. He led his fellow bondmen to believe that he was acting under the order of Heaven. In proof of this he alleged that the singular appearance of the sun at that time was a divine signal for the commencement of the struggle which would result in the recovery of their freedom. This insurrection resulted in the death of sixty-four white persons, and more than one hundred slaves. The Southampton was the eleventh large insurrection in the Southern States, besides numerous attempts and revolts.

[29] In March, 1790, the General Assembly of France, on the petition of the *free* people of color in St. Domingo, many of whom were intelligent and wealthy, passed a decree intended to be in their favor, but so ambiguous as to be construed in favor of both the whites and the blacks. The differences growing out of the decree created two parties—the *whites* and the people of color; and some blood was shed. In 1791, the blacks again petitioned, and a decree was passed declaring the colored people citizens, who were born of free parents on both sides. This produced great excitement among the whites, and the two parties armed against each other, and horrible massacres and conflagrations followed. Then the Assembly rescinded this last decree, and like results followed, the blacks being the exasperated parties and the aggressors. Then the decree giving citizenship to the blacks was restored, and commissioners were sent out to keep the peace. The commissioners, unable to sustain themselves, between the two parties, with the troops they had, issued a proclamation that all blacks who were willing to range themselves under the banner of the Republic should be free. As a result a very large proportion of the blacks became in fact free. In 1794, the Conventional Assembly *abolished slavery* throughout the French Colonies. Some years afterward the French Government sought, with an army of 60,000 men to reinstate slavery, but were unsuccessful, and then the white planters were driven from the Island.

British history, though not connected with slaves, was more in point. In that case, only about twenty were admitted to the secret; and yet one of them, in his anxiety to save a friend, betrayed the plot to that friend, and, by consequence, averted the calamity. Occasional poisonings from the kitchen, and open or stealthy assassinations in the field, and local revolts extending to a score or so, will continue to occur as the natural results of slavery; but no general insurrection of slaves, as I think, can happen in this country for a long time. Whoever much fears, or much hopes for such an event, will be alike disappointed.

In the language of Mr. Jefferson, uttered many years ago, "It is still in our power to direct the process of emancipation, and deportation, peaceably, and in such slow degrees, as that the evil will wear off insensibly; and their places be, *pari passu,* filled up by free white laborers. If, on the contrary, it is left to force itself on, human nature must shudder at the prospect held up."[30]

Mr. Jefferson did not mean to say, nor do I, that the power of emancipation is in the Federal Government. He spoke of Virginia; and, as to the power of emancipation, I speak of the slaveholding States only. The Federal Government, however, as we insist, has the power of restraining the extension of the institution—the power to insure that a slave insurrection shall never occur on any American soil which is now free from slavery.

John Brown's effort was peculiar. It was not a slave insurrection. It was an attempt by white men to get up a revolt among slaves, in which the slaves refused to participate. In fact, it was so absurd that the slaves, with all their ignorance, saw plainly enough it could not succeed. That affair, in its philosophy, corresponds with the many attempts, related in history, at the assassination of kings and emperors. An enthusiast broods over the oppression of a people till he fancies himself commissioned by Heaven to liberate them. He ventures the attempt, which ends in little else than his own execution. Orsini's attempt on Louis Napoleon, and John Brown's attempt at Harper's Ferry were, in their philosophy, precisely the same. The eagerness to cast blame on old England in the one case, and on New England in the other, does not disprove the sameness of the two things.

And how much would it avail you, if you could, by the use of John Brown, Helper's Book, and the like, break up the Republican organization? Human action can be modified to some extent, but human nature cannot be changed. There is a judgment and a feel-

[30] *Vide* Jefferson's Autobiography, commenced January 6th, 1821. Jefferson's Works, vol. 1, page 49.

ing against slavery in this nation, which cast at least a million and a half of votes. You cannot destroy that judgment and feeling—that sentiment—by breaking up the political organization which rallies around it. You can scarcely scatter and disperse an army which has been formed into order in the face of your heaviest fire; but if you could, how much would you gain by forcing the sentiment which created it out of the peaceful channel of the ballot-box, into some other channel? What would that other channel probably be? Would the number of John Browns be lessened or enlarged by the operation?

But you will break up the Union rather than submit to a denial of your Constitutional rights.[31]

[31] "I am not ashamed or afraid publicly to avow, that the election of William H. Seward or Salmon P. Chase, or any such representative of the Republican party, upon a sectional platform, ought to be resisted to the disruption of every tie that binds this Confederacy together. (Applause on the Democratic side of the House.)"—*Mr. Curry, of Alabama, in the House of Representatives.*

"Just so sure as the Republican party succeed in electing a sectional man, upon their sectional, anti-slavery platform, breathing destruction and death to the rights of my people, just so sure, in my judgment, the time will have come when the South must and will take an unmistakable and decided action, and then he who dallies is a dastard, and he who doubts is damned! I need not tell what I, as a Southern man, will do. I think I may safely speak for the masses of the people of Georgia—that when that event happens, they, in my judgment, will consider it an overt act, a declaration of war, and meet immediately in convention, to take into consideration the mode and measure of redress. That is my position; and if that be treason to the Government, make the most of it."—*Mr. Gartell, of Georgia, in the House of Representatives.*

"I said to my constituents, and to the people of the capital of my State, on my way here, if such an event did occur,"—[*i.e.*, the election of a Republican President, upon a Republican platform,] "while it would be their duty to determine the course which the State would pursue, it would be my privilege to counsel with them as to what I believed to be the proper course; and I said to them, what I say now, and what I will always say in such an event, that my counsel would be to take independence out of the Union in preference to the loss of constitutional rights, and consequent degradation and dishonor, in it. That is my position, and it is the position which I know the Democratic party of the State of Mississippi will maintain."—*Gov. McRae, of Mississippi.*

"It is useless to attempt to conceal the fact that, in the present temper of the southern people, it" [*i.e.*, the election of a Republican President] "cannot be, and will not be submitted to. The 'irrepressible conflict' doctrine, announced and advocated by the ablest and most distinguished leader of the Republican party, is an open declaration of war against the institution of slavery; wherever it exists; and I would be disloyal to Virginia and the South, if I did not declare that the election of such a man, entertaining such sentiment, and advocating such doctrines, *ought to be resisted by the slaveholding States.* The idea of permitting such a man to have the control and direction of the army and navy of the United States, and the appointment of high judicial and executive officers, POSTMASTERS INCLUDED, *cannot* be entertained by the South for a moment."—*Gen. Letcher, of Virginia.*

"Slavery *must* be maintained—in the Union, if possible; out of it, if necessary: peaceably if we may; forcibly if we must."—*Senator Iverson, of Georgia.*

"Lincoln and Hamlin, the Black Republican nominees, will be elected in No-

That has a somewhat reckless sound; but it would be palliated, if not fully justified, were we proposing, by the mere force of numbers, to deprive you of some right, plainly written down in the Constitution. But we are proposing no such thing.

When you make these declarations, you have a specific and well-understood allusion to an assumed Constitutional right of yours, to take slaves into the federal territories, and to hold them there as property. But no such right is specifically written in the Constitution. That instrument is literally silent about any such right. We, on the contrary, deny that such a right has any existence in the Constitution, even by implication.

Your purpose, then, plainly stated, is, that you will destroy the Government, unless you be allowed to construe and enforce the Constitution as you please, on all points in dispute between you and us. You will rule or ruin in all events.

This, plainly stated, is your language. Perhaps you will say the Supreme Court has decided the disputed Constitutional question in your favor. Not quite so. But waiving the lawyer's distinction between dictum and decision, the Court have decided the question for you in a sort of way. The Court have substantially said, it is your Constitutional right to take slaves into the federal territories, and to hold them there as property. When I say the decision was made in a sort of way, I mean it was made in a divided Court, by a bare majority of the Judges, and they not quite agreeing with one another in the reasons for making it;[32] that it is so made as that its

---

vember next, and the South will then decide the great question whether they will submit to the domination of Black Republican rule—the fundamental principle of their organization being an open, undisguised, and declared war upon our social institutions. I believe that the honor and safety of the South, in that contingency, will require the prompt secession of the slaveholding States from the Union; and failing then to obtain from the free States additional and higher guaranties for the protection of our rights and property, that the seceding States should proceed to establish a new government. But while I think such would be the imperative duty of the South, I should emphatically reprobate and repudiate any scheme having for its object the separate secession of South Carolina. If Georgia, Alabama and Mississippi alone—giving us a portion of the Atlantic and Gulf coasts—would unite with this State in a common secession upon the election of a Black Republican, I would give my assent to the policy."—*Letter of Hon. James L. Orr, of S.C., to John Martin and others*, July 23, 1860.

[32] The Hon. John A. Andrew, of the Boston Bar, made the following analysis of the Dred Scott case in the Massachusetts legislature. Hon. Caleb Cushing was then a member of that body, but did not question its correctness.

"On the question of possibility of citizenship to one of the Dred Scott color, extraction, and origin, three justices, viz., Taney, Wayne and Daniels, held the negative. Nelson and Campbell passed over the plea by which the question was raised. Grier agreed with Nelson. Catron said the question was not open. McLean agreed with Catron, but thought the plea bad. Curtis agreed that the question was open, but attacked the plea, met its averments, and decided that a free born col-

avowed supporters disagree with one another about its meaning, and that it was mainly based upon a mistaken statement of fact—the statement in the opinion that "the right of property in a slave is distinctly and expressly affirmed in the Constitution."[33]

An inspection of the Constitution will show that the right of property in a slave is not "*distinctly* and *expressly* affirmed" in it. Bear in mind, the Judges do not pledge their judicial opinion that

---

ored person, native to any State, is a citizen thereof, by birth, and is therefore a citizen of the Union, and entitled to sue in the Federal Courts.

"Had a majority of the court directly sustained the plea in abatement, and denied the jurisdiction of the Circut Court appealed from, then all else they could have said and done would have been done and said in a cause not theirs to try and not theirs to discuss. In the absence of such majority, one step more was to be taken. And the next step reveals an agreement of six of the Justices, on a point decisive of the cause, and putting an end to all the functions of the court.

"It is this. Scott was first carried to Rock Island, in the State of Illinois, where he remained about two years, before going with his master to Fort Snelling, in the Territory of Wisconsin. His claim to freedom was rested on the alleged effect of his translation from a slave State, and again into a free territory. If, by his removal to Illinois, he became emancipated from his master, the subsequent continuance of his pilgrimage into the Louisiana purchase could not add to his freedom, nor alter the fact. If, by reason of any want or infirmity in the laws of Illinois, or of conformity on his part to their behests, Dred Scott remained a slave while he remained in that State, then—for the sake of learning the effect on him of his territorial residence beyond the Mississippi, and of his marriage and other proceedings there, and the effect of the sojournment and marriage of Harriet, in the same territory, upon herself and her children—it might become needful to advance one other step into the investigation of the law; to inspect the Missouri Compromise, banishing slavery to the south of the line of 36°30′ in the Louisiana purchase.

"But no exigency of the cause ever demanded or justified that advance; for six of the Justices, including the Chief Justice himself, decided that the *status* of the plaintiff, as free or slave, was dependent, not upon the laws of the State into which he had been, but of the State of Missouri, in which he was at the commencement of the suit. The Chief Justice asserted that 'it is now firmly settled by the decisions of the highest court in the State, that Scott and his family, on their return were not free, but were, by the laws of Missouri, the property of the defendant.' This was the burden of the opinion of Nelson, who declares 'the question is one solely depending upon the law of Missouri, and that the federal Court, sitting in the State, and trying the case before us, was bound to follow it.' It received the emphatic endorsement of Wayne, whose general concurrence was with the Chief Justice. Grier concurred in set terms with Nelson on all 'the questions discussed by him.' Campbell says, 'The claim of the plaintiff to freedom depends upon the effect to be given to his absence from Missouri, in company with his master in Illinois and Minnesota, *and this effect is to be ascertained by reference to the laws of Missouri.*' Five of the Justices, then, (if no more of them,) regard the law of Missouri as decisive of the plaintiff's rights."

33 "Now, as we have already said in an earlier part of this opinion upon a different point, the right of property in a slave is distinctly and expressly affirmed in the Constitution. The right to traffic in it, *like an ordinary article of merchandise and property*, was guaranteed to the citizens of the United States in every State that might desire it for twenty years."—*Ch. J. Taney*, 19 *How. U.S.R.*, p.451. *Vide* language of Mr. Madison, note 35, as to "*merchandise.*"

such right is *impliedly* affirmed in the Constitution; but they pledge their veracity that it is "*distinctly* and *expressly*" affirmed there—"distinctly," that is, not mingled with anything else—"expressly," that is, in words meaning just that, without the aid of any inference, and susceptible of no other meaning.

If they had only pledged their judicial opinion that such right is affirmed in the instrument by implication, it would be open to others to show that neither the word "slave" nor "slavery" is to be found in the Constitution, nor the word "property" even, in any connection with language alluding to the things slave, or slavery, and that wherever in that instrument the slave is alluded to, he is called a "person;"—and wherever his master's legal right in relation to him is alluded to, it is spoken of as "service or labor which may be due,"—as a debt payable in service or labor.[34] Also, it would be open to show, by contemporaneous history, that this mode of alluding to slaves and slavery, instead of speaking of them, was employed on purpose to exclude from the Constitution the idea that there could be property in man.

To show all this, is easy and certain.[35]

[34] Not only was the right of property *not* intended to be "distinctly and expressly affirmed in the Constitution;" but the following extract from Mr. Madison demonstrates that the utmost care was taken to avoid so doing:—

"The clause as originally offered [respecting fugitive slaves] read 'If any person LEGALLY bound to service or labor in any of the United States shall escape into another State," etc., etc. (Vol. 3, p. 1456.) In regard to this, Mr. Madison says, "The term '*legally*' was struck out, and the words 'under the laws thereof,' inserted after the word State, in compliance with the wish of some who thought the term 'legally' equivocal and favoring the idea that slavery was legal in a moral point of view."—*Ib.*, p. 1589.

[35] We subjoin a portion of the history alluded to by Mr. Lincoln. The following extract relates to the provision of the Constitution relative to the slave trade. (Article I, Sec. 9.)

25th August, 1787.—The report of the Committee of eleven being taken up, Gen. [Charles Cotesworth] Pinckney moved to strike out the words "the year 1800," and insert the words "the year 1808."

Mr. Gorham seconded the motion.

Mr. Madison—Twenty years will produce all the mischief that can be apprehended from the liberty to import slaves. So long a term will be more dishonorable to the American character than to say nothing about it in the Constitution.

* * * * * * * * * * * * * * * * * * * *

Mr. Gouverneur Morris was for making the clause read at once—

"The importation of slaves into North Carolina, South Carolina, and Georgia, shall not be prohibited," &c.

This, he said, would be most fair, and would avoid the ambiguity by which, under the power with regard to naturalization the liberty reserved to the States might be defeated. He wished it to be known, also, that this part of the Constitution was a compliance with those States. If the change of language, however, should be objected to by the members from those States, he should not urge it.

Col. Mason, (of Va.,) was not against using the term "slaves," but against

When this obvious mistake of the Judges shall be brought to their notice, is it not reasonable to expect that they will withdraw the mistaken statement, and reconsider the conclusion based upon it?

And then it is to be remembered that "our fathers, who framed the Government under which we live"—the men who made the Constitution—decided this same Constitutional question in our favor, long ago—decided it without division among themselves, when making the decision; without division among themselves about the meaning of it after it was made, and, so far as any evidence is left, without basing it upon any mistaken statement of facts.

Under all these circumstances, do you really feel yourselves justified to break up this Government, unless such a court decision as yours is, shall be at once submitted to as a conclusive and final rule of political action? But you will not abide the election of a Republican President! In that supposed event, you say, you will destroy

---

naming North Carolina, South Carolina, and Georgia, lest it should give offence to the people of those States.

Mr. Sherman liked a description better than the terms proposed, which had been declined by the old Congress, and were not pleasing to some people.

Mr. Clymer concurred with Mr. Sherman.

Mr. Williamson, of North Carolina, said that *both in opinion and practice he was against slavery; but thought it more in favor of humanity, from a view of all circumstances, to let in South Carolina and Georgia, on those terms, than to exclude them from the Union.*

Mr. Morris withdrew his motion.

Mr. Dickinson wished the clause to be confined to the States which had not themselves prohibited the importation of slaves, and for that purpose moved to amend the clause so as to read—

"The importation of slaves into such of the States as shall permit the same, shall not be prohibited by the Legislature of the United States, until the year 1808," which was disagreed to, *nem. con.*

The first part of the report was then agreed to as follows:

"The migration or importation of such persons as the several States now existing shall think proper to admit, shall not be prohibited by the Legislature prior to the year 1808."

* *

Mr. Sherman was against the second part, ["but a tax or duty may be imposed on such migration or importation at a rate not exceeding *the average of the duties laid on imports,*"] as acknowledging men to be property by taxing them as such under the *character* of slaves.

* *

Mr. Madison *thought it wrong to admit in the Constitution the idea that there could be property in men.* The reason of duties did not hold, as slaves *are not, like merchandise,* consumed.

* *

It was finally agreed, *nem., con.* to make the clause read—

"But a tax or duty may be imposed on such importation, not exceeding *ten dollars* for each PERSON."—*Madison Papers,* Aug. 25, 1787.

the Union; and then, you say, the great crime of having destroyed it will be upon us! That is cool. A highwayman holds a pistol to my ear, and mutters through his teeth, "Stand and deliver, or I shall kill you, and then you will be a murderer!"

To be sure, what the robber demanded of me—my money—was my own; and I had a clear right to keep it; but it was no more my own than my vote is my own; and the threat of death to me, to extort my money, and the threat of destruction to the Union, to extort my vote, can scarcely be distinguished in principle.

A few words now to Republicans. *It is exceedingly desirable that all parts of this great Confederacy shall be at peace, and in harmony, one with another. Let us Republicans do our part to have it so. Even though much provoked, let us do nothing through passion and ill temper. Even though the southern people will not so much as listen to us, let us calmly consider their demands, and yield to them if, in our deliberate view of our duty, we possibly can.*[36] Judging by all they say and do, and by the subject and nature of their controversy with us, let us determine, if we can, what will satisfy them.

Will they be satisfied if the Territories be unconditionally surrendered to them? We know they will not. In all their present complaints against us, the Territories are scarcely mentioned. Invasions and insurrections are the rage now. Will it satisfy them, if, in the future, we have nothing to do with invasions and insurrections? We know it will not. We so know, because we know we never had anything to do with invasions and insurrections; and yet this total abstaining does not exempt us from the charge and the denunciation.

The question recurs, what will satisfy them? Simply this: We must not only let them alone, but we must, somehow, convince them that we do let them alone. This, we know by experience, is no easy task. We have been so trying to convince them from the very beginning of our organization, but with no success. In all our platforms and speeches we have constantly protested our purpose to let them alone; but this has had no tendency to convince them. Alike unavailing to convince them, is the fact that they have never detected a man of us in any attempt to disturb them.

These natural, and apparently adequate means all failing, what will convince them? This, and this only: cease to call slavery *wrong*, and join them in calling it *right*. And this must be done thoroughly—done in *acts* as well as in *words*. Silence will not be

[36] Compare this noble passage and that at page 18 [*i.e.*, p. 535, *supra*], with the twaddle of Mr. Orr, (note 31,) and the slang of Mr. Douglas, (note 38.)

tolerated—we must place ourselves avowedly with them. Senator Douglas's new sedition law must be enacted and enforced, suppressing all declarations that slavery is wrong, whether made in politics, in presses, in pulpits, or in private. We must arrest and return their fugitive slaves with greedy pleasure. We must pull down our Free State constitutions. The whole atmosphere must be disinfected from all taint of opposition to slavery, before they will cease to believe that all their troubles proceed from us.

I am quite aware they do not state their case precisely in this way. Most of them would probably say to us, "Let us alone, *do* nothing to us, and *say* what you please about slavery." But we do let them alone—have never disturbed them—so that, after all, it is what we say, which dissatisfies them. They will continue to accuse us of doing, until we cease saying.

I am also aware they have not, as yet, in terms, demanded the overthrow of our Free-State Constitutions.[37] Yet those Constitutions declare the wrong of slavery, with more solemn emphasis, than do all other sayings against it; and when all these other sayings shall have been silenced, the overthrow of these Constitutions will be demanded, and nothing be left to resist the demand. It is nothing to the contrary, that they do not demand the whole of this just now. Demanding what they do, and for the reason they do, they can voluntarily stop nowhere short of this consummation. Holding, as they do, that slavery is morally right, and socially elevating, they

[37] That demand has since been made. Says MR. O'CONOR, counsel for the State of Virginia in the *Lemon Case*, page 44: "We claim that under these various provisions of the Federal Constitution, a citizen of Virginia has an immunity against the operation of any law which the State of New-York can enact, whilst he is a stranger and wayfarer, or whilst passing through our territory; and that he has absolute protection for all his domestic rights, and for all his rights of property, which under the laws of the United States, and the laws of his own State, he was entitled to, whilst in his own State. We claim this, and neither more NOR LESS."

Throughout the whole of that case, in which the right to pass through New-York with slaves at the pleasure of the slave owners is maintained, it is nowhere contended that the statute is contrary to the Constitution of New-York; but that the statute and the Constitution of the State are both contrary to the Constitution of the United States.

The State of Virginia, not content with the decision of our own courts upon the right claimed by them, is now engaged in carrying this, the Lemon case, to the Supreme Court of the United States, hoping by a decision there, in accordance with the intimations in the Dred Scott case, to overthrow the Constitution of New-York.

Senator Toombs, of Georgia, has claimed in the Senate, that laws of Connecticut, Maine, Massachusetts, Michigan, New Hampshire, Ohio, Rhode Island, Vermont, and Wisconsin, for the exclusion of slavery, conceded to be warranted by the State Constitutions, are contrary to the Constitution of the United States, and has asked for the enactment of laws by the General Government which shall override the laws of those States and the Constitutions which authorize them.

cannot cease to demand a full national recognition of it, as a legal right, and a social blessing.[38]

Nor can we justifiably withhold this, on any ground save our conviction that slavery is wrong. If slavery is right, all words, acts, laws, and constitutions against it, are themselves wrong, and should be silenced, and swept away. If it is right, we cannot justly object to its nationality—its universality; if it is wrong, they cannot justly insist upon its extension—its enlargement. All they ask, we could readily grant, if we thought slavery right; all we ask, they could as readily grant, if they thought it wrong.[39] Their thinking it right,

[38] "Policy, humanity, and Christianity, alike forbid the extension of the evils of free society to new people and coming generations."—*Richmond Enquirer, Jan.* 22, 1856.

"I am satisfied that the mind of the South has undergone a change to this great extent, that it is now the *almost universal belief* in the South, not only that the condition of African slavery in their midst, is the best condition to which the African race has ever been subjected, but that *it has the effect of ennobling both races, the white and the black.*"—*Senator Mason, of Virginia.*

"I declare again, as I did in reply to the Senator from Wisconsin (Mr. Doolittle,) that, in my opinion, slavery is a great moral, social and political blessing —a blessing to the slave, and a blessing to the master."—*Mr. Brown, in the Senate, March* 6, 1860.

"I am a Southern States' Rights man; I am an African slave-trader. I am one of those Southern men who believe that slavery is right—morally, religiously, socially, and politically." (Applause.) * * * * * * * * * * * * *
"I represent the African Slave-trade interests of that section. (Applause.) I am proud of the position I occupy in that respect. I believe the African Slave-trader is a true missionary and a true Christian." (Applause.)—*Mr. Gaulden, a delegate from First Congressional District of Georgia, in the Charleston Convention, now a supporter of Mr. Douglas.*

"Ladies and gentlemen, I would gladly speak again, but you see from the tones of my voice, that I am unable to. This has been a happy, a glorious day. I shall never forget it. There is a charm about this beautiful day, about this sea air, and especially about that peculiar institution of yours—a clam bake. I think you have the advantage, in that respect, of Southerners. For my own part, I have much more fondness for your clams than I have for their niggers. But every man to his taste."—*Hon. Stephen A. Douglas's Address at Rocky Point, R. I., Aug.* 2, 1860.

[39] It is interesting to observe how two profoundly logical minds, though holding extreme, opposite views, have deduced this common conclusion. Says Mr. O'Conor, the eminent leader of the New-York Bar, and the counsel for the State of Virginia in the Lemon case, in his speech at Cooper Institute, December 19th, 1859:—

"That is the point to which this great argument must come—Is negro slavery unjust? If it is unjust, it violates that first rule of human conduct—'Render to every man his due.' If it is unjust, it violates the law of God which says, 'Love thy neighbor as thyself,' for that requires that we should perpetrate no injustice. Gentlemen, if it could be maintained that negro slavery was unjust, perhaps I might be prepared—perhaps we all ought to be prepared—to go with that distinguished man to whom allusion is frequently made, and say, 'There is a higher law which compels us to trample beneath our feet the Constitution established by our fathers, with all the blessings it secures to their children.' But I insist—and that is the argument which we must meet, and on which we must come to a conclusion that shall govern our actions in the future selection of representatives in the Congress of the United States—I insist that negro slavery is not unjust."

and our thinking it wrong, is the precise fact upon which depends the whole controversy. Thinking it right, as they do, they are not to blame for desiring its full recognition, as being right; but, thinking it wrong, as we do, can we yield to them? Can we cast our votes with their view, and against our own? In view of our moral, social, and political responsibilities, can we do this?

Wrong as we think slavery is, we can yet afford to let it alone where it is, because that much is due to the necessity arising from its actual presence in the nation; but can we, while our votes will prevent it, allow it to spread into the National Territories, and to overrun us here in these Free States? If our sense of duty forbids this, then let us stand by our duty, fearlessly and effectively. Let us be diverted by none of those sophistical contrivances wherewith we are so industriously plied and belabored—contrivances such as groping for some middle ground between the right and the wrong, vain as the search for a man who should be neither a living man nor a dead man—such as a policy of "don't care" on a question about which all true men do care—such as Union appeals beseeching true Union men to yield to Disunionists, reversing the divine rule, and calling, not the sinners, but the righteous to repentance—such as invocations to Washington, imploring men to unsay what Washington said, and undo what Washington did.

Neither let us be slandered from our duty by false accusations against us, nor frightened from it by menaces of destruction to the Government nor of dungeons to ourselves. LET US HAVE FAITH THAT RIGHT MAKES MIGHT, AND IN THAT FAITH, LET US, TO THE END, DARE TO DO OUR DUTY AS WE UNDERSTAND IT.

Speech at Providence, Rhode Island[1]

February 28, 1860

Mr. Lincoln began by alluding good naturedly to some remarks of the *Press* and the *Post*, which he had read on his way hither in the cars. Having with characteristic humor and wit, made a few comments upon the words of the *Press*, he proposed to take as the main subject of his speech topics suggested by the quotation which the *Post* made from one of his former speeches. He defended the position which he took in that speech, that this country cannot permanently endure half slave and half free. He gave the context in which his cited words were found, and discussed his subject with great fairness, earnestness and ability. He showed that he occupied only the ground which was taken by the founders of our government, and triumphantly vindicated himself and the Republican party against the false charges which are so unscrupulously brought against them.

[1] *Illinois State Journal,* March 7, 1860, copied from the Providence *Journal,* February 29, 1860.

Speech at Manchester, New Hampshire[1]

March 1, 1860

One of the best points of his speech, (and this was among the first,) was the answer to the question—What will satisfy the demands of the South upon the subject of Slavery?—Simply this, said the speaker, we must not only let them alone, but we must convince them that we do let them alone. This is no easy task. In all our speeches, resolutions and platforms, we have constantly protested our purpose to let them alone; but it has had no tendency to convince them. Alike unavailing to convince them is the fact that they have never detected a man of us in any attempt to disturb them.

These natural, and apparently adequate means, all failing, what will convince them? This, and this only; cease to call slavery *wrong,* and join with them in calling it *right.* And this must be done thoroughly—we must place ourselves avowedly with them. Douglas's new sedition law must be enacted and enforced, suppressing all declarations that slavery is wrong, whether made in politics, in presses, in pulpits, or in private. We must arrest and return their fugitive slaves with greedy pleasure; we must pull down our Free State Constitutions, inasmuch as they declare the wrong of slavery with more solemn emphasis than do all other sayings against it. If we throw open the Free Territories to them, they will not be satisfied; we know this from past experience, as well as from present controversy.

Another point considered was the charge that the Republican party is sectional. The democracy say we are sectional because our party has no existence in the South. The *fact* is substantially true; but does it prove the issue? If it does, then in case we should, without change of principle, begin to get votes in that section, we should thereby cease to be sectional. You will soon find that we have ceased to be sectional, for we shall have votes in the South in the glorious year of 1860. Some of you delight to flaunt in our faces the warning against sectional parties given by Washington in his Farewell Address. Yet, less than eight years before Washington gave that warning, he had, as President of the United States, approved and signed an act of Congress, enforcing the prohibition of slavery in the North Western Territory, which act embodied the policy of the government upon that subject up to, and at the very moment he penned that warning.

Again; the speaker showed that every one of the exciting questions upon slavery now before the country were thrown upon us by those very men who taunt the Republicans as being radical and sectional. *We* stick to, and contend for, the identical old policy which was adopted by the fathers of the Republic; *you* reject, and scout, and spit upon that old policy, and insist upon substituting something new. Some of you are for reviving the African slave trade; some for a congressional Slave Code for the Territories; some for Congress forbidding the Territories to prohibit slavery within their limits; some for maintaining slavery in the Territories through the Judiciary; and some for Popular Sovereignty principle, which means, if one man would enslave another, no third man should object. Not one of these various plans can show a precedent or an advocate in the century within which our government originated. Consider, then, who is conservative, your party, or ours. The speaker said, let us not be slandered from our duty by the false accusations against us, nor frightened from it by menaces of destruction to the Government, nor of dungeons to ourselves.

[1] Manchester *Daily American*, March 2, 1860. This is the most adequate report of the speech available. Lincoln spoke at Concord, New Hampshire, in the afternoon and at Manchester at night, but no available newspaper report gives even a summary of the speech at Concord.

Speech at Dover, New Hampshire[1]

March 2, 1860

Mr. Lincoln spoke nearly two hours and we believe he would have held his audience had he spoken all night. He gave a brief sketch of the course of the democracy, in reference to the slavery question, showing how they had made it the prominent and almost the only question in National politics—how their leading statesmen had all been compelled to bow to the slave power and become its obedient vassals. In reply to the charge of sectionalism, raised against the republicans, he said, we deny it. That makes an issue, the burden of proof is upon you, the democracy. You produce your proof; and what is it? Why, that the republican party has no existence in the South. The fact is substantially true, but does it prove the issue? If it does, then in case we should, without change of principle, begin to get votes there, we should thereby cease to be sectional. There was no escape from this conclusion, and if the democracy would abide by it, they would find that the republicans would get votes at the South this very year. Northern democrats were fond of saying to the opponents of slavery, why don't you go South and preach your doctrines where slavery exists, not oppose it here, where it does not exist. Frank Blair of Missouri, a democrat, did raise the standard of opposition in the very heart of slavery—and when he was defeated, did his brother democrats of the North sympathize with him? "Not one of them," said Mr. Lincoln. Their only greeting to him was "H-u-r-r-a-h for the D-i-m-o-c-r-a-c-y!" The republicans were charged with being responsible for the John Brown raid, yet a Committee of Congress, with unlimited powers, had failed to implicate a single republican in his Harper's Ferry enterprise. If any republican is guilty in that matter, you, the democracy, know it or you do not know it. If you do know it, you are inexcusable not to designate the man and prove the fact. If you do not know it, you are inexcusable to assert it, and especially to persist in the assertion after you have tried and failed to make the proof. The republicans who remained steadfast to the principles of the fathers on the subject of slavery, were the conservative party, while the democracy, who insisted upon substituting something new, were the destructives. But the South were threatening to destroy the Union in the event of the election of a republican President, and were telling us that the great crime of having destroyed it will be upon us. This is cool. A highwayman holds a pistol to my ear, with "stand and deliver, or I shall kill you, and then you will be a murderer." To be sure the money which he demands is my own, and I have a clear right to keep it, but it is no more so than my vote, and the threat of death to extort my money, and the threat of destruction to the Union to extort my vote, can scarcely be distinguished in principle. To satisfy them, said Mr. Lincoln, is no easy task. We must not only cease to call slavery *wrong*, but we must join with them in calling it *right*. Silence will not be tolerated. Douglas's new sedition law must be enacted and enforced. We must arrest and return their fugitive slaves with greedy pleasure. We must pull down our Free State Constitutions. The whole atmosphere must be disinfected from the taint of opposition to slavery, before they will cease to believe that all their troubles proceed from us. Wrong as we believe slavery to be, we should let [it] alone in the States where it exists, because its extirpation would occasion greater wrongs, but we should not, while our votes can prevent it, allow it to spread over the National Territories and over-run us in the Free States. Neither should we be diverted by trick or stratagem, by a senseless clamor about "popular sovereignty," by any contrivances for groping for some middle ground between the right and the wrong—the "don't care" policy of Douglas—or Union appeals to true Union men to yield to the threats of Disunionists, which was reversing the divine rule, and calling, not the sinners but the righteous to repentance—none of these things should move or intimidate us; but having faith that right makes might, let us to the end, dare to do our duty.

[1] Dover *Inquirer*, March 8, 1860.

To Isaac Pomeroy[1]

Isaac Pomeroy, Esq | Exeter N H
Dear Sir: | March 3 1860.

Owing to my great itineracy in this region, yours of the 28th. ult has just reached me. I have already spoken five times, and am engaged to speak five more. By the time these engagements shall be fulfilled, I shall be so far worn down, and also will be carried so far beyond my allotted time, that an immediate return home will be a necessity with me. At this very sitting I am declining invitations to go to Philadelphia, Reading, and Pittsburgh in Pa. You perceive I treat you no worse than I do others. The near approach of the elections in N.H. Conn. & R.I. has been the means of their getting me so deeply in here. I hope I may yet be able to visit New-Jersey & Pa. before the fall elections. While at New-York a Mr. William Silvey got a promise from me that I would write him whether I could visit, & speak at New-Ark. Will you please show him this? Yours Respectfully A. LINCOLN

79. Cedar St. N.Y.

[1] ALS-F, ISLA. Isaac Pomeroy, writing from New York City as a member of the Young Men's Working Club of the Republican Party at Newark, New Jersey, asked Lincoln to make a speech at Newark (DLC-RTL).

To James A. Briggs[1]

[March 4, 1860]

Yours of the 29th ult. covering check for $200, was received . . . Since I left New York I have spoken at Providence, R.I. and at Concord, Manchester, Dover & Exeter, in this State; and I still am to speak at Hartford, Meriden . . . Then I close, and start for home . . . Much as I appreciate your kindness allow me to beg that you will make no arrangement to detain me. . . .

[1] Parke-Bernet Catalog No. 829, January 20, 1947. This partial text is all that is available.

To Mary Todd Lincoln[1]

[Exeter, N.H. March 4, 1860]

I have been unable to escape this toil. If I had foreseen it, I think I would not have come east at all. The speech at New York, being within my calculation before I started, went off passably well and gave me no trouble whatever. The difficulty was to make nine others, before reading audiences who had already seen all my ideas in print.

[1] James Schouler, "Abraham Lincoln at Tremont Temple in 1848," *Proceedings of the Massachusetts Historical Society*, XLII (1909), 81. Robert T. Lincoln in a letter to Schouler (January 29, 1908) quoted this passage from "a letter written by my father to my mother on March 4th [1860], at Exeter, N. H."—*ibid.* Efforts to locate the original letter or a complete copy have failed. Lincoln was visiting his son Robert, who was attending Phillips Exeter Academy, and spoke at Exeter on March 3, but no adequate report of the speech has been located.